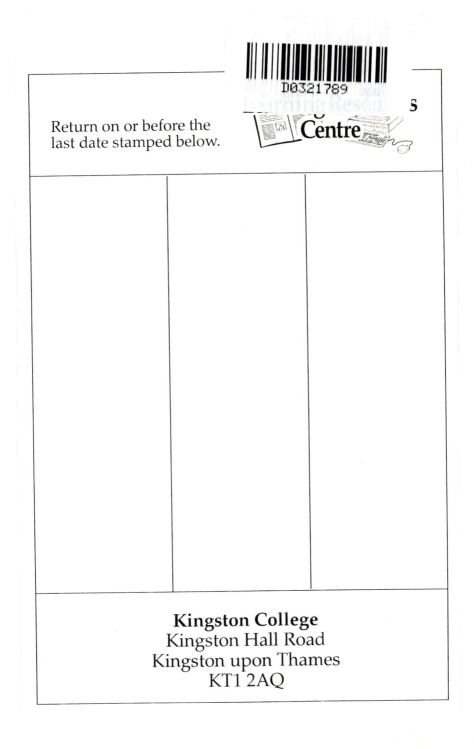

Return on or before the
last date stamped below.

Centre

Kingston College
Kingston Hall Road
Kingston upon Thames
KT1 2AQ

Keith Joseph

Also by Mark Garnett and published by Acumen

Alport: A Study in Loyalty

Keith Joseph

Andrew Denham & Mark Garnett

First published in 2001 by Acumen

Acumen Publishing Limited
15a Lewins Yard
East Street
Chesham
Bucks HP5 1HQ

www.acumenpublishing.co.uk

ISBN: 1-902683-03-X

British Library Cataloguing-in-Publication Data
A catalogue record for this book is available
from the British Library.

Designed and typeset in Bembo
by Kate Williams, Abergavenny.
Printed and bound by Biddles Ltd., Guildford and King's Lynn.

For Patricia and Dilakshi

Contents

Acknowledgements

Many people have assisted us in our research for this book. Some have helped to such an extent that the hackneyed phrase "Without whom . . ." should apply; several have merely suggested other people who could provide more information. Others who have helped preferred that we should not acknowledge their part in this undertaking. We hope that in private communications (or in the relevant footnotes) we have made our special obligations clear. But we would like to extend our thanks to: Lord Aberdare; Leo Abse; Catherine and Ian Aitken; the late Lord Aldington; Richard Aldrich; Michael Alison; the late Lord Alport; Lord Ashley; Norma Aubertin-Potter; Alan Bacon; Simon Bailey; Lord Baker; Ruth Barden; Richard Barker; Correlli Barnett; Greig Barr; the late Lord Beloff; Tony Benn; Bob Bessell; Lord Biffen; Lord Blake; William Blake; Andrew Bond; Colette Bowe; Sir Rhodes and Lady Florette Boyson; Lord Brittan; Sir Samuel Brittan; the late Sir Nigel Broackes; John Brocklehurst; Robert Butler; Ronald Butt; John Campbell; Sir Peter Carey; Brian Carlisle; Sir Raymond Carr; Lord Carr; Baroness Castle; Leslie Chapman; Kenneth Clarke; Nigel Cochrane; J. L. Cohen; John Cole; Sir Frederick Corfield; Sir Patrick Cormack; Patrick Cosgrave; Philip Cowley; Bernard Crick; Michael Crick; the late Sir Julian Critchley; Robin Darwall-Smith; Lord Dean; Lord Deedes; James and Mary Douglas; Major Tony Eeles; John Ehrman; Keith Feldman; Frank Field; Sir Charles Fletcher-Cooke; Michael Foot; Sir Norman Fowler; Milton Friedman; Peter Fullerton; Neville Gaffin; John Kenneth Galbraith; Andrew Gamble; Rita Gibbs; Roy Gluckstein; Geoffrey Goodman; William Hague; Morrison Halcrow; Sir David Hancock; Michael Hargreave; Colin Harmsworth; Colin Harris; Lord Harris of High Cross; Brian and Betty Harrison; Sir Graham Hart; David Hartshorne; Sir Edward Heath; Simon Heffer; Peter Hennessy; Paul Heywood; Peter Hill; Richard Hoggart; Simon

Hoggart; Chris Holmes; Sir John Hoskyns; Anthony Howard; Greville Howard; Lord Howe; Lord Howell; Miles Hudson; Lord Hurd; Sir Bernard Ingham; Peter Jay; Lord Jenkin; Kate Jenkins; Lord Jenkins; Vivian Jennings; Anthony Joseph; Judith Joseph; the late Lord Joseph; Rex Joseph; Veronica Kendon; Nicola Kennan; Sir Ludovic Kennedy; Lord Lamont; Julia Langdon; Lord Lawson; Charles Leadbeater; Hugh and Penny Lee; Oliver Letwin; Jeremy Lever; Peter Lilley; the Earl of Lisburne; Ian Little; Douglas Lyne; Sir Donald MacDougall; Michael Mates; David McKie; Frank McLynn; Sir Ferdinand Mount; Tom Mullen; Lord Murray; Virginia Murray; Pam Nicole; John Oakley-Smith; Hiran Odedra; Matthew Parris; Biddy Passmore; Chris Patten; Baroness Pike; Lord Plant; Lord Prior; Wilfred Proudfoot; Lord Quinton; Giles Radice; Gary and Ming-Yeh Rawnsley; Vicky Rea; John Redwood; Lord Renton; the late Sir Robert Rhodes James; David Richardson; Sir Adam Ridley; Alexandra Rocca; Andrew Roth; the late Anthony Salmon; Anthony Seldon; Madron Seligman; Brendon Sewill; Stuart Sexton; Richard Shepherd; Rob Shepherd; Christopher Sheppard; Jill Sherlock; Sir Alfred Sherman; the late Zuzanna Shonfield; Michael Simmonds; John Smith; Jill Spellman; Ian and Carole Taylor; Lord Tebbit; Lady Thatcher; Lord Thomas of Swynnerton; Polly Toynbee; Sir Guenter Treitel; Lord Vinson; Lord Waldegrave; George Walden; Lord Walker; Robert Walsha; Sir Alan Walters; Alan Watkins; Charles Webster; Richard Weight; Robin Wendt; Lord Wilberforce; Peter Wilby; Max Wilkinson; David Willetts; Ted Wragg; and Lord Young of Graffham.

For bearing with us during the longer than expected gestation period of this book, we should like to thank our editor, Steven Gerrard. The first draft was read by John Ramsden and an anonymous referee; we are most grateful for their comments, which have proved to be very helpful in making our final revisions. Allan Garnett, Lord Gilmour, Peter Robinson and Francis Wheen were kind enough to read the whole manuscript in the later stages of the process. Andrew Denham would like to thank the Research Committee of the School of Politics, University of Nottingham and the Arts and Humanities Research Board (AHRB) for the award of an extended period of study leave in 1998–9. Above all, he is indebted to Patricia, Nadine, Elizabeth, Anjelica and Rachel for their forbearance. Mark Garnett would also like to record his gratitude to his family for their invaluable support. On a controversial and complex subject our informants have often provided conflicting testimony. Although we are most grateful to all those who have helped in whatever capacity, we alone are responsible for any errors of fact or interpretation which may remain.

Andrew Denham & Mark Garnett
Nottingham
December 2000

Preface

Keith Joseph was almost the only senior Cabinet minister of the 1980s who did not write a memoir. There were several offers from publishers but he rejected them all. He was an intensely private man, anxious to protect his family from intrusion. If this were not enough to ensure his silence, he was also excessively modest. As Education Secretary during the 1980s, when almost everyone with an interest in British politics regarded him as either a Saint or a Satan, he continued to assume that the people he met – even those with a professional interest in the work of his Department – would not know who he was without a formal introduction. In retirement he was never a candidate for the television chat-show or the after-dinner circuit. Unusually for a politician, he disliked speaking of himself; almost uniquely, he was very uneasy even when his name was mentioned in public. But if he was painfully shy, he appeared to be remarkably candid on those occasions when he allowed himself to reminisce. In particular, he was critical of his ministerial record. As he admitted in a revealing interview at the time of his retirement from the House of Commons, "I know my own capacities. Adequate for some jobs, but not for others". Instead of regretting that he never became Prime Minister, he thought that "it would have been a disaster for the party, country and me" had he done so. The burden of leading the Opposition, let alone the crushing responsibility of running an administration, would have been too much for him. Leaving aside other intriguing questions about Joseph, this self-deprecation alone makes him one of the most interesting and attractive senior figures in post-war British politics.

Coaxed by friends, Joseph did give several lengthy interviews to Morrison Halcrow who published a biography in 1989. But the fall of Mrs Thatcher, Lord Joseph's frequent absences in America during his last years, and his own tendency to play down his contribution to public life combined to make him a relatively neglected figure in the early 1990s. His death in December 1994 brought the usual tributes and respectful obituary articles; but the press interest was not sustained. By that time the Conservative Party was tearing itself apart over Europe, and although Joseph had strong views on that subject his name was primarily linked to the controversy over "monetarism" which had dominated the early 1980s. The battle within the Conservative Party between the "wets" and the "dries" had apparently been settled in favour of the latter when Joseph died; the media was now only interested in the clash between "Eurofanatics" and "Europhobes". The Public Records Office had begun to release papers relating to Joseph's career as a minister in the Macmillan–Home years, but no one took much notice. As a character he was beginning to fade in the public memory; if any impression remained, it was his reputation for agonised deliberation, which earned him during the 1970s the nickname of "The Mad Monk".

But while Joseph's name and personality were increasingly obscure his legacy was growing in importance. His speeches in the mid-1970s aroused fierce controversy, but twenty years later their themes had become the stock assumptions of British politics. The overriding priority of controlling inflation; the dangers of state interference; the central importance of the entrepreneur and the value of skilled managers; the need to strengthen the family and to raise educational standards: all of these, and more, were taken for granted in the élite political discourse of 1994. Joseph was not an original thinker, but on some of these subjects he was among the first post-war politicians to provoke a debate. Others he promoted with more assiduity even than Enoch Powell – in many respects a comparable figure.

In 1975 Joseph baffled commentators with an appeal for the Labour Party to join the Conservatives on what he called "common ground". He hoped that a new "consensus" could be reached between the major British parties, but thought that during the post-war period the initiative had passed to Labour. The Conservatives had lost touch with voters. If they re-established this contact they could "reverse the trend" and force Labour to adopt a more constructive approach to wealth creation. By the time of Joseph's death bipartisan agreement on basic principles – at least among senior figures – was becoming as familiar in Britain as ideological conflict had been in the 1970s and 1980s. Tony Blair, the newly elected Labour leader, had embarked on a course which would make the 1997 general election a personality contest, rather than a clash of ideas. But those who believed that Britain had witnessed "the end of ideology" were mistaken; rather, "New" Labour was the product of a belief that a single ideology had "won" the "battle of ideas". In reforming his party Blair was acting on the assumption that free market ideas had defeated socialism. Now he offered the country a blend of economic efficiency and social compassion – precisely the agenda that Joseph had advocated throughout his political career.

Ironically, by driving Labour to accept a great deal of "common ground" with the Conservatives Blair helped to ensure a devastating defeat for the party which Joseph served for almost forty years. Probably this would not have worried Joseph too much; he had rarely allowed himself to be constrained by narrow partisan interests, although he might have regretted the narrow Conservative defeat in Leeds North-East in 1997, the constituency he won easily on nine occasions after 1956. The fact that Joseph's convictions have become even more influential now that his own political generation has passed is scarcely surprising; his chief aim was to change what he called "the climate of opinion", and those who were developing their political outlook at the height of his campaign were most likely to be affected by his message.

At the end of the twentieth century it was fashionable to muse on the comparative influence of various political figures. People differed in their personal rankings, and political loyalties were bound to affect their judgements. But on any measure of "influence" – a concept that eludes precise definition – the half-forgotten Keith Joseph had strong claims for consideration. Facile generalisations about cause and effect have no place in serious political commentary, and the relative importance of "events" and "ideas" can be end-lessly debated. But there is clear evidence to support the view that Joseph's role in changing Britain's post-war "consensus" was as great as (if not greater than) that of any other individual. Margaret Thatcher's part in this process was complementary to his, but she rarely expounded her creed in theoretical terms, and without Joseph her rise to the Conservative leadership might not have happened. Joseph never held any of the highest offices in government; but neither did three other twentieth-century politicians of acknowledged influence, Joseph Chamberlain, Tony Benn and Enoch Powell. Unlike them, Joseph was a man who could not hope to attract a following by virtue of a dominating character; his importance rests entirely on more enduring qualities.

This is not to say that Joseph's record as a practising politician disproves Powell's dictum that all such careers end in failure. After first becoming a government minister in 1959 he was in office for more than fifteen years, and served in five departments, before retiring from the front-bench in 1986. He was not the only well-informed commentator to find fault with his performance during that time (even if he was among the harshest of the critics). It was often assumed that Joseph was too much of an intellectual to succeed in politics. But if Powell was right, and failure is the common lot of politicians, then there is no need to single out intellectuals as a particularly hapless group. It was only in the mid-1970s that Joseph began to be regarded as "a deeply impractical man". When he left office in 1964 after his first spell as a Cabinet minister he was seen as a politician who had been able to combine his intellectual interests with rigorous attention to the day-to-day problems of a department. Only after the second consecutive defeat for the Conservatives, in 1966, did he begin to show signs that his love of ideas might present a problem to his colleagues. Back in office after the 1970 general election he returned to his previous form, and was hailed as one of the most successful ministers of the Heath Government. But a further defeat (combined with illness, financial problems, and difficulties within his family) ushered in a five-year period during which he ignored the promptings of political calculation. Although his thinking reflected a wider disillusionment with the British post-war "consensus", the image of a political maverick – "The Mad Monk" – was quickly established, and he never shook this off. Thus when he again returned to office those of his actions which deviated from his stated beliefs were interpreted as evidence of failure, whether or not they produced the desired results in practice. The decision to continue subsidies to state industries like British Leyland (for example) would have been greeted as a sign of healthy pragmatism in any other minister. By his own conduct in Opposition, Joseph ensured that it would be derided as a "U-turn". It is only fair to point out that while Mrs Thatcher was judged by her words, as a departmental minister Joseph had to make his words and actions compatible. Equally, the biographer cannot overlook the extent to which he brought this dilemma on himself.

Many politicians have embarked on political careers with strong academic credentials. Lord Hailsham – Joseph's front-bench colleague for a quarter of a century – was, like him, a Fellow of All Souls, and even Joseph's warmest admirer would admit that Hailsham had the more powerful intellect of the two. Hailsham never secured the premiership, but a penchant for abstract thinking was hardly a factor in the decision of leading Conservatives to reject him in 1963. It seems, in fact, that politicians are usually categorised as "intellectuals" when, having delivered persistent challenges to "accepted wisdom" in philosophical language, they alienate a significant proportion of their colleagues. While this does not mean that an assumption of political "failure" is built into the definition of "intellectual", in a political culture like that of Britain, where promotion depends on a broad conformity with "the rules of the game", the odds are stacked against those who earn an "intellectual" reputation. In Joseph's case the key point is the *nature* of his intellect. Above all, he was a man of intellectual *enthusiasms*. For most of his life he was blessed with a formidable memory, and he never lost his thirst for knowledge. Certainly he had many intellectual habits, but there was little sign of the *scepticism* normally associated with the term. At first he was convinced that strenuous inquiry and debate would yield an answer to every political problem; after his "conversion" he believed that the right answers could be found by reference to the doctrine of economic liberalism. This unusual trait explains his strong appeal to Conservatives who agreed with his later thinking – to them he epitomised the intellectual as hero. But the same characteristic also accounts for the fact that many colleagues (like Hailsham himself) considered Joseph to be "dotty", however much they liked him as an individual.

When Joseph left school a friend described him as "an enigma"; at his memorial service his son remembered that as a young boy he could never understand "how such a clever man could get into *so* much trouble". To some extent this remarkable character will always remain elusive. But while preparing this book we have been impressed by the extent to which Joseph's quest for truth was linked to a search for an unambiguous sense of self – a settled *identity*. His political career cannot be explained without an examination of his background and upbringing which is as thorough as the records allow; to an unusual extent, we believe, this provides a key to understanding the policies he upheld, and the fervour with which he promoted them. His need for secure roots was not satisfied by becoming a Conservative MP, or even a Cabinet minister; he wanted to feel that he represented a cause rather than merely a party, and this craving was only satisfied in his mid-fifties. The political quality he admired above all was what he called "moral courage", and he felt that up to 1974 he had not shown enough of it. Afterwards he more than compensated for any shortcomings on this score, but his character had not really changed. Rather, in early 1974 he felt a new confidence in the ideas which he had advocated in the past, and this enabled him to show the courage he had always possessed. His psychological need for ideological certainty explains features of his life which would otherwise remain a puzzle: why this shy man forced himself to encounter derision and personal danger in an exhausting series of speeches; why a politician who thought that the need to feel "loved" motivated most members of his profession found himself among the best-hated people of his time; and why this man of deep (if not indiscriminate) compassion never dissociated himself from policies which greatly increased the poverty that he had set out to "eliminate". It took enormous courage for Joseph to make the public confessions of error which marked his speeches in the late 1970s; to deliver a new series of admissions after all his work on behalf of the monetarist doctrine was asking too much of any human being. Finally, without exploring the roots of Joseph's complex personality it is impossible to explain why even his opponents felt a twinge of regret on his retirement, and why when he died his enemies mixed their criticisms with tributes.

While we contend that Joseph's ideas still exert a powerful influence on British politics, whether or not this influence has been wholly beneficial is an entirely separate question. It is hoped that the following pages will contribute something to an understanding both of "Thatcherism" (in theory and practice) and of government initiatives since Mrs Thatcher's departure from office. We have not refrained from critical comment, particularly on the coherence of Joseph's ideas. Joseph himself never spared his intellectual opponents, and the extent to which his ideas deserve critical scrutiny is a tribute to his continuing relevance. Apart from the difficulty of penetrating behind Joseph's own reticence, our main challenge has been to combine this critical spirit with something of the respect and affection for our subject which has developed during the course of our research. While this has always been our goal, it must be confessed that the task would have been simplified had it not been for the feeling that, after 1974, circumstances were constantly conspiring to ensure that Joseph's ideas were tried out in practice. In turn, our approach has been conditioned by a recognition that, for a character like Keith Joseph, an electoral victory for his party based on a minority of the popular vote could only be the beginning of the battle. Few politicians have shown less inclination to rest on their laurels; none has accepted self-sacrifice more eagerly.

It is no part of our brief to provide a detailed account of the course which the Thatcher Governments *should* have taken after 1979. But we believe that damaging mistakes were made, both of policy and of presentation, and that these are mostly attributable to the adherence by senior figures to the monetarist theory. Lurking behind this doctrine, with which the Thatcher Governments are so intimately associated, was a problem of how radical economic change could be reconciled with the desire for social stability which Joseph himself shared with so many Conservatives. As the Government's leading theoretician – and as someone whose fascination with economics was matched by a deep interest in society – Joseph could have been expected to address this difficulty. But he never did; and although it played no direct part in Mrs Thatcher's own downfall it can be argued that the failure to weave the various strands of "Thatcherism" into a coherent basis for political action made a vital contribution to the catastrophic Conservative defeat of May 1997.

Morrison Halcrow's biography remains the only other published book about Keith Joseph. In part, its relative brevity reflects the daunting task of writing about a person who always preferred to discuss ideas than to divulge anecdotes about his past. His close friends were protective of this shy man, and his personal courtesy ensured that there are no stories of rows with political opponents which would shed new light on his character. Since Joseph's death, however, much new information has become available, and new perspectives have opened. A considerable tranche of valuable material relating to Joseph's years in Opposition between 1974 and 1979 – the period when he rightly thought that his greatest contribution was made – has been catalogued by the Bodleian Library. The official papers for Joseph's time at the DHSS have formed the basis of a painstaking study (by Charles Webster), and some documents have been made available in the Public Records Office before the expiry of the usual thirty years. Restrictions still apply to Joseph's later spells at Industry (1979–81) and Education (1981–86). But the Thatcher Governments in general were as leaky (and leaked against) as any administrations in British history, and since Joseph was so controversial much of the information which reached the public domain related to his activities. After their release it is unlikely that these documents will force a radical rethink of Joseph's record as a minister, even if some interesting details are added. Most of Joseph's colleagues have now retired, and are available to provide their recollections. Many surviving friends from his early days have been most helpful to us. Joseph did not keep a private collection of papers, which makes it unlikely that there will ever be an "official" biography. But Joseph's family placed no obstacles in our way and rebuffed our advances with great courtesy. Above all, although Joseph's role in post-war politics is still the subject of debate, sufficient time has now passed to attempt to reach an authoritative judgement on a career which has been the subject of myths, both favourable and otherwise, ever since his announcement that he was only "converted" to Conservatism in April 1974.

"... with our good intentions, we have tried to improve life; but sometimes, to our mortification, we have seen the unintended ill consequences of our good wishes apparently make things worse"

Lord Joseph of Portsoken, 22 May 1991

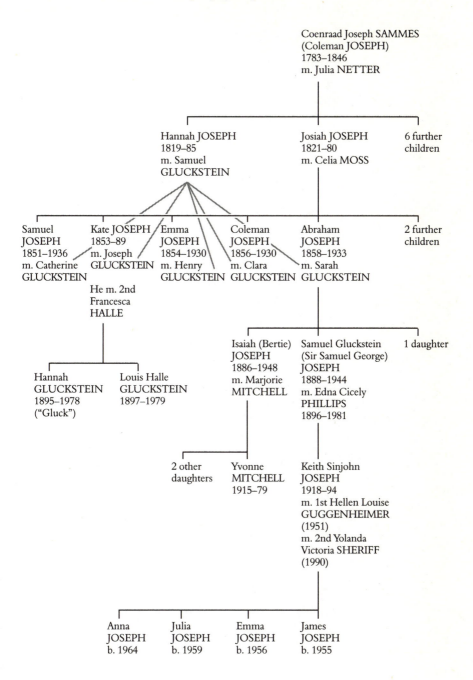

Coenraad Joseph SAMMES
(Coleman JOSEPH)
1783–1846
m. Julia NETTER

Hannah JOSEPH
1819–85
m. Samuel
GLUCKSTEIN

Josiah JOSEPH
1821–80
m. Celia MOSS

6 further
children

Samuel
JOSEPH
1851–1936
m. Catherine
GLUCKSTEIN

Kate JOSEPH
1853–89
m. Joseph
GLUCKSTEIN

He m. 2nd
Francesca
HALLE

Emma
JOSEPH
1854–1930
m. Henry
GLUCKSTEIN

Coleman
JOSEPH
1856–1930
m. Clara
GLUCKSTEIN

Abraham
JOSEPH
1858–1933
m. Sarah
GLUCKSTEIN

2 further
children

Hannah
GLUCKSTEIN
1895–1978
("Gluck")

Louis Halle
GLUCKSTEIN
1897–1979

Isaiah (Bertie)
JOSEPH
1886–1948
m. Marjorie
MITCHELL

Samuel Gluckstein
(Sir Samuel George)
JOSEPH
1888–1944
m. Edna Cicely
PHILLIPS
1896–1981

1 daughter

2 other
daughters

Yvonne
MITCHELL
1915–79

Keith Sinjohn
JOSEPH
1918–94
m. 1st Hellen Louise
GUGGENHEIMER
(1951)
m. 2nd Yolanda
Victoria SHERIFF
(1990)

Anna
JOSEPH
b. 1964

Julia
JOSEPH
b. 1959

Emma
JOSEPH
b. 1956

James
JOSEPH
b. 1955

Chapter One

"Rather an Enigma . . ."

Keith Sinjohn Joseph was born on 17 January 1918. Between his conception and his birth the world which lay in wait for him underwent a dramatic and lasting change. In November 1917 a Bolshevik government was installed in Russia. Just nine days before Keith's birth the US President Woodrow Wilson, in his "Fourteen Points", advocated self-determination and open negotiation at a League of Nations against the old ways of secret diplomacy and hostile alliances. After more than three years of carnage in Europe the beginning of 1918 brought a mixture of fear and confidence for the opposing forces; the Germans believed that the conclusion of a separate peace with Russia would lead to a rapid victory, while Britain and its allies sought to stave off collapse until American troops arrived to swing the conflict their way. A. J. P. Taylor stressed the importance of January 1918 in world history; in that month, he wrote, "Europe ceased to be the centre of the world . . . there began a competition between communism and liberal democracy which has lasted to the present day". That pregnant verdict was published in 1956 – the year in which Keith Joseph became a Conservative MP. More flippantly, the authors of *1066 and All That* lamented this period as one in which Britain lost its status as "Top Nation" and history came to a full-stop. Joseph lived to see another major reordering of world forces, and the apparent end of conflict between the competing ideologies of 1918. But the upheavals of January 1918 produced the context which dominated his political career.[1]

The world crisis had a more immediate and direct impact on Keith Joseph's family. His father, Samuel Gluckstein Joseph, was a Lieutenant in the 5th Battalion of the Royal Irish Regiment, on active service in France when Keith was born. Yet the natural anxiety of Samuel's devoted wife Edna was tempered by her knowledge that if the child's father never returned there would be other friends to help launch him into the new, insecure world. Keith was born in the billiard room of 63 Portland Place, the elegant home of his maternal grandfather, Philip A. Solomon Phillips. Portland Place, to the north of Regent Street, was perhaps the best example of eighteenth-century architecture in London. Phillips' four-storey house boasted an interior designed by Robert Adam, and had been occupied between 1893 and 1898 by the author Frances Hodgson Burnett. Another celebrated literary figure, John Buchan, lived across the road in number 76, where he completed *The Thirty-Nine Steps* (1915); at the time of Keith Joseph's birth Buchan was writing another novel, *Mr Standfast*, while serving as Director of the Department of Information and dodging occasional Zeppelin raids near his home. The Earl of Shrewsbury had his London residence two doors away from Phillips; the road also housed several diplomatic legations, and the homes of three serving MPs.[2]

The expense of maintaining and heating number 63 had been a constant worry for Mrs Hodgson Burnett, whose resources were also drained by the servants, carriages and horses which a Portland Place lifestyle demanded. But while Hodgson Burnett relied on her pen to support herself, Keith Joseph's maternal grandfather enjoyed far greater security. Born in 1867, Phillips had been a partner in Crichton Brothers, a Bond Street firm of antique silversmiths. Before he reached the age of fifty he had earned enough to retire in comfort. In his later years he amused himself by examining archival records concerning Anglo-Jewish and Huguenot jewellers; this agreeable pastime resulted in several learned articles and two books. Like his famous grandson he was an assiduous (if not obsessive) contributor to the correspondence columns, and although he particularly favoured *The Times* he was always ready to send a note wherever he felt that his expertise might be of interest. For example, in 1929 readers of *The Connoisseur* were invited to share his regret that "snuff-boxes *qua* snuff-boxes have not so far found a historian". Judged by his writings, Phillips was a courteous and diffident scholar. Before his death in January 1934 he had moved to an even more fashionable London address, Park Lane; his estate was

---

1. A. J. P. Taylor, *The Struggle for Mastery in Europe 1848–1918* (Oxford University Press, 1971), 568.
2. Janet Adam Smith, *John Buchan* (Rupert Hart-Davis, 1965), 199–200, 206; information from Post Office Directory for 1918. Number 63 Portland Place is now part of the headquarters of the Chartered Institute of Management Accountants. We are most grateful to Tom Mullen for information about the building.

valued at almost £60,000 in 1934 – comfortably over £1 million in today's values.[3]

In one of Keith Joseph's favourite novels, C. P. Snow's *The Conscience of the Rich,* the narrator observes that his wealthy young friend Charles March "often envied that simplification, that compulsory simplification, which being poor imposed upon my life".[4] The circumstances of Keith's birth ensured that he would never know that fortunate "simplification", and it had also been denied to his parents. Samuel Joseph was born in 1888 at 50 High Street, Notting Hill.[5] When Keith's grandfather, Abraham Joseph, died aged seventy-four in 1933 his gross estate was worth £23,840. This hardly placed him at the summit of the wealth league – the net worth of the economist John Maynard Keynes in 1936 has been estimated at over £500,000 – but Abraham Joseph shared with Philip Phillips a comfortable mid-table position at a time when only the best-paid industrial workers earned as much as £4 per week. Dying within a year of each other both Joseph and Phillips were buried at Willesden, in the Orthodox section of what has been called "the Rolls Royce among London's Jewish cemeteries".[6]

Samuel Joseph and Edna Phillips, who married while the former was on leave in 1916, had no reason to fear the financial consequences of starting a family. But more valuable even than the comfortable circumstances of Keith Joseph's parents was his inherited membership of an influential and affluent network of relatives. Philip Phillips belonged to a long-resident Anglo-Jewish family – an important consideration in itself, since refugees from the pogroms of Eastern Europe trebled the Jewish population of Britain in the three decades after 1890 and the newcomers were regarded with some aversion by the established families.[7] But while Phillips had been content to assure himself of the leisurely lifestyle of a gentleman the Josephs were part of an extended and astonishing clan whose entrepreneurial drive was matched only by a penchant for inter-marriage which resulted in a highly complex family tree (p. xvii).

The first member of the Joseph family to use that surname was born Coenraad Joseph Sammes in 1773. A merchant by trade, at some point he dropped the "Sammes" and changed his first name; afterwards he was known

---

3. Ann Thwaite, *Waiting for the Party: The Life of Frances Hodgson Burnett 1849–1924* (Secker & Warburg, 1974), 150–1; *The Connoisseur*, Vol. LXXXIII (January–June 1929), 29; *The Times* obituary of P. A. S. Phillips and reader's letter, 29 and 31 January 1934; details of will, *The Times* 14 April 1934.
4. C. P. Snow, *The Conscience of the Rich* (Penguin, 1961), 46.
5. The address is now 50 Notting Hill Gate; the original building is mostly occupied by a bank.
6. Details of will, *The Times* 5 June 1933; Robert Skidelsky, *John Maynard Keynes: The Economist as Saviour 1920–1937* (Macmillan, 1992), 524; Hugh Mellor, *London Cemeteries* (Scolar Press, 3rd edition, 1994), 184.
7. Figures for Jews in the UK: 1891 – 101,189; 1921 – 300,000. Taken from *Jewish Year Book*, selected years, and reprinted in A. H. Halsey (ed.), *British Social Trends Since 1900* (Macmillan, 1988), 602.

as Coleman Joseph. In the early nineteenth century his family was based in Amsterdam, then moved to Whitechapel in London's East End. From there one of Coleman's four sons, Keith Joseph's great-grandfather Josiah (born Tobias Joseph), ventured into the New World. Abraham Joseph, the sixth of Josiah's seven children, was born in Philadelphia in 1858. By 1885 he had migrated to London, and in November of that year he married Sarah Gluckstein in Paddington. Either Abraham had succumbed to an irresistible hereditary attraction or the match had been expected of him. Four of his siblings had already married into the Gluckstein family. Feelings must have been running high in 1885; earlier in that year Abraham's brother (another Coleman Joseph) and his sister Emma had both paired off with Glucksteins.

The patriarch who supplied all these spouses was Samuel Gluckstein, who had emigrated to London from Rheinberg, Germany in 1840. For him wedlock with a Joseph was part of the natural order of things. On his first arrival Gluckstein had stayed with the Joseph family in Whitechapel. The arrangement produced a lodging-place for his heart, and five years later he married his land-lord's daughter, Hannah Joseph.[8] Abraham Joseph's wife Sarah was among twelve products of this union; they, and all the other Josephs and Glucksteins who fell for each other, were thus first cousins.

Samuel Gluckstein prospered in the tobacco trade, undercutting his rivals with cleverly advertised cigars ("The more you smoke, the more you save"). One of his enthusiastic customers was another émigré from a Jewish background, Karl Marx.[9] In 1904 the main family firm, Salmon & Gluckstein (a relative by marriage, Barnett Salmon, having joined Samuel Gluckstein's three sons in running the company) was sold to Imperial Tobacco for over £600,000 – a prodigious sum in those days. By this time the family's business interests had diversified. In his travels on behalf of the tobacco concern Samuel's son Montague Gluckstein was impressed by the lack of refreshment facilities for "respectable" families, who were equally repelled by pubs and by dirty cafés. In the last years of the century a chain of teashops was established, including the ornate Trocadero in Piccadilly and a branch opposite the Stock Exchange. The venture was dominated by the family although it traded under the name of a friend and more distant relative, Joe Lyons. This measure was taken because while cigar-making was considered to be a respectable trade the family's good name might be jeopardised by an advertised connection with the dubious tea-shop business.[10]

---

8. On this point see Diana Souhami's well-informed account in *Gluck 1895–1978: Her Biography* (Pandora Press, 1988), 23. She states that the Glucksteins and the Josephs were already related in 1840, but we have been unable to trace the connection. She also writes that Samuel Gluckstein found lodgings with his *aunt*, but this is rather odd since Hannah's father Coleman Joseph was still living in 1840.
9. Francis Wheen, *Karl Marx* (Fourth Estate, 1999), 294.
10. Maurice Corina, *Trust in Tobacco: The Anglo-American Struggle for Power* (Michael Joseph, 1975), 79.

No wistful account of London between the wars would be complete without a mention of Lyons' teashops, with their white-and-gold façades and their waitresses (or "Nippies") in their distinctive red uniforms. For many years the venture was a phenomenal success; by the 1930s it employed over 30,000 people throughout its various branches, which included factories producing tea and cakes. In the late 1940s the Joe Lyons food laboratory at Hammersmith hired a young research chemist called Margaret Roberts, shortly before she became the second wife of Denis Thatcher. Yet the key to its initial prosperity – the close co-operation between gifted relatives – threatened its permanence. The family already knew what might happen if personal feuding broke out, and had taken a dramatic step to guard against friction. The founder of the tobacco company, Samuel Gluckstein, was a "violent and overbearing" man whose temperament dragged the family into an extended and almost ruinous law-suit. After his death in 1873 the new partners had agreed to establish an arrangement known as "The Fund", under which family members pooled their assets. The Chair of the company would be held through seniority rather than ability, and the proceeds would be shared on the basis of need, regardless of individual contributions. The arrangement would cover any children, as well as the adults. Even relatively trivial business decisions were to be taken only after extensive debate between the (male) members of the family.[11]

Stephen Aris has described The Fund as a bizarre marriage between contradictory ideologies, with "arch-exponents of the capitalist system" yoked together in something approximating to a Bolshevik Soviet.[12] Alternatively it can be seen as an extreme expression of two familiar Victorian dogmas – those of self-help and of the family. Whatever the nature of its inspiration, an arrangement which guaranteed financial security could also be stifling and helped to produce some notable characters. One of Keith Joseph's cousins, the noted painter, Hannah Gluckstein (who adopted the name "Gluck"), once exclaimed "How I hate [my relatives] with their money and general bloodiness!". Much to the embarrassment of her conventional parents, Gluck enjoyed flaunting her non-comformity. She made no secret of her sexual orientation and "for a time turned androgyny into high fashion . . . [she] got her shirts from Jermyn Street, had her hair cut at Truefitt gentleman's hairdressers in Old Bond Street, and blew her nose on large linen handkerchiefs monogrammed with a G". On a theatre visit in 1918 she sported a Homburg hat and a dagger in her belt. But she learned to live with her hatred of the money, and continued to draw upon The Fund. Another cousin, Yvonne (the daughter of Samuel Joseph's elder brother Bertie) became a well-known actress and writer after reverting to her mother's maiden name of Mitchell. The qualities of the family are best illustrated by the career of

---

11. Stephen Aris, *The Jews in Business* (Jonathan Cape, 1970), 176–185; Souhami, *Gluck*, 23–4.
12. Aris, *Jews in Business*, 180.

Gluck's brother, Louis Halle Gluckstein, who took a path which was outwardly conformist but whose inexhaustible drive to work for good causes and to earn honours marks him as the most eccentric of the lot. Gluck's biographer has noted of the mainstream members of the family that "They earned knighthoods, CBEs, OBEs, MBEs, mayoralties and medals. They were QCs, MPs and Councillors". On his own, Louis Gluckstein had worked his way through the whole of this list by his mid-sixties, exchanging an earlier CBE for the even grander GBE (Knight of the Grand Cross of the British Empire). In his next decade he started up a new collection, becoming in 1969 a *Commendatore* of the Italian Order of Merit. To round off his improbable attributes, Louis was also a man of striking appearance even in his seventies. Kenneth Baker, who encountered him in one of his less exacting roles (President of the St Marylebone Conservative Association) retained a vivid memory of Louis's "immensely tall and stooped courtly figure".[13]

When the family pact was established in 1873 Keith Joseph's paternal grandfather, Abraham, was just fifteen years old. Although The Fund is often mentioned in books about the Anglo-Jewish business community the family (for understandable reasons) has not been anxious to publicise all of the details. But the story proved irresistible for Yvonne Mitchell, who in 1967 published a partly fictionalised account in her novel *The Family*. In an author's note Mitchell made an explicit disclaimer, writing that she loved her family and that "None of its members will, I think, recognise themselves or one another in this book, for none of them, even the generations which I know, have been deliberately portrayed. There will be some similarities, no doubt, and near parallels in the story . . .". Most authors include this type of self-denying ordinance only to break it in some places. Thankfully for the historian, Yvonne Mitchell was unusually forgetful of the restraints. There are one or two obvious fictions in the novel; for example, while Yvonne's own father Bertie Joseph is barely disguised in the character "Albert", no one among the over-crowded cast can be identified with Bertie's real-life brother (and Keith's father) Samuel. But the character "Nathaniel Coleman" is clearly Keith's grandfather Abraham Joseph; like Abraham, he is fifteen at the time of the meeting which produced The Fund, and he even lives in later life at the Royal Palace Hotel, Kensington, a family property in which Abraham Joseph and his wife Sarah lived for many years. Any chance that the family would have approved of Yvonne's book was dissipated by the dust-jacket summary, which praised her "haunting lyrical style [which] brilliantly evokes the miseries of comfortless childhood". Despite Yvonne's protestations of love for the family the only character to emerge with much

---

13. Souhami, *Gluck*, 10–11, 22, 25, 27; Kenneth Baker, *The Turbulent Years: My Life in Politics* (Faber & Faber, 1993), 32–3; see the entry for Louis Halle Gluckstein in *Who Was Who 1971–1980* (A. & C. Black, 1981). Gluck's father Joseph Gluckstein had a different take on his relatives, telling his future wife's parents that "We pride ourselves on being the most united family in the whole world".

credit is the one representing her favourite uncle, the irresistible Louis Gluckstein. Her own father is presented as "in turn a monster, a figure of fun, a man of minor tragedy", bitterly resentful of his status as merely "a highly salaried employee" in the family business, in contrast to his relatives who could depend upon "what his mind envisaged as a bottomless river of treasure". He "cursed deeply and daily" the fact that his fate had been determined twenty-two years [sic] before he was born – when his father "Nathaniel" [Abraham] decided *not* to participate in the Fund.[14]

In 1873, Mitchell relates, Nathaniel is working for a kosher butcher from a stall on Petticoat Lane market. He is portrayed as a handsome dreamer, who dominates his younger brother Benjamin.[15] Everyone agrees to the idea of pooling their resources until Nathaniel has his chance to speak:

"I think you're all mad", said Nathaniel, in his gentle, good-natured voice, "to saddle yourselves while you're young wiv one another's poverty.[16] I think we should all go our own way. I don't like the feeling of being 'emmed in . . . And anyway", he added, "it won't work, and you'll all be un'appy and quarrel with each other, and the taste will go out of friend-ship an' family feeling"

"'Ear 'ear", said little Benjamin, gazing at his handsome brother with awe and love, "'ear 'ear".

"And", continued Nathaniel, "you talk of everyone benefiting but what you 'aven't thought of is that 'im that works 'ardest will 'ave to drag along 'im that works least".

"That's the beauty of it", said Samuel [Montague Gluckstein].

"And what's more, if most of you fails, you all fail", said Nathaniel.

"That's the beauty of it", repeated Samuel . . .

So the partly fictional Abraham Joseph goes to South Africa, prospecting for gold; on his return to England he sets up with his brother as a trader in linen and cotton goods, in order to keep his business affairs separate from the family firm "Appleby's" [Joe Lyons]. But the tentacles of the Family are not so easily evaded; Appleby's expands into the hotel business, the hotels need linen and cotton, and Abraham's firm is the obvious supplier for these commodities.[17]

---

14. Yvonne Mitchell, *The Family* (Heinemann, 1967), dust-jacket notes, 6. While Mitchell writes that her fictional "Albert" is born in 1895, the real life Bertie Joseph was born in 1886.
15. "Benjamin" typifies Mitchell's preference for mixing up facts, rather than using her imagina-tion. The character is clearly based on Abraham's real-life *elder* brother, Coleman, but while Coleman lived until he was seventy-three "Benjamin" dies at fifty-nine – the same age as Mitchell's own father Bertie.
16. Apparently Abraham's accent owed more to the East End than to his native Philadelphia.
17. Mitchell, *The Family*, 3–18, 131.

The notion that Abraham Joseph tried his hand at gold-prospecting in South Africa before returning to London to set up a linen business fits with known facts about his life. Although the naturalisation papers he lodged in 1901 include a claim that he had been resident in Britain for thirty years – implying that he left America in his early teens - he was certainly out of the country at the time of the 1881 census. He left extensive property in southern Africa to his grandson; and along with his elder brother Coleman he set up in business as a general merchant, including linen among his wares.[18] Mitchell's account of the fateful meeting also has an authentic ring; it sounds like a tale told often and with regret in the house of Bertie Joseph, where Yvonne grew up. But the story is one of her few departures from thinly disguised fact. Some doubt must remain because no one took minutes at the meeting. But members of the Gluckstein family have pointed out that Abraham was not entitled even to take part in the 1873 discussion, which was restricted to the six "founding fathers" – the *existing* sons or sons-in-law of the first Samuel Gluckstein. Abraham did not achieve that status until he married Sarah in 1885 – twelve years after the original meeting.[19] It does, though, seem reasonable to conclude that Abraham's attitude towards the Fund was faithfully reflected in "Nathaniel's" recorded speech, and that his feelings reflected a desire to assert his independence from the rest of the family. This impression is supported by the fact that surviving relatives remember his reputation for flawed judgement.[20]

After attending the City of London School between the ages of ten and fifteen Abraham's son Samuel Joseph did exploit his connections to the extent of taking his first job in Lyons' works department. But he seems to have been biding his time, looking for a chance to avoid being "'emmed in" by the wider family. In 1908 an opportunity arose, when ill-health forced a Mr Charles William Bovis to put his construction company on the market. A cousin of Samuel Joseph, Sidney Gluckstein, bought the firm which soon proved adept at winning building contracts in what was then a highly competitive market. Significantly, Sidney Gluckstein's father Henry had rebelled against the rest of his family to the extent of emigrating to South Africa for some years; Sidney's son has noted Henry's "lifelong determination to remain independent", which was passed down the generations. It seems that Henry was especially close to

---

18. See Government Papers, Public Records Office, PRO HO/144/619: B35, 825; interview with Anthony Salmon. In 1901 Abraham was living in West Hampstead.
19. The Fund was established on a legal basis in 1893; the document was signed by three of Samuel Gluckstein's sons, and three of his sons-in-law, but not by Abraham Joseph. His brother Samuel, who married Catherine Gluckstein five years after the founding of the Fund, had been allowed to join; but special circumstances seem to have inspired this concession. Letter to authors from Roy Gluckstein; David Richardson, "The History of the Catering Industry, with special reference to the development of J. Lyons & Co. Ltd to 1939" (unpublished PhD thesis, University of Kent, 1970). We are most grateful to Dr Richardson for his assistance on this point.
20. Private information.

Abraham; they were buried side-by-side at Willesden, well away from any other male Gluckstein. Sidney was an ideal partner for Samuel Joseph, who began to acquire practical experience of joinery, carpentry and quantity surveying. In 1910 Bovis bought another building firm, and in July of that year Samuel replaced Sidney's original partner on the Bovis board.[21]

In later years Keith Joseph frequently praised the model entrepreneur as someone who begins with nothing, mortgaging his house to raise start-up capital. In one of his last speeches he referred to entrepreneurs as magical, mysterious beings: "They do not come because of good education, and they do not come of good birth. They do not come because of happy homes or unhappy homes. We do not know how they come . . .".[22] In conformity with this image he was inclined to play down the initial prospects of his father's business, joking about its minuscule resources. At the time of the Bovis purchase the building industry was in the doldrums. Yet, being a reputable firm based in London's fashionable Marylebone district – which included Portland Place – the company was an astute acquisition. Family legend put the price of the deal at just £500. In fact Sidney Gluckstein and his first ally (a shadowy figure called Alfred Grace) paid the ailing Mr Bovis £750 – by no means a fortune, but somewhat above the going rate for what the romance of hindsight transformed into nothing more than "a horse and cart, a ladder and a telepho-nist". Actually there was a yard, a shop, offices and some stables. The element of risk was reduced further by the knowledge that the new partners could always return to Lyons if their venture failed. Samuel Joseph's delayed entry into the business might be interpreted as a further exercise of caution on his part, but more likely it was part of a prearranged plan that he should pass a brief interlude gaining the kind of practical knowledge which Bovis would require. His brother Bertie later joined the Bovis board. Ironically, even in their act of outward rebellion the young entrepreneurs conformed to the family view that relatives make the best business partners, and both of their fathers (and their own wives) spent time on the board.[23]

Samuel Joseph was a man of energy and courage. When he returned from the First World War he had been mentioned in despatches twice, having served in Salonika and Egypt (where he was wounded) before his time in France. He seems to have enjoyed the social aspects of the military life; he gave his son the unusual middle name of "Sinjohn" in a (mis-spelt) tribute to a member of his unit, and just before his death he received a friendly letter from a fellow soldier who still remembered that they had occupied neighbouring beds in an Alexandria hospital

---

21. Peter Cooper, *Building Relationships: The History of Bovis, 1885–2000* (Cassell, 2000), 18. We are indebted for additional information on Bovis to John Oakley-Smith and Andrew Bond.
22. *House of Lords Debates*, vol. 536, col. 325, 26 February 1992.
23. Morrison Halcrow, *Keith Joseph: A Single Mind* (Macmillan, 1989), 3; Cooper, *Building Relationships,* 20, 28–9.

a quarter of a century before.[24] Keith Joseph later recalled that Sidney Gluckstein and his father had agreed that it would be foolish for both of them to volunteer for service abroad, so Gluckstein stayed at home after they had tossed a coin. This is another family myth (or at least an embroidery of the truth) which fosters the impression of two virile young men with a gambling outlook on work and war. The truth is more prosaic. The historian of Bovis has shown that Samuel volunteered for service at the beginning of 1915, and that pragmatic counsels within the family persuaded Sidney to drop the idea of following his cousin's example. They would have known better than to try to deflect Samuel Joseph once his mind was made up; he was among 10,000 members of the Anglo-Jewish community who enlisted before conscription was introduced in May 1916.[25]

Bovis had made modest progress by 1914, acquiring new headquarters in Berkeley Street after taking over another building firm. But its best days lay ahead. In the 1920s the company redeveloped much of Regent Street; other projects included work at the London School of Economics, Bush House, Africa House, several major offices in the City of London, and numerous cinemas. Although Bovis apparently did little work for J. Lyons[26], a fruitful and lengthy association with another Anglo-Jewish firm, Marks & Spencer, began in 1926. For personal reasons, Gluckstein and Joseph might have been most proud of Bovis's role in building the Liberal Jewish Synagogue in St Johns Wood Road, to which both Samuel and the Glucksteins belonged; bombed in the Second World War, the building was later restored by Bovis. Samuel and Sidney were remembered as model employers, maintaining the level of wages during economic down-turns in the expectation that this would cement the loyalty of their workers. Mutual respect and understanding arose from the fact that the bosses had gained practical experience on site. In an industry well accustomed to rapid staff turnover, Bovis proved an exception; many of the early employees stayed with the company throughout their careers. By 1928 the net assets of the firm stood at £167,252; average profits for the preceding three years were £40,206. The cousins were ready to take the bold step of floating their company on the London Stock Exchange. The days of the "horse and cart" were long behind them; as early as 1919 Samuel Joseph conducted his business with the help of a company-owned Chevrolet car. At the time he was drawing £2,000 per year from the company.[27]

---

24. Letter from H. de Vere Bass, 6 January 1943, Mansion House Papers 10a, 11. The colleague who inspired Keith Joseph's middle name, Lieutenant J. P. St. John Pike, had been awarded the Military Cross earlier in the conflict.
25. Halcrow, *Joseph*, 2–3; Cooper, *Building Relationships*, 28; V. D. Lipman, *A History of the Jews in Britain since 1858* (Leicester University Press, 1990), 140.
26. The source of this information was Sidney Gluckstein's nephew Harry Vincent. Bovis's historian is rather sceptical, since it is difficult to explain the company's early progress unless it had won contracts from Lyons. It may be significant that the company's first AGM (1910) was held in Lyons's Trocadero (which Bovis redeveloped in the 1980s). Cooper, *Building Relationships*, 21–2, 137.
27. *Ibid.*, 46, 29.

But even the best management could make mistakes, and the construction industry was highly vulnerable to down-swings in the wider economy. Keith Joseph remembered that Bovis was brought to the verge of bankruptcy by an ill-advised deal in the mid-1920s, and that when business was quiet his father would be irritated to find that he could tour all of the company's sites and still return home in time for a late breakfast. Bovis advertised itself through large billboards on which the company name was very prominent, unlike most of its competitors who cluttered their signs with other details. Joseph remembered that his father "was particularly keen to see that the Bovis nameboards were cleaned". In another anecdote calculated to demonstrate Samuel's ability to combine close attention to detail with innovation, Joseph related that his father had designed a wardrobe "in answer to my mother's complaint that she thought there must be something better in which to hang clothes than a bare cupboard". The result of Mrs Joseph's grumbling, Keith claimed, was the "Compactom" wardrobe, which quickly proved a very lucrative side line for Bovis. No doubt Samuel played some part in this, but the credit for designing the Compactom has also been awarded to Vincent Gluckstein (later Vincent Vincent), one of Samuel's numerous cousins.[28]

In later years Keith Joseph recalled that his childhood had been very happy, thanks to the material comfort of his home and the indulgence of his parents. Several schoolfriends who visited the family have confirmed this impression. One friend remembered Edna Joseph as a rather slight figure; this might have led to a decision by the couple to limit their family once a single heir had been produced (although Samuel Joseph might have looked at the soaring and entwining branches of the family tree and concluded that, in this sphere, small is beautiful). Edna was a popular woman, whose slender frame concealed an abundance of quiet determination. She worshipped the husband for whom she spent thirty-seven years in mourning. Every year she visited the Grand Hotel, Eastbourne, where the couple had spent their honeymoon; the staff made every effort to make the room look as it had done back in 1916, even down to the furniture coverings.[29]

In 1973, when asked whether his thinking on the emotional deprivation of the young owed anything to his own childhood experiences, Keith Joseph replied "It obviously owed a lot . . .". It seems that, for once, he was caught off guard in this interview.[30] Usually he avoided giving even an obscure hint that he had felt starved of affection when young, describing his father as someone who was very good with children. Certainly Samuel was a generous host

28. *Ibid.*, 44, 50; see obituary of Vincent Vincent, *The Times*, 17 January 1971. While other Harrow school boys made do with a "battered hanging rack", Keith's room boasted a Compactom; letter to the authors from Hugh Lee.
29. Halcrow, *Joseph*, 6; interviews with Madron Seligman, Michael Hargreave and Greig Barr; private information.
30. KJ, interview with Terry Coleman, *Guardian*, 12 November 1973.

whenever Keith was visited by school friends. But Samuel's work, and the circumstances of his son's schooling, obstructed the development of any close bond. To his first biographer, Morrison Halcrow, Keith observed (although "certainly not in any pejorative way") that Samuel was not a well-read man. This might be dismissed as nothing more than a factual statement – after all Samuel had little time for reading and Keith was the first Joseph to attend university. Yet it was still a rather odd remark to make to a biographer, and it indicates a disagreement between father and son on an important issue since Keith believed that education was a life-long process. This was a symptom of underlying temperamental differences between the two characters. For example, Samuel Joseph earned the reputation of a decisive (indeed *too* decisive) man, reaching his conclusions without feeling any obligation to review the question from all conceivable angles. His son was never a person to make snap decisions, even on relatively trivial matters, and by the end of his career the furrowed brow had become his trademark.[31]

On behalf of his young son, Samuel Joseph took decisions which were designed to secure him a prosperous and peaceful future in England. His own father had applied for British citizenship in 1901, in what seems to have been a prudent response to agitation for restrictions on "alien" immigration. The then Prime Minister, the Marquess of Salisbury, was a prominent supporter of such legislation, but nothing was done until the passage of the 1905 Aliens' Act. Anti-Semitic feelings were fuelled after the war by the prominence of Jewish businessmen among those who were alleged to have exploited the conflict for personal gain, and during a well-publicised libel trial of 1919 a journalist had claimed that "A man can't be both English and a Jew".[32] The patriotic Samuel Joseph refused to accept that his own parentage had saddled him with divided loyalties, and he was determined that no such accusations could be levelled at his son. Leo Abse recalls being told by Keith Joseph (his "pair" in the House of Commons) that his father "denied him" his barmitzvah, which should have been celebrated on his thirteenth birthday in January 1931. This was most unusual, and almost certainly overprotective on Samuel's part. Besides depriving the boy of a good party, a chance to show off his remarkable ability to memorise texts, and the expensive presents which would have rewarded his efforts, the absence of a barmitzvah distanced Keith from Anglo–Jewry without bringing him closer to any other community. Sir Alfred Sherman thought that Joseph "had no Jewish knowledge to speak of", and that this was a serious handicap to his political career. According to Sherman, a more solid grounding in Judaism would have "made him more philosophical, giving him a broader

---

31. Halcrow, *Joseph*, 3.
32. On 1905 Aliens' Act, see Geoffrey Alderman, *The Jewish Community in British Politics* (Clarendon Press, 1983), ch. 5; Francis Beckett, *The Rebel Who Lost His Cause: The Tragedy of John Beckett, MP* (London House, 1999), 53–4.

and longer perspective, and made him less easily ruffled". Sherman had strong views on this subject – and an idiosyncratic notion of what "a broader and longer perspective" would have revealed to Joseph. But he was not the only observer who detected this weakness. After Joseph's retirement from the Cabinet a correspondent in the *Jewish Chronicle* complained that he had failed to bring to his work at the Department of Education "a fraction of traditional Jewish respect for teachers and for learning, of Jewish intellectual humility and flexibility".[33]

Whether or not these critics had a point, Joseph's background did not provide him with a secure sense of religious and cultural identity. Towards the end of his life he characterised his immediate family as "minimally observing, but maximally acknowledging, Jews". As members of the Liberal Jewish Synagogue rather than the Orthodox branch to which Keith's grandparents had belonged the Josephs were half way to being "assimilated", but no more than half way. In religion, as in their connection with "The Family", they were neither one thing nor the other. Many other Jews of their class were "quite content to observe traditions that did not overly inconvenience them"; it was fairly common to eschew "spiritual enthusiasm" and to concentrate instead on "reasonable behaviour, fraternal responsibility, ethnic loyalty, intellectual courtesy, and communal charity". But failing to hold a barmitzvah for their only son placed the Josephs at the lower end even of the "minimalist" scale. As an adult Keith Joseph was reported to be a member of both the Liberal Jewish Synagogue in St John's Wood and the Orthodox synagogue near his Chelsea home; this, at least one friend thought, emphasised the problem of identity rather than resolving it. He was an infrequent attender of either synagogue, and did not obey the dietary laws of his religion; but he did worship on what he called "the imperative days" and fasted on the Day of Atonement. He was keen to question acquaintances who had been brought up in closer accordance with the Jewish tradition, and more than one observer thought that he regretted his father's decision to "deny" him the barmitzvah.[34]

The lack of regular contact between Samuel Joseph and his only child was the result of another conscious decision by a father who was determined to give his son a solid English upbringing. Keith's first school, Gibbs Wagner's in Sloane Street, was local, but at the beginning of 1926 the eight year-old boy was sent out of London, to Lockers Park School, Hemel Hempstead. This well-regarded prep school was close enough to home for regular visits. It was not

---

33. Interview with Leo Abse; *Jewish Chronicle*, 19 September 1986, 16 December 1994.
34. Halcrow, *Joseph*, 2; Todd M. Endelman, *Radical Assimilation in English Jewish History 1656–1945* (Indiana University Press, 1990), 84; interviews with Leo Abse and Geoffrey Goodman; private information; KJ interview with Anthony King, "Talking Politics", BBC Radio 4, 4 August 1973 (transcript kindly supplied by the BBC). Cf. C. P. Snow's March family, whom Sugana Ramanathan has described as 'on the surface completely assimilated but at the core tenacious about their Jewishness': see *The Novels of C. P. Snow: A Critical Introduction* (Macmillan, 1978), 23.

unusual for children of Joseph's class to sleep away from their parents during term-time, but his sense of isolation must have been increased by the fact that when he first arrived he was the youngest boy by a year. The earliest photograph of Joseph at the school gives a hint of his feelings; a tiny figure sitting at the extreme right of the front row, he seems both vulnerable and pugnacious. This gives added interest to a face which already shows signs of the handsome youth which Keith Joseph became. In later life he seems to have been proud of his childhood good looks; for a profile of senior Conservatives published in 1970 he was almost the only member of the Shadow Cabinet to supply old photographs.

Many years later, as Secretary of State for Education, Joseph noted the effects of racial bullying on school children. It could "sap the individual's self-confidence and ability to concentrate on their [sic] learning"; it attacked "much that the child holds dear – parents, the wider family, and the tradition in which he or she has been brought up".[35] The restrained language could mean either that he had never experienced this problem himself, or that he was struggling to distance himself from painful memories. The latter is far more likely. When interviewed in retirement, Joseph remembered that he had been subjected to "a certain amount of verbal bullying" at Lockers Park because he was a Jew. The school had been patronised for many years by affluent Jewish families; when Joseph first arrived the ten year-old Edmund de Rothschild was just two forms above him. But victimisation was common enough at prep schools, and the liberal outlook of the staff at Lockers Park could be no guarantee against anti-Semitic prejudices picked up by boys at home. A student of the Jewish experience in England has noted that Jewish youngsters at public schools "were made aware that they were not the same as everybody else", and sometimes this feeling was awakened with brutal violence. Edmund de Rothschild remembered being kicked at Lockers Park by the young thug who had been assigned to him as a "mentor". He was so traumatised that shortly afterwards he tried to jump out of an upstairs window. Edmund records that his tormentor called him "dirty little Jew"; by coincidence, his cousin Victor (later Lord Rothschild) had been welcomed to his own prep school, Stanmore Park, with kicks to the shins and the identical insulting remark. Victor Rothschild was disagreeably surprised by this treatment, since religion had scarcely figured in his previous life at home. A secular upbringing had given him no reason to feel very different from other boys, and this, coupled with his natural resilience, enabled him to bounce back. But Keith Joseph was a more sensitive child. Having begun life in an intense family environment he now knew how it felt to be an outsider.[36]

---

35. *Evening Standard*, 21 March 1984.
36. Halcrow, *Joseph*, 4; Endelman, *Radical Assimilation*, 98–100; Edmund de Rothschild, *A Gilt-Edged Life* (John Murray, 1998), 31; Lord Rothschild, *Meditations of a Broomstick* (Collins, 1977), 13.

When the Gentile narrator of *The Conscience of the Rich* first visits the home of the Anglo–Jewish March family he is far more impressed by the trappings of wealth than by any outward signs of their religious beliefs; yet he "had already seen the meaning which being Jews had for both Charles and Katherine [March]". In a later conversation Charles March makes that meaning explicit, telling his friend that:

> I haven't enjoyed being a Jew. Since I was a child I haven't been allowed to forget – that other people see me through different eyes. They label me with a difference that I can't accept. I know that I sometimes make myself feel a stranger, I know that very well. But still, other people have made me feel a stranger far more often than I have myself. It isn't their fault. It's simply a fact. But it's a fact that interferes with your spirits and nags at you. Sometimes it torments you – particularly when you're young.

March's "self-contempt" was a common reaction for young Jews in the face of "popular stereotypes and snobbish prejudice".[37] The best form of compensation for this acute discomfort was positive recognition by others. March confides that during his years at Cambridge he had been "aching . . . to be liked for the person I believed myself to be", and threw himself into the effort of making intimate friends. By the end of the novel March achieves something like a resolution of his inner torment, but he continues to feel a wound which the narrator recognises as being far keener than his own (relative) poverty. March undergoes a dramatic "conversion", and embarks on a new course under the spell of a woman with extreme political views. Without drawing too much significance from a work of fiction – even one that Keith admired – it seems reasonable to suggest that the self-revelations of Charles March struck a chord with him. One observer noted of the Joseph family that "The fact that they were rich and paternalist is more important than that they were Jewish". But, like Charles March, Keith Joseph seemed to be acutely aware that other people saw him "through different eyes". As a rising politician he was reported to have said that he felt the need to "fire on all six cylinders at once" because he was a Jew, and although he denied saying those exact words he once admitted that "It's the kind of remark I'd like to have made". Some early acquaintances sensed an "aching" for friendship (although unlike March Joseph was too reserved to make the first move towards intimacy).[38]

---

37. Snow, *Conscience*, 56–7, Endelman, *Radical Assimilation,* 101.
38. Snow, *Conscience*, 49; interview with Geoffrey Goodman; *Spectator*, 19 May 1979; private information. For "six cylinders" story see, for example, Michael Harrington, "Sir Keith Joseph", in T. Stacey & R. St Oswald (eds) *Here Come the Tories* (Tom Stacey, 1970), 78; interview with Morrison Halcrow; *The Times*, 18 January 1970. Other versions have him firing on "all *four* cylinders".

As Secretary of State for Education Joseph was convinced of the value of regular testing for children, and fortunately for the historian Lockers Park took the same view. Throughout his time at the school he was among the youngest of his class, but in December 1928 he was placed eleventh out of thirteen for his overall work, finishing below four boys of comparable age. After a sluggish start there seems to have been a spurt; he was placed second out of his whole class in July 1929, and in July 1930 he had climbed to the top. This remarkable intellectual boom was followed by a spectacular slump; he was bottom of his class list in September 1930, at the time of his thirteenth birthday in January 1931 he was back in eleventh out of thirteen, and on the final league table of his Lockers Park career (May 1931) he had only struggled up to eighth of twelve.[39]

Joseph's lowly final position in the class lists is probably a sign that he could not complete all of the work assigned to him. On top form he was as able as any other boy in the school; he came second in the spelling competition of December 1930, and won this outright in March 1931. Illness is the most likely explanation for his erratic performance. Along with their obvious advantages establishments like Lockers Park offered their inmates something like a crash course in childhood maladies, and the intrusion of a more serious bug could bring the normal life of a school to a halt. For example, the *Lockers Park Magazine* for the summer term of 1931 reports a serious epidemic of whooping cough, which, along with injuries to outstanding players, hampered the performance of the school's cricket teams after the first two matches. Keith Joseph was among the victims; he "was unable to play at all after the first three weeks". But the whooping cough outbreak of 1931 cannot explain a decline in academic performance which had begun in the previous autumn, and the *Lockers Park Magazine* shows that while he was struggling in the classroom Joseph was taking part in other activities which would have been ruled out by a virus.[40]

A Lockers Park pupil of the previous generation was Basil Henriques (born 1890), who later became a noted philanthropist and a champion of Liberal Judaism. Although no instances of bullying are recorded in his biography, he was plagued by "digestive problems" when he attended the school. The trouble recurred later, when he attended Harrow School and Oxford University. Almost certainly the underlying cause was nervous tension.[41] This kind of problem is often concealed by sufferers, both at the time and in later years. But there is good evidence to suggest that Joseph was afflicted by a similiar condition – more of a threat to long-term contentment than childhood coughs and sneezes. When Joseph left Harrow John Brocklehurst, a boy from his House (Moretons) noted that "most of his illness was of his own invention.

---

39. Academic records held in Lockers Park School archives.
40. *Lockers Park School Magazine 1930–1*, 24.
41. L. L. Loewe, *Basil Henriques: A Portrait* (Routledge & Kegan Paul, 1976), 7.

This is borne out by the fact that when he became more self-confident during his last two years, he was hardly ill at all". Rather than "inventing" his difficulties, Joseph was displaying classic symptoms of a psychosomatic disorder. Although he was far more reticent in later life than other Jews who were miserable at Lockers Park, their testimony, combined with Joseph's startling academic inconsistency, is enough to suggest that his long history of ill-health began at that school.[42]

Joseph took part in most of the activities offered by Lockers Park. In December 1930 he acted in a French play, *Un Quartier Tranquille*, which provided a typical opportunity for prep school cross-dressing. Joseph received a favourable notice for his portrayal of Anastasie, "a very amusing maid, whose imperturbable nature drove her mistress almost frantic".[43] He specialised in serving wenches; at Harrow he played a similar (and virtually mute) role in *The Merry Wives of Windsor*. Apparently he did not excel at boxing but at least he took part, and he played the special Harrow brand of football (see below) for the school Second XI. In the summer of 1929 he could finish no better than third in an egg-and-spoon race; perhaps this was just a shade too frivolous for a contemplative boy. Yet Joseph did show a lighter side to his character at Lockers Park. In the school *Magazine* of Christmas 1928–9 a poem entitled "Ode to Lockers Park" appeared under the names of Keith Joseph and a school fellow, A. F. A. Carlisle. A set of couplets based on the alphabet, the poem celebrates the more illustrious members of the school in a jaunty doggerel style typified by the opening lines:

A's for the alphabet, which now I begin,
B's for the boys, who inhabit therein[44]

Superficially, this juvenile exercise suggests that Joseph had adapted to life at the school. But if he did become more happy over time, the damage caused by initial misery could recur at even a minor provocation; and both in subject matter and style the poem can be interpreted as an attempt to "fit in". This might also explain his participation in such unlikely activities as boxing and egg-and-spoon racing; feeling vulnerable for other reasons, he would be anxious to take part in every physical activity to avoid being branded as "wet", like so many public school weaklings. Even if he was accepted in time, a concerted strategy of this kind could

---

42. John Brocklehurst's assessment of Keith was written in the Moretons House Book for 1935–8, held in Harrow School archives.

43. *Lockers Park School Magazine 1930–1*, 7–8.

44. "An Ode to Lockers Park", *Lockers Park School Magazine*, Winter Term 1928–9, 10. Carlisle went up to Harrow with Joseph, but was placed in a different House – in those institutions, tantamount to a severance of previous friendship. But when Joseph joined the Heath Cabinet in 1970 his poetic collaborator was Deputy Chief of Economic Intelligence at the Bank of England.

become an ingrained habit, and in the closed environment of a boarding school there could be no escape from the stress.

Yet Joseph was resourceful enough to seek distractions from his troubles. Even at this early age he had become obsessed with cricket. In lamenting his absence for most of the 1931 season, the *Lockers Park Magazine* noted that he had "promised to be the best bat in the XI". The scorecards support this view to some extent; on 2 July 1930 he notched up an undefeated 67 in a match against Elstree, and he reached double figures on two other occasions. But his cricketing exploits fluctuated as wildly as his academic efforts; in the remaining matches before the advent of whooping cough his successive scores were 0, 1, 0, 0, 1, and 0. Joseph, it seems, would invariably march to the crease with aggressive intentions; provided that he survived the first couple of deliveries he would serve his team well, but it was more likely that his dashing approach would bring about a rapid departure. Fortunately for a boy with a mania for the game, his active participation would not close with a forlorn trudge back to the pavilion. He was an agile fieldsman, and a match rarely passed without him taking at least one catch. He also bowled occasionally, with an "unorthodox" action which one observer has compared with that of Bob Willis, the England paceman of the 1970s and 1980s.[45]

Recently it has become fashionable for historians to argue that at least part of the reason for Britain's twentieth-century decline was the tendency of successful businessmen to send their children to public schools in order to turn them into the sort of "gentlemen" whose hallmark was a disdain for entrepreneurial activity. The theory appealed very strongly to Keith Joseph himself.[46] But Bovis had won many contracts through the ability of its senior executives to charm potential clients, and Samuel Joseph must have calculated that his son would be of greater value to the firm if he learned upper-class manners with the offspring of rich men. Lockers Park was something of a nursery for Harrow; of the ten boys who left the school with Keith Joseph in May 1931, four were heading for the same North London destination. They reached their new residence before Joseph, who did not arrive until early in 1932. He spent at least part of the interval with a "crammer" to help him recover the ground which he had lost in his final months at Lockers Park.

Stories about the experience of Jewish boys at Harrow would not have improved Joseph's appetite for the school. Charles de Rothschild, who attended in the 1890s, wrote after his escape that "If ever I have a son he will be instructed in boxing and ju-jitsu before he enters school, as Jew-hunts such as

---

45. *Ibid.*, 24; detailed scorecards held in Lockers Park School archives; letter to the authors from Hugh Lee.
46. For a brilliant exposition of this thesis, see Correlli Barnett, *The Collapse of British Power*, (Eyre Methuen, 1972); also Martin Weiner, *English Culture and the Decline of the Industrial Spirit 1850–1980* (Pelican, 1985).

I experienced are very one-sided amusement". From his experience in the following decade Jawaharlal Nehru – a very sensitive witness – recalled that "there was always a background of anti-semitic feeling" among the boys. Victor Rothschild, who attended the school in the 1920s, hinted at "many hideous aspects of life at Harrow".[47] But these were not the barbarous days of the 1850s, when new boys of all faiths and of none were hung up by their heels in front of the fire and "roasted". Keith Joseph's time at Harrow coincided with the rise of Hitler in Germany and the rioting associated with Oswald Mosley in England. It would be unrealistic to suppose that anti-Semitic feelings were unknown in the school during the 1930s, but it seems that the boys now refrained from any violent manifestations of their feelings towards "outsiders". Provision for Jewish worship had been allowed (rather grudgingly) in Victor Rothschild's time; Joseph attended both the Anglican chapel and "a classroom known as the Tin Tabernacle". He could hardly have avoided some bullying at Harrow, but his suffering was probably little worse than that of other boys subjected to the system known as "fagging". This custom took different forms in the various Harrow Houses; among the duties remembered by Joseph's contemporaries were lighting fires, running errands, waiting at table, cleaning shoes and making toast for the older House Monitors (the prefects) who were the lords of that small piece of earth. Some boys fared much worse at the hands of their school fellows, who had plenty of opportunities for a range of sadistic practices in the first year when four would share a room. But no one remembers that Joseph was singled out in this way, and although in one letter, written when he was a senior boy, he gave a sympathetic account of a bullied child who screamed in his sleep he offered no hint that he had ever been in a similar plight.[48]

Victor Rothschild has left some light-hearted anecdotes about homosexual practices – at which his own Harrow contemporary and fellow opening batsman Terence Rattigan was adept. From his letters it seems that Joseph was no different from most adolescents isolated at public school from mixed company. He was quite prepared to indulge in banter, but a letter which includes a jocular reference to "the usual crop of minor offences" shows that his real preferences lay elsewhere. Just after his eighteenth birthday he met the twenty year-old cousin of a friend and boasted that "as far as I can make out, there was mutual 'clicking'". The girl had promised to visit Harrow again soon, an encounter anticipated with relish by Joseph who considered her to be "the goods!"[49]

47. Endleman, *Radical Assimilation*, 98–9; Rothschild, *Broomstick*, 14.
48. Viscount Templewood, *The Unbroken Thread* (Collins, 1949), 141; Information supplied by John Campbell, Madron Seligman, William Blake and Hugh Lee; KJ to Michael Hargreave, 12 February 1936 (letters in private possession; we are most grateful to Major Hargreave for allowing us to consult this correspondence). The boy who cried in his sleep was Peter Minoprio, who years later joined the Conservative Research Department and worked closely with Joseph.
49. Rothschild, *Broomstick*, 14; KJ to Michael Hargreave, 31 January 1936.

Academically Joseph was more consistent at Harrow than he had been at Lockers Park, although there were two hiccups – evidence of "invented" illness, perhaps – when he was "not placed" in the Easter examinations of 1932 and 1933. Like the other boys, he followed a curriculum in the lower school comprising Divinity, English, history, geography, Latin, French, mathematics and science. Much to his subsequent regret, he learned very little from the latter course of instruction. Later he specialised in modern languages. Until the upper fifth he hovered on the edge of the top five in his class; in the school certificate exams which occupied his final two years he was rated as Class II. None of his marks indicated that he would win first-class honours at university. Joseph's perform- ance was accurately summarised by his friend John Brocklehurst, in the informal "report" he wrote to mark his departure from the school: "His brain, though not anything out of the ordinary, was above the average, and he always worked hard". His most notable achievement came within his first year, when he secured the Shakespeare Prize for the Lower School. This involved memorising a passage from Shakespeare and reciting it in the Speech Room, a magnificent building modelled on a Greek theatre. The prize had eluded Winston Churchill; that great Old Harrovian, then languishing on the Westminster back-benches, had only come fourth. Keith Joseph won another similar award, the Crompton Prize for clear speaking; but he was no match for his old friend from Lockers Park, A. F. A. Carlisle, who left Harrow with at least five prizes and scholarships. Joseph did win approval for his general conduct, being appointed in his final year as one of Harrow's petty tyrants – the Monitors. Even this was clouded by a slight setback. A few days before securing the honour he had been disappointed in his hope to be chosen as at least Second Head of Moretons House. Joseph was remembered as an easy-going Monitor, taking his leniency so far as to light his own fire. One of the privileges which came with his new status was the right to cycle around the whole of Harrow Hill. Informing a friend that he had taken advantage of this and bought himself a bike "of incredible size" he added, typically, that he must have looked "a hell of a fool" while riding it.[50]

As at most of Britain's public schools sport was a central aspect of life at Harrow, and could provide an easy route to popularity. Activities included swimming, musketry and the variety of football unique to the school. Harrow football had been devised because the playing fields were often waterlogged; the school invented the word "soccer" to distinguish the more familiar game from its own version. The ball, "the shape of a much flattened globe", was larger than a football; a "base" was scored when this object was kicked at any height between two upright posts. The rules combined some of those from both rugby

---

50. Records in Harrow School archives; Randolph S. Churchill, *Winston S. Churchill: Volume I, Youth 1874–1900* (Heinemann, 1966), 118; KJ to Michael Hargreave, undated letter of 1936, letter of 31 January 1936 (correspondence in private possession); correspondence between authors and Hugh Lee.

and soccer, but no contact between players was allowed. One of Keith Joseph's contemporaries recalled that long stretches of the game would be occupied by the opposing full-backs hoofing the ball to one another across the field, to the exclusion of other players. But Joseph was able to dribble with the ball in one of the House matches of his final year, and his "inspired" performance was recognised by the award of a fez with a tassel on it. Despite this exploit Brocklehurst considered that Joseph was "not a great athlete", and noted that he had been disappointed by a narrow failure to be picked for Moretons' rugby team.[51]

Not surprisingly, Brocklehurst recorded that Joseph's "best game was cricket, and this he took very seriously". Even so, "he was not a born cricketer", and battled against this handicap "by dint of hard work and concentration". The obvious goal for any Harrow schoolboy with cricketing ambitions was to play for the First XI against Eton at Lords; in 1929 this had been achieved by Victor Rothschild, who included cricket amongst his improbable array of gifts. In his attempts to reach the required standard Joseph could depend on help from the former England star Wilfred Rhodes, at that time a member of the Harrow staff. Not even the best coach could overcome defects of temperament; an earlier pupil, Sir Samuel Hoare (later Viscount Templewood) took extra lessons during the school holidays but in matches he was crippled by "over-anxiety". In the case of Keith Joseph the evidence is inconclusive; in fifth form House matches he was accused of too frequently losing his wicket "playing careless and stupid shots", which might have been inspired either by too much or too little anxiety. His record for Moretons House in his last two years was fairly unimpressive; he always got off the mark and his highest score was 47, but out of ten innings four ended in single-figure scores. Much later he recalled that he was captain of the school second team, but his performances at that higher level were no better, the apparent highlight being a knock of 23 against Dulwich which was brought to an end by a run-out.[52]

According to friends Joseph was frustrated by his shortcomings, and given his craving for recognition his failure to play for the Harrow First XI must have been a significant blow. But instead of quenching his love of cricket the disappointment seems to have driven it to a new intensity. Some of his remarks leave the impression that his feelings went beyond a desire to excel at a gentleman's game, and that at one time he dreamed of a career as a professional "player". In 1973 Joseph told Anthony King that he no longer played the game, and had even stopped following it in the newspapers. But the armchair interest, at least, seems to have been rekindled when the pressure of ministerial life was removed. Morrison Halcrow remembered that when he discussed cricket after

51. Information contained in Harrow School Prospectus; letter to authors from John Campbell.
52. Templewood, *Unbroken Thread*, 143; cricketing records in Harrow School archives.

his retirement from the political field Joseph's eyes would become unusually bright. They must have gleamed when he related how in two innings at Harrow he struck sixes off the first ball he faced. His memory cannot be tested against the existing scorecards, which lack detail, but it confirms the impression of a cavalier cricketer.[53]

After Harrow Keith Joseph knew that he would never play cricket for England, but in other respects when he left in the summer of 1936 his career options had been greatly increased. Rather than bearing out the theory that the ethos of the public school was antagonistic towards private enterprise, Joseph planned only a slight deviation from his father's path. Brocklehurst stated with (misplaced) confidence that "he is to be an architect". Beyond his choice of profession, Joseph had been groomed by Harrow as one of society's future leaders. If political ambitions developed in him over the coming years his school had provided a very solid foundation. After listing the cricketing stars nurtured by Harrow some school boys might have remembered that the nineteenth century Prime Ministers Spencer Perceval, Sir Robert Peel, Lord Aberdeen and Lord Palmerston had also been there. A more recent inmate, Stanley Baldwin, had been flogged as the author of some juvenile pornography. Even so, in 1923 Baldwin told his successors at the school that he had made it a priority as Prime Minister to form "a Government of which Harrow should not be ashamed"; apart from himself there were five old Harrovians in his first cabinet. When Keith Joseph left the school Baldwin was Prime Minister once again.[54]

The list of Harrovian politicians is hardly a roll-call of radicalism, but the school which produced Lord Byron could not be described as a production line for conformity. A plaque which Joseph must have passed almost every day at the school supposedly records the spot where, in the early-nineteenth century, the young Anthony Ashley Cooper, later famous as the philanthropic Lord Shaftesbury, witnessed "with shame and indignation" a pauper's funeral (the "indignation" was provoked by the drunken state of several mourners rather than their rags). Towards the end of his life Keith Joseph revealed that he had been exposed to poverty as a very young boy at his first school in London. Every day he had seen the same beggar in the area of Sloane Square, and regularly sneaked food out of his house to feed the man. Although Shaftesbury was always a Tory, times had changed and this type of youthful social concern fitted Keith Joseph into the mould of another ex-public schoolboy – Clement Attlee, who became

---

53. KJ interview with Anthony King; interview with Morrison Halcrow; Halcrow, *Joseph*, 4.
54. Stanley Baldwin, *On England* (Philip Allen, 1927), 267. During Joseph's own Cabinet career Harrow had less reason for pride. In his first spell (1962–4) only two of his colleagues (William Deedes and John Profumo) had been to the school. Joseph was a minister for a further eleven years (1970–4, 1979–86), but during that period he was the only Harrow representative in the Cabinet.

leader of the Labour Party in 1935. The resemblance continued during Joseph's stay at Harrow. The school had a mission in London's East End, which he visited (though "not to excess"), and in March 1936 he told a friend that "to salve my conscience, I intend to do some sort of social work" in Eastbourne over the holidays. Beneath his light-hearted phrases in this letter there is a more earnest note of self-criticism: "I feel I might as well try to do something for somebody other than myself for once". For the time being, however, Joseph showed no sign of wanting to "salve his conscience" through political activity.[55]

John Brocklehurst concluded his long essay on the departing Keith Joseph with a sunny prediction: "Whatever he does, he will make a success of it". Samuel Joseph must have thought that his money – over £200 a year in fees alone – had been wisely invested, and the fact that Keith sent his own son to Harrow is an indication that he retained a high opinion of the school. Yet the detail of Brocklehurst's appraisal offered grounds for further consideration. Certainly his first words were at variance with the optimism of his conclusion. "K. S. Joseph", he wrote, "was rather an enigma the whole time he was here". Having rehearsed the story of Joseph's regular illnesses, his sporting activities and his prizes, Brocklehurst observed that:

> At first he was thought to be rather "priggish", and though he got over that, he never cured his greatest fault properly. This was that he would take everything far too seriously. Whenever he talked, he would talk seriously rather than listen to or try to make lighter conversation. Anything of this kind seemed to bore him all too soon. This is not to suggest that he was entirely lacking any sense of humour. It merely means that he preferred to be serious [rather] than frivolous. This caused him to be rather misunderstood by those who did not know him well, and who sometimes were embarrassed by his frankness and his apparent inability or unwillingness to discuss any topics other than intimate ones.

Evidently Brocklehurst had difficulty in giving up his attempt to unravel the "enigma" that was Keith Joseph. He went on to offer the distinctly double-edged opinion that his friend:

> was a good actor, off the stage as well as on, and gave the impression that he was acting most of the time he was talking to one, perhaps to create an effect, or to drive his point home. He was conscious of his serious outlook on life, and though it was not the least derogatory to him, he was always trying to get over it. It did, in actual fact, lead to fits of depression and nerves, which did not help him.

---

55. Halcrow, *Joseph*, 3; KJ to Michael Hargreave, 15 March 1936.

Most of the profile-writers of the 1970s and 1980s groped towards similar conclusions about a person who sustained with uncanny accuracy Wordsworth's dictum that the child is the father to the man. Unfortunately Brocklehurst's penetrating analysis breaks off at this point. The penultimate paragraph adopts a more cheering mood:

> However, [in] his last two or three terms – he was made a Monitor in 1936 – he came on enormously, and made a number of friends, including several very intimate ones, among whom I am more than glad to count my name. I think in conclusion I can fairly say that Harrow did him good, and that Harrow is better for having had him.

Of all the faults that Keith Joseph could have brought away from Harrow, taking everything too seriously might be regarded as a very minor peccadillo. But Brocklehurst had portrayed an introverted young man, who had overcome his difficulties only to the extent that he could relax when his status was assured and when he was in the company of his closest friends. It was said at Harrow that Joseph paid the local barber five extra shillings per term for refraining from conversation while he was cutting his hair.[56] He wanted to be popular, but his natural reserve, combined with definite ideas about propriety in relations with others, meant that outside his intimate circle he could be seen as prim and humourless. As a defence mechanism he had adopted an exaggerated style of self-deprecation which would not always be taken as a sign of genuine humility. This was the key element of what Brocklehurst described as "acting" – the only point, incidentally, which was missed by the many journalists who tried to solve the Joseph enigma. But while Joseph may have been aware of his own foibles, effecting a real change in his character was another matter. The underlying reasons for his unease – his Jewish origins, an exaggerated feeling of under-achievement, and a vague sense of guilt which accompanied his privileged upbringing – would always lurk beneath the superficial polish which his character acquired at Lockers Park and Harrow.

---

56. Letter to authors from Hugh Lee.

Chapter Two

Triumph and Tragedy

Samuel Joseph had provided his only child with a head-start in life, but he had no thought of sitting back and exulting in the glorious prospects of the next generation. Samuel was occupied with his own course, and had been driving hard on at least six cylinders ever since he left school. As a politician Sir Keith Joseph liked to refer to those who worked too hard as "the ulcer people". This label would do less than justice to Samuel, who by the 1930s could already be identified as a "heart-attack person". Sir Keith remembered that his father was struck down several times by such life-threatening illnesses, but Samuel was not the kind of man to be deterred by bodily weakness.[1]

Samuel Joseph's temperament was not ideally suited to every aspect of public service; for example, the full details of contracts won by Bovis in the 1920s were never recorded in the minutes of board meetings because he found that kind of bureaucratic practice "excessively tedious". But his other qualities overrode any petty drawbacks. In standing as a candidate for office in London Samuel was arguably furthering his firm's interests to some extent, but the overall impression is that of a man with a high estimation of his abilities and an equal determination to place them at the disposal of his fellow citizens, whether or not he received any material reward. It was a dominant family trait.

---

1. Halcrow, *Joseph*, 5.

Surrounded by so many people who shared that outlook, the young Keith Joseph could be forgiven for assuming that a zest for public service was a common (if not universal) human characteristic.[2]

In this race the Glucksteins had made the early running; they were represented on Westminster City Council as early as 1906. Samuel began his attempt to catch up in the Bovis heartland of St Marylebone. In 1922 he was elected to the Borough Council, and he served twice as Mayor of St Marylebone (in 1928 and 1930). The flotation of Bovis in 1928 transferred his attention to the City of London; a member of the Cutlers' Company, he was admitted to the Freedom of the City in April 1929. Two years later he became a Common Councilman for the Castle Baynard ward, a position he held until October 1933 when he moved another step up the ladder, being chosen to represent the ward of Portsoken as one of its two Aldermen in succession to another member of London's Jewish community, Isidore Nathan Jacobs. The mainly residential Portsoken ward lay on the extreme south-east of the City – indeed, it was outside the walls and only returned Aldermen due to a medieval dispensation. But it bordered on the Whitechapel area which had a strong connection with London Jewry and with the Gluckstein–Joseph families in particular; it contained Petticoat Lane, where Abraham Joseph had once worked. The fact that Abraham had recently died added to the poignancy of his son's election.

Despite the world economic slump and the decision of the National Government to take Britain off the gold standard in 1931, London retained its leading position as a financial centre; as a building contractor Bovis had shared in its prosperity during the 1920s. Samuel's elevation to the position of Alderman gave extra prestige to the company, to compensate for the additional call on his time. As a magistrate Samuel again showed symptoms of irritation against inflexible procedures, along with an occasional dash of social compassion. During the Second World War, for example, he presided over the case of a middle-aged woman accused of stealing a few items of clothing. The woman was distressed, and Samuel protested against the police's "distasteful" decision to keep such a minor offender on remand in prison.[3]

Before he joined the Court of Aldermen Samuel had taken on an even heavier responsibility. In June 1933 an election took place for two Sheriffs of London, each to serve for one year. There were three candidates for the positions; Samuel Joseph, Alderman Jacobs, and Mr Arthur Leonard Bateman, MP. With 2,698 votes Samuel topped the poll, followed by Jacobs with 2,581. Bateman, the Unionist MP for North Camberwell, attracted only 489 votes.

The margin of his defeat was a humiliation for Bateman, who had served in London local government and was a Freeman of the City. Having based his

---

2. Cooper, *Building Relationships*, 36.
3. *City Press*, 4 June 1944.

campaign on anti-Semitism, Bateman's sole consolation was that the result could be presented as proof that his conspiracy theories were true. After the figures had been released he advertised his hatred of Jews while attempting to disguise his bitter disappointment at the result:

> I am not complaining. I am going to the House of Commons to tell the Attorney-General and Mr Ramsay MacDonald that I will stand again next year – even though they put another two Jews against me.
>
> The position is getting serious. I tell you we have lost the City of London to the Jews. They will hold it.
>
> Before long we shall have to declare war on them as they have done in Germany . . .
>
> Do you realise that they had 100-odd cars against my 28? Do you realise that the whole of Jewry was organised against me?
>
> If things do not change I am going to talk as Mosley talks, and, if necessary, I shall change my party.
>
> But, mark you, I'm not complaining at losing . . .

Bateman's extreme views and volatile temperament had ensured his defeat. In an editorial comment the *City Press* claimed that the final outburst could "have only one effect – that of increasing the feeling of indignation aroused by [Bateman's] attitude in recent weeks". The real "war" against the Jews in Germany had scarcely begun, but Hitler was consolidating his power as Chancellor and his intentions were well known in London. A month before the poll the *Press* carried a report of a speech by another MP, Walter Greaves-Lord, who described Bateman's conduct as "horrible" and invited the City to elect Joseph and Jacobs in order to confirm its belief that "Whether a man be Jew or Gentile, so long as he is a true and loyal citizen, he is equally entitled to Civic rank". Yet the newspaper's report from the election painted the failed candidate in a more flattering light: "He never flinched or gave the least sign of concern. The Livery was opposed to him. No one can say that he did not show pluck!" The reporter noted the City's long tradition of religious toleration – the first Jewish Lord Mayor had taken office back in 1855 – but instead of presenting a positive case for the principle he merely described religion as "a matter fraught with such dreadful possibilities that no one who has even a glimmering of historical knowledge would lightly raise it".[4]

Whether or not a sizeable proportion of his audience privately agreed with him Bateman had ended his chances of advancement in the City. He carried out his threat to stand again in October 1933, when Jacobs, who had been ailing at the

---

4. *City Press,* 12 May, 30 June 1933. See also Richard Griffiths, *Fellow Travellers of the Right: British Enthusiasts for Nazi Germany 1933–39* (Oxford University Press, 1983), 82.

time of the June election, stood down. Despite the absence of Jewish candidates in the field this time Bateman was even more heavily defeated, finishing a distant last of the five who stood. In the following year he tried again, with a similar result, and he lost his parliamentary seat in 1935. But Bateman had merely given voice to a belief which was held far beyond the East End that provided Oswald Mosley with his rowdiest recruits. His nomination papers had been signed by six Conservative MPs – and by Field Marshall Lord Allenby. The views of this broader racist constituency are expressed by the well-heeled lawyer Herbert Getcliffe in *The Conscience of the Rich,* when he informs the narrator that "The boys on the Jewish upper deck are doing a bit of pulling together. Don't you wish you were in that racket . . .?". In referring to the number of cars placed at the disposal of supporters of Jacobs and Joseph, Bateman was identifying the contest as another example of the "Jewish upper deck" "pulling together". He expected that those who read his remarks would equate the cars with wealth, and conclude that Jacobs and Joseph had bought their positions. In real terms this meant nothing more than that Bateman's opponents were more popular and better organised; few City electors would have lacked the means to transport themselves to the poll.[5]

Some might have quailed before Bateman's onslaught, and the wider swamp of ill-feeling which it symbolised, but Samuel Joseph was contemptuous of prejudice whether vocal or unspoken. He explained his personal approach to racist bigotry during the Second World War, in a letter to a Jewish woman who had overheard anti-Semitic comments while queueing for a new ration book. Someone in the line expressed her hopes "that Hitler would come over and burn all the Jews", and that "the Jews little knew what was coming to them when the War was over". Presumably these sentiments had been voiced in the full knowledge that there were Jews in the queue; they reflected a widespread belief that Jews were making profits on the black market, and that Jewish shop-keepers gave preferential treatment to their co-religionist customers. Samuel was quite sympathetic to the outraged feelings of his correspondent, but his reply also contained a reproach for her passive response at the time:

if, with your experience, you come up against such an incident again . . . you should immediately open up a conversation and ask what justification such an individual has for making such remarks. You should say that you would very much like the opportunity to discuss the matter with her, and as many others as would like to join in the discussion. It is[,] I am positive, absolutely necessary to grab any statement of such a nature wildly made, and nail it to the mast instantly. For a Jew to hide behind somebody else because he is afeared of criticism is the weakest and most

---

5. Snow, *Conscience*, 46.

absurd reply . . . No – I have nothing but contempt for the paltry, absurd slogans which the ignorant people spread, and it is up to the person who does know, to refute them in a bold, open and clear manner.[6]

This was magnificent stuff – even if in practice it would call for much more than common courage. Regrettably, it seems that even Samuel made a trivial compromise when the pressure was at its greatest. In 1937, with the German Nazis confiscating Jewish-owned businesses and thousands of East End voters registering their support for Mosley's anti-Semitism in London's municipal elections, several of the Bovis chiefs decided to change their names for reasons of personal security. Some of their efforts seem rather comical today; but these were practical men, and their move must be regarded as a symptom of rising panic. Sidney Gluckstein became Sidney Glyn, possibly because of the proximity of these surnames in the London telephone book. His brother Vincent Gluckstein was even less original; he was known in the firm as "Mr Vincent", so he dubbed himself "Vincent Vincent". Another brother, Samuel Gluckstein, refused to change his name but his sons decided to relaunch themselves as Harry and Neville Vincent.[7] At the time of his birth Samuel Joseph's middle name was recorded as "Gluckstein", and he was still using this at least as late as 1929; but by the late 1930s he was known as Sir Samuel George Joseph (having been knighted after his term as Sheriff). In Sir Samuel's defence it must be allowed that he would have been an unusual family member had he not changed his name at some point. Coenraad Sammes' switch to the surname Joseph set a precedent for his son Tobias, who decided that he would prefer to be known as Josiah Joseph. Evidently there was some resistance to the name Isaiah, which was discarded by two family members, including Sir Samuel's brother Bertie.

Keith Joseph, at Harrow when the Shrieval election took place, must have been aware of the unpleasant circumstances whether or not his family kept him informed, since Bateman's inflammatory speech was reported in the national press. His immediate reaction is unknown, but it probably did little to change his position at the school – it may even have increased his desire to invite friends into his home. During 1936 his letters reveal a sensitivity to the situation of Jews abroad. When a friend went to live in Munich for a few months to learn German Keith suggested that he might come over for a visit, but wanted to know "as soon as you discover it, the reaction to Jews in Germany". In another letter he wondered half-jokingly what "general reaction there would be if I was announced by my surname at a public function there?". But there was no move to change his name to Keith Sinjohn Keith.[8]

---

6. Mansion House Papers, 10a, 11, Elsa Cohn to Samuel Joseph, 3 March 1943; Samuel's reply, 7 March 1943.
7. Cooper, *Building Relationships*, 62.
8. KJ to Michael Hargreave, 12 February 1936.

In April 1936 Joseph sat the entrance examination for Magdalen College, Oxford, cheerfully telling his friends that he expected to fail. His forecast was inaccurate, and he went up to study for a degree in Jurisprudence. This was a surprising choice for an aspiring architect, although a qualification in law would do no harm for a more general career in business and his older cousin Louis Gluckstein had taken the same degree. Following Louis' example turned out to be the most significant choice of Keith Joseph's early life.[9]

Magdalen College did not enjoy a high reputation for the teaching of law in the mid-1930s. This situation changed with the election in 1936 of John Morris as a college Fellow and Tutor. Morris, a young man who had won an Oxford First and practised for a short time at the Bar, was an excellent teacher whose lectures "were models of lucidity, elegance and intellectual rigour". He demanded hard work – indeed, his *Times* obituarist claimed that without realising it "he could be terrifying to his pupils" – yet he was always ready with sympathy when they encountered difficulties on academic or personal matters. This dominating "father figure" must have held special attractions for Keith Joseph; anecdotes about his own treatment of students in later years suggest that he based his variety of "teaching" on Morris's approach. No doubt the feeling was reciprocal to some extent, since most tutors retain memories of their first promising students and Joseph had far more aptitude for the subject than the four other Magdalen men who took the degree with him. According to another obituarist, Morris "was proud of the achievements of his former pupils; he liked to make lists of those who held high judicial office or who had achieved success in other fields". Keith Joseph's career must have given him special pleasure, even when his former charge became Education Secretary and helped to provoke a rebellious mood in Oxford. Just three months after Morris's death in 1984, the University refused to award an honorary degree to Margaret Thatcher.[10]

Long after his schooldays were over Joseph implied that he had not worked very hard at Harrow because he felt no pressure to excel academically; he thought that he had only done well at Magdalen because he had "caught up with his reading during vacations". These self-appraisals sound like the typical apologies of the person who, years after the event, is still fearful of being branded as the school swot. John Brocklehurst had testified that Joseph "always worked hard" at Harrow to compensate for an intelligence which was "above the average" without being extraordinary. Of his life at Oxford one is forced to conclude that unless Joseph studied hard during term time he must have struggled to fill up the days. Sport could keep him occupied to some extent; an admiring friend remembers him going for early morning runs, there would be

---

9. KJ to Michael Hargreave, 16 April 1936.
10. *The Times*, 2 October 1984; obituary of John Morris by Sir Guenter Treitel, *Magdalen College Record*, 1985.

a certain amount of cricket in the summer, and he played a little "soccer", tennis and squash.[11] Joseph maintained his interest in acting, calling the theatre his "weekly debauch and relaxation". But the surviving evidence shows that, if anything, he had more distractions from work during his holidays. In an undated letter, probably from his first term, he told a friend that he was "going on a farm next holidays – I mean that I am going to do some sort of work: – it may be building, you know, laying bricks". The same letter also discussed plans for convivial meetings as soon as term was over. During the 1936 Christmas holiday he asked the friend to stay with him at the Grand Hotel, Eastbourne; an Oxford acquaintance was already there.[12]

Other recollections of Joseph's conduct at Oxford echo the more positive aspects of Brocklehurst's Harrow report. One cloud which threatened briefly at school had been kept at bay: Joseph was not considered to be at all "priggish". But the overwhelming characteristic was still serious-mindedness; "he did not partake in rowdy undergraduate parties, prevalent in pre-war days", and Robert Blake remembered that he had already "acquired a certain tortured expression".[13] Another serious-minded youth, Edward Heath of Balliol College, was busily engaged in music and student politics, but Joseph used neither of these outlets for his surplus time. As a schoolboy Heath had excelled at almost every academic subject; yet, deciding to broaden his activities at Oxford, he could scarcely dream of securing a First. Keith Joseph had been a good second-rater at Harrow, but now, thanks to his enthusiastic tutor and his own application, he laid the first bricks of an intellectual reputation. He was so enthusiastic about his subject that he conceived an interest in a career at the Bar; apparently his architectural ambitions were now forgotten.[14]

Joseph's correct behaviour at Magdalen persisted throughout his three years there. It seems that he spurned the opportunity for even a one-off under-graduate caper, and there is no record of any serious flirtations while his fellow student of Jurisprudence, Woodrow Wyatt of Worcester College, was spending most of his time in amorous adventures. Keith Joseph's lack of interest in undergraduate politics was surprising, leaving aside any assumptions based on his later career. Between 1936 and 1939 the Oxford Union was particularly vibrant, featuring such notable near-contemporaries as Edward Heath, Denis Healey and Roy Jenkins. Joseph's Harrow friend Madron Seligman, a year behind him at Balliol, was very keen and eventually rose to the Union presidency. But although they remained in touch Seligman's feelings failed to infect Joseph. During one vacation Joseph stayed with a miner's family near

---

11. Halcrow, *Joseph*, 4; letter to authors from Lord Blake. Even so, one of his Magdalen friends could not remember Joseph taking the slightest interest in sport, and was astonished when he learned that his old friend had been a member of the MCC; interview with Greig Barr.
12. KJ to Michael Hargreave, undated letters of 1936, letter of 27 December 1936.
13. Letters to authors from the Earl of Lisburne and Lord Blake.
14. Letter to authors from Lord Blake.

Rotherham as part of a project organised by a Quaker group; this practical experience of poverty, he told Morrison Halcrow, had a similar effect on him to his early encounters with the beggar in Sloane Square. Working for a week in the mine produced admiration for (if not an intimate understanding of) those who existed under conditions which he had only read about.[15]

Joseph seems to have been fairly popular at Oxford but his attempts to fit in with at least one convivial group of undergraduates were only successful to a point. One of his Magdalen contemporaries was the left-wing Andrew Shonfield, later renowned as a Keynesian economist. According to Shonfield's widow Zuzanna, Joseph (one of the fortunate few to possess a car) was persuaded to drive several enthusiasts for Republican Spain to greet some refugees who had arrived at Harwich. During the journey Joseph "seemed to exude benevolence and a desire to participate but simply didn't understand much of what these left-wingers were talking about, and he certainly couldn't join in the songs they sang in the car".[16]

It seems that this was another illustration of Joseph's combination of a desire for close friendship and an excessive timidity which obstructed any overt display of his feelings. The left-wing jargon might have acted as an extra deterrent, but he understood the issues under discussion. Although there is no precise date for the incident it must have taken place at a time when events in Spain were engrossing the attention even of the most insular undergraduates. And Joseph was certainly not insular. The family was capable of venturing beyond Eastbourne in the holiday season, and Switzerland was a favourite destination ("Switzerland was swell", he reported after one jaunt – although he felt that his skiing was hopelessly inept). In September 1936 Joseph wrote to a friend from Geneva, having just witnessed a dramatic session at the League of Nations. The Italian delegation was trying to persuade the League to recognise the conquest of Abyssinia, which it had completed in May after eight months of war. Among the delegates whom Joseph saw at close quarters were the exiled Abyssinian Emperor Haile Selassie, the British Foreign Secretary Anthony Eden, and Litvinov, the Soviet People's Commissar for Foreign Affairs; he noticed that "in the long corridors, whispering groups walk slowly up and down: it is there that politics are made". His observations on the "fine scene" contrive to be both engaged and detached, but his excitement at being present is obvious – high-level diplomacy was so absorbing that he even declined to give the details of an episode which had led to him being "crossed in love". Joseph was well aware that these discussions were highly significant to his own generation. A few months earlier he had told the friend that "People in the School seem to think that our next field day will be held on the plains of France or Germany",

---

15. Halcrow, *Joseph*, 5.
16. *Ibid.*

adding in the flippant tone typical of his letters that he was "terrified" at the prospect.[17]

Possibly Joseph had mixed feelings about Spain; the Republicans were fighting Hitler, but they were also regarded as a threat to private property and the singing in his car was more concerned with the general war between the classes than with the conflict in Spain. Shonfield, himself a Jew, was less reticent, in keeping with an outgoing character which Joseph envied; but then Shonfield's father had not changed his middle name out of fear of the fascist menace. Joseph even refrained from activity during the Oxford by-election of September 1938, fought over the issue of appeasement, although Lord Blake remembers him as a private supporter of the anti-Chamberlain candidate A. D. Lindsay, who stood against the Conservative Quintin Hogg in that famous struggle.[18]

Joseph's quiet commitment was shown in other activities. Attachment to the Officer Cadet Training Corps was expected of every Harrow schoolboy over fifteen, and although there were exemptions for sickly specimens it is likely that he at least picked up the rudiments of "musketry" on the War Office course for which all the boys were entered. As the international situation darkened during Joseph's time in Oxford, he enrolled with the City-based Honourable Artillery Company (HAC). This was an unhappy experience; horse-riding was involved, and Joseph explained many years later that a leg injury (suffered during a "soccer" game) would have hampered him in this role even if he had been an experienced rider, which he was not. He left the HAC and decamped to the Oxford Territorials. His membership of this body meant that at the declaration of war with Germany in September 1939 he reported for duty.[19]

The deepening international crisis overshadowed Joseph's graduation from Magdalen in the summer of 1939 as one of six Oxford candidates to receive First Class honours in Jurisprudence. Woodrow Wyatt had been told by his tutor – like John Morris, an enthusiastic and youthful academic – that a First was within reach provided that he settled down to some work. Instead of heeding this advice Wyatt "delayed trying to memorise yards of facts" until his final term had begun, and was handicapped by an inability to produce legible writing at high speed; even so, he emerged with a Second. But even if Joseph's performance can be attributed to relentless feeding on textbooks and relatively clear handwriting, it was a tribute to an excellent memory and notable self-discipline. Under normal circumstances the First would have been a marvellous boost to the self-confidence of someone who, until that time, had seemed like the eternal "B" candidate in everything that he did. Yet the threat of war, with all its implications for Jewish people, placed an ominous barrier between

---

17. KJ to Michael Hargreave, undated letter of 1936, 22 October 1936, 15 March 1936.
18. Private information; letter to authors from Lord Blake.
19. KJ to Michael Hargreave, undated letter of 1936; Halcrow, *Joseph*, 5.

the young graduate and the impressive range of opportunities which lay before him. In the meantime he agreed that for 1939–40 he would share lodgings off the Iffley Road with Robert Blake, who had graduated a year earlier with a First in Politics, Philosophy and Economics (PPE) – unless war came, in which case neither would take advantage of their academic credentials to accept non-combatant duties.[20]

Strictly speaking, Joseph was fated to be a "non-combatant" for most of the war; indeed, he was only in action for a year. For about six months he was stationed at Aldershot, with a small group of Oxbridge "Firsts" in an Officer Cadet Training Unit (OCTU). One of his Magdalen friends also attached to this Unit remembered that he showed himself to be thoroughly competent. Joseph performed well in his training course, and was remembered to have been something of a leader in organising social activities. But he still left the impression of holding himself slightly aloof, possibly because he drank only in moderation and never smoked (which was most unusual).[21] He had joined the Royal Artillery – like his friend Blake – and seemed poised to plunge into the fight as a member of the British Expeditionary Force (BEF). On Friday 3 May 1940, writing from the RA headquarters at Woolwich, Joseph told a friend that he would be sailing for France on the following Monday. But just a week later the Germans opened their *Blitzkrieg* in Western Europe; by the 20th they had reached the Belgian coast, and on the 27th the evacuation began of British troops stranded at Dunkirk. There is no record of Keith Joseph having been involved in the evacuation; presumably his journey to France was postponed before being cancelled forever by events across the Channel.[22]

For the next three years Joseph continued his training for the action which he had so narrowly missed. He hated having to kick his heels in Britain while the fate of Europe hung in the balance. Denis Healey, another Oxford "First" who joined the Royal Artillery, discovered the joys of second-hand bookshops during his own protracted spell of training; for several months his talents could be put to no better use than counting the passengers on trains. The more restless Joseph asked to be trained as a parachutist – an idea vetoed by a senior officer. Having excelled in his own training, he was offered a post as an instructor at Aldershot, but turned this down on the assumption that it would deny him any chance of more active service.[23]

Keith Joseph rarely spoke about his war, and there is little in the official records to fill in the early gaps. But a war diary for October 1943, now in the Public Records Office, mentions his arrival as a Captain in the 154 Battery of the

20. Woodrow Wyatt, *Confessions of an Optimist* (Collins, 1985), 76; letter to authors from Lord Blake.
21. Interview with Greig Barr.
22. KJ to Michael Hargreave, 3 May 1940.
23. Halcrow, *Joseph*, 6; Denis Healey, *The Time of My Life* (Michael Joseph, 1989) 52.

172 Field Regiment, RA. At that time the Battery was in Italy. It had left Britain early in 1943, as part of the 46th Infantry Division. The ship containing the Battery's guns and vehicles had been torpedoed off Algiers, and it took part in several sharp actions before Tunis fell in May 1943. After exercises on the Tunisian coast, in September the Battery, now in support of the 128 (Hampshire) Infantry Battalion, joined the Allied invasion of Italy and landed near Salerno.[24]

What Joseph had been doing in the months before he joined the Battery cannot now be traced, but he had not previously seen action. He did not think that he was particularly brave, once remarking in his own defence that the ability to overcome fear was as meritorious as raw courage. But he earned a reputation for bravery (if not recklessness) by volunteering for the most dangerous missions. His Battery pushed northwards, towards the German "Gustav" line which followed the rivers Garigliano, Rapido and Sangro. The focal point of Allied attacks was the town of Cassino, near the centre of the line. In preparation for this operation the 154 Battery was involved in an attempt to secure two "steep pimples" to the south, Monte Trocchio and Monte Porchia. In December 1943 Captain Joseph was engaged in reconnaissance work; his frequent reports show that he had a keen appreciation of military movements. On 3 January 1944 he was given the task of directing his Battery's fire on to Monte Trocchio, to create a smoke-screen in support of American troops hoping to drive away German units who were holding up the Allied advance. Although he was targetted by enemy shells, within a few days his objectives were achieved. But German attacks persisted, and Joseph was wounded at the beginning of February. He was hit in the leg – probably by shrapnel, which claimed several lives in the Battery during this phase of the campaign. But it was not a serious wound, and he spent only a few days in a field hospital. While he was away from his unit the fighting intensified; at the end of the first week in February two of his comrades were evacuated, suffering from exhaustion.[25]

After this burst of reported activity Captain Joseph was re-absorbed by the fog of war. His Battery was not involved in the main fighting for Monte Cassino, which culminated in a furious (and unsuccessful) air and artillery assault in mid-March. The aerial bombardment of the historic monastery had begun in February; fortunately for him, it seems that Joseph had no part in this "useless piece of destruction".[26] Neither was he present when, assisted by an enveloping smoke-screen, Polish troops occupied the remnants of the monastery on 18 May. On 16 March the 154th had been taken out of the line and sailed for Egypt, where the whole division rested. Then there was training

---

24. See War Diaries in PRO WO166/7055 and WO169/9532.
25. Operational orders for 172 Field Regiment, 3, 4, 10 January 1944, in PRO WO170/979.
26. Peter Calvocoressi and Guy Wint, *Total War: Causes and Courses of the Second World War* (Pelican, 1974), 511; see de Rothschild, *A Gilt-Edged Life*, 112, in which it is implied that Joseph was actually present in the crucial phase of fighting at Cassino.

in Palestine and Syria. Possibly it was during this lull that Joseph taught short-hand to the men under his command, in an exercise apparently designed to make him learn the skill himself. He had already taught himself Italian. He was not the only Oxford graduate who whiled away war-time hours in a quest for new accomplishments; Denis Healey, for example, tried to teach himself elementary Russian. Joseph was only unusual in his method of study. His remarkable memory for literary texts, and his ability to switch his thoughts rapidly from one language to another, enabled him to absorb Italian by reading a translation of Shakespeare.[27]

The Battery returned to Italy on 3 July 1944, disembarking at Taranto in the far south. Their objective was to join in a new attack, on the "Gothic" line established by the Germans in Tuscany. They made steady progress but were hampered by autumn rain and heavy resistance; on 11 September three members of the unit were killed, and seven wounded. The Battery was still in action on 16 October, when Joseph was recalled to Britain. He never saw action again. He must have left behind his military career with mixed feelings. Lord Blake believes that the experience scarred him – "a certain sombreness of outlook eclipsed his undergraduate gaiety" – but Blake was one of very few to have witnessed the frivolous side of Joseph's nature before the war. Blake's remark certainly supports the impression gained from other sources – that Joseph left the army without having imbibed the spirit of companionship which transformed the outlook and character of so many fellow-intellectuals (Joseph himself acknowledged that the war "didn't mature me as much as it matured many others").[28] After all, when he joined the Battery its members had already shared the bonding experience of fighting together in North Africa; a relative newcomer, his activities often took him away from the main body of the unit. Compared to the experience of the average Oxford "First", his war had been fairly active and the brevity of his fighting experience was not his fault. But given his father's proud record, it must have been disappointing for him to leave with a relatively junior rank and no decoration (he was, however, mentioned in dispatches). There was a story that his mastery of the smoke-screen earned him the sobriquet "Smokey Joe", but an RA officer with his surname was pretty sure to encounter this joke before he had fired a single shell and at least one of his comrades remembers winning the same accolade after a practice exercise back in England.[29]

---

27. Halcrow, *Joseph*, 6; Healey, *Time of My Life*, 51–2; correspondence between authors and Major Tony Eeles; private information.
28. Letter from Lord Blake to authors; KJ interview with Anthony King.
29. See *London Gazette*, January 1945; Halcrow, *Joseph*, 6; interview with Major Tony Eeles. When invited by Anthony King to speak about his war, Joseph confirmed the "Smokey Joe" story, but instead of referring to his courageous conduct merely added "I hope the smoke-screen did its job – that's all" (KJ interview with Anthony King).

On a personal level, for the Joseph family the story of the Second World War was one of triumph and tragedy. After his stint as a City Sheriff Sir Samuel continued his hectic schedule, amassing a collection of jobs and offices which would have been very notable in any English family which did not also contain Louis Gluckstein (who fought in both world wars and ended up as a Colonel and a Deputy Director at the War Office). Apart from his role of Chairman and Managing Director of Bovis and his positions in the City hierarchy, at one time or another Sir Samuel was an underwriting member of Lloyds, an Extraordinary Director of Scottish Equitable Life, and a governor of several City hospitals.

Sir Samuel's spell as a London Sheriff qualified him for the office of Lord Mayor, the greatest prize of all, which descended in a rough line of seniority through those who had been both Aldermen and Sheriffs. Clearly the subject was discussed with some excitement within the family after he had won the controversial Shrieval election; Philip Phillips changed his will, asking that a seventeenth-century tobacco box be presented to the Guildhall if his son-in-law ever became Mayor.[30] On the one hand the war had stripped the Mayoralty of some trappings; the pageantry of the Lord Mayor's Show was curtailed and the Guildhall was gutted at the end of 1941. But if anything the job was more important than ever; at the height of hostilities the Mayor was a potent rallying point for the morale of Londoners, and as thoughts turned towards peace he would be fully occupied in planning the restoration of the battered capital. These responsibilities meant that war-time Mayors needed to be reasonably sure of their physical fitness. Hence in September 1940 it was announced that the two senior Aldermen, Sir John Laurie and Sir Frank Pollitzer, had both declined to be considered for the office – the first on medical advice, the second because he felt that at his age he would be unequal to the duties at such a critical time.[31]

In the following year the refuseniks of 1940 found themselves sufficiently reinvigorated to form the shortlist of two candidates which, by tradition, was submitted to the Court of Aldermen meeting in secret. Laurie, a Harrow man and a senior Freemason, emerged as the winner. As the *City Press* newspaper reported, the name of Sir Samuel Joseph had been greeted with cries of "Later on!" when it was read out during the preliminaries, when the field was whittled down to two by the assembled Liverymen of the London Guilds. The majority had shouted "Next time!" when Pollitzer's name was called – and, by the informal rules which governed the process the unsuccessful candidate on the 1941 shortlist would be a guaranteed winner on his next outing.[32]

---

30. Details of Phillips's will, *The Times*, 14 April 1934.
31. *The Times*, 24 July 1940.
32. *City Press*, 3 October 1941.

But these were revolutionary times in the City of London. When Laurie's successor was chosen in September 1942 the attendance was greater than it had been for several years. Sir Samuel Joseph had moved up the ladder, and along with Pollitzer he was placed on the shortlist. It was noted that some feeble cries of "No, No" had mingled with the approving yells for Sir Frank. When after a surprising interlude of twenty minutes the Aldermen trooped back into the Guildhall Sir Samuel was walking beside the Mayor in the procession – a sure sign that he had won out of turn and become the sixth Jewish Lord Mayor, the first since 1902. The waiting Liverymen registered their shock with appropriate decorum; as the *City Press* put it, "a slight murmur filled the hall" when the result was known.[33]

The issue of the *City Press* which carried the news of Sir Samuel Joseph's elevation also contained a letter from Pollitzer. He offered his "sincere appreciation and thanks" to the Liverymen who had shouted "All, All!" on his behalf. His endorsement of the successful candidate could have been more resounding: "I am sure", he wrote, "that Sir Samuel Joseph will discharge his duties to the satisfaction of the City". Pollitzer's wounded feelings were understandable; but two years had passed since the time when he declared that he was too old to undertake the Lord Mayor's duties, and those who doubted his fitness for the job lacked the foreknowledge that he would live to the age of eighty-one. Back in 1940 Sir John Laurie had picked a much better excuse when he ducked out through illness. Indeed, had Pollitzer brought health into the question he might easily have won in 1942, because no respectable doctor would have endorsed Sir Samuel Joseph's decision to stand. According to Keith Joseph, his mother had "pleaded" with Sir Samuel to disobey the voice of duty, with the usual result.[34]

Once again, a victory for Sir Samuel was greeted by expressions of anti-Semitism, both public and private. Pollitzer's evident unhappiness was not inspired by racism, because he himself was a Jew. However, the contest between the co-religionists provided an excuse for mischief-making by the notorious Nazi broadcaster William Joyce ("Lord Haw-Haw"). More insidious was the remark recorded in his diary by Montagu Norman, the long-serving Governor of the Bank of England, in May 1942. Norman had discussed the issue of the Mayoralty with the incumbent, Laurie. "W[oul]d they be wise to elect a Jew?" he asked himself. "I say NO". These undercurrents must have dampened spirits a little on 9 November, the date of the new Lord Mayor's Show; crowds were relatively thin, and the Mayor himself was absent from the procession, standing to take the salute at St Paul's Cathedral. There is no evidence that Keith Joseph was present, although he was in England at the time. But Winston Churchill put in an appearance, encouraged by positive developments in the war. On the night

---

33. *City Press,* 2 October 1942.
34. Halcrow, *Joseph,* 5.

of 4 November 1942 the BBC had told its listeners to expect "the best news for years" soon after midnight. The Germans had been defeated at El Alamein, and at a City of London meeting on the day after the Lord Mayor's Show Churchill hailed what was at least "the end of the beginning".[35]

It seems, however, that taking up the post of Lord Mayor marked the beginning of the end for Sir Samuel Joseph. Despite the heart attacks he had already suffered he drove himself at such a frantic pace that his secretary was forced by exhaustion to apply for leave. Apart from ceremonial occasions, such as hosting dinners for Churchill and General de Gaulle, Sir Samuel held more informal gatherings every Saturday afternoon at the Mansion House, for up to 1,200 service men and women at a time. He and the Lady Mayoress would talk to the guests and sometimes show a selected few around the building. He also threw himself into charitable work, often in response to news of overseas disasters, and some progress was made in the planning of a post-war London. As reported in the *Jewish Chronicle*, Sir Samuel's last public act as Lord Mayor was to open a temporary replacement for the bombed Great Synagogue in Duke's Place.[36]

When his year-long term of office expired in November 1943 the *City Press* paid Sir Samuel a handsome tribute. He had, the paper recorded, "displayed that genius for organisation which characterises the members of his family", and his role had been performed with equal energy and dignity. But on the next page of the newspaper a different light was cast on Sir Samuel's year in office. Under the ominous heading "Lord Mayor's Farewell – Unusual Speech", the *Press* reported that, after acknowledging that almost everyone had been most helpful to him, Sir Samuel had suddenly lashed out against the "four or five" exceptions: "he was satisfied that whatever he had done would have been unsatisfactory. From the inception they disliked the colour of his eyes". Possibly the troubles encountered by Sir Samuel would have affected anyone in his position, since after the enforced unity of the Blitz City men now enjoyed the luxury of squabbling about the future. But Montagu Norman had recorded in his diary that Sir Samuel had heard about his anti-Semitism, and the views of such a powerful figure were sure to influence others in the City. The surviving papers at the Guildhall are predictably silent, and even though the war-time tide had turned in Britain's favour the *City Press* was unlikely to publish unedifying details of faction-fighting. Whatever the provocation, the incident proves that Sir Samuel Joseph was a man who saw no reason to disguise his feelings, in public or in private. It was the kind of outburst which would have made a Harrow schoolboy shudder.[37]

---

35. Halcrow, *Joseph*, 5; David Kynaston, *The City of London, Volume III: Illusions of Gold, 1914–1945* (Chatto & Windus, 1999), 485; Angus Calder, *The People's War: Britain 1939–1945* (Jonathan Cape, 1969), 304.
36. *City Press*, 30 July, 5 November, 1943; *Jewish Chronicle*, 13 October 1944
37. *City Press*, 5 November 1943; Kynaston, *Illusions*, 485. Bizarrely, Norman convinced himself that the rumours which had reached Sir Samuel were untrue.

After leaving office Sir Samuel returned to his work at Bovis, and was chairing board meetings as late as August 1944. In the following month, however, it was reported that on medical advice he would be taking a period of complete rest. On 4 October he succumbed to a final heart attack, after just a week of disorientating inactivity.[38]

Sir Samuel Joseph was in his fifty-seventh year when he died. In a frank obituary published by the *City Press* there is some suggestion of what it must have been like to be the son of such a man:

> No one could say that he was an easy man to serve, for all his life he had set before him a model of efficiency that was as exacting as it was his own. Everything he did had to be done not merely well but more than well; and with this he combined unquenchable energy surprising in a man who never really enjoyed perfect health. No detail was too small for Samuel Joseph, and if he took much out of himself, he expected much from those in his service. His judgements were quick – often hasty – and he seldom stopped to take advice.

A 1964 profile of Sir Keith Joseph noted that "He drives himself without mercy and expects his aides to accept his merciless approach to work". But the remark about hasty judgements is an almost surreal indication of the enormous gulf between the characters of father and son. And few people thought the latter difficult to serve. One reason for this might have been that when Sir Keith was irritated by a display of incompetence his outbursts were "immediately succeeded by an apology if he [thought] that he may have been too harsh".[39]

The news of Sir Samuel's death reached the 154 Battery on 14 October. Joseph was granted compassionate leave and set off for England, only arriving after the funeral and two memorial services had been held. He inherited the baronetcy which his father had received at the end of 1943, as the Mayoral equivalent of a carriage clock. But the legacy was more potent than this. Contact with his father had been unusually rare, but Sir Samuel was the kind of man who did not need to be present to make his influence felt and it is most unlikely that the tendency to make excessive demands was a trait that he reserved exclusively for professional dealings. Other members of his family had retired relatively early, and it is just conceivable that (had he lived) the ex-Mayor could have followed this course. In (relatively) mellow old age he might have acted as a friendly support to his only son. But after 1944 all that remained was the vivid memory of his years of whirlwind activity, sustained without regard to his health, and his "exacting" standards. Oxford or the army could

---

38. Cooper, *Building Relationships*, 77–8.
39. *City Press*, 13 October 1944; *The Times*, 22 September 1964.

have provided Sir Keith Joseph with alternative role models; but Morris, the most influential figure of those years, in many ways resembled his father and Joseph seems to have lost contact with his comrades in the 154 Battery.[40]

In 1974 an interviewer asked Joseph whether "you feel that you have to prove something to your father, to yourself". "No, good Lord no", he replied. This only suggests that the influence had been so strong that Joseph was not conscious of it; it had become a central feature of his own nature. Moments earlier Joseph had referred to his father's death through overwork "in his early fifties" – "in his mid-fifties", he hastily added. At the time of the interview Joseph was just four months short of his own fifty-seventh birthday. His father's working methods had shown that there was a great deal to do in life; his premature death suggested that there might not be much time in which to do it. Instead of saying that he had to "fire on all six cylinders" because he was a Jew, Sir Keith could have attributed the need for this extraordinary effort to the fact that he was the son of Sir Samuel Joseph, Bart.[41]

---

40. There was, however, at least one reunion gathering of the promising graduates from the Aldershot OCTU; letters to authors from Greig Barr.
41. KJ interview with Llew Gardner, "People and Politics", Thames Television, 24 October 1974.

Chapter 3

"Altruism and Egotism"

The newly dubbed Sir Keith Joseph continued to serve his country in the period immediately after his return from the Italian front. But for the biographer the evidence relating to his activities is just as patchy as for the period of his training. In a 1970 profile Michael Harrington mentioned that Joseph "was posted to the Ministry of Works as personal assistant to Duncan Sandys". This is confirmed by the memories of some friends, and others who worked in the ministry, but it never featured in his *Who's Who* entry, or any other of the numerous Joseph profiles.[1] The connection with Sandys would have been of considerable value to Joseph in later years, yet it seems to have been broken as soon as he relinquished the post. Since Sandys was Churchill's son-in-law the experience might have kindled political interests, but Joseph never alluded to this period when explaining his ambition to enter the Commons. Other members of his family had been connected to government departments; Louis Gluckstein made his inevitable contribution, and his brother Montague was a catering adviser to the Ministry of Food throughout

---

1. Harrington in *Here Come the Tories*, 77; interviews with Greig Barr and Leslie Chapman. Joseph's name does not appear in the *Imperial Calendar* listing civil servants within the ministry, which implies that Sandys hired him in a personal capacity; a trawl through relevant files in the PRO and the Sandys Papers at Churchill College, Cambridge, has also failed to turn up his name.

the war. Bovis had been contracted by the government for numerous building projects during the conflict, and the Ministry of Works was represented at Sir Samuel's memorial services. Sir Keith Joseph's close links to the firm reinforced his status as an Oxford "First" to make him an excellent candidate for a position in the ministry.

The idea of Sir Keith as a ministerial aide is an intriguing one, given his later Whitehall experiences. An observer writing in 1964 thought that Joseph had "the habit of mind of a first-class administrative civil servant". But there was no chance at this stage of him being "captured" by the bureaucratic mind, and his attention had probably turned to other fields long before the German surrender. The death of Sir Samuel Joseph had acted as a dramatic wake-up call for his son. In October 1944 Sir Keith could reflect that he had a first-class degree to his credit, while his father had not even been a "well-read man". But this academic achievement could be traced back to the influence of Sir Samuel, who had planned and paid for his expensive education. For a young man who had already shown that he could suffer under stress, the idea that he should "prove" himself must have been unappealing at first. But if Joseph had any private misgivings about devoting the rest of his adult life to the appeasement of his father's ghost, his mother, preparing herself for long years of mourning, was always there as a living rebuke to his doubts. Looking over the list of Joseph's activities in the immediate post-war years it seems that the necessary effort became addictive, and every increase in the dosage brought him closer to disaster.[2]

Unfortunately it is impossible now to give an exact chronology of Joseph's various labours. But some of them must have been tackled simultaneously, creating a burden which not even Louis Gluckstein or Sir Keith's own father could have shrugged off without difficulty. In one obvious respect Joseph could show himself the deserving child of such a father by direct imitation of his example: he could contribute something solid to the family firm, rather than lapsing into a manager with a grand title and influence out of proportion to his qualifications for work in the construction industry. This course was open to him; he had inherited 65,000 Bovis shares from Sir Samuel. But the latter had proved well worth his senior place in the firm by gaining practical experience before joining the board, and Sir Keith now followed the same route, qualifying as a licentiate of the Institute of Building. This involved both practical work on building sites as well as the application of his formidable memory to the relevant textbooks. Joseph's experiences at this time offered a congenial opportunity to indulge in self-deprecation; he told one interviewer that he "must have been the worst bricklayer in Britain", and Morrison Halcrow was entertained with the story of how, while the Baronet was digging furiously in a

---

2. *The Times*, 22 September 1964.

muddy trench at the British Plaster Board factory at East Leake, the Bovis foreman took him aside and reminded him that the quicker the job was done the less his workforce would be paid.[3]

Even if Joseph's bricklaying really was incompetent and his digging over-enthusiastic he had at least gained some insights into the mentality and practices of his company's staff. At the same time he was reading for his Bar examinations, resulting in a call to practice at the Middle Temple (which he chose to ignore). In November 1946 he won promotion at Bovis, being appointed to a committee established to assess the efficiency of the company's plant department. But by that time he had proved himself in a far more demanding field, becoming an All Souls Fellow in June 1946.

To win a Prize Fellowship at All Souls College, Oxford, is to join a very select group. The financial reward – initially £400 per year (around £10,000 in today's money) – was dwarfed by the prestige of winning one of the most coveted positions in Oxford academic life. Joseph's decision to compete for a Fellowship was a sign of growing confidence in his intellectual powers, but also of his independent spirit. His tutor, John Morris, encouraged him to consider a career as a full-time academic. But Morris' own failure to win an All Souls Fellowship had helped to create a lasting antipathy to the college; he thought that the buildings would be better employed as University offices. Joseph stuck to his own preferences; the life of an ordinary college tutor was not for him, but he was unable to resist the challenge of the All Souls competition.[4]

It was the beginning of an association with All Souls which lasted until his death (with an eleven-year gap between 1960 and 1971). Joseph's connection with the college was of inestimable value to him over the coming decades. His status ensured that his views were regarded as those of an "intellectual", even by opponents. Some people automatically developed an inferiority complex, and at least one of his later parliamentary colleagues could hardly believe that an All Souls Fellow would speak to him at all. But as Joseph had found at Harrow his unfailing courtesy, and a native modesty which was at least a match for his intellect, protected him from the reputation of being unduly "priggish".[5]

In normal years All Souls elected two Fellows, and in the pre-war and immediate post-war years one of the places was often won by a lawyer. Some notable representatives of the legal profession had secured Fellowships before the war, among them the brilliant Quintin Hogg (later Lord Hailsham). There was, though, a feeling that it was easier to succeed in the Law competition than to secure the other post. Naturally this idea was most common among the non-

---

3. Graham Turner in *Sunday Times*, 6 May 1979; Halcrow, *Joseph*, 9. Joseph also tried his hand at house painting, but insisted that he proved no more adept at that; KJ interview with Anthony King.
4. *The Times* obituary of John Morris, 2 October 1984; letter to the authors from Jeremy Lever.
5. Interview with Brian Harrison.

lawyers, but they might have had a point; the list of failed candidates from other fields includes Harold Wilson, one of the brightest Oxford graduates of the century. The denigration of Law as a subject was based partly on the unsettling fact that it was linked to a vocation; another grievance was that even at this level the successful candidate depended on memory far more than on creative thinking or judgements based on concise logical argument. The disparagement of Law Fellowships could be dismissed as the unappealing voice of intellectual snobbery, but the existence of the opinion should be recorded.[6]

Joseph was faced with three specialised Law papers and one general paper; in addition, he was asked to translate passages from French and Latin into English, and to dine in college with all the Fellows. Then the candidate had to write an essay with a one-word title. Joseph was invited to speculate on the theme of "Tragedy", which would have activated his interest in drama and his ability to quote reams of Shakespearian blank-verse. Even so, it might have been more interesting for him if he had tackled a topic which had baffled A. L. Rowse before the War – "Possessions".[7]

In 1946 All Souls was below its full complement of Prize Fellows; there had been no awards between 1939 and 1944. To begin to rectify this situation, in 1946 two competitions were held (in June and October); a total of six Prize Fellowships were awarded, and Joseph took one of two Law awards. Lord Wilberforce, who first met Sir Keith at the time of his examination, recalled that the competition in June was unusually strong, because of the pent-up demand. The precise number of Joseph's rivals has not been recorded, but nineteen scholars took the examination of October 1946 and this was roughly the total number of entrants in a normal year.[8]

Given that his active military service had been truncated Joseph might have held a slight advantage over some of his contemporaries. The war must have claimed a number of potential competitors (of the sixty-seven boys who went up to Harrow with Joseph in September 1931, thirteen died between 1939 and 1945). Then again, some of his rivals in June 1946 would have spent the whole of the conflict in "reserved" occupations, with far more opportunity to shake off any academic rust. To win an All Souls Fellowship of any kind, at any time,

---

6. Jeremy Lever (elected in 1957) has pointed out to us that some eminent lawyers have gained Prize Fellowships after sitting the examination as historians.

7. A. L. Rowse, *A Cornishman at Oxford* (Jonathan Cape, 1965), 241–3; for general advice on All Souls questions, we are most grateful to Dr Norma Aubertin-Potter, Sir Raymond Carr, Lord Quinton, Lord Wilberforce and Jeremy Lever. The procedure has varied over the years and Jeremy Lever has suggested that Joseph might have taken two specialised and two general papers. Rowse recorded that the oral translations were particularly stress-inducing; David Cecil fled from the room after one glance at the task ahead of him. The additional "social test" of dining with the Fellows could also be taxing: the candidate was bound to feel that he was being scrutinised for any breach of table etiquette, and despite the plentiful wine he had to resist any temptation to over-indulge.

8. Lord Wilberforce's, speech at All Souls College, Oxford, memorial service for KJ, 3 June 1995.

demands intellectual power well above even that of the average Oxford graduate. Having laboured in the academic mid-field at Lockers Park and Harrow,
life at Oxford had made Joseph pick up the bit and the War had done nothing
to stop his momentum. This picture of a "late developer", ironically, is
supported by two anecdotes which, at first sight, might be regarded as grounds
for questioning the value of Joseph's success. On hearing of the Fellowship
Joseph's old French Master from Harrow expressed amazement, but added
"True, only a Law Fellowship" as if this resolved the mystery. The master in
question was apparently alone in referring to Joseph as "Black Joe" – possibly a
sign that their relationship had not always run smoothly. Years later the eminent
historian John Ehrman (who had been Joseph's junior at Lockers Park) was
greeted with the jocular observation that "I never thought that you would
become a Fellow of Trinity [Cambridge]". Ehrman countered by telling Joseph
that "No-one could have foreseen that you would be a Fellow of All Souls".[9]

Even if no one foresaw it, Joseph's Fellowship had been won and he could
enjoy his admission to what a colleague, Sir Arthur (later Lord) Salter,
described as "a singularly desirable club, for those admitted to it the best in the
world". Unlike Salter, Joseph spent most of his time in London, but many
other Fellows were in the same position and it did not prevent him from
forging some useful friendships. Apart from Salter himself, Joseph got to know
Lionel Curtis, in pre-war days a prime mover behind the Royal Institute of
International Affairs. In 1950 Curtis published *The Open Road to Freedom*, a
passionate treatise which argued that the best way to avoid future wars would be
"for free nations to pool their resources under one federal government". Before
the book went to press Curtis showed the manuscript to the members of an *ad
hoc* committee, which included Joseph, and their comments were included in
the printed version. There was also a robust private exchange with Isaiah Berlin
(the first Jew to win a Prize Fellowship) over the latter's essay "Jewish Slavery
and Emancipation" which had appeared over several issues of the *Jewish Chronicle*. When the piece was reprinted in a collection, Joseph praised "its noble plea
for tolerance", but revealed that Berlin had touched a tender spot:

> Let those, however, not already self-conscious and those apt to be
> influenced by analyses of motives keep away, for its analogies are such as
> to make most of us feel – whatever we do – guilty, either of being too
> obviously Jewish or of trying too obviously not to be. These analogies are
> for talk and not for print.

In short, Berlin had confronted Joseph with the key question of identity, in
brutal terms: the offending analogy was between a Jew and a hunchback. Berlin

---

9. Letters to authors from Hugh Lee and John Ehrman.

seems to have accepted Joseph's forceful argument; the essay did not reappear in any of his subsequent collections. The idea that colleagues could freely and forcefully exchange ideas and opinions was not the least of the lasting benefits which Joseph took away from All Souls; it affected him so deeply, indeed, that he tended to treat everyone he met as a potential member of a study-group. He also appreciated the chance to consult acknowledged experts on subjects which interested him, sometimes asking them to recommend the best introductory books. He still enjoyed the company of long-established Oxford friends, including Robert Blake who had become a Christ Church don.[10]

The full £400 All Souls Fellowship was guaranteed for two years. After that period, those (like Joseph himself) who had decided that academia would be no more than a part-time interest had their stipends reduced for the remaining five years. Even these "weekenders", or "London Fellows", were expected to conduct some research. It was typical of Joseph that he embarked on a project which would have taxed even a full-time scholar. The topic of his thesis was "political, racial, and religious tolerance, setting out to distinguish between toleration and indifference". Many years later it was reported that he had kept some of his notes, although he feared that the exercise was "a little pretentious". No trace now remains of what would have been a fascinating inquiry, in a field of obvious interest to Berlin himself. The fact that it was never completed did nothing to tarnish Joseph's reputation at All Souls, and his obvious semi-detachment from academia was accepted without any difficulty. The College was always welcoming to those who looked likely to succeed in public life.[11]

The All Souls Fellowship showed that Sir Keith was more than just his father's son; no doubt Sir Samuel would have been proud of his success while questioning the necessity of devoting even more of his time to the ivory towers. But it would take Joseph more than one bound to free himself from the Lord Mayor's legacy. In February 1946 the *City Press* announced that he had been co-opted to fill a vacancy among Portsoken's Common Councillors. This was merely an early staging-post on the road which his father had taken. In October Sir Keith was elected unopposed as an Alderman for the ward. Returning thanks for the welcome given to him, he "said he was taught by his father to aim at the high ideals of service expressed by the Court of Aldermen". The *City Press* enthused that "To have been awarded a Fellowship at All Souls, Oxford, and to have secured an Aldermanry of the City of London at the age of 29 [sic] is a remarkable achievement. Indeed it is to be doubted whether the Court of Aldermen has ever been called upon to admit so young a man".[12]

---

10. Lord Salter, *Memoirs of a Public Servant* (Faber & Faber, 1961), 242; Michael Ignatieff, *Isaiah Berlin* (Chatto & Windus, 1998), 185; KJ, review of *Hebrew University Garland* in *Jewish Chronicle*, 24 October 1952; private information. Joseph and Berlin remained on friendly terms for the rest of their lives, and the philosopher attended Joseph's All Souls memorial service.
11. KJ interview with Terry Coleman; interview with the late Lord Beloff.
12. *City Press,* 2 February 1946; *Jewish Chronicle*, 22 November 1946.

This was praise sufficient to foster an arrogant streak in most people. But Joseph's head was not for turning. Better than anyone else he knew that this additional honour could not be compared with his Fellowship; it owed little more to his personal merits than his baronetcy had done.[13] Whether or not he was a reluctant candidate in the first place, before long he had reason to regret his City responsibilities. Beneath the Alderman, Fellow of All Souls, qualified barrister and licenciate of the Institute of Building, the Keith Joseph who had suffered from nervous illness at school could still be identified.

At first Joseph was a model member of the Court of Aldermen. After attending his first meeting of the Court on 3 December 1946 he missed just two of the next thirteen sessions up to April 1948, even though these were rather tedious and formal occasions mainly occupied with rubber-stamping the creation of City freemen. Aware that an active Alderman should engage in charitable work, Joseph plunged headlong into this field, joining several worthy bodies and helping to establish a new charity for the elderly, the Three Score Club. Throughout this period he also put in his hours on a couple of rather unimportant sub-committees, undertook some prison visits, and sat on the magistrate's bench. In November 1948 he was appointed to the City's Juvenile Court. But this decision was made in his absence. By 12 October 1948 he had failed to turn up to six of the monthly meetings in a row. On that day the Town Clerk was requested "to convey to Alderman Sir Keith Joseph, Bt., the sympathy of his brethren of this Court and their hopes for a speedy recovery from his illness". Two months leave of absence was granted, and this was soon extended to six months.[14]

The Joseph explanation for "his illness" is a curious one. According to Morrison Halcrow, Sir Keith "had come home from the Army plumper than he felt he should be", so he "put himself on a near-starvation diet". Halcrow rightly suggests that this can only be a partial explanation, and hints that Joseph had decided to try to live on as little money as possible: "Whatever the motivation, he had to live with the physical consequences. He developed an ulcer, which gave him hell, on and off, for the next ten years". He drank large quantities of milk to alleviate his symptoms, but this unbalanced his body chemistry and eventually he went into hospital where half of his stomach was removed. This drastic (and all too common) surgery worked, and "by the time he became a public figure his health was in fact reasonably good".[15]

This was a very painful episode for Joseph, and it must have been difficult for him to allude to the subject (particularly since he remained prone to

---

13. Ironically in an otherwise excellent profile based on an interview with Joseph Terry Coleman wrote that he had taken the Fellowship because "it was offered to him" (*Guardian*, 12 November 1973).
14. *Minutes of the Court of Aldermen*, London Guildhall Library, various dates.
15. Halcrow, *Joseph*, 8.

digestive problems of various kinds for the rest of his life). He was anxious to avoid the impression that "mental over-exertion" was responsible for his impaired health, and backed up his denial by dating the beginning of his difficulties back to the time when he left the army – i.e. when his real "exertions" had scarcely begun. But this account only succeeds in making the state of his mind seem worse than the plight of his stomach; we would have to accept that, despite suffering acute discomfort from his ulcers, he voluntarily subjected himself to the stresses of various examinations, took on new responsibilities at Bovis, and felt fit enough to stand for office in the City of London.

Perhaps Joseph did think that he was too "plump" when he came back from the war, and the near-starvation diet injured his stomach. But his extreme reaction suggests an obsessional outlook, in itself a possible symptom of "mental over-exertion". In any case, the evidence shows that his condition deteriorated through the years in which he pushed himself hardest, to the extent that by the autumn of 1948 something had to give. He suffered a physical breakdown. With the period of leave running out, on 15 March 1949 his resignation from his Portsoken ward was accepted. For the record the Court noted that he "always took the keenest interest in the work of the Corporation and conscientiously and efficiently discharged his duties in this Court . . . His brethren realise, therefore, what a great disappointment it must be to him to be obliged to abandon a career in public life which was so full of promise". Typically he had approached more than one friend in the hope that the vacancy at Portsoken could be filled without delay.[16]

In March 1949 the *City Press* merely reported the remark of the former Lord Mayor, Sir George Wilkinson, that the Court regretted the end of Joseph's *civic* career. But the rest of the article lent support to the view that, having bitten off more than he could safely chew, Sir Keith would never again nibble at public service of any kind. He had been advised by his doctors "that he would be unable to handle the Aldermanic work as well as that of normal business without grave risk of making himself a permanent invalid". Since the work of an Alderman was hardly exhausting – Sir Samuel, after all, had combined it with his senior position in Bovis – this seemed to rule out Sir Keith from any future meaningful activity outside the firm. Certainly none of the Aldermen who met to approve Joseph's letter of resignation can have imagined that within a decade he would be a junior minister of the Crown. They would have been flabbergasted by the suggestion that such a man would ever be considered as a potential leader of the Opposition. The experience probably explains why in later years Joseph found it difficult to admit to illness, even when the symptoms were affecting his behaviour in a manner which aroused unflattering press speculation.[17]

16. *Minutes of the Court of Aldermen*, 15 March 1949.
17. *City Press*, 18 March 1949.

In retirement Joseph's memory was not as precise as it had been in his younger days, and his reference to *ten* years of "hell" caused by the ulcer can be questioned. It seems more likely that the major stomach surgery took place in 1968, twenty years after his resignation from the Court of Aldermen. Presumably after less drastic treatment in 1949 he recuperated for some time with his mother, who continued to live in Claridges Hotel, the residence which Sir Samuel had chosen during his Mayoralty as an alternative to the damaged Mansion House. Having watched her beloved husband succumb to overwork, the protective Lady Joseph had good reason to advise her only child to take things easy for a while. According to at least one account Joseph had not chosen full-time business over civic life; he gave up both for the time being, although he continued an association with the Bovis subsidiary Gilbert-Ash. It was not until 1951 that he took an executive role on the main company board, which his father had done in his early twenties.[18]

During his days of frantic activity Joseph had lacked one obvious source of potential stability. Generally members of his family did not marry early: they could bide their time until the inevitable Gluckstein or Salmon crossed their paths. But Sir Samuel Joseph had taken the radical step of marrying someone who was not also his cousin; this followed the remarkable initiative of Louis Gluckstein's father, who in 1894 had married an American after the death of his first wife Kate Joseph. The results of this experiment were mixed, since Louis' flawless record was balanced by the trail of havoc left by his sister, the painter "Gluck". But Sir Keith had no intention of throwing himself back into the bosom of "The Family". No one remembered him having a girlfriend at Magdalen, but amidst his other commitments he found time for at least one brief romantic liaison before quitting the Court of Aldermen.[19] By the early 1950s the combination of his impeccable manners, his Fellowship, his wealth and his good looks were guaranteed to make him irresistible to someone.

In 1951 Hellen Guggenheimer was a twenty year-old New Yorker, planning to spend a year at London University after studying in the United States. According to the *Jewish Chronicle* her subject was Literature (although she later told Richard Crossman that she had not read a novel before the age of twenty-three).[20] She first met Joseph at a tea-party held by Rabbi Israel Mattuck, leader of the Liberal Jewish movement (and private chaplain to Samuel Joseph during his Mayoralty), soon after the Baronet's thirty-third birthday. Hellen was a very striking young woman – she was compared with justice to the film star Audrey Hepburn. Of equal importance to Joseph was the fact that Hellen was very serious-minded,

---

18. The breakdown "compelled him to leave the directorate of a building firm in the City when he was just past the age of 30"; *The Times*, 22 September 1964. The resignation from Portsoken is not mentioned in this profile.
19. Interview with Greig Barr; private information.
20. *Jewish Chronicle*, 27 January 1955; Richard Crossman, *Diaries of a Cabinet Minister, Volume II, Lord President of the Council and Leader of the House of Commons 1966–68* (Hamish Hamilton & Jonathan Cape, 1976), 398.

passionate for self-improvement. Most observers agreed that she surpassed even Sir Keith in her tendency to see life as an intellectual challenge. Contrary to some press reports Hellen was not an heiress; in fact her father Sigmar, having fled from Nazi Germany, worked for a pickle manufacturer.[21] But this was no great obstacle to Joseph, and since Hellen was Jewish there could be no objection on that side. The similarity in their temperaments apparently overcame any problem which might have arisen from the thirteen-year disparity in their ages. On paper it looked like an ideal match. The couple were married at the West London Synagogue on 7 July 1951, about six months after their first meeting. Sir Basil Henriques (who had probably encountered Joseph through their common interest in charitable work on behalf of Boys' Clubs) gave an address at the Claridges' reception; Joseph kept his own remarks to a minimum. After the wedding the couple took a honeymoon at Agay on the French Riviera. Before his marriage Joseph was living with his mother (who had by this time moved to the Grosvenor House Hotel). The newly weds originally planned to live in St John's Wood, but later chose Chelsea for their home, settling at 23 Mulberry Walk, an impressive Queen Anne-style house on a street which had been built just before the First World War.[22]

Opinions were divided from the start about the wisdom of the marriage. Some people found Hellen and Sir Keith an intimidating team; one acquaintance thought that they had "an aura of unstoppable success" and seemed "sleek" and "glossy". Others interpreted Lady Joseph's aloofness as a sign of excessive self-esteem, a judgement which might have been inspired in part by confusion over her origins. People who thought that she was a member of the super-rich American Guggenheim family were bound to misread her character. Some who knew better were critical of Sir Keith for failing to correct the story that his wife was fabulously wealthy, but he seems to have taken the view that it was none of his business if people made false assumptions. Before Joseph's marriage the future Conservative Party Treasurer Alistair McAlpine met him for the first time (in the company of his beautiful cousin Yvonne Mitchell). McAlpine's parents thought that Sir Keith "was really rather pompous", and were not alone in doing so (although their son eventually came to a different conclusion). Stories about the prodigious application of Hellen and Sir Keith – including a rumour that they had drawn up reading lists to help them fill any gaps in their knowledge – were unlikely to encourage people to relax in their company. As if to compensate, Joseph took to accosting old friends with exaggerated *bonhomie* – an approach which only increased their discomfort.[23]

---

21. Private information.
22. William Clark papers, Bodleian Library, 95, fol. 180. It seems that Joseph's mother played a significant role in the choice of Mulberry Walk; private information.
23. Simon Hoggart, "Mrs Thatcher's Man-in-Waiting", *Guardian*, 21 July 1980; Alistair McAlpine, *Once a Jolly Bagman: Memoirs* (Phoenix, 1998), 14; letter to authors from Hugh Lee. When the reading list story came up during the interview with Anthony King, Joseph did not deny it.

Inevitably the change in Joseph's status had a knock-on effect on his other relationships, and most of his pre-war friends saw less of him after 1951. Presumably Joseph himself was too happy – or too busy – to notice. It was no coincidence that his commitments both inside and outside Bovis began to increase from the time of his marriage; either his health had benefitted from a period of relative relaxation, or he had learned to cope with the problem. His new domestic arrangements provided him with a secure launch pad for a new beginning. In September 1951, for example, the *Jewish Chronicle* noted that he was part of the Council of the Mermaid Theatre, St John's Wood; in the following April he became Joint Treasurer of the Friends of the Hebrew University of Jerusalem. In November 1953 his All Souls Fellowship was renewed for a further seven years, in a departure from the normal practice of the time which was to deny such extensions to married Fellows.[24] He was more selective in his choice of activity – the theatrical connection, for example, marked a return to one of his early tastes, which was shared by his artistic wife. His obsession with cricket was not forgotten; soon after his return from war he had been elected to the exclusive Marylebone Cricket Club (MCC).[25] Despite his false start he could see a way to make a valuable contribution to public life while finally joining the board of the family firm, now restructured as Bovis Holdings Limited.

The Bovis connection also provided Joseph with opportunities for travel. He visited Gibraltar on business, and in May 1953, accompanied by Hellen, he toured Southern Rhodesia and South Africa on behalf of Gilbert-Ash which had embarked on several projects in the region. As Joseph told Lionel Curtis, he had a more personal reason for his journey; he hoped to visit "Joseph's Block", "a completely undeveloped stretch of 26,000 acres" in Southern Rhodesia. This modest property had been left to Sir Keith by Abraham twenty years before, but it seems that this was the first time that its owner had inspected it to see whether it had any potential for development. It was another indication that marriage had brought with it a new sense of purpose.[26]

Joseph's African trip interrupted negotiations for a new venture which he had embarked upon at the beginning of 1953. He had decided that he should become a Member of Parliament.

After Lionel de Rothschild had been prevented several times from taking his seat as MP for the City of London, the bar against Jewish members of the House of Commons was lifted in 1858. The first six Jewish MPs belonged to

---

24. The circumstances of Joseph's re-election are not clear; possibly, as Jeremy Lever has suggested, there was a dearth of young Fellows because of the war-time gap. But it seems fair to suggest that Joseph would not have been re-elected had he not been well regarded by his colleagues; letter to authors from Jeremy Lever.
25. He never represented the Club on the field during a thirty-year connection; information kindly supplied by the MCC.
26. KJ to Lionel Curtis, 27 February 1953, MSS Curtis, 95, fols. 101–2, Bodleian Library.

the newly founded Liberal Party, and the first Jewish Conservative did not appear in the House of Commons until 1874. But the automatic association of Jews with Liberal politics, though often made at the time, was an unsound generalisation. In the late 1870s Gladstone's stance on the "Eastern Question" alienated many Jews including, crucially, the Rothschilds. At this time the tobacco firm of Salmon & Gluckstein was beginning to prosper, and presumably the family started to take a close interest in politics at a time when London Jews were becoming more sympathetic to Conservatism. When Abraham and Coleman Joseph applied for British citizenship at the turn of the century both cited the right to vote in elections as the only reason for their applications.[27]

Once the loyalty had formed it was difficult to shake, so that when Joseph was asked late in life to give reasons for his commitment to the Conservative Party he merely replied that "It never occurred to me to become a member of any other party". In 1929 three members of his family stood for Parliament in the Conservative interest. Isidore Salmon was already MP for Harrow, a seat which he held from 1924 up to his death in 1941; thus, while Keith Joseph was at school, his local MP was a close relative. Judged from his voting record, Salmon was a supporter of Neville Chamberlain and the policy of appeasement. Samuel Gluckstein, who had been defeated at North Hammersmith in 1924, contested Plymouth Devonport in 1929 against another Jew, Leslie Hore-Belisha, and lost again. The unstoppable Louis Gluckstein fought Nottingham East for the first time in 1929; after winning the seat in 1931 he retained it in 1935, and joined Salmon in supporting Chamberlain over Munich. Buried under the Labour landslide at the next general election in 1945 he was thwarted in his attempt to wrest back Nottingham East in 1950. Then he looked further north, being mentioned as a possible candidate for the safe constituency of Penrith and the Border, later to be won by William Whitelaw. This came to nothing, however, and he turned his attention back to London and the marginal seat of Holborn and St Pancras, where, after another defeat in 1955, even he decided to give up the parliamentary struggle although he remained very active in Conservative circles.

Sir Samuel Joseph never stood for Parliament but he shared the family preference for the Conservatives to the extent of joining the Carlton Club. Perhaps he was most attracted by the social benefits arising from a connection with the party: some of his decisions as a magistrate suggest more radical views, and one of his "unusual speeches" gives the true flavour of his ideas. The *City Press* reported an address he gave as Sheriff of London to a Rotary Club luncheon:

---

27. See Alderman, *Jewish Community in British Politics*, 14–46; PRO HO/144/619: B35, 825. Of course, Abraham and Coleman were unlikely to have stated another pressing reason for their applications – namely the fear of deportation as "aliens".

he touched on the problem of unemployment. There were, he said, those who considered that shorter hours and bigger pay would be good for all. He was inclined to agree with that . . . He suggested that we should look towards giving encouragement to those who were prepared to back a 30-hour week at the present rate of pay. We must then educate everybody to enjoy leisure (Laughter). "Educate the workers to spend freely. Let them have cinemas and theatres and motors and fur coats" (Laughter) . . . What was to stop our giving luxury to the workers and enabling everyone to have a motor car? It would give employment to everyone in turn, and would cost nobody anything. (Laughter). It was a subject which was worth a lot of thinking about before they turned it down.[28]

The sounds of merriment which punctuated the speech indicate that Sir Samuel's listeners assumed that all of this was a joke; but the reported words show that he was earnest. Without the benefit of an Oxbridge education Sir Samuel had outlined – if in a crude form – a Keynesian approach to economic management. It was not the kind of speech which would often be heard in the Carlton Club; if the audience had not thought that Sir Samuel was joking they might have ensured that he never became Lord Mayor. The *City Press* published on the following Friday gave a reassuring explanation for those who were worried that the speech was sincere. Under the headline "Invalids", the newspaper reported that "[Sir Samuel's] temperature is still high, and he is likely to remain in bed for some days".[29]

As Lord Mayor, Sir Samuel Joseph continued to betray unorthodox thoughts about economic management, treating with brisk indifference considerations which would horrify any politician who – like his own son in later years – was a stickler for "monetary continence". Referring to the restoration work in the City of London, he exhorted his audience not to allow "the fear of expense" to deter them in their aims. "Throughout history", he continued, "money has invariably lessened in value, and capital expense, which may look excessive one day, is easily met thereafter. With this in mind, does it really matter if our replanning costs a few millions more or less?"[30]

While his relatives seemed happy enough to sit on the same Westminster benches as A. L. Bateman, Sir Samuel's more personal experiences at the hands of Tory anti-Semites must have dampened some of his relish for the party. Had he been an enthusiastic believer in Conservative policy before the war one might have expected his son to have shown a little more interest at Oxford. According to Lord Wilberforce, who first met Sir Keith Joseph in 1946, he was at that time "interested in wide issues but not identifiably political". Lord Blake

28. *City Press*, 9 March 1934.
29. *City Press*, 16 March 1934.
30. Quoted in *The Builder*, 13 October 1944.

remembers that they shared misgivings about the nationalisation policy of the Attlee government. But Sir Keith's official link with his chosen party was delayed until 1948, when he joined the Young Conservatives. Significantly, perhaps, his decision was taken after the publication of the *Industrial Charter* (1947), a statement of policy which showed that the Conservatives had endorsed the broad outlines of Labour's post-war programme while opposing further state intervention in industry. He was not remembered as an active member, but this might not mean very much because he was already ill when he joined.[31]

By 1953 Joseph's health had improved and he had gained a wife – that indispensable asset for an aspiring Tory candidate. Any doubts he might have had about his aptitude for politics must have diminished when Lionel Curtis asked him for his views on the most pressing issue of the day. He also found that he could establish a rapport with powerful political figures. Armed with an introductory letter from Curtis he spoke for more than an hour during his African trip with Sir Godfrey Huggins, shortly to become the first Prime Minister of the Central African Federation; Huggins discussed the problems of Rhodesia "with frankness and cogency". Significantly, at about this time Joseph asked another All Souls Fellow, the historian Raymond Carr, for a reading list on democracy; Carr remembers discussing with him the pros and cons of a parliamentary career, the impression being that Joseph had already made up his mind.[32]

Having taken so long to enter the political pool, Joseph started to swim vigorously. In a wide-ranging 1987 interview (with Anthony Seldon) he explained his motivation with his characteristic self-deprecation: "The usual mixture of altruism and egotism". If any "egotism" was present, it was of an unusual kind – the assumption that he really could make a difference through political activity, rather than trying to help others through his existing position as a private individual with plentiful means. Another man would have called this "idealism". As for the "altruism", he repeated his aim more than once so that there should be no mistake: "My main motivation was then, as it has been since, the escape of a society and of individuals from poverty . . . I had arrived anxious to *eliminate* poverty . . . I simply arrived in Parliament full of good-will, with passionate concern about poverty". It was an aim which Joseph shared with many young Conservatives after the war. In most cases, the social concern had been fuelled by the solidarity of all ranks in the armed forces. But in explaining his feelings Joseph revealed an intensity which was unusual – if not unique. In his case the war seems to have reinforced emotions which had

---

31. Lord Wilberforce, speech at KJ memorial service; letter to authors from Lord Blake.
32. KJ to Lionel Curtis, 28 May 1953, MSS Curtis, 74, fol. 155, Bodleian Library; interview with Sir Raymond Carr.

formed early in his life. Since the Churchill government elected in 1951 stood for economic progress and social harmony, there were positive reasons for his decision to stand as a Conservative, over and above his rejection of socialist principles. Yet the impression remains that he regarded the party primarily as a suitable vehicle for effecting beneficial reforms. When Margaret Thatcher wrote that she was "both by instinct and upbringing . . . always a "true blue" Conservative" she introduced a valid distinction. His upbringing was sufficient to determine Joseph's political allegiance, but there is no evidence that he felt anything like the instinctive, almost "tribal" loyalty which so often develops in partisan families. Baroness Thatcher has also recorded her excitement at the sudden contrast between Oxford University, where Conservatism was deeply unpopular, and her first party conference, where she met "hundreds of other people who believed as I did". His abstention from student politics meant that Joseph could never share this experience. Unlike near-contemporaries such as Enoch Powell and Iain Macleod, he never gained insights into the soul of the party by working inside the organisation. In many respects Joseph was an idiosyncratic Conservative, and perhaps the oddest thing about him was his evident conviction that his lack of real "roots" in the party made no difference to his attractions as a candidate.[33]

Joseph began his overtures to Conservative Central Office early in 1953, and inquiries were made as to his suitability for the candidate's list. Typically, he made no use of his family connections. His All Souls colleague Sir Arthur Salter described Sir Keith as "a very fine person, of deep and strong convictions and an unmistakable sincerity which adds to [the] force and persuasiveness of his arguments" – not a bad recommendation from one of the great public servants of the century. Salter, and the other two referees, were obviously keen that the party should not miss the chance of recruiting such a promising young man, and in their anxiety on his behalf they made some tactical departures from the truth. Viscount Long, grandson of a Tory Cabinet minister, offered the inaccurate recollection that Joseph had been head of his son's House at Harrow and "did extraordinarily well there"; but Long could be forgiven this lapse since his son Walter, slightly junior to Sir Keith at Harrow, had been killed in the war and was unavailable to prompt his father's memory. Salter thought that Joseph had resigned from the Court of Aldermen "to devote more time to his business". In fact the party was made aware of the real reason for the resignation, but it made little difference given the avalanche of testimony in the candidate's favour.[34]

Officials made the predictable assumption, without having met Sir Keith, that he must be "a man of above average intelligence as a Fellow of All Souls". That

---

33. KJ interview with Anthony Seldon, *Contemporary Record*, **1**(1), Spring 1987, 26 (our italics); Margaret Thatcher, *The Path to Power* (HarperCollins, 1995), 28, 48.
34. See correspondence in candidate file (CAND) 7, Conservative Party Archive (CPA), Bodleian Library.

impression was confirmed during interviews, and the party professionals were agreeably surprised to find that Joseph had other advantages. The Conservative Vice-Chairman for Candidates, John Hare, noted that Sir Keith had urged him to meet Lady Joseph: "I see his point in so doing, because she seemed to me to be a very charming young American, who I am sure would be an electoral asset". Hare made another interesting point in Joseph's favour, minuting that "There is a good deal of talk about anti-Semitic prejudice within the Party and his adoption, therefore, by some constituency would be helpful also for this reason". There was room for differences of opinion here; John Morrison, who was the first person to interview Joseph (on 10 February 1953) suggested that "As a Jew I suppose he is not every constituency's man and, therefore, his placing would need care".

Joseph himself had been thinking about his ideal "placing". Morrison recorded that "He is definitely not interested in anything to do with an agricultural constituency".[35] The vetting process was interrupted by the African visit, and when Joseph returned in July he declared a specific preference for the West London seats of Ealing North and East Fulham. Failing one of these, he "would take on more or less any seat in the London area with a view to gaining experience"; he would not object "if the majority against us is substantial". The following month brought a further relaxation of his conditions; he told Hare that he would "go further afield", even to distant Lancashire – provided that the seat was not contaminated by a significant rural element. It was an impressive tide of enthusiasm, but the party professionals refused to be carried away on it. In particular they could not miss the lack of previous commitment to the party, which two of Joseph's referees had addressed with sheepish replies. The exception (Salter) placed him on the "progressive" wing of the party; but despite his long record of loyalty to Churchill Salter was suspect on this point, having only in 1950 discovered that he was a Conservative. Misgivings were expressed through a concentration by the officials on Joseph's inexperience as a platform speaker – even though he must have pointed out that his oratorical skills had won him prizes at Harrow. For Joseph the objection acted as a spur for further efforts to prove himself; he arranged to undertake open-air speaking engagements in London.

The residual doubts meant that Joseph was placed on the "B" list of potential Conservative candidates. For someone who had no record of party activism this was the highest grade he could expect, although had he known of it he might have reflected wryly that he was back to the status which had become familiar to him at Harrow. At least it meant that he would have the chance to earn an "A-plus" in the field. The Conservative constituency association chairman at East

---

35. This stipulation marked Joseph off as one of the new generation of Conservatives; he had little or no experience of rural life, and clearly this was one area in which he had no impulse to accumulate knowledge.

Fulham, a seat held for Labour since 1945 by the ex-minister Michael Stewart, was impressed by Joseph's CV and placed him on a list of those "worth considering", along with the former candidate for Dartford, Margaret Thatcher.[36]

Bordering on the familiar territory of Chelsea and Kensington, East Fulham was just about the ideal seat for Joseph to fight, and when in October 1953 he emerged as the Prospective Conservative Candidate he told John Hare that he had been "surprisingly lucky" to land in such congenial territory. Possibly he was too lucky for his own good; most of his contemporaries (including Mrs Thatcher) had trailed the country looking for an opportunity, and had learned much about the nature of their party as a result. At least Joseph knew that he should lose no time in starting a canvass of the area, and he devised an ambitious strategy for winning over undecided voters for whom he planned to hold meetings addressed "by a prominent TV personality such as Robert Boothby or Hailsham". Practical steps could also be taken to exploit legislation passed by the "Socialist" Attlee government; Joseph expressed his anxiety "to start up a scheme in E. Fulham to take advantage of repair grants available under the Housing Acts of 1949".[37]

This enthusiasm helped Joseph over an early obstacle. The constituency of East Fulham disappeared in the boundary changes of 1954. A new seat, Barons Court, swallowed roughly equal portions of East Fulham and South Kensington, with a smaller segment drawn from West Fulham. The territory was just as Joseph would have wished; it was "entirely residential". By January 1955, when the Conservatives chose their candidate, he had already canvassed around 2,000 voters. His diligence ensured that there was no acrimony when he was selected to fight Barons Court, for a general election which was called for 26 May 1955 soon after Anthony Eden succeeded Winston Churchill as prime minister.[38]

The fact that the remodelled constituency was classed as a marginal seat ensured that it would receive special attention from the press and from academic observers. In an attempt to ratchet up the excitement, some London papers dubbed the local campaign "The Battle of Barons Court", but the circumstances of 1955 dictated that this would be a low-key general election and the "Battle" turned out to be "a clean, rancourless engagement". Joseph was backed by the larger army – estimates of his voluntary helpers, most of whom came from neighbouring constituencies, ranged between 700 and 1,000. Their manoeuvres began well before polling day; thirty-one party members were

---

36. Memorandum by E. Anslow-Wilson, 26 August 1953, CCO 1/10/10, CPA, Bodleian Library. In the same month the birth of twins brought a temporary halt to Mrs Thatcher's political ambitions; see Thatcher, *Path to Power*, 80–81.
37. KJ to John Hare, 2 October 1953; memorandum of 27 May 1954, CAND 7, CPA, Bodleian Library.
38. All information about the campaign in Barons Court is drawn from Robert McKenzie's study in David Butler, *The British General Election of 1955* (Frank Cass, 1969), 118–19.

assigned the task of keeping in touch with supporters who had either moved house or gone off on holiday. One of the most active of Sir Keith's foot-soldiers was Lady Joseph, who had given birth to their first child, James Samuel, in time for this essential recruit to the campaign team to be featured in publicity photographs. She compiled a list of 2,000 undecided voters and recruited thirty personal friends to pester this crucial group.

Joseph's approach to the Barons Court campaign removed any concerns that he might alienate voters by talking above their heads. At the same time, although friends had joked that the constituency should be renamed "Baronet's Court", the candidate was anxious to avoid being denounced by his Bevanite opponent as a haughty aristocrat. One incident recorded by Robert McKenzie in a special study of the constituency is a vivid evocation of Joseph in action: ". . . he showed considerable originality in his use of a visual aid designed to compare the Conservative record since 1951 with that of the Labour government during its last three and a half years in office. He had a collection of lengths of cane painted alternately red (for Labour) or blue (for Conservative)". The canes were used to compare the records of Conservative and Labour governments on a range of key domestic issues.

> As Sir Keith was handed each cane by Lady Joseph, he spoke for a minute or two on its significance and then stuck the cane into a frame. It then became in effect a statistical diagram showing, as the candidate explained, the superior achievements of the Conservatives. This admirable device misfired on at least one occasion when, to the amusement of the audience, Sir Keith got his canes mixed up. Otherwise it undoubtedly had the effect of relieving the traditional tedium of campaign oratory.

Joseph also displayed on cards some "dire warnings about the consequences of Conservative victory uttered by Labour speakers in former years", but no one at the back of the hall could read them. Elsewhere Joseph asserted that the Opposition had "lost their old kindness and progressiveness, they are a party of the past, empty of all but hatred and prejudice". Among Labour's "lies intended to fool YOU" (as Joseph put it in his campaign literature) had been the claim before 1951 that a Conservative government would create a million unemployed. Instead, after four years of Tory rule employment was "Fuller than before at higher wages". Taxation had been steadily reduced, spending on social services was up, and the cost of living had risen more slowly than it did under Labour. A re-elected government would keep up this good work, and go further in some areas; Conservatives would "not rest until every family has a decent home", and they would also work through the United Nations to abolish nuclear weapons.[39]

---

39. KJ publicity leaflet for Barons Court election, 1955, London School of Economics (LSE) archives.

In later years Joseph played down his hopes of winning Barons Court, suggesting that, in view of his happy association with Leeds North-East, he had been fortunate to lose his first contest. Yet it is a very eccentric politician who dismisses a defeat in a constituency so close to his existing home as a stroke of luck, and at the time there was an intensive effort from all concerned with the Conservative campaign. This lasted until polling day when pledged supporters were reminded on at least three occasions of their duty to vote. Those who seemed to be repenting of their promises were visited by "the most attractive feminine canvassers". But the response of the party's high command was rather disappointing; Eden made only a token appearance, and the largest gathering (of 450 people) was addressed by the vigorous but relatively obscure Minister of Transport, John Boyd-Carpenter. On balance, it seems that Labour was more anxious to retain a marginal seat than the Conservatives were to win the "Battle"; Clement Attlee and Nye Bevan both turned up to speak to an audience of 900 at Hammersmith's King's Theatre (Attlee, fighting his last campaign as leader, found the stage door locked and had to be helped over the footlights by Bevan).

The result showed that Joseph had just failed to pull off a notable victory: he lost by only 125 votes. The bare figures suggested a highly creditable first effort, and presented Joseph as the kind of "unlucky loser" who deserved a shot at a more promising seat. Only one observer thought that the Conservatives had lost because of a blunder by the candidate. Typically, this harsh witness was Joseph himself. The main local issue was the recent decision of Hammersmith Borough Council to take the income of its tenants into account when calculating rents. A campaign of non-payment began in opposition to the scheme, and as a result thirty tenants were evicted. The controversy threatened to damage the prospects of Tom Williams, the Labour candidate, since his party controlled the Borough Council and most of the tenants were potential supporters. At a public meeting two weeks before polling day he attempted a desperate compromise, combining criticism of the Council with some sympathetic noises about the reasoning behind its approach and a plea that he could not be held responsible. Unlike Williams, Joseph had no reason at all to appease the Council, and an instinctive politician would have bid for some cheap votes among the tenants by attacking the details of the plan while keeping quiet about the principle. Instead he made the mistake of being honest, taking voluntarily the line of argument which had been forced on Williams. His decision turned what might have been a resounding victory into a scoreless draw. "In retrospect", Robert McKenzie recorded, "[Joseph] was inclined to wonder whether this action in itself may have made the difference between victory and defeat". He was aware, in short, of the need for tactical ploys; but at this stage, at least, he found them alien to his nature.

If the election as a whole had produced a Conservative defeat there might have been a serious inquest into a result at Barons Court which was a fairly poor return on the special effort made by the local party. But the Conservative government was returned to power with an overall majority of 58 and this made everything seem rosy. After the election John Hare consulted with Colonel Urton of the London Area Office about the next step for Joseph. Hare had developed a high opinion of the vanquished candidate. In June he advised that Joseph should accept readoption at Barons Court, but only on the under-standing that he would be free to change horses if a better opportunity came along over the next two years. In his reply Joseph revealed that his rejection at the altar by Barons Court had only increased his political ardour; he asked to be considered for "any 'safe' vacancy wherever it might be". Geographical considerations had been flung out of the window, but his aversion to the rural population remained: to the last he stipulated that the seat should not be "mainly an agricultural constituency". The prejudice remained with him to the end of his career in the Commons; in April 1986 he told a student audience that he was willing to answer questions "on any topic except agriculture".[40]

Joseph only had to wait for a few months before his chance arrived. In early January 1956 the Conservative MP for Leeds North-East, Osbert Peake, was elevated to the peerage as Viscount Ingleby. Peake, until December 1955 the Minister for Pensions and National Insurance, had enjoyed a majority of over 9,000 and although the boundaries of his constituency had changed before the 1955 general election, Leeds North-East was regarded as a safe seat. It was predominantly residential, and its few business concerns were on a small scale: farmers and representatives of the landed aristocracy were wholly absent. Out of twelve councillors who represented the four city wards included in the constituency nine were Conservatives. Until the shock of the 1945 general election Peake had rarely visited Leeds North-East and had felt no need for an extensive canvass; although he had stepped up his efforts in recent years the local voters were not accustomed to being courted for their favours, and this was still considered to be natural Tory territory.

The Leeds North-East by-election was fixed for 9 February 1956. On 13 January the Conservative selection committee was presented with a choice between two candidates: Sir Keith Joseph, and Miss Mervyn Pike. As the local agent reported to Conservative Central Office this line-up was deeply resented by some members of the constituency party (who had received the news of a by-election so soon after the national poll as "a nasty shock"). The ill-feeling arose partly because even for a shortlist it was excessively truncated; but more wounding to the local Conservative Association were the facts that neither of the candidates was local, and that "the two finalists consisted of a Jew and a woman". Robert McKenzie had reported that at Barons Court Joseph made no

---

40. John Hare to KJ, 13 June 1955; KJ to Hare, 14 July 1955, CAND 7, CPA, Bodleian Library; Richard Kelly, *Conservative Party Conferences: The Hidden System* (Manchester University Press, 1989), 109–10.

secret of his religious background, and apparently did not suffer as a result. There was a sizeable Jewish community in Leeds; *The Times* thought that this element was "sufficient to maul savagely, or even to upset, with a blaze of inflamed feeling, the comfortably majority which Mr Osbert Peake enjoyed". But there was also a vocal element which had not been converted to multi-culturalism. Presumably the decisive factor in this choice between two misfits was Mervyn Pike's additional blunder of having avoided marriage for thirty-seven years – a state of affairs which some members of the committee might have attributed to a nightmarish outlook on life. In addition, Joseph was fortunate in that his main opponent, Labour's Harry Waterman, was also a Jew. The Conservative constituency chairman, Mr C. W. Mustill, undertook the task of reconciling the party faithful to a candidate who was at least recognised as being "most enthusiastic and able". But discontent rumbled on, and the issue of Joseph's London roots would have been aired in a leading article of the staunchly Conservative *Yorkshire Post* if the Area Publicity Officer had not issued a timely instruction for the newspaper to behave itself.[41]

It was an unpromising beginning to Joseph's relationship with Leeds, and there was no comfort to be gained from the national picture. On 7 December 1955 Clement Attlee resigned from the Labour Party leadership, and one week later Hugh Gaitskell, the former Chancellor, won a decisive victory over Nye Bevan and Herbert Morrison after an election campaign which was surprising for its lack of acrimony. Just before Christmas Frederic Bennett held Torquay for the Conservatives in a by-election, but the party's share of the vote was down by nearly 10 per cent. A government reshuffle had been expected for some months; now, on 20 December Eden dashed into what proved to be a disastrous reconstruction of his team, replacing Rab Butler at the Treasury with his most unscrupulous rival, Harold Macmillan. Another victim of this sudden blood-letting was Osbert Peake, whom Eden had privately identified as ripe for removal from the front-bench as long ago as 1945.[42]

After waiting so long to turn his love affair with the British people into a marriage Eden had been denied a protracted honeymoon. Newspaper comment in January ensured that for the Prime Minister 1956 began almost as badly as it was to end. On 2 January *The Times* opened the campaign with a leading article predicting that the government would lose office unless it began to reveal a sense of purpose. The *Daily Mail* chipped in on the following day. The authoritative voice of Conservatism was in danger of being left behind in the rush of condemnation, but the *Daily Telegraph* made up for lost time by delivering the most effective blow of all in Donald McLachan's leading article,

---

41. *Manchester Guardian*, 2 February 1956; *The Times*, 6 February 1956; Report of 17 January 1956 and undated report on Leeds North-East by-election in CCO 1/11/1, CPA, Bodleian Library; see footnote 6, Chapter 5.
42. Robert Rhodes James, *Anthony Eden* (Papermac, 1987), 311, 422–3.

"The Firm Smack of Government", which both reflected and increased grass-roots dismay. This intervention "drew from the Prime Minister a pained and pungent oath". Foolishly, Eden issued an official denial to rumours that he would stand down in the summer, and received a notably lukewarm vote of confidence from Butler when that aggrieved minister was asked whether Eden might be called "the best Prime Minister we have got".[43]

When the selection committee for Leeds North-East met on 13 January its members were already disgruntled, although as Eden gratefully recorded in his diary the *Yorkshire Post* had provided him with a lonely voice of support. But before the Prime Minister departed for talks in the United States he had time to jeopardise his party's prospects in the coming by-election by choosing Bradford as the venue for a misguided counter-attack against the press. In the speech, delivered on 18 January, he lambasted "cantankerous newspapers", and vowed to see out his full term of office "If God Wills". But Eden's God was powerless against the rival deities who had marked him out for the familiar process of madness and destruction.[44]

In his election address Joseph proved how much he had learned from his defeat at Barons Court by dealing adroitly with the Eden problem, praising the Prime Minister's contribution to world peace without mentioning him by name. He emphasised social issues, pointing out the government's achievements in clearing slums and increasing benefits while ensuring a general rise in the standard of living. He set himself the target of taking this positive message to at least 1,000 homes, and was not deterred by the limited turn-out at the public meetings. One of these events was opened by the chairman with the words "The eyes of the world are on North-East Leeds", a claim which rather exaggerated the importance of the "dozen or so people (press and officials included)" who heard it. It was thought that even the few who had merely "attended out of curiosity to see the Candidate about whom there had been so much controversy within the Association". But Joseph made a point of delivering at least one campaigning speech every night; *The Times* was impressed by the way in which he "deal[t] briskly with even the most recalcitrant and verbose old-age pensioner sitting on the front row". The *Manchester Guardian* chose appropriate cricketing metaphors when describing the candidate; he would have to be careful batting "on the pitch that Sir Anthony [had] prepared for him", and his only "flashing shot" had been an assault on "dogmatic Socialist nationalisation".[45]

---

43. Lord Butler, *The Art of the Possible*, (Hamish Hamilton, 1971), 183; Richard Lamb, *The Failure of the Eden Government* (Sidgwick & Jackson, 1987), 13.
44. Rhodes James, *Eden* 425–6.
45. "Conservative Policy is the Right Policy . . ." (1956 election leaflet); *Manchester Guardian*, 2 February 1956; Report on Leeds North-East by-election in CCO 1/11/1, CPA, Bodleian Library; *The Times*, 6 February 1956.

The latter comment was rather unfair; throughout the campaign Joseph showed plenty of aggression. But given his later remarks about his priorities on entering politics he chose a surprising theme for his key speech, delivered on 20 January at Harehills County Primary School. Instead of attacking poverty he concentrated on the interests of the self-employed, calling for an extension of pension rights and urging that "what this country needs is a sufficient supply of inventors". As the chastened *Yorkshire Post* reported:

> He believed that what the people wanted more and more was an age of freedom of choice where they would be economically free and by virtue of extended education, free socially to choose the things they wanted to do . . . Calling for a fair deal for the middle classes, Sir Keith said this section of the community had not only done much for the country by their work but they had played a large part in the cultural life of their particular neighbourhood. They had not, however, been able to regain the standards of life they enjoyed in the past.

No doubt this implied rebuke to his own party – which had evidently ignored the sufferings of the middle classes through its five years in power – went down well at this "well-attended meeting" of discontented Tories. In an article designed to answer questions from the voters Joseph placed "The encouragement of efficiency and competition in industry" at the top of a list of subjects he would raise if elected. His second cause would be the introduction of "Better 'differentials' for skilled craftsmen, supervisors and those with responsibility, and fairer treatment for the self-employed, for professional people and for the middle classes". The social services, education and housing were the last items on his list, featuring below the candidate's thoughts on the Commonwealth.[46]

Despite Joseph's well-pitched rallying cry to the bourgeoisie, when on 7 February the party's General Director Stephen Piersenné visited the constituency he found alarming evidence of apathy about the election and vigorous back-stabbing within the local party. Piersenné knew the area well, having formerly been based in Leeds as the Central Office Agent for Yorkshire.[47] His local knowledge added to the vigour of his complaints to Oliver Poole, the Chairman of the national party. "There is no evidence of any determined effort by the City organisation", he noted. "The Chairman is ill and the Vice-Chairman is away. The Chief Agent [for the City of Leeds] is unimpressive, lacks leadership and is not popular. The Agent for North East Leeds is elderly, disgruntled and apt to resent advice" (to add to those short-comings the latter

---

46. *Yorkshire Post*, 21 January, 6 February 1956.
47. We are grateful to Professor John Ramsden for pointing this out.

official was another pillar of the party to be prostrated by illness at the start of the campaign). It had been decided that no help should be requested from neighbouring constituencies, a contrast with the Battle of Barons Court which Joseph was quick to bring to Piersenné's attention. Indeed, the General Director thought that the candidate was "a trifle temperamental", and he recorded his fears that Joseph's religion would do more harm than good. Recognising that "anti-Semitic prejudice is strong", he concluded that many Conservatives would withhold support and that these lost voters would not be replaced by non-Conservative Jews since "the Jewish community as a whole is hostile to the Government". Waterman, the Labour candidate, had already tried to exploit this by criticising the Government for allowing an arms build-up to increase the instability of the Middle East; Joseph had countered on 3 February by reminding voters that Waterman came from the party of Ernest Bevin, a determined anti-Zionist. He would not have alluded to the race question had it not been raised by his opponent; he himself came from a background which was at best tepid in its enthusiasm for the state of Israel, and in any case such matters were a distraction from the domestic issues on which he based his campaign message.[48]

Piersenné thought that the Conservatives could expect a majority between 2,500 and 4,000, depending on the size of the poll. It was a gloomy forecast, but at least there was no thought of defeat. Presumably the Labour Party agreed with this assessment, and its approach to the by-election indicated that it was happy to see the fulfilment of its gloomy prophecies. After the election the Conservatives judged Waterman's campaign to have been "badly organised and conducted without evident enthusiasm". The local Labour newspaper, the *Leeds Weekly Citizen*, provided skimpy coverage after an opening plea for a vigorous fight (which appeared along with a recognition that the Conservatives had fielded "a good candidate"). The lackadaisical mood transmitted itself even to the newly crowned Labour Party leader who decided not to put in an appearance even though he represented a Leeds constituency. Given the Government's difficulties, its recent poor performance in by-elections and the controversy surrounding Joseph's selection, Labour's attitude is difficult to understand. The Opposition even had a specific local grievance, because the Conservatives had chosen an early date for the poll in order to avoid having to fight on a revised register, which would have nullified their traditional advantage in organising postal votes. It was estimated that around 20 per cent of the voters on the existing register no longer lived in the constituency. But Leeds North-East was different from the constituencies in which the government had suffered recent set-backs; there was no Liberal candidate. At Torquay the

---

48. Stephen Piersenné to Oliver Poole, 9 February 1956, CCO 1/11/1, CPA, Bodleian Library; *Evening Post*, 3 February 1956.

Liberals had taken 23.8 per cent of the poll, and only a week after Joseph's result the party notched up 36.4 per cent at Hereford. Leeds North-East was not natural Liberal territory, but the absence of a candidate from that party deprived potential Conservative protesters of their obvious outlet and may well have saved Joseph from a very damaging reversal.[49]

Although it was claimed that Sir Keith and Hellen hit their target of visiting 1,000 houses, their attempts to drum up enthusiasm for polling day were impeded by freezing weather which lasted throughout the three-week campaign, and by Lady Joseph's bout of influenza. Clad in "snow boots and with his trouser bottoms pushed into his socks", Sir Keith defied the "slush and drizzle" on his canvassing rounds to charm the faithful with a courtesy which marked his dealings in every milieu. His obvious good nature was not assumed for the occasion – it reflected his ingrained wish to avoid giving offence – but it would not have been noticed so much in a man without a title. The *Yorkshire Post* found a housewife who declared that "it speaks volumes for him turning out on a day like this", as if only an over-developed sense of *noblesse oblige* could prise a Baronet away from his fireside on a chilly day. The newspaper even thought it worthy of favourable comment that the aristocratic couple left slips of paper signed plain "Keith Joseph" or "Hellen Joseph" when their canvassing targets were away from home. Even the *Weekly Citizen* had a good word for Lady Joseph, who refused to take part in a "photo call" on nomination day when she realised that Waterman's wife had not been invited to attend.[50]

Certainly the arctic conditions provided many Labour supporters with a conclusive reason to stay indoors. Turn-out on 9 February was derisory and despite the government's unpopularity the Conservative share of the poll actually increased (compared to the 1955 figure) by almost two per cent. When the result was announced at 11pm Joseph had received just over 14,000 votes, a drop of more than 10,000 on Osbert Peake's tally at the general election; the Conservative majority was 5,869, representing a numerical fall of 3,410. In his speech of acceptance Joseph looked forward to a long association with his new constituents, and now that the victory was secure he interpreted his win as a ringing endorsement of Sir Anthony Eden.

Stephen Piersenné, preparing in Taunton for another by-election test of the Prime Minister's public standing, confessed that the outcome "was a good deal better than I had dared to hope for". But the Chief Agent for Leeds, F. Goulding, replied that he had been shocked by "the appalling poll", over-looking the influence of the redundant electoral register. Goulding pointed to an all-out effort over the last three days of the campaign as a decisive factor in the victory. The party's report on the election, however, damned Goulding and

---

49. Chris Cook and John Ramsden (eds), *By-Elections in British Politics* (Macmillan, 1973), 194; *The Times*, 6 February 1956; *Leeds Weekly Citizen*, 27 January, 3, 10 February 1956.
50. *Yorkshire Post*, 27 January 1956; *Leeds Weekly Citizen*, 17 February 1956.

everyone else concerned with the campaign – except the Josephs, who had "proved to be a very powerful team and created a good impression. Sir Keith Joseph is hardworking, able, and a good speaker". His only fault was an inability to comprehend why the organisation in the constituency was so ramshackle; despite the furore which greeted his selection he could not see why Central Office had not simply barked orders to local officials on his behalf. But any displays of temperament had been overlooked by a cheer-leading press, who agreed that Joseph came over to the public as "jolly, breezy and emphatic".[51]

Within three generations the Joseph family had moved from Petticoat Lane market to the House of Commons, and it had made the journey under its own steam. Sir Keith had become only the second Jewish Conservative to be elected to the House of Commons since 1945.[52] He could look forward to many happy years with a beautiful and supportive wife, a growing family – a daughter, Emma, was born at the end of 1956 – and constituents who would not make too many demands on him. With what looked to be a safe majority and influential friends within the party he could concentrate his efforts on making an impact at Westminster, with some reason to hope for a ministerial position before too long. Meanwhile he could contribute to his varied outside interests, in particular to the firm which his father had helped to transform into one of the country's leading building operations. There were many pleasing prospects for Sir Keith Joseph in February 1956, but perhaps most appealing was the thought that the man who had been written off at the age of thirty-one could now stand comparison with the most talented members of his extended family – even with his demanding father.

51. See correspondence in CAND 7, CPA, Bodleian Library.
52. The other, Henry d'Avigdor Goldsmid, had also been educated at Harrow and Oxford. Geoffrey Alderman has written that "neither was remotely typical of the Anglo–Jewish community"; see "Converts to the Vision in True Blue", *Times Higher Education Supplement*, 10 July 1987.

Chapter Four

The Start of an Innings

S ir Keith Joseph entered the House of Commons in February 1956 as a representative of a Conservative Party in transition. Joseph's colleagues on the
Conservative back-benches bore a similar profile to their pre-war counterparts,
with a large contingent from landed families and the world of big business. Yet
things were slowly changing. The post-war reforms recommended by the
Maxwell Fyfe committee had reduced the financial contributions which had
been demanded from most parliamentary candidates. While the immediate
impact of this change can be exaggerated – in Joseph's day only two Tory MPs
could be described as "working class" – at least the party had recognised in
principle that it should spread its social net more widely to refresh its stock of
talent. In this context Joseph himself belonged both to the past and to the
future. His business background, the paternalistic activities of his family, and
his education fitted him into the old mould. But his religion, his apparent lack
of any sympathy for the "landed interest", and his meritocratic outlook encouraged commentators to regard him as one of a new breed of Tories. In this
respect, as in so many others, Joseph was a somewhat ambiguous figure.[1]

---

1. Joseph himself seems to have thought that he represented a break with the Conservative past.
   This is suggested by his refusal to consider fighting an agricultural constituency, and his
   remark in a 1973 interview that there had been "no county element" in his family background; KJ interview with Terry Coleman.

Despite its hard-nosed image from inter-war days there was no need for the Conservative Party to engage in a radical reappraisal of priorities to accept the thinking behind Labour's welfare reforms. In social affairs there was substantial continuity between the Churchill coalition and the Attlee government. It was accepted that there had to be at least a "safety net" to protect the poorest in society from destitution.[2] But suspicion of an over-mighty state was endemic – a legacy of the steady infiltration of many Liberals into the Conservative Party which had started before 1900 – and many back-benchers feared the increase in governmental responsibilities entailed by Labour's policy. A few gave voice to their concerns; Enoch Powell, for example, claimed that Conservatives should be cautious of using the term "welfare state", since welfare was "something which ought to flow from the nature and organisation of the community itself" rather than from the anonymous and distant state. But Powell, on this as on so many issues, was unusually outspoken. The majority of Conservative MPs, believing the new system to be at best a troublesome necessity, showed their feelings by deserting the Commons' chamber when social policy was under discussion. Even they realised, though, that the parliamentary party needed to recruit people with expertise and enthusiasm. As a result, young Conservative MPs could win esteem for themselves without doing much more than sitting through debates on White Papers and ministerial statements on the work of Commissions.[3]

This reluctance on the part of most Conservatives to immerse themselves in the detailed workings of the welfare state explains, at least in part, the immediate impact created in 1950 by the One Nation group of MPs. Not all of the group's members were preoccupied with social policy, but it was a central concern for Powell, Iain Macleod, and Angus Maude, who provided the greatest intellectual impetus in the early days of One Nation. Macleod soon won government office for an attack on Bevan which showed off both his knowledge of the Health Service and his polemical skills. Neither Powell nor Maude were as "clubbable" as Macleod and both had to wait longer for promotion. The original members were never as united in their thinking as the later use of the "One Nation" slogan implies – and those who used it in the 1980s as a rallying cry against "Thatcherism" overlooked the fact that Macleod and Powell were as keen to protect the taxpayer as they were to bring succour to the needy. But the group's early publications (*One Nation* (1950) and *Change is Our*

---

2. As Harriet Jones has written, in 1945 the Conservatives had advocated "the rationalisation and extension of the social services, contingent upon financial circumstances": "The Cold War and the Santa Claus Syndrome", in Martin Francis and Ina Zweiniger-Bargielowska (eds), *The Conservatives and British Society 1880–1990* (University of Wales Press, 1996), 245.
3. Enoch Powell, "Conservatives and the Social Services", in *Political Quarterly*, Vol XXIV No. 2, April–June 1953, 156–66. In the interview with Anthony Seldon, Joseph explained his rapid rise within his party by reference to the fact that he "didn't have much competition on social issues" (*Contemporary Record*, Spring 1987, 26).

Ally (1954)) developed a distinctive approach to the "welfare state", offering the party some fertile suggestions for reform and giving the lie to the socialist jibe that Conservatives lacked constructive ideas.

Those members of One Nation who heard Joseph's maiden speech would not have instantly recognised a kindred soul. The new MP waited for three months before making his parliamentary debut, and he chose a prestigious occasion: the annual debate on the Finance Bill. On 17 April 1956 the Chancellor Harold Macmillan had delivered his only budget, increasing some taxes and pledging to cut government expenditure by the then impressive figure of £100 million. These attempts to squeeze domestic demand followed a rise in interest rates to 5.5 per cent – the highest level for twenty-five years. It was a fairly chilly message for Macmillan – an expansionist by nature – to deliver, and he offered an apparent contradiction of his own strategy by asserting that "The problem of inflation cannot be dealt with by cutting down demand; the other side of the picture is the need for increasing production". But Macmillan spiced up the dish by announcing the introduction of Premium Bonds, and his skilful presentation won a positive response from commentators.[4]

Sir Keith Joseph rose to give his views on Macmillan's measures on 9 May. He opened with the traditional appeal to his audience for tolerance, and the compulsory (contrived) reference to his constituency. What followed was praised by the next speaker (Labour's Arthur Blenkinsop) for its clarity and logic, and the newcomer was commended from the Conservative benches by Sir Edward Boyle, summing up the debate as Economic Secretary to the Treasury. Understandably nervous, Joseph had for the most part stuck to familiar territory. He had welcomed the budget; his only criticism, that it would be better to increase supply than to stifle demand, was an almost perfect echo of Macmillan's own comment. The distinctive part of the speech rehearsed arguments which would have been familiar to anyone who had followed the Leeds North-East by-election. Management, Joseph stressed, should be properly rewarded because managers took the brunt of any criticism when things went badly; in particular, incentives had to be improved for senior managers in the nationalised industries. Workers should realise that productivity increases would benefit the whole community rather than threatening jobs. There should be more labour mobility, and although Joseph was concerned that the process should be "humanised" he did not specify how this could be achieved.[5]

In short, Joseph's maiden speech was the work of a businessman loyal to the interests of his own kind and to the Conservative government. At least the ordeal had passed without an obvious slip, but the adrenalin was now surging through the Baronet and a few minutes later he tried to intervene during a

---

4. Alistair Horne, *Macmillan, 1894–1956* (Macmillan, 1988), 382–3.
5. *Hansard*, vol. 552, cols 1283–8, 9 May 1956.

speech by Labour's Ian Mikardo. A seasoned debater would have hesitated before taking on such a sharp-witted speaker, and Mikardo treated Joseph to a most appropriate rebuke: "The hon. member for Leeds, North East must get his eye in and get used to the bowling before he starts bouncing about like this. He has only recently been at the wicket for the first time".[6]

This light-hearted advice may have had an effect on Joseph, who now fell silent in the Commons for six months. It was an interesting time for a serious student to analyse the parliamentary "bowling". During the summer and autumn of 1956 tension was rising in the Middle East, with the ill and irritable Eden growing ever more enraged at the nationalist aspirations of the Egyptian leader Colonel Nasser. When in March 1956 the young King Hussein of Jordan sacked the British commander of the Arab Legion, Eden blamed the influence of Nasser. In this he was mistaken, but he was facing criticism from right-wing Tories for having negotiated the removal of British troops from Egypt and he needed a convenient outlet for his feelings. Eden had won his original reputation for his refusal to appease Mussolini. Hoping now to retrieve his position through dramatic activity, he seems to have convinced himself that in Nasser the Axis dictators were reincarnated – a familiar delusion for post-war British leaders.[7]

In July 1956 the American Eisenhower administration withdrew promised financial assistance for the Egyptian Aswan Dam. In view of later events this was a strange piece of provocation, more likely to drive Nasser into the arms of the Soviet Union than to inspire a more constructive attitude towards the West. Eden had conceived his personal hostility for Nasser because the latter's actions implied that Britain was no longer capable of independent action on the world stage; now he showed that Nasser had a point by eagerly following the US lead and cancelling assistance for the crucial dam. The Colonel's response was to announce the nationalisation of the Suez Canal Company. This action Eden knew to be perfectly legal. However, the British government was itching for a showdown and at a meeting of the Cabinet's Egypt Committee on 30 July ministers agreed that Nasser must be deposed.

In early August Harold Macmillan – acting more as an ex-Foreign Secretary than as the current Chancellor – suggested that Israel could be induced to attack Egypt as a safer alternative to direct British action. Apparently Eden was "very shocked" to hear this; that would have been the proper reaction, because the proposed pretext for an Israeli assault was to be an imaginary fear of Egyptian

---

6. *Hansard*, vol. 552, col. 1326, 9 May 1956. The sporting imagery implies that MPs were already aware of Joseph's youthful passion. As late as February 1959 the *Finchley Press* referred to him as a "cricketing MP", although there is no evidence that he played competitively after the war; John Campbell, *Margaret Thatcher: Volume One, The Grocer's Daughter* (Jonathan Cape, 2000), 117.

7. This section follows the argument in Ian Gilmour and Mark Garnett, *"Whatever Happened to the Tories?"* (Fourth Estate, 1997), chapters 4 and 5.

aggression. But Eden rapidly recovered from his shock and began to think that dragging Israel into his feud with Nasser might be helpful. A junior minister at the Foreign Office, Lord Reading, was authorised to test the likely reaction from British Jews to strong measures against the Egyptians – as if this would provide an infallible guide to the likely policy of the State of Israel. In September Edmund de Rothschild told Reading that the Jewish community was divided over Egypt but that there would be general support for firm action by the British. This was not enough for Eden, who had managed to convince himself that Israel's survival was in the balance and that in withholding a blank cheque from the Government British Jewry was playing hard to get. His emotional condition is best illustrated by the contrast with a note from the (otherwise belligerent) Marquess of Salisbury, who reminded him that "we sh[ou]ld be very chary of letting [British Jews] feel that we need them too much". Nevertheless the Prime Minister continued to hope that the Jewish community would bombard the press with angry letters and pressurise the restive Hugh Gaitskell into meek support for the government line.[8]

As a Jewish Conservative MP Sir Keith Joseph became a natural focus of interest in this feverish atmosphere. Morrison Halcrow notes that at some point during these critical months Joseph was treated to lunch by the Chancellor of the Duchy of Lancaster, the Earl of Selkirk. Although it is unclear whether this meeting took place before or after the Suez débâcle, it may well have been another attempt by the government to decipher the real thinking of the Jewish community in advance of action. If the desire for such information was the motivation for Selkirk's friendly gesture, it can only have resulted in another disappointment for Eden. Having been brought up outside the Orthodox Jewish faith Joseph was admirably placed to reinforce Rothschild's message that there was no uniform "Jewish lobby" in Britain. Being well-informed on the existing balance of forces in the Middle East he must also have known that Egypt was unlikely to attack Israel at least in the near future; presumably the meeting with Selkirk reinforced his view that any instability in the region would be highly regrettable – it could easily bring the Soviet Union into existing quarrels – and that Britain certainly must refrain from any hasty action.[9]

As informed observers would have anticipated, after Israel invaded Sinai on 29 October its well-equipped troops made rapid progress. In line with a concerted and secret plan, Britain and France then presented an ultimatum to both Egypt and Israel to stop fighting; understandably Egypt treated this with scorn, and although Israel announced its acceptance its forces pushed on. Despite almost unanimous support for a US-sponsored resolution in the United Nations demanding a ceasefire, the British stuck to their dishonourable

---

8. Horne, *Macmillan,* 400–1; Papers in PRO PREM 11/1115.
9. Halcrow, *Joseph,* 14–15.

agreement, attacking Egypt with bombers and then with ground troops who landed with the French at Port Said on 5 November. In the meantime their Israeli allies had achieved their objectives and were now anxious for a ceasefire under United Nations supervision. On the following day Eisenhower won a decisive victory in his presidential election, leaving him free to orchestrate an attack on sterling which was rapidly draining Britain's currency reserves.

Eden's deeply laid plans had resulted in a fiasco, and his government was tottering. On 5 November – the day that the Soviet Union took advantage of the international disarray and moved to crush an uprising in Hungary – Sir Edward Boyle left the Treasury and it was announced that Anthony Nutting, the Minister of State at the Foreign Office, had resigned from the government. Walter Monckton, the Minister of Defence, stepped down from that post as soon as he heard of Eden's proposed action, although he agreed to stay in the Cabinet as Paymaster-General. Even Eden's Press Secretary, William Clark (a long-standing acquaintance of Sir Keith's) resigned after being ordered to say that Nutting had intended to go anyway for personal reasons. Defections at the heart of government were serious enough, but with Labour united in opposition behind Gaitskell the Prime Minister could not afford widespread unrest on the Conservative back-benches. On 5 November, as the British troops were disembarking, Eden learned that a group of MPs, meeting at the home of Sir Alec Spearman in Queen Anne's Gate, had decided to make a protest. The Chief Whip, Edward Heath, was shown a letter signed by eleven Conservatives; the letter demanded that British troops should be placed under the orders of the United Nations. Among the signatories were Spearman, Robert Boothby, Nigel Nicolson, the former Cabinet minister Walter Elliott – and Sir Keith Joseph. Heath had his own deep reservations about the Suez misadventure, but he dutifully recorded the names of the dissidents.[10]

Joseph's behaviour during the Suez crisis could be seen as the first instance of him marching for a distance up the hill of principle before effecting a swift pragmatic retreat. In fact, his signature of the protest letter was highly courageous. When he put down his name he could have had no idea that events would shortly save him the trouble of taking matters any further. The rebels had no safety in numbers; there were enough of them to cause profound irritation, but alone they were not strong enough to threaten Eden's majority. The clandestine transmission of the letter to the Prime Minister suggests an attempt to force the government into a climb-down without a Commons vote, but if Eden and his ministers were pugnacious enough to bomb Egypt they could be expected to defy a handful of back-benchers. Joseph had hardly made a fearsome parliamentary reputation, with just a quietly received maiden speech to his name. At the very least he was putting in jeopardy his chances of early

---

10. Edward Heath, *The Course of My Life* (Hodder Headline, 1998), 171–2.

promotion; at worst, given the discontent which had surrounded his original selection for Leeds North-East, he had embarked on a course which could lead to his being dumped by his constituency party.

Why did Joseph take this risk? During the meetings at Spearman's flat (where the rebels reclined on Regency chairs and sipped whisky while uttering "terrible things" about Eden) a variety of arguments were deployed. Spearman himself had emphasised the likely economic consequences at a meeting of the 1922 Committee in September.[11] These effects looked likely to extend far beyond the immediate sterling crisis triggered by Eisenhower; apart from the prospect of UN-approved sanctions Britain's relations with oil-rich Middle East countries would be strained for the foreseeable future. To an economic expansionist like Joseph these considerations carried their own conclusions; that Harold Macmillan at the Treasury was able to disregard them for a crucial period is one of the deepest mysteries of Suez. Robert Boothby concentrated his arguments on Britain's future in the world of diplomatic alliances. According to his biographer, Boothby "condemned Eden's tactics and objectives, and particularly the failure to secure American complaisance"; this ineptitude drove him to oppose the Government despite his warm affection for Israel. On this point Joseph's confidence that Eden's policy was more likely to harm than to benefit Israel would have been reinforced by the fact that of Labour's seventeen Jewish MPs only Manny Shinwell and Harold Lever showed the remotest sympathy with the objectives of the British Government. Finally, the fact that Joseph helped to organise a Commons' motion on Hungary in the following month suggests that he regarded Nasser as an unnecessary distraction from the direct communist threat.[12]

Any mixture of these motives would be sufficient to explain Joseph's partial rebellion. That it never came to its logical conclusion in a defiance of the government whip is explained by events soon after Heath saw the letter. After a prolonged Cabinet meeting on the morning of 6 November the offensive was brought to a halt in spite of furious opposition from the French. Finally the penny – or rather, the £100 million which had been lost from Britain's reserves – had dropped with Macmillan. More than two thousand Egyptians had been killed in the ill-conceived allied offensive; British losses were slight in terms of men and machines but the damage to its international reputation was as severe as the critics had expected.

On 8 November the Government faced a vote of censure for its months of madness. Before the debate Heath informed the known Conservative rebels

---

11. Nigel Nicolson, *Long Life* (Phoenix, 1998), 164.
12. Hugh Thomas, *The Suez Affair* (Pelican, 1970), 163, 155; Robert Rhodes James, *Bob Boothby* (Headline, 1992), 382–3. The historian of Suez (and later Chairman of the Centre for Policy Studies), Lord Thomas of Swynnerton, first met Joseph at Spearman's home in 1966, and recalls that the crisis was much discussed by his fellow guests; letter to authors from Lord Thomas.

that on the following day the UN would assume responsibility, thus satisfying the demand put forward in their letter. His biographer claims that Heath also pleaded for a return to the fold on the grounds that a significant show of dissent might leave the party in the hands of its right wing; to Spearman, at least, he hinted that his seat might be in danger if he pressed his opposition any further. Heath does not recall having to talk to Joseph; in his own memoirs Anthony Barber, the whip who liaised with Yorkshire members, indicated that he, rather than Heath, persuaded the recalcitrant Baronet "not to rock the boat". Since Joseph had got what he asked for it is unlikely that he would have taken much persuading from anyone. In the end only eight die-hard rebels abstained. The mood of the party can be gauged from the fact that the unrepentant Boothby almost lost the backing of his constituency members despite his earlier popularity; Nigel Nicolson was deselected even though he received strong backing from Heath and others. If *Searchlight*, the newsletter for Leeds Conservatives, is a reliable guide the same fate might have befallen Joseph had he broken cover and failed to support the government in the vote; the issue for May 1957 asserted that time had proved Sir Anthony Eden to be right in his Suez policy. But there is no evidence that his stance provoked a rift.[13]

This was not quite the end of Suez as far as Joseph was concerned. In a futile gesture of defiance a total of 130 Conservative MPs – including many regarded as moderates – signed a motion on 27 November condemning the USA for "gravely endangering the Atlantic Alliance". On the following day twenty-six of their colleagues, including Joseph, Sir Edward Boyle, Walter Elliott, and Spearman, put their names to a riposte, which called on ministers "to do everything within their power to bring about a restoration of active cooperation between our respective Governments". The evening of the 28th saw a stormy meeting of the back-bench Foreign Affairs Committee, at which Joseph was noted among the strongest of the government's critics. The fault-lines in the Conservative Party were starkly exposed.[14]

Before these symptoms of civil war were displayed to the public Joseph witnessed the remarkable meeting of the 1922 Committee on 22 November when, with Eden *en route* to Jamaica, his senior lieutenants Rab Butler and Harold Macmillan attempted to rally the demoralised Tory troops, with very contrasting results. Butler had been unhappy about Suez from the start, while Macmillan had switched from hawk to dove almost overnight; as such, the latter was more in tune with the majority of Conservative back-benchers who were now learning that the policy they had once cheered had been a frightful mistake.

---

13. John Campbell, *Edward Heath: A Biography* (Jonathan Cape, 1993), 95, interview with Sir Edward Heath; Anthony Barber, *Taking the Tide* (Michael Russell, 1996), 105; *Leeds Searchlight*, May 1957.
14. *The Times*, 28, 29 November 1956; Andrew Roth, unpublished memorandum on KJ. We are most grateful to Mr Roth for his help on this and many other points.

Macmillan's discourse on great empires was enlivened by gestures which almost propelled Butler out of his chair; the latter, who in Eden's absence was carrying the main burden of government in difficult times delivered a constructive but dull lecture. When Eden stepped down on 9 January 1957, against his wishes Macmillan was chosen as his successor. In retirement Joseph thought that the 1922 meeting had been "one of the dominating ingredients of the Conservative party decision in [Macmillan's] favour", and marvelled at the way in which "He peppered his brilliantly effective monologue, if you can apply peppering to silences, with long pregnant silences in which you could have heard a pin drop in the packed committee room". Joseph had always been a connoisseur of oratory; by the end of his career he was also aware of the difference between a "pregnant silence" intended for dramatic effect and one induced by a frustrating search for the right words.[15]

By the time that Macmillan took the premiership Joseph had been chosen to fill his first post within the parliamentary party. In November 1956 he became honorary secretary of the back-bench Health and Social Services Committee. As he cheerfully admitted, this position was "not very strongly disputed", and nothing in Joseph's maiden speech would have led his colleagues to think that he would have offered himself for the unglamorous job.[16] But once the Suez invasion had been called off Joseph began to speak more frequently, and to specialise on the subjects which dominated the rest of his parliamentary career. During the remainder of the 1955–9 Parliament his contributions included thoughts on housing, the health service, and the elderly.

Two general features characterised Sir Keith's speeches. It was impossible to hear his views without being struck by the remarkable research effort which lay behind them. He constantly referred to the sort of publication which the majority of his colleagues would set aside after scanning the contents page – learned books and pamphlets, and closely printed reports both official and unofficial. Quite possibly the six-month gap between his first two parliamentary speeches was occupied by a concentrated burst of reading (although during these months he was also acting as secretary to a group of MPs who in December 1956 published a pamphlet on technological change, *Automation and the Consumer*).[17] Whenever he managed to fit in his research, Joseph had prepared himself for the role of Fact Finder-General to the Conservative Party on social matters; and his

---

15. KJ interview with Anthony Seldon, 27.
16. *Ibid.,* 26. Among the proposals put forward by the committee at this time was the idea that National Health Service prescription charges should be doubled; see *Sunday Times*, 6 July 1958.
17. The brief introduction to this pamphlet acknowledged that Joseph had undertaken most of the editing. The text contains several familiar Joseph themes; for example, it welcomed the Ministry of Labour's "efforts to obtain statistics and information on mobility of labour", and appealed for improved management standards in nationalised industries; see *Automation and the Consumer* (CPC, 1956), 34.

excellent memory meant that he could at will call up the recommendations and criticisms of all the relevant authorities. As he grew more confident in this role he was able to chastise those who failed to turn up to debate such vital subjects, and to goad the Opposition's own specialists when they showed that their home-work had not been as thorough as his own. Of one report, he complained that there were "not quite enough statistics to get one's teeth into".[18]

If Joseph's approach would have been warmly approved by Mr Gradgrind, in his speeches the sentiments of that archetypal Victorian were mingled with traces of feeling which another Dickensian character would have traduced as "humbug". Joseph's second general characteristic was a tendency to move beyond his rows of figures and to reveal some tenderness. For example, he showed himself to be moved by the plight of the elderly – particularly those who were lonely, isolated from their families – and referred back to his experi-ences with the Three-Score Club which had provided "cheerful circumstances and surroundings for old people who could not afford them on their own". Noting the extra heating costs incurred during winter months, in one speech he hinted that a supplement to the old-age pension might be justified – an anticipation of the Christmas bonus introduced by the Heath government nearly twenty years later. In a debate on disability which he had instigated himself he told the sparsely populated House that some disabled people had said to him: "If only we had known before the disability occurred to us what some of our colleagues were suffering, how much we would have tried to do for them".[19] It was a moving and effective message to deliver to people who themselves might become disabled at some stage – all the more poignant with hindsight, since Joseph himself spent his final years in a wheelchair.

Joseph's usual answer to these problems was more efficient delivery of services, not extra resources. He was obsessed by what he saw as poor co-ordination between welfare agencies, and toyed with the idea of a super-ministry to ensure that each branch knew what the others were doing; in this way the situation could be dramatically improved, he thought, without calling on the taxpayer. He showed a marked deference to the "expert", recommending that there should be a Social Service Staff College to which administrators from all government levels would be sent; there might also be a think-tank on the (Lionel Curtis-inspired) Chatham House model to provide ideas on better services. Convinced that a good deal of poverty persisted because potential benefit claimants were ignorant of their due he repeatedly urged better public-ity, and recommended that officials should be given more discretion in the awards they made.[20]

---

18. *Hansard*, vol. 571, cols 1590–1, 7 June 1957.
19. *Hansard*, vol. 565, cols 930–5, 4 February 1957; vol. 571, cols 1587–94, 7 June 1957.
20. *Hansard* vol. 565, cols 930–5, 4 February 1957; vol. 567, cols 253–9, 19 March 1957; vol. 604, cols 103–8, 20 April 1959; vol. 608, cols 494–501, 15 July 1959.

Joseph's faith in the virtues of the management consultant was also on display when he discussed the National Health Service. In a typical contribution he told the House that among 100,000 employees ICI employed 1,500 "work study experts"; the NHS had a pay-roll of 424,000, but this figure included only nine of these specialists. Better management techniques, he averred, would "enable fewer people at higher wages to do the same work to the better satisfaction of the client". Thankfully this process would be painless; NHS staff numbers could be reduced through natural wastage. Joseph proceeded to deluge his listeners with statistics showing vast efficiency differentials between NHS units in various parts of the country.[21]

Better than any other speech this one captures Sir Keith Joseph in his first years as an MP. His earnest inquiries were potentially invaluable, and an audit of this kind was apposite as the NHS entered its second decade. But there was a definite tendency to take his approach too far, and a failure to recognise the underlying factors that could explain discrepancies in performance. In his eyes statistical information was the only reliable guide to the existence of a problem. Once the need for reform had been established the invariable solution was to summon "work study experts" or similar luminaries; no difficulty could stand for long against a few clear-headed individuals with relevant qualifications from respected institutions. Since the answers to administrative questions seemed to be so easy Sir Keith became an avid seeker after malfunctions of the bureaucratic system. But these were subjects in which he readily acknowledged a central role for government. Outside the welfare services another system was appropriate – one which required the minimum of meddling because in some mysterious way it regulated itself. For Sir Keith Joseph, the entrepreneur was an even greater idol than the management consultant, and for the creation of wealth he placed unquestioning trust in the free market.

Joseph's best-known remark from these years was made during the debate on the 1958 budget, when he declared that "As Tories, we want more competition, production and, to be quite brutal, more bankruptcies". He repeated this many times over the years (although he dropped the admission that the remark was "quite brutal"). Equally revealing was a lyrical tribute in May 1957 to "the people who make the wealth, the dynamos of mind, energy and personality in public enterprise or private enterprise who invent, administer, organise and run things". That Joseph allowed the possibility of finding such people at work in the public sector is rather surprising, since a regular refrain in these early years was the need to raise salaries for the captains of nationalised industry in order to recruit the right people; and since the taxpayer cushioned them from the salutary fear of bankruptcy they could not hope to match the frenzied efforts of their free-market counterparts even if their pay was appropriate. Regardless of

---

21. *Hansard*, vol. 587, cols 142–6, 28 April 1958.

where they worked, Joseph thought that these highly remunerated heroes would suddenly down tools if taxes were raised. The secret was to find a level of taxation which would fund essential public services without making the ulcer-ridden "dynamos of mind, energy and personality" lose all motivation – or emigrate.[22]

Since the Conservative Party had traded successfully under the banner of economic freedom throughout the 1950s this kind of talk was commonplace. But there was something curious about Joseph's praise of entrepreneurs. The language was both flamboyant and highly abstract; unlike some of his speeches on ageing or disability there were hardly any personal touches or anecdotes to bring life into the picture. The forces in his world of Social Darwinism had nothing to do with real people; there were only teeth, claws, and blood. There was no reference to the social responsibilities associated with wealth, although so many of the businessmen known to Joseph were active supporters of charities. Almost everything he said about economics during this Parliament had the same flavour of abstraction. There was a single remark in a debate of February 1959 on Fuel and Power, when he remembered his work in a coal mine and admitted that "One week was quite enough for me"; but the same speech also featured fine examples of Joseph's "brutal" phrasing, notably his denial that governments could ever "protect producers of products made obsolete by newer, more convenient, more acceptable and more demanded materials". He went on to warn that communities which were over-dependent on a single product should never be complacent, then contradicted his previous thoughts on freeing the labour market by praising the Soviet Government's programme of "redeploying human beings for optimum progress".[23]

At a time when nice "Mr Butskell" was supposed to preside at the Treasury Board it seems strange to read speeches by a thoughtful politician whose ideas yoked Adam Smith to Stalin. But the key to understanding Joseph's economic views at this time was the context of generally rising living standards, and his status as a self-professed "passionate expansionist". The healthy economic outlook explains his remark of March 1959 that "any Government that failed to achieve full employment, generally speaking, would not remain long in office" – although to cover himself he added "unless there were such a world depression that no Government could do anything about it". Spreading affluence meant that it was possible to envisage a shorter working week and better holidays (as Joseph's father had once done); the retirement age might be raised, although (typically) he thought that there was a need for more research on this point. If the economy kept on expanding there would be more resources for the unlucky few whose independent efforts were not enough even in a society

---

22. *Hansard*, vol. 586, cols 487–93, 17 April 1958; vol. 569, col. 1048, 8 May 1957.
23. *Hansard*, vol. 599, cols 780–4, 6 February 1959.

brimming with opportunities. These unfortunates would have to remain the responsibility of a (well-managed) state bureaucracy; the rest could relish the freedom of the market, knowing that there would always be another job to go to if things went wrong at their existing workplace. Joseph's reference to the forced movement of labour was a far-sighted appreciation of the one grey cloud on a golden horizon. In some areas – particularly mining districts – technological change or cheaper imports might bring an entire industry to its knees. For that eventuality government and workers alike would have to be prepared, and if necessary cherished freedoms would have to be sacrificed on a temporary basis for the greater good.[24]

The Harrow prize-winner had certainly become a thoughtful and interesting parliamentary performer. At this time the satirical magazine *Punch* acclaimed his "fluency, pleasant manner[and] constructive criticisms"; one of his speeches on the social services, it was felt, had been "a model of what a Parliamentary speech should be and so rarely is". From time to time, however, there were lapses that a skilled politician – rather than an earnest lecturer – would have avoided. In one debate on NHS contributions Joseph interrupted a Labour speaker to confirm that health spending had recently diminished as a percentage of national income, but he went on to say that the government was still being more generous than its Labour predecessor because Britain's overall wealth had expanded so impressively under Conservative rule. The Labour MP, Sir Frederick Messer, coolly ignored the second part of Joseph's interjection and thanked him for "making my case for me". A few minutes later there was a baffling incident, when during his own speech Sir Keith refused to give way to Margaret ("Peggy") Herbison, the Labour MP for Lanarkshire North. Normally debates on social questions were good-tempered; the regular handful of participants on all sides regarded each other with the affection which often develops between people who recognise each other's eccentricity. This time Joseph was in full flood and had no patience with a potential diversion; he asserted with some asperity that Herbison had not extended a similar courtesy to him earlier in the debate, and dismissed her protestations that she had, in fact, given way to him during her speech. "Not to me today", snapped Sir Keith, "that was last month". In fact Herbison was right; she had allowed Joseph to intervene without hesitation while she was speaking that day. But a week earlier she had only relented at the third time of asking. It seems that on this occasion the excitement of dealing statistical blows to Labour on the subject of their beloved NHS had caused a temporary short-circuit in Joseph's formidable memory banks.[25]

---

24. *Hansard*, vol. 601, cols 773–86, 6 March 1959.
25. Quotation from *Punch* (undated) in Roth memorandum; *Hansard*, vol. 569, cols 1042, 1045, 8 May 1957; vol. 569, cols 215, 216, 217, 1 May 1957.

Despite his unremarkable maiden speech Joseph's real interests soon came to the notice of the One Nation group. His membership was proposed at the meeting of 14 June 1956, and he attended for the first time two weeks later. Apart from its serious work the group met for convivial dinners every week while Parliament was sitting, and for all his addiction to statistics Joseph was perfectly at home in this atmosphere. A founder member, "Cub" Alport, once wrote that One Nation took him back to the atmosphere of his Cambridge college, and to Joseph it must have seemed like Westminster's closest approximation to All Souls.[26]

In accordance with the rules of the One Nation group Joseph's membership was interrupted whenever he held a government position. But he always went back when the Conservatives returned to opposition, although his attendance was sporadic between 1964 and 1970. The main fruit of his early association was *The Responsible Society*, which appeared in March 1959. The main impetus behind this lengthy pamphlet came from Joseph and William Deedes, formerly a junior minister at the Ministry of Housing and Local Government. The original plan was for a more specialised study which would have advocated a share-holding, home-owning, high-investment society, and Joseph was the chief instigator of intensive consultations with experts in finance and business. However, this idea was dropped in favour of a more generalised pamphlet; even this might not have come to fruition had the authors not been stimulated by the likely publicity arising from what would be the 200th publication issued by the Conservative Political Centre (CPC). Political differences between individual members was a serious handicap to progress, and the final version owed much to the CPC Director, Peter Goldman. As in the case of the original *One Nation* no names were appended to the individual chapters, but there is no mistaking the style and ideas of Joseph in the contribution on the social services. He rehearsed most of the arguments which had informed his Commons' speeches: there was a need for better co-ordination among welfare services; inflation must be minimised to protect the value of benefits; the elderly deserved more generous treatment; private pension arrangements must be encouraged, etc.[27]

The new elements were a concern about the effect of welfare on the character of individuals – and an explicit recognition that "The social services for the most part are here to stay". On the first point, Joseph began by contesting what he assumed to be a general opinion: that the social services "tend to make people irresponsible". The great jurist A. V. Dicey (whose works were edited by Joseph's old tutor John Morris) wrote in 1905 that the proposition

---

26. Information on KJ and One Nation group derived from the papers of Sir John Rodgers and kindly supplied by Robert Walsha; Mark Garnett, *Alport: A Study in Loyalty* (Acumen, 1999), 105.
27. We are most grateful to Lord Deedes, Brian Harrison and Lord Carr for discussions on this pamphlet; information supplied by Robert Walsha.

"State help kills self-help" was an "undeniable truth".[28] Joseph disagreed. "Security", he wrote, "even automatic and unearned, is not necessarily demoralising. It is as much a spring board for vigour and family devotion as [is] insecurity". The reference to unearned security could be applied to Joseph's own background; as he put it with refreshing honesty, "Surely it is not seemly for critics – sometimes secure other than by their own efforts and seldom thereby demoralised – to seek to deny some share of security to their fellow citizens". More surprisingly, he declared that "social services enlarge the scope and the freedom of the individual". This reads like a clear endorsement of the "positive" view of liberty (the notion that freedom is meaningless unless an agent is assured of certain resources) most often associated with progressive Liberals in the early part of the twentieth century.[29] But Joseph discarded this outlook later in the chapter when he wrote that "Any individual, institution or industry receiving a grant of Government money suffers in a sense a restriction of liberty". There was also a threat to liberty in the growth of bureaucracy. As *The Times* noted in its review of the pamphlet, the issue of freedom was central for each of the contributors; the various authors had regarded "the past eight years of Conservative Government as a period during which some progress has been made in halting and indeed reversing the trend towards State domination and giving the individual back some share of initiative". But Joseph's indecision on this key issue was left unresolved at the end of his chapter, when he confessed that it was too early to judge the overall effects of the social services on the national character and refused to prophesy the ultimate outcome of state intervention in this sphere.[30]

The detail of Joseph's chapter, though, suggested that he felt the Conservatives could do more to "reverse the trend" in its policy towards the social services. His acknowledgement that they were a permanent fixture was qualified by his belief that there must be reform. Echoing previous One Nation writings he called for better targetting of help to those in greatest need, namely "the elderly and the chronic sick, particularly those who have no family: and especially those who, hovering between health and disability, can neither keep themselves nor come within the scope of public or private benefits". This list seems deliberately to exclude the pre-Victorian category of "able-bodied poor"; but at this time, at least, Joseph's attitude merely reflected the expectation of continuing full employment in Britain which would ensure worthwhile jobs for all those who wanted to support themselves. Part of the answer to the plight

---

28. A. V. Dicey, *Law and Opinion in England* (Macmillan, 1914), 258.
29. In a speech to the British Medical Association (BMA) of April 1959 Joseph repeated his argument, claiming that the Welfare State had "increased personal freedom and the scope for responsibility"; quoted in Nicholas Deakin, *The Politics of Welfare: Continuities and Change* (Harvester Wheatsheaf, 1994), 45.
30. One Nation group, *The Responsible Society* (CPC, 1959), 31, 32, 35, 41; *The Times*, 24 March 1959.

of the sick and elderly, as he had suggested several times in the Commons, was to give more discretion to officials of the National Assistance Board; he hoped for a gradual move away from universal benefits, which gave help to those who were able to fend for themselves, towards means-tested awards. Over time he was fairly confident that rising living standards would enable the majority of citizens to provide for old age or sickness through private insurance, resulting in a mixture of "private" and "public" benefits.[31]

Without containing anything very radical Joseph's chapter consolidated his reputation as a thoughtful student of the social services. One Nation pamphlets did not constitute party policy, but new recruits were usually regarded by the whips as potential front-bench material. By the time that *The Responsible Society* appeared Joseph had taken his first step towards ministerial rank, and his membership of One Nation almost certainly helped him on his way.

As part of the post-Suez government reshuffle, in January 1957 "Cub" Alport was moved from his position of Assistant Postmaster-General to act as Lord Home's deputy at the Commonwealth Relations Office. Since his boss was a peer Alport became the Commons' spokesman for his department, and he would need a Parliamentary Private Secretary to keep an eye on the back-bench mood. He asked the whips to suggest a suitable candidate, and Joseph's name was suggested. Alport had never heard of him, but when he received the news that Joseph was both a member of One Nation *and* a Fellow of All Souls he had no hesitation in taking the whips' advice. The fact that Joseph had never spoken a word in the House on Commonwealth subjects was no deterrent; and at least he had visited the Central African Federation, which occupied much of the CRO's time in the late 1950s.[32]

On paper it was scarcely a glittering appointment for Joseph, an impression lent inadvertent support by the fact that the *Leeds Searchlight* misinformed its readers that Alport was a Secretary of State (rather than a mere Under-Secretary). But at that time Commonwealth affairs enjoyed a much higher profile than social services – even if for the wrong reasons. Alport had always dreamed of working in this field but Suez had brought an abrupt end to his positive ideas of constructive partnership between the former peoples of the British Empire. Britain's overseas role provided Labour with an opportunity to put the Government on the back foot, and although Alport was unhappy with the general direction of policy his job was to offer some kind of defence. According to Morrison Halcrow, Joseph remembered some gloomy times in the Smoking Room after Alport had endured morale-sapping bouts with the Opposition: "It hadn't gone very well, Alport would say. What did you think, Keith? No, it didn't go well, Keith would reply bleakly. Not at all well".[33]

---

31. *Ibid.*, 34, 40.
32. Garnett, *Alport*, 134; interview with Lord Alport.
33. Halcrow, *Joseph*, 19.

Many years later Alport recalled giving some frank advice when his former PPS moved to his first ministerial position: "Always remember, Keith, that you have no political judgement".[34] This might have been what Alport *wished* that he had said; but whether he said it or not he certainly felt with hindsight that he had made a poor appointment. He was in need of someone with twitching antennae, not a hyperactive brain. When Patrick Cormack served as Joseph's PPS in the early 1970s, he explained that "a prudent Minister like Sir Keith Joseph must keep in very close touch with opinion in the House, and that is one of my principal tasks".[35] Even if he had been an instinctive politician, after only a year in the Commons Joseph was too much of a novice to detect the unspoken thoughts of his Conservative colleagues after his minister had endured the parliamentary bear-pit. As his own anecdote shows, all that Joseph could do was to confirm the pessimistic judgements which Alport had instantly made for himself in the Commons' chamber.[36]

But if Alport came to regret his choice Joseph had good reasons for contentment. In November 1956 he had made himself known to the whips as a potential rebel on a vital international question, but within a few months the power brokers had decided that he was reliable enough to act as an aide to a minister who held perhaps the most difficult government position in the field of foreign affairs. To complete the rosy picture for Joseph, his unpaid appointment meant that his membership of One Nation did not lapse, and he was free to pursue his real interests. At Blackpool on 7 October 1958 he made his first contribution at a Conservative conference (albeit at a gathering concerned with local government, which met on the day before the main proceedings). Joseph's subject was not the Commonwealth but the NHS, which he described as "a great national blessing enabling people to live longer and happier lives". He spoke once again of the need to eliminate waste, and to institute "a social services college or, if all else failed, a national health service inspectorate". His talk was later published as a CPC pamphlet. In the following month no sooner had Alport retired wounded from a bitter encounter on Commonwealth matters than Joseph stood up to second a Private Member's Bill on Family Allowances. He had already gained another platform for his ideas when he joined the Parliamentary Select Committee on Nationalised Industries, recruited by his One Nation colleague Sir Toby Low (later Lord Aldington). He

---

34. Interview with Lord Alport.
35. Cormack quoted (anonymously) in Donald Searing, *Westminster's World: Understanding Political Roles* (Harvard University Press, 1994), 291.
36. When Leo Abse entered the Commons after a by-election in 1958 Joseph approached him rather tentatively and asked whether he would consider being his parliamentary "pair". If Abse was right in thinking that Joseph had not reached an arrangement with any other Labour member before this, the anecdote would be a striking confirmation of Joseph's unsuitability as a PPS; exchanging relevant gossip with a "pair" is probably the most obvious way in which a ministerial aide can help his boss; see Leo Abse, *Margaret, Daughter of Beatrice: A Psycho-Biography of Margaret Thatcher* (Jonathan Cape, 1990), 158.

proved a most energetic member, missing only six out of fifty-five meetings and badgering the witnesses with questions. And while Alport's chances of proper relaxation were greatly reduced by the knowledge that a crisis might blow up at any time his PPS was able in September 1957 to leave for a nine-week visit to America. Not that he was planning a leisurely break beside a swimming pool: as the guest of the English Speaking Union and the Ford Foundation he went out "to look, listen and learn" on economic matters. When he returned he wrote a gushing article for the *Yorkshire Post* on lessons which Britain could derive from the USA – notably that it should establish more graduate schools for budding managers. In the following year he was off to Israel and Greece; presumably for at least part of that month he allowed himself to behave like a normal tourist, although what seems to have been his first trip to the Holy Land offered the chance for research in the wake of Suez.[37]

In March 1957, two months after Macmillan replaced Eden, the Marquess of Salisbury resigned from the Cabinet, thus striking a blow which many expected to prove fatal to the Government. In that month the Conservatives trailed Labour by 10 per cent in the Gallup Poll. But a slow recovery set in, and by August 1958 the two main parties had drawn level. In the following month the Government pulled ahead. Macmillan was as surprised as anyone by the resurgence, particularly since he had to deal with another well-publicised Cabinet crisis in January 1958 when the Chancellor of the Exchequer Peter Thorneycroft resigned with his two junior ministers, Nigel Birch and Enoch Powell. The Treasury ministers departed when their colleagues could not agree to their preferred figure for cuts in public spending. In later years Joseph became a friend of Powell's, and a supporter of his economic views; in 1958, however, he was far more likely to sympathise with the majority view in the Cabinet, because although he thought that general taxation was too high he hoped that the level might come down as a result of economic growth rather than a reduction of spending on essential services. There was never any question that on this occasion Joseph would even deliver a warning to the whips that his loyalty was in doubt.[38]

Thorneycroft's resignation – dismissed by Macmillan as "a little local difficulty" – proved to be no more than a temporary blip for the Government. The throw away line which Macmillan used in a speech at Bedford in July 1957 – "most of our people have never had it so good" – was not so much a hostage to electoral fortune as an accurate depiction of Britain's mood at this time, combined with a warning that the good times might not last. As the Parliament drew to a close Macmillan was most concerned about developments in the

---

37. Minutes of 1958 Conservative Conference, 155; *The Times*, 8 October 1958; private information; David Coombes, *The Member of Parliament and the Administration* (Allen & Unwin, 1966), 86, 92; *Leeds Searchlight*, September 1957; "Training for Management", *Yorkshire Post*, 28 November 1957.
38. For the background to this period, see John Ramsden, *The Winds of Change: Macmillan to Heath, 1957–1975* (Longman, 1996), chapter 1.

Central African Federation, where it proved impossible for him to square demands for self-government from the African population with assurances given to the white-dominated Government of Sir Roy Welensky. Fortunately for the Tories this issue proved to be less important to the voters than their general sense of well-being; hire-purchase debt (a sure barometer of the "feel-good factor") rose by a third between 1958 and 1959. Thorneycroft's replacement Derrick Heathcoat Amory cut income tax in the 1959 Budget. At the general election of 8 October the Conservatives were returned for the third consecutive time, with an overall majority of 100. For the fourth election in a row the party's represen-tation in the Commons had increased; Labour, which had hoped for much better and ran a solid campaign, seemed to be destined for permanent opposition.[39]

At Leeds North-East Sir Keith Joseph had a majority of 11,531, winning almost two-thirds of the vote. By the time of the election Leeds Conservatives had realised that (whatever their initial misgivings) they had a potential star in their midst, someone worthy of profound respect if not quite the favourite of their hearts. It was obvious that he had made a good start in Parliament, and the *Leeds Searchlight* acknowledged Joseph's growing prominence by noting the television programmes in which he was asked to appear. The marked increase in television ownership over the decade was among the clearest evidence that "Tory Freedom" had worked (although the evidence was lacking in the case of Joseph, who never allowed a set into his house). In the days before the election, the crucial new audience was treated to a Conservative broadcast in which an "unsmiling and intense" Joseph lambasted Labour's proposed pension reforms as an attempt to cheat the elderly. The other participants were Edith Pitt, a junior minister at Pensions, and Rab Butler. Even if Joseph had only been asked to appear as the token young(ish) back-bencher to illustrate the depth of talent in the party it was a flattering invitation.[40]

Despite the many calls on his time Joseph fulfilled his constituency duties and spoke at local party gatherings, such as a conference on the empire held at Leeds University and courses run by the Conservative Party at the nearby Swinton College. Elsewhere his responsibilties were growing; in 1958 he became Chairman of Bovis and a third child, Julia, was born in the following year. But now he seemed strong and confident enough to take on anything that life might throw in his way. Ten years after his breakdown and his resignation from the Court of London Aldermen Sir Keith Joseph looked the epitome of a successful modern Conservative. When Harold Macmillan appointed him Parliamentary Secretary at the Ministry of Housing, Local Government and Welsh Affairs after the election, the *Economist* commented that he was "clearly being tried out for higher office".[41]

---

39. Gilmour and Garnett, *Whatever Happened,* 150.
40. *Leeds Searchlight*, September, November 1958; *The Times*, 24 September 1959.
41. *Economist*, 31 October 1959.

Chapter 5

The Man in Whitehall

When Richard Crossman became Minister of Housing and Local Government in October 1964 he realised that:

the name "Ministry of Housing and Local Government" is an extra-ordinary misnomer. In fact the Ministry does no house building at all. The people who build are either the local authorities or private-enterprise builders. Our Ministry is a Ministry for permissions, regulations, an administrative Ministry where the Minister should be someone passion-ately interested in the judicial activities of making decisions or giving planning permissions for the future of New Towns.

Crossman was a keen observer of government machinery, but this corner of Whitehall had escaped his special scrutiny because he had expected to be sent to the Department of Education and Science. Consoled by the Prime Minister Harold Wilson with the thought that he "was to lead the housing drive", Crossman soon grasped that he was in no position to drive anything. His predecessors at the ministry, he felt, had done little more than:

add up the figures and take credit for the creation of houses which are largely the responsibility on the one side of the Ministry of Public

Building and Works, who deal with the housing industry, and on the other of the Chancellor of the Exchequer, who fixes the rate of interest which largely determines how many private-sector houses are built.

This realization was an unfortunate start to his relationship with the ministry. Crossman was only cheered by the expectations that the Government's target for house building would be met regardless of his decisions – and that he was unlikely to stay at Housing for very long.[1]

Like Crossman, Sir Keith Joseph was a newcomer to Whitehall when he was despatched in 1959 to the same ministry. But while Crossman "shot straight in with a complete lack of confidence in civil servants" and was later accused of having behaved like "a bull in a china shop" rather than a minister, Joseph settled into his new routine as if he were an old hand. His background in the construction industry was an obvious advantage, but this was only one aspect of his work. After making his first speech from the front-bench on 11 November he dealt comfortably in the House with the bewildering assortment of issues which came across his desk. The volume of work must have been a little higher than it was in Crossman's day, because after 1964 Welsh Affairs was extracted from a very miscellaneous department.[2]

Before the end of his first year in office Joseph could include caravan sites, noise abatement, water pollution and radioactive substances among the list of topics he had addressed in Parliament under the single rubric of local government affairs. These issues rarely grabbed the national headlines, but they could not be treated lightly; each attracted its troop of interest groups, demanding or opposing government intervention. As a measure of the Ministry's overall workload, at the 1961 Conservative Party conference the Housing Minister, Henry Brooke, was called upon to answer thirteen out of the twenty-one questions which were posed to the full complement of Cabinet ministers by the enthusiastic audience.[3]

Much of Joseph's work was ideal for a man who loved to sail on a sea of statistics. Less than four months into his job, for example, he was happy to correct a Member who had produced alarmist figures about a rubbish tip:

It is thought that the tip will take about 60,000 cubic yards of refuse, but this will involve not, as my hon. friend thought 50,000 tons; it will involve about 25,000 tons of refuse, and it will therefore take a shorter time to fill, because it is expected that about 200 tons of household refuse

1. Richard Crossman, *Diaries of a Cabinet Minister: Volume 1, Minister of Housing 1964–66* (Hamish Hamilton and Jonathan Cape, 1975), 25, 43; Anthony Howard, *Crossman: The Pursuit of Power* (Jonathan Cape, 1990), 265.
2. Howard, *Crossman*, 266–7.
3. Minutes of Conservative Party conference, Brighton 1961, 127–35.

will be deposited each week, instead of the 400 tons that he expected, and that 200 tons will occupy between 800 and 1,000 cubic yards . . .

A ministry with at least nominal responsibility for housing the nation in reasonable comfort might also have been better situated; located at the junction of Whitehall and Great George Street, it was described by a previous inmate as "a vast oppressive building . . . ugly, inconvenient, and without a trace of personality". These unfortunate drawbacks seem to have escaped the notice of Sir Keith Joseph, whose mind was focused on the business at hand. For the first time he could rely on a team of diligent civil servants to unearth reassuring information about rubbish tips, etc. – and unlike Crossman he was always glad of their assistance, which relieved him of the burden of making personal decisions on the myriad routine issues which cropped up. The hours were long; his immediate predecessor Reginald Bevins recalled with a shudder that the normal working day lasted from 9.45am to either 11pm or midnight, and if his performance in other posts is any guide Joseph probably worked even harder than that. It was rumoured in Whitehall that on at least one occasion civil servants had asked Lady Joseph to come to the office and calm her husband down. This was no way for a person to behave while nursing an ulcer; Joseph was sick before at least one speech. When he sat down after his first appearance at the dispatch-box, Harold Macmillan (another sufferer from pre-match nerves) is said to have offered a soothing thought: "If it's any consolation, it will get worse".[4]

If Joseph's parliamentary duties had involved nothing more than regular factual recitals this job would have been the perfect apprenticeship for him. But while much of the ministry's legislative programme could pass on the nod of dozing heads there were some issues which caused a serious stir both within and outside Parliament, and in addition to the usual partisan controversies Joseph had to be alert to attacks from his own back-benches. For example, many Conservatives deplored the rating system that along with national taxation provided the funding for local government. In February 1960 Joseph defended the rates, noting that in real terms the local tax burden had scarcely risen since the war even though "local authority services have expanded, are expanding, and will expand". But with a revaluation of properties looming – and values rising steeply in affluent areas – the Government was obliged to adopt a defensive line to appease its own natural supporters.[5]

More than a quarter of a century later the rating system became the most notorious casualty of Margaret Thatcher's protracted battle with local

---

4. Charles Hill, *Both Sides of the Hill* (Heinemann, 1964), 214; *Hansard*, vol. 617, cols 1569–70, 19 February 1960; Reginald Bevins, *The Greasy Pole: A Personal Account of the Realities of British Politics* (Hodder & Stoughton, 1965), 49; private information; Halcrow, *Joseph* 22.
5. *Hansard*, vol. 618, col. 606, 25 February 1960.

government. It was during Joseph's first stint at Housing, Local Government and Welsh Affairs that Mrs Thatcher first got to know him well, although they had met briefly before she entered the House as MP for Finchley in 1959. For a constituency with a sizeable Jewish population Joseph was an obvious choice when Mrs Thatcher invited colleagues to speak on her behalf between her (somewhat controversial) adoption meeting and the 1959 general election.[6] Joseph was reported in the local press as having defended individual liberty against encroachments by the state; Mrs Thatcher's own speeches at this time echoed the strong support for free enterprise which Joseph had demonstrated during his first campaigns at Barons Court and Leeds North-East. The pair encountered each other again early in the Parliament, when Mrs Thatcher came runner-up in a private members' ballot and decided to introduce a Bill which would prevent local councillors from denying the press access to their meetings. Having foreshadowed such legislation in the 1959 manifesto the Government was sympathetic to Mrs Thatcher's case, especially since the issue had recently resurfaced when some Labour authorities excluded journalists working for newspapers which were involved in an industrial dispute. The minister whom Mrs Thatcher consulted on technical matters during the course of the Bill was Sir Keith Joseph.[7]

Mrs Thatcher was taking a conscious risk with her Bill, because she had yet to speak in the House and by tradition a maiden speech should sidestep party controversies. But when the Bill was read for a second time, on 5 February 1960, the débutant made a favourable impression. Joseph had already taken an opportunity to signal his approval for the principle in a debate a week earlier. When the third reading took place on 13 May he replied to the debate on behalf of the Government in terms of unmistakable personal warmth. After congratulating Mrs Thatcher he noted that the subject of the Bill was contentious but felt certain that it would pass because of the "cogent, charming, lucid and composed manner of my hon. Friend. I am sure", he added, "that we all hope that this will not be her last venture into legislation". Joseph's visible support ensured Mrs Thatcher's lasting gratitude. But the key factor in ensuring the success of a Private Members' Bill is the allocation of parliamentary time, and this had been secured behind the scenes by Henry

---

6. The previous MP for Finchley, Sir John Crowder, accused Central Office of hoping to force the constituency to choose between "a bloody Jew [Peter Goldman] and a bloody woman". But despite this eerie echo of the controversies surrounding Joseph's own adoption at Leeds North-East, the battle this time took place on different lines. On this occasion the constituency selection panel had decided for tactical reasons not to put up a Jewish candidate. There was a misogynist clique in Finchley, but unlike Mervyn Pike, Joseph's unsuccessful opponent of 1956, Mrs Thatcher was married with young twins and only five members dissented from her adoption; see Campbell, *Grocer's Daughter*, 112–14; Thatcher, *Path to Power*, 98.
7. *Ibid.*, 111; Campbell, *Grocer's Daughter*, 117–18.

Brooke, Joseph's senior colleague at the ministry, in consultation with Rab Butler in his capacity of Leader of the House of Commons.[8]

By the time that Mrs Thatcher's Bill had passed through Parliament the right of the press to attend council meetings was far from being the most contentious issue facing Joseph's ministry. The Government's housing policy was at the centre of a swelling political storm. One of the great triumphs of the post-war Churchill Government had been the fulfilment of a rash target of 300,000 housing completions in a single year – an achievement which boosted the political career of the then Housing Minister, Harold Macmillan. But in the second month of Macmillan's premiership his Cabinet made a fateful decision, when it agreed to persevere with a controversial Bill which would remove rent control from houses let above a certain value. Rents which remained under control were also permitted to rise, and through "creeping decontrol" the rent for these houses would be freed from restrictions as soon as there was a change of tenant.

The 1957 Rent Act produced howls of rage from Labour. Michael Stewart, who confronted Joseph in numerous debates on the subject, summed up the case against decontrol in his memoirs: "What relaxation of rent control means is that those who are already adequately housed find it easier to improve their position, while those less well off and already cramped find their situation becoming desperate". The typical Conservative response to this view was to dismiss it as a predictable exercise in socialist alarmism. Pointing out that most rents had been fixed by wartime legislation, they argued that rising prosperity since 1939 meant that all tenants were now paying much less than they could afford. The Conservative Party stood for a "property-owning democracy" (a slogan popularised by Anthony Eden), and rent control was a powerful disincentive to people who would otherwise save to buy their own homes. Those with a special interest in the subject attributed a chronic shortage of privately owned houses for rent to the fact that landlords would rather sell their properties than receive a pittance from residents who enjoyed security of tenure. There was another element within the party – best represented by Enoch Powell, who led for the Government on second reading – which acknowledged the practical arguments but also supported decontrol on the ideological ground that economic activity of any kind ought to be as free as possible from state intervention.[9]

Joseph had made one of his first parliamentary speeches during the second reading of the controversial Bill, on 21 November 1956. Having declared an

---

8. *Hansard*, vol. 614, cols 1350–8, 756–60, 5 and 1 February 1960; vol. 623, cols 836–7, 13 May 1960; Butler to Brooke, 9 March 1960, PRO FO 1109/227. The politicians may have been helpful, but Mrs Thatcher's initiative was criticised within Joseph's ministry by the Permanent Secretary, Evelyn Sharp; see Campbell, *Grocer's Daughter*, 128.
9. Michael Stewart, *Life and Labour: An Autobiography* (Sidgwick & Jackson, 1980), 114.

interest as a Bovis director, he planted himself in the camp of ideological supporters of the measure. The ultimate goal, he asserted, should be "the creation of a really free market in housing accommodation". If landlords were permitted to charge a market rent the private sector would be saved, and the available stock would increase; the legislation would also help labour mobility. Just over a year later Joseph was ready to claim that there was now "no housing problem in the country thanks to the Rent Act", even if there had been a few early teething problems. But the party leadership was less complacent. The Act had included some safeguards which meant that the full impact of its provisions was unlikely to be felt until after the next general election, and while the likes of Powell or back-benchers who agreed with him were free to acclaim it as a triumph in itself, more cautious ministers knew that they would have to clean up the mess if the legislation caused problems once the 1959 election had been won. On taking over the ministry from Duncan Sandys in January 1957 Brooke was alarmed by the volume of complaints, which were arriving at the rate of 250 letters per day even at that early stage in the Bill's progress through Parliament. A large proportion of these letters were forwarded by Conservative back-benchers, who often enclosed covering messages implying that they had never supported the legislation in the first place. Even when the correspondents were not themselves lifelong Conservatives they indicated that the Rent Act would be highly damaging to the party. For example, the Tenants' Association of St Marylebone (an area with strong Joseph connections) thought that the Government would "have no chance whatsoever" of winning the next election unless it took immediate remedial action; the Act had been "a base betrayal" of Conservative voters. In the face of this barrage it was decided that the issue must at least be neutralised, and the 1959 manifesto ruled out an extension of decontrol. The tactic was successful. In a poll conducted at the time of the general election Gallup found that although "housing and rents" was one of only two issues on which Labour was seen as more competent than the Conservatives, only 9 per cent named this as the most important problem facing the country.[10]

By the time that Joseph joined the Government there was plenty of evidence to confirm the gloomy picture painted in the letters. The number of private properties available for rent had not risen after all. There was a decline of around 300,000 houses between 1958 and 1964, which at best meant that the rate of shrinkage in the privately rented sector had been reduced by the Act. Even the free market zealots had to take notice of this, because a further decline of supply combined with even stable demand would increase the upward pressure on rents. As a group landlords have rarely been popular and there will

---

10. *Hansard*, vol. 560, cols 1817–20, 21 November 1956; Simon Heffer, *Like the Roman: The Life of Enoch Powell* (Weidenfeld & Nicolson, 1998), 211; Malcolm J. Barnett, *The Politics of Legislation: The Rent Act 1957* (LSE, 1969), 235; correspondence in PRO HLG 41/146.

always be individuals who live down to the image; the press began to pick up stories of hard-hearted capitalists exploiting the legislation to grind the noses of their vulnerable tenants. Actually, despite its sizeable mail-bag, the ministry had little idea of the overall impact of its own policy at the time; the redoubtable Permanent Secretary, Dame Evelyn Sharp, later admitted that "no-one thought it feasible to collect worthwhile information on a national scale about so diverse and private a matter". This did not prevent Joseph – usually an avid collector of statistics – from theorising on the subject. On 26 February 1960 he told the House that the evidence of unhappiness was "not surprising", because tenants had "not been trained to a market rent". After they had received a little "training" they would appreciate the benificient effects of the Act. Most landlords had behaved reasonably, thought Joseph. In the same debate, however, Brooke was more outspoken, showing a sensitivity to the mood of the House derived from his longer experience in front-line politics; he "deplore[d] the occasional abrupt and inconsiderate clutching at the last penny" by some landlords.[11]

Decontrol might have "crept" at first, but it gathered speed and discontent accelerated with it. As three-year leases signed after the 1957 Act came up for renewal in the summer of 1960 tenants were hit by increases of up to 200 per cent, and organised protests began. Cases of real hardship resulting from the increases were brought to the attention of MPs of all parties, and the pressure intensified on Brooke and Joseph. As the careful historian of the Act has noted, the worst-affected groups were young families, large families, and the elderly, who could not afford "market" prices and also found it difficult to obtain council housing. By June Joseph was compelled to admit in the House that sudden rent increases "can be a desperate and frightening shock to the people concerned", but he thought that if rents had never been controlled in the first place the process would have generated far less pain. Joseph's tone suggests that he had convinced himself that the policy of rent control was the exclusive preserve of socialists determined to restrict the operations of the market for their own ideological purposes, but over the century such legislation had been introduced by governments of every colour, in the face of clear evidence that tenants would be exploited if they were left unprotected. Indeed the Conservative Government of Neville Chamberlain had passed the 1939 Rent Act which imposed the system of restrictions partially lifted by the legislation of 1957. In any case, the problem was not to be solved by tracing its origins.[12]

By August 1960 the rent controversy was causing profound concern at the highest levels of Government. On the 4th Brooke told Macmillan that "we must soldier through"; he saw the advantage of taking the "odium" of the policy upon himself rather than handing a poisoned chalice to a new minister. The

---

11. Evelyn Sharp, *The Ministry of Housing and Local Government* (Allen & Unwin, 1969), 244; *Hansard*, vol. 618, cols 798, 800, 26 February 1960; vol. 582, cols 951–5, 17 February 1958.
12. *Hansard*, vol. 624, cols 384–5, 21 June 1960; Barnett, *Politics of Legislation*, 254.

Government could not appear to be confessing a major error, so there was no possibility of repealing the Rent Act; Brooke satisfied himself by drafting the 1961 Housing Act, which tinkered around the edges of the problem by putting more onus on landlords to keep their properties in good repair.[13]

This approach was satisfactory to Joseph, who submitted a memorandum of his own to the Prime Minister later in August. Explaining that the problem was largely confined to London, he said that the 1957 estimates of the rate of decontrol had been too low. Many good landlords were selling out "to less reputable people, who are now out to drive very hard bargains with the tenants already in possession". To judge from his parliamentary rhetoric at this time, Joseph was puzzled rather than angered by the activities of the landlords, and the main effect of the continuing saga was to undermine his initial confidence in the problem-solving powers of government. During a July debate on land-use, for example, he adapted a political cliché to make his point: "Sometimes the market judges wrong, but it judges a great deal better than any Whitehall gentleman".[14]

Associated with the rent problem was a growing disquiet amongst Conservatives – and revulsion, both real and synthetic, on the Labour benches – at the rising cost of land and the inflated profits of speculators. There were awkward debates on this subject in March, April and July 1961, during which the Opposition produced some startling statistics. For example, one piece of land in Banstead, Surrey, was reported to have shot up in price from £2,500 to £250,000 in just eight years. The issue was particularly useful for Labour because a hint of corruption could be implied, if not openly alleged. If land was offered for sale with planning permission already granted it would be far more valuable – and the responsibility for planning decisions rested with ministers in the department. But at this stage Joseph refused to contemplate any government action on the problem, sticking to his line that the market decided values and that the recent increases represented nothing more than "a process of adjustment" to rising living standards.[15]

Amidst these troubles there were lighter moments in the parliamentary routine. Sometimes Joseph himself tried to inject humour into his speeches, with mixed results. Replying to a debate on rural water and sewerage, for example, he congratulated the Conservative MP Sir Gerald Wills who was an assiduous campaigner on the subject, noting that "great men are sometimes commemorated by fountains. My hon. friend will find that his name is writ not in water but in pipes". In June 1961, on the second reading of the uncontentious Public Health Bill, he produced a more successful piece of word-play, saying that the legislation covered a range "from rags to rinks, from cellars to

---

13. PRO PREM 11/3389, Brooke to Macmillan, 4 August 1960.
14. PRO PREM 11/3389, KJ to Macmillan, 26 August 1960; *Hansard*, vol. 627, col. 164, 18 July 1960.
15. *Hansard* vol. 644, col. 1590, 20 July 1961.

chimneys, from skiing to skittles, and from pigeons to parks". When the Bill had passed through the Commons a Labour member confessed that Joseph had "steered us through, comparatively amicably, with one or two exceptions, to a safe port at the end". In the same debate the Conservative Dame Irene Ward hailed Joseph as "a most sympathetic Minister and a most competent Parliamentary performer".[16]

Joseph's political stock had risen slightly but at Housing and Local Government he was stuck in an unpromising market-place and the thought of a move would not have been unpleasant to him. The chance came in October 1961, as a result of difficulties in a very different area of government activity.

Despite his triumph in the 1959 general election and subsequent rumours that the Labour Party was finished as a party of government, Harold Macmillan was never free from the insecurities which attend high office. Given his record as an early disciple of Keynes he was an unlikely figure to be placed on the right wing of his party by well-informed observers, but the long-standing grudge against Butler's role in appeasement meant that when the choice was made between the two men in 1957 Macmillan drew significant support from the right. Understandably he remained highly sensitive to signs of discontent from that restive element of the party, and by the autumn of 1961 there was unmistakable evidence of simmering trouble on two key issues. In July Macmillan announced that Britain was applying for membership of the European Economic Community (EEC) – a move which signalled a belated recognition of the country's more modest status in the post-war world. This sudden dose of realism was swallowed with great reluctance by the right – the more so because it had serious implications for Britain's ties with the Commonwealth. These were already causing concern in Downing Street; the Prime Minister had been pursuing a policy of disengagement from Britain's overseas territories and right-wing back-benchers who much preferred the *status quo* were protesting that the process was moving far too rapidly.

At the centre of this controversy was the Minister for Colonial Affairs, Iain Macleod. The right regarded Macleod as an unprincipled gambler, a view given memorable expression in Lord Salisbury's phrase "too clever by half". In October 1961 Macleod was pressing ahead with radical constitutional reform in the Central African Federation, and even Macmillan (who had encouraged his general approach) began to take alarm at the stirrings within his party. Macleod was far too dangerous to sack, so after some tough negotiations he was made Leader of the House of Commons and Chairman of the Conservative Party – a dual role which looked like a promotion but which in reality weakened Macleod by depriving him of a strong departmental base. The main victim of

---

16. *Hansard*, vol. 645, cols 822, 797, 28 July 1961; Charles Bellairs, *Conservative Social and Industrial Reform* (CPC, 1997), 77.

the changes, however, was Rab Butler, Macleod's former mentor, who had held the Leadership of the House and the party chairmanship in an uncomfortable combination with the Home Office.

To replace Macleod, Macmillan took Reginald Maudling away from his post of President of the Board of Trade – a choice which quickly disillusioned the right, because the new Colonial Secretary merely continued with his predecessor's radical policy. Maudling's move set off a limited game of musical chairs within the Government. Frederick Erroll, the junior minister at the Board of Trade, was promoted to the Presidency, and Sir Keith Joseph stepped into Erroll's old role of number two in the Department. There was a complete changing of the guard at Housing, Local Government and Welsh Affairs. Henry Brooke made his escape to the Home Office, to be replaced by Dr Charles Hill whose desire to run his own ministry after several years as Chancellor of the Duchy of Lancaster overcame any reservations he might have had about inheriting one of the Cabinet's hottest seats.[17]

When offered the post of Vice-President of the Board of Trade in 1841, the thirty-one-year-old William Gladstone protested that "governing packages" fell a long way short of his present ambitions. But he ended up enjoying the job. For Joseph more than a century later it represented a promotion. He was still a deputy, but at the Board of Trade this gave him the rank of Minister of State, rather than the more humble-sounding Parliamentary Secretary. His interest in trade was less personal than his feelings towards housing, but he certainly did not lack interest; it was reported that he would sometimes work as late as 2am, in a department with a long tradition of support for the principle of free trade. On the face of it there was less parliamentary drudgery; at least, there were fewer set-piece debates and they tended to be less heated because everyone agreed that exports should be encouraged. Even so, the subject matter was often complicated; during the debate on Joseph's first piece of legislation, an Export Guarantees Bill, the Conservative One Nation stalwart Sir John Vaughan Morgan joked that the new minister would "find himself studying briefs for which it is essential to have an ice pack on the head and aspirins to hand". These were the kind of briefs which made Joseph's mouth water. But at every ministerial question-time he would have to be ready to reel off his statistics, and to master all of these for Britain's trade with every country in the world was a challenge even for someone with his absorbant qualities. These occasions also encouraged controversy, since they gave MPs from all sides the chance to contest the government's opinion that membership of the Common Market would greatly improve Britain's trading position.[18]

---

17. Hill, *Both Sides*, 213–4.
18. Roy Jenkins, *Gladstone* (Macmillan, 1996), 67; *Observer*, 25 November 1962; *Hansard*, vol. 648, col. 1304, 10 November 1961.

Joseph's own favourable views on European co-operation were long-standing. When he contributed constructive criticisms to Lionel Curtis's book *The Open Road to Freedom* back in 1950 he had warned that the pursuit of a Federation including mainly the western powers would be "hideously difficult", but he approved warmly of the ideal. In one of his first speeches after his appointment to the Board of Trade, at Roubaix in Northern France, he insisted that although there would be significant economic gains if Britain joined the EEC the political advantages would be even greater; a united Europe would be "a strong force for peace", whereas a divided Europe "would be a danger to itself and to its allies". Against those within his own party who assumed that Britain had to choose between Europe and the Commonwealth, Joseph argued that "on the contrary our entry into the Common Market provides an opportunity to bring the Commonwealth and Europe closer together".[19]

Britain was already a member of the European Free Trade Area (EFTA), although this was now regarded as a poor second-best, excluding as it did the most powerful continental economies. Even so, British membership of the organisation involved Joseph in a good deal of travel. At the end of November 1961 he visited Geneva with the Lord Privy Seal, Edward Heath, to whom Macmillan had entrusted negotiations with Brussels. In April 1962 he went back to Switzerland with Heath for another meeting, and in July he travelled to Copenhagen. EFTA was not the only reason for his journeys abroad; in March he was in Luxembourg and he visited Paris in June. A skiing holiday over Christmas 1961 provided some relief, although since the venue this time was the Alps in Switzerland it was scarcely a clean break with his travelling itinerary.[20]

At Housing, Local Government and Welsh Affairs Joseph had won a reputation for the energetic conduct of his duties. On a typical visit to a housing estate he would dart into the nearest house and flush the toilet in order to gauge the quality of the building's amenities. The habit stuck; even on social visits in later life he would comment on the facilities offered by his hosts. He would rarely be seen without a notebook and pencil – tools that accompanied him for the rest of his ministerial career and into retirement. At the Board of Trade his behaviour was similar. On visits to factories he would quiz managers on their apprenticeship schemes and their design departments. Although the interrogation would include a more welcome inquiry into any extra help the Government could offer, *The Times* delicately hinted that some captains of industry might be irritated by an inquisitorial minister who "probes and criticises as well as offering praise where it is due". It was reported that in the first three months of 1961 Joseph infiltrated

19. KJ in Lionel Curtis, *The Open Road to Freedom* (Basil Blackwell, 1950), 72; *The Times* 25 November 1961.
20. *Leeds Searchlight*, December 1961, February, April, July 1962; *The Times*, 27 June 1962.

"some 50 firms" across Britain in this fashion; he calculated that, in addition, he had discussions with about 500 businessmen at his London office. But it was not entirely one-way traffic; his department claimed to be receiving 1,000 enquiries every day from British exporters.[21]

On one of his inspections, of a Meccano factory in Liverpool, Joseph tactfully conceded that he had yet to encounter an inefficient management set-up on his tours. Yet his purpose was to exhort even (or especially) the efficient firms to increase their exports. Once again the prospect of joining the Common Market provided the motive force for his efforts; if Britain's factories could not compete with their continental rivals, entry would be an economic disaster. Joseph invariably warned his hosts that "as the tariffs come down, they [would] find themselves in a tougher world and [would] have to change their policy". Industries which had been performing well on world markets would be reprimanded if their performance in Europe fell below standard. Presumably inspired by his experiences at Housing, Joseph went public with a target for British industry of £1 million additional exports per day.[22]

In a thoughtful speech to the League of Jewish Women in March 1962 Joseph alluded to "the evil of boredom" as one of the greatest misfortunes of the human condition. His working methods allowed little scope for boredom, but they were hazardous for a person whose health had broken down in the late 1940s under far less pressure. His headlong pace was symbolised by one of the few anecdotes about his time at the Board of Trade, when in February 1962 he turned up for a tour of Edinburgh without his luggage: "he had to buy another razor and scribble another speech". But his energetic approach to business was attracting notice. In March he delivered an unpublicised speech at "a private meeting of Tory MPs"; according to Andrew Roth, Joseph "held them spellbound", and this was reported back to Downing Street. Other sources confirm that he was an excellent performer in front of the small groups who attended Conservative back-bench committees. Macmillan – who was beginning to doubt whether "young people today have learned how to work" because some of his more youthful ministers seemed to be flagging – was sure to be impressed by what he heard. The only question seemed to be which department would provide a suitable harness for all this enthusiasm. The meteoric minister was still without a place in the Cabinet, and he would soon be diverted back onto a familiar course.[23]

Macmillan was already brooding on the prospects for his party, and in March the Liberals stormed home by almost 8,000 votes in the "safe" Conservative seat of Orpington. This result the Prime Minister considered to be a "staggering

---

21. *The Times*, 28 March 1962.
22. *The Times*, 28 March, 12 January 1962.
23. Speech at Woburn House, London, reported in *Jewish Chronicle*, 9 March 1962; Roth memorandum; Harold Macmillan, *At the End of the Day* (Macmillan, 1973), 56; private information.

blow".[24] Other by-elections in the spring told a similar story – of an electorate flocking to the Liberals to register their protest against a tired Government. Macmillan and Macleod looked to the Chancellor, Selwyn Lloyd, for a Budget fillip; instead, Lloyd produced a dull package which was remembered only for its introduction of a new tax on sweets and ice cream. The Government continued to limp in the opinion polls. On 11 July Macleod warned the Prime Minister that the party had to steel itself for a thumping defeat in a forthcoming by-election at Leicester North-East, and that it was time for an urgent reconstruction of the Government. On the same day, Butler inadvertently gave the press advance notice that the Chancellor was to be dropped from the Cabinet.

Many observers were mystified by the fact that Selwyn Lloyd had survived the fall of Anthony Eden, since he had been Foreign Secretary (at least in name) during the Suez fiasco. His move to the Treasury in July 1960 did not arrest the decline in his political fortunes. At the end of his first year in his new office he jolted the complacent beneficiaries of the "affluent society" by pointing out that wages were outstripping productivity improvements, and instituting a "pay pause" to help correct the imbalance. The Tories had ridden high on the tide of prosperity; now it seemed that they were about to sink as the familiar post-war economic pattern of "stop-go" reasserted itself. After the announcement of the pay pause Selwyn Lloyd became the most unpopular Chancellor since the war.

When news of Lloyd's imminent departure leaked out the supposedly "unflappable" Macmillan panicked. He seemed to have a guilt-complex about his Chancellor; in addition, he had convinced himself that members of the Cabinet were preparing themselves for his own removal from office. The chief plotter was supposed to be Butler; the Prime Minister's mistaken assumption that he was preparing to strike was based on an accurate calculation of the injuries he had caused to that mistreated minister. Butler could be humiliated again by a further demotion, but he could not be turned out of the Cabinet with safety. The blows had to be aimed elsewhere. On the day that the voters of Leicester North-East went to the polls Macmillan sacked seven ministers in a ferocious cull which immortalised 12 July 1962 as "the night of the long knives". Lloyd was taken aback; he had presented a routine economic review to the Cabinet that morning without any sign from his leader that by the end of the day he would be relieved of his heavy cares. Although he now despised Macmillan Lloyd declined to air his grievances in public. Most of the other victims had clearly been selected because they had outlived their usefulness – an imputation which caused widespread resentment. Macmillan thought that the axed Lord Chancellor, Kilmuir, had been "splendid" when told of his

---

24. Macmillan, *End of the Day*, 57.

dismissal, but the fallen minister (the former Sir David Maxwell Fyfe) was merely saving his resentment for his memoirs. The Education Secretary Sir David Eccles, who at fifty-nine was ten years younger than his leader, was a strange person to be placed in the ranks of the superannuated; he protested that he had been "sacked with less notice than a housemaid". By contrast Dr Charles Hill, the popular wartime "Radio Doctor", claimed in his own auto-biography that he had long expected his job at Housing, Local Government and Welsh Affairs to come to an end before the next election.[25]

If Macmillan had botched his butchery he proved to be much more shrewd in his constructive work. Among those who now took Cabinet rank were Enoch Powell (who remained at Health) Sir Edward Boyle (Education) – and Sir Keith Joseph, who took over from the "Radio Doctor" at the head of his old ministry. Including such able politicians as Macleod, Maudling (Lloyd's replacement as Chancellor), Heath, Hailsham and Butler, this has been called with justice "the most intellectually gifted Conservative Cabinet of the century". It was also potentially volatile; three of its members (Boyle, Powell and Peter Thorneycroft) had recent experience of resignation, and when he was at the Colonial Office Macleod had developed the habit of threatening to leave the Government whenever he wanted to force the Prime Minister's hand. But at the first meeting of the new Cabinet Macmillan felt "a sense of freshness and interest" from his colleagues. Explaining his changes to the Queen, he wrote that Boyle and Joseph represented "active and energetic youth". At forty, Boyle was Joseph's junior by four years.[26]

Although the new appointees received less press attention than their slaughtered predecessors it was generally agreed that Macmillan had strength-ened his team. Joseph was hailed by *The Times* as "one of the party's progressive intellectuals", although it noted that "he is not the most Bravura performer at the Dispatch Box". The *Sunday Express* went still further and its enthusiasm induced an historical error: "Sir Keith is the first Jew for more than twenty years to enter a Tory Cabinet. He could well become the first Jew since Disraeli to form one".[27] For a man who had only been a Member of Parliament for six and a half years it was a remarkable rise. A reminder of where it all started was a letter (among 500 messages of congratulation) from his old CRO boss "Cub" Alport, now High Commissioner to the Central African Federation. Joseph replied that "To think back these last few years makes me, and probably you, dizzy".[28]

The compliment to Joseph was all the greater because Macmillan, remember-ing his own experiences, put housing near the top of his list when he thought of

25. Hill, *Both Sides*, 100; Gilmour & Garnett, *Whatever Happened*, 173.
26. *Ibid.*; Macmillan, *End of the Day*, 98.
27. *The Times*, 14 July 1962; *Sunday Express* quoted in Roth memorandum. The last Jewish Cabi-net minister was Leslie Hore-Belisha; while Disraeli had been born to a Jewish family (and continued to acknowledge his ancestry) he had been christened at an early age.
28. KJ to Alport, 23 July 1962, Alport MSS, Box 17.

the issues which could win (or lose) an election. If Joseph had not previously been aware of this, the point was made forcibly enough in a Prime Ministerial memo of 23 August which identified significant scope for "imaginative and necessary improvements". In October Macmillan's over-heated imagination conjured for the Cabinet the vision of a new town in London which would be built on derelict land purchased by central government: "Would like Minister of Housing to look at this. Think big. £500 million for a start". By the end of the year Macmillan had calmed down a little, but was still hectoring Joseph: "You must (and will) recreate the spirit of 1951–4". Rather than endorsing Crossman's pessimism Joseph would have agreed with Charles Hill's identification of "the tremendous scope that a Minister of Housing and Local Government has for contributing to the country's faster social and economic modernisation". But he knew enough about the existing situation to feel that his Prime Minister was asking a great deal of him; and he already put too much pressure on himself to relish the thought that an ex-Minister of Housing was pinning so much on his performance. By February 1963 he had become so defensive about his ministry that he told the Party Chairman that housing was far less important in electoral terms than education and leisure.[29]

Joseph soon found himself under pressure from Macmillan in other ways. One possible complication to cloud his happy prospect as a new Cabinet minister (and privy counsellor – he was the first in his family to achieve either of these distinctions) was his position as a major shareholder in Bovis. Given the responsibilities of the department there was a strong likelihood that the Opposition would try to argue that there was a conflict of interest. Indeed, there had been some investigation by the press into this question when Joseph first joined the government in 1959, at which time he had relinquished the Bovis chairmanship. Oddly, though, this did not become a problem for several months after Joseph entered the Cabinet. Then, in February 1963, he was asked by the Prime Minister to clarify the situation. Possibly this was a response to recent press reports of a £600,000 deal for Bovis to rebuild Marks & Spencer's Reading store. Certainly one of Joseph's colleagues recalls being troubled at the time by the minister's close association with the Sieff family which controlled the retail firm.[30] To Macmillan's memo Joseph replied with what would soon become a fateful phrase in a different context; there was "no impropriety whatsoever in the present position" regarding the 52,000 shares controlled by himself and Lady Joseph. "I do not see myself any conflict of interest here", he told Macmillan; he had been advised at each stage of his career that he had no reason to sell the shares – nor, apparently, to take any other kind of action.

---

29. KJ to Harold Macmillan, 4 February 1963, PRO PREM 11/4942; Macmillan to KJ, 23 August, 12 December 1962, PRO PREM 11/4297; Hill, *Both Sides*, 229; CPA CRD/52/9, Bodleian Library, Chairman's committee meeting 4 February 1963.
30. Private information.

Sir Keith's defence was that the shares owned by Lady Joseph and himself amounted to no more than 2–2.5 per cent of the total – hardly a controlling interest. Even so, it was a substantial block of shares and it was well known that Joseph had a strong sentimental tie with the company. A reply drafted for Macmillan gives a clear answer to the question which Joseph's letter studiously avoided: whether or not he had placed the shares in the hands of trustees. He had not. Now he was asked to do so, and to "sever any continuing connection which you may have with the management of Bovis which might be construed as enabling you to advise them about their affairs". Furthermore, he was not to deal with any business within his ministry which directly affected Bovis. In a rather huffy reply to the Prime Minister Joseph pointed out that he had already severed his formal connections with Bovis, and that he had arranged for Henry Brooke to deal with any business which might affect the firm's interests.[31]

Even at first glance this is a curious story, although its implications seem more serious today, after so many stories of ministerial skulduggery in financial affairs. The business background which made Joseph an ideal candidate for his office also placed him at the centre of a possible (if minor) scandal. Of course, there was nothing to prevent him from gossiping with his former colleagues (and relatives) at Bovis about forthcoming developments, whether or not he maintained a formal connection. That connection was pretty certain to be re-established when he left office, and since the decision-making process within the ministry was notoriously slow he would continue to possess valuable inside information for months (if not years) after he relinquished his post. Joseph obviously regarded any suggestion that he might exploit his office in this way as a slur on his character. His conduct must be taken as a striking example of his honesty – and of his naïveté. In response, he briefly swung to the opposite extreme and became excessively cautious. In the summer of 1963 Lord Alport returned from Africa to find that promises of new political office were not being honoured. When he asked Joseph if he could help to find some work for him through his business contacts, the latter showed his usual generosity. But he decided not to ask Geoffrey Rippon to see if anything could be arranged through his PPS Albert Costain, because this would be "indirectly an approach to a building organisation" since Costain's family were major players in that business. He suggested that Alport should write directly to the Chairman of Costain's. The irony in the fact that Rippon, responsible for so many of the government's building plans, should have appointed for his PPS a member of the Costain family was apparently lost on Joseph.[32]

---

31. Memorandum from Macmillan to KJ, 13 February 1963; KJ to Macmillan, 4, 18 February 1963, PRO PREM 11/4942
32. KJ to Alport, 9 August 1963, Alport MSS; Patrick Dunleavy, *The Politics of Mass Housing in Britain, 1945–1975* (Clarendon Press, 1981), 20.

Yet there is an even more baffling postscript. When discussing Joseph's *initial* government appointment back in 1959 Morrison Halcrow relates a story – provided during an interview with Joseph himself – which cannot be squared with the documentary evidence. After noting that the accepted practice on being appointed to a closely related department was to place shares with trustees, Halcrow continues:

> When [Joseph] was summoned to the Prime Minister's room at the Commons he had omitted, in the excitement of being offered a job, to raise the matter [of the shares], which occurred to him only as he emerged into the corridor. He paused, wondering whether he ought to go straight back in. In the corridor, as he recalled, there was one of those fatherly policemen who are part of Commons folklore, who looked at the hesitant figure and decided he needed advice. "Never 'esitate, sir", he said. "Never 'esitate".[33]

The story seems the more convincing for its Josephite flavour of self-deprecation. But nowhere in the government record is there any suggestion that the shares had been discussed with Macmillan prior to Joseph's entry into the Cabinet in 1962 – three years after the policeman supposedly helped to convince him to make a full disclosure. In his first letter to Macmillan Joseph alluded to advice taken on previous occasions, which would have given him an ideal pretext to remind his leader that the matter had been dealt with satisfactorily in 1959. But in what he clearly regarded as a comprehensive defence of his conduct Joseph offered no hint that he had previously brought the shares to the Prime Minister's attention. In fact, although guidelines for share-ownership had first been drawn up at the time of the Marconi Scandal when Asquith was Prime Minister, there had been several revisions since then. The latest version had been written by Butler in response to a press campaign against the Transport Secretary Ernest Marples in 1960 – i.e. *after* Joseph joined the government as a junior minister. The fact that a new, more rigorous attitude to business interests had arisen since his first appointment offers an entirely innocent explanation for Joseph's failure to mention the shares during his interview with Macmillan. But the quaint story of the cockney bobby is more suggestive of residual guilt over the episode than a lapse of memory.[34]

Before his first month was over Joseph was given a striking reintroduction to the passions aroused by housing in Britain. Around 250 residents of Bethnal Green nursing grievances against their landlords paid a visit to Mulberry Walk. Sir Keith was out at the time, but the police allowed four protestors to knock at

---

33. Halcrow, *Joseph*, 21
34. For guidelines on shares see PRO PREM 11/4945. Butler's memorandum was drawn up on 28 January 1960.

the door and Lady Joseph invited them in to await her husband. The *Daily Express* reported that the crowd "recognised him at once" when Joseph returned ten minutes later – a sign of an enhanced profile which could have been given under more gratifying circumstances. When he heard that the four-man deputation was in his house he said "I hope they haven't woken the children", a typical piece of solicitude which only encouraged the besieging army to renew its chanting. Stepping inside he found the protestors helping themselves to drinks in his drawing-room. The refreshment was all that they got out of the minister, who told them that he could promise nothing because the issue was still being considered. But they did not have to wait for long; as the *Leeds Searchlight* reported in September, among Joseph's early decisions in his new post was to authorise the issue of compulsory purchase orders against the Bethnal Green landlords. Uncharacteristically the minister seems to have taken some notice of this useful lesson in public relations; before the end of the year he had invited three representatives of London's homeless to Mulberry Walk and encouraged their children to join Lady Joseph's "tea, milk and biscuit party around the electric fire". But the family had not seen the last of such demonstrations; there was a similar siege (this time by sixty pensioners) in March 1973.[35]

The size of Joseph's task was emphasised by a memorandum drawn up by the Conservative Research Department at his request. Entitled "Tory Housing Discontents", it listed eight problem areas, including rates, the shortage of housing, the failure to deal with land speculators, and the impact of the Rent Act. The "feeling that there is not enough house building to meet present and prospective requirements" meant that "we are tending to lose the initiative on the housing front". Displeasure at rent increases was combined in some areas with envy of council house occupants whose rents were heavily subsidised even when they were relatively affluent. The memo struck a shrewd note in illustrating the sort of grievance held against the operation of the Rent Act; it cited cases of elderly couples who had spent money on maintaining their property now being faced with a choice between paying more rent or buying the house – neither of which they could afford. The elderly – particularly those who had exercised "thrift" during their lives – were always likely to arouse Joseph's sympathies.[36]

Yet before returning to his old department Joseph had demonstrated that his affection for the Rent Act still outweighed his sympathy with aggrieved tenants, and his priority was further decontrol, not an attempt to modify the legislation in order to protect its victims. At a meeting of the Party Chairman's committee two months before his appointment he had argued that "creeping decontrol" had been far too slow: "Supposing you freed the lot so that commerce would

---

35. *Daily Express*, 30 July 1962; *Leeds Searchlight*, September 1962; Roth memorandum.
36. Memorandum, 17 July 1962, CPA CRD 2/23/24, Bodleian Library.

come in and buy up?" Iain Macleod replied that such blind obedience to the precepts of economic liberalism would be to commit electoral "*hara-kiri*". Later Joseph returned to the charge, urging that a policy of total decontrol should be combined "with refuge shelters and threats against the landlords"; this would ensure "a sensible system of housing" and "renew the housing of this country". This time the response of "political suicide" came not just from the wily Party Chairman but from all the members of his committee.[37]

At the time of that meeting Joseph cannot have expected to return so soon to his old ministry, and it was more difficult to let down his ideological hair once he had been landed with overall responsibility for housing. From the start he struck a realistic note, at least when discussing the outlook with colleagues. Before his departure Hill had tried to respond to his leader's urgings, but judging from the official records it seems that his language had been all too sober for Macmillan's taste. Joseph's approach must have convinced the Prime Minister that he had made a shrewd appointment, even if the diagnosis was still bleak. His first memorandum to the Cabinet reads like a rehearsal of Labour complaints – but at least the prose was more dynamic than anything the weary Radio Doctor could now manage. "We need a new impetus in housing", Joseph informed the Cabinet of 2 October:

> The 4 million post-war houses – 3 million of them under Conservative administration – have been largely absorbed by the rise in the number of households, caused by changing habits and prosperity . . . So that, in spite of all we have done, housing is still desperately short in many places; hundreds of thousands of families are living in slums, many more in houses grossly ill-equipped . . . most people it is true are better housed today than ever before; but this only sharpens the contrast with the rest. Housing, high-lighted now by the ugly phenomenon of homelessness in London, is a source of bitter and constant criticism of the Government – from all directions.

In general terms, Joseph sketched what he felt to be the most promising way of breaking through the gloom. "We ought not to be content with anything less than the maximum practicable effort", he wrote, and (apeing the entrepreneurial language he admired so much) "we shall never make progress unless we take risks". There should be more productivity in the building industry because pre-fabricated units of reasonable quality could now be mass-produced, home improvements should be encouraged through additional grants, slums could be cleared within ten or fifteen years, and a target of 350,000 new houses per year should be set. London was (correctly) identified as the biggest problem; the

---

37. CCO CRD 2/52/9, 7 May 1962.

Government should encourage the relocation of offices from that booming area.[38]

On the afternoon of 10 October Joseph gave his first speech as a Cabinet minister to a Conservative Party conference, which met in Llandudno that year. In Wales Joseph could claim to be on home ground; at the Eisteddfod earlier in the year he had already proved equal to the task of singing *Land of My Fathers* in Welsh (a test which a later minister comprehensively failed). The motion on 10 October called on the government to speed up slum clearance and house building, and the debate was lively. Graham Page, the MP for Crosby, demanded a target of half a million new homes a year for the next five years, while a speaker from Huddersfield argued that slum clearance should be less of a priority than home improvements – a position which a later speaker called "disgraceful".

The conference required from Joseph an acknowledgement of the problems, followed swiftly by an assurance of better things to come. It was a challenge to which he responded with great skill, producing a brisk, businesslike perform-ance, not only promising progress but also explaining how this might be achieved. He rehearsed his hopeful arguments about new industrial techniques. Two more new towns were "on the horizon", and a more determined search could be made for building space in existing urban areas. There were no precise targets (as yet), but he heralded "the biggest slum clearance drive ever. We shall aim to double or treble the rate of clearance in some of the areas where the slum blight lies heaviest". The conference rewarded him with a spontaneous standing ovation – the first that year – and the resolution was passed unani-mously.[39]

The press identified Joseph as the star of the show. The *Economist* welcomed his "air of ruthless determination", and in other papers he was singled out as "the most vigorous and forceful" of the new ministers. Lengthy profiles began to appear in the heavyweight papers, furnished from the cuttings library with the dubious stories – about "Smokey Joe" and "firing on all cylinders" – which would be repeated in almost all such articles over the years. In the *Sunday Express*, "Crossbencher" noted that his reputation "has soared astoundingly"; the column also acknowledged his "bustling brilliance". Typically, Joseph was troubled rather than elated by the praise, knowing that the reception of his speech had raised expectations which would be difficult to satisfy or restrain. It had, in fact, been a lacklustre first day of the conference, and it was fairly easy to shine out against such a dull background.[40]

Housing was more than enough for one person to worry about, but there was a good deal of unfinished business on other matters. "Crossbencher" had

38. CAB(62)143, 2 October 1962.
39. Minutes of Eighty-First Annual Conference (1962), 33–39.
40. *Economist*, 13 October 1962; *Observer*, 25 November 1962; *Sunday Express*, 18 November 1962.

noted that Joseph "has been smartly harvesting the credit for many of the projects prepared by his predecessor at Housing, Dr Charles Hill". As if to answer this charge, in the spring of 1963 Joseph wrote privately to Hill, expressing the hope that "I leave in train for my successor as much in hand as you left for me". However, he noted that some of this business he would have preferred to do without. Ironically he instanced the rates and the reorganisation of London government, both of which were headaches inherited by Hill from Brooke and Joseph when they left the ministry back in 1961. There was widespread dismay when the new rates bills arrived in 1963 – Joseph's own rates for Mulberry Walk rose by 50 per cent. In July he asserted that "We all value local government independence, and we all know that rates are the only means by which local government draws an independent source of money". But the clamour was too loud, and much of it came from those who had retired on fixed incomes to seaside resorts – the last resting-places of many Conservative voters. Hill had set up a committee to examine the situation once the revaluation was in place, and when it reported Joseph had to rush through legislation to cushion those hardest hit with subsidies raised from central taxation. It was not lost on Labour that the action in this case was lightning-fast compared to the response to the impact of rent increases which mainly affected working-class people.[41]

The Rates (Interim Relief) Act could never be more than a plaster stuck over a wound which would continue to fester. By contrast the London Government Bill which Joseph introduced as one of his first duties was intended to produce lasting benefits. In the name of efficient, modern administration it took responsibility for many services from the London Boroughs, and replaced the London County Council (LCC) with a directly elected Greater London Council (GLC). Bringing suburban areas under the London umbrella meant that while the LCC had often been controlled by Labour the electorate for the new body seemed likely to favour the Conservatives. As such, the legislation was fiercely opposed by Labour. This gave Joseph an opportunity to denounce the Opposition for failing to move with the times, and for falling short of their democratic aspirations: "One would have thought", he mocked, "that this proposal that Londoners should have an effective say in the shaping of their own environment would have an obvious appeal". The Government had to resort to a guillotine motion curtailing debate, which brought its own democratic credentials into question. More seriously, the "obvious appeal" of the reorganisation failed to register with many suburban Tories, who were appalled by the idea of being spatchcocked into London boroughs.[42]

The Government's decision to ignore its supporters and press ahead with the London reforms was matched in other parts of the country, where historic

---

41. *Ibid.*; Hill, *Both Sides*, 221; *Hansard* vol. 682, col. 199, 29 July 1963.
42. *Hansard*, vol. 669, col. 53, 10 December 1962; Ramsden, *Winds of Change*, 178.

jurisdictions such as the Soke of Peterborough were to be stitched onto neighbouring counties. Joseph understood the attachment to ancient names, but he felt that the country had to be "modernised" whether or not the changes were popular. Privately he suggested that the number of local authorities should be halved "(though one dare not say this in public)". As such, he pressed hard for the acceptance of a recommendation that the tiny county of Rutland should be absorbed by Leicestershire. As early as 1960, when he made his debut at a Conservative Party conference, he had joked uneasily about the level of opposition to this reform, but that was during the period of phoney war over Rutland which had come to an end by 1963.[43]

In March Joseph steeled himself for a battle over Rutland, which he called "the linchpin" of the reorganisation programme. Marshalling his arguments for the Government's Home Affairs Committee, he began with an attempt at a disarming admission: "It is not easy; and indeed I would dodge it if I could". But reorganisation was necessary, and Rutland's champions missed the point: "When small authorities say 'we are efficient' they mean that they do well the little things they do – and that is often true. But they can only do little things . . .". The logic was impeccable, but Joseph resisted its most radical implication – that the existing local government bodies should be capped by a handful of regional authorities. In any case, the voice of logic contradicted the promptings of political calculation. The Committee deferred a decision, and in April Joseph returned with a concession: the announcement could be postponed for a few months. This was still not enough to win the support of his colleagues.[44]

Joseph's stubborn defence of the proposal alarmed his party chairman, who had clearly marked him as one of the Government's most dangerous fire-hazards. Macleod told Macmillan that he had long ago "put it to the Minister that on the whole it would be easier for us to push our local government proposals . . . if at the same time, we gave a convincing demonstration that we were not just governed by statistics". With a flexibility of mind – some might call it cynicism – which was impossible for one of Joseph's temperament Macleod inverted the usual logic. Rutland might only have a population of 25,000, but this actually strengthened the case for saving it in order to sneak the other reforms past a party faithful with a nostalgic attachment to the traditions of old England. Macleod had too many guns for Joseph, who retired from the field after further bloody encounters at Home Affairs and before the whole Cabinet in July. On 1 August Joseph had to explain to the Commons why Rutland was really a different case from those of the Soke of Peterborough and other districts that now disappeared from the map. While it is not unusual for

43. KJ to Alec Home, PRO PREM 11/4856; 79th Conservative Party conference (1960).
44. HA (63) 36, 25 March 1963; HA (63) 51, 23 April 1963. For Joseph's negative views on a regional tier of government, see record of his conversation with Alastair Hetherington, 17 March 1964, Hetherington Papers 6/20, LSE archives.

ministers to defend in the House decisions which have been forced on them behind the scenes, Joseph departed from typical practice by ensuring that Kenneth Lewis, the local MP, was told where the credit really belonged for "saving" Rutland.[45]

Joseph's part in the Rutland affair is a reasonable indication of his political development after his first year as a Cabinet minister. For all his many virtues he still had an underdeveloped sense of politics as "The Art of the Possible". In one sense he had been unlucky, in that he was a member of a government which by the summer of 1963 had been in office for twelve years. Joseph might try to blame the Attlee government for some of his problems, but by now this line of argument could hardly raise a cheer even from Conservative back-benchers. For the most part Joseph was burdened by the legacy of his own party, which greatly reduced his chances of wriggling out of a tight spot. In particular, for a time after Suez ministers seemed to have developed the habit of thinking that they could not possibly win the next general election, so that risks could be taken in some areas and Royal Commissions established in others in the expectation that someone else would be on lookout when the sky grew dark with chickens coming home to roost. 1957 was a particularly fateful year for Joseph; it saw the passage of the Rent Act, and the establishment of the committee which recommended the Rutland *anschluss*. The habit died hard. For the Ministry of Transport 1960 was an *annus horribilis*; the much-maligned Dr Richard Beeching was appointed to head an inquiry into the railway network just before Christmas.

At the end of January 1963 the Government received a fresh blow when its application to join the EEC was vetoed by General de Gaulle. Ironically this reversal exposed a mistake made before Suez – Anthony Eden's decision to stay out of the talks which originally established the Community. By this time the signs of government decay were unmistakable to most observers. The next election could not be called later than October 1964; up to that date the Conservatives could expect more bad news, but Macleod rightly felt that they should guard themselves against fresh mistakes which would alienate their core supporters. Joseph's view that ministers should do the right thing regardless of the consequences was all very well in good times but potentially disastrous for his party in the circumstances of 1963. Even when the Government was distracted from constructive suggestions by a wave of scandals he was causing irritation with unseasonal ideas, minuting to Macmillan in May 1963 that there should be a Cabinet committee on general issues of social policy. Although the Prime Minister gave a patient reply it was far too late in the Parliament to think of such a thing. Joseph, in short, was almost the ideal minister for fair weather

---

45. PRO PREM 11/ 4339; *Hansard* vol. 682, cols 662–8; Nigel Fisher, *Iain Macleod* (Andre Deutsch, 1970), 216.

– but, as one of the Government's back-bench critics later said, under Macmillan it could never be "glad confident morning again".[46]

If Joseph's political nose was still under-developed even he felt it twitching by the end of March. On the 21st of that month Standing Committee F was discussing the London Government Bill for the twenty-first time. At about five o'clock Ben Parkin, the Labour MP for North Paddington, rose to speak about the capital's sewerage system. To the surprise of those who had remained to debate this worthy subject on what was the last day of the Bill's committee stage, a discourse about the problem of storm water took a sudden diversion into what Parkin described as "the case of the missing model". Parkin was making a mischievous allusion to rumours that the Minister for War, John Profumo, had been party to the disappearance of Christine Keeler, a Crown witness who had been involved in a shooting incident. The perplexed chairman of the committee interjected that "I do not think there is anything about a missing model in this schedule", whereupon Parkin made an obscure attempt to demonstrate the relevance of his remarks to the matter in hand. He sprinkled his excuse with technical jargon, which evidently satisfied Sir Keith Joseph who congratulated him on his contribution. But the press had been alerted to the fact that Labour was about to break its parliamentary silence on the Profumo Affair.[47]

On the same evening the freedom of the press was debated by the Commons, and this presented Labour's George Wigg with a more promising opportunity to refer to the matter than London's sewage problems had done. A few days later Ben Parkin was approached in a lobby by a visibly agitated Minister for Housing, who asked him to confirm that his musings on the missing model had not really been about sewage. By this time the political storm water was flooding over the Government. After Wigg's speech, which had been supported by Crossman and Barbara Castle, five ministers interrogated Profumo who denied any "impropriety" in his relationship with Keeler. On 22 March Profumo misled the House of Commons by repeating this denial. He did not admit his fault and resign until 4 June; the delay allowed the press plenty of time to feed on the rumours, and ensured maximum damage to the Government's image, already tarnished by the scandal surrounding the spy John Vassall.[48]

Ministers who had been scattered across the world reassembled for a Cabinet meeting at Admiralty House on 12 June. When they left the press was massing outside. Joseph pleaded to be allowed through the throng because he had a lunch engagement. Some of his colleagues showed by their demeanour that it had been an unhappy gathering. Speculation immediately centred on

---

46. PRO PREM 11/4109.
47. Clive Irving, Ron Hall and Jeremy Washington, *Scandal '63: A Study of the Profumo Affair* (Heinemann, 1963), 97–8.
48. *Ibid.*, 98.

Enoch Powell, the Health Minister, but the London papers that evening named three others who were said to be deeply dissatisfied with the Prime Minister's explanation of the handling of the Profumo Affair. These were Henry Brooke, Sir Edward Boyle and Sir Keith Joseph. Revelling in the image of an incorruptible member of a decadent administration, Powell did not signal his decision to stay in office for three days: with encouragement from Downing Street, the others issued immediate statements of support for Macmillan. Joseph, assisted by Macmillan's press secretary Harold Evans, admitted that like his colleagues he was dismayed by the course of events but protested that he had no idea how rumours of his intention to resign could have started. Unconscious of the dangers of being seen to protest too much, he repeated his denial in a speech to his constituents.[49]

For the second time in his career it seemed that Joseph had picked up the standard of rebellion only to lay it down again. In fact, on this occasion he probably never thought of touching it. In the summer of 1963 he was working closely with Powell on a scheme to guarantee a minimum income for pensioners; presumably it was this experience which inspired his sincere and lasting respect for Powell's intellect, although from the outset he had been attracted by what he later described as "that marvellous voice I can't hope to match".[50] But far from being involved in some sort of conspiracy, it seems that Joseph was only linked with Powell on this occasion by uninspired guesswork. Powell and Brooke were the last to leave the Cabinet meeting, having remained behind to press the Lord Chancellor, Dilhorne, for further information. Once the over-heated reporters had realised that at least one minister was apparently considering his position anyone else who had left the Cabinet meeting with a worried expression – or failed to make a statement supportive of the Prime Minister – was assumed to be in the resigning mood. Joseph wore an expression of this kind even when the government was popular, and his desire to hurry off to lunch could be misread as a wish to think through his position before saying anything. Even so, Joseph was genuinely unhappy about the implications of Profumo. Possibly the pain was increased by his knowledge that the disgraced minister had been a near-contemporary at Harrow. Although the Cabinet minutes for 12 June are even less informative than usual, Powell's concern was that the five ministers who interviewed the War Minister had failed so miserably to uncover the truth as to arouse suspicions that they had been trying to suppress it. The Prime Minister's own honour was not involved directly – indeed his aloofness from the matter was held to be a sign that he was out of touch with modern life. Ditching the pilot at the height of the storm and at such a late stage in the Parliament was hardly calculated to improve the

---

49. *Ibid.*, 155; PRO PREM 11/4370.
50. Robert Shepherd, *Enoch Powell: A Portrait* (Hutchinson, 1996), 252; John Ranelagh, *Thatcher's People* (HarperCollins, 1991), 138.

party's chances of clinging to office. But Joseph, more anxious than most that his ministerial work should not be ended by electoral defeat, was sure to be infected by the gloomy mood of the meeting.

Joseph was soon involved more deeply in another embarrassing episode for the Government. A well-publicised participant in the Profumo scandal was Peter (originally Perec) Rachman, who had died in November 1962 but whose legacy earned him a bizarre afterlife of notoriety. Rachman had been numbered among the many lovers of Keeler's friend, Mandy Rice-Davies; so deep was his affection for the girl that, soon after his marriage to a different lady, he presented her with a white Jaguar car. He had already been the subject of media attention for his activities in the London housing market; after Profumo he became the archetype of the grasping landlord. From 1963 onwards "Rachman-ism" has been a shorthand notation for the shady and oppressive dealings of some landlords in the wake of the 1957 Rent Act.

Rachman had limited physical appeal; he was described as "short, plump and balding". Yet like another protagonist in the Profumo Affair, Stephen Ward, he had an ability to charm members of both sexes. Not the least of his attractions was his opulent lifestyle; for him, white Jaguars were the equivalent of the average suitor's bunch of roses. As in the case of the corrupt foreign financier Melmotte in Anthony Trollope's *The Way We Live Now*, the suggestion of sharp practice did nothing to deter his admirers; anyway it was offset by a carefully constructed catalogue of good works. It seemed to increase media interest that Rachman was Eastern European by origin, and a Jew.

Rachman began his work by purchasing a house off the Harrow Road in the mid-1950s. The eight-roomed property was cheap because all but one of the rooms was subject to rent control. The enterprising landlord rented the other room to eight West Indians, who had been selected because of their musical enthusiasm. He told his new tenants that he was very liberal-minded and would not object if they held regular parties. The other tenants soon left, allowing Rachman to re-let their rooms on new terms as allowed by the Rent Act. As Rachman's empire spread through Paddington, Bayswater and North Kensington his methods became more spectacular; when the tenants of one house proved difficult to shift he hired some workmen to "repair" the roof, and after stripping the tiles they never returned.[51]

When the *Sunday Times* published the results of an investigation into Rachman's activities on 7 July 1963 the newspaper knew that it had netted a scoop; only a month after Profumo's resignation the public was still thirsty for tales of misdeeds by "fashionable" people. Joseph was mentioned in passing; sharing Rachman's apparent enthusiasm for housing associations, he had donated £25 towards one of the tycoon's schemes. On 22 July Labour tried to

---

51. *Sunday Times*, 7 July 1963.

exploit the situation by staging a vote of no confidence in the Government's housing policy. Harold Wilson claimed that "there must surely be honoured places for portraits of a Macmillan, a Sandys, a Brooke, a Hill and a Joseph" at Rachman's headquarters. This typical Wilsonian sally produced another myth in the Joseph story; before long it was being reported that pictures of Brooke and Joseph really *did* adorn the walls of Rachman's Hampstead home. There were other palpable hits at the minister; Wilson's researchers had dug up the story of a victimised tenant with the surname of Joseph, who deserved to enjoy "the same rights under our laws [as] any of his kinsmen".[52]

The Conservatives desperately needed a strong reply from Joseph. Macmillan was unavoidably absent from the debate, but he had sent his minister a note which was intended to boost his morale: "I am sure you will do well on Monday . . . you have *done* a lot to improve things and I feel sure that you will be able to get this over to the House and – very important – the Press". If the wording made Joseph feel that Macmillan's confidence in him was less than absolute he would have been right; on the same day his leader asked the Chief Secretary to the Treasury, John Boyd-Carpenter, if he might postpone a trip to Germany to ensure that the debate had "a powerful wind-up" speech. Joseph had yet to encounter the Labour leader in debate, but he was buoyed up by the memory of a clash with Michael Stewart in early May, when he had attacked Labour's "panaceas" on housing which added up to "shifty, shifting, vote catching, double talk". At the end of that speech his colleagues had rushed from the back-benches to pat him on the back.[53]

Joseph's performance on 22 July was less spectacular, but it was still a sound effort given that he was batting on a very sticky wicket. His task was to defend the Rent Act and to deny that Rachman's activities had arisen from that legislation, while admitting that London was a problem which merited some urgent action. Quoting figures produced by the housing expert Professor David Donnison, he claimed that whereas in the past houses and flats were almost all sold as soon as a tenancy ended, four-fifths of them were now being re-let. Even if the rents were now much higher, this meant at least that the Act had slowed down the rate of decline in the private sector, preserving a "third way" for tenants who could obtain neither council accommodation nor a property of their own. He showed his distaste for the activities of Rachman and his kind, but argued that these had begun before the passage of the Rent Act and that there would have been prosecutions had tighter laws been available at the time.

Joseph was certain in his own mind that the Rent Act should not be blamed for Rachman's activities, although no one could deny that its terms must have increased the landlord's takings. The most effective passage of the speech came

---

52. *Sunday Times*, 7 July 1963; Keith Banting, *Poverty, Politics and Policy: Britain in the 1960s* (Macmillan, 1979), 25–6; Halcrow, *Joseph*, 30; *Hansard*, vol. 680, col. 1064, 22 July 1963.
53. PRO PREM 11/ 4297; *The Times*, 3 May 1963.

when he switched from defence to a brisk attack on Wilson. Pointing out that the Labour leader had shown little interest in housing before some connection had been established with the Profumo affair, he contrasted Wilson's conduct with that of the "diligent, capable and very conscientious" Michael Stewart who had refused to drag this serious issue down to the level of a "general smear" on the Government. Unfortunately he over-egged his portrait of Wilson as an opportunist. In pointing out that Labour knew all about the problem of tenant intimidation long ago, Joseph inadvertently let it slip that Ben Parkin had briefed him on the subject back in 1960. Since Labour was arguing that the Government should have taken sterner action without delay, Joseph had gone some distance towards making their case for them. He also announced the establishment of a committee to look into London's problems, to be chaired by Sir Milner Holland. He was right to assert that such a committee had been in contemplation for some months, but as the official papers show the process had at least been accelerated because of the furore over Rachman.[54]

At the end of his speech Joseph noted that "The only main answer is more houses", and as usual he upheld the present government's record as superior to anything that Labour had done in the past or was capable of doing if it returned to office. It was enough to keep his own benches fairly happy, but it showed the real weakness of the Rent Act. The "Gentleman in Whitehall" had proved equally fallible when relaxing regulation as he had done when it was imposed. It was perfectly true that most tenants were enjoying a bargain deal by 1957, and some could afford to pay considerably more. Supporters of the Bill had genuinely believed that it would increase the supply of rented housing. But when Conservatives like Powell (and Joseph) chose to support the Bill on ideological grounds they ensured that Labour would place it high on the list of measures to repeal if it won the next election – and back in 1957 this had seemed more likely than not. Landlords were unlikely to start a frenzy of new building in these circumstances; instead they could be expected to squeeze as much as possible out of their existing stock. In short, the Conservatives should have built in far more safeguards from the start – that they did not proved that on this occasion ideology triumphed over electoral calculation. When the blow fell they could argue that the worst abuses were concentrated in London – but this only meant that they were sure to attract the maximum, damaging publicity. Once in place the Rent Act became such a shibboleth of the party that it could not be repealed without a humiliating volte-face; the result was a series of palliative measures, introduced too late to protect ministers from the consequences of their own blunder. It should have been an instructive lesson, but it was ignored by Margaret Thatcher who inflicted an even more deadly wound on her party when she pushed through the Poll Tax. When that decision

---

54. See correspondence on the appointment of Milner Holland in PRO PREM 11/4297; *Hansard*, vol. 680, cols 1077–92, 22 July 1963.

was taken Joseph was about to leave office for the last time, but in supporting her policy he showed himself to be equally forgetful of the nightmares which the Rent Act had caused him. By that time, indeed, he looked back on the Rent Act as a well-intentioned measure which had not gone far enough.[55]

Although Joseph had fought off his critics the Rachman scandal had been a disagreeable distraction from the constructive tasks which he had set himself. His hopes centred on a White Paper which was published in June 1963. The main proposal was the establishment of a Housing Corporation, with funds of £100 million, to lend on attractive terms to people who wanted to club together to build houses. This built on a more modest scheme introduced in the 1961 Housing Act; it promised an alternative means of providing cheap accommodation without enhancing the powers of local government. Other sections of the White Paper, however, were clearly designed to redress the balance between tenant and landlord which had been tilted too far by the infamous Rent Act. The most controversial proposal was to compel landlords to improve run-down properties. When brought before the Cabinet in May 1963 this notion provoked a damning memorandum from Enoch Powell, who accused Joseph of acting on a principle which could only be familiar to socialists. Commenting on Powell's paper, Iain Macleod deplored Joseph's "appalling hostages to fortune" which were "revolutionary" and "objectionable to a Tory": "we should be in no doubt with what horror these Fabian proposals will be greeted by many of our party". With the battle for Rutland raging on in other Cabinet committees Macleod was more convinced than ever that Joseph was a loose cannon on the Government's deck. But this time the battle went against the Party Chairman – Joseph's proposals only had a few teeth extracted before the publication of the White Paper. More predictably he received strong support from Macmillan; this secured the Cabinet's backing for a target of 350,000 houses per year, against Powell's furious complaints.[56]

The new Housing Bill had to wait until the Government's legislative programme of 1963–4, which party managers knew could settle the outcome of the next general election. Despite the crippling setbacks of De Gaulle's veto and the Profumo affair Macmillan had decided that he would lead the Conservatives into the fight with a resurgent Labour Party. The key battleground would be the question of which party could best modernise Britain, and it was obvious that the issue of housing would be well to the fore. But before Joseph had the chance to explain his plans for the future to the House of Commons the modernising Macmillan had been replaced as Prime Minister by a man whose opponents lampooned him as a relic from the feudal system.

---

55. *Ibid.*; KJ interview with Anthony Seldon, 28.
56. For Cabinet papers by KJ and Powell see CP (63) 80 and 84; for Macleod memorandum (15 May 1963) see PRO PREM 11/4297; for discussions in Cabinet see CC 63 (32), 16 May 1963.

Chapter 6

"Blind"

S ir Keith Joseph arrived in Blackpool for the 1963 Conservative Party conference knowing that he was unlikely to repeat his triumph of the previous
year. But at least he had won another Cabinet skirmish over his housing plans,
and could give his audience something to cheer. The Chief Secretary to the
Treasury, John Boyd-Carpenter, had doubted the wisdom of raising the annual
target for housing completions once more. Joseph now wanted a figure of
400,000 per year for 1965–70 – despite the fact that in his White Paper of June
he had deliberately omitted a definite deadline even for the 350,000 target – and
Boyd-Carpenter had objected that this would overstretch capacity in the building industry. Persuading Macmillan of the need for higher housing targets was
never very difficult, and Joseph overcame any reluctance the Prime Minister
might have felt this time by predicting that an early announcement would steal
the thunder of Labour, who seemed likely to unveil a similar figure as their goal
if they won the next election. Besides, bad weather at the start of 1963 meant
that this was going to be a poor year for completions, so there was even more
ground to make up.[1]

The debate went well for Joseph, whose ambitions appeared more moderate
and attainable once the Crosby MP Graham Page had repeated his attempt to

---

1. Boyd-Carpenter to KJ, 4 October 1963; KJ to Macmillan, 7 October 1963, PRO PREM 11/
   4297.

raise the bidding to half a million houses per year. Joseph also predicted that his Housing Bill would be "very unpopular with bad landlords who exploit the housing shortage". An earlier speaker had pointed out the urgent need for action in the wake of the Rachman scandal: "We are identified with [bad landlords]. The mud is on us all. And make no mistake about it, it will remain on us until we tackle this business as it should be tackled". The other current public bogeyman – the land speculator – was also threatened in a section of Joseph's speech which hinted that the state might acquire land for major developments and cream off the profits when it was resold. Joseph distinguished his idea from the Land Commission proposed by Labour; this, he said, would go much further and would enmesh even the small property-owner in a bureaucratic nightmare. As usual, Joseph defended the Rent Act and denounced Labour's plans to repeal it.[2]

Joseph's speech was well received and the anodyne resolution he supported was passed unanimously. But, as *The Times* reported, the official proceedings of the 1963 conference very rarely "flared to life". Before the opening session on 9 October the Chairman of the National Union announced that the Prime Minister had been taken ill and would not be travelling to Blackpool. On the previous day Macmillan had presided over a Cabinet meeting in great discomfort from what turned out to be a relatively minor prostate problem. At that stage only Enoch Powell among his colleagues openly suggested a change of leader, but once Macmillan had been told that an operation was necessary and that he could not travel to the conference everyone's thoughts turned to the identity of his successor. As a result, the atmosphere on the first day of the conference was one of "bemused unreality", and the platform was often half-empty as some of the less bemused Cabinet ministers considered their next moves in privacy.[3]

The winning side in "The War of the Macmillan Succession" adopted brilliant tactics. As his sympathetic biographer has written, "Alec Home played the part of reluctant candidate to perfection", and although Macmillan was able to choreograph the process from his hospital bed only a skilful operator could have secured such a position after appearing somewhat irrelevant when it became clear that he would have to resign. But the strategic thinking was gravely flawed. Although the supporters of Lord Home calculated that his quiet charm made their man the "unity" candidate, a contrived campaign on his behalf opened the prospect of prolonged recrimination after the choice had been made. Another obvious question for those who pushed Home forward was his ability to handle Wilson in Commons clashes; this was less of a problem with Macmillan's previous preference, Lord Hailsham (Quintin Hogg), who

---

2. Minutes of Eighty-Second Annual Conservative Party Conference (9–12 October 1963), 29, 31–3.
3. *The Times* 10 October 1963.

had also been in the Lords for many years but was known as a bruising and quick-witted debater. From an electoral perspective the relatively new television factor was crucial, and while loyal Conservatives might deplore the shallow showmanship of Wilson there could be no guarantee that the voting public would prefer "the old governing class at its best" when it entered British living-rooms in the shape of Alec Home.[4]

Had the party been given an opportunity for prolonged reflection instead of being stampeded into a decision one important consideration would have been whether or not to choose a leader from the rising generation of politicians. The Chancellor Reginald Maudling (forty-six) was thought to be among the front-line contenders, but he had never been Macmillan's choice and his outside chance was torpedoed by a lame speech to the conference. Edward Heath, one year older than Maudling, had been strongly tipped early in the year but his public profile had faded after the failure of the EEC talks.

By October 1963 another member of this talented generation had emerged as a possible runner. A handful of Conservatives – mainly those connected with the "modernising" Bow Group – upheld the claims of Sir Keith Joseph. Their ideas were summed up in a book written in 1964 by Timothy Raison, the former editor of the Bow Group's magazine *Crossbow*. Raison attacked Labour for placing their emphasis "on the redistribution rather than the creation of wealth, on security rather than drive, on curbing the powerful forces of the market rather than on taking advantage of them, on constraining rather than liberating". By contrast, Conservatives recognised that "the real drive in any economy which is largely dependent on capitalism must always come from the individual. It is the entrepreneur whom we must encourage and breed". But Raison also envisaged a creative role for the state in the economy; for example, he argued that "only the most bigoted adherent of *laisser-faire* is likely to object to a system of common consultation on industrial and economic problems between government, industry, unions, and other parties". Although he shied away from the level of intervention involved in French economic planning, he noted that this had been instrumental in securing post-war recovery. On welfare, Raison believed that the state should be more selective, but more generous where its assistance was really needed. He accepted that countries such as West Germany had "managed both to operate successful competitive economies and to provide generous welfare services"; regrettably Britain's economy was too weak for this as yet, and there was always the underlying problem of whether excessive generosity would lead to "dependency". But the title of Raison's chapter, "Progressive Welfare", was an apt slogan for his preferred policy.[5]

---

4. D. R. Thorpe, *Alec Douglas-Home* (Sinclair-Stevenson, 1997), 294.
5. On the Bow Group, see Ramsden, *Winds of Change*, 53–4; Timothy Raison, *Why Conservative?* (Penguin, 1964), 46–7, 51, 66.

What they lacked in numbers the young "modernisers" made up for with their enthusiasm, and, exemplified by the future Cabinet minister David Howell, they tended to be among the most able of the young Conservatives.[6] Howell recalled that Joseph was something of an idol for the Bow Group, with his hatred of inefficiency, his obvious social concern, and his well-groomed appearance. Presumably it was a Bow Grouper who told a *Daily Mail* reporter at about this time that Joseph could become "the Tory Jack Kennedy". One seasoned observer recalled that members of the Joseph lobby would take political correspondents to one side and say "Brilliant mind, old boy. Young. Extremely good in debate. The new image the party needs". In 1963 such talk was premature; even if his generation had been given a free run at the leadership Joseph could not have beaten Maudling or Heath. And whereas the latter pair had joined the Commons in 1950, Joseph was still a relative newcomer. But there was plenty of time to catch up – if his ambition matched his obvious abilities.[7]

In retirement Joseph remembered his own opinion of the battle between his senior colleagues. He saw Lord Home as "the right choice, simply in terms of integrity". Joseph "still had not fallen under the spell of Butler. As for the other candidates who had been flaunting their talents at Blackpool, he admired but had reservations about Quintin Hogg; he was suspicious of Reginald Maudling". Joseph had found the scenes at the conference "very vulgar" – when Hogg disclaimed his peerage amidst great enthusiasm he was reported as looking "embarrassed" on the platform. He was happy to escape back to London to discuss the situation with Macmillan on 16 October.[8]

If the Conservative Party was the main long-term casualty of the 1963 leadership battle, truth was a very early (and predictable) victim. Macmillan and his allies were determined to keep Butler out, even though he was the clear favourite among the electorate. There was no formal procedure within the party at the time, but it had to appear that there had been some element of consultation to "prove" that Butler did not command the support of the party. The soundings of MPs and peers taken by the Chief Whip Martin Redmayne would not have satisfied the most cavalier market researcher. Redmayne, who had been encouraging Home to consider making himself available for the leadership since the summer, designed his questions in order to elicit the preferred answer – that Home had the fewest enemies.[9] This conclusion was apparently supported by the Cabinet, which was canvassed by the Lord Chancellor, Dilhorne. But amongst those whom Dilhorne recorded as making

---

6. Raison's book appeared in a series outlining the philosophy of the competing parties before the 1964 general election.
7. Roth memorandum; interview with Lord Howell.
8. Halcrow, *Joseph*, 32–3; Dennis Walters' diary, quoted in Thorpe, *Douglas-Home*, 286.
9. Thorpe, *Douglas-Home*, 289.

Home their first choice for leader were Iain Macleod (who later resigned in protest at the *coup d'état* before writing for the *Spectator* a scathing account of Dilhorne's role) and Sir Edward Boyle (who would have followed Macleod out of the Cabinet if Butler had held firm and refused to serve under Home). Macleod's reputation as a man of deep calculation has allowed Dilhorne's defenders to suggest that he might have given his "vote" to Home as part of some labyrinthine plot to advance his own interests. If so, his later conduct was incomprehensible, and the theory does nothing to explain the presence on the list of Boyle who had no conceivable motive for such antics.[10]

Dilhorne's "findings" survive in the Public Records Office. Not everything he wrote down was inaccurate; so long as he had forged a clear majority for Home he could afford to list the real choices of at least some of those whose loyalties were too obvious to misrepresent. Thus, for example, Enoch Powell was correctly recorded as a Butler man, and the "vulgar" Hailsham was allotted Peter Thorneycroft, thus doubling his tiny Cabinet retinue. A little-noticed oddity of the list is the treatment of Sir Keith Joseph. At first he was put down as a "Home man", but, uniquely on the list of first choices Dilhorne later scratched out his name and allocated him to Maudling. The same amendment occurs on other lists, in which various candidates are assumed to be out of the running but Home and Maudling are in "opposition".[11]

The fact that Dilhorne took the trouble to revise his list suggests that Joseph made his real position very clear to the Cabinet's creative accountant. But the *Economist* subsequently claimed that Joseph had been staunch in support of *Butler*. Significantly, the article placed him in this camp along with Boyle and Powell, thus reuniting in print the troublesome triumvirate who were alleged to have contemplated resignation over Profumo. When he discussed the question with Macmillan on 16 October Joseph indicated that a Butler premiership, with Home continuing as Foreign Secretary, would be a solid arrangement. Confessing himself to be "torn between safety and growth", he added that if Butler proved unacceptable he would prefer a jump to the next generation.[12]

The record of the Macmillan–Joseph interview does not necessarily bring Dilhorne's list into further discredit. Once Joseph learned that Butler really was "unacceptable" he might have stated a preference for Maudling among the younger candidates. But clearly Home was never his first choice. This attitude was hardly surprising; Joseph had no love for the landed aristocracy, and Home's grouse-moor image was the last thing that would excite a man who had refused to contemplate fighting an agricultural seat. Both had been attached to the Commonwealth Relations Office between 1957 and 1959, but Joseph had

---

10. Rob Shepherd, *Iain Macleod: A Biography* (Pimlico, 1995), 326–7.
11. See list in PRO PREM 11/5008; Gilmour & Garnett, *Whatever Happened*, 198–9.
12. *Economist*, 19 October 1963; Thorpe, *Douglas-Home*, 305.

limited interest in that sphere, which for Home was a rival obsession to field sports. The fact that Joseph was happy to jump a generation – despite any "suspicions" he might really have had about Maudling – reveals the depth of his own integrity back in 1963. While Home was never likely to be more than an interim leader Maudling was only a year older than Joseph, and if fortune favoured him he might have led the party for long enough to scupper any leadership ambitions that any of his present colleagues might have been nursing. But once the party's choice had been made – or manufactured – Joseph did not feel strongly enough to make an issue of it. During the crucial hours Powell heard a report that "Joseph had said Home would be as good a Prime Minister as any other", so when he tried to rally the discontented behind the wavering Butler he made no effort to contact Sir Keith. Their good relations survived the crisis, which resulted in another resignation by Powell. But Powell's memory of October 1963 was better than Joseph's proved to be, and when a few more grievances had been added to his list it helped him to conclude that Joseph, however honourable and intelligent, was irresolute.[13]

If Home had been allowed to dictate policy after Macmillan's departure his elevation would have been a disaster for the young "modernisers" in the Cabinet. When asked to produce a statement of his beliefs by the Research Department, the new Prime Minister owned up to the heretical view that he had "never really believed that the well off society is the answer to everything". Joseph could echo Home's concern that Britain "must be in the first XI" and high in the batting order, but he would have winced at his leader's eulogy on the "instinct" that was the great virtue "of countrymen who living close to nature have a sixth sense of what is possible and impossible". Home was not the sort of man to fight for the abolition of the county of Rutland – or, for that matter, to acquiesce in the destruction of the Soke of Peterborough.[14]

But Home was tractable on most areas of domestic policy, as befitted a man who joked that he did sums with the aid of matchsticks. Two unexpected bonuses for Joseph arising from the change at the top were the resignations of Macleod and Powell; the first seemed to have made a point of opposing every suggestion made by the Housing Minister, while the second could be a ruthless critic of proposals which deviated from his own interpretation of Conservative orthodoxy. The loss even of Macmillan had a silver lining. He is said to have quipped in later years that Joseph was "the only boring Jew I have met", but this jaundiced judgement was more discreditable to himself than to his former colleague. At the time their relations were reasonably good, and the Prime Minister was normally helpful to Joseph up to a point. But his support would evaporate once he began to fret about the electoral considerations which were a lower priority for Joseph. Everything now depended on the ability of the

---

13. Heffer, *Like the Roman*, 330.
14. PRO PREM 11/5006.

modernisers to manage Home; if they could sway him the balance of the Cabinet would actually have tilted their way. Although Joseph would never have made such a calculation at the time of the Blackpool conference, he was astute enough to make the best of the party's "decision". Just a few days into the new regime he launched his own campaign, acquainting Home with the unwelcome tidings that "we will, I think, have to face public acquisition [of development land] on a large scale". As Joseph told the new Party Chairman Lord Blakenham (the former John Hare), he was "much concerned about the way in which housing is proving a trump in Socialist propaganda". He sensed that the advent of Home would give him the freedom to rebut Labour's "vote-catching double talk".[15]

Macmillan had been an enthusiast for land acquisition, even suggesting a month before his resignation that one of Joseph's minutes on the subject should be circulated to other ministers as a model of its kind.[16] But one piece of controversial legislation which Macmillan would have prevented was the abolition of Resale Price Maintenance (RPM), a measure which was approved, after much debate, at the Cabinet meeting of 15 January 1964. The system of RPM allowed manufacturers to fix a standard selling-price for their goods, thus preventing competitive price-cutting by shops. It was fiercely opposed by the big retailers, but small shopkeepers regarded it as a guarantee of their livelihood and they represented a vocal and numerous element among the party's grass-roots. Various attempts had been made since the war to outlaw RPM, but as recently as 1963 ministers had backed away in fear of the electoral consequences. In July of that year Macmillan and Maudling had agreed that it would be too risky to alienate crucial supporters as an election loomed; in the previous summer Macleod had sounded out opinion and reached a similar verdict. The adoption of the proposal in what had to be an election year is testimony to the determined advocacy of the Secretary of State for Industry, Trade and Regional Development, Edward Heath. Home was very uneasy, but Maudling now decided that on balance it was reasonable to proceed. Another of Heath's key backers was Sir Keith Joseph. Repeal was strongly favoured by officials at the Board of Trade; presumably Joseph had been attracted by the scheme when it was discussed during his own stint at that department.[17]

15. Julian Critchley, *The Palace of Varieties: An Insider's View of Westminster* (Faber & Faber, 1989), 127; KJ to Home, 23 October 1963, PRO PREM 11/5144; KJ to Blakenham, 6 November 1963, CCO 20/1/11, CPA, Bodleian Library.
16. KJ to Macmillan, 13 September 1963; Macmillan note, 14 September 1963, PRO PREM 11/5154. Rather touching evidence of Sir Keith's insecurity in the face of Labour criticism is the fact that he attached his memorandum when writing in defence of his policies to the new Party Chairman in November 1963, adding that Macmillan had approved of it; KJ to Lord Blakenham, 28 November 1963, CCO 20/1/11, CPA, Bodleian Library.
17. On KJ and RPM see Jock Bruce-Gardyne and Nigel Lawson, *The Power Game: An Examination of Decision-Making in Government* (Macmillan, 1976), 100; interview with Sir Peter Carey. For 1962–3 deliberations, see PRO PREM 11/4536.

From the outset RPM abolition was deeply unpopular with Tory back-benchers and after an acrimonious meeting of the 1922 Committee on 23 January Redmayne (who himself opposed the Bill) warned that unless it made concessions the Government would be defeated. But the bandwagon had gathered too much momentum, and by the summer it had crashed through the resistance after only a few minor detours. While the Bill was travelling through the Commons the modernisers kept up the pressure. In February Joseph laid before the Cabinet his plans for the state acquisition of land. Redmayne protested that this was a step too far; "I hope", he moaned to Home, "that the enthusiasm of younger Ministers will not once again rush us into action before we are sure that it will not cause further alarm and despondency in the Party". Joseph's colleagues Boyd-Carpenter and Geoffrey Rippon (who was supposed to be working in tandem with Joseph at the Ministry of Public Works) were both deeply unhappy at the proposed policy, and Home himself regarded it as a "vexed question". As late as June 1964 Redmayne told the harrassed Prime Minister that Joseph's plans for local government reorganisation in Yorkshire and the North Midlands were "nonsensical"; Home's only comment was "I fear it must go on". Just three days before writing this weary minute the cowed Prime Minister had referred to Joseph in Leeds as "our splendid young imaginative Minister of Housing".[18]

The "splendid" Joseph was now oblivious to any "alarm and despondency" which might be spreading among less dynamic Conservatives. Privately he had serious doubts about his party's chances at the next election; even if it won, there would have to be changes. To Sir Edward Boyle he lamented "the lack of any clear set of explicable priorities [for government expenditure]". If Home remained as Prime Minister after the election he would need to be advised by "some sort of 'Herbert Morrison' figure with an oversight of domestic policy". Joseph was not suggesting that he himself should hold this position, but the *ersatz* Herbert Morrison would have to share his own desire for the better co-ordination of government activity: "Our struggles now with bits and pieces of the social implications of modernization – redundancy, higher unemployment – all show the lack of a unifying domestic policy", Joseph pointed out.[19]

Whatever the next election might bring, Joseph seized the opportunities for immediate action which were offered by his present post. Despite constant assurances to the Commons that the Green Belt was sacrosanct he began to think that it should be loosened a little in order to release more land (a notch had been let out in the Lea Valley in the previous year). The erosion of the Green Belt was another way in which the embarrassing hike in the price of land

---

18. Redmayne to Home, 18 February 1964, and other correspondence in PRO PREM 11/5142; Home note of 15 November, PRO PREM 11/5144; Redmayne to Home, 22 June 1964; Home note of 22 June 1964, PRO PREM 11/4903.
19. KJ to Boyle, 2 April 1964, Boyle Papers, MSS 660/24078.

might be halted through an increase in supply. But to denude these protected areas on the necessary scale would cause outrage amongst natural Tories, and Joseph had to consider an even more effective foe in Dame Evelyn Sharp, a consistent champion of the Green Belt.[20] As he revealed in a private conversation with the journalist Alastair Hetherington, Joseph was not convinced that all of the protected land was genuinely "green", and he hoped that local authorities would take the initiative in exploiting any loopholes. More ambitiously, in conjunction with Heath Joseph planned more legislation based on an official study of the South-East region, which was acting as a powerful magnet for employment even though migrants found it almost impossible to find decent housing at an affordable price. The number of London's homeless had been registered at 1,000 in 1957; now it was 4,725. In the past commissions had been set up to allow governments to put off awkward decisions, and published reports were stored away until they were sufficiently dusty. Now the modernisers jumped into action while the ink was drying. The eager ministers agreed that to contain the problems of the South-East massive state planning would be required; government offices would be moved out of London and private firms encouraged to follow suit. Many new towns would have to be built in any case, to house over a million more people in the London area by 1981. Joseph told Hetherington that he believed the expansion to be "the greatest planning for new cities and towns ever undertaken in the world".[21]

Joseph explained the principles which would underlie this new phase of government activity on 4 December 1963, when replying to a debate on Regional Development. He stressed the importance of local government reform, rejecting the idea of a directly elected regional administrative tier but suggesting that some planning should take place at that level. The "Man in Whitehall" should also play an enhanced role. As Joseph acknowledged, "The central Government have great responsibilities and great power to create employment, both directly by their social policies, and by their financial priorities". The overall objective was a piece of social engineering – "to achieve the fuller use of national resources and a more even spread of prosperity". Joseph went on to deliver his ritual rebukes to socialists who had failed to recognise the need for change in the modern world, and he characterised the proper function of government as that of providing the framework in which

---

20. Dame Evelyn, though, did recognise the need for flexibility at a time of rising demand. Once she had persuaded Joseph to tread carefully in this area (on the well-chosen ground that any general statements about relaxing restrictions would cause alarm, "coming from a new Minister known to be appointed to push housing") she was faced with the new problem of talking him out of issuing guarantees about the Green Belt which could easily prove to be unrealistic. See Sharp memoranda of 1 and 24 October, and KJ memorandum of 19 October, 1962, in PRO HLG 143/1.
21. Memorandum by Heath, CP (64) 44, 14 February 1964; *Hansard*, vol. 684, col. 634, 18 November 1963 (homeless figures); KJ interview with Alastair Hetherington, 17 March 1964, Hetherington Papers 6/20, LSE archives.

free enterprise could prosper. But even before Joseph had risen to speak James Callaghan had disentangled the real message from the partisan rhetoric and teased him on his new outlook: "The right hon. Gentleman is not fully a Socialist yet, but he is coming along". Some Conservatives shared this view; regional development plans were singled out by Enoch Powell for criticism in an anonymous series of articles in *The Times*. In a speech at Glasgow Powell claimed that "the party of free enterprise seems ready to throw its principles and beliefs overboard" in an unthinking response to the imbalance of regional prosperity. The new line handed another "trump card" to Labour; in February 1964 Harold Wilson noted how often Joseph had adopted modified versions of Labour policy, and dubbed him "Little Sir Echo".[22]

Reflecting on his record as Minister of Housing in a 1987 interview with Anthony Seldon, Joseph confessed sadly that "I was at that time a statist . . . I went along with the then fashionable policies". This was unduly modest. The official records of the time show that Joseph was not a follower but a leader, along with Heath and Wilson, of "fashionable" thinking. The nature of this thinking was "statist" to a degree, but it was certainly not "Socialist" by any rational definition; Wilson himself, after all, had started life as a progressive Liberal and had only ever posed as a man of the left when it suited him. Some of the clashes between front-bench spokesmen seem farcical today; in one debate on Welsh Affairs, for example, Joseph claimed that there was "all the difference in the world" between the overall annual growth target of 4 per cent produced by the National Economic Development Council (NEDC) and Labour planning which would introduce targets for individual industries. Neither system would involve compulsion; the only penalty for falling short would be continued relative economic decline. But the extreme right of the Conservative Party was not interested in the question of whether Labour had moved as far from its ideological moorings as the Conservatives had done; the near-coincidence in the policies of the two parties was sufficient to condemn the Government in their eyes. To his credit Joseph denied that his hand had been forced by his officials, notably Dame Evelyn Sharp. This gave the lie to another Joseph myth – that throughout his career he was "a lion in opposition and a lamb in government", taking office full of "good intentions" but being ground down by "statist" civil servants. Rather, it was Joseph who ground down his staff, with a frenetic routine which one victim calculated as taking twenty hours out of every day.[23]

---

22. *Hansard*, vol. 685, cols 1267–82; John Wood (ed.), *A Nation Not Afraid: The Thinking of Enoch Powell* (Batsford, 1965), 87; Harold Wilson, *The New Britain* (Penguin, 1964), 60.
23. KJ interview with Anthony Seldon, 27; *Hansard*, vol. 697, col. 655, 25 June 1964; KJ's PPS Wilfred Proudfoot, cited in Roth memorandum. Explaining his own poor relationship with Dame Evelyn Sharp, Richard Crossman told Alastair Hetherington that she "preferred a young man like Keith Joseph, whom she could direct and steer". But this was not entirely convincing; as Crossman himself admitted, there were other good reasons for Dame Evelyn's antipathy towards him. See Howard, *Crossman*, 268–9.

In April 1963 Rab Butler recorded a discussion on the economy during a weekend strategy meeting held at Chequers. He had asserted that "a managed economy is here to stay" against "those with Sir Keith Joseph" who had upheld the free market.[24] Whatever he might have said in private meetings, Joseph had been badly rattled by Rachman, and after the summer of 1963 his ministerial decisions were determined by a range of uncongenial developments. His underlying instincts remained those of a free market man but the problems which had piled up in his department since the passage of the Rent Act were not amenable to instinctive solutions. In most cases they represented the downside of the prosperity which had kept the Conservatives in power for over a decade. The growth in population was far greater than anyone had anticipated, and the people of the "Affluent Society" were more demanding than their predecessors. Above all the Government was confronted by that unique twentieth-century phenomenon, the "generation gap". Young people wanted independence from their parents much sooner than they had done before the war, and were marrying earlier; hence the insatiable demand for housing. The 1959 report of a Conservative committee on Arts and Amenities on which Joseph had served lamented that "The emancipation of the adolescent . . . has taken everyone by surprise".[25] If "Conservative freedom" had brought this about it would have to be reined in by the state unless a situation approaching anarchy were to break out in the South-East; Joseph's responsibilities confronted him with the contrasting problem of Wales, where action was needed to create jobs as older industries declined. That even a convinced economic liberal like Joseph was overwhelmed by circumstances is a sign of how difficult things were becoming, not an indication that his commitment was weak. Joseph had been driven to this "statist" position by the summer of 1963, but he was so busy that he could be forgiven for being less than fully conscious of the process which had forced him there – even though he had to offer reasoned defences of his policy in the Commons. His future intellectual

---

24. Butler memorandum, 28 April 1963, Butler MSS, G40, Trinity College, Cambridge. James Margach, who reported that the Chequers' meeting was seen by ministers "as the long-term launching pad for the recovery of the Government and the party", was told that Joseph gave a "brilliant" presentation on "his conception of future housing and social needs, redevelopment on an imaginative scale embracing old urban areas and new towns". This talk had been marked by Joseph's "mastery of detail" rather than ideological arguments. See James Margach, "Enoch's Weekend", in *Sunday Times*, 5 May 1963, and Ramsden, *Winds of Change*, 181–2.
25. "The Use of Leisure", Report of Conservative Policy Committee on Recreation, Arts and Sports (1959), CRD 2/52/13, CPA, Bodleian Library. We are most grateful to Dr Richard Weight for bringing this committee to our attention. The final report was published as *The Challenge of Leisure* (CPC, 1959). The minutes suggest that Joseph soon became a dominant figure within the committee of nine who drafted the report. But his colleagues turned down his suggestion of a 200 word section on "boredom", which described that condition as "one of the privileges of those no longer absorbed in the struggle to survive. . . The privilege of boredom has now become nearly universal". All that remained was the recognition that the arts were "a bulwark against boredom". However, *The Times* was more complimentary about a similar Labour document, published at the same time; see *The Times*, 31 August 1959.

development now hinged on the fortunes of his party; if it could beat Labour again Joseph would be exposed to more of the pressures of high office, and his journey towards "statism" (if not, *pace* Callaghan, "socialism") might be completed. But if the Conservatives lost and Joseph had to oppose a new government wedded by conviction to "statist" solutions he was sure to feel a renewed pull from his underlying instincts, whatever Shadow post he might be given.

Given the circumstances of his arrival at Number Ten, the short time before the next election, and his anxiety not to be the man who brought a run of three victories to an end, Home was understandably anxious to get his timing right. From his colleagues he received almost as many opinions as potential polling dates. In December 1963, when he first asked ministers for manifesto suggestions, Home preferred the following May or June. But Nigel Lawson from the Research Department advised that the economic outlook pointed to October – the latest possible month. From the same evidence the Chancellor reached the opposite conclusion. Economic growth, at an unsustainable 6 per cent in the early part of 1964, dictated some harsh measures. But few shared Maudling's preference for a spring election which would allow him to postpone the necessary "austere" budget until the votes had been cast. Harold Macmillan urged his successor to choose October, and to announce this quickly. At a meeting in early April Joseph proffered his own advice. His preference for October was influenced by the assumption that the furore over RPM would have died down a little by then – and that the public would grow tired of Wilson the more they saw of him. Ironically in view of later "Thatcherite" recrimination against Maudling Joseph also predicted that the 1964 Budget would be strong and would pay dividends by the autumn. As a result of these deliberations Home compromised and on 9 April – the day that the Tories took a trouncing in the first GLC elections – he announced that there would not be a spring election. It was a fateful decision, not least because it left Maudling with no choice but to introduce an April budget which was nowhere near as stringent as the circumstances demanded. In his memoirs he was surprisingly reticent about the genesis of an economic package which by the 1980s had made his name a byword for mismanagement; at the time he was reported as saying in private that his party had "ceased to govern".[26]

The GLC result, in which the Conservatives took only a third of the seats, was a personal setback to Joseph. In particular, feelings ran high in the suburban areas where the results indicated that many Conservative parliamentary seats were now under threat. Local activists fumed against the reorganisation, under Joseph's London Government Act, which had marooned them in Labour-controlled

---

26. See correspondence in PRO PREM 11/4755; Reginald Maudling, *Memoirs* (Sidgwick & Jackson, 1978), 130; Michael Stewart, *Politics and Economic Policy in the UK since 1963: The Jekyll & Hyde Years* (Pergamon Press, 1978), 17 and note.

boroughs. At least Sir Louis Gluckstein survived (along with Sir Samuel Salmon and two other Conservative representatives for Westminster), and eventually became Chairman of the GLC. But there was no time for Joseph to brood over the poor result. His parliamentary schedule was as demanding as ever; while the country waited for Home to fire the starting gun for a national contest there were Bills on Rates and Housing to guide through the Commons. By this time Joseph and his Labour Shadow Michael Stewart had developed a mutual respect, although inevitably this was qualified by the need to keep scoring party points. During the third reading of the Housing Bill, for example, Stewart ironically congratulated Joseph on having used the Rachman outcry to force reform on his reluctant colleagues. There were occasional eruptions of ill-temper, largely caused by Joseph's frustration at being forced so often on to the back foot. Almost every month the Opposition chose housing for set-piece debates which merely reheated the old arguments. Joseph would close his speeches with attacks on Labour which sounded as though he, rather than Stewart, was the Shadow Minister. Having clutched his own 400,000 target out of the air to cheer his party conference he used it to jeer at Labour, which delayed for a while before matching the figure. Given the limited direct power of the ministry this was a pointless war conducted on the back of envelopes; when Stewart duly came up with his own 400,000 target Joseph accused Labour of beguiling the electorate with "panaceas" – a favourite word which was equally appropriate as a description of his own visions. As Joseph later confessed, "I was just a 'more man'. I used to go to bed at night counting the number of houses I'd destroyed and the number of planning approvals that had been given . . . Just *more*".[27]

At least this futile jousting was punctuated by some moments of humour. When for the umpteenth time Joseph argued that more housing was needed because the birth-rate had "rocketted" since the Rent Act Labour's Denis Howell intervened to "point out to the right Hon. Gentleman that the children born in 1958 do not yet need houses". Joseph's own attempts to liven things up merely showed the strain he was under. Towards the end of a June speech on land values he joked that the Opposition's scorecard:

> should read: cheap interest rates for housing, bowled Harold Wilson; land commission out by a method not known to *Wisden*[;] caught by the *Economist*, run out by Mr Denman, stumped by Mr Alan Day, and bowled by *Socialist Commentary* and many others . . .

Even MPs aquainted with all the gentlemen and publications cited by Joseph must have been baffled by this sporting imagery. Unrealistically measuring

---

27. Ramsden, *Winds of Change*, 225; *Hansard*, vol. 693, col. 195, 13 April 1964; KJ interview with Terry Coleman.

himself against venerated figures like Shakespeare who could summon a killing line at will, Joseph was still conscious of his limitations as a parliamentary wit. After one exchange with Callaghan he exclaimed to friends that he had composed a succinct and cutting reply, but the inspired phrase only came into his mind when the debate was over.[28]

Humour was in short supply behind the scenes. The Treasury was soon regretting Maudling's electioneering budget. In May 1964 Boyd-Carpenter invited ministers to find departmental cuts for the coming year; his suggested figure for Housing was £13 million. Joseph wanted an increase rather than a reduction in his budget, and argued that without extra funding construction would grind to a halt in the North-East – an area of special sensitivity to the Government. A Cabinet meeting of 12 May reached a predictable compromise; the Treasury's shears were kept away from Joseph's department but there would be no increase. Meanwhile Joseph was increasingly anxious for guidance from his colleagues on land values. In July he circulated two possible conclusions to a draft statement on the subject. The first promised that the Treasury would look for a way of taxing the profits of speculation, while the second argued against an inquiry because such taxes were always counter-productive. Nothing better illustrates the division within Joseph, between the voice of his instincts and the call of pragmatic calculation. Not for the last time he presented two contradictory cases at a meeting of ministers, pointing out that even Conservative voters wanted some action against the speculators but following up with an admission that a tax would involve the party contradicting all that it had said and done since 1951. The Cabinet refused to help him out of his internal wrestling match; it thought that some hint of action should be given but that nothing concrete could be proposed without stirring up more trouble.[29]

These Cabinet discussions took place as ministers were cobbling together ideas for the 1964 manifesto, eventually published with a title (*Prosperity with a Purpose*) which was more hopeful than descriptive. In April the Director of the Conservative Research Department (CRD) Sir Michael Fraser had identified Housing as one of the "main minuses in terms of policy subjects", and the relevant manifesto sections reflected the pessimism of Central Office. The record since 1951 was set out, but the impressive figures – an overall average of 300,000 houses built per year (and an estimated 370,000 for 1964), 44 per cent owner-occupation, 130,000 older houses modernised each year – were interlaced with admissions that there was more to do on virtually every front. The last of the nine subsections comprised a sheepish pledge that "we shall take no

---

28. *Hansard*, vol. 691, col. 1412, 18 March 1964; vol. 695, col. 1502, 5 June 1964; Graham Turner in *Sunday Times*, 6 May 1979.
29. KJ memoranda, CP (64) 97, 8 May 1964, CP (64) 159, 28 July 1964; Cabinet minutes CM (64) 27, 12 May 1964, CM (64) 44, 30 July 1964.

further steps to remove rent control", and a commitment to introduce more protection for tenants if the Milner Holland report into London conditions was sufficiently damning. The full impact of the great Rent Act which Joseph had defended so stoutly was now open to assessment, and the implicit verdict was that it had proved a disaster. All of the agonising about land values was condensed into a spineless promise that "In considering any further measure to tax land transactions, the test must be that it should not adversely affect the price or the supply of land". The authors of the Nuffield election study quoted one "influential figure" within the party (Joseph himself?) who had told them that land was certain to be a vote-loser whatever the Conservatives did, and that if they had rushed a detailed plan into the manifesto it could only have been "half-baked". In other areas of Joseph's responsibility the message was equally subdued; there was no attempt to brag about the local government reforms, and the paragraph on future plans for reorganisation was brief, imprecise and anodyne. Meanwhile the rating system which he had always found satisfactory was threatened by a recognition that "a reform of the rates is required", although here again nothing specific was proposed.[30]

On 15 September 1964 Home finally announced that the election would take place a month from that day. Although his party was worried about the housing issue Joseph himself took a prominent part in the campaign. On 17 September he appeared in a televised debate with Michael Stewart. The possibility of such a "confrontation programme" had been discussed by Fraser and Blakenham as far back as November 1963, and the two officials had reached "no firm conclusions, there being arguments against as well as in favour of this approach". In the event Stewart and Joseph fought out what was regarded as a fairly amicable draw. At least this was a different result from a previous "confrontation", at the Oxford Union in May, when Stewart had gained a comfortable victory for the proposition that another election victory for the Conservatives would be "a national tragedy". But at Central Office it was felt that the broadcast had been a serious mistake; in particular, land values had been exposed as the party's Achilles' heel, with Joseph tacitly admitting that the manifesto phrasing was "nebulous and meaningless".[31]

Joseph also featured in two party political broadcasts, once in the guise of a building site foreman. At every opportunity he lambasted Labour's plans for a Land Commission, its supposed threat to abolish owner-occupation, and its pledge to repeal the Rent Act. It was ludicrous, he told a Huddersfield audience, that Labour should pose as a rational "planning party" when its policies would increase housing demand while reducing the supply. The Conservatives,

30. Michael Fraser to Lord Blakenham, 23 April 1964, CCO 20/1/12; *Prosperity with a Purpose*, (CCO, 1964); David Butler and Anthony King, *The British General Election of 1964* (Macmillan, 1965), 89.
31. Fraser to Blakenham, 28 November 1963, CCO 20/1/11, CPA, Bodleian Library; *The Times*, 22 May 1964; Anthony Howard in *New Statesman*, 25 September 1964.

by contrast, believed in "a realistic policy of planning by persuasion and by co-operation"; they rejected Labour's George Brown's proposed National Plan for the economy because "it is just not practicable in a world which changes so rapidly to predict what industry and what firm will be able to sell next year in all the markets of the world". But despite a typically energetic campaigning effort by Joseph he could do nothing to convince the electorate that housing was safe in Conservative hands; Gallup found that Labour led the Tories by 41 to 31 per cent on the issue.[32]

On 4 October Joseph spoke in his own constituency, stressing that the Tories "had always thought that the result of the election would be close. They thought it would be a hard fight, but they would win". Indeed there was a fragile confidence in the government camp, based on a narrowing gap in opinion polls over the year. But three days after the speech Labour's Anthony Wedgwood Benn learned that "Sir Keith Joseph, amongst others, was completely dejected by the way the campaign was going and thought it might be a Labour landslide", a view which received apparent confirmation in an NOP poll of marginal seats, and the fact that, when challenged by a heckler to wager £5 on the outcome of the election, Joseph replied, "Make it 5s. and I'll take you on". From the start of the campaign the Conservatives had received only bad news. In late September disappointing balance of payments figures indicated that Maudling had been right in his forebodings about the economy. On 8 October Home was jostled and shouted down when he spoke at the Birmingham Bullring. The *Daily Express* published the following morning reported Rab Butler's belief that "things might start slipping" from the Conservatives towards the end of the campaign. One thing which certainly slipped away was the bold theme of "modernisation"; apparently this had little impact on the voters, at least when conjured by Alec Home, although the Prime Minister's fortitude during the campaign was widely admired.[33]

The 1964 general election could have been decided by a little slippage either way. With 317 seats Labour was returned with an overall majority of only four, and if a few hundred votes over the country had changed hands the Tories (304 seats) would have won. In Leeds, where Joseph and Sir Donald Kaberry (North-West) were the only sitting Conservatives, there was no change. Joseph's majority fell to 8,325; as the meticulous *Leeds Searchlight* noted, the adverse swing of 3.3 per cent in Leeds North-East meant that he had performed better than all but four Cabinet ministers (the worst being Henry Brooke (Hampstead) who suffered a 10 per cent swing). Only Tony Barber and Geoffrey Rippon were ousted from the Commons but every minister had lost

---

32. Butler and King, *British General Election of 1964*, 173; *The Times*, 9 October 1964.
33. *The Times*, 5, 15 October 1964; Tony Benn's Diary, 7 October 1964 (his informants were David Butler and Anthony King, who were gathering information for their Nuffield election study). We are most grateful to Mr Benn for allowing us access to his unedited diaries.

his Cabinet seat. The "thirteen wasted years" depicted in Labour propaganda were over, and Harold Wilson now had the chance to waste some himself.[34]

An Opposition MP for the first time, Joseph could not avoid reflecting on his performance in office. The Housing Corporation was a legacy of real importance, and he could take some compensation from a reasonable election result in Wales, where his policies had helped to reduce unemployment and where the Conservatives suffered a net loss of only one seat to Labour. But he knew that there was material in the pending tray, notably the Milner Holland report on London, which would add voices of criticism to his own nagging sense of failure. The only way to suppress this feeling was to throw himself into new tasks, and soon he was as busy as ever.

If Joseph had given himself more time to ponder he might have taken comfort from the fact that commentators were far from writing him off yet. One pre-election profile spoke of a "mind that operates like a high-powered searchlight", and his "radiation of a clear conviction that to waste time is a sin". Admittedly the article did not spare Joseph's over-wrought personality, characterising him as "taut of visage and fiery-eyed". But the tone of the piece was admiring; it implied that his difficulties had been understood, and his relative failure forgiven.[35]

Joseph delivered his own verdict in two interviews in the 1970s and 1980s. It could all be summed up in that unpleasant word: "statist". Admittedly he was "full of goodwill, full of diligence, earnest, well intentioned". But he had been "blind" to failings which were now obvious to him and his benevolent motives had produced only "the worst of results":

> Heaven help us, I used to think myself a public benefactor in all that slum clearance and all those high blocks of flats which were then fashionable. Looking back, I think that these were all understandable short cuts which went in the wrong direction . . . We broke up communities, we broke up long-standing architecture and relationships, and all with the best intentions. Mind you, there wasn't much criticism at the time.[36]

For Leo Abse, this kind of talk confirmed his impression of Joseph as a masochistic politician; he added wryly that "unfortunately the buildings could not be dismantled as easily as [Joseph's] original support for them". But Joseph's final point, at least, was a fair comment. Although there had been ominous disasters (notably one in Birkenhead) during Joseph's time as Parliamentary Secretary, the subject of high-rise flats which became "ghettos in the sky" almost as soon as they were opened was scarcely mentioned either

---

34. *Leeds Searchlight*, November 1964.
35. *The Times*, 22 September 1964.
36. KJ interview with Terry Coleman.

inside Parliament or in the press until after 1964. Even at the end of the decade John Major, Lambeth Council's Housing Chairman, thought that some high-rise building was justified. Like virtually everyone else, Joseph was carried away by the idea that these buildings could be built with great speed: "It was prefabrication and, Heaven help me, high blocks". Superficially this social disaster seems to be a greater stain on Joseph's record even than Mr Rachman. But given the shortage of land most ministers would have succumbed to this alluring solution. As Nicholas Timmins has pointed out, the ministerial blame should be shared with Duncan Sandys, who in 1956 began to pay out additional subsidies for high-rise developments. The other guilty men were the "town planners, builders, engineers and architects, together with local councillors who believed they were doing their best". This army of middle-class profes-sionals acted in "An unintended conspiracy" which blighted the lives of many working-class families. However important a part Joseph might have played in the "conspiracy" he certainly was not a lone gunman.[37]

The remainder of Joseph's account of these years was a prelude to a typical piece of self-flagellation. If "statist" solutions went in the wrong direction, the right route must have been the free market:

> I was convinced intellectually that the way to get rid of Rachman was to get rid of rent restriction. But it required a great deal more moral courage than I had at the time . . . I regret it certainly, but I think it would have been a titanic moral task to persuade colleagues, the Conservative Party, Parliament and the country, including the intellectuals, of the right course.[38]

In 1987, when he gave this revealing interview, Joseph took it for granted that, given sufficient "moral courage" in its votaries, an idea will always triumph. When his colleagues had scoffed at his idea of freeing up the entire rented sector he had backed down. By contrast, Edward Heath had forced his will on the Cabinet over RPM (although in this 1987 interview Joseph spoke as if the repeal, which he had supported at the time, might have been a mistake). But while Joseph had dimly glimpsed a kind of truth in 1962–4, by 1987 he was almost completely "blind" to the political realities which had faced him at Housing. Once the practical results of the Rent Act became clear there was no chance that anyone even with the moral courage of a Gandhi could have persuaded more than a rump of doctrinaire Conservative MPs – let alone the country – to support a further risk of that nature. Certainly Heath was a more robust character than Joseph, but he was able to argue on behalf of his

---

37. Abse, *Margaret*, 157; Nicholas Timmins, *The Five Giants: A Biography of the Welfare State* (HarperCollins, 1995), 184–5.
38. KJ interview with Anthony Seldon.

legislation that his hand was forced by a critical report on monopolies and mergers which was about to appear, while John Stonehouse had lined up a Private Member's Bill on the subject. No back-bench MP – not even Enoch Powell who continued to see rent control and housing subsidies as "two giant evils"– was suicidal enough to call a debate on ending rent control, and all of the reports were suggesting that the 1957 legislation had been a failure. Finally, to focus on that peculiar phrase "moral courage", the worst effects of the Rent Act had been felt amongst the poorest in society, while the small shopkeepers who opposed Heath were unlikely to have to sleep in the streets once he got his way. To accelerate the removal of rent restriction would ensure further hardship for the poor, at least in the short-term. The conscious infliction of suffering in pursuit of an ideological "panacea" is not normally held to be the product of "moral courage".[39]

From the outset Joseph had regarded his political life as a moral calling. According to the flattering 1964 pre-election profile, the nature of his ethical outlook was obvious; the headline was "Convinced Tory with an Active Social Conscience".[40] In later years his approach to social questions was often explained by reference to a sense of "guilt" arising from his own privileged background.[41] But to accept that this played some part in shaping Joseph's political approach is not the same thing as assuming that it dominated his thinking on all social questions. The solid evidence of his early parliamentary career proved that he sympathised deeply with the *genteel* poor, particularly those who were elderly. He was also an unswerving champion of the disabled, at a time when others were content to look the other way. Yet in his speeches Joseph had shown himself to be unmoved by those who had suffered from Rachman and his kind. Convinced that a free housing market was in everyone's long-term interests, he was slow to recognise that short-term difficulties could cause lasting pain. Meanwhile he showed a tendency to regard the low-paid and the unemployed – i.e. the "able-bodied poor" – as problems to be dealt with rather than as human beings with their individual problems, dreams and fears. He despised inefficiency, of course, and he loathed poverty; but he had given no real sign as yet that he understood those who (for whatever reason) lacked the self-motivation to "better themselves".

The other reason for the praise of Joseph's conscience was his assumed support for the social reforms of the 1960s. In 1964 this impression seems to have been based on his membership of organisations such as the Howard League for Penal Reform, rather than his parliamentary record. "On controversial issues such as hanging, homosexuality, abortion, or family planning, Joseph

39. On this point, see Peter Walker in *Crossbow*, April 1975, 15–16; Wood (ed.), *A Nation Not Afraid*, 90.
40. *The Times*, 22 September 1964.
41. See, for example, *Sunday Mirror*, 25 March 1973.

lined up with the liberals", one historian has written.[42] But although Joseph consistently voted against the death penalty, on the other "permissive" issues of the 1960s (including divorce reform) he abstained, and his overall record shows him to have been less "liberal" than at least one Conservative often written off by opponents as a reactionary. For example, while Enoch Powell supported David Steel's Medical Termination of Pregnancy Bill in July 1966, Joseph either abstained or was not present. The only exception was a vote cast in favour of Leo Abse's motion to *bring in* a private member's Bill on homosexuality; but Joseph abstained in the division on the substance of the Bill in February 1966.[43] On none of these subjects did Joseph make a single speech in the Commons, even though the debates were invariably free from normal parliamentary discipline. Of course there was room for disagreement on all these matters, and Joseph could scarcely be blamed if commentators assumed that he was an unflinching advocate of "progressive" measures in every aspect of social policy. But although he felt more deeply than others when his emotions were fully engaged, Joseph's attitude here as elsewhere was characterised by *selective* support.

"The problem with Keith", a back-bench colleague reflected many years later, "is that he thinks you can solve bloody well everything . . . Why can't someone din it into him that there are no broad and sweeping truths?" This tendency, rather than an undiscriminating social conscience, marked Sir Keith Joseph as a most unusual Conservative during his early career. In October 1964 the generous assessment of his performance in office by media commentators could not distract him from the feeling that the problems of his department could have been solved if only he had applied himself with more diligence. For many Tory MPs, Opposition was a new and disorientating experience. Joseph's personal sense of failure gave him extra impetus, as he began his quest for certainty.[44]

42. Charles Webster, *The Health Services Since the War: Volume II, Government and Health Care: The National Health Service 1958–1979* (HMSO, 1996), 375.
43. See *Hansard*, vol. 713, col. 618, 26 May 1965; vol. 724, col. 870, 11 February 1966. Abse's own views underline the hazards of drawing general inferences from attitudes on specific "permissive" measures; while his Homosexual Reform Bill was proceeding through the Commons he was trying to restrict the terms of David Steel's Medical Termination of Pregnancy Bill. See Leo Abse, *Private Member* (Macdonald, 1973), 226–33.
44. Simon Hoggart, "Mrs Thatcher's Man-in-Waiting", *Guardian*, 21 July 1980.

Chapter 7

The First Crusade

Introspection was in vogue for the British during the first half of the 1960s, and the public disliked the results of their self-analysis. The intoxicating affluence of the late 1950s had been followed by the usual morning-after feeling; in contrast to the general war-time mood, the British were now prosperous enough to grumble that they were not matching the performance of some of their neighbours. Penguin Books published a successful series with the general title *What's Wrong With . . .?*; invariably these tracts uncovered a great deal that was wrong, affecting industry, the trade unions, the church and almost every other aspect of British life. In the wake of the Profumo affair *Encounter* magazine asked whether Britain's post-war history amounted to "The Suicide of a Nation". Christopher Booker has condensed the arguments of the "What's Wrong With . . .?" school:

> Britain was being "strangled" and "suffocated" by "complacency", "inefficiency", "outworn attitudes", "archaic institutions", the "class system" and "amateurism". The remedies, only too obvious, were "dynamism", "professionalism", "ruthless competition", "tough-mindedness", "more research", "more investment", "more roads", "more monorails to speed Britain's traffic", more tough ruthless professionalism in every direction.[1]

1. Christopher Booker, *The Neophiliacs: A Study of the Revolution in English Life in the Fifties and Sixties* (Collins, 1969), 153–4. The authors are most grateful to Brendon Sewill for reading and commenting on this and the following three chapters.

In the long term this mood – and some of the authors who voiced it – would help to destroy the "consensual" post-war approach to British politics. But at the time it seemed to have narrowed still further the gap between "Left" and "Right". Both of the main political parties produced manifestos for the 1964 general election that promised radical revitalisation. Having been in Opposition for so long Labour could afford to underline the theme with a suitable title – *The New Britain* – while Harold Wilson dazzled audiences with his talk of a white-hot technological revolution. The Conservatives had the more ticklish task of making the case for urgent modernisation while arguing that they had been doing their best to keep up with developments during their thirteen years in office.

Gloom might have been the dominant emotion among commentators in the early 1960s but not everyone felt that way. One of the main attractions of the Institute of Economic Affairs (IEA) was its refusal to succumb to the wide-spread sense of malaise – a defiant attitude which it symbolised in the spring of 1964 with the publication of a book of essays entitled *The Rebirth of Britain*. Founded in 1957 to counter what its supporters discerned as an alarming post-war growth in the powers and activities of the British state, the IEA represented the antithesis of what Sir Keith Joseph later dismissed as "fashionable thinking". It was the kind of perverse organisation which might have preached doom if the rest of the world was dancing for joy. By the 1980s it had been joined by other coteries of economic liberals, but in 1964 it was a lone voice and exulted in this isolation; its associates were proud of the label Graham Hutton had given them – "the awkward squad". Although its pamphlets focused on the "dismal science" of economics the IEA encouraged its authors to punch home their messages with a polemical style which made its output accessible to the non-specialist. Its publications had a very respectable sale, and must have reached many more readers than the figures suggest. It had no party affiliation, and despite its free market zeal its weekly lunches were open to anyone with interesting things to say. Socialists were particularly welcome, as potential converts – the same was true of Conservatives who had recently lapsed into the ways of "statism". Only moderation and mediocrity were frowned upon. There was no bar against politicians (or even ministers) although they were regarded with suspicion as people only too ready to buy up electoral support with reckless promises.

Shortly after the 1964 general election Sir Keith Joseph made his first appearance at the IEA's offices (then situated in Eaton Square, Belgravia, not far from the residence of Enoch Powell who contributed to *The Rebirth of Britain*). Joseph's striking good looks made an immediate impression, but it was also noted that he was sniffing a good deal. Ferdinand Mount, working at that time in the Conservative Research Department, remembered that Joseph "seemed to have a cold most of that Autumn . . . there was a flourishing of handkerchiefs, a seismic nose-blowing, an unrestrained show of misery which didn't, however, interfere with his appetite for work". The reason for this lingering condition, as so often with Joseph, was probably stress: and his solution, as usual, was to work even harder. Through his handkerchief he muttered something to the effect that he had heard of interesting and radical work being done by the IEA, then noticed a display of pamphlets on a nearby table. He "studied them earnestly", and having picked up a considerable pile asked Ralph Harris, the Institute's Director, how much they cost. Harris replied that the IEA was an educational charity and that MPs, more than anyone else, needed to be educated. He remembered that Joseph waved a copy of Professor Frank Paish's attack on incomes policy (*Policy for Incomes* (1964)) and asked for advice on the best publications giving an opposing view. When Harris in reply ventured to warn against the work of the Keynesian Andrew Shonfield Joseph defended his old acquaintance, adding that Shonfield was a co-religionist and that his wife Zuzanna was a vigorous charity worker. Harris, an affable man who never allowed personal friendship to cloud his judgement, was disappointed by this response. Years later in the House of Lords Joseph recalled their first meeting, and confessed that Harris had been right about Shonfield. In any case the slightly awkward initial exchange of views did not prevent Joseph from becoming a regular visitor, anxious to learn rather than to preach any message of his own.[2]

As an obsessive consumer of political tracts Joseph must have come across the IEA's work before 1964. One of the Institute's most notable early publications was Basil Yamey's pamphlet on RPM (1960); this was far from being the only contribution to the debate, but when the controversy was at its height it would have been natural for Joseph to consult a well-argued piece which supported his own views. The same could be said for A. R. Ilersic's thoughtful and balanced review of local government finance, *Relief for Ratepayers* (1963). If Joseph did not stumble upon this literature independently he was on friendly terms with at least two Conservatives who had forged links with the IEA: Enoch Powell and Geoffrey Howe. Howe, at that time chairman of the party's Bow Group, remembered that his organisation and the IEA "quite quickly gravitated into contact with each other"; Harris and his co-director, Arthur Seldon, became regular contributors to the journal *Crossbow*. Howe's rather dour public image disguised an inquiring mind and – to use Joseph's phrase – a substantial streak of "moral courage". In 1956 he had co-written a pamphlet on housing that anticipated the 1957 Rent Act, and he continued to push for a more ideological line while the government was hoping to shove this issue onto

---

2. Ferdinand Mount in *Spectator*, 5 January 1980; Richard Cockett, *Thinking the Unthinkable: Think-Tanks and the Economic Counter-Revolution 1931–1983* (HarperCollins, 1994), 167–8; Interview with Lord Harris of High Cross. We are most grateful for Lord Harris's generous help, here and elsewhere.

the back burner during the early 1960s. Whatever his private views even Joseph had learned enough from handling the legacy of the Rent Act to realise that further reform on these lines would have to wait. Howe remembered Joseph putting through a telephone call at this time "from a pub somewhere in mid-Glamorgan", in an unavailing attempt to dissuade *Crossbow* from putting forward radical ideas on housing.[3]

Joseph had left university without even a basic knowledge of economics. At All Souls he at least showed enough interest to inquire about a suitable text-book, and was advised to read the then standard work, by the American Keynesian Paul Samuelson.[4] Judging by his early speeches Samuelson's book had a limited effect on his thinking. But prior to 1964 Joseph's arguments for economic liberalism had been relatively unsophisticated; they had arisen chiefly from instincts which, while not exactly untutored, lacked the support which years of specialised study would have lent to them. Contact with the IEA provided him with "an intellectual back-up system and a sounding-board". The psychological boost given to Joseph by the knowledge that an enthusiastic body of economic experts agreed with him and could clothe his instincts with de-tailed argument can scarcely be exaggerated; presumably Margaret Thatcher received the same feeling of "ideological reinforcement" when she began to frequent the Institute at around the same time. Yet Joseph's early visits to Eaton Square only intensified his internal struggles; that which made the IEA bold made him more drunk and disorientated. As a front-line politician he still knew that he had to take political realities into account, and if he ever forgot this his colleagues were on hand to issue prompt reminders. His attitude at this time is typified by a letter to Arthur Seldon from 1965, on the subject of health charges. Having agreed with Seldon that this reform could "draw back into practice extra doctors who are now either giving up medicine or this country" he noted that the benefits of the market "would take a little time to prove and the first year of any such scheme would be bound in fact to reduce the amount of medi-cal attention available to the public. I want to put into your head the political difficulty of the short term . . .". In exasperation Seldon wrote in the margin "Is this a plea for painless change? Isn't it the politician's job (paid) to educate and lead?". If Joseph had seen this note he might have wearily agreed, but he had to accept that it would be hard enough to "educate and lead" the Shadow Cabinet when Harold Wilson might call a general election at any moment. A more elegant expression of this thought had just been published by the IEA itself: "Those whose business it is to think, to study and to criticise have a positive duty to follow the *Logos* where it leads them; it is the business of others (or of the same people in another capacity) to speculate on what might be "politically practicable", and how, at any particular moment of time."

3. Geoffrey Howe, *Conflict of Loyalty* (Macmillan, 1994), 30–2; interview with Lord Howe.
4. Letter to the authors from Ian Little.

The author, Powell, had then noted that the boundaries of the "politically practicable" were always shifting. But the IEA went further than this, tending to despise those politicians who recognised that boundaries existed at all, whether moveable or fixed. For someone like Powell, with settled convictions of his own, this made the Institute a congenial venue for bracing discussion. Joseph, whose mind was in constant flux, must have visited Eaton Square with a mixture of exhilaration and fear.[5]

Thus the early phase of Joseph's relationship with the IEA revealed the mis-understandings that could arise between extra-parliamentary campaigners and senior political figures. But at least this new influence provided a more thoughtful element to his Opposition speeches, and his reputation as a "technocratic" minister under Macmillan and Home began to be superseded by an image of one who was at home with ideas as well as with practical problems. During his re-education he was taking new initiatives far removed from the ivory tower (in addition to his connection with Bovis which he rejoined as Deputy Chairman after the election). In 1960 he had been instrumental in setting up the Foundation for Management Education (FME), a body which aimed to promote management as "a field of intellectual endeavour which should be encouraged and fostered at British universities in the urgent interest of the nation's economic and industrial performance". The original idea for the Foundation had been germinating in Joseph's mind since his work on the 1956 pamphlet *Automation and the Consumer*; he received further inspiration during his fact-finding visit to the United States in 1957. On his return he contacted John Bolton, a Harvard graduate and businessman who was a staunch advocate of management training. In the colourful words of the Foundation's historian, when Joseph first met Bolton "the gods sow[ed] the seed from which the tree of FME inexorably grew". Like-minded figures from business and politics were recruited, and Joseph played a major part in keeping the tree watered by drawing up an appeal for funds. He also contributed to a study of the feasibility of setting up the new institutions. However, his direct role in the organisation was short-lived; he resigned the chairmanship on his promotion to Minister of State at the Board of Trade, presumably because this new government job required him to get the best out of existing British management while the premise of the FME was that the quality of personnel was so inadequate that a major educational effort was required. After the fall of the Home government Joseph was invited to rejoin the council of the Foundation. But having recruited him to sow the first seeds, the gods were less demanding of his energies in this second stint and he left the council in 1967. Although with typical modesty Joseph did nothing to publicise his role, by the end of his life

---

5. Cockett, *Thinking the Unthinkable*, 168; Enoch Powell, "Is it Politically Practicable?" in *The Rebirth of Britain: A Symposium of Essays by Eighteen Writers* (Pan, 1964), 262–3.

he could look back on a remarkable achievement; however grudging their acceptance by the mainstream academic community, business schools had been established as a part of many British universities.[6]

On leaving office Joseph made a further attempt to do good by stealth, recruiting a group of friends from business and charitable backgrounds (including Zuzanna Shonfield and Nigel Broackes of Trafalgar House) to help him run a housing association. Given his general aversion to publicity – and the nature of the work involved – it was curious that Joseph should name the association "The Mulberry Trust" after the road on which his own comfortable home was situated. But this rather oblique self-reference was justified because the Trust set out to demonstrate the benefits of his most ambitious reform. Mulberry used funds made available by Joseph's Housing Corporation and charities to refurbish properties in the Paddington area, and let them on very reasonable terms to people referred to the Trust by Westminster Council and local Citizen's Advice Bureaux. In addition, the Trust provided information and assistance to its tenants, eventually establishing a nursery to help mothers seeking work.

Joseph once remarked with justifiable pride that "my charitable work hasn't been limited to merely tagging along behind other people's endeavours. I've tried to find gaps of various sorts and fill them in".[7] Although political commitments meant that he could not devote as much time to charity as he would have liked, his ministerial work also revealed some "gaps" which demanded immediate action. The Mulberry Trust was Joseph's final battle with the ghost of Peter Rachman. The properties on its books (which eventually numbered around 800) were concentrated to the north of the Harrow Road, close to the centre of the corrupt landlord's operations. Many of the clients were recent arrivals from the Caribbean, who had been portrayed in lurid terms by the media during the Rachman years. Without interference from Joseph his colleagues on the board established a policy which was liberal even by the standards of the 1960s; there was no discrimination, for example, against people in same-sex relationships.

Like other similar bodies which sprang up in London at this time, Mulberry helped to save a significant number of people from misery and exploitation. But a constant theme in the memories of those who worked with Joseph is the extent of his naïveté. He was too sanguine about the potential scale of the Trust's activities, and his disappointment was clear when, by necessity, it decided to cut corners rather than conform to all of the exacting housing standards laid down by the recent Parker-Morris report. Impressions of Joseph in this role confirm the message conveyed by many of his speeches – that his

---

6. Philip F. Nind, *A Firm Foundation: The Story of the Foundation for Management Education* (Foundation for Management Education, 1985), 1–17; "Educating the Managers", *Economist*, 20 August 1960.

7. KJ interview with Anthony King.

sympathy with the life of the poor was essentially abstract. He could not imagine how people functioned without the resources that he took for granted. While Mulberry struggled to find decent accommodation for people who had been sharing a lavatory with twenty others, Joseph around this time spent £11,000 on a "space age" refurbishment of his own kitchen. As so often, rather than appraising the situation at the "human" level, he founded his views on statistics; it was remembered that he was particularly doleful when it was discovered that the rate of divorce was higher in Mulberry properties than amongst those on the Trust's waiting-list. The possibility that the long-desired security of a home might give couples the chance to think clearly about their relationships seems not to have occurred to Joseph. On the micro level this was a symptom of the general error which had condemned the Conservatives to electoral defeat – the mistaken assumption that social stability and individual happiness were the inevitable products of greater prosperity.[8]

Joseph had a personal reason to brood over these questions in the later 1960s. His fourth and final child, Anna, was born in July 1964. Although Joseph spoke of the enjoyment he and his wife had found in parenthood, he added that "we had to work at it. There was a lot of work involved". He certainly loved young people. After spending the night at the home of a colleague in the early 1970s, he surprised his host by sitting on the stairs reading *The Tale of Peter Rabbit* to the family's two young children. But his attitude to child-rearing was of a piece with his general outlook. Greatly impressed by the responsibilities involved, his sense of duty conquered all. Years later Joseph was astonished when John Redwood told him that he had never read a book on child-rearing, relying on his own instincts instead. "I admire your certainty", he replied. For Joseph, the existence of offspring was another stimulus to exhaustive research. Friends with older children would be badgered for information about the rate of development that could be expected at particular ages. According to one story, the Joseph children were not allowed to read strip cartoons; they certainly would have found it difficult to watch much television, since their parents did not own a set. Hellen agreed with her husband, at least in thinking that child development was no subject for levity. When Richard Crossman met Lady Joseph for the first time, he was surprised that instead of making the usual small-talk this "extremely grave, good-looking, middle-aged woman" opened "a serious discussion on children's health".[9]

Interviewed in 1973 when he was once again a minister, Joseph spoke of his concern for "the unknown millions" of children who were emotionally deprived, whatever the material circumstances of their parents. Mothers, he felt, should not start a family unless they had "a flair for maternity" and were

8. Private information.
9. Interview in *Sunday Mirror*, 25 March 1973; interview with Sir Patrick Cormack; interview with John Redwood; Crossman, *Diaries: Volume II*, 398.

prepared to take trouble with their children. There was an equal responsibility for fathers. "They've got to involve themselves in play with the child", he declared. "Play is *crucial*". But play also had to be useful; it was "the natural preparation for school", valuable for teaching the child "to use words, and its fingers even, to co-ordinate, to focus . . .". To illustrate his theme, he revealed that he had given up an hour and a half to the eight year-old Anna on the previous Sunday; after "ping-pong" and drawing he took her for a walk. At other times he could attend to his own work while she practised on the violin (Sir Keith's own love of music was marred by his feeling that he could not master it at an intellectual level, but all of the Joseph children were encouraged to play instruments by Hellen). It was a touching account, but he seemed to have wandered away from his point about *emotional* deprivation. To create this kind of bond with a child takes time; and that was something which Joseph could never afford while he was in front-line politics. He was clearly conscious that his own experience with his father might be repeated; the question was whether anything could be done to prevent this. In addition to the well-being of his children, his own emotional health was involved in his closest relationships. As he told another interviewer in 1973, he loved reading aloud, and it was clearly a matter of regret to him that his wife and children "preferred to read to themselves". In another respect there was room for improvement in Joseph's domestic arrangements; one visitor received the impression that the children ate their meals with their nanny, in a part of the house which almost seemed cordoned-off from the adult quarters.[10]

Although Sir Keith valued his privacy outsiders were certainly not excluded from the Joseph household. For example, the future Chancellor Kenneth Clarke remembered being invited to Mulberry Walk for drinks with a party of students in the early 1960s. There was no feeling that Joseph was talking down to his guests; he seemed genuinely interested in the replies to his questions. Even so, one feels that he was treating the gathering as yet another fact-finding opportunity. Dinner parties would be much more intense, being regarded as an ideal setting to discuss pre-selected books rather than to unwind over too many glasses of wine (Joseph was still a moderate drinker, as he had been in the army). For long-term acquaintances this was nothing extraordinary, but at some point (probably in the mid-1960s) even they noticed that the tension in the air had increased still further.[11]

For understandable reasons friends are reluctant to speak about the breakdown of Joseph's first marriage. Those who offer an opinion tend to have heard the first news of trouble at different times; in any case, it is often difficult even for couples in that predicament to give a precise date for the start of their problems. When Richard Crossman first met Lady Joseph he assumed that Sir

10. Interview in *Sunday Mirror*, 25 March 1973; private information.
11. Interview with Kenneth Clarke; private information.

Keith must have become "such a difficult tense man" because he had "a difficult tense wife".[12] He failed to consider that the original cause of these symptoms might have been Joseph himself – or that the married couple might have been equally "difficult" and "tense" when they first met. But when two driven personalities have contrasting obsessions they can rarely live amicably under one roof. Lady Joseph had never been bitten by the political bug which, by 1964, had provoked a raging fever in her husband; she had, after all, married a businessman with vague political aspirations rather than an established MP. As Sir Keith's fortunes rose his wife's distaste for his chosen profession was probably sublimated. Just a few months after the birth of their fourth child, however, a blow fell. The election propelled Sir Keith out of office, but not out of frantic activity as Lady Joseph had reason to expect. The difference between the workload of a minister and a "shadow" need not be great – particularly when that shadow minister is someone with the remorseless application of Sir Keith Joseph. Indeed, the absence of civil servants – and of the rigid demarcation imposed by Whitehall departments – gave Joseph scope to make himself busier than ever. The main difference was the disappearance of routine ministerial visits from his diary; physically Sir Keith could spend more time in London, but he would still be preoccupied with politics and his presence would only remind Lady Joseph of the distance between them.

Joseph was well-known for his mild manners, but when sufficiently provoked he was quite capable of showing irritation, as industrialists and councillors had discovered during his ministerial career. When personal matters were at the root of his distress, it was understandable that he occasionally lost control of his temper. Acquaintances have hinted that 23 Mulberry Walk was the scene of such displays during the 1960s, and since Lady Joseph was as highly strung as her husband it is unlikely that all of the fireworks were set off by one side. Other political couples could survive gross misdemeanours with minimal fuss, but the Josephs were the kind of people who were capable of magnifying trivial disagreements into prolonged running battles. This was evidence of the strain they were both under, and suggests that beneath the surface tension were deep reserves of love which only served to make matters worse. Joseph's sense of duty banished any idea that he should give up his present course to save his marriage, and given the depth of his commitment there was no prospect of a compromise which would satisfy both parties. The only realistic prospect was for a further deterioration in the relationship, with Joseph devoting even more time to his work as a means of escape from his domestic unhappiness.

There was no question of a separation as yet – apart from any other consideration the eldest child, James, was only ten in 1965, and Lady Joseph

---

12. Crossman, *Diaries: Volume II*, 398.

was devoted to her family. But on one point, at least, she seems finally to have put her foot down. The presence in Leeds North-East of the woman who was regarded as the prettiest of all parliamentary wives had always been recorded by the *Leeds Searchlight*, and considering her private feelings she had done more than her duty in accompanying her husband on most of his journeys north. After 1964 the reported visits of the local MP (almost invariably headlined "Sir Keith has a busy day in Leeds") contain very few references to Lady Joseph. Her absences must have been very awkward for a sensitive man like Joseph, whose excuses were limited by the fact that someone with his wealth could easily afford a babysitter even if the usual nanny was unavailable. By now Hellen was earning a reputation as a sculptress, but this was no reason for her to be detained in London every time Joseph travelled to his constituency. A hidden hand must have been at work when Joseph chose the topic of an address to the North-East Leeds Luncheon Club on 7 October 1969; he "kept members enthralled" while ruminating on the divorces of Henry VIII.[13]

Within the Conservative Party, at least, there was a spirit of reconciliation after the 1964 general election. Powell and Macleod were welcomed back into the Shadow Cabinet, from which Rab Butler departed (to take up the Mastership of Trinity College, Cambridge) in January 1965. As before, the real moving spirit was Edward Heath, who became Shadow Chancellor; equally significant was Heath's appointment to yet another of Rab's old jobs, the Chairmanship of the Advisory Committee on Policy (ACP), which gave him control of a major policy review exercise. Harold Wilson obviously hoped to call an election at a time which would maximise his chances of being returned with a workable majority, but if things went badly he might be forced to go to the country through a series of by-election defeats or a rebellion on his own side provoked by the mishandling of a crisis. To imagine that the Opposition policy exercise could make much difference to the outcome of an election called under any of these scenarios required an act of faith. Fortunately Heath possessed an abundance of this quality, and he also knew that after thirteen years in office the party needed to unveil some fresh proposals for its supporters. Thanks to Heath's energetic management by the summer of 1965 around thirty groups were at work, generally chaired by the appropriate Shadow minister and staffed by a mixture of MPs and non-parliamentary experts.[14]

Although he had only been in Cabinet for two years Joseph had established himself as a key front-bencher. If not the first on the team sheet he had moved beyond the middle-order, and it would be more difficult for sceptics like Macleod to question his judgement in future. After the election he was finally moved away from Housing and given responsibility for the Social Services and

---

13. *Leeds Searchlight*, November 1969.
14. John Ramsden, *The Making of Conservative Party Policy: The Conservative Research Department since 1929* (Longman, 1980), 238.

for Wales. Ironically the Housing portfolio went to John Boyd-Carpenter who as Chief Secretary to the Treasury had tried to scupper most of Joseph's ambitious housing plans. Richard Crossman, Joseph's successor at Housing and Local Government, soon encountered similar problems with Labour's Chancellor James Callaghan, but although there was little sign of the heralded "housing drive" the Wilson government could still make the running on this subject. Joseph's cherished Rent Act was quickly repealed, although there was no return to the old rigid controls. Overriding the objections of Evelyn Sharp, Crossman opted for a middle course, introducing a system of flexible "Fair Rents" to be assessed by local officials, while bolstering security of tenure. As a reinforcement for his case the minister released the Milner Holland report in March 1965, to coincide with the second reading of his own Bill; the report, he told Wilson, provided "overwhelming evidence of the disastrous consequences of the 1957 Rent Act, so far at least as London is concerned". The evidence, indeed, was rather *too* overwhelming, and Crossman was inclined to play it down rather than provoke pressure for additional reform. Backroom deals were struck, and the Opposition allowed an unopposed second reading for Crossman's Bill. When Milner Holland was debated in the Commons the temperature had subsided. In his own contribution Joseph managed to sound at least semi-detached, claiming the credit for setting up the committee rather than admitting any responsibility for the mess he had failed to clear up in office.[15]

The link between his old ministry and Social Security (and his involvement with Mulberry) meant that Joseph could still gnaw at the old unappetising bone of housing. One of his speeches on the subject was published as a party pamphlet in 1967, and as late as 1968 he was submitting his thoughts to the Shadow Cabinet. But his removal from direct political responsibility at least freed him from possible trouble arising from his Bovis connection; as the *Economist* reported, the profits of the family firm soared from £200,000 to over half a million pounds during 1963, and during the course of Joseph's final year at the ministry the value of his shares more than doubled. In March 1963 *The Times* reported that a trust arrangement had been set up for his children; his solicitor pointed out that this would entail "a considerable saving in estate duty". Had he kept the housing portfolio questions might have been asked over the appointment of Evelyn Sharp to the Bovis board on her retirement from the civil service in 1967. On Social Services Joseph could think and speak without disturbance from the rattle of skeletons in his cupboard; furthermore the appointment gave him the chance to dust down some of the suggestions he had made in his first years as an MP without having to worry at this stage about their practical implications.[16]

---

15. Crossman to Wilson, 3 March 1965, PRO PREM 13/377; Crossman, *Diaries: Volume I*, 153–4, 262–3; *Hansard*, vol. 709, cols 158–70, 22 March 1965.
16. Sir Keith Joseph, *Changing Housing* (CPC, 1967); *The Times*, 30 March 1963; *Economist*, 31 October 1964, 534.

Few people could have been better formed for a policy review than Sir Keith Joseph in the mid-1960s. His fertile mind had not always been appreciated by busy ministerial colleagues, but Heath's wide-ranging exercise provided him with a licence to think. The nature of his ideas had also changed. Thanks largely to the input of the IEA the internal wrangling between the ideologue and the calculating politician was more frantic than ever, but for a year or two the competing elements produced creative results. During his first nine months shadowing Social Services Joseph benefitted from the assistance of Margaret Thatcher, who had been a junior minister at Pensions and National Insurance from 1961 to 1964 and continued to serve the party in that capacity after the election. The pair worked very quickly in harness, producing in early February a paper on pensions which formed the basis for party policy in the 1966 general election and beyond. Joseph's fingerprints were evident in the suggestion that the Ministries of Health and of Pensions and National Insurance should be merged into a Department of Health and Social Security (DHSS), thus ensuring the enhanced co-ordination of services which he had so often recommended; the same drive for administrative neatness produced a proposal (later adopted by Labour) to place the National Assistance Board (NAB) under the umbrella of the Ministry of Pensions and National Insurance. The special needs of the disabled were also recognised, in line with Joseph's long-held sympathies. The other major proposal was to retain the basic state pension, but to work towards a situation where almost every worker could also draw from an occupational scheme after retirement rather than relying on the graduated state pension which had been introduced by the Macmillan government. Occupational schemes already covered around two-thirds of working adult males. If the whole population could be included in some way, holding pension rights which could be transferred on every change of job, individual responsibility would be upheld, the state's role would be reduced, and people could still avoid a serious drop in income when they retired. In addition, they would be encouraged to keep working after retirement age through a further relaxation of the rule which at that time permitted earnings of up to £5 per week before any loss of pension was incurred. These ideas obviously owed something to the work of the IEA; they were lent extra credibility at the time because of the assumption (clearly shared by Joseph and Mrs Thatcher) that conditions of full employment would continue, ensuring that almost everyone would be able to keep up their payments. Even so, although there was talk of some required minimum standards the plan remained suspiciously sketchy up to the election; Joseph was particularly unconvincing when challenged in the Commons about coverage for the low paid.[17]

---

17. See LCC (65) 14, meeting of 2 February 1965, and paper on pensions LCC (65) 12, Bodleian Library. The plans were modified slightly in May. For an excellent background discussion see Rodney Lowe, "The Replanning of the Welfare State 1957–1964", in Martin Francis and Ina Zweiniger-Bargielowska (eds), *The Conservatives and British Society 1880–1990* (University of Wales Press, 1996), 255–73.

The blossoming of Joseph's political alliance with Mrs Thatcher was also apparent in parliamentary exchanges. His junior partner was already regarded as a doughty debater and drew plenty of Labour's fire upon herself. Joseph often seconded her counter-attacks, and acted as a chivalrous champion against her assailants. In July 1965, for example, he sprang to her defence when Will Griffiths, the MP for Manchester Exchange, accused her of making a speech which was "full of hypocrisy and humbug". In his private dealings Joseph was habitually courteous to women. But his warmth towards the Member for Finchley contrasted starkly with the acerbic treatment he meted out to his old sparring-partner "Peggy" Herbison, who now re-crossed his path as Minister for Pensions and National Insurance. The antagonism between these two reached a peak during the debate on a Private Members' Bill introduced by the Tory MP for Abingdon, Airey Neave. Neave proposed that pension rights should be extended to 250,000 elderly people who were not covered by contributions. The Government wanted to kill this legislation; it would be expensive, and in addition to the genuine needy it would benefit people who had been affluent enough to opt out of National Insurance after the war. But Labour's managers were aware that some back-benchers were sympathetic to the principle. George Wigg came up with the solution of talking out the Bill, while Herbison promised that the Government would introduce its own measures to iron out the anomalies. The debate went on through the night of 22 March and deep into the following morning; even towards its close Joseph was still leaping from his seat to interrupt Herbison. His conduct would have been more defensible had not the Shadow Cabinet itself been caught in two minds about Neave's measure; as the party spokesman on pensions Joseph had doubts about a costly reform which he would have to endorse as official party policy if the Conservatives threw their weight behind it. The thwarted Neave was undeterred by his March setback, and two months later Joseph told the Shadow Cabinet that he "would see Mr Neave and try to get him to play down his campaign, but he felt he was unlikely to be successful". His hunch was right; Neave was still agitating for reform at the end of the year and his idea appeared among the plethora of Conservative pledges in the 1966 manifesto.[18]

By the time of their last parliamentary confrontation Peggy Herbison was moved to protest that "each time that [Joseph] comes to the Dispatch Box he seems to be in a raging temper about something". She was not alone in facing an abrasive Joseph during the first year of the Wilson government. On 28 July 1965 he led for the Opposition in a debate on the cost of living. Summarising the Conservative goal as that of "a high earning, low-cost, competitive,

---

18. *Hansard*, vol. 715, cols 1509–22, 6 July 1965; vol. 709 cols 1148–58, 25 March 1965; Edward Short, *Whip to Wilson: The Crucial Years of Labour Government* (Macdonald, 1989), 137–8; see paper on Neave's Bill by KJ and Heath, LCC (65) 19, and minutes of LCC (65) 53, 2 June 1965, Bodleian Library; *Action Not Words* (CCO, 1996), 10.

compassionate society", he savaged Labour for its broken promises. A range of taxes were up, interest rates were higher than under the previous Government, and although Joseph admitted that prices had risen during the Conservative years the trend had accelerated since October 1964. He kept the speech reasonably short, and packed his peroration with violent imagery: "The Government have smashed their election pledges . . . It is a smash and grab, stop, stop, stop Government. Not go with Labour, but Labour should go – and the sooner the better". It was a rousing performance, even if Douglas Jay, for Labour, could reply that the Government was merely having to deal with the economic consequences of Mr Maudling. Indeed most commentators agree that Wilson should have devalued sterling to ease the balance of payments situation as soon as the election was over. But memories of Labour's previous devaluation of 1949 stayed the Prime Minister's hand, and the Government was hamstrung by his decision until it gave way in ignominious circumstances three years later.[19]

Wilson had no intention of "going", and at the end of June he had taken some of the wind out of Opposition sails by announcing that there would be no general election that summer. It was the Conservative leader who had already decided to go. Wounded by criticisms of his style and by rumours that colleagues were lining up to replace him, Home informed the 1922 Committee of his resignation on 22 July. Under new rules introduced after the fiasco of October 1963 the next leader would be elected by the parliamentary party. The list of candidates presented Joseph with an awkward choice, between Maudling (his probable preference of 1963 and the public favourite), Powell (the politician he most admired) and Heath, who in recent months had proved his leadership qualities and who was, of the three, most in tune with Joseph's current approach. Despite the background buzz in his favour last time round Joseph himself was not a candidate. Instead he canvassed on Heath's behalf; among his last-minute converts was Margaret Thatcher, who as a parliamentary "neighbour" to Reginald Maudling might otherwise have voted for the ex-Chancellor.[20]

Ever since this inaugural secret ballot for the Conservative leadership voting behaviour has been subject to improbable rumours (often spread by Labour MPs who are always fascinated by the faction-fights of their rivals). It has been suggested that in spite of his declared position Joseph actually cast his vote for Powell, and given the confusion surrounding his conduct in 1963 the story deserves inspection. He was quixotic enough to be tempted to vote for Powell in an attempt to save him from humiliation (in the end Powell attracted only fourteen supporters). Yet the contest between Maudling and Heath was too close to call until the result was announced, and Joseph certainly wanted the

---

19. *Hansard*, vol. 724, col. 1369, 16 February 1966; vol. 717, cols 487–97, 28 July 1965; Ben Pimlott, *Harold Wilson* (HarperCollins, 1992), 350–2.
20. Thatcher, *Path to Power*, 133–6.

Shadow Chancellor to win despite a lack of personal rapport. The idea that he might have gone round telling people to vote for Heath in the hope that this would make it safe for him to follow his heart rather than his head is highly implausible.[21]

On 27 July – the day before Joseph launched his parliamentary attack on Labour's economic record – Heath won the first ballot in the leadership election by 150 votes to Maudling's 133. The latter declined to take advantage of the provision in the new rules that there could be a second ballot if the leading candidate failed to secure a 15 per cent margin of victory. The general verdict was that in Heath the Conservative Party had selected a champion to unhorse Wilson using the same weapons. Like Wilson, Heath came from a relatively humble home, both were tough-minded, and it was assumed that they shared an addiction to the tactical side of politics rather than strategic visions. But Joseph's own decision was swung by what he saw as the *contrast* between Heath and Wilson. While he distrusted the Prime Minister's motives, he explained to Mrs Thatcher that "Ted has a passion to get Britain right". The country was like a business which needed turning round; Heath was the ideal Chairman of the Board, but Wilson would merely keep the shareholders entertained while their assets continued to depreciate.[22]

Joseph's own "passion" could never be disputed, but the change from Home to Heath stirred him to even greater efforts – despite the loss of Margaret Thatcher who was shuffled to Housing by the new leader. Joseph retained his responsibility for policy on the Social Services, but now added to his burdens the Labour portfolio which would have been quite enough on its own for most people. The 1964 Conservative manifesto had promised "an early inquiry" into possible trade union reform – a subject which had been relatively neglected since the war. The spur for this new interest was a series of decisions in the courts, notably the House of Lords' ruling of January 1964 (in *Rookes v Barnard*) that trade unions were liable for damages arising from industrial disputes. Labour did not mention the subject in its manifesto and in September 1964 Wilson told the TUC that there was no need for such a time-wasting exercise as a special inquiry. The perspective of office induced rapid second thoughts, and in February 1965 he announced the establishment of a Royal Commission.

The Conservatives were naturally resentful of Wilson's behaviour and made it a priority to seize the initiative themselves before the Commission (chaired by Lord Donovan) completed its work. Joseph was able to take over ideas for union reform already developed by the relevant policy group, which had been influenced by the pamphlet *A Giant's Strength* (1958) written by a group of young Conservative lawyers. A newcomer to the subject, Joseph added little to this work in his contribution to *Putting Britain Right Ahead*, the Conservative policy

---

21. Interview with Leo Abse.
22. Thatcher, *Path to Power*, 136.

document published before the 1965 party conference. There would be "a range of new Industrial Courts" to adjudicate on intra-union disputes and breaches of workplace agreements on the part of either unions or employers; unions would also be required to apply to a registrar for official recognition, subject to their satisfaction of certain conditions. As an incentive for the unions to co-operate it was also suggested that, if a majority of the workforce so desired, employers would be compelled to recognise a union as an official negotiating body. Ever watchful, in Shadow Cabinet Enoch Powell branded this idea "a big departure from principle" with serious implications for individual liberty; it would encourage the development of "closed shops" – workplaces where employees had no alternative but to join a union. After further thought Joseph shared these misgivings, but there was little else that he could offer to appease the unions. In his speech to the 1965 conference he compromised by referring to the concession as one "long sought" by the unions, but he dismissed it in two sentences after explaining at length all the other aspects of the policy.[23]

The search for incentives symptomised the Conservative dilemma over the presentation of union reform. Recent Ministers of Labour (notably Macleod and Heath himself) had tried to build constructive relations with the unions, but their efforts could not entirely erase the old impression that the Tories were the bosses' party. The first policy group, which issued its report in July 1965, had pointed out the danger of producing proposals which looked as if they were "directed against the trade unions"; by implication, the ideal was a policy which would have the effect of limiting union power while appearing to be even-handed. Joseph himself drew attention to this problem, arguing that it would be unwise to "allow the unions to pose as political victims or martyrs in a class war" and advocating additional concessions including protection against unfair dismissal and employee membership of the (toothless) "supervisory boards" of companies above a certain size. But although *Putting Britain Right Ahead* claimed that the Conservative goal was "fairness" at work, and that the union reforms should be seen in the context of an overall package to make industry more competitive, there was a marked contrast between the detailed proposals on union reform and the cursory, generalised suggestions for attacking the restrictive practices of employers. Evidently the Conservative leadership felt that it was time to make amends to the supporters who had been infuriated by the repeal of RPM.[24]

Joseph had been chosen for the Labour post because he had a more dynamic image than his predecessor, Jo Godber, whose preference for a piecemeal approach to the union question had already been rejected by the policy group in favour of an all-encompassing Bill. If Heath calculated that the new

23. For Powell, see LCC (65) 65, 15 September 1965, CPA, Bodleian Library.
24. Report 2 July 1965 CPA, CRD/3/17/20, PG/20/65/45; KJ's paper "Trade Union Policy", LCC (65) 70, 8 December 1965, Bodleian Library; *Putting Britain Right Ahead* (CCO, 1965), 12.

spokesman would content himself with a vigorous sales pitch on behalf of the existing product he was mistaken. Once the policy document had been published Joseph began to push for an even harder line on the unions, introducing the question of "overmanning" in industry and suggesting that a commissioner should be empowered to bring "flagrant" cases before the Industrial Courts. The bizarre notion that a government appointee might tour the country advising firms to sack a proportion of their workers could only occur to someone with approximately equal disdain for management and men. Believing that British managers needed to knuckle down to their responsibilities, Joseph also revised the Industrial Relations proposals to ensure that companies would prosecute unions for contractual breaches, rather than leaving this to the state as originally envisaged. But his ultimate loyalties were obvious, at least to his colleagues. In a covering note for a paper submitted to the Shadow Cabinet in December 1965 – after he had held the relevant portfolio for almost six months – he noted that he had consulted "a relatively large number of employers, personnel specialists and academics", but had yet to see a single trade union leader. His approach dismayed Godber. But the latter was now marooned at Agriculture and Heath saw no reason to overrule his hyperactive colleague – even though many of the industrialists who had been consulted had (predictably) opposed the idea that they, rather than the government, should take unions to court.[25]

Talk of "overmanning" – a word which was probably intended as a euphemism but which managed to sound more ugly than any alternative – suggested a topic which the Shadow Cabinet was reluctant to debate. *Putting Britain Right Ahead* included sharp criticism of industrial atttitudes which were still "conditioned" by the 1930s, yet this passage was coupled with a restatement of the party's commitment to full employment. It was assumed that any retreat from this position would have disastrous electoral consequences, but in any case most of the Shadow Cabinet (including Heath) had themselves been "conditioned" by the 1930s and their commitment was heartfelt. They were consoled by the assumption – easy enough to make at the time – that if firms tackled the problem of "overmanning", the cast-off workers would soon find new jobs. Under the Conservatives Britain would be offered the prospect of painless change.

With hindsight it looks as though Shadow ministers were ducking the obvious questions. If British prosperity were really so precarious as they claimed, surely the necessary reforms would be followed by at least a transitional period in which

25. "Industrial Relations Policy: Matters for Further Consideration", memorandum for Policy Group on Trade Union Law and Practices, 1 January 1966, CRD/3/17/20, CPA, Bodleian Library; Keith Middlemas, *Power, Competition and the State Volume 2, Threats to the Postwar Settlement: Britain, 1961–74* (Macmillan, 1990), 270–1; Lewis Johnman, "The Conservatives in Opposition, 1964–70", in Richard Coopey, Steven Fielding and Nick Tiratsoo (eds), *The Wilson Governments 1964–1970* (Pinter, 1993), 193.

unemployment would be much higher than the post-war average? If union power was great enough to demand radical action, would not a brief interlude of high unemployment be a good thing, to bring Britain's workers to their senses? In their next two periods in office Conservatives had to confront these questions, and the answers depended on their appreciation of the experience of unemployment. In the mid-1960s there were few indications of the position that Joseph would take, although in his 1965 conference speech he referred with feeling to "the shock of a man going home to tell his wife that his job has come to an end". But he went on to banish this miserable vision, stating with confidence that there would be few redundancies and that the few who found no market for their existing skills would benefit from an ambitious re-training programme. The need was not for higher unemployment, but for a situation in which there was a close match between advertised vacancies and the number of people out of work. The logic of this view (often heard at the IEA) was that a country could be said to enjoy conditions of "full employment" if there was even one unfilled vacancy, no matter how many people registered as jobless. There was no sign of outright hostility to the unemployed, but flashes of sympathetic understanding were very rare. In one of his few parliamentary speeches which touched on the subject Joseph replied to fears that earnings-linked unemployment benefit might encourage people to "malinger":

> That may be so – I do not know. I have never been one who believed that malingering should be over-stressed. There is an element of malingering, and I think that over-generous treatment could encourage it, but I also think that we are wrong to put it as our first consideration.

This was the Sir Keith Joseph who had contributed in the 1950s to *The Responsible Society*; he felt that the jury was still out on whether or not a generous welfare state would give rise to a "dependency culture", and, as on most issues concerning poverty, he displayed a tendency to confuse statistical facts with psychological insights. For the moment, at least, the figures suggested that the state could maintain existing benefit levels.[26]

The initial response from Labour and the trade unions to the industrial relations proposals was fairly muted, presumably because their attention was riveted on the Donovan Commission which was still taking evidence. But unexpected and unwelcome criticism came from the Conservative frontbencher Angus Maude, who in January 1966 wrote an article for the *Spectator* which implored his party to "stop pussyfooting" on industrial relations and called for more radicalism in social services. Joseph had good reason to feel

---

26. *Hansard*, vol. 720, col. 195, 10 November 1965. Minutes of Eighty-Third Conservative Party conference (1965).

mortified by the allegation that he had failed in both his areas of responsibility, but the damage was not confined to him. A close ally of Enoch Powell, Maude felt that his own party was "a meaningless irrelevance" in the eyes of voters – despite the fact that under Heath's leadership Conservative support in the Gallup polls had never fallen below a third of the electorate. Heath himself was lagging behind his party (and Wilson) in the polls, but regardless of his popularity rating he had no alternative but to sack the insubordinate Maude. The ill-judged *Spectator* article appeared only a month after another Tory own goal, when the party divided three ways in a vote on oil sanctions against the illegal Rhodesian government led by Ian Smith. In February Labour won a hard-fought by-election in Hull, helped in part by the timely announcement of a new bridge over the Humber. The economy remained a serious worry but the voters could be reassured by a little short-term window-dressing. Wilson was keen to avoid Home's mistake of 1964; this time an awkward budget would be postponed until after the general election. Soon after the Hull result he decided to go to the country at the end of March.[27]

During the 1966 campaign an American journalist asked "Are all English elections dull like this?". A low-key contest was no help to Heath, who tried to raise the temperature with a series of speeches in which he predicted economic disaster if Labour was returned. The leader's sense of urgency was reflected in the Conservative manifesto, *Action Not Words*, which overpowered the reader with its "staccato orders for a massive offensive on all conceivable fronts". Yet Wilson managed to convince a majority of voters that there was no need for a change in command; he would do the job very well once he had secured a reasonable number of parliamentary reinforcements. The poll of 31 March gave him an overall majority of 96. The Conservatives (on 253 seats) suffered a net loss of 51 MPs.[28]

Like Gaitskell in 1959, Heath found that a demoralising defeat for his party did little to harm his own image, at least with the press. But for Sir Keith Joseph the 1966 general election campaign had no silver lining. While he predicted a Labour victory at a One Nation dinner held just before Parliament was dissolved he underestimated its scale, believing that there would be a majority of only 30. This disappointment was compounded by the fact that his personal message hardly registered with the voters. Early in March eight trade unionists at a depot in Cowley were "tried" for refusing to join an unofficial strike; it was reported that a hangman's noose was dangling in the background as their case was heard, while the lynch-mob chanted "hang the bastards". For Joseph this was a perfect illustration of the need for reform, but it was next to useless as a weapon against Labour because it allowed Wilson to talk tough himself,

---

27. Angus Maude, "Winter of Tory Discontent", *Spectator*, 14 January 1966.
28. Heath, *Course of My Life*, 281; Gilmour & Garnett, *Whatever Happened*, 225.

without offending the majority of trade unionists who were appalled by the stories. The Conservatives presented the trade union policy as the centre-piece of their campaign but Joseph's speeches were rarely reported; even the party broadcast on industrial relations was entrusted to Macleod and Quintin Hogg. Joseph's attempts to interest the public in his party's plans for the social services were equally ineffectual.[29]

In Leeds the situation remained unchanged after the election; the Conservatives retained their outposts in the northern part of the city. But Joseph's majority was cut again, this time by more than 3,000 votes. He had never taken his constituency for granted, but with his lead over his Labour rival now below 5,000 he would have to be even more assiduous in future. It should have been a relief to discover that in the post-election reshuffle Heath took away one of Joseph's responsibilties, giving the social services job to Miss Mervyn Pike (who more than a decade earlier had fought Sir Keith for the Leeds North-East nomination). But the Chief Whip William Whitelaw was deputed to provide a soothing explanation of the new arrangement, which Joseph probably regarded as an example of front-bench "overmanning".[30]

Joseph soon compensated himself for the loss of social services. He was still accumulating jobs outside Parliament, and in July 1966 became Chairman of the Research Board of the Institute of Jewish Affairs. Besides, his remaining post offered scope for additional work. Since trade union reform was seen as the key to economic revival Joseph was entitled to a say in this wider field and the official Treasury spokesman, Macleod, raised no objection to his input. During the election Heath had claimed that people who voted Labour would have to pay later, and he did not have long to wait before he had the grim satisfaction of seeing his prophecy verified. Only a few days after the election James Callaghan's budget introduced the Selective Employment Tax (SET), an impost on service sector jobs which was advertised as a boost to manufacturing industry but was really a desperate bid to raise money. Despite a run on sterling over the summer Wilson still preferred the perceived alternative – savage deflation – to devaluation. In July bank rate and indirect taxes were raised, public expenditure cut by £150 million, the personal travel allowance was reduced to £50, and a six-month freeze on prices and incomes was announced to replace the previous voluntary guidelines. The inevitable consequences of "the biggest deflationary package ever" were "rising unemployment, stagnant output, and the complete abandonment of the National Plan" (which in the previous year had set the ambitious economic growth target of 25 per cent over six years).[31]

29. One Nation minutes, 2 March 1966; *General Election 1966: Daily Notes* (CRD, 1966), 64–5.
30. Undated memorandum, "Leader's Committee as at present planned", Heath Papers.
31. Stewart, *Jekyll & Hyde Years*, 72–3.

Prices and incomes policy was a Conservative invention, but it had not figured among the multitude of proposals contained in *Action Not Words*. There were few active enthusiasts for the policy; even those who supported it did so on the grounds that it might be the only weapon against inflation in desperate times. For free-market ideologues such as Powell and the IEA a voluntary policy was mainly harmful in that it was a symptom of unsound thinking on the real causes of inflation. But Labour's version, which put the restraint of pay and prices on a statutory basis, was the devil's work, bringing in its train an army of bureaucrats. In the Shadow Cabinet Joseph took the initiative, submitting a paper at the first sign of government action in May 1966. The document bore unmistakable traces of the contest for Joseph's soul between the IEA and Machiavelli, which in this instance produced some alarming gyrations. On the same page as the assertion that "The Bill is dirigiste *and* won't work", creating "an administrative nightmare, with so many loopholes as to be a joke", Joseph speculated that "Perhaps we shall one day want to operate some such policy". In the Shadow Cabinet discussion of 4 July he concentrated on the practical arguments: "he believed that the Bill would not have its desired effect, that the Bill would not touch earnings, and that therefore we should oppose it. The policy in the Bill could only be effective in deflationary conditions which would in themselves make the Bill unnecessary".

There was no ambiguity in Joseph's treatment of the issue in the Commons in August; he lambasted "an evil and unnecessary Bill" which was "a new instrument of tyranny" in the hands of a doctrinaire government. Yet this harsher language reflected the fact that the measure had been made even more "dirigiste" after a Cabinet meeting of 20 July. Unlike the more inflexible ideologues Joseph defended Selwyn Lloyd's "Pay Pause", in line with the view expressed in the Shadow Cabinet that "a voluntary incomes policy had a useful role to play" in certain circumstances. Presumably this was the line Joseph had taken during an argument with Powell at a One Nation dinner in February (although the precise nature of their disagreement was not minuted). Machiavelli was still winning – if only by a short head – and Joseph's incautious language disguised a position very close to that of Macleod and Heath.[32]

In fact the freeze proved to be reasonably popular, and over the year from July 1966 wages and prices rose by only 2 per cent. Britain's balance of payments moved into surplus. But this gave only temporary respite to sterling, and the squeeze on demand caused other problems. By February 1967 unemployment (though still only around 2 per cent of the workforce, the level recommended by Frank Paish) was more than double the rate it had been when the deflationary measures were introduced. In his attacks on Labour's

---

32. LCC (66) 92, KJ's paper on "Early Warning" Bill, 20 May 1966; minutes of LCC meeting, 4 July 1966, LCC (66) 116, CPA, Bodleian Library; *Hansard*, vol. 733, cols 1731–42, 10 August 1966; One Nation minutes, 9 February 1966; Shepherd, *Macleod*, 444.

record Joseph enjoyed saying with heavy irony that Harold Wilson was Britain's first Prime Minister with first-rate economic qualifications. Given Wilson's record in office this might have been regarded as a good reason for Joseph to keep away from academic economists, but around the time of the July crisis he embarked on a series of working lunches and interviews, mostly with IEA associates such as Professor Colin Clark. Enoch Powell once told Iain Macleod that it might be helpful if he knew some economics; this was only half a jest and less than half an insult, since Macleod thought that economics should be subservient to political calculation. Joseph was beginning to reach the opposite conclusion, and whenever he was troubled by his own ignorance of a subject he sought out what he considered to be the best sources. At All Souls he had read recommended textbooks. Now he could supplement his reading by talking to the authors, and in the existing political context he was sure to choose economic liberals, rather than Keynesians like his old friend Shonfield (at that time an active member of the Donovan Commission). Always susceptible in the company of an acknowledged expert, Joseph was the more willing to absorb the message of people who reinforced his instincts, and used the kind of entrepreneurial language which was so congenial to him.[33]

The sterling crisis erupted again in April 1967, after the release of adverse balance of payments figures. There now seemed to be no alternative to a devaluation of the pound, and Joseph was busy canvassing opinion amongst his new allies who, on balance, favoured a floating exchange rate (as did Wilson). In normal circumstances economic liberals would have been gleeful at the prospect of the currency being allowed to find its "true" market level, but these were abnormal times and instead of "floating" sterling was certain to sink, with dire consequences both for the British economy and for the country's international prestige. There seemed to be no easy short-term answer, since there was no prospect of an early general election and Joseph was convinced that the first trained economist in Downing Street was an inveterate bungler. But was there any assurance that the Conservatives would retrieve the situation after three or four years of pain under Labour? Joseph could not suppress his doubts. Despite his promptings few of his colleagues seemed anxious to lap up the wisdom of his new friends in the economics profession. In early February 1967 he arranged a two-day seminar to discuss Professor Paish's ideas on the link between unemployment and inflation, but of the front-bench team only Powell and Anthony Barber turned up. Heath had established an Economic Policy Group, but its most powerful members (Boyle, Maudling, Macleod and Heath himself) were all antipathetic to free market evangelism. On Heath's instructions Joseph was sent copies of all the group's papers, but not until

---

33. Stewart, *Jekyll & Hyde Years,* 79; see Powell's contribution to symposium on Conservative policy making 1965–70, *Contemporary Record*, February 1990, 38.

November 1967 was he informed that he could attend any meetings which might interest him.[34]

Soon after the ill-attended seminar Joseph was shuffled by Heath from Labour to Trade and Power. The ostensible reason for the new change was Tony Barber's move from Trade to the party chairmanship, but there was an implied slight in Joseph's loss of the key union policy to Robert Carr, who was keen to restore a less confrontational approach. Joseph's last Shadow Cabinet paper at Labour had suggested that the Conservatives might deal with the political contributions of trade unions, reversing the existing situation where members had to make the effort to "contract out" if they did not want to help fund the Labour Party. The party was already committed to reforms which required delicate presentation; adopting a further measure with such an overt political purpose would discredit the whole package. In January 1964 Joseph himself had opposed a proposal emanating from his party's National Union to move against the political levy, on the grounds that it would undermine good indus-trial relations. Although Shadow ministers agreed with Joseph that the link between Labour and the unions was a major obstacle to economic progress, they knew that any reform would call attention to the cosy Conservative alliance with the business community. When his new paper was discussed on 13 February 1967 it was given a polite reception by his colleagues but nothing further was heard of it. Clearly it was time to give his energies a new outlet.[35]

Joseph's first economic crusade, which opened with a speech at Reading on 26 April 1967, thus began against a background of personal frustration and growing concern at Britain's plight. Evidently the press had been tipped off that this would be something more than the usual ritual of rallying the local troops; *The Times* reported that Joseph was planning "a series of speeches in which he redefines a Tory philosophy and relates it to some of the main political issues of the day". The reference to "a Tory philosophy" must have set off alarm bells in Central Office; Angus Maude had earned his dismissal by alleging the lack of such a creed. Yet Maude had an unparalleled trouble-making reputation, having resigned his seat and emigrated to Australia in disgust after the Suez climb-down. Joseph had exhibited occasional symptoms of a restive nature, but he had always stayed on the leash. Perhaps he was intending to perform a valuable service to the party, and would claim that Heath's policies had always been backed by a coherent philosophy if anyone cared to look for it.[36]

If this really was Joseph's purpose, he bungled the exercise. Under the ominous headline "Tory errors confessed", Sir Keith was quoted as indicting

---

34. See correspondence in CRD 3/7/6/7, CPA, Bodleian Library.
35. Ramsden, *Winds of Change*, 280–1, 219; KJ's paper "Trade Union Funds", LCC (67) 126, and minutes of Shadow Cabinet meeting of 13 February 1967, LCC (67) 155, CPA, Bodleian Library.
36. *The Times*, 27 April 1967.

"successive Conservative Governments since the war" for having betrayed the true faith. They had:

> made the mistake of failing to let private enterprise work properly. When we took over the Government in 1951 we found private enterprise totally shackled by the socialists. Our error was that we only half freed it . . . We made life at once too easy and too hard for private enterprise. Too easy because to keep unemployment far lower than it is now, we kept demand too high, and businessmen therefore had full order books. Too hard because we kept many of the socialist shackles and added new ones of our own, and because we taxed profits and high earnings very heavily.

In the past Joseph had struggled to find the neat soundbites which would drive home a positive message or put down an opponent. On this occasion he had been able to prepare the clinching phrase in advance. "Private enterprise has not failed", he declared: "it has not been properly tried". It was certainly an eye-catching remark – a mirror image of the socialist claim that their own "panacea" had never been given a fair chance. And like the socialists, Joseph was begging the question of *why* his party had done little more than to pay lip-service to its boasted beliefs. An obvious reason was a well-founded fear that the voters would take fright at a radical break from established policies; but the relative freedom of opposition had effaced Joseph's memory of the need for restraint in office.

The content of the speech must have surprised the Shadow Cabinet, who less than a year before had been told by Joseph that "we should run a market economy but . . . we shall not be understood or forgiven by the public if we appear to rely solely on market forces". From the point of view of the current party leadership the most galling aspect of Joseph's analysis was the attribution of blame. Albeit from a very different perspective, a front-bench Conservative had apparently confirmed Harold Wilson's accusation that the Tories had presided over "thirteen wasted years". The personal role of Joseph in the Conservative failure was also left irritatingly obscure. By his repeated use of the word "we" he seemed to be accepting his own share of guilt. But the alleged "betrayal" had begun in 1951 – before he had even been accepted as a Tory candidate. The implication of the speech was that the main responsibility rested with the Churchill government of which Joseph (unlike Heath and Macleod) had never been a member. Their initial failure to dismantle "Socialist" controls (some of which, of course, had been introduced by the war-time coalition led by Churchill himself) had set the trend for the misdeeds – or reprehensible inaction – of Eden, Macmillan and Home. Joseph had slipped at least a partial alibi for himself into what purported to be a candid confession; it was an early draft of what developed into an admission that he had merely followed "fashionable thinking" in the early 1960s. In fact no one who knew Joseph could accuse him of underhand dealing; but the fact that his choice of words had been innocent only made the speech more ominous. Anxious to paint his own previous record as black as possible, and full of enthusiasm for the new truths which had broken in on him, he completely overlooked the possibility that he would leave others looking much worse than himself. His ingrained honesty meant that he was certain to repeat this offence at some point. A shrewd gambler could already anticipate that this would happen when his party was next in Opposition, after he had committed more sins which could be exaggerated and inadvertently reflected onto his colleagues. Indeed, the first manifestation of the habit had come within months of the Conservatives losing office in 1964, when in a little-noticed speech to his constituents Joseph attacked Labour's record on exports before admitting that "In 13 years we never solved the problem".[37]

The short-term effect of Joseph's crusade was to alert the press to the fact that there was more than one "Powellite" in the Shadow Cabinet, and that they could now speak in terms of an ideological rift rather than the existence of one eloquent dissident. In May an editorial in *The Times* exposed the factions: "there are those like Mr Maudling or Sir Edward Boyle who are economic interventionists, willing to use the power of the state for constructive ends. There are others like Mr Enoch Powell or Sir Keith Joseph who are virtually laisser-faire economists". The newspaper went on to pronounce that "no one who reads Conservative speeches can find a convincing answer to the problems which [from] 1960 to 1964 plainly defeated them". Clearly the leading British organ of opinion had been left cold by Joseph's "redefinition" of Conservatism; its sympathies lay with the "constructive" Boyle and Maudling. Instead of a valiant crusader Sir Keith had proved to be a very errant knight – the Don Quixote of Eaton Square.[38]

Joseph felt that *The Times* editorial could not be allowed to pass without a reply. Claiming that he and others had been "puzzled" by the phrase "virtually laisser-faire", he reminded the paper's readers that he had been "campaigning for two main causes both of which depend on strenuous state action". The causes were "more help for people in need", and a reinvigorated free enterprise system, which could only be guaranteed if the state took action to enforce competition. "The purpose is to release energies for another, but this time a humane, industrial revolution. Surely these are not 'virtually laisser-faire' policies?" When spelling out the argument in this way Joseph had a valid point; although "*laisser-faire*" tends to be used as a term of abuse that escapes precise definition, any government truly worthy of the label would abjure all forms of

---

37. KJ's paper "Early Warning Bill", LCC (66) 92, 3, 20 May 1966, CPA, Bodleian Library; *The Times*, 5 December 1964.
38. *The Times*, 20 May 1967.

economic intervention. Even so, *The Times* had been careful to call him "*virtually* laisser-faire"; it was inconceivable that any post-war British politician of the front rank would advocate the doctrine in unqualified form. And Joseph had not clarified his remark about the betrayal of private enterprise by *all* Conservative governments since 1951. Stripped of the soundbites, his preferred approach sounded identical to the modernising drive which *had* been tried (notably by Heath over RPM), and which the party had offered to the voters in its 1966 manifesto. The real "puzzle" was why Joseph should dress up what amounted to an endorsement of the party's *existing* "philosophy" as an appeal for a radical *re-think*. His initiative was all the more vexing because the Conservatives had just made strong gains in local elections, had won a parliamentary by-election at Glasgow Pollok on 9 March, and had established a significant lead in the opinion polls for the first time since June 1965.[39]

The best clue to Joseph's thinking at this time is a book review which appeared a few weeks after the Reading speech. It was a remarkable piece, which included a prediction that the labour force in manufacturing would steadily decline, to be replaced by the service sector as the main employer in Britain. But other passages were more provocative than far-sighted. The tone of the first two paragraphs echo that of Angus Maude's suicide note. Joseph opened with the claim that the "real political struggle" in Britain was between "those who believe in a collectivist economy with a relatively small private enterprise sector" and "those who believe in a private enterprise economy with a relatively small public sector". Most of his colleagues would have been happy to submit to this ideological test, but the next paragraph revealed that on current form they would fail it in Joseph's eyes:

> Conservatives as well as Socialists tend to regard much of our present public sector as permanent; but the detachment of Opposition may give us the chance to see clearly the failure of many of our public enterprises. What we need above all before Conservatives are returned to power next time is a clearer understanding of the economic, social and legal framework which will enable private enterprise to serve the public properly.

Like Maude before him, Joseph implied that he had already developed that "clearer understanding", and was out to prove that his days of "pussyfooting about" were behind him. But, also like Maude, he had jumped to the false conclusion that, because he himself needed ideological clarity his colleagues must have similar requirements. The Shadow Cabinet had yet to recognise "the magic qualities of competitive private enterprise" (a starry-eyed rhapsody that could have been penned by Powell himself). As Maude would have put it, they

---

39. *The Times,* 22 May 1967.

"talked like technocrats" on economics; Joseph thought that they should be preaching from the gospels of Adam Smith. It might have consoled them to learn that they were not alone in their failure properly to rebut socialist claims. Among the contributors to the book Joseph was reviewing (*The Case for Capitalism*), the former Marxist Alfred Sherman was praised for "a fine passage on capitalism and liberty". But even passionate economic liberals like the born-again Sherman failed to measure up, because they refused to "question the common assumption that public not private enterprise is the more socially just; or is better at providing housing or medical treatment". Joseph seemed to be suggesting that the next Conservative government should abandon the present National Health Service, based on a public service ethos, and replace it with the "magic" of the profit motive. If he was prepared even to dream of this there could be no limit to a Conservative programme of de-nationalisation.[40]

The fact that both Maude and Joseph were admirers of Powell suggested that all this was more than a coincidence – as did the fact that, like Maude, Joseph published his insubordinate musings in the *Spectator*. But the Reading incident had underlined the differences between Powell and Joseph.[41] On economic matters the former was doctrinaire, consistent and determined. Fuelled by honourable ambition, he calculated that his populist speeches would help both his cause and his career, and he was well aware of the differences between Heath's thinking and his own. Joseph had certainly developed an ideological mind-set which marked him off from the majority of his colleagues, who believed that their goals would be threatened, not secured, by a doctrinaire approach to political questions. But unlike Powell Joseph was vulnerable to the influence of others. Ian Gilmour once applied a quip of Stanley Baldwin's to Powell, who had "a Rolls Royce brain without a chauffeur". By comparison Joseph's mind was a Mercedes-Benz with several erratic passengers wrestling for the wheel.[42] He represented a style of politics which placed honesty far above guile; but in the Britain of Harold Wilson his personal code of morality made him seem like a hopeless amateur. A startling example of his approach came in December 1966, when he told a meeting of the Child Poverty Action Group (CPAG) that poverty could be abolished "relatively quickly if we get our priorities right". He went on to predict that if "one tenth of the moral energy generated by members of Parliament about Vietnam" was redirected into this battle, poverty could be conquered. In the context of 1966 it was an outburst

---

40. *Spectator*, 19 May 1967.
41. In retirement Powell described Joseph as a "butterfly" who delivered a message that "could only be said by a hawk if they were to have any effect". Although this was a serious under-statement of Joseph's influence, the implicit comparison of the "butterfly" Joseph with the "hawkish" Powell is very apt. See Ranelagh, *Thatcher's People*, 137–8.
42. Ian Gilmour, review of Heffer's *Like the Roman*, *Evening Standard*, 20 November 1998.

reminiscent of the speeches that his father had delivered to dumbfounded audiences in the 1930s and early 1940s.[43]

Unlike Powell Joseph had not thrown himself into politics on his return from war. By comparison, he had little understanding of the party to which he belonged, and the broader context of Conservative support. While Powell well knew that his was a radical voice, it simply did not occur to Joseph that hard-line economic liberalism was alien to the pragmatic tradition of Conservatism; having discovered the teachings of the IEA he wanted to share them with others, oblivious to the likely consequences. With Joseph, personal advance-ment would always be at most a secondary consideration. His speeches and writings in 1967 gave the first clear sign that he was both more different and more dangerous than had been thought.

Joseph's eccentricities – and lack of media appeal compared with that of Powell – probably saved him on this occasion. The same behaviour which marked clear conspiratorial intentions in a Maude or a Powell could only give rise to speculation when Joseph was the agent in question. Heath does not recall having to rebuke his colleague at any time in the Opposition period. The only evidence that words had been exchanged on the subject is a somewhat apologetic reference to his contacts with the IEA in a letter from Joseph to his leader of early April 1968. In private, however, Heath gave free expression to his annoyance.[44] His own major contribution on economic policy, delivered at Carshalton on 8 July 1967, showed that on this subject he would be guided by pragmatic considerations, not ideology. He spoke at length of the need to give more scope to free enterprise, but re-affirmed his own acceptance of the mixed economy and emphasised that government had a duty to do more than simply to set the right framework for competition. Under his leadership the party would be radical, but never "doctrinaire" like Labour. There was no need for a philosophical rethink because the correct line had been established in 1963.[45]

For Joseph, the shock of *The Times* editorial was serious enough to calm him down, despite the lack of response from the leadership. The stir caused by the Reading speech soon died away. But some MPs had taken note of the outburst. Sir Richard Body, a back-bencher first elected in 1966, told Morrison Halcrow that while Joseph was regarded as part of the Heath "establishment", there was a "ginger group" of economic liberals which saw him as an ally. At the time,

43. *The Times*, 19 December 1966. More orthodox members of Joseph's party agreed with the official US line that the war in Vietnam was essential to the survival of the free world. Although the worst incidents of the conflict lay ahead, by the end of 1966 critics could already feel that they had some issues worth airing. In May, for example, Nicholas Tomalin of the *Sunday Times* had interviewed an American General who described his enjoyment of shoot-ing from his helicopter "at any Vietnamese seen running for cover" (Philip Knightley, *The First Casualty* (Prion, 2000), 425).
44. Interview with Sir Edward Heath; KJ to Heath, 3 April 1968, CRD 3/7/6/7, CPA, Bodleian Library; letter to authors from Brendon Sewill.
45. Edward Heath, press release of speech at a Conservative meeting, Carshalton, 8 July 1967, 17.

with the party dogged by division over issues like Rhodesia, economic differences were not the all-absorbing topic of discussion that they later became. Ironically, when the "Powellite" challenge to Heath's authority came to dominate the headlines it was race, not economics, which brought conflict into the open.[46]

---

46. Halcrow, *Joseph*, 39.

Chapter 8

"Inflammatory Filth"

After Reading Joseph continued his planned round of speeches. But there was little press interest, and the chastened crusader had dropped the ploy of hacking through his own ranks. He was taciturn in the Commons over the next few months, and the minutes of Shadow Cabinet meetings suggest that his interventions were rare and subdued at this time. In July 1967, for example, the Shadow team discussed a Research Department paper on "Strategy and Tactics". The debate revolved around the question of whether there were recognisable movements (or "watersheds") in public opinion. An active crusader would have taken this as an invitation to seize his lance, but Iain Macleod set the tone of the discussion by asserting that the public was not ready to listen to the Conservatives with no immediate prospect of an election. Joseph merely observed that the party should establish a few broad principles, such as "we were in favour of thrift in public spending, and that we sought to look after the needy and the disabled". Despite all the work of the policy groups it was felt that the party should not go beyond this; even Powell felt that movements of public opinion were difficult to predict or control, and warned against offering hostages to fortune at this stage in the form of detailed policy pronouncements. Joseph would have to keep his armour in storage, at least for a year or two.[1]

---

1. See Shadow Cabinet discussion in LCC (67) 185, 17 July 1967, CPA, Bodleian Library.

Despite the downbeat mood of the meeting voters were still turning to the Conservatives as the economic outlook worsened. On 21 September 1967 the Opposition took Cambridge, and Clement Attlee's old seat of Walthamstow West (on a swing of over 18 per cent). There was a further gain for the Conservatives at Leicester South-West on 2 November. On the same day the Government's economic adviser Sir Alec Cairncross told Wilson that he would have to abandon his three-year battle to prop up sterling; the trade deficit had reached record levels and currency reserves were draining off in the fight with the speculators. The decision to devalue sterling from $2.80 to $2.40 was taken on 13 November. The Prime Minister compounded the damage with a perky television broadcast which assured the public that "the pound in your pocket" was unaffected. In December the Gallup poll showed a Tory lead of more than 10 per cent.[2]

In the debate on devaluation Joseph made a thoughtful contribution which eschewed narrow partisan rhetoric. While Heath had fulminated against Wilson's dishonest betrayal of British interests Joseph recognised that devaluation could benefit the country, provided that it was accompanied by a new dose of deflationary measures. He was rewarded with fewer interruptions than usual, although when he expounded the Conservative policies for economic revival one Labour member asked him to "put a new record on". The new moderate tone remained on show in February 1968 – the month after Joseph celebrated his fiftieth birthday. Labour's Industrial Reorganisation Bill, piloted by Anthony Wedgwood Benn, was designed to provide substantial funds for investment through the Government's Industrial Reorganisation Corporation (IRC). This was the kind of interventionist strategy which economic liberals abhorred, and Joseph did condemn both the excessive powers granted to the Corporation and the temptation it would offer for the minister to use "tax-payers' money [to support] industrial lame ducks and white elephants". But, as Benn noted, the speech marked a definite shift in Joseph's position; his strictures fell a long way short of a commitment to abolish the IRC itself when the Conservatives returned to power. Joseph's affection for the IRC was also revealed to the Shadow Cabinet. In June 1968 he told his colleagues that "some of its activities could be considered useful, and he wondered if we wanted to attack it or if we might wish to keep it in being when we returned to office". There followed an interesting example of a supposed ideologue being outflanked on the right by pragmatists; the majority view was that having opposed the IRC at the outset the party might as well pledge to abolish it, but Joseph remained unconvinced.[3]

2. Clive Ponting, *Breach of Promise: Labour in Power 1964–1970* (Hamish Hamilton, 1989), 289–91.
3. *Hansard*, vol. 754, cols 1252–9, 21 November 1967, vol. 757, cols 1592–1605, 1 February 1968; LCC (68) 246, Shadow Cabinet meeting 26 June 1966, CPA, Bodleian Library.

Joseph's *Spectator* book review of May 1967 had implied that nothing should be ruled out as a candidate for return to the private sector. By the end of the year this subject was causing trouble for Heath. The leader had invited Nicholas Ridley to chair the policy group on nationalised industries, and Ridley had packed it with his right-wing allies. As Heath's private secretary John MacGregor pointed out, the two members with the most practical experience on the subject (Lord Nugent and Sir Keith's friend, Sir Henry d'Avigdor-Goldsmid) were also the most sceptical about the radical line that was developing within the group. When he saw the preliminary report on Nationalised Industries in November 1967 Heath found it "alarmingly naïve and even half-baked"; confronted with the opening suggestion that state industries should be "run on strictly commercial lines, with the sole task of maximising their profits" he noted in dismay, "How can you [do this] when they have such a large monopoly element in them?". Wiser counsellors intervened. When Ridley was invited to a meeting of the Economic Policy Group on 8 February 1968, Joseph joined forces once again with the Shadow spokesman on Fuel and Power, Margaret Thatcher. Mrs Thatcher developed Heath's theme; public utilities, she declared, "could never be run on straight commercial lines. One could not have two rival enterprises seeking to sell electricity in competition one with another". Joseph's contribution at the meeting was to give another outing to his current hobby-horse, a state holding company in the mould of the IRC. He saved his most dramatic intervention for a meeting of the Nationalised Industries policy group later in February, when he predicted that the recently renationalised steel industry would be impossible to sell off in the short-term. Asking the group to keep his remarks confidential, he warned that "we might have to accept that some parts of the industry would remain nationalised for some considerable time". This showed an awareness of practical considerations based on extensive consultation, but Joseph's preference for private industry was still evident. In a private conversation with the economic writer Duncan Burn, he expressed the view that a reorganisation of steel based on regional groups rather than the old companies could increase efficiency, and that this would make it easier for the industry to be sold off in the future. The idea that a state enterprise could be a national asset simply did not occur to him, even if it made a profit.[4]

Contrary to the myths of later years, Heath's objection to the work of the Nationalised Industries group was not that it recommended the sale of state holdings, but that the members had failed to do their homework. The result of

---

4. Memorandum from John MacGregor to Edward Heath, 7 November 1967; Report of the Policy Group on Nationalised Industries, with annotations by Edward Heath, 13 October 1967, Heath papers; Minutes of meetings of Policy Groups on Economic Policy and Nationalised Industries, 8 and 19 February 1968, Heath Papers; record of KJ discussion with Duncan Burn, 21 March 1968, Burn Papers 4/5 (31), LSE archives.

Ridley's botched job was that the Conservatives went into the 1970 election inadequately prepared in what was always bound to be a very complicated (and controversial) policy area. The 1970 manifesto could go no further than promise that a Conservative government would "progressively reduce" the involvement of the state in industry – a pledge that scarcely elaborated on Iain Macleod's remark in Shadow Cabinet that it was "politically important to denationalise something. The question was what?". Heath knew that the state sector could only be reduced significantly if industrialists had enough confidence to buy the nationalised firms. He envisaged a programme of privatisation which would extend over more than one Parliament, gathering momentum as Conservative policies encouraged investors to take greater risks. That the momentum never developed was due in large measure to events, but Ridley's committee played its part in ensuring a disappointing outcome.[5]

At least the right-wingers on the Nationalised Industries policy group were planting the seeds of future trouble in secret. In April 1968 a more familiar source of ideological conflict, Enoch Powell, caused an immediate problem for Heath amid unprecedented publicity. His "Rivers of Blood" speech on immigration was also a serious blow to Joseph, both as a personal admirer of Powell and as the Shadow Cabinet member with the greatest personal interest in racial questions. Indeed, if one can speak of "turning points" in a political career which rarely ran straight, then Powell's speech may be regarded as the most important of all the diversions encountered by Sir Keith Joseph.

The growing trend towards legislation in the field of race relations had already troubled Joseph. On 12 April 1965 the Shadow Cabinet discussed Labour's Race Relations Bill, which outlawed incitement to racial hatred but failed to deal with discrimination in housing or employment. With his experience at Housing fresh in his mind Joseph no doubt felt that the Bill was only objectionable in that it did not go far enough, but his colleagues disliked the proposed criminal sanctions. Joseph pointed out that if the Conservatives voted against the Bill they would antagonise members of the Jewish community, and offered to set up a meeting between the Home Affairs spokesman Peter Thorneycroft and Jewish leaders. Once his main argument had been rejected, however, he told Thorneycroft that such a meeting would be pointless, in a letter which was presented as a final attempt at persuasion but which was really a warning that he could not follow the party in voting against the Bill. His temper at full stretch, Joseph adopted the approach – and the violent language – which his father had used when discussing racism during the war. While even an outspoken opponent of racism like Iain Macleod could base his opposition to the Bill on the grounds that it threatened free speech, Joseph denied that it would have any such effect because "the Courts will rightly limit

---

5. Macleod in LCC (68) 254, 24 July 1968; *A Better Tomorrow: The Conservative Programme for the Next 5 years* (CCO,1970), 14.

it to the sort of sustained unprovoked inflamatory [sic] filth to which argument, however racial, need never descend". Like his father Sir Keith thought that racist views should be contested by reasoning, patient but firm; confident that this would lead to the intellectual defeat of racism, his priority at this time was how to deal with the problem of those who tried to stir up unthinking prejudice.[6]

In the second reading vote on 3 May 1965 Joseph carried out his threat, and defied a two-line Whip by abstaining on the Race Relations Bill along with Sir Edward Boyle. This was a serious step, given the slender Labour majority in the Commons. But resignation never seems to have crossed his mind, and by refraining from public exposure of his views he guarded himself against disciplinary action. In any case the issue was soon defused, if only temporarily; in order to secure bi-partisan support the Home Secretary Sir Frank Soskice agreed to a Conservative amendment which extracted the few remaining teeth from the measure, and on 21 July 1965 (in the absence of Powell) the Shadow Cabinet "agreed that it would be a great mistake to oppose this Bill as it would offend certain communities and do a great deal of harm to the party". The third reading passed without a division.[7]

After his rebellion Joseph made every effort to show that he was an inflexible champion of free speech. During ministerial questions on 31 May the Tory MP Peter Griffiths, whose victory in 1964 at Smethwick on an anti-immigrant platform had done much to stoke up the demand for legislation, was attacked for his views by a Labour member in fulfilment of Harold Wilson's promise to treat Griffiths as a "parliamentary leper", whatever the subject immediately under discussion. Joseph intervened to ask the Speaker whether it was in order "for the hon. gentleman to make a gratuitous comment like that in answering a question on the order paper". In recognition of the limits on free speech imposed by the conventions of the House, the offending remarks were withdrawn.[8]

The issues of immigration and race relations resurfaced in 1967, with the prospect that large numbers of Kenyan Asians would wish to claim their right to settlement in Britain under existing laws. In the face of pressure from Conservatives (notably Duncan Sandys and Powell), at the end of February 1968 the Labour government rushed through legislation to ensure that future immigration would be limited to those "with close ties to the country of birth, naturalization or descent". Obviously the new restrictions would fall more heavily on black people wishing to settle in Britain than on whites, even if they had been born in the same hospital. This breach of previous undertakings to

---

6. Zig Layton-Henry, *The Politics of Immigration* (Blackwell, 1992), 49–50; LCC (65) 45, 14 April 1965; KJ to Peter Thorneycroft, 14 April 1965, CAND 7, CPA, Bodleian Library.
7. LCC minutes (65) 63, 21 July 1965, Bodleian Library.
8. *Hansard*, vol. 713, col. 1172, 31 May 1965.

members of the Commonwealth was too much for Macleod's stomach; he voted against the Government alongside thirteen Conservative rebels. Robert Carr and Sir Edward Boyle toed the line but only on the understanding that the party would not vote against further legislation on race relations which had been promised by the Government as a sop to those who were outraged by its capitulation to Powell and Sandys. There is no record that Joseph added his voice to those of Carr and Boyle; treating immigrants well once they were in Britain was one thing, but letting in substantial numbers from abroad, in his view, would exacerbate the situation.[9]

Roy Jenkins, who became Home Secretary in December 1965, shared none of Soskice's private reservations about Britain's black and Asian communities and his liberal views were reinforced by detailed research into the racial problem. His Bill covered the existing loopholes on housing and employment, although "conciliation procedures" were still preferred to legal action against offenders. When it considered the new proposals on 10 April 1968 the Shadow Cabinet divided on the previous lines, except that Joseph now joined Boyle and Carr in arguing that the party should not be seen to oppose the Bill. The trio reserved their position until a sub-committee had drafted a "reasoned amendment". Carr and Boyle were both members of this committee, as was Powell (but not Joseph); eventually the group came up with the formula that the Bill should be opposed because "on balance", it would "not in its practical application contribute to the achievement of racial harmony".[10]

On 20 April, two days before the Shadow Cabinet was due to consider the matter again, Powell delivered his notorious speech in Birmingham. Back in February Macleod and Quintin Hogg had expressed their distaste for an earlier Powell oration; this time they were staggered by the provocative language, and by what they regarded as conduct incompatible with membership of the Shadow Cabinet. For Powell's supporters the latter point was the crucial weakness in his critics' case; the rules governing the behaviour of Conservative front-benchers out of office were informal to start with and it was not the invariable practice to seek advance clearance for speeches from the relevant Shadow minister (in this case Hogg). Furthermore, Powell believed that Heath had given him a general licence to speak outside his subject area. He also asserted that he was merely stating party policy. *Action Not Words* had pledged the Conservatives to "Ensure that all immigrants living in Britain are treated in all respects as equal citizens and without discrimination", yet Powell claimed that the Race Relations Bill proposed to give them something *better* than equal treatment. But although he made a cursory reference to the official policy his apocalyptic tone could not be squared with it. While the press concentrated on the more lurid passages taken from a constituent's letter, it was far more

---

9. Layton-Henry, *Politics of Immigration*, 52; Shepherd, *Macleod*, 498.
10. LCC (68) 231, 10 April 1968, CPA, Bodleian Library.

damning that Powell had reported without any qualifying comment the alarmist view that Britons were being "made strangers in their own country". If delivered to a small group of like-minded intellectuals Powell's speech might have been decoded as an appeal for an end to immigration, but outside this select company it could be interpreted (by supporters and opponents alike) as an attempt to increase ill-feeling towards the existing immigrant population, and to encourage demands for forcible repatriation. Powell had recently been reported as telling a *Sunday Times* journalist that he included arresting phrases in his speeches in order to make it impossible for Heath to sack him. Later he denied making this remark, but to his opponents it seemed the only plausible explanation for his behaviour. Had he restrained his flair for publicity he might have escaped the consequences of his action – like Joseph in May 1965 (and April 1967). Instead his fate resembled that of his friend Maude; he broke no written rules, but by his conduct he had put himself beyond the pale.[11]

When Heath consulted his colleagues he found that Macleod, Hogg, Boyle and Carr shared his own view that Powell had to be sacked. Although the apparent desire of these (and of unnamed others) to resign if Heath failed to act was never put to the test, the leader's hand would have been forced by the threats even if he had not already resolved to dismiss the man who had been a consistent source of trouble in his allotted area of Defence. By contrast, when Boyle decided that he could not support the Shadow Cabinet's reasoned amendment after the Commons debate on 23 April he was not sacked (or, as Powell's sympathisers noted, even "carpeted"). Such was the wrath of the Right at this apparent application of double standards by Heath that a history of the party written from that viewpoint made the false assertion that Boyle and his friends "broke with their party and voted with the Government".[12] They did no such thing, and, unlike Powell, Boyle had kept within bounds by making no public statement of his position. Still, it was a difficult time for Heath. He had been a very effective Chief Whip during the Suez crisis, keeping the party united despite his obvious sympathy for those who opposed Eden's policy. Now, as leader, he was under fire from both sides and his patience with rebels of any colour was fraying. In June the current Chief Whip, William Whitelaw, confided his fears that "people felt very strongly" about race relations, adding that "there was a feeling that the Party had been going too far Right on too many issues". Whitelaw rarely poked his head above the parapet in this fashion, and it was promptly bitten off by his leader who fumed "that the Left did not realise the simple political truth that if they insisted on voting with the

---

11. Full text of speech in Humphrey Berkeley, *The Odyssey of Enoch: A Political Memoir* (Hamish Hamilton, 1977), appendix.
12. See, for example, T. F. Lindsay and Michael Harrington, *The Conservative Party 1918–1970* (Macmillan, 1974), 257. But, oddly enough, Margaret Thatcher thought that Joseph, Carr and Boyle had all voted *for* the amendment (she was correct in Carr's case); Thatcher, *Path to Power*, 146.

Government the Party was bound to move to the Right. It had been the same with Rhodesia". In recognition of his leader's difficulties (and dismay at what he regarded as increasing prejudice in the party ranks) Boyle abandoned his political career in the following year.[13]

Joseph might not have thought that Powell's outburst fell into the category of "inflammatory filth", but classical allusions to the River Tiber foaming with blood was not the epitome of rational argument in the context of race relations.[14] The overwhelming response to the speech – notably the marches by dockers from the East End of London – must have been particularly disturbing to someone who had once referred to those who were "guilty, either of being too obviously Jewish or of trying too obviously not to be". He decided to express his feelings in a private letter to the man who in the previous October had been chosen as guest speaker at the Leeds North-East annual dinner. Powell sent a suitably lofty reply: "We have been friends for a long time. But, now, we are looking through different windows".[15] This kind of talk always rattled Joseph. "Rivers of Blood" marked the beginning of the strangest interlude in his political career. He did not vote after the Commons debate on the Shadow Cabinet amendment, but incurred none of the opprobrium that was visited on Boyle. He failed to attend Shadow Cabinet again until 12 June – an absence of ten meetings – and on the same day he reappeared at a One Nation dinner after a similar gap. Even the beam of the *Leeds Searchlight* failed to locate him during this period. The only trace of an explanation in the party archives is the bald statement that he was too ill to attend the Economic Policy Group on 8 May, but the ailment was unspecified. When he reappeared in the Commons to speak on 27 June, he again referred to illness. In early April he had been laid up with a very painful shoulder injury which might have recurred towards the end of the month. He was prone to accidents – in 1965 he had suffered a broken finger when he trapped his right hand in a door at the House of Commons and later he damaged his neck carrying books to and from Westminster. But it seems unlikely that a new injury could have been serious enough to excuse him from all parliamentary business for almost two months, or that he would have described the problem as an "illness".[16]

The extent and timing of Joseph's absence after "Rivers of Blood" in itself provides scope for speculation. Even if Joseph was unlikely to feign illness, was it possible that he was exaggerating the symptoms while he contemplated resignation? No hint of this appeared in the press. But Simon Heffer has revealed that in July 1968 Joseph sent a further message to Powell, inviting him

13. LCC (68) 244, 19 June 1968, CPA, Bodleian Library.
14. In a statement published by the *Daily Express* (25 April 1968) Heath wrote that "most people will admit it was inflammatory talk".
15. *Leeds Searchlight*, February 1967; Powell's letter to Joseph quoted in *Spectator*, 22 July 1972.
16. *Hansard*, vol. 767, col. 941, 27 June 1968; for shoulder injury and news of mystery illness, see CRD 3/7/6/7, CPA, Bodleian Library; private information.

to a dinner party and claiming that he had not been consulted by Heath before Powell was dismissed. At the very least, this indicates that Joseph was troubled as much by the leadership's reaction to Powell as he had been by the original speech – with every reason, since Powell had been sacked on the only major issue which could produce a serious disagreement between the pair. The incident continued to preoccupy Joseph, and eventually he felt that he had to speak out in public. In a BBC television interview of January 1969 he asserted that he was proud to belong to the same party as Powell, referred to their long-standing friendship, and praised his ex-colleague for airing a subject which previous governments had been too weak to tackle. There was a familiar ring to his explanation of this error. Through "honourable short-sightedness" the last Conservative administration had allowed in "a flood of immigrants". He later clarified his position to the extent of denying that he would have used the kind of phrases which had marked Powell's speech, but talk of a "flood of immigrants" was impeccably Powellite and his "clarification" undermined his whole conciliatory case since it was the wording of the speech which had angered his colleagues.[17]

The Conservatives had toughened their stance on immigration since April 1968, but the name of Powell had never sounded sweet in Heath's ears and Joseph cannot have been proferring an authorised olive branch. The usual question arises: was Joseph's intervention a calculated move; had his emotion overcome his own stock of rationality; or was he acting on a mixture of both these impulses? If the first explanation was the right one, Joseph had performed a strategic master-stroke. Powell remained a hero to the economic liberals, but his prospects of ever leading the party were no longer realistic. Even if he occasionally deviated from the script, Joseph was emerging as the most likely understudy on offer for the role which Powell could no longer perform. At the very least, his interview sent a signal to the Powellites that his loyalty to the economic message made him overlook any frailties in the messenger; the implication was that despite his origins he could be trusted to be tough on immigration, using more tact than Powell to promote action where the Prophet had produced only sound and fury. And while Powell's parliamentary follow-ing was probably no greater than thirty, Joseph had the potential to reach out beyond this constituency.[18] Without ever "drivelling and drooling that he cared" (in Margaret Thatcher's contemptuous phrase from later years) he had won a reputation for social concern which Powell had never contended for, and this, combined with his background, enabled him to make forthright pronounce-ments on race without provoking any outcry. In the terminology of the 1980s Joseph stood for "dry" economics and "wet" social policies – already a potent combination with thoughtful Conservatives. To an extent his departure from

---

17. Heffer, *Like the Roman*, 458, 505.
18. On Powell's parliamentary following, see Ramsden, *Winds of Change*, 296.

the Shadow Cabinet would annoy both wings of the party, so he could stake out this ground without any fear of the sack from Heath – who would in any case begin to look accident-prone if another senior colleague fell overboard.

Not even the most unworldly Conservative could entirely overlook the divisions within the party after "Rivers of Blood". Consecutive resolutions on "The Party and the Future" at the 1968 conference illustrated the dilemma which confronted Heath and his allies. One called on the Conservatives to stop drifting to the left, while the other echoed Whitelaw's warning that they had alienated progressive opinion by concentrating exclusively on being anti-socialist. The resolutions were moved by members of the same constituency party, Southend East. There were also eighty resolutions on race.[19] Powell's sensational departure from the Shadow Cabinet crystallized existing disagreements within the party, not least because some economic liberals now hated Heath even more than they despised Wilson. But instead of regarding this as an opportunity for his own advancement, Joseph found himself emotionally torn. Speculation about his suitability as the candidate to bridge the growing gulf in the party certainly began at about this time, but not in his own mind. In retirement Joseph claimed that all politicians "are looking for love". In the spring of 1968 he was certainly in no condition to bear with equanimity a blunt rejection from Powell. To Ralph Harris, Joseph seemed to be "obsessed" with Powell, constantly wondering what the party could do without him on the front-bench. Whatever else he might have intended by his broadcast of January 1969 his words read like an appeal for Powell to give their private friendship another chance. He hoped that he might be allowed to look through "the same windows" again. Given the issue at stake, a more general (and even more personal) consideration must have been involved. Judging by the public response, it seemed to Joseph that Powell had "spoken for England"; as he put it in the January 1969 interview, he had drawn attention to "a problem where popular demand was violently against what the politicians were doing". If Joseph's own identity was brought into question by some of Powell's more extreme supporters – such as the dock-workers who intimidated MPs when they marched to the Commons at the height of the controversy – the only way to demonstrate his true loyalties was to make a public statement of broad support for Powell. But Joseph still admired Heath, and he wanted to keep on standing beside the party leader. In the past, severe emotional stress had provoked genuine illness in Joseph. The most likely explanation of his mysterious disappearance after "Rivers of Blood" is that the same thing happened again; his digestive problems worsened, and he entered hospital for an operation which demanded a prolonged period of recuperation. In a 1974 interview he referred to such an operation, and although he said that the surgery took

---

19. See resolutions 103 and 104, and 471 to 550 in Programme of Eighty-Sixth Conservative Party conference (CCO, 1968).

place "seven years ago" this must have been a slip; during 1967 he was never absent from the Commons for more than a few consecutive days.[20]

After Joseph's strange sabbatical he ensured that the case for more radical policies was aired, while avoiding unnecessary fuss. Three months after Powell's departure, for example, he suggested tentatively that the Education Policy group might explore the IEA's favourite idea of replacing the existing funding system with "vouchers" which, in theory, could expand parental choice. The group, however, had already concluded that such a system would be "administratively complex and expensive"; the worst impact, it was thought, would fall on the poorest areas. Joseph also spoke up for a tax regime which would benefit middle-class "wealth creators" rather than the holders of investment income, but he made his case calmly and changed the subject when it became clear that Heath supported Macleod in preferring Arthur Cockfield's scheme of treating all forms of income alike for tax purposes. He even felt able at this time to praise the philosophy which underlay the party's existing policies, as if his request for a rethink in the previous year had been a temporary aberration. Only at the Economic Policy group meeting of July 1968 did Joseph seem restive, wondering aloud when the group was actually going to get round to talking about economic policy. There were also opportunities for sounding statesmanlike in the Commons. In a debate on the long-delayed Donovan Report, for example, he gave the findings of the Royal Commission a broad welcome but singled out the dissenting report by Andrew Shonfield for particular praise and recommended to the House the Conservative policy on industrial relations, recently published in the pamphlet *A Fair Deal at Work*. His 1968 conference speech exalted competition, but only as "the best means yet devised by mankind to serve the needs of the public" – a back-handed tribute from a person who had recently spoken of the magical qualities of free enterprise.[21]

Yet Joseph was too vulnerable to outside forces to keep up his delicate balancing act. At any time the pressure of events and personalities could coincide, to bring back the messianic model unveiled in April 1967. The three forces pushing him in that direction as an election approached were Britain's economic plight under Labour, the increasing likelihood of a Conservative government, and the developing ideas of Enoch Powell.

At the Conservative conference of October 1968 Powell was attacked over race by Quintin Hogg. While the party was digesting this message at Blackpool,

---

20. Heffer, *Like the Roman*, 505; KJ interview with Llew Gardner; interview with Lord Harris of High Cross; Andrew Denham, interview with KJ, April 1991 (politicians "want to be loved").
21. LCC (68) 251, 254, 15 and 24 July 1968; Economic Policy Group, Twenty-Sixth meetings, 27 June and 26 July, 1968, CPA, Bodleian Library; *Hansard*, vol. 798, cols 1362–71, 16 July 1968; report of KJ speech in October 1968, cited in Roth memorandum; minutes of Eighty-Sixth Conservative Party conference (1968), 99–101; Johnman in Coopey, Fielding and Tiratsoo (eds), *The Wilson Governments*, 194.

Powell himself was opening a new flank at a nearby resort. Powell's "Morecambe Budget" was a breathtaking intellectual exercise, containing among other things a demand that the official Budget should consider taxation and expenditure together. On the basis of government figures Powell claimed that the existing rate of income tax could be almost halved without taking a penny from "Education, health, [and] the whole system of social security benefits". To balance the account he proposed the abolition of various interventionist bodies. Investment grants would disappear, along with assistance to "development areas". The IRC would be abolished, along with the Prices and Incomes Board, the Shipping Industry Board, the Land Commission, and other institutions erected in recent years whether by Labour or by the Macmillan government of which he had been a part. Overseas aid would be scrapped, and more than a billion pounds spent on the nationalised industries could be saved "simply by eliminating losses and transferring the great profit-makers to private management".[22]

Powell's programme was savagely attacked. In the *Sunday Telegraph* Patrick Hutber recalled causing pain to his readers in the past by "saying that Mr Powell knew no economics and, what is worse, was unaware of this important fact". After Morecambe he felt that his strictures had been vindicated. The *Yorkshire Post* was one of the few newspapers which gave Powell's ideas sympathetic consideration, arguing that radical change was needed even if the Morecambe programme was vulnerable to detailed criticism. Although Joseph made no immediate comment, the tone of his January 1969 interview on Powell suggests that he agreed with the *Yorkshire Post*. Certain proposals he could not accept; for example, Powell had consigned both the IRC and Joseph's own Housing Corporation to the scrapheap without pausing for breath. But in his opening statement Powell had announced a general purpose which was close to Joseph's own heart. "The trouble with this nation", he said, "is that we have been brainwashed for years into believing that 'it can't be done'. Britain has become the 'Mr Can't' of the modern world". One did not have to agree with the entire Morecambe programme to applaud Powell's attempt to break out of the "fashionable" mind-set which seemed to accept decline (and ever-higher taxes) as inevitable. To Joseph, the speech must have seemed a demonstration of the highest "moral courage".[23]

Yet as Powell had noted, he had delivered his speech "untrammelled by spokesmanship"; Joseph's situation was more delicate. On 3 March 1969 he was due to speak in a debate on Barbara Castle's White Paper on Industrial Relations (*In Place of Strife*). The proposed legislation went further than Donovan without endorsing all the proposals contained in *A Fair Deal at Work*.

---

22. Enoch Powell, *Income Tax at 4'3 in the £* (Tom Stacey, 1970), 25–38 (including Hutber and *Yorkshire Post* quotations).
23. *Ibid.*, 39–49, 25; Heffer, *Like the Roman*, 484–7.

Joseph rehearsed the official Shadow Cabinet line – that the White Paper was a step in the right direction which was far too insignificant to deserve support. In passing he made a cool reference to Powell's contribution earlier in the debate, selecting the only point on which he could tactfully express public agreement. But the next speaker, Labour's Harold Walker, was closer to the truth when he described Powell's intervention as "a brilliant, scintillating, witty, intellectual speech". Powell had scorned the idea that trade unions caused inflation. The belief in this "mythical connection" could "do nothing but harm", he announced. The real connection – which Powell hinted at in his speech without naming it – lay between inflation and the money supply, which the Government had a duty to control.[24]

Admiring Powell's economic thought as he did, Joseph could not be unaffected when it was expressed with such vivacity. There is good evidence that the two had been conferring outside their usual meeting-place of the One Nation group. On 3 March Powell denounced productivity agreements at factory level as a "will-o'-the-wisp . . . which cannot be made intelligible in terms of a wage award and which dissolves upon examination". The only figures that mattered, in Powell's view, were those of overall national income and productivity. Three weeks earlier, during a Shadow Cabinet discussion on the wording of a new policy document, Joseph remarked that "we should be wary of any title that contained the word 'productivity'". Productivity agreements, he felt, meant nothing and were simply a means for employers to look as if they were getting something in return for pay rises extorted by the unions. This was a new (and short-lived) theme for Joseph.[25]

Since Powell's departure from the Shadow Cabinet Heath's allies had been keeping an eye on his activities.[26] But apart from private dinner parties Joseph could still enjoy Powell's company at the offices of the IEA, now situated very close to the Commons in Lord North Street. The journalist Patrick Cosgrave later recalled seeing both men at an IEA event in late 1969; presumably that was not an isolated occasion. At the meeting attended by Cosgrave the case for economic liberalism was expressed with such vigour that the scales fell from his eyes, and he left Lord North Street as a true believer.[27] Joseph was already familiar with the road to Damascus, but the significance for him of close consultations with Powell and the IEA in early 1969 cannot be overstated. If Powell's analysis of 3 March was right the Conservatives had crafted the wrong keystone for their industrial strategy – and Joseph had helped with the work.

---

24. Powell, *Income Tax*, 22; Hansard, vol. 779, cols 149–53, 83–93, 3 March 1969.
25. LCC (69) 282, 12 February 1969, CPA, Bodleian Library: *Hansard*, vol. 779, col. 863, March 1969.
26. After a heated argument over immigration between Powell and Rippon at the One Nation meeting of 25 November 1968 details of the encounter were leaked to Whitelaw; see Heffer, *Like the Roman*, 499.
27. Patrick Cosgrave in *Spectator*, 22 January 1977.

The only chance of retrieving the situation was to press harder the case for sound economic management, which might produce a context in which the proposed union reforms could be helpful. But now Powell had gone Joseph was more aware than ever before of his isolation in a Shadow Cabinet dominated by pragmatic politicians. Tax cuts were certain under a new Conservative government, but Joseph had already urged that the planned 6d. reduction in the standard rate would provide an insufficient incentive for middle-managers (it represented barely 10 per cent of the tax cut proposed by Powell). In her Conservative Political Centre speech at the October 1968 party conference Margaret Thatcher had called for greater attention to the money supply, an economic indicator of growing interest to the IEA which had been quick to note the recent pronouncements of the Chicago economist Milton Friedman on this subject. But no one else in the Shadow Cabinet matched Mrs Thatcher's enthusiasm. With the Conservatives more than 20 per cent ahead in the NOP polls there was no chance that Wilson would call an election in 1969, so there was still time for the mass conversion of Joseph's colleagues. But if nothing had changed by the end of that year something would have to be said. He ended a contribution to the *Leeds Searchlight* in December 1968 with a firm pledge: "Above all, we shall make our economic philosophy and policies clear".[28]

A harsher rhetorical line now emerged in Joseph's speeches outside Parliament. Less than a fortnight after hearing Powell on productivity he let a newborn cat leap out of his bag in an address to the annual Conservative conference on local government. In 1965 he had defended an increase in unemployment benefit, playing down the incidence of "malingering". At the local government conference he was asked to explain his current thinking on this point. Already Joseph had privately signalled a dramatic change. At a meeting of the Conservative Steering Committee in March 1968 he had suggested that "the 19th Century distinction between 'the worthy poor' and 'the feckless poor' had some relevance to present conditions, though one would have to find some new words . . . he thought the Party should try and close the loopholes through which the feckless exploited the social services". By March 1969 he was ready to go public with this Victorian vocabulary. In the first part of his reply at the conference Joseph echoed his old position, saying that the level of benefits was satisfactory, and that the real problem was inadequate reward for those in work. But, taking care to claim that his leader agreed with his thinking, he went on to predict that under a Conservative government "People will have to be challenged: take a job or else". *The Times* reported that the Tories evidently had devised a "scheme to challenge the work-shy". They

---

28. For KJ's strictures on the planned tax cuts, see minutes of Economic Policy group, 27 June and 26 July 1968, CPA, Bodleian Library; for Thatcher speech, see *Path to Power*, 148–9; KJ, "Socialist Schizophrenia", in *Leeds Searchlight*, December 1968.

had not, but Joseph's confrontational language was echoed in the 1970 manifesto which talked of "the whole system being brought into disrepute by the shirkers and the scroungers", and promised a crackdown.[29]

At the time of his renewed contact with Powell Joseph was writing a paper for the Shadow Cabinet on state intervention in industry. This was completed in late February 1969, but was not discussed until April. Once again Joseph picked over the arguments for and against the IRC; his paper sided with his colleagues' view that it should be abolished, although the old flame was still flickering and in the discussion he made another attempt to change their minds. The residual realist in Joseph also surfaced with a statement which makes interesting reading in view of Thatcherite criticism of Heath's subsequent actions. He noted that there was a strong case for state intervention "when a significant industry, closely linked to government, sinks into trouble beyond its own repair". But while these passages justify Robert Taylor's view of this paper as "prudent and pragmatic", elsewhere it seemed that after bracing himself for the slaughter of the IRC Joseph had developed a taste for blood-letting. In a new departure he urged that the "Little Neddies" – bodies which provided a forum for employers, officials and unions to discuss the structure of particular industries – should be scrapped. The overarching tripartite organisation, the National Economic Development Council (NEDC) could be retained, but Joseph gave no reason for sparing it and his brusque treatment was apparently designed to offer his colleagues the option of putting it to the sword along with all the other "corporate" institutions. Significantly, all of these bodies had been marked down for slaughter by Powell at Morecambe; but they had been set up under Macmillan and Home. The Shadow Cabinet ignored Joseph's subtle hint on the NEDC, and Heath would only suggest that a few "Little Neddies" might share the fate of Little Nell. A disheartening discussion for Joseph was rounded off by Barber and Macleod, who stressed that Opposition thinking was incomplete on these subjects and that it would be unwise to hold a Commons' debate. Recalling occasions like this, one back-bench colleague said in 1970 that "Old Joseph would have good ideas, but so often he would trail back a week later from his Shadow Cabinet [meeting] to say that he had been overruled".[30]

While Joseph was waiting for signs that his own colleagues would come to accept at least some of Powell's economic analysis, by the summer of 1969 he was disorientated again by the knowledge that the Labour government had been

---

29. SC/68/4, steering committee meeting of 18 March 1968, Heath Papers, box 412; *The Times*, 17 March 1969; *A Better Tomorrow*, 22.
30. KJ's paper "Government Intervention in Industry", LCC (69) 221, 28 February 1969; Robert Taylor, "The Heath Government, Industrial Policy and the 'New Capitalism'", in Ball and Seldon (eds), *The Heath Government 1970–74: A Reappraisal* (Longman, 1996); discussion of 21 April 1969, LCC (69) 296, Bodleian Library; Powell, *Income Tax*, 30; Andrew Alexander and Alan Watkins, *The Making of the Prime Minister 1970* (Macdonald Unit 75, 1970), 104.

forced to adopt one of its key elements. In May Roy Jenkins (who had succeeded James Callaghan as Chancellor after devaluation) despatched the Government's second "letter of intent" to its creditors at the International Monetary Fund (IMF). In return for their support of sterling he promised a severe restriction (which ultimately proved to be a contraction) of the money supply for 1969–70. Leading for the Opposition in the subsequent Commons' debate, Iain Macleod drew attention to the fact that in pursuing the "monetarist" theories of Milton Friedman the Chancellor had embarked on a dangerous experiment.

As Shadow spokesman on Trade and Power Joseph also contributed to the debate. He had been introduced to Friedman's ideas at the IEA, and was naturally interested to monitor the progress of an "experiment" which would introduce the dose of deflation for which he had been calling. Yet partisan considerations prevented him from offering unequivocal backing to the policy. Joseph opened with an explicit comparison of Friedman's importance with that of Keynes, and an expression of relief that while the previous generation had been "slow to heed the teaching of Keynes" there were members of the House on both sides who had taken an early interest in monetarism. But this first public signal of his sympathy for Friedman's ideas was followed by a vigorous statement of support for Macleod. He agreed with his colleague that:

> though there is great persuasiveness in the arguments of Professor Friedman, we in this country know nothing about the potential effects on our special conditions. *We are not like America.* We share with America the characteristic of providing a great international trading currency. But, unlike America, we are in an open and exposed economy with a far higher proportion of trade being international. Alas, unlike America, we also have a very large public sector. Clearly, the Government have committed the country to the full imposition of a *dogma* of whose implications for our life no one yet can be sure . . .[31]

Thus Sir Keith Joseph delivered himself of words which would have been heartily approved by any opponent of the early economic policy of the Thatcher governments. After this blast it was easy to overlook more positive noises dressed up as warnings, notably an insistence that the Government could not "cure the troubles of this country *entirely* by the discovery of money supply and holding down growth" – a view which Joseph developed years later into one of his most celebrated speeches, "Monetarism is not enough".

Despite the clear difference of emphasis between Macleod and Joseph the latter's speech on this occasion could not have been described as "Powellite". In

---

31. *Hansard*, vol. 785, cols 1617–25, 25 June 1969 (our italics).

any case, disagreement over the relative value of economic theories could be overlooked as the Wilson government faced disaster in other fields. In June 1969 it withdrew *In Place of Strife* under trade union pressure. Even so, when in the autumn Sir Edward Boyle gave up his position as Opposition spokesman on Education an opportunity presented itself of solving the Joseph problem without an unseemly purge. Although Whitelaw suggested that in the interests of continuity Joseph should stay at his present post, he was made the first choice to succeed Boyle in a Shadow role which would send him well clear of economic policy-making. Margaret Thatcher, who eventually took on Education, was later told that the original plan had broken down only because Reginald Maudling refused to move to Trade and Power in place of Joseph. Mrs Thatcher's informant might have got hold of a garbled story – Maudling was not the only plausible candidate for Joseph's job – but Whitelaw's note supports press speculation at the time that Joseph was being considered for a position which he had not, up to this time, shown any signs of coveting. He had no wish to move anywhere; indeed he was becoming more involved in general economic questions, chairing a policy group on the balance of payments which did not report until the time of the next election, and immersing himself in policy work on regional development. In September 1969 he renewed his interest in the social services, writing to ask Professor Peter Townsend of the Child Poverty Action Group (CPAG) for relevant and up-to-date information. But this inquiry was only part of his attempt to broaden the economic case against the Government; in November 1969 he used the latest statistics to claim that the low-paid had fared as badly as everyone else under Labour.[32]

By this time the opinion poll gap had narrowed dramatically, and at the end of the year NOP found the Conservatives only three points ahead. The Opposition had to gear itself up for an election in the near future, and arrangements were made for the Shadow Cabinet to discuss their policies in the New Year at the Selsdon Park Hotel near Croydon. Meanwhile Joseph was making preparations of his own. In 1968 he had asked Alfred Sherman of the *Daily Telegraph* to look over one of his speeches. Within a few minutes Sherman had suggested improvements which delighted Joseph, who was the harshest critic of his own speech-writing. At the end of 1969 he asked Sherman to help him again, this time on another ambitious series of speeches beginning with a discourse on economic policy.[33]

Joseph began his second crusade with a speech to Tory trade unionists on the Saturday before the Selsdon Park meeting. The text showed that he had learned

---

32. Whitelaw, undated note in Heath Papers (box 723); Thatcher, *Path to Power*, 156; for press reports, see e.g. *Financial Times*, 21 October 1969; KJ to Peter Townsend, 10 September 1969, Townsend Papers, University of Essex; *Hansard*, vol. 790, cols 761–71, 3 November 1969.

33. Cockett, *Thinking the Unthinkable*, 232; interview with Sir Alfred Sherman. Joseph had first met Sherman in 1963, when the latter produced some searching criticisms of Joseph's policy on New Towns.

something from his experience of 1967. Although some commentators noted that he spoke in the language of Powellism the lyrical praise of the market was tempered by a new note of criticism, possibly derived from a reading of Adam Smith: "Competition is a bold concept – and a highly artificial state of affairs. Left to themselves, most businessmen would share the market and keep newcomers out". Therefore there was a need for "determined, tireless Government action", and although the state should stick to what it did best Joseph described his vision as being "poles apart from laissez-faire" in an attempt to avoid the criticisms he had faced in 1967. As the *Guardian*'s economics editor Anthony Harris put it, Joseph seemed to be more realistic than some Tories who spoke as if the market-place "were some noble state of nature"; but being more realistic he was "more threatening. In fact, he is a revolutionary".[34]

Harris believed that Joseph was an *authorised* revolutionary, since he was merely echoing the line laid down by Heath when he abolished Resale Price Maintenance. In the same newspaper the well-informed Ian Aitken said much the same thing, while drawing attention to passages in the speech which sounded like Powell. In fact, the timing – perfect, if he wanted to influence the Selsdon Park discussions – suggests either that Joseph was acting without full permission, or that once he had gained clearance for the speech he took steps to ensure press coverage which was more extensive than Heath had anticipated.[35] What seems to have happened is that Joseph showed a draft of a speech to James Douglas of the Research Department in November 1969. Douglas noted that Joseph's intended criticisms of the last Conservative government sounded familiar, and could be quoted out of context. He suggested that Joseph should look around for someone to help with his speeches, undoubtedly thinking that such a person would iron out the passages in the draft which were open to misinterpretation. Joseph took the advice and consulted Sherman, thus beginning a celebrated partnership with a man whose respect for cautious utterance was limited in the extreme. Ironically, it seems that Joseph assumed that he had approval for the general message of the speech, and had no need to discuss the matter any further with Douglas.[36]

It was reported months later that Joseph's initiative had "unnerved" several Shadow ministers. Heath was not named, but as in 1967 he gave vent to his feelings in private.[37] Yet Joseph and Sherman had ensured that the main substance of his speech was in line with party policy. The displeasure arose from the dogmatic tone which characterised the speech – and from the associated press reporting, which looked as if Joseph had been giving some underhand briefings in addition to more formal interviews (including a chat

34. *Guardian*, 26 January 1970.
35. One senior official in the Research Department thought that the speech was "unauthorised", although excerpts were published by the party as a press hand-out.
36. James Douglas to KJ, 28 November 1969, Joseph Papers, 30/1, Bodleian Library.
37. *The Times*, 22 June 1970; letter to authors from Brendon Sewill.

with the *Observer*'s Nora Beloff in which he expressed the hope that the Conservatives would abolish the Prices and Incomes Board). One article, published in advance of the speech, stated that "He admits to agreeing with Enoch Powell very largely on *home* [economic?] affairs". The author of the piece then made the flattering (and surprising) judgement that "Joseph is not a reckless politician" before eulogising his "beautiful American wife" and hinting archly at future ambitions: "As soon as he was an MP, he wanted to be a Minister. And now? He has simply not thought about being Prime Minister, it is such a remote possibility. But he has been reading with much appreciation Robert Blake's life of Disraeli".[38]

Rather than allowing historians accurately to reconstruct Joseph's intellectual development, reports over the years of the prodigious feats of reading performed by the All Souls fellow produce new puzzles. Ferdinand Mount once quipped that Joseph was "inclined when in doubt to call for more paper as looser men will call for more wine".[39] The remark applied to Joseph's habit of delaying a decision until all the arguments had been rehearsed (and often repeated). But it also suggests something of his more general thirst for the written word. Referring in 1973 to the fact that Joseph never listed any "recreations" in his *Who's Who* entry, Anthony King asked "Is there a blank there because you don't have any?", then quickly corrected himself: "Clearly you do – you read". Like Gladstone (with whom he shared more character traits than he did with Disraeli) Joseph snatched every spare moment for this "recreation".[40] Even as a minister he managed to plough through "about a book a week"; apart from political and historical works, he read Russian novels in translation and enjoyed Proust in the original French.[41] The subject of books was always likely to come up in an interview with such a man; the temptation to tease, or to mention a long-standing favourite as his current choice, must have been difficult for him to resist. But on this occasion the reporter had reason to be intrigued. As an old friend of the author Joseph might have been expected to have read Blake's celebrated biography of the Jewish-born premier soon after its publication – in 1966. Why start reading it now – when his chances of emulating Disraeli were so much greater than they had been three years before? Others felt that Joseph was unduly preoccupied at this time. Andrew Roth, a perceptive observer who had frequent contact with Joseph, made a private note that:

---

38. "Sir Keith as Tory evangelist", undated cutting in Roth archives [Dec 1969/Jan 1970].
39. Quoted in Halcrow, *Joseph*, 90.
40. KJ interview with Anthony King. Also like Gladstone, Joseph was an eclectic reader. While Chancellor of the Exchequer, Gladstone perused *On the Application of Machining to the Manufacture of Rotating Chambered-Breach Fire-Arms and their Peculiarities* (by Henry Colt) – undeterred by his lack of interest in pistols. Lord Wilberforce recalled at Joseph's memorial service that Joseph had borrowed a book on cosmology physics from the House of Lords library, and only returned it (heavily annotated) three months later. Jenkins, *Gladstone*, 179; Lord Wilberforce, speech at KJ memorial service.
41. KJ interview with Anthony King.

Whenever you are with him, although he is spasmodically very charming, you come away with the feeling that midway in the meeting, you "lost" him because you were "wasting" his time. This is a common experience of those who meet the redoubtable Sir Keith Joseph, Bt.[42]

Shortly after the 1970 election *Private Eye* carried a provocative item concerning Joseph. In August 1970 the satirical journal claimed that Joseph had travelled to Edinburgh to visit an eminent psychiatrist, Professor George Carstairs. The article stated that he had asked "which personal traits and characteristics he ought to emphasise and which to suppress in order to look the part of a future Prime Minister". The *Eye* was deliberately vague about the date of this supposed interview, but there *was* a relevant matter about which Joseph might have sought professional advice in mid-1970. In speculating about the identity of Boyle's successor at Education some unnamed Tory MPs had told the *Daily Express* that Joseph was not a "sufficiently forceful" parliamentarian for the post – a particularly hurtful allegation for Joseph who had not even wanted the job in the first place.[43]

The story should be taken with the ration of salt essential for *Eye* readers. If the interview took place *after* the 1970 general election it could have been part of another Joseph fact-finding mission – especially since Joseph shared Enoch Powell's view that the Health Service needed to pay more attention to the needs of mental patients. Carstairs specialised in child development, which may have provided Joseph with a personal reason for consulting him – a reason which, for understandable reasons, he would not be keen to divulge in a public correction. But the fact that the staff of *Private Eye* were ready to believe that Joseph was calculating his chances of leading the party – to the point of obsession – is in itself significant. It fits with the other evidence which suggests that in late 1969/early 1970 Joseph felt at least a few nudges from the ambition that circumstances had been thrusting upon him since the "Rivers of Blood" speech. If Heath were to lose the next election he would have to go, and a profile in *Time and Tide* made the point that Joseph was better placed than Powell to be the candidate of a right-wing which was likely to be boosted by a further defeat for the party on a non-ideological platform.[44]

It stretches the notion of Joseph's naïveté much too far to argue that he was not aware of his leadership prospects when he launched his second crusade (even if he disparaged speculation on his behalf). *The Times* joined the chorus of praise, labelling Joseph "a non-doctrinaire Tory", and noting that Wilson had privately identified him as the Conservative front-bencher "who would provide

---

42. Roth memorandum.
43. *Private Eye*, 227, 'Colour Section', 28 August 1970; undated *Daily Express* cutting, Roth archives.
44. "Sir Keith – a man who talks true Tory policy", *Time and Tide*, 29 January 1970.

the greatest leadership challenge to Labour". The paper introduced some new, even more flattering errors about Joseph's background: his degree was inflated to a "double first", his business experience was exaggerated, and it was claimed that his father had "founded" Bovis. He was described as standing at the top of "a powerful-looking pyramid of the next generation"; a twelve-strong team of brilliant young MPs was preparing to assist him when he returned to government. The chapter on Joseph in a book designed to promote the whole Shadow Cabinet directly contradicted the anonymous Conservative MPs by calling him "one of the most forceful and articulate of contemporary Conservatives". He was "in no sense a shy or retiring man. Far from it". The author predicted that Joseph would be Chancellor one day, and could easily be the man to take the leader's place if he "should be run over by the traditional bus". *Time and Tide* seemed to be hoping for such an accident, pleading that "If he is not to be Prime Minister in the next government then he should be Chancellor of the Exchequer". Joseph's Oxford contemporary, the Labour MP Woodrow Wyatt, told readers of the *Sunday Mirror* that "To think of him in connection with any vice would be an unpardonable offence". Clearly the hedonistic Wyatt would not have chosen him as a dining companion, but he was unable to conceal his admiration.[45]

In his speech of January 1970 Joseph had not travelled very far from the official route, but he had driven much too fast. If anyone cared to look closely there were signs of unhappiness in the party high command; the monthly *Notes on Current Politics* published by Conservative Central Office failed even to mention in passing what was billed in the newspapers as a "definitive" Opposition contribution on economic matters. But a direct rebuke was ruled out. It was difficult for Heath's supporters to devise even a non-attributable whispering campaign against a senior figure like Joseph with an election likely to be called at any time. The assumption that he was speaking with full authority was soon transformed into a journalistic commonplace. As one commentator put it, "Since he has not been sacked from the Shadow Cabinet one must presume that he speaks with the backing of Mr Heath".[46]

Reports that Wilson feared Joseph as a parliamentary foe were probably exaggerated; more likely, he wanted to talk up Joseph's importance as a means of scaring the voters. Anthony Wedgwood Benn had provided the cue for his leader, suggesting at an inner Cabinet meeting of 2 February that the Selsdon Park meeting had been helpful to Labour and signalling his intention of answering Joseph's "pure and unadulterated nineteenth-century Powellite speech". After the Shadow Cabinet conference the Prime Minister branded the

---

45. Harrington, "Sir Keith Joseph" in Stacey and St Oswald (eds), *Here Come the Tories*, 75; *Time and Tide*, 29 January 1970; undated *Sunday Mirror* cutting, Roth archives.
46. Harrington in *Here Come the Tories*, 82.

Opposition as economic Neanderthals, with Heath as their living embodiment – "Selsdon Man", who was planning "a wanton, calculated and deliberate return to greater inequality". According to Wilson "The new Conservative slogan is: Back to the free-for-all. A free-for-all in place of the Welfare State: a free-for-all market in labour, in housing, in the social services". Labour, housing and social services were all areas on which Joseph had made notable recent speeches, and Wilson singled out the housing contribution as one which had featured "words ominously close to those of Enoch Powell". Wilson continued to keep a close watch on Joseph's speeches and articles; in May he attacked a recent *Spectator* piece on regional investment as "a prescription for a great decline in development areas".[47] For the next three decades Thatcherites talked nostalgically about the "Selsdon programme", lamenting the fact that Heath was so weak as to abandon it in office. But there was no such "programme". Wilson was only able to talk about Conservative economic intentions at all because of the stir caused by the speeches of Sir Keith Joseph – the "guru" of Thatcherism, and the man who first spoke out against the Government of which he had been a part. For tactical reasons it was useful for Labour to claim that Heath himself was the archetype of "Selsdon Man" – and, having refused to distance himself from Joseph's speeches, he left himself open to the jibe. At the time, Barbara Castle saw no reason to pull the punches which were aimed at the Tory leader. But in later years she recognised that "we were attacking the wrong man".[48]

Heath's team is often hailed as the best-prepared Shadow Cabinet in history. This would be true if the relevant criterion is the amount of time spent on policy-making, but not if it means being armed with a practical programme behind which everyone is united. On that score the Conservatives were not much better prepared in 1970 than they had been in 1966 or 1964. The minutes of the over-hyped Selsdon meeting reveal the extent of the disarray. Instead of weaving together the various threads of the policy exercise, Shadow ministers were soon tangled up in the details, and were often diverted from the main themes by the sudden intrusion of new ideas. Joseph was one of the main culprits here. In the debate on Health he brought up a suggestion that the Government might reduce capital expenditure by encouraging private enterprise to build hospitals which would then by rented by the state on long-term leases. At first Heath seemed attracted by an idea which anticipated the Private Finance

---

47. *Daily Telegraph*, 7 February 1970; Tony Benn, *Office Without Power: Diaries 1968–72* (Hutchinson, 1989), 232. For Wilson on regional development, see *The Times*, 13 May 1970. Joseph's *Spectator* article ("State intervention, Tory style", 21 March) followed party policy by advocating a move from investment grants to tax allowances for industry; but it also contained the subversive remark that "no convincing evidence has been published that investment incentives actually increase the quality of investment". Powell was able to quote Joseph's speech at the 1969 party conference as proof that his own position on investment grants had been officially adopted; see Powell, *Income Tax*, 30 n.
48. Interview with Baroness Castle of Blackburn.

Initiative (PFI) of the 1990s, but Geoffrey Rippon called it "very silly . . . Better for country to build rather than rent buildings". Joseph's recorded response was "Agreed", and thus the conversation ended. Rippon also clashed with Joseph over the latter's plan for a commission to enforce competition; Rippon dismissed this idea as "the height of lunacy". On another occasion Joseph backed Margaret Thatcher in asking that the party's manifesto should include a pledge of support for the IEA's idea of a privately funded university. This time Heath was less interested, to Joseph's evident surprise and dismay. The leader thought that the Government was sure to be dragged in to backing its warm words with money if the project fared badly; the whole point, for Joseph and Mrs Thatcher, was that complete financial independence from the state would make the proposed institution a beacon of academic freedom.[49]

Typical of the unsatisfactory nature of the Selsdon exercise was the final session on the first day (Saturday 31 January), which Heath opened with the disheartening news that there were only ninety minutes remaining in which the Shadow Cabinet had to reach concrete decisions on several separate policy areas. More than half of the time was consumed by the first subject, family allowances, which turned into a running battle between Iain Macleod (seconded by Tony Barber), and Lord Balniel, the social services spokesman, who was supported by Joseph.

Rarely can a debate between senior members of the same party have been conducted so much at cross purposes. Macleod's intention was to save money to finance the substantial tax-cuts which he had explained in detail earlier in the day; in that session Joseph had repeated his concern that Macleod was being too generous to investment income, and made a fruitless attempt to refloat the idea of a wealth tax to redress the balance. Like Balniel, he now voiced his concern for those families who earned too little to be liable to tax in the first place; since Macleod's proposal of a Value Added Tax (VAT) would increase prices their position was likely to deteriorate further. The Shadow Chancellor wanted to abolish family allowances – an idea which frightened some electorally conscious colleagues but which opinion polling suggested the party could survive because, as Mrs Thatcher helpfully pointed out, middle-class women did not relish going into the Post Office to collect the money. The measure would save the Treasury up to £250 million. Less than half of that amount (£100 million) would be ploughed back as increased help to the low-paid. Balniel was concerned about the political implications of disbursing this money in benefits which involved some kind of means test. Joseph was simply concerned to help "5 million people living under supplementary benefit level, 1 million of them children". He stressed the inevitable knock-on effects; poverty, he reminded his colleagues, was linked "with crime, squalor, and poor

---

49. Minutes of Selsdon Park conference, 31 January 1970, Fourth Session, 16, CPA, Bodleian Library.

housing". The conversation went back and forth without any sign of a compromise. Lord Jellicoe suggested that there might still be a year before the election to allow a new policy group to come up with a solution. Joseph, however, thought that anything agreed in Opposition could be no better than a stop-gap solution. The somewhat sketchy minutes record that he was insistent to the point of repetition on the need for comprehensive research: "Must wait for help from the Civil Service when in office. Cannot do any more until we have the Civil Service to help".[50]

Thanks primarily to Macleod – who prompted Heath to tell the assembled press about law and order policies which had never been discussed at the conference – Selsdon probably made the Conservative team look sufficiently tough to enthuse right-wing voters.[51] If so, the opinion polls indicated that this was more than balanced by revulsion felt by moderates. After a good start to the year, helped by Heath's victory in the Sydney–Hobart boat race, the party began to slip back towards Labour. Dismayed by the "Selsdon" image presented by the media, Heath complained privately that "It's all gone mad". But Joseph was determined to complete his new series of speeches, and having opened it with a fanfare from the press he wanted to end on an high note. After the final speech in March (delivered at the unglamorous venue of the Young Conservatives national advisory committee) the heavyweight newspapers devoted many column inches to Joseph and his programme. The *Sunday Times* proclaimed this as "The 20 Steps to Civilised Capitalism". Again, the packaging and the personalised publicity rather than the charted course would have "unnerved" Joseph's colleagues. Most of the "steps" had been traced in earlier speeches, but he was ready with some unfamiliar slogans, which had become ubiquitous by the end of the Thatcher years: he spoke of "the virtues of a social market philosophy, of free enterprise in a civilised context", and of the need to start "rolling back the public sector". In the *Financial Times* he turned visionary, talking of a "middle-income society" in which everyone would play golf, listen to music, read books and employ a stockbroker. "Everyone", it turned out, excluded the "10 per cent" who, through no fault of their own, would always have to rely on state assistance.[52]

The press reaction to all this was mixed. Nicholas Faith in the *Sunday Times* noted that few capitalists relished the prospect of "the cold blast of competition" which Joseph expected them to enjoy, and for the *Guardian* Victor Keegan doubted the wisdom of Joseph's policy towards the Little Neddies

---

50. Minutes of Selsdon Park conference, 31 January 1970, Sixth Session, CPA, Bodleian Library; Rodney Lowe, "The Social Policy of the Heath Government", in Stuart Ball & Anthony Seldon (eds), *The Heath Government 1970–74: A Reappraisal* (Longman, 1996), 200.
51. Shepherd, *Macleod,* 517. Sir Edward Heath has suggested that the fateful suggestion came from Hogg; see *Course of My Life*, 301.
52. Heath's remark reported by Lord Aldington, quoted in Middlemas, *Power, Vol. II*, 283; *Sunday Times*, 8 March 1970; *Financial Times*, 17 March 1970.

(which he had now decided to prune rather than completely uproot). Indeed what was trumpeted as a "blueprint" was still more of an outline to be filled in as a Conservative government went along. When in a *Financial Times* interview David Watt admitted that he was not clear about the meaning of "a rollback of the public sector", Joseph interjected "You're not meant to be". To the further question "How far [do] you think this is really feasible?", the answer was "We obviously want to leave our options open".[53]

Yet Joseph was closing up his party's options in one crucial sense. Faith was able to predict with reasonable accuracy the key factors which led to the Heath government's so-called "U-Turn". He wrote:

> What is very relevant is whether the Tory policies would not hurt existing Tory voters so sharply that either the policies would have to be watered down because of their possible effect, or whether, if applied, they would not create great tensions within the Tory party . . . Sir Keith assumes that there is a great mass of entrepreneurial talent at present buried, mostly presumably in smaller businesses, straining at the leash, which would respond immediately to changes, particularly to reductions in direct taxation. This is completely unproven, and indeed unprovable.[54]

In short, by allowing Joseph a decisive voice in the development of competition policy the Tories were pinning all their faith on his entrepreneurs. The party envisaged a society in which there would be more millionaires and more bankrupts. What they failed to appreciate was that if their policies produced more bankrupts than millionaires the Conservative Party would end up sharing the costs – along with a new army of the unemployed. Joseph's contacts with industrialists had helped to make him a little more cautious – but not enough to provoke him into thinking up a contingency plan in case the whole project ground to a halt. Fortunately for Joseph, he no longer had any responsibility for economic policy when the Heath government was forced into a frantic search for Plan B. With hindsight, this was extremely unfortunate for Heath himself.

To a great extent Heath brought his problems on himself, writing a foreword to the 1970 manifesto which emphasised his inflexible principles in order to point up the contrast with Wilson. His principles and his ultimate goals were indeed inflexible, but contrary to the manifesto message he was always prepared to contemplate tactical alternatives. Ironically, in view of what followed, Joseph himself drew attention to this gap between rhetoric and reality when the Shadow Cabinet discussed a draft of the manifesto in March 1970. As so often Macleod rejected his concerns. Indeed, Macleod's gambling streak came to the

---

53. *Sunday Times*, 8 March 1970; *Guardian*, 9 March 1970; *Financial Times*, 17 March 1970
54. *Sunday Times*, 8 March 1970.

fore in the run up to this crucial election. The Shadow Cabinet was uncertain of the correct line on a compulsory prices and incomes policy. Although hindsight suggests that the issue was avoided because of divisions in the party, this is highly misleading; after all, even Joseph had acknowledged that in the last resort statutory action might become unavoidable. Rather, the failure to engage in lengthy debate about prices and incomes policy typified the general failure of the Heath Shadow Cabinet to establish contingency plans. But according to Peter Walker, Macleod thought that the party had to take a stance one way or another. It should rule out an incomes policy, "And if the time comes when events make us change our view, OK we'll have to change our view". As a result, the manifesto stated bluntly that "Labour's compulsory wage control was a failure and we will not repeat it". By the time that "events" made the party change its view, Macleod was no longer around to explain how such a *volte-face* could be presented to the public.[55]

When Wilson called a general election for 18 June 1970 it seemed unlikely to most observers that the Conservative policies would ever be tested. Labour had just done well in the borough elections, and only 21 per cent of the public expected a change at Number 10. On the day before Wilson announced the election date Gallup reported that the government was 7.5 per cent ahead. This was a shattering blow to Conservative morale. Joseph later recalled that Macleod "was very confident that we would win and he said so all the way through", but Whitelaw and others saw through this outward show of bravado. Although candidates were soon able to report that the picture was very different on the doorstep, preparations were in hand to tell Heath that he could not continue as leader after his second consecutive defeat as leader.[56]

The 1970 general election campaign was more lively than that of 1966, but Joseph was again consigned to a supporting role. He made no appearance in the television broadcasts (which were dominated by Heath), and although he addressed something like thirty meetings around the country, indoor and out, his speeches were rarely reported in the national press. The Nuffield study placed him in the third rank of audience-pullers; along with Tony Barber and Mrs Thatcher he usually attracted 200 or more. The most vivid account of Joseph during this campaign described a visit by the former Minister for Welsh Affairs to Haverfordwest. First he addressed some unresponsive farmers "amid the acrid smells of the cattle auction ring". He moved on to the main square, where the reporter watched "a lightly-built tense man with a stare like a laser beam" pacing around, rehearsing his speech "as if it were an opening night". When his turn came the actor *manque* tried to warm up his audience with some humour, but this was a mistake:

---

55. On incomes policy, see Brendon Sewill's remarks in *Contemporary Record* vol. 3, no. 3, February 1990, 38; Shepherd, *Macleod*, 519; *A Better Tomorrow*, 11.
56. Ramsden, *Winds of Change*, 307; Shepherd, *Macleod*, 525.

jokes do not come eas[il]y to him and an expectant pause after the first one produced no results. "I was Minister for Wales once," he said. "I was paid half what the present Minister is getting, but I built more houses and there were 50,000 more jobs here then." There was neither laughter nor applause.[57]

Joseph had never thrived in a rural setting, and elsewhere his message carried more punch. At Nottingham on 2 June he accused Labour of conducting a "vendetta" against small businesses; a week later, in Brighton, he predicted that if Wilson were re-elected Britain would become "the slum of Europe". Perhaps his most effective speech, however, concerned social services. "We do not wear our hearts on our sleeves like many Socialists", he declared; "we don't hawk our social consciences around to cover up the vagueness of our ideas. But this doesn't mean that we care any less than those who shout more". Although "we are not for a single moment smug", this was one area in which the Conservatives could be proud of their record up to 1964, because they had increased spending on social services "significantly faster" than Labour had done even though they had cut taxes at the same time. His last major contribution to the campaign was an article for the *Daily Telegraph*, in which he once again rejected the idea that his party believed in *laissez-faire*, and called for the creation of "a balanced society: free and humane; collectively responsible but not collectivist; dynamic but stable; patriotic but not parochial". In keeping with the mainstream Conservative tradition, he described society as "a living organism", not a random collection of jostling individuals or, as the socialists believed, a laboratory for ideological experiments. Although he attacked the "indiscriminate" bailing-out of companies in trouble, he made the prescient acknowledgement that "Rescues there must sometimes be". The only abrasive note in the text was another attack on "the undeserving poor – the shirkers", who had allegedly enjoyed "a field day" under Labour. Even so, for moderates the overall effect was tarnished by the headline: "We are the radicals now".[58]

Three months before the election Joseph had pointed out that he disagreed with Enoch Powell on at least one issue. Instead of just relying on market forces to correct the problem of London as Powell had consistently argued, Joseph felt that government should take some action to prevent the "obscene" social consequences which would arise if the capital continued to grow. Even in expressing disagreement, however, Joseph managed to give the impression that Powell was a mighty oracle, while during the election campaign Heath came as close as he tactfully could to including Powell and his supporters in a list of

---

57. Unsourced cutting in Roth archives, 10 June 1970.
58. David Butler and Michael Pinto-Duschinsky, *The British General Election of 1970* (Macmillan, 1971), 316; speeches at Nottingham, Brighton and Denton, 2, 10 and 2 June 1970, *General Election 1970: Daily Notes* (CRD), 9, 12, 4 June 1970.

people who "do our country no service". When Tony Benn referred to Belsen concentration camp in the course of an outspoken attack on Powell even Heath defended his former colleague, but Joseph added a personal edge to his own remarks, accusing Benn of "toady[ing] to a left-wing bunch of students".[59] Yet in spite of his continuing preoccupation with Powell Joseph differed from him on the fundamental point of the campaign. He hoped that his party would win the election. Given that he had to divert his energies from Leeds North-East it was understandable that Joseph was heartened by Iain Macleod's cheery predictions of victory. His worries proved to be unfounded, although he fared significantly worse than his Leeds colleagues. His proportion of the vote and margin of victory was almost exactly what it had been in 1966, while Sir Donald Kaberry in the safer North-West seat increased his majority by almost 2,000 and there were more substantial pro-Conservative swings in the constituencies held by Labour. Joseph's response to this relative disappointment was highly characteristic. Shortly after the election he wrote to Sir Richard Webster, the Director of the Party Organisation, to ask why he had been "so far as I can see . . . the only Tory who had virtually no swing". "I am very ready to accept that this may be due to something personal", he added, although his agent had reassured him that he had only detected "residual dislike" of his recent Commons' vote to confirm the abolition of capital punishment. In his reply Sir Richard calculated that there had been a small swing in Joseph's favour – around 0.5 per cent – and speculated (without a hint of irony) that the outcome in Leeds North-East might have been adversely affected by "Rivers of Blood".[60]

But at least Joseph was home and dry – as was the national party, with an overall majority of 30. The state of the economy had been perhaps the decisive factor. Balance of payments figures released on 15 June showed a deficit of £31 million, suggesting that the painful devaluation had not solved this problem. Pollsters found that the public anticipated another economic crisis, and the balance of payments statistics apparently succeeded where Joseph's speeches had failed. On this key point a majority now felt that they trusted the Tories more than Labour, helped to that conclusion by the former Governor of the Bank of England, Lord Cromer, who launched a savage attack on Wilson. Yet it remained doubtful that voters perceived much difference between the detailed policies of the two parties; they still had not fallen in love with Heath, but they decided that on balance he was a better pilot for troubled waters than Wilson had proved to be.

On Fleet Street the alchemy of the ballot box transformed careful analyses of the Tory defeat, and political obituaries for Heath, into waste paper overnight. Two journalists composing an instant history of the campaign on the

59. *The Times*, 5 June 1970.
60. KJ to Sir Richard Webster, no date, Webster to KJ, 29 June 1970, CCO 500/24/272, CPA, Bodleian Library.

assumption that Wilson would win had to rewrite the whole book in a hurry. But London's weekly *City Press* was printed before the election result was known, and remains a helpful guide to what the papers *would* have said after the expected Labour victory. The editor placed the blame squarely on Selsdon Park, identifying Joseph's policy areas along with law and order as themes which damaged the party. "Keeping government out of industry" had made no appeal to voters; furthermore, "Conservative talk of selectivity in the social services is not based on any well conceived plan, and where it has aroused comment the reaction has been unfavourable". Understandably, parties like to think that they win elections for positive reasons, and in the aftermath of victory this ominous verdict was forgotten. Later events convinced economic liberals that there had been a fully worked-out "Selsdon programme" congenial to them, which had been knowingly endorsed by the voters. Joseph himself tended to think on these lines; in 1990 he said that "It remains true as I recall that there were in that Selsdon document the seeds of much of what we still wanted to do and more or less carried out after 1979". He was too modest: the "seeds" were in his own speeches, not in any "Selsdon document".[61]

Heath began to put together his Cabinet with Whitelaw and Francis Pym as soon as he reached Downing Street. Wherever possible the new Prime Minister merely appointed members of his team to the role they had been shadowing; Mrs Thatcher, for instance, took Education, and Macleod became Chancellor (apparently to his own surprise). But Heath decided to make an exception with Joseph, who (after a reorganisation of ministries by Wilson) had fought the election as Shadow spokesman on Technology. The Cabinet equivalent was offered to Geoffrey Rippon, from the Right of the party but, as *The Times* put it, "not so near or as publicly committed as Sir Keith" to Powellite policies. One well-placed observer suggested that the switch was made because of "the possibility of a policy clash" between Joseph and Macleod. Rippon had never got on with Joseph, and had made several sarcastic interjections at Selsdon Park. Among these was a mocking response to Joseph's last-ditch attempt to save the IRC; the Corporation was abolished in one of Rippon's first actions in government.[62]

---

61. *Financial Times*, 15 March 1970; Butler and Pinto-Duschinsky, *Election of 1970*, 163, 167; Stewart, *Jekyll & Hyde Years*, 116; *City Press*, 12 June 1970; KJ quoted in *Contemporary Record*, vol. 3, no.3, February 1990, 36; cf. Norman Tebbit, *Upwardly Mobile* (Futura, 1989), 134.
62. For Rippon's earlier clash with Powell, see note 26 above. Joseph had been at the One Nation meeting of 25 November 1968 but left before the row took place. He had taken part in a discussion on exchange rates, on which his views were judged to be "as usual obscure". Samuel Brittan has suggested that the anticipated "policy clash" arose from Joseph's committee on the balance of payments, which was about to make a case for floating exchange rates. Although this policy was later forced on the government it was certainly unwelcome to the leadership in June 1970; see Brittan, *Capitalism with a Human Face* (Edward Elgar, 1995), 15. Heffer, *Like the Roman*, 499; private information; *The Times*, 22 June 1970; Jock Bruce-Gardyne, *Whatever Happened to the Quiet Revolution?* (Charles Knight, 1974), 14.

"After some thought" Heath decided to offer Joseph the consolation of the DHSS, even though this meant disappointment for his friend Robin Balniel who was left out of the Cabinet. Heath's biographer thought that "there was probably no significance" in a decision which gave Joseph the chance to show that the Conservatives could deliver results, while the socialists merely talked, on the subject widely thought to be closest to his heart. Yet an ambition to help the poor does not necessarily inspire the wish to become Secretary of State for Social Services. Joseph had always believed that the battle against deprivation could be won only in the context of a healthy economy. As such, the Chancellor of the Exchequer was the real minister for the sick, the elderly and the poor. At Technology Joseph could have been a useful *aide de camp*; but at Departments like Education and the DHSS one was dependent on ammunition and tactics decided by more senior officers. If the Conservatives had won in 1966 Joseph would have been happy to take on this subsidiary role, but he thought that he had won his economic spurs since then and some important commentators agreed with him. On his own reckoning he could only regard the appointment to the DHSS as a demotion, however delighted he might sound when talking to the press in the days after the election.[63]

---

63. Heath, *Course of My Life*, 310–11; Campbell, *Heath*, 381.

Chapter 9

A Titanic Job

On returning to Whitehall as Secretary of State for Social Services Joseph was reunited with the chauffeur, Molly, who had driven him when he was at Housing. Coincidentally Richard Crossman, who had inherited Molly from Sir Keith in 1964, was the departing minister at the DHSS. On his last day in office Crossman's current driver was away, so Molly picked him up from Paddington Station. Crossman reflected in his diary that Molly used to enjoy working for Sir Keith, because she could "mother" him. He was glad that Joseph had been picked as his replacement; "He is a civilised, cultivated man, who is certainly intelligent enough". But Crossman wondered whether he could stand up to the strain. His misgivings were confirmed when he encountered Molly again some time later. Asked if she was glad to be working once more for her favourite minister, she shook her head sadly and replied, "At least *you* were never sick, sir". This time round Molly would have to be more nurse than mother. Joseph had at least one minor operation during this period, but the nature of the problem was not disclosed to the press, then or later.[1]

Apparently Joseph's health had been reasonably good in the run-up to the election, but Crossman must have been watching him more closely than the

---

1. Crossman, *Diaries of a Cabinet Minister, Volume III, Secretary of State for Social Services, 1968–70* (Hamish Hamilton and Jonathan Cape, 1977), 953–4; interview with Alan Watkins; *The Times*, 3, 7 January 1972. We are most grateful to Sir Graham Hart, Penny Lee, Dr Charles Webster and Robin Wendt for their advice on this chapter.

commentators who saw him as someone who could withstand even the pressures of the premiership. It was a stressful job that Joseph had undertaken, comparable to his first Cabinet post. Like Housing, Local Government and Welsh Affairs, Health and Social Security (created in 1968) combined the work of departments which on their own would stretch a minister's stamina; the load could only be tolerated if the incumbent was able to delegate tasks to his or her junior ministers.[2] For almost the whole of his term of office Joseph was served by three able men – Lord Aberdare, Paul Dean and Michael Alison. But the feeling of overall responsibility for such a large field of domestic policy was not something that Joseph could delegate, and, as ever, he drove himself relent-lessly. To one close aide he seemed addicted to work, paying obsessive attention to minor matters and showing signs of frustration whenever spaces appeared in his diary.[3] He was naturally keen to prove the viability of the new "super-ministry", for which he and Margaret Thatcher had argued in Opposition as a means of co-ordinating the social services. Yet the DHSS has been described as "Harold Wilson's folly, put together for no greater purpose than satisfying the ministerial ambitions of Dick Crossman". Soon after its establishment the civil servants who had influenced Wilson's decision told the Prime Minister that he should have ignored their advice and combined social services with the Home Office instead. The survival of the DHSS until 1988 (when it was dismantled by Mrs Thatcher herself) was regarded by informed observers as a minor miracle.[4]

The Department's newly built headquarters, south of the Thames at London's Elephant and Castle, had not been designed as an aid to relaxation. The building was twelve stories high; one commentator suggested that there was some poetic justice in the fact that Joseph was finding out what it was like to spend much of his day in "an appalling high block overlooking other new and already grubby concrete blocks". If anything the building (Alexander Fleming House) was even less appealing than the Ministry of Housing and Local Government. Crossman thought that the site was "ghastly". It had been chosen for its low cost, but most of the savings had to be spent on double-glazing and air-conditioning because otherwise the staff would have been deafened by trains which ran directly beneath and to the side of the building. There had been some compensation for the shortcomings of the Ministry of Housing, in that it was close to the centre of things in Whitehall. But while the House of Commons was visible from the top of Alexander Fleming House, if the traffic was heavy the journey to Westminster could take up to twenty

---

2. An audit carried out in the late 1980s – after Health and Social Security had been separated once again – found that these were the two busiest ministries in Whitehall; in combination they were responsible for almost 10,000 parliamentary questions, and they received 37,500 letters requiring a ministerial reply; Peter Hennessy, *Whitehall* (Fontana, 1990), 422–4.
3. Private information.
4. Hennessy, *Whitehall*, 419, 421.

minutes. Thwarted in his attempts to move somewhere more congenial, Crossman in his brighter moods could tell himself that it was "quite a nice ivory tower" after all. But he soon reverted to private rants about "the beastliness of this absolutely characterless and formless building".[5]

At least the atmosphere inside this depressing structure was improved by the exchange of Crossman for Joseph. In 1969 the latter had hinted darkly that senior civil servants were a potential obstacle to change, but this seemed to be forgotten as soon as he was back in office. The memoranda which have been released by the Public Records Office indicate that his (frequent) frustrations were not directed against individual officials; rather, he was aware that obstruction would come somewhere down the line, either from other parts of the Whitehall machine or from competing pressure groups.[6] DHSS officials have no memories of the stressed-out, unwell minister who was sighted at this time by journalists, some politicians, and his ministerial driver. An Assistant Secretary, Penny Lee – wife of Sir Keith's Harrow near-contemporary Hugh – thought that Joseph was:

> unusually accessible, with none of the pomp of office I remembered from some of his predecessors. He was alarmingly well informed – if there was a recent study of a topic under discussion he had often read and digested it, even if his officials hadn't yet got hold of it. And he was exceptionally open minded and ready to pick up ideas wherever he could.

Though admired for his intellectual ability, Crossman was widely disliked within the ministry for his regular displays of rudeness and bad temper. He was also felt to have "dillied and dallied" over proposed reforms, and by comparison Joseph was appreciated as both an able and a decisive minister. Certainly the memories of civil servants contradict the contemporary view expressed in the *Guardian*, namely that by contrast with the new Education Secretary, Margaret Thatcher, Joseph "dither[ed] over decisions". The main difficulty arose because of his "open mind". Joseph's notebook and pencil could appear on improbable occasions. To make conversation, the journalist Alan Watkins once mentioned to the Secretary of State that it was rather a pity that highly trained doctors should have to spend so much time on mundane matters, such as patients suffering from the common cold. "Sir Keith stared for some seconds and then wrote something down on a piece of paper. 'I'll raise this with the Department', he said". In her final days in May 1971 Joseph visited Lady

---

5. KJ interview with Terry Coleman; Crossman, *Diaries, Vol. III*, 7, 605, 791.
6. For example, in an undated memorandum from his first year in office Joseph asked an official to explore the possibility of inducing the BMA to revise consultants' terms of employment. Concerned by evidence of "idleness" and "inefficiency" within the profession, he wrote that "I know the difficulties, but it is the public who suffer". See PRO BN13/1631.

Reading, the indomitable founder of the Women's Royal Voluntary Service (WRVS). Among her many initiatives, Lady Reading had provided the inspiration for the "meals on wheels" service – a particular favourite with Sir Keith – and after the war she had set up "knitting groups" to stave off boredom for elderly women. Soon after Joseph's visit an Under-Secretary received a minute in which the Secretary of State conveyed Lady Reading's last suggestions, concerning the help that prisoners and down-and-outs could be made to give to more "deserving" members of society. The plan would have cost several million pounds but it captured Joseph's imagination and he asked for a considered report. Other civil servants dreaded Monday mornings, when they would find the fruits of Joseph's weekend researches waiting for them on green slips. Returning to work one Monday Mrs Lee was greeted by five of these slips, most of which conveyed ideas for helping the homeless.[7]

This was the kind of thing that Joseph liked best – starting up initiatives to fill perceived "gaps" and enlisting others to see them through to fruition. It was an approach to business which depended on officials sharing his personal visions and his vigour; if they did not (and had some instinct for self-preservation) they found that they could conveniently forget to implement Joseph's instructions in the knowledge that the Secretary of State would soon be distracted by his next brainchild. Apparently Lady Reading's valedictory suggestions never emerged from the Under-Secretary's desk drawer. The official in question was approaching retirement and could afford to protect both himself and his immediate colleagues from the Joseph whirlwind. According to rumour others were less fortunate, and Joseph was not the only denizen of the Department to suffer from stress-induced health problems during his term of office. The Secretary of State already knew many people working in health and welfare; naturally he wanted to consult these, and the meetings could bring to light a host of new contacts who might be called in to bring their expertise to bear on topical questions. Nobody was spared at the meetings. One Social Services Director remembers discussions (ranging over "pensions, the Health Service [and] the role of voluntary organisations") that were "intensely invigorating and exhausting"; after one working dinner a young colleague said that as an intellectual exercise it was "more strenuous than his Finals at Cambridge". In his desire to secure "superb treatment" for all those who used the NHS, Joseph was as demanding as ever on his tours of inspection. "When I go to a hospital", he told one interviewer, "and am shown a patient, the question I ask the doctors is: 'If he were a *millionaire* what more could you do for him than you're doing now?'". But those who rode out the storm looked back on Joseph's spell at the DHSS with growing affection. One

---

7. Interview with Robin Wendt; letter to authors from Penny Lee; Campbell, *Grocer's Daughter*, 212; Alan Watkins in the *New Statesman*, 18 October 1974.

official went so far as to hail him as "a sort of folk-hero" within the department.[8]

Heath ran into criticism for encouraging his ministers to take holidays in August 1970. It was an early sign that relations with the press would be uneasy, because in every respect bar public relations the decision was perfectly justified. The government had published an ambitious legislative programme, and ministers needed some refreshment before tackling this work. Already the stress of office had claimed a notable victim. Iain Macleod returned to Number 11 on 19 July, less than two weeks after abdominal surgery. The economic outlook was worse even than the Conservatives had claimed during the election campaign, and when he should have been recuperating the new Chancellor fretted over an enforced decision to increase electricity prices, contrary to his own promises. Macleod died from a massive heart attack on the second evening after his return to Downing Street.[9]

Macleod's original illness had been a bad enough set-back to the Government. Before his operation the Chancellor had given an unconvincing performance in the Commons, helping to create the impression that the dynamic new team had been thrown off balance by the true state of Britain's finances. But his death had more serious repercussions for his colleagues – and for Joseph in particular. Heath had expected to move Macleod from the Treasury after a couple of years, but the necessity of an immediate reshuffle was unwelcome to say the least. The Prime Minister, determined to minimise the changes within the existing team, gave a Cabinet post to John Davies, the former Director-General of the Confederation of British Industry (CBI). Davies had only been in the Commons for a month, and as a representative of big business he was sure to be roughly handled by Labour before he had learned to cope with even the ordinary demands of the House. Heath later acknowledged that Davies was "not an inspired appointment". His ministerial career was most notable for an ill-judged attack on Britain's "lame ducks" – a phrase previously deployed by Joseph.[10]

Macleod had always been wary of Joseph, and after his death it was no longer possible to disguise the fact that his reservations were shared by others. The then Employment Secretary Robert Carr remembers that the reshuffle was discussed by Heath and his closest colleagues on the journey home from Macleod's funeral at Gargrave in Yorkshire. Joseph was never mentioned. Yet his claims to the Treasury were certainly comparable to those of Heath's preferred candidate, Anthony Barber, and at least one newspaper had confidently expected Joseph to be the choice. Worse still, Barber's promotion left a

---

8. Private information; letter to authors from Bob Bessell; Timmins, *Five Giants*, 291; *Sunday Mirror*, 25 March 1973.
9. Shepherd, *Macleod*, 534.
10. Heath, *Course of My Life*, 321.

vacancy in the position of Chancellor of the Duchy of Lancaster (with special responsibility for European matters). This was filled by Rippon, the Minister of Technology, who was succeeded by John Davies even though Joseph had attracted so much attention while shadowing that post.[11]

Hindsight might suggest that the Prime Minister was determined to keep Joseph's hands off economic policy whatever the cost. But at the time Heath thought that the instant promotion of Davies was a calculated risk, not a dangerous gamble. A frustrated Chancellor himself, he had made a virtue of his necessity; in Barber, he now had a close personal ally at the Treasury, and Davies could be expected to be more compliant than Rippon. But if the Prime Minister's purpose was to consolidate his own position in control of economic policy, there must be significance in the fact that someone as well qualified as Joseph was not even considered either for Technology or the Treasury. No rumour of discontent reached the press, but this was the man who had been tipped as the next Chancellor (if not Prime Minister) even before Macleod's death and his silence shows how well he had learned to bite his tongue. Nevertheless, Joseph allowed an unconscious hint of disappointment to drop out from time to time. Although the Home Secretary, Maudling, was officially number two in the Cabinet (just as he had been Deputy Leader in Opposition), as Chancellor Joseph would have been *de facto* vice-captain. The Ministry of Technology was about to move higher up the batting order under its new title, the Department of Trade and Industry. By contrast, in an interview after he had been in the post for over three years Joseph bracketed the DHSS with Housing and Local Government as no better than a "top Second XI job". He compared his political career to his record as a Harrow cricketer, and as usual denied that he had ambitions for further ascent. But talking of his schooldays earlier in the interview Joseph had left his stumps unguarded, admitting that failure to break into the first eleven "makes one hate one's fellow boys". On the page this looked like a joke, but Joseph's Harrow letters betray the true depth of his resentment when he was overlooked at school. Although his present job did provide him with the opportunity to make life more comfortable for millions of people, the prospect of being stuck in the Government reserves for as long as Heath picked the team must have vexed him.[12]

There were also serious policy complications for Joseph arising from Macleod's death. The tangled family allowances plot began as far back as January 1970. In the same week that the Shadow Chancellor rejected the case for an increase in the allowance at Selsdon Park, Richard Crossman was visited at the Cabinet Office by Peter Townsend and Frank Field of the CPAG.

---

11. Interview with Lord Carr; *Daily Express*, 22 July 1970; *Evening Standard*, 23 July 1970.
12. KJ interview with Terry Coleman. In fact Joseph was ranked eighth in the Cabinet hierarchy; Crossman had been fifth. We are most grateful to Robin Wendt for this point.

According to Field, Crossman's behaviour on 27 January was in keeping with his surname; he put on "an extraordinary 'performance'. He banged the table, he shouted, and he mocked. There was an endless machine-gunning of sarcastic jokes to which the civil servants responded as if part of a medieval court".[13]

Crossman's outburst was not surprising, since the CPAG delegation had visited him in order to attack the Labour government on "our most sensitive point, our humanity".[14] Field, who had become Director of the Group in the Autumn of 1969, felt that it should adopt "a more radical political stance" if it wanted to influence the Labour government. His first move was an attempt to shame ministers into raising family allowances. Before the ill-tempered meeting Crossman was presented with a CPAG memorandum which purported to show that far from improving the position of the poor as it had promised, over five years Labour had allowed their situation to deteriorate relative to that of the average worker. In the long term no one emerged with much credit from the incident; Field himself later admitted that the CPAG's claim was based on flimsy evidence. But, as Crossman confided to his diary, the immediate political cost was borne by himself, since on television the same evening he all but confirmed the CPAG argument. He had been caught off guard by Field's new aggressive tactics. Before the meeting even started the media had been given advance notice of the memorandum, together with a press release headlined "Poor Worse Off Under Labour".[15]

Macleod had been quick to seize this chance to marry the two sides of his political persona – the sincere believer in "the brotherhood of man", and the cynical opportunist. The direct electoral benefits to his party of posing as the true friends of the poor might be slender, but it would undoubtedly hit the morale of Labour's constituency-workers and help to foster a general impression of government failure. But as co-founder of the charity for the homeless, "Crisis at Christmas" (later "Crisis") Macleod was sure to be moved when he heard passionate arguments for more generous allowances. On 23 March Joseph raised once again the necessity of presenting coherent proposals on an issue which had been "a big failure [for] the present government". Two days later Macleod met Field and Townsend, who were startled to find him an easy convert. The commitment to increased family allowances which he made at the meeting was soon repeated in the Commons, where he pledged £30 million of new money for the purpose. Just before the election Heath confirmed in writing the Conservative acceptance of the view that "the only way of tackling family poverty in the short-term is to increase family allowances and operate the claw-back principle". During the campaign Heath regularly

13. Frank Field, *Poverty and Politics* (Heinemann, 1982), 33.
14. Crossman, *Diaries, Vol. II*, 791.
15. Field, *Poverty and Politics* 31, 34.

taunted Labour with their broken promises in respect of the poor, although the Conservative manifesto merely promised to "ensure that adequate family allowances go to those families that need them" – a sign that Macleod was packing a parachute in case his new plane encountered turbulence. Field later told Nicholas Timmins that the controversy "may have contributed marginally" to Labour's defeat; certainly some activists thought it was a factor, and up until the 1979 election hecklers called him "Judas".[16]

Joseph had attended CPAG meetings since the mid-1960s. He may not have been a benefactor of the Group himself, but Bovis Holdings provided funding (ironically, their sponsorship began after talks between Field and the Chairman, Sir Keith's cousin Neville Vincent, which took place within a few days of Macleod's announcement).[17] Field and Townsend thought that they could rely on Joseph to abide by Macleod's promises, and did not meet the new Secretary of State until September. They came away feeling that their confidence was justified; as Townsend later reminded Joseph, "Any disagreements between us seemed to have been properly limited to the *kind* of family allowance increase which the Government might approve". But alarm bells were triggered at a second meeting, held during the Conservative Party conference at Blackpool. It seemed to the CPAG that Joseph had raised objections which their existing scheme had been designed to meet; in effect, that he was attacking a straw doll to disguise his true intention, which was to save money for the Treasury.[18]

On 27 October Barber delivered a major statement on public expenditure. This included an announcement that instead of the promised increase in family allowances, a means-tested Family Income Supplement (FIS) would be introduced for low-paid workers. When Joseph spoke in support of the new legislation two weeks later, he explained that, having looked more carefully at the figures, he had realised that an increase in the family allowance would not help the poorest after all. About a third of the relevant families had only one child, but the allowance was restricted to households with two or more. Furthermore, since Labour had allowed tax thresholds to decline in real value, the great majority of the population would immediately lose any extra money in tax. Joseph had calculated that if the Government increased the allowance by an overall £180 million, £174 million would automatically return to its coffers through "claw-back", leaving only £6 million to help the poorest. He felt that it would be nonsensical for a tax-cutting government to increase bills in this way. To give genuine help to the poor through the family allowance would involve "astronomic" expenditure. The FIS, by contrast, would be specifically

---

16. *Ibid.*, 38–40; Heath to Field, 1 June 1970; *A Better Tomorrow*, 22; Timmins, *Five Giants*, 278–9; LCC (70), 357th meeting, 23 March 1970, CPA, Bodleian Library.
17. Interview with Frank Field; Neville Vincent to Frank Field, 1 April 1970, Townsend Papers, Box 65.
18. Townsend to KJ, 26 October 1970, Townsend Papers, Box 65.

targeted, to boost the annual income of the most needy 180,000 families by up to £150, costing a maximum of £8 million per year. Due to administrative problems, however, it would not be possible for this money to be paid out until 1 August 1971.[19]

Joseph held out a limp olive branch to the CPAG, promising that its views would be taken into account in a comprehensive study of family poverty. But the Group's reaction was apoplectic. Townsend told Shirley Williams that her colleagues within the Parliamentary Labour Party were "bound to feel that the Bill is [so] derisory and harmful as to deserve only contempt"; clearly this was his own view, which he expressed to any member of the press who would listen. The means test was anathema to the CPAG because the perceived stigma discouraged the poor from claiming their full entitlements; in this context the intensive campaign of public education promised by Joseph might actually prove counter-productive, by broadcasting the fact that claimants were in special need. The ultimate irony was that FIS was based on a scheme which Labour had rejected when in office. By their public denunciations of the Wilson government the CPAG had helped to extract the poor from Labour's frying pan only to douse them in Conservative flames.[20]

It seemed to Townsend (and to Field at the time[21]) that Joseph had proved a broken reed. To make room for its cuts in direct taxation the Treasury had been looking for departmental savings – a campaign whose most serious casualty was the image of Margaret Thatcher, the "Milk-Snatching" Education Secretary. Unable to believe that Joseph might willingly have agreed to implement FIS, the activists assumed that, robbed of Macleod's support, he had meekly surrendered. His presentation of the Family Income Supplements Bill on 10 November was apologetic enough to encourage that view. But some of his objections to family allowances had been raised at Selsdon Park – notably the discovery that many poor parents had only a single child, either because the mother had been deserted or because one member of a stable partnership had suddenly lost earning capacity. Joseph had tried to forewarn his colleagues that meaningful relief for the working poor would be very expensive, but he had already lost the last phase of his battle with Macleod for a tax on investment income which could have paid the bill without endangering the tax cuts for the middle class that he favoured as a matter of principle. Above all, Joseph had no objection to means tests; indeed, as a consistent advocate of "selective" benefits he had every reason to favour them. His true opinion of the unselective alternative is suggested by the fact that when Barber raised the tax threshold in his next budget Joseph decided not to exploit the opportunity of increasing the family

---

19. *Hansard*, vol. 805, col. 45, 27 October 1970; vol. 806, cols 217–21, 10 November 1970.
20. Townsend to Shirley Williams, 9 November 1970, Townsend Papers, Box 65.
21. Later Field revised his view, thinking that the CPAG should have concentrated its efforts on asking the government to increase tax thresholds; interview with Frank Field.

allowance. Whenever the subject was raised he excused himself by referring to "technical difficulties". In reality, he was waiting for the Treasury to work out the details of a "negative income tax" which would unify the taxation and benefit systems, but this really did suffer from "technical difficulties"; the complexities meant that it remained a Conservative aspiration for the general election of February 1974 and beyond.[22]

Joseph had spent the late 1960s lamenting his own record as a minister. Granted a second chance to prove himself, his first major decision had caused the government acute embarrassment. FIS was prominent among the 1970 decisions which caused an internal Treasury review team to reflect that "The critics had a fair measure of success in presenting the Government's public expenditure policies as harsh and unfair". Attacked by Roy Jenkins on the broken promise, Barber became so flustered that he referred to Wilson as if he were still Prime Minister – a lapse which continued to make him shudder a quarter of a century later. When the Labour leader replied to the Government's spending programme on 5 November he characterised it as "a total denial, a betrayal, of every promise the Conservatives made in the election", and put the decision on family allowances at the top of his charge sheet. Under the circumstances Crossman was restrained in his denunciation of FIS as "a dirty little Bill" which had been foisted on his successor by civil servants. More than a year after the introduction of the new benefit Joseph was confronted at first hand with the dismay which his decision had caused among social workers. At what he described as a "disastrous" meeting with thirty representatives of the profession, his audience was unmoved by the familiar explanations. He used a Departmental official as an outlet for his feelings. "They did seem naïve and ignorant", he minuted, adding hastily that the social workers must have felt the same way about him. Provoked by their attitude, he had suggested at the meeting that better rewards were needed in order to attract more talented staff – implying that the existing professionals were below standard – and as soon as he returned to the Elephant and Castle he began a pointed inquiry into the reading lists on social work courses.[23]

Yet the most damaging assault on Sir Keith came from his own backbenches. In debate Enoch Powell pointed out the similarities between FIS and the "Speenhamland" system, introduced in the late-eighteenth century to subsidise the wages of agricultural labourers. Although Powell acknowledged that the parallel could not be exact in the very different context of the 1970s he lashed out against a device which departed from the principle "that a man should receive as near as may be the full value of his work in cash". Powell

---

22. *Hansard*, vol. 806, cols 217–30, 10 November 1970. Brendon Sewill, who first brought the negative income tax to the Conservative Party's attention in 1967, was surprised when Joseph gave a fairly cool response to the new idea; letter to authors from Brendon Sewill.
23. Webster, *Health Services*, Vol. II, 393; *Hansard*, vol. 805, cols 55, 1277, 27 October, November 1970; Barber, *Taking the Tide* 102; KJ memorandum of 16 October 1971, PRO BN 13/1631.

failed to mention that Speenhamland had undoubtedly saved many labourers' families from starvation. There was no attack on Joseph by name – this was unnecessary, so clear was Powell's implicit message that his policy contravened one of the key tenets of economic liberalism. He had no doubt that the Bill would pass, but predicted that "many of those who vote for it or let it go through will live to regret what we have done". In practice Powell's predictions proved to be exaggerated, but the results were bad enough. To activists in the field of child poverty, FIS made the scandal of the high-rise flats look like a molehill. Take-up was abysmal. Although Joseph despatched letters to every social worker in Britain to mobilise the army of claimants, by the end of 1971 fewer than half of the potential recruits had enlisted. At least Joseph had helped to introduce a memorable phrase to the British political vocabulary, but it hardly flattered his policy. According to Frank Field and David Piachaud, the FIS had caught the poor in a "poverty trap", because the detailed workings of the new benefit meant that funds were progressively withdrawn as the earnings of low-income families increased. In extreme cases, this could mean that a substantial pay rise would actually leave a family worse off.[24]

In the immediate aftermath of FIS Joseph told Field that the new system "is certainly not perfect but it will bring substantial help to the poorest of the poor, including one-child households". In his later parliamentary speeches he took to praising his policy with one breath then undermining it in the next. The publicity campaign to increase take-up, he told the Commons in November 1972, had been "dramatically successful – although, we admit, not successful enough". In private meetings his tone was even more pessimistic, and he soon found himself having to introduce revisions to his own system. Originally designed as a stop-gap measure, FIS remained on the statute book up to 1988 (when it was superseded by Family Credit). But if it was unrepealed it was also unloved. Sir Keith Joseph, the advocate of selective benefits, had produced some telling evidence to support the prosecution case. Despite the distaste many Tories felt for the alternative universalist approach to social welfare, "no new means-tested benefit of any significance was introduced by the Conservatives for almost twenty years" after 1970. At least Joseph had the satisfaction of a partial *rapprochement* with CPAG; at the group's 1971 Annual General Meeting he was given a warm reception, inspired by his courage in attending and also by a recognition that he had done his best in difficult circumstances.[25]

The furore over FIS was not the only problem Joseph encountered in his first few months of office. In July he had the pleasure of at last rewarding Airey Neave

---

24. *Hansard*, vol. 806, cols 265–6, 10 November 1970; Timmins, *Five Giants*, 283–4; on Speenhamland see Brian Inglis, *Poverty and the Industrial Revolution* (Panther, 1972), 75–85.
25. KJ to Field, 12 November 1970, Townsend Papers, Box 65; *Hansard*, vol. 845, col. 653, 6 November 1972; Timmins, *Five Giants*, 284; Frank Field, "Social Policy: A Thirty-Year Journey" (Second Keith Joseph Memorial Lecture, CPS, 1998), 1.

for his patience, extending pension rights to those who had not been covered by the 1948 National Insurance Act. He also borrowed an idea from his Labour predecessors, introducing a £4 per week tax-free Attendance Allowance for severely disabled people requiring 24-hour care, and widows aged between forty and fifty were newly provided for. But even these apparent acts of generosity bore clear traces of the parsimonious Treasury; Attendance Allowance, for example, would not be payable for six months while the claimant proved that his or her disability was sufficiently drastic. Elsewhere the Government's desire for economies bore even harder on Joseph, who wanted to boost his budget in other areas. After discussions in July and August he agreed a package which included significant increases in charges for dental and opthalmic services, and the raising of prescription charges from two shillings and sixpence to four shillings. Eye tests, however, remained free; it took another two decades for the Conservatives to form the view that it was appropriate to charge for this crucial service. The predictable result of the new price list was a drop in demand. In the first year the issue of prescriptions fell by 10 per cent, and presumably the most needy constituted a majority of those who decided to try to restore their health without medical help. Yet Joseph's reputation as a compassionate minister was scarcely touched by all this. Instead, critical comment focused on the cuts affecting school children, which were held to be all the more shameful because they had been introduced by a woman. The *Sun* even doubted whether Mrs Thatcher was a human being. The fact that the Education Secretary had fought successfully to save the Open University – perhaps the noblest initiative of the Wilson years – was considered to be far less newsworthy than her Treasury-enforced confiscation of school milk.[26]

The spending cuts of Autumn 1970 showed that Heath had dealt Joseph an almost unplayable hand when he appointed him to the DHSS. An enemy of high government spending in general, Joseph hoped that economic growth would enable the state to protect the "worthy" poor. If the government's economic strategy succeeded, in a few years the DHSS would be an idyllic place from which the fruits of economic growth would be dispensed to grateful, self-respecting clients. But even on the most optimistic forecasts there was sure to be a transitional phase during which the department would be restricted to handing out sticking-plasters. Since economic recovery was held to be dependent on tax cuts, even the supply of Band-Aids was under threat in the short-term. The fact that the press seemed to understand his dilemma was no consolation for Joseph. He was in a catch-22 position which had already exposed the frailty of his approach to politics – his combination of economic rigour with social tenderness. Something dramatic had to be done, and quickly.

---

26. Webster, *Health Services, Vol. II*, 395; Thatcher, *Path to Power*, 180–2.

Joseph's attempt to break free began almost on the day that he took office. In June 1970 he asked his officials to examine the possibility of relieving the taxpayer of at least some of the cost of health care. Existing studies (notably the IEA's *Choice in Welfare*) suggested alternatives, through introducing charges for services currently free at the point of use, or through a system of compulsory insurance. The leading Conservative proponent of a radical new approach, Geoffrey Howe, was invited to make representations, and in October a working party was established (despite Treasury protests) with an unrestricted brief to examine "alternative methods of financing health and welfare services in the public and private sectors".[27]

Before the 1970 general election a well-informed source had told the newspaper proprietor Cecil King that Joseph resembled Harold Wilson at least in the respect that he would never do anything unpopular. This was another version of Sir Keith's familiar self-criticism, that he lacked "moral courage". But the funding problem provided a chance for him to make up for his failures in the early 1960s. It was heartening that the IEA and Howe (who had worked on a study published by the British Medical Association (BMA)) supported radical change, and this was one initiative of which Powell would approve. But every time Joseph had flown the kite of private funding in Opposition the strings had been cut by colleagues, and now the challenge was more daunting. Even before his ideas could be presented in Cabinet they had to be subjected to civil service scrutiny. The precedents were deeply inauspicious. In 1963 the options urged by the IEA had been examined and rejected by a range of affected departments, including Powell's Ministry of Health. At least on that occasion powerful figures in the Treasury had expressed some sympathy. This time one official dismissed the updated *Choice in Welfare* as containing "99 per cent rubbish".[28]

From an early stage Joseph had sent out signals that his "moral courage" would again be found wanting. Before the working party began to meet he had (rightly) doubted "whether the Government had a mandate to switch the NHS fully to an insurance-based system". At least that left the possibility of *partially* funding the Health Service by private means, but even this would have come as a surprise to many people who had just voted Tory. By the end of November Joseph had scampered away from the field of battle, acknowledging that the current system of funding would remain in place. But the press had caught wind of the working party, and *The Times* of 21 December 1970 ran a front-page article with the deadpan headline "Disbanding health service is considered". Joseph was reported to favour in principle a compulsory system of health insurance, but due to Treasury objections the new favourite was the idea of

---

27. Webster, *Health Services, Vol. II*, 386–8.
28. Cecil King, *Diary 1965–1970* (Jonathan Cape, 1972), 319–20; Webster, *Health Services, Vol. II*, 388, 903n; Andrew Denham and Mark Garnett, *British Think-Tanks and the Climate of Opinion* (UCL Press, 1998), 94.

"hiving off" NHS activities "on such a massive scale that nothing but a residual safety-net for the destitute would be left". With the political temperature already raised by the second reading of the highly contentious Industrial Relations Bill on 14–15 December, this kind of publicity was the last thing that the new government wanted. Joseph was summoned to Chequers on New Year's Eve for a conversation with Heath, during which he repeated his seasonal resolution not to privatise the NHS. It would have looked too craven prematurely to wind up the working party, but when this reported in July 1971 it reached the self-evident conclusion that "short of a major revolution in the whole NHS system, there was very limited scope for any changes whose benefits would outweigh the practical difficulties to which they would give rise". Joseph had already told the Conservative Advisory Committee on Policy (ACP) that "It was a temptation to see private enterprise as the answer . . . but insurance did not of itself increase resources". He admitted that "one clearly would not devise the social services on the present pattern, but one had to start from the point to which history had led us".[29]

In a radio interview broadcast in August 1973 Joseph reflected that in his job "one frequently finishes up being damned by both the progressives and by those who disagree with the progressives".[30] In his first months in office he had damaged his reputation with the CPAG; now it was the turn of the IEA to feel badly let down. Immediately after the election Arthur Seldon had told Joseph that the Conservatives really could "break Labour's hold on the working class and destroy Socialism for all time". This beatific vision quickly faded, as Joseph proved himself to be just another "Mr Can't". Three months later Seldon sent Joseph a report on private health care in Australia – the model which was explicitly rejected at the ACP meeting – "with some sadness mixed with cynicism". He had gathered from a recent conversation with the Secretary of State that he was sure to compromise in the end. His only remaining hope was that this would be merely a tactical retreat, and that unlike other Tories Joseph would remember that public opinion could be changed over time. By February 1972 Seldon was writing in anger, not in sorrow. Joseph, he raged, had "given nothing to those who expected something different". In *Crossbow* he praised Joseph as "a high-principled Minister with a kindly disposition", but went on to chastise him for showing insufficient resolution. Oddly enough, at about the same time the IEA's *bête noire* Richard Crossman echoed Seldon's advice to keep

29. Webster, *Health Services, Vol. II*, 388–92; minutes of ACP meeting, 9 June 1971, Bodleian Library.
30. KJ interview with Anthony King. Joseph was even attacked by Barbara Robb, the founder of the pressure group Aid for the Elderly in Government Institutions (AEGIS), which campaigned for the better treatment of the elderly in government institutions. After an intervention by Joseph's advisor Brian Abel-Smith a letter accusing the Secretary of State of failing to study AEGIS' proposals was never sent. Since Joseph's record on this subject was far superior to that of any of his predecessors the incident illustrates the thankless nature of his job. See correspondence in AEGIS 2/5/A, LSE archives.

fighting for specific policy ideas when Joseph chose to confide his worries to his predecessor in the unlikely setting of a *New Statesman* party.[31]

Seldon was a little more favourable towards Joseph's plan for pensions, but even this he described as "a half measure", which might end up helping Labour to implement its own scheme. After much delay, in 1969 Crossman had introduced legislation for a wage-related state pension based on graduated contributions. This plan was strongly redistributive; it guaranteed a pension equal to at least half of average earnings, which would be uprated in line with inflation. In opposing the measure, the Conservatives deplored its disincentive effect on people who would otherwise pay into occupational schemes. Assisted by Margaret Thatcher, Joseph had devised an approach which turned Crossman on his head. Contributions to the state pension would still be wage-related, but the payments after retirement would be made at a flat rate. As Nicholas Timmins has pointed out, this element of Joseph's scheme was, ironically, "more redistributive than Crossman's": hence Seldon's complaint. But the arrangement would be attractive only to the lowest paid workers, and, contrary to the provisions of the Crossman Bill, under the Conservative plan high earners would be encouraged (though, it was decided after much debate, not compelled) to "contract out" into non-state schemes. The intended result was that the great majority of the population would in future rely on occupational schemes to top up their income in retirement; the value of the state pension would be linked to prices, but over time it would become no more than a fall-back for the poor.[32]

To the great relief of the powerful pensions industry Crossman's Bill lapsed with the 1970 General Election, although it had completed its committee stage in the Commons. When Joseph unveiled his own White Paper in September 1971 the press response was generally favourable, drowning out Labour's predictable protests and disappointed noises from the IEA, which had hoped that those able to afford private provision would have been forced to insure themselves.[33] In her memoirs Barbara Castle described the Conservative plan as "pathetic", and remembered the fun she had at Joseph's expense during the committee stage. But her efforts to amend the legislation were in vain, and the Bill became law in 1973. Joseph had fared better than Crossman, but not much. In 1975 Mrs Castle enjoyed what she thought was the last laugh, when her Social Security Pensions Act replaced Joseph's plan. In its turn this reform was reformed by the 1986 Social Security Act which bore some resemblance to Joseph's ill-fated scheme. One crucial difference was that Joseph had insisted on strict minimum standards for private pensions. In the different climate of

31. Cockett, *Thinking the Unthinkable*, 169, 206–7; Arthur Seldon, "Conservatives and the Welfare State", *Crossbow*, August–September 1972; interview with Alan Watkins.
32. Timmins, *Five Giants*, 348.
33. Michael Piltch, "Saving for Retirement", in Rhodes Boyson (ed.), *Down with the Poor: An Analysis of the Failure of the "Welfare State" and a Plan to End Poverty* (Churchill Press, 1971), 79.

the mid-1980s many insurance companies seized the opportunity of defrauding their customers through the operations of a truly "free" market.[34]

Even before the end of 1970 the IEA had published a book of essays which scarcely spared a single aspect of the new government's social policies. The editor, the ex-socialist Dr Rhodes Boyson, pointed out the contrast between ministers who had promised so much, and his contributors who refused to "trim or trifle".[35] Joseph had always known the IEA to be a demanding friend, and he could bear the Institute's recriminations – at least while he retained the loyalty and affection of his civil servants. There were also understanding allies in the media. In *The Times* Ronald Butt provided a favourable gloss for the retreat over Health Service funding, claiming that Joseph had shared the Treasury's reservations all along and blaming any problems on the Conservatives' "failure to do their homework" on the social services, for which Joseph himself was only marginally responsible. Butt acknowledged that Joseph was "a highly doctrinal non-interventionist", a "vocal believer in the platonic beauty and efficiency of the free and unimpeded market" whose economic views were "little short" – again that tactful qualification – "of Powellism". But he would do nothing very radical in his present position because he believed that "economic efficiency and social concern are two quite different things which, for the good of each, must be treated separately". Even this sympathetic piece, written by a perceptive and well-informed journalist, depicted Joseph as a man of many paradoxes. There were hints that, rather than arising from settled principle, his current caution was the product of his "nervous" disposition. He had, Butt recognised, a reputation for grasping "rashly at some appealing idea without measuring the consequences". Although Butt thought that he was now "more self-assured", this said little for his previous condition because he was still characterised as "a shy, intense and rather guarded man".[36]

Butt made no reference to the FIS controversy, but he did predict that Joseph was ready to make another of his personal detours. In Barber's first economic statement it had been envisaged that charges for NHS prescriptions would continue to rise until they represented half the real cost up to a maximum of 50 pence. For once the Treasury was pleased with this idea. But it troubled Heath, who thought that people might regard it as an attack on the founding principles of the NHS. It also threatened to make life more complicated for the drug manufacturers, for doctors and for pharmacists. Opposition from these quarters – coupled with worries about the inflationary consequences – forced Joseph to drop his proposal by July 1971.[37]

---

34. Barbara Castle, *Fighting all the Way* (Macmillan, 1993), 464; on the 1986 Act, see Andrew Marr, *Ruling Britannia* (Michael Joseph, 1995) 143–50.
35. Boyson, "Prologue", in *Down with the Poor*, v.
36. Ronald Butt in *The Times*, 6 May 1971.
37. Webster, *Health Services, Vol. II*, 394.

Ronald Butt greeted this as a "sensible retreat" by the Secretary of State. Yet the climb-down marked the end of Joseph's creative options on the question of financing the NHS. He had no alternative but to fall back on the familiar post-war model of ministerial conduct, bidding high in each spending round in the hope that the Treasury would meet him somewhere near half-way. In this he was reasonably successful. As he emphasised in his speech to the 1973 party conference, "The real buying power of the National Health Service and the Local Authority Social Service Departments in our current four years, is rising from year to year at a rate of 40 per cent higher than it was in Labour's central four years, year by year". He translated this exciting message for his audience: "In other words, we are spending more in real terms than Labour ever managed to do and increasing our rate of spending on these services faster than Labour did". Plans for public expenditure for the five-year period up to 1975/6 anticipated an overall increase of £1.5 billion (allowing for inflation) for the health and personal social services.[38]

Joseph's time at the DHSS is best remembered for the amount of money he spent, which explains his "folk-hero" status within the Department. Ronald Butt's view at the time was that Tony Barber had "refused Sir Keith almost nothing"; later John Campbell characterised him as "one of the most open-handed Secretaries of State the social services have ever had". Opponents would later dwell on the delicious irony that Joseph, the scourge of profligate government, had himself launched repeated raids on the Treasury. Yet criticism of Joseph on this score is almost – if not quite – as unfair as the right-wing fantasies about Selsdon Park. Any Secretary of State for Social Services was bound to spend a great deal of money. When Heath appointed Joseph to the DHSS, he did so in the knowledge that (like Powell) the new minister believed that government generosity in these fields was justified, however penny-pinching it should be elsewhere. The 1970 Conservative manifesto had complained that "The fundamental problem of all Britain's social services . . . is the shortage of resources", and boasted about the party's previous record. In the summer of 1969 Maurice Macmillan had informed his colleagues that an extra £500 million per year was needed to maintain the Health Service in anything like an acceptable condition.[39] When Joseph reviewed the situation from his new vantage point at Elephant and Castle, he told the Cabinet that:

What we said in our Manifesto was not an exaggeration . . . Hospital buildings are not only outdated but under-equipped and inadequately maintained. Standards of service in different parts of the country are still markedly unequal. Nurse recruitment is dropping. The doctors are

---

38. *Financial Times*, 16 November 1971; *Minutes of Ninety-First Conservative Party Conference, 1973*, 98; *Guardian*, 3 January 1973.
39. *The Times*, 6 May 1971; Campbell, *Heath*, 381; *A Better Tomorrow*, 19; Advisory Committee on Poverty (ACP) (69) 100, 11 June 1969, CPA, Bodleian Library.

restive because they lack the resources to give their patients the most modern treatment. Standards in psychiatric and geriatric hospitals are scandalously low.[40]

On this view, continued underfunding of the NHS was not an option; the service would simply fall apart if nothing was done. With a recruitment crisis looming Joseph had to approve fairly generous pay settlements for NHS staff, ensuring that between 1970 and 1972 the number of nurses rose by 30,000. Limited resources prevented Joseph from pushing Britain to the forefront of new medical developments, such as heart transplantation. He concentrated his attention on what he called the "Cinderella" services – those which catered for his long-held concerns, the elderly, the mentally ill, the mentally handicapped and people with permanent physical problems (or "afflictions") such as deafness. Once again, these groups had been singled out as deserving special attention in the 1970 manifesto, and Crossman tacitly confirmed that they had suffered undue neglect in the past when he told *The Times* that Joseph had been much more successful than he had been in persuading the Treasury to provide the cash to make necessary improvements to long-stay hospitals. In his campaign to make life more comfortable for the inmates of these hospitals Joseph's deep sympathy for the patients was seconded by his eye for detail; he even initiated changes to bedroom furnishings in these institutions. The plight of the disabled was high-lighted during Joseph's time at the DHSS by the tragic results of the fertility drug Thalidomide. When he became aware of the problem (rather belatedly) in the winter of 1972 he was deeply moved, and impressed by the "dignity, spontaneity and vitality" of the affected children. As he pointed out in debate, adequate compensation was due from the manufacturer, Distillers, rather than the Government. But although he stressed that victims could benefit under the new Attendance Allowance, in November 1972 he provided an additional £3 million to relieve the short-term problem and promised that he would keep the situation under review. To Labour's Jack Ashley, who led the parliamentary campaign on behalf of the children, the announcement was "an irrelevance" because the new money was not specifically earmarked for Thalidomide cases. But the grant developed into what became known as the Family Fund which, Ashley conceded, "has helped thousands of children" since 1972.[41]

---

40. Quoted in Webster, *Health Services, Vol. II*, 392.
41. *A Better Tomorrow*, 22; *The Times*, 9 August 1972; Michael Alison speech at KJ memorial service; *Hansard*, vol. 846, cols 191–4, 14 November 1972; vol. 847, cols 432–47, 29 November 1972; Jack Ashley, *Acts of Defiance* (Reinhardt Books, 1992), 199. As a determined campaigner Ashley tended to regard all ministers as "Scrooges", and attributed their apparently generous decisions to his own persistence. Thus, for example, when Joseph announced that behind-the-ear devices for the deaf were to be made available free of charge Ashley clearly thought that nothing would have been done were it not for the embarrassment caused by his Commons' interventions. More likely, Ashley's tactics helped Joseph to secure agreement for a measure which he would have wanted anyway; see *Defiance*, 345.

Some of Joseph's decisions led to a degree of expenditure which had not been anticipated. For example, his implementation of the Labour-commissioned Seebohm Report, which established Social Service Departments to co-ordinate the social work carried out by each local authority, was expected to involve some additional costs. But the reform was allowed to fuel "an expansionist frenzy", with annual growth rates of around 12 per cent between 1970 and 1973. Joseph had expounded his long-held views on the better co-ordination of welfare services to the Seebohm Committee. In this instance his desire to back his judgement did get the better of his caution over public spending; his largesse seems all the more misguided because, in the short-term at least, the "uncontrolled"expansion produced more friction than co-ordination within the new Departments and there was a second upheaval when local government was reorganised in 1974. But elsewhere Joseph was criticised for not being generous enough – notably in his resistance to attempts by the House of Lords to ensure that family planning supplies were offered free of prescription charges. As we have seen, FIS caused a political storm, even though it provided new money for the poor. Joseph's decision to uprate the state pension every year, instead of the previous biennial increase, was enforced by rising inflation, and the overall pension bill was on an upward trend anyway as life expectancy increased. The resulting rise in the number of elderly Britons also meant extra costs for the NHS. In the face of ever-increasing expenditure Joseph took every opportunity to encourage a greater contribution to welfare services from the voluntary sector – "to an extent", thought one Labour MP, "that is unrealistic and verges on excuse-making for the failure of Government to accept its necessary share of responsibility".[42]

It would be wrong, then, to describe Joseph as inordinately profligate. At first sight there seems to be more mileage in the complaint that he *boasted* about the spending of his Department, in a fashion which consorts badly with his pronouncements after he had returned once again to Opposition. But the braggart Sir Keith was born out of a weakness which affected the whole of the Heath government: its failure to master public relations. At a meeting of the Advisory Committee on Policy (ACP) in June 1971 it was noted that a recent poll showed that the party was still regarded as being "fairly hard-headed but also hard-hearted . . . even Conservative achievements in the social field – such as the introduction of pensions for the over-80s – were ascribed by a majority of the public to the Labour Party". Joseph had been shown this research in April, and commented that it revealed "an unsurprising but distressing lack of awareness of what we are up to". He told the ACP that he was planning a series of "major speeches" but not until the autumn because he sensibly felt that "the right time to propound ideas was when they could be validated with examples of things done".

---

42. Timmins, *Five Giants*, 293; John Grant, *Member of Parliament* (Michael Joseph, 1974), 177.

In the short-term, of course, the best way to show a caring face was to brandish a burgeoning wallet, and Joseph's speech at the October conference featured a heavy emphasis on the £110 million which he had prised out of the Treasury to fund the "Cinderella services". The need for more effective presentation had been suggested earlier in that month by Heath himself, who had commented "Excellent stuff, but we have to put it across" on a Joseph memo outlining ideas for the next party manifesto. By November 1972 the ACP was still lamenting that Labour was seen as the caring party. Now it was felt that parliamentary Conservatives had failed to support the efforts of the Secretary of State in pushing the good news. But senior colleagues continued to denigrate Joseph for his own poor presentation. After the election of February 1974 Lord Carrington complained to Cecil King that "Joseph had managed to give a great deal of money to the Social Services without securing any benefit for the Party". The real problem, as Joseph admitted to an interviewer in rather untypical language, was that the aspects of the Health Service which he had benefitted most lacked "sex appeal".[43]

Joseph's critics are on firmer ground when they attack his reorganisation of the National Health Service. This was another policy which had been inherited from Labour. Although the need for reform had initially been suggested by the Porritt Report as long ago as 1962, a Green Paper was not published until 1968 and this was revised by Richard Crossman whose own effort appeared in February 1970. The protracted delay should have acted as a warning; it had been caused in part by changes in the plan to reorganise local government, but also by the competing demands of several vocal interest groups. In particular, Crossman had been thwarted in his desire entirely to abolish the Regional Hospital Boards which had been set up by Bevan in 1948. He also had to agree that the members of his proposed Area Health Authorities would be appointed in equal proportions by the health profession, local government, and the Secretary of State (who would also appoint the Chairman).[44]

At first Joseph confessed to feeling taken aback by the scale of the task confronting his Department, and as early as April 1971 he was regretting the "uncertainty" which the Seebohm changes had already inflicted on the providers of health and personal social services.[45] But gradually he began to warm towards the prospect of remounting one of his old hobby-horses – the cause of better management. If the DHSS could pull off its difficult assignment, efficiency savings might be significant enough to help solve the funding crisis

---

43. *Minutes of the Eighty-Ninth Conservative Party Conference, 1971,* 103; ACP (71) 112 Meeting, 9 June 1971; ACP (72) 120 Meeting, 6 November 1972, CPA, Bodleian Library; Ramsden, *Winds of Change,* 320–1; Heath to KJ, 5 October 1971, SC 1971 (Folder 9), CPA, Bodleian Library; Cecil King, *The Cecil King Diary, 1971–74* (Jonathan Cape, 1975), 367; *Sunday Mirror,* 25 March 1973.
44. Rudolf Klein, *The Politics of the National Health Service* (Longman, 1983), 92–3.
45. See memorandum of 1 April, 1971, in PRO BN 13/1631; "The Department should have realised it. *I* should have realised it".

in the NHS. Joseph was soon calling meetings, commissioning papers, and "instituting pressing investigations on questions of minor detail". His eagerness was not invariably appreciated by officials. For example, he formed the notion of perching an NHS Chief Executive on the top of his proposed structure, despite admitting that the job of such an overlord would be "Titanic". Tactful civil servants ensured that this plan was dropped at any early stage. Another personal initiative, to introduce the Health Service equivalent of a Queen's Award for Industry, made the same journey from drawing board to filing cabinet. On more substantial points Joseph found the road blocked by his political colleagues. At first he wanted the power to appoint all the members of the regional authorities, who in turn would select the area boards. Taken aback by the strength of opposition within the Cabinet (particularly from the Environment Secretary Peter Walker), Joseph reluctantly agreed that three local government representatives should be included in each of the area authorities.[46]

To counter the hubbub arising from vested interests and pressure groups Joseph hired the management consultant firm, McKinsey, and asked for advice from a group based at Brunel University. But after the years of delay the reorganisation was rushed through, to fulfil Joseph's promise that it would coincide with Walker's revision of local authority boundaries. The legislation, introduced in February 1973 and passed in July, established 14 Regional, 90 Area, and 200 District Health Authorities. The first were given responsibility for planning, and the second were linked to the new local government bodies. The District Health Authorities, in charge of policy implementation, would be monitored by Community Health Councils, whose powers were augmented late on in response to representations from many sources, including the Consumer's Association, Conservative Central Office, the House of Lords, and Joseph's colleague Michael Alison. The idea that representatives of the local community could have an effective voice in the running of the NHS made limited appeal to health professionals; it also dismayed Joseph, who was troubled by the thought that these bodies afforded scope for unqualified "people who will make careers and names out of mischief and distortion".[47]

Thanks to the management consultants, at least the legislation was adorned with high-sounding slogans. There was to be "maximum delegation downwards", coupled with "maximum accountability upwards". But beyond this Joseph's expert advisors had little to contribute; he might with more profit have consulted the works of Franz Kafka. In practice the slogan ought to have been "maximum confusion everywhere". The result of all the consultations was "an attempt to please everyone [which] satisfied no-one". For Labour, John Silkin made the best quip: "If you have tiers, prepare to shed them now". As Rodney

---

46. Webster, *Health Services, Vol. II*, 454–5, 466–7.
47. KJ minute of 19 October 1972, quoted in Webster, *Health Services, Vol. II*, 518–9.

Lowe has observed, Joseph had put together "a Byzantine structure in which there were too many tiers of administration and in which senior executive officials were responsible to authorities which might include among their members one of their subordinates". In a machine which was more Heath Robinson than Heathite, no one could take an independent decision; morale among staff, already low, sank further. There were now far more bureaucrats to feel depressed; the reorganisation made a significant contribution to the swelling of the ranks of public employees under Heath. In the year after the Government fell the post-war civil service peaked at 747,000 employees; staff numbers in the health and social services reached almost one million. It was easier to count this impressive army than to work out exactly what it was supposed to do; when the Act came into operation it was discovered that no one had sent a circular laying down the functions of each tier, and when the relevant documents were requested at DHSS headquarters no file was discovered. A circular had to be drawn up within 24 hours, causing the official drafted in to oversee the reorganisation to dub the whole process "an absolute shambles". Unlike the pensions scheme, at least the reorganised Health Service was not still-born, and to an extent Joseph was protected from bad publicity by the fact that Tory voters were far more exercised by Walker's changes in local government (which included what proved to be the temporary excision of Rutland county). But its life was even shorter than that of the FIS; the great Health Service reorganisation found its euthanasia under the first Thatcher Government.[48]

Crossman, who accused Joseph of exhibiting "terrifying" managerialism, also predicted that the regional authorities would become "satrapies". In a similar vein the *Guardian* thought that these bodies "would become self-perpetuating oligarchies with no time to listen to the customers". The patronage powers of the Secretary of State were extensive enough even after Walker's intervention. One official later complained that "Once you had run through [Sir Keith's] friends, you had no one else" to appoint. This was slightly unfair, since Joseph had very extensive contacts within the worlds of business and management; if his "friends" (and all of his relatives) had been excluded the pool of available talent would have been seriously drained. But in his anxiety to appoint people who shared his priorities Joseph showed under Heath a tendency to overlook sensitivities about the boundaries between the proper and improper uses of political patronage. Before the end of 1970 the Prime Minister had been forced to dissuade him from bringing in "a consultant from a large building construction firm with which he was associated" (as the historian of the NHS tactfully put it) to advise on the hospital programme. More seriously for the Secretary of State, *Private Eye* tried to involve him in its campaign against

---

48. Lowe, "The Social Policy of the Heath Government" in Ball and Seldon (eds), *Heath Government*, 206, 191n; Hennessy, *Whitehall*, 261; Rodney Lowe, *The Welfare State in Britain since 1945* (Macmillan, 1993), 186; Klein, *Politics of the NHS*, 99; Timmins, *Five Giants*, 295–6.

the corrupt architect John Poulson. The *Eye* was able to show a strong connection between Poulson and Bovis – notably in the partnership venture which produced a tourist centre at Aviemore in Scotland. But the investigation, which in the summer of 1972 claimed the scalp of Reginald Maulding, did nothing to hinder Joseph's career. After a while the *Eye* even dropped its habit of referring to its intended victim as "Sir Keith Bovis".[49]

Joseph was often treated harshly in parliamentary debates during these years. If he felt that he never received sufficient praise for his significant acts of compassion, he certainly was greeted with a full quota of odium for the relatively small cuts in the benefits bill which he regularly announced in the Commons. The same minister who cost the taxpayer millions in his botched and bureaucratic reorganisation of the NHS had earlier abolished the Social Security Local Advisory Committees, recouping for the Treasury the princely sum of £130,000. In tandem with this measure, Joseph informed MPs that he was bringing to an end retrospective payments of benefit for the first three days of sickness, injury or unemployment for workers. The saving here, at an estimated £19 million per year, was far more substantial. But the offence caused still outweighed any gain for the elephantine social security budget, and Shirley Williams was able to protest that Joseph's statement had been leaked in advance to the press. Telling evidence of his weariness of all the barracking is the fact that much of the committee work on the reorganisation Bill was left to junior ministers, although Sir Patrick Cormack remembers that in the first couple of years Joseph had invariably taken the leading role at all stages of important legislation, showing a remarkable attention to detail.[50]

The fact that the cuts package of March 1971 was unveiled while the controversy over the Industrial Relations Act was at its height showed just how much room for improvement there was in Joseph's presentation of bad news. Within a few days of the announcement he was shown the opinion survey which branded the Conservatives as "hard-hearted". But he pressed on with measures which could do little to propitiate his party's critics. In 1971 he asked Sir Henry Fisher (who had won an All Souls Prize Fellowship in the same year as Joseph and was now a retired judge) to head a committee looking into the procedures for checking abuses of the benefit system. When the committee reported in March 1973 Joseph announced the appointment of sixty additional inspectors; special efforts would be made to track down people who continued to work while claiming supplementary benefit. As one element of a balanced approach to all kinds of fraud this would have been unexceptionable. In an editorial comment *The Times* pointed out that "the belief that abuse is considerable and

---

49. Webster, *Health Services, Vol. II*, 511, 383; Klein, *Politics of the NHS,* 96, 98; private information; *Private Eye,* 24 April 1970, 9 February 1972. We are most grateful to Francis Wheen for his help with the *Eye* archives.
50. *Hansard*, vol. 814, cols 1151–61, 29 March 1971; interview with Sir Patrick Cormack.

relatively unchecked provides a political obstacle to devoting sufficient re-sources to social security". But when Joseph was asked in the Commons to advocate equally strong action against those who evaded income tax he studiously ignored the question and referred instead to claimants' unions who betrayed "a hectoring approach to public officials who are carrying out their hu-mane duty". His comments had a personal edge; in response to a crackdown which they felt to be unduly intrusive the East London Claimants' Union had pledged itself to investigate Joseph's own financial affairs and to mount a round-the-clock surveillance of Mulberry Walk.[51]

When Barber's drive for economies bit hard in the 1973 spending round, pensioners and people on invalidity benefit were given more substantial benefit increases than the temporarily sick and the unemployed, and Joseph explored the possibility of taxing (what were assumed to be) "short-term" benefits. The historian of the welfare state, Nicholas Timmins, notes that Joseph's tenure of office coincided with the beginning of "harsher treatment for the unemployed relative to other claimants", but he adds that the Secretary of State did not draw an *explicit* distinction between the "deserving" and the "undeserving" poor. As we have seen, though, Joseph had been using even more emotive language to mark this supposed distinction since 1968 at the latest – although he saved those words for more secluded settings.[52]

Yet Joseph's personal reputation emerged unscathed from all this: so much so that in January 1974 Edward Heath chose to praise him for his "imaginative social policies", which proved how far the party had changed since 1945. On the Labour front-bench Barbara Castle was a severe critic, but she was one of the few members of her party who felt that way. Another opponent was the Conservative Sir Gerald Nabarro, whose Private Member's Bill against smoking was talked out on the orders of an embarrassed Secretary of State. Joseph himself was a "militant" anti-smoker who chewed his handkerchief rather than lighting up when particularly nervous (he also refreshed his spirit by consuming enormous quantities of chocolate – rather a perilous pastime for one of his constitution). But although he described the results of smoking as "without exaggeration, a holocaust of human life" he was reluctant to legislate against the powerful tobacco lobby, which was as good a friend to the Conservatives as the pension industry. He negotiated a voluntary code which resulted in the first health warn-ings to appear on cigarette packets, but this did not satisfy Nabarro who, as a recently reformed smoker, outstripped even Joseph in his militancy. He was still campaigning for tougher action when he died in November 1973.[53]

---

51. *The Times*, 29, 30 March; *Hansard*, vol. 856, cols 184–5, 8 May 1973.
52. Timmins, *Five Giants*, 287–8.
53. Webster, *Health Services, Vol. II*, 424; Sir Gerald Nabarro, *Exploits of a Politician* (Arthur Baker, 1973), 171–200. Joseph also earned the lasting resentment of Lord Longford, for refusing a request to have the imprisoned Moors Murderer Ian Brady switched to Broadmoor, where he could be treated for psychological disorder; see Lord Longford, *Diary of a Year* (Weidenfeld and Nicolson, 1982), 115.

There was a general feeling that Joseph meant well – a sentiment which was reinforced by his speech to the October 1973 party conference, in which he stood up to demands from the rank-and-file for the withdrawal of benefits from strikers. Actually this proposal had been discussed several times within the Cabinet, and Joseph had no objection to it in principle.[54] As for the "shirkers and scroungers" whom he had denounced in Opposition, he told the conference "to face the fact that there are a large number of people who are not employable". He asked whether his audience really wanted to inflict starvation on the children of those "who cannot manage their lives effectively, too inadequate to hold down jobs". Confronted with real evidence, as opposed to the claims of right-wing activists, Joseph had discovered that the population of "shirkers and scroungers" was somewhat smaller than he had thought, even though the existence of such people was "absolutely infuriating". Compared with the cynical conference performances of some of his Conservative successors in his job it was a meritorious speech, acclaimed by the *Spectator* as an "oratorical revelation". Joseph's treatment of sensitive questions evidently reflected his habit of allowing civil servants to guide him for set-piece speeches. But his keepers were not on hand when he addressed the Maidstone Women's Conservative Association in June. "Unfortunately we cannot shoot them", he had jested after deploring the activites of benefit cheats.[55]

Just one meticulously prepared speech had been enough to leave Joseph invulnerable to the charge that he was personally uncaring. On 29 June 1972, at the Church House in Westminster, he addressed a conference organised by the Pre-School Playgroups Association. The text of the speech had been passed around within the DHSS for some time, in the expectation that it would be well publicised and, hopefully, set off a public debate.[56] The Secretary of State had also organised a three-day seminar at All Souls as part of his preparation (he had been elected by the College as a Distinguished Fellow in 1971, eleven years after his previous "London Fellowship" had expired). In the first section of his speech Joseph went through the usual rituals, praising the work of the Association, totting up the various grants provided by government, and promising that apart from giving subsidies the state would make no attempt to interfere in the detailed work of this commendable voluntary organisation. In the second section, however, he opened his real theme. "The family", he declared, "is the basis sanctified by the main sources of our western religious traditions for the healthy development of children. Yet the family is under attack . . . There are many forces at work to discourage and distort priorities and attitudes. Many

---

54. Private information.
55. *CPC Monthly Report*, No. 94, January 1974; *Minutes of the Ninety-First Conservative Party Conference, 1973*, 98; *Yorkshire Post*, 30 June 1973; *Spectator*, 20 October 1973.
56. Timmins, *Five Giants*, 289.

parents had no chance when they were children to learn what a happy home can be".[57]

Thus Joseph introduced the main problem of society as he saw it, and he had a snappy phrase on hand to catch the attention of the media. Many families in Britain were trapped in what he called a "Cycle of Deprivation". By "deprivation" he meant "circumstances which prevent people developing to nearer their potential – physically, emotionally and intellectually – than many do now". These circumstances, he argued, tended to be transmitted from parents to children. Joseph was careful to ensure that he was not misunderstood; he was saying that "in a proportion of cases, occurring *at all levels of society*, the problems of one generation appear to reproduce themselves in the next".[58] Despite this qualification he acknowledged that "the most vulnerable are those already at the bottom of the economic ladder", and that the problem had become more evident since the war because some had been left further behind while average living standards had risen significantly.

To support his case, Sir Keith buried his audience under the usual avalanche of research findings, concluding after his exhaustive review that there was a clear need for additional studies. Having identified the difficulty, the obvious question was what could be done about it? Part of the answer was to find additional resources, and Joseph allowed himself a surprising tribute to his own FIS which constituted "a frontal attack on family poverty". But then he trespassed on treacherous ground. "There is no doubt", he said, "that, if effective family planning were more widely practised and if those most in need of advice could be reached, the size of the problem – that is, the numbers caught up in the "cycle of deprivation" – could over the years be kept below what it would otherwise be". Although he was careful to point out that "large families can have great strengths and value", on the other hand there was:

> a positive association [between such families and] delinquency, low intelligence and poor reading skills – factors likely to propel people into the "cycle" . . . It may be that there is less time for conversation between parents and children, for reasoned explanation and for individual support for each child . . . where parents with large families are immature and in danger themselves of marital breakdown, the more so when they are also poor and badly housed, the children are virtually sure to be deprived.[59]

---

57. The concept, sometimes called "the cycle of degradation", had been the subject of debate almost from the beginning of Joseph's time at the Department. KJ, "The Cycle of Family Deprivation", in *Caring for People* (CCO, 1972), 31.
58. *Ibid.*, 33 (emphasis added).
59. *Ibid.*, 37–8.

Joseph noted that he was reviewing family planning policies in co-operation with Margaret Thatcher at Education.[60] In fact discussions within the DHSS had begun in September 1970, when Joseph asked his officials to prepare plans for a programme of sterilisation in the case of "really bad problem families". In February 1971 he had provided funds for a free family planning service in socially deprived areas, and later instigated pilot schemes in Leicestershire and Cheshire for a co-ordinated drive to publicise the virtues of birth control. Family planning, however, would not be enough, and Joseph urged that more effort should be made to teach people parenting skills, beginning with school lessons on the subject.[61]

The family had become the focus of another Joseph crusade. It was hardly a new departure for him. In a 1966 article he had referred to the problems arising from "low income families with several children, and from households with self-inflicted wounds". He wrote then that these "often form in turn the same sort of household from which they came, and the cycle repeats itself".[62] Even earlier, in his policy work on Arts and Amenities in the late 1950s he had noted that young people lacked a "sense of purpose and of personal responsibility", and now this generation was itself raising children. Back in 1959 Joseph had suggested that work camps, or youth clubs held in redecorated church halls, might offer outlets for the surplus energy of adolescents.[63] Now the situation seemed far more urgent. From Joseph's perspective at the DHSS the problems of the family seemed to underlie the full range of Britain's present difficulties, from social disorder to economic stagnation. There were specific threats to the work of his own Department; he was well aware, for example, that the plight of the "Cinderella services" would be far worse if family members stopped caring for their sick, disabled or elderly relatives at home. Now possible solutions had suggested themselves. The Secretary of State had been greatly impressed when one social services director told him that nearly all the problems in his town of 20,000 households were caused by 800 families. Among other things, these figures suggested that a relatively limited, well-targetted effort by the state could greatly reduce (if not eradicate) the worst problems. The civil servants who moved over from the Home Office when the children's department was transferred to the DHSS were informed that, rather than "running approved schools" as they had expected, they "were going to put the family right". One

---

60. However, Mrs Thatcher was far more wary of this field. When asked in 1974 by a "senior backbencher. . . with Central Office backing" to explore the population problems she "refused to have anything whatsoever to do with them, and ensured that they never came near to surfacing as party policy". As usual, her instinct served her very well. See Ramsden, *Winds of Change*, 441–2.
61. Webster, *Health Services, Vol. II*, 418; Timothy Raison, *The Tories and the Welfare State: A History of Conservative Social Policy since the Second World War* (Macmillan, 1990), 81.
62. KJ, "Help for the really needy", *Daily Telegraph*, 22 March 1966.
63. Third draft of report on Arts and Amenities, CRD 2/52/13, CPA, Bodleian Library (additional comments by Joseph kindly supplied by Dr Richard Weight); *Guardian*, 4 June 1973.

of them recalled that "Our jaws dropped somewhat". Joseph's own jaw was kept very busy by the family over the years; although it caused him more trouble than any of his other crusades, he chose the subject as the theme of his last public speech. The "cycle" concept was well received at the time, across the political range from the *Guardian* to *The Times*. According to Timmins, it "brought forth profoundly different interpretations. To some on the left it looked like an appeal for community action. To others it appeared an attempt to blame the individual and deny the state's responsibility. To the right it appeared to be a defence of the family. To many it seemed just common sense".[64]

For Peter Townsend at the CPAG, however, the speech was a new version of an old thesis; namely that "many of the poor are poor because they do not conform with prevailing social values and need to be disciplined or taught so to conform for their own good". As such, it had to be recognised as no more than "a piece of ideological special pleading". The ideology in question was nineteenth-century liberalism of the type which had produced the notorious New Poor Law of 1834. In making his speech, Townsend thought, Joseph had unwittingly exposed the double-standards inseparable from his own creed. Liberalism of this stamp combines a theoretical tolerance of all beliefs and lifestyles with a practical discouragement of noncomformity outside well-defined parameters; it talks loudly about letting people run their own lives as they choose, but uses the full power of the state to indoctrinate those who lack sufficient resources to exercise real choice. Townsend believed that Joseph had betrayed his real thinking by concentrating on relatively cheap remedies for poverty. Had he been serious about alleviating (let alone "eliminating") poverty, he would have come out in favour of massive redistribution away from the rich, but he belonged to a government which had concentrated its efforts on reducing taxes for the affluent.[65]

Townsend was certainly justified in ignoring Joseph's qualifying remark which identified problems at all levels of income; in his private correspondence within the Department the minister was far more explicit in his references to "probably-doomed children" being produced by "the least accessible elements of the population".[66] But the thinking behind "the cycle of deprivation" was far more complex than Townsend allowed. As one profile-writer put it, "It is easy to parody the concept. It is much harder to fault the thinking or mock the compassion behind it". Although he had never wholly accepted the positive theoretical case for economic redistribution Joseph acknowledged that more resources should be devoted to the poor. And whereas nineteenth-century liberalism depended on the existence of a sizeable pool of ill-educated,

---

64. Timmins, *Five Giants*, 289–90.
65. Peter Townsend, "The Cycle of Deprivation – A Social Indictment", 30 March 1974, Townsend Papers.
66. See, for example, KJ's memo of 16 September 1971, in PRO BN 13/1631.

impoverished workers, Joseph really did want to eradicate poverty. What critics could not know is that the speech, and associated press interviews, required a great deal of courage. In one article he remarked that "What terrifies one is the home in which parents don't talk to each other and this occurs across the class barriers". Whether or not he was thinking of his own home when he said this, he seems to have been trying to compensate for falling below the standards of parenting which he had laid down. There are several anecdotes from this year which illustrate his attentiveness to other people's children. One Sunday Joseph rang his Principal Private Secretary, Graham Hart, to arrange a talk about a forthcoming speech. Hart went round to Mulberry Walk, taking with him his five-year-old son. At the sight of the child Sir Keith's eyes glinted. At one point, while he was going over the draft, Hart glanced over to see the Secretary of State and the boy playing "matching pairs" on the floor with a pack of cards. In his own home, however, his wife was able to spend far more time with the children, and the antagonism between the couple was sure to spill over into a feeling of something like estrangement between Joseph and the children he loved so much.[67]

Whether or not he was a consistent ideologue at this time, Joseph was totally sincere in his desire to help break the "cycle of deprivation" – which in itself was a most useful concept for others who wanted to publicise Britain's social problems. The difficulty was that Joseph's diagnosis had betrayed enough of his own preconceptions to make researchers wary. Even if Sir Keith was sincere, would their follow-up work on the subject be twisted by others within his party to provide superficial backing for a right-wing social agenda? The research groups which Joseph set up at the time of his speech demonstrated a counter-vailing bias, away from the individual family and towards more substantial social structures. A published summary of the findings concluded that "famil-ial continuity" was only part of the problem which Joseph had identified. Detailed research revealed that more than half of the children born in "deprived" homes actually broke out of the "cycle". More important were geographical factors. Some regions were disproportionately affected, and within regions inner-city areas showed particularly high levels of delinquency and illiteracy. There were also "socio-cultural" disparities; black people, for example, "continued to be disadvantaged in educational attainment, employ-ment and housing". In conclusion, although the studies supported Joseph's contention that poverty was not the sole cause of the problem, his further point that deprivation could co-exist with rising national prosperity prompted the unwelcome hint that what really mattered was not low incomes as such, but "relative deprivation" – the gap between the rich and the poor. The authors distanced themselves from the view that "nothing short of massive social

---

67. *Guardian*, 4 June 1973; interview with Sir Graham Hart; private information.

change" would be effective, but they were clearly sympathetic to further distribution of wealth, and a significant rise in public expenditure. As a final irritant
to Joseph, they preferred to use the word "disadvantage" rather than his own
"deprivation".[68]

Differences of perspective, in both methodology and ideology, made
constructive dialogue unlikely between Joseph and the researchers. But at best
the findings on the family had introduced complexity to what had seemed a
very neat theory about the transmission of "disadvantage"; indeed, it seemed
that in many cases a background of economic or emotional distress could act as
a spur to effort.[69] In contemplating possible remedies, Joseph was confronted
once again with the puzzle he had tried to address in *The Responsible Society*.
Despite their obvious good intentions, had the architects of the "welfare state"
only made matters worse, by removing incentives for self-improvement? Since
his early days in the One Nation group Joseph had felt the attraction of the
simple answers which could provide the basis for decisive action. After the
difficulties he had encountered at Housing he was more than ever torn between
his desire to reach firm conclusions and the need to think things through at
length before stating his position. Hence the "cycle" speech, which was not so
much a call for an open debate as an invitation to researchers to find empirical
support for ideas which he held already. On social matters broad generalisation
was unusually hazardous, but as Joseph grew older and his opportunities for
action began to slip away he was increasingly tempted to run the risks. He
acknowledged his ignorance of the poor at the 1971 party conference, when he
admitted that "no-one knows very much about motives at this level of income".
But the absence of satisfactory knowledge on the subject offered him a free
licence for speculation. In his own mind, the division between the "deserving"
and the "undeserving" poor was becoming clearer than ever; in reality it was
blurring still further, as the era of guaranteed full employment came to an end.

Joseph was able to cut through these dilemmas when a problem could be
brought home by the plight of a particular individual. Just after the 1971 party
conference William Compton Carr, a former Conservative MP, received an
eighteen month jail sentence for fraud. It was noted in court that he had been
forced to borrow money from banks and from friends to meet the expenses of
Westminster life, but eventually he "found himself in the clutches of a money-
lender", which started his downfall. Until 1964 Compton Carr had been MP
for Barons Court, where Joseph fought his first election; the Secretary of State
was one of the unnamed generous friends, and unlike the rest of his colleagues

---

68. Michael Rutter and Nicola Madge, *Cycles of Disadvantage: A Review of Research* (Heinemann, 1976), 1–2, 325–7.
69. Joseph himself later recognised that there was no connection between a solid upbringing and a desire to succeed in business; by that time he had been influenced by Samuel Smiles, whose work implied that poverty was the best forcing ground for entrepreneurs; see *House of Lords Debates*, vol. 536, col. 325, 26 February 1992.

he continued to stand by Compton Carr in his time of adversity. Years later Joseph asked the newly elected MP George Walden to act as his PPS. Despite his passionate interest in education Walden was unhappy at the thought of losing his political independence, and made the excuse that this unpaid position would prevent him from supplementing his earnings from journalism. To Walden's dismay Joseph arranged for him to meet the Party Treasurer, Lord McAlpine. The result was a generous commission to write some pamphlets (Walden sent back the money but decided that he could no longer refuse the position). Yet Joseph's largesse extended well beyond his parliamentary colleagues. At the DHSS he often intervened personally to support requests for special help from the public. As a minister he was well placed to cut through red tape when it was delaying the supply of medical equipment. But he was also ready to assist when confronted with a difficulty unrelated to his post at the DHSS. Among many unpublicised acts of charity, he once offered to pay for the repair of a musical instrument belonging to a man he had encountered at a hostel for the homeless in his constituency. He took the instrument to London, and when he discovered that it could not be mended he bought a new one.[70]

In short, while Joseph's sympathy could easily be engaged in certain instances he was still a mixture of enthusiasm, compassion, and ignorance on the subject of poverty. After the "cycle of deprivation" speech another ingredient was added; a degree of confidence that he had something worthwhile to say about the plight of the poor, so long as he used a few eye-catching phrases to advertise his message. It was to prove a fateful combination – for Sir Keith Joseph, and for his country.

---

70. *Minutes of the Eighty-Ninth Conservative Party Conference*, 1971, 102; *The Times*, 22 December 1971; private information; George Walden, *Lucky George: Memoirs of an Anti-Politician* (Allen Lane, 1999), 266; interview with Pam Nicole, whose letter to Joseph concerning a delay in the supply of an artificial leg to a relative brought a swift response from Joseph; letter to authors from Richard Barker (Conservative Party agent for Leeds North-East).

Chapter 10

"Not a Conservative"

Edward Heath proved to be a most unlucky Prime Minister – above all, in the enemies he collected. Ranging from Enoch Powell on the Right to Arthur Scargill on the Left, many of Heath's detractors were as eloquent as they were sure of the truth of their various convictions. Vehemently opposed to what they regarded as a flabby post-war "consensus", they despised Heath as its living embodiment – even more so after he negotiated Britain's entry into the EEC. Throughout Heath's premiership Powell and his allies maintained an opposition ostensibly based on principle, although Powell's critics pointed out that he had only discovered a threat to British sovereignty in EEC membership after leaving the Shadow Cabinet. Yet the Government's majority was large enough for its internal critics to be ignored with safety, even on the European issue where shrewd tactics and the co-operation of Labour's own dissidents ensured the passage of the necessary legislation. The formation of the Economic Dining Club (1972) and the Selsdon Group (1973) revealed that some right-wing Conservative MPs were so disillusioned with government policy that they were prepared to sacrifice their prospects for future advancement.[1] Ultimately, though, it was the Left which brought Heath down,

---

1. For the Economic Dining Club and the Selsdon Group see Cockett, *Thinking the Unthinkable*, 211–16.

even if the Right proved much more enthusiastic in kicking him after he had lost power.

From a right-wing perspective the story of the Heath Government is a melodrama in two acts. In the first, the Prime Minister talks of a "quiet revolution" and attempts to carry it out, clutching his "Selsdon Programme". But the opening act is tragically brief. After the interval a new character emerges. Unnecessarily frightened by rising unemployment, Heath becomes a semi-socialist (at least), nationalising everything in sight, losing all control of the money supply, and finally capitulating to union power. During this disastrous period Heath listens only to people who think as he does; wise counsellors are available to him, but he makes sure that they have no say over the crucial decisions and sacks at least one of them (the martyred Nicholas Ridley, dismissed from a junior post at Trade and Industry). At the end of the play the wise people rise up and depose Heath, amid the relieved applause of the audience; he exits stage left, sulking.

Ideological factions invariably produce mythological accounts of the past, complete with a cast of heroes and villains; this helps to foster a sense of their own cohesion. It was understandable that the Conservative Right should attempt to rewrite recent history after the disaster that befell the party in February 1974. As we have seen, Heath laid the foundations of the enduring Selsdon Park myth through his pronouncements in the run-up to the 1970 general election, culminating in the manifesto foreword which contrasted his inflexibility with Wilson's opportunism; after winning the election, his inability to deploy the skills which had made him such a successful Chief Whip left his decisions vulnerable to the distortions of others. Heath and his colleagues were genuinely troubled as unemployment approached (and then briefly topped) one million. Undoubtedly some of them experienced visions of the 1930s, and imagined privations which subsequent welfare reforms had largely rectified.[2] But for the Prime Minister mass unemployment was only a terrible symptom of an underlying malady – the failure of industrialists to invest in Britain's future, notwithstanding the incentives his government had provided. Heath's frustration is usually illustrated by his well-known attack on Lonrho as "the unacceptable face of capitalism" but a more detailed picture is provided by a speech to the Institute of Directors in the autumn of 1973. Making no concessions to the feelings of his listeners, he reminded them that:

---

2. In some cases it seems that ex-ministers emphasised this point for political reasons – i.e. to demonstrate the contrast with the Thatcher governments. Not only did this obscure the underlying reasons for Heath's reflationary policy, it was also a tactic of dubious value, since after 1983 it was evident that Mrs Thatcher could hold on to power even though unemployment had risen to levels unimaginable in the early 1970s. See, for example, Jim Prior's remarks quoted in Phillip Whitehead, *The Writing on the Wall: Britain in the Seventies* (Michael Joseph, 1985), 82.

> When we came in we were told that there weren't sufficient inducements to invest. So we provided the inducements. Then we were told people were scared of balance-of-payments difficulties leading to stop-go. So we floated the pound. Then we were told of fears of inflation: and now we're dealing with that. And still you aren't investing enough.[3]

For their part, the captains of industry and their financial backers thought they had every reason to hold back, at least until Heath had beaten Labour for a second time. In particular, they rightly suspected that the trade unions would not co-operate with a Conservative Government so soon after they had fended off Barbara Castle's attempts to restrain their power. Investors were free to make their profits in other countries, which kept no unemployment statistics but had plenty of prisons for strikers. Before Heath fell from office they were provided with a new opening for their funds, when Chile's Augusto Pinochet began to conduct his experiment in economic liberalism and social repression.

The investment strike caught Heath unawares, and when he wrote his uncompromising foreword to the 1970 manifesto he had also failed to take full account of the extent to which British industrialists had been conditioned by Labour's economic strategy. Rolls Royce had negotiated a very tight contract with the American company Lockheed, in the expectation that the Wilson Government which had overseen the deal would be around to bail them out if things went wrong. At first Heath offered financial support, but when this proved inadequate he encouraged the company to call in the receiver and, when no private firm would take on the responsibility, his Government nationalised its aero-engine division as a temporary measure. In later years this prudent decision became a horror story for the Conservative Right; later decisions to help Upper Clyde Shipbuilders and to introduce an Industry Act which greatly increased state powers of economic intervention were taken as "proof" that the Prime Minister had discarded his earlier principles. But Heath's objective had not changed. He wanted an economy which was strong enough to compete in European markets. Those who deplored Britain's entry into the EEC tended to forget that the domestic economy would still be subjected to these pressures even if Heath's negotiations had failed. At a time of rapid technological change there was an urgent need for heavy investment to maintain even Britain's reduced post-war economic status. If private individuals and institutions were unwilling to do the job, it was felt that the Government should arm itself with sufficient powers to step into the breach. Priority was given to existing industries of strategic importance, and to technological innovation. Similarly, it was only after the CBI and the trade unions had failed to agree a voluntary deal

---

3. Quoted in Harold Wilson, *Final Term: The Labour Government 1974–1976* (Weidenfeld and Nicolson, 1979), 4.

on prices and incomes in the autumn of 1972 that the Government legislated for them; as Tony Barber's advisor put it "almost all Conservative Ministers detested [this] as much as their subsequent critics".[4]

At first Barber's economic measures were cautious, but pessimistic growth forecasts persuaded Heath to switch to an ambitious strategy of reflation, beginning in the summer of 1971.[5] The Government's timing proved disastrous. In the first quarter of 1972 world commodity prices began a steep rise which culminated in the quadrupling of the cost of oil after the outbreak of war in the Middle East. For a year economic growth was very impressive by post-war British standards, but it was accompanied by rising inflation (almost 10 per cent for 1973). While the oil crisis grabbed the headlines, few people noticed that the cost of food imports increased by almost 20 per cent during 1973; the problem for Britain was accentuated by the breakdown of the Bretton Woods system of currency management, which after July 1972 caused the "floating" of the pound (downwards). The statutory incomes policy had to be made increasingly flexible (and complicated) as the British economy was rocked by successive blows. When the coal miners began an overtime ban in November 1973, to support their claim for a pay increase which broke the terms of Stage Three of the Government's policy, the country's plight was brought home by nightly power cuts and by the introduction of a three-day working week (during which there was a suspiciously small decline in national output). Heath came under increasing pressure from some colleagues to call a general election; only after the miners voted for an all-out strike on 5 February 1974 did he give in, and call what became known as the "Who Governs?" election for 28 February.

Always keen to place the worst interpretation on Heath's decisions, Enoch Powell claimed that the election was a "fraudulent" attempt to exploit a temporary crisis, since the Prime Minister had a workable parliamentary majority and his mandate had more than a year still to run. This argument might have pleased constitutional purists – and those who felt that inflation has nothing to do with the size of wage increases – but coming from Powell it was a cloak for his fear that the Conservatives would win the election, thus ending his own leadership chances forever. Within the Cabinet, Whitelaw and Francis Pym spoke up against an early poll at the first of two meetings held to discuss the subject. The views of two former Chief Whips were weighty enough to encourage anyone else with serious doubts to speak up, but no one did and at

---

4. Brendon Sewill, in R. Harris and B. Sewell, *British Economic Policy: Two Views* (IEA, 1975), 51.
5. Although one well-informed observer remembers a "sudden change in November 1971", Heath's memoirs confirm that Barber's mini-budget of July 1971, which set an annual growth target of 4.5 per cent, was the real turning point. See *Course of My Life*, 345–6; cf. Donald MacDougall, *Don and Mandarin: Memoirs of an Economist* (John Murray, 1987), 188, which focuses on a Chequers meeting on 3 November 1971. This was certainly an event of real importance, but it is best regarded as the occasion on which Heath first presented his existing policies as a grand economic strategy.

a second meeting there was unanimous agreement. To his constituents Sir Keith Joseph countered Powell's attack, saying that a new electoral mandate was needed to fight "extremists". He did not add the further point which had occurred to his colleagues: that if the party lost at least they could feel that they left office with their honour intact.[6]

While a poll in February 1974 might have worked to the advantage of a Wilson, for Heath it was the worst possible time to go to the country. Voters were left in no doubt of the difficulties which lay ahead, or the sacrifices which would be required of them. But many felt that they had elected Heath in 1970 precisely to avoid this ordeal and now blamed the country's plight on the Prime Minister rather than their own conduct. As usual the Liberal Party offered a tempting refuge for disgruntled Conservatives. Powell introduced a new option, by declaring that his principles would not allow him to stand as a candidate of his old party, and, later, that he had cast a postal vote for Labour. His supporters could follow his example – ignoring the fact that the Opposition had compiled its most left-wing manifesto since 1945, and justifying their actions to themselves because Wilson had made a transparently "fraudulent" promise to renegotiate the terms of Britain's entry to the EEC.

The Conservative manifesto, *Firm Action for a Fair Britain*, neatly summarised Heath's dilemma in February 1974. He had to appear both tough and compassionate – the pilot who would weather the storm and hand out seasickness tablets before the boat reached calmer waters. It was decided that in this task Sir Keith Joseph would have to be called to the bridge. Well in advance of the election a poster campaign was launched; two of the advertisements, with the slogans "Doing Something for Everyone" and "For all the People", relied heavily on Joseph's record at the DHSS. During the campaign itself he featured in the second Conservative television broadcast, along with grateful nurses and pensioners. The section of the manifesto devoted to Health recorded numerous achievements and promised more of the same. On Social Security faith was still pinned on progress towards a negative income tax, for which legislation was promised in the next Parliament. As a first step, child tax credits would replace the existing system of allowances, and for the first time families with only one child would be included. After the storm over the Family Income Supplement, it was thought advisable to stress that the new

---

6. *Yorkshire Post*, 14 February 1974. In July 1984 Joseph told Geoffrey Goodman that both he and Mrs Thatcher had spoken up at a Cabinet sub-committee, strongly questioning the need to hold an election at all. Goodman wrote up the story for his weekly *Daily Mirror* column, but the newspaper's proprietor Robert Maxwell demanded that this should be removed from later editions. Goodman was told that Maxwell disbelieved the story; probably he was also concerned that the appearance of the article might undermine his self-appointed role as an honest broker in the 1984–5 dispute. Goodman rightly believed that the honesty of his source (which he refused to reveal at the time) was unimpeachable, but Joseph's disclosure is not substantiated in Lady Thatcher's memoirs and the truth will not emerge until the release of full Cabinet records for 1974. Interview with Geoffrey Goodman; cf. *Path to Power*, 232–3.

system would bring help to those in need without subjecting them to a means test.[7]

The record of the DHSS under Joseph's stewardship was upheld with pride by many Conservatives. Nigel Lawson was among the candidates in February 1974 who reported that the party message was going down well among pensioners.[8] If anything the tactic of holding up Joseph as the exemplar of caring Conservatism worked *too* well. The *Sunday Mirror* reported that he was referred to in Downing Street as "our statutory humane minister"; whether this was true or not, it reinforced the impression that Joseph was far too good for a Conservative Cabinet. Joseph's speech to the 1973 party conference had been warmly received, provoking talk among delegates of his potential as a future party leader; it was noted that when Heath mentioned Joseph by name as he closed the conference there was a roar of approval from the audience. Before the election *The Times* acknowledged that Joseph had "contributed more than most to the Tory Party's prospects of success". Yet by February 1974 some of the gilt had been rubbed from the record. In June 1973 Joseph had described many of Britain's hospitals as "archaic museums", painting this dire picture only to highlight the improvements that would be made under his "record building programme". After December 1973, when Barber announced a particularly heavy hit against capital spending on hospitals in his package of public expenditure cuts, Joseph's earlier rhetoric left his party exposed to additional criticism. Replying to an Opposition motion which deplored the "savage" cuts, Joseph said that he regretted this necessary decision but characterised the changes as a temporary "abatement of the rate of acceleration" in expenditure. While attacking the government's policies, the next Labour speaker excepted the Secretary of State from his indictment of a callous government.[9]

As we have seen, Joseph had never disguised his view that in social matters some cases were far more "deserving" than others. But when Labour's Brian O'Malley lashed both the Secretary of State and his pension policy in November 1972, he was forced to acknowledge that not only "hon. members opposite but people in all walks of life" considered Joseph to be "a compassionate man who cares about the problems of the underprivileged". Joseph could not be blamed for his virtual immunity from personal attack; neither was it his fault that he tended to be given credit for specific decisions of the whole Cabinet. Yet it was a remarkable irony that the man who had done most to create the

---

7. David Butler and Dennis Kavanagh, *The British General Election of February 1974* (Macmillan, 1974), 39–40, 75, 159.
8. Eight months later, fighting the unwinnable seat of St Pancras North for the second time, John Major stressed the "Cinderella services" when explaining his beliefs to canvassers; Anthony Seldon, *Major: A Political Life* (Phoenix 1998), 44–5.
9. *Sunday Mirror*, 25 March 1973; *Leeds Searchlight*, Nov 1973; *Yorkshire Post*, 30 June 1973; Spectator, 20 October 1973; *Hansard*, vol. 868, col. 122, 28 January 1974. When Labour returned to power in February 1974 the budget cuts were cancelled.

hard-faced "Selsdon Man" image should have escaped so lightly while the rest of his colleagues were damned for their alleged inhumanity. As a minister he had continued to shun publicity for acts which others would have flaunted. For example, it was remembered that one night he decided to investigate the work of a charity for the homeless on London's Embankment. "He just went, anonymously, no press, no TV. He just put on his coat and scarf and went down there on his own".[10] Of course, these surreptitious missions were bound to become public knowledge in the end; and when they did so they tended to win for Joseph more public esteem than if he had organised splendid photo-opportunities every time he ventured outside his Department. There was absolutely no calculation in this; neither was Joseph trying to promote himself when he deliberately drew media attention to his "cycle of deprivation" speech, or to the problem of child abuse, highlighted by the tragic case of the murdered Maria Colwell.[11] But Joseph's image sometimes gave rise to assumptions which were at odds with reality. For example, the introduction in 1972 of a £10 Christmas bonus for pensioners was widely assumed to be a personal initiative of the soft-hearted Baronet. He had foreshadowed this idea in one of his first speeches as an MP, but from the Whitehall perspective it had looked less attractive to him. When a one-off payment of this kind was suggested by Barber's advisor Brendon Sewill, Joseph had shown no enthusiasm for a benefit which would go to rich and poor alike; he also opposed it in Cabinet, on administrative grounds. At a press conference before the election of February 1974 Heath was accused of having forced his Secretary of State to include in the manifesto the proposal to reduce supplementary benefit for strikers. Clearly irritated, Heath claimed that Joseph had supported even tougher measures. Indeed, in February 1971 *Private Eye* reported that the Secretary of State had instructed his officials to cut off the benefits of striking postal workers, only to be told of "possible counter-productive effects".[12]

The national focus on Joseph's work at the DHSS seems to have helped him at local level. In 1970 he had been worried about his own seat, and by February 1974 the situation looked even more doubtful despite a very good showing by Leeds Conservatives in the local elections of the previous year. For the first time since 1950 the Liberals fielded a candidate in Leeds North-East. The Labour candidate believed that this would work to his advantage, and that recent minor boundary changes would not affect the outcome. In public the Conservative agent expressed the usual confidence, claiming that he had been "inundated" with offers of help. But there was an additional factor clouding Joseph's

10. *Hansard*, vol. 847, col. 261, 28 November 1972; *The Times*, 20 February 1974; Robin Wendt's recollection quoted in Timmins, *Five Giants*, 290.
11. For an examination of Joseph's key role in publicising the Colwell case, see Nigel Parton, "The Natural History of Child Abuse: A Study in Social Problem Definition", *British Journal of Social Work*, vol. 9 (1979), 427–51.
12. Interview with Brendon Sewill; Heath, *Course of My Life*, 414; *Private Eye*, 12 February 1971.

prospects of winning, in the month which marked the eighteenth anniversary of his entry into Parliament. Britain had remained studiously neutral during the Arab–Israeli Yom Kippur war, imposing an arms embargo on each side. Many within the Jewish community felt that in practice this would damage Israel more than its Arab enemies, and the British Zionist Federation compiled a list of MPs who had failed to vote against the government. The culprits included Joseph, and in February 1974 he depended more than ever on the loyalty of his Jewish constituents. According to her memoirs, both Margaret Thatcher and Joseph were "intensely irritated" by the government's position. This may well be true, but Lady Thatcher does not reveal whether or not the dissident duo gave voice to their feelings during what she claims were "difficult discussions" in Cabinet (and Heath does not remember hearing their views at the time). In any case, Joseph had always distanced himself from Zionism.[13]

The *Leeds Searchlight* noted that, as in 1956, Joseph often defied freezing weather to meet as many constituents as possible during the campaign. On polling day they registered their gratitude by giving Joseph an increased majority of 7,260 (on a turnout nearly 10 per cent up on 1970). The *Searchlight* exulted that this "resounding majority and vote of confidence" had been achieved despite Joseph's commitments in the national campaign, and the help that he had given to the Conservative candidate for York. The outcome was "a tribute to his many years' service as a devoted constituency member and his proud record of achievement as a leading Minister". In fact the increased majority concealed an adverse swing of 6.1 per cent in Leeds North-East, but the detailed picture supported the *Searchlight*'s assertion that Joseph had built up a personal following. Research suggested that over the country as a whole the Liberals took votes almost equally from Labour and the Conservatives in this election, yet Joseph's share of the poll fell less than that of his Labour opponent – despite the attentions of the British Zionist Federation, which seems to have made inroads on Mrs Thatcher's Finchley stronghold.[14]

Nationally the Liberals achieved almost 20 per cent of the vote, although only fourteen MPs were returned. But they were not the most notable victims of Britain's disproportional representation. The Conservatives received the most votes, but had only 297 MPs compared to Labour's 301. Fittingly, their fate was sealed by Heath's determination to put his country's interest above his party. His attempts to solve the crisis in Northern Ireland broke the historic Tory link with Ulster Unionism, depriving the Conservatives of up to eleven seats. In the negotiations which followed what was a "hung" election result,

---

13. *Yorkshire Post*, 14 February 1974; Butler and Kavanagh, *Election of 1974* 227; Thatcher, *Path to Power*, 230; interview with Sir Edward Heath. A former President of the Conservative Friends of Israel remembered that Joseph took no interest in the activities of the organisation; letter to authors from the late Sir Robert Rhodes James.
14. *Leeds Searchlight*, March/April 1974; Ramsden, *Winds of Change*, 382.

Heath offered the party whip to only seven (moderate) Unionists, who refused to co-operate while their four hard-line colleagues were excluded. This meant that any deal with the Liberals would still leave the Conservatives short of an overall majority, and exploratory talks with the Liberal leader Jeremy Thorpe led nowhere. In short, had Heath been willing to lay down his principles for his political life he could have clung on in Downing Street. Yet his fulfilment of the constitutional duty of trying to form a government before submitting his resignation was held against him in some quarters. Margaret Thatcher wrote years later that the "horse-trading" alienated the public which hated a "bad loser" – exactly the image which she and her allies created for Heath after 1975.[15]

Ian Gilmour has recalled that Sir Keith Joseph was the only member of the Cabinet who seemed uneasy about the "horse-trading" while it was going on. Probably this arose not from any sense that Heath had behaved improperly, but from a new disillusionment with the government's record which made him reluctant to carry on the fight. Since the turn of the year, while the rest of the country had been obsessed with the struggle between the miners and the elected government, Joseph had been preoccupied by a problem which threatened to destroy the only certainty in his life – his financial security.[16]

The humbling of Bovis is an instructive illustration of the economic history of Britain between 1970 and 1974. At first the company's profits rose, buoyed up by a boom in the housing market. Financial institutions saw property as a hedge against inflation, and poured money into building and development projects. Close relationships were forged between companies in these sectors. The Bovis board committed itself wholeheartedly to the trend in 1971, acquiring the Brighton-based Twentieth Century Banking Corporation which Harry Vincent saw as "a logical extension of our operations". Bovis also engaged in a bitter, prolonged and ultimately unsuccessful takeover bid for the shipping group Peninsular and Orient (P&O). In September 1972, when this deal was discussed, Bovis was valued at £160 million. In 1973 its share price rose to 362p. But by the end of that year high interest rates had caused a slow-down in the building industry; the property "bubble" had been pricked. Twentieth Century Banking was brought close to collapse, as similar institutions were hit by an "unprecedented withdrawal of deposits". On 20 December 1973 the Bovis share price plunged to 83p, prompting the management to announce that new takeover talks were under way. Public statements concealed the extent of the problem. An audit by the National Westminster Bank indicated that the plight of Twentieth Century Banking was far worse than the Bovis board had thought, and the parent company "faced closure within twenty-four hours". In their panic the board turned to P&O which as a major

15. Thatcher, *Path to Power*, 239.
16. Gilmour and Garnett, *Whatever Happened*, 288–9.

shareholder had an interest in the survival of Bovis but nevertheless drove a hard bargain, valuing its former predator below £25 million. Three days before the general election Joseph's cousin Neville Vincent advised shareholders to accept an offer which spelt the end of Bovis's history as an independent company. Unsurprisingly, the response was positive.[17]

The lesson of Bovis's downfall was obvious. Although a background role had been played by government policy – which included, ironically, the easing of controls on the financial sector in line with economic liberal thinking[18] – individuals within the company had miscalculated badly. As the company's historian has written, "Bovis had succumbed to the get-rich-quick philosophy"; a significant role in the disaster was played by three young entrepreneurs recruited in 1969. The problem extended beyond the cavaliar approach to new acquisitions. Supremely confident that the property bubble would continue to inflate, Bovis had started work on ambitious new construction projects without even opening negotiations with potential buyers and lessees.[19] Presumably Joseph's personal role in all this was insignificant; even if he discussed developments informally, the board was no longer dominated as it had once been by his close relatives. But his share in the disaster threatened to engulf his comfortable lifestyle.[20] Having talked rather flippantly of millionaires and bankrupts, he almost found himself plummeting from one status to the other overnight. He confided to friends that his fortune had been cut to a third or a fourth of what it had been, and interviewed on television later in the year he fended off repeated questions about his wealth with rueful references to his reduced circumstances. Of course, other members of his family were involved in the misfortune; in the interview Joseph made reference to "a whole network . . . of relatives" who had suffered major losses.[21]

During all the controversy which surrounded Joseph during 1974, the press never made an explicit connection between his behaviour and the Bovis crash. Under the new regime, indeed, the company recovered relatively quickly. But

17. *The Times*, 21 December 1973, 26 January 1974; *Sunday Times*, 27 January 1974.
18. See Noel Thompson, "Economic Ideas and the Development of Economic Opinion", in Richard Coopey and Nicholas Woodward (eds), *Britain in the 1970s: The Troubled Economy* (UCL Press, 1996), 73.
19. Cooper, *Building Relationships*, 96. In response to an intervention by Dennis Skinner in May 1979, Sir Keith claimed that the Heath government had "created credit conditions which led businessmen to expect that the boom would *not* last for ever" (*Hansard*, vol. 967, col. 709, 21 May 1979; italics ours). Since his own company had operated on precisely the opposite expectation, the word "not" seems so bizarre as to lead one to suspect a misprint. But it is confirmed from contemporary news reports. The only explanation is that Sir Keith had blotted anything discreditable to business from his personal history of that crucial period.
20. However, the error of recruiting the entrepreneurial "whiz-kids" had taken place before his return to office in 1970, and it seems that he was playing a central role in the development of Bovis's strategy at that time. His Mulberry Trust associate, Sir Nigel Broackes, recalled that Joseph set up a meeting early in 1970 with a view to arranging a merger between Bovis and his own firm, Tra-falgar House. See Nigel Broackes, *A Growing Concern* (Weidenfeld & Nicolson, 1979), 119.
21. KJ interview with Llew Gardner.

it was not surprising that the blow knocked Joseph off-balance, and that when the loss of office was added to the impact he began to behave like a man desperate for some safe anchorage in a strange world. If the cost could be restricted to pounds and pennies on a balance sheet, the collapse of Bovis would have been easier to take. But the proud and reputable firm built up by his father – from just a horse, a cart and a telephonist, according to Joseph's inaccurate memory – had suddenly become the lamest of all lame ducks. It had also been affected badly by industrial action during the Heath years. Another of Joseph's concerns, the Mulberry Trust, had ceased operating as an independent venture in the early 1970s, amidst claims of financial malpractice unconnected to board members. At the same time, Joseph's painstaking efforts at the DHSS were endangered by the threat of electoral defeat. He needed an explanation for all this: preferably (and understandably) one that was simple enough to apply across the whole range of problems which had suddenly crowded in upon him. Even before the election Joseph had consulted Alfred Sherman on the subject of Yom Kippur. But Sherman also deployed his rhetorical skills in persuading Joseph that the British economy faced bankruptcy. According to one account Sherman added a clinching personal challenge: "You have to do something about the state of the country".[22]

Sir Alfred Sherman has no recollection that Bovis was discussed at this time, but the recent calamity must have been in Joseph's mind and a plausible explanation was at hand. Monetarists believed that the secondary banking crisis was the result not of numerous mistakes by firms like Bovis, but the inevitable culmination of "a world-wide monetary binge" in which the British government had fully participated; as such, they took it as an excellent argument for their own case.[23] Joseph was unlikely to struggle for long against this sweeping logic, containing as it did a strong suggestion that the problem, at root, was a moral one (significantly, he would later characterise his preferred economic policy as one which guaranteed "monetary continence"). Joseph had more reason than most to question the argument in detail; why, for instance, had other construction firms (like Sir Nigel Broackes's Trafalgar House) emerged from the crisis bloodied but unbroken? His brooding led to the conclusion that the Heath government had been as bad as any of its post-war Conservative predecessors – if not worse. While he had been shunted into a siding at the Elephant and Castle the money supply had been allowed to spiral out of

22. Ranelagh, *Thatcher's People*, 174. According to Sherman, two articles he wrote for the *Daily Telegraph* in the summer of 1973 triggered off Joseph's brooding about the economic situation. Sherman also attacked the "social engineers" who had undermined community through the New Towns of the 1960s. Joseph was well acquainted with Sherman's views on this subject, but he might have been impressed by a personal attack on the "creators and propagandists" of the New Towns who "characteristically" had not been forced to live in them; see Cockett, *Thinking the Unthinkable*, 232–3.
23. Sherman in *Jewish Chronicle*, 16 December 1994; David Smith, *The Rise and Fall of Monetarism* (Penguin, 1987), 43–4. Interview with Sir Alfred Sherman.

1. "Both vulnerable and pugnacious . . .": KJ (front row, far right) during his first year at Lockers Park *(by kind permission of Lockers Park School)*.

2. "An introverted young man . . .": KJ at Harrow *(by kind permission of the Keepers and Governors of Harrow School)*.

3. "A man of unquenchable energy": Sir Samuel Joseph as Lord Mayor of London, with Winston Churchill. Lady Joseph (Keith's mother) is in the background *(private collection)*.

4. The war "didn't mature me as much as it matured others": KJ as an officer of the Royal Artillery *(private collection)*.

5. "An aura of unstoppable success": Sir Keith and the first Lady Joseph *(by kind permission of NE Leeds Conservative Association)*.

6. Fighting the Trend: KJ campaigning in Leeds North-East during the ill-fated 1966 Conservative general election campaign *(by kind permission of NE Leeds Conservative Association)*.

7. "The Tory Jack Kennedy": a dynamic and good-natured KJ charms his constituency supporters, 1966 (©Yorkshire Post).

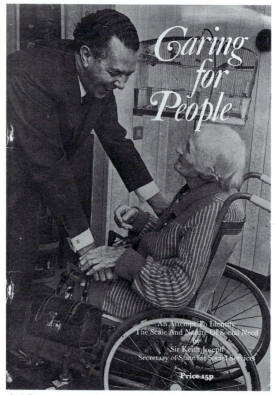

8. "Our statutory humane minister": KJ as Secretary of State for Social Services *(by kind permission of CPA, Bodleian Library)*.

9. Every Prime Minister needs a Willie . . . and a Keith. William Whitelaw, Margaret Thatcher and Sir Keith Joseph at a meeting of the Shadow Cabinet, 1975 *(by kind permission of CPA, Bodleian Library).*

10. "Mrs Thatcher's 'svengali'": KJ, April 1978 (©Yorkshire Post).

11. The bogey men of British politics, 1979.

12. Leeds, July 1981: Another business closes as monetarist policies hit home (© Yorkshire Post).

13. "A toff down on his luck": after the Brighton bomb and back-bench uproar over student loans, KJ faces more protests, December 1984 (© Yorkshire Post).

14. "It was as if he had been granted an extra life": Lord Joseph with Yolanda *(courtesy of Lord Harris of High Cross)*.

control, bringing ruin to the British economy. Joseph now believed that the expansionary policy of the Heath Government had not only been excessive; it had never been necessary in the first place. Unemployment had risen because of the sharp monetary squeeze under Jenkins; if Heath and Barber had been patient, the economy would have picked up momentum anyway. A different politician would have consoled himself with the thought that, at least, he bore no direct personal responsibility for the disaster. But Joseph could not satisfy himself so easily. He had been a relatively senior member of the Cabinet. Although his speeches before the 1970 election had shown his attachment to a more rigorous brand of economic management – and he had pointed out the likely effects of the Jenkins "squeeze" at the time – he could now blame himself for having shown inadequate "moral courage".[24]

It was greatly to Joseph's credit that he could fight an election campaign in the midst of great personal anxiety; indeed in January 1974 he scored one of his greatest parliamentary successes, fending off an attack by Michael Foot after casting aside his prepared speech.[25] But his victory at Leeds North-East provided only a temporary respite from misery, from which he could no longer hope to find a refuge at home. Before the election Tony Barber had decided to leave politics, and back in Opposition Heath required a Shadow Chancellor. As late as January there had been press speculation that Joseph would succeed Barber at the Treasury. But a month after the election his party leader denied him for a third time. The shadow job went to Robert Carr, who had been Home Secretary for the last twenty months of the Heath Government. Heath's intended offer to Joseph is not known; presumably, in the belief that he had done well at the DHSS, he would have asked him to shadow the post he had just vacated. But Joseph made it clear that if he were not to become Shadow Chancellor no other portfolio was of interest to him. Instead he demanded a roving policy role; in addition, he wanted an immediate and radical review of economic policy. Heath turned down the latter proposal, having just fought an election on a platform which he believed to be right. As yet there was no personal animosity between the two men, but after Joseph's demand for a rethink they could no longer consider themselves to be friendly colleagues.[26] According to Sherman this had been one of the most important meetings in post-war British history: "If [Joseph] had got the Shadow Chancellorship, there would have been no 'Thatcher Revolution'", he claimed. The feeling that

24. Roth memorandum; Cockett, *Thinking the Unthinkable*, 233; for an eloquent and concise expression of the monetarist critique of the Heath government, see Ralph Harris's contribution to *British Economic Policy 1970–74*, esp. 12–13. For Joseph on Jenkins, see *The Times* report of speech in Dudley, 31 October 1969.

25. *Hansard*, vol. 867, cols 1219–27, 21 January 1974.

26. Even after the events of 1974–5 Heath remained puzzled rather than angered by Joseph's conduct, describing his former colleague as "A good man fallen among monetarists"; "Prophet without Honour", *New Statesman*, 29 October 1976.

Joseph should have been given the job was not restricted to the right wing; it was enhanced at the beginning of April, when he delivered an attack on the Chancellor Denis Healey which was regarded as almost the only exception in a series of subdued speeches from the Opposition front-bench. But the real opportunity had been missed in July 1970. If Joseph had been chosen to replace Macleod he would have been securely tied into the government's evolving economic policy. Contrary to Sherman's view, it is highly unlikely that Joseph would have proved equally malleable if Heath had appointed him Shadow Chancellor in the circumstances of February 1974.[27]

After the election Joseph hoped to "pick up old friendships" among economic liberals. But his cycle of disillusion was completed when he called on Alan Walters at the London School of Economics. Walters, a regular author for the IEA, had been introduced to Joseph by Enoch Powell many years before, and advised him for a short time at the DHSS; later he wrote a paper arguing that the Heath government had retreated from its original virtue. Joseph had forwarded this document to the Prime Minister; when he reported back to Walters he said that Heath had "convinced him that the policies [stood] a good chance of succeeding" and the consequences of inaction would be much worse. Now, when the ex-minister visited Walters at the LSE he received an icy reception. Walters did not go so far as to refuse a hand shake, but Joseph recalled that he was "very scornful, scarcely willing to talk". Whatever his merits as an economist, Walters clearly had a sound grasp of psychology. If he had thrown his arms around Sir Keith he would not have commended himself half so well. Before long he swallowed his grievances against his obsequious visitor, and agreed to meet Joseph and Sherman for discussions in the latter's flat off Kensington High Street. Suitably impressed by the tirades of these strong characters against his former colleagues – and by the certainty with which they spelled out the course which the government should have taken – Joseph enticed Mrs Thatcher and his old Bow Group friend David Howell to hear the critique in further meetings at Mulberry Walk.[28]

After the Walters brush-off, Joseph was ready for trouble from the IEA, but he disarmed Ralph Harris by saying "I'll understand if you think it's a waste of time. I came to see you ten years ago, and we've been discredited in between". Later Joseph gave a dinner for the forgiving Harris and Seldon at Locketts (now Shepherd's) restaurant near the IEA's offices in Westminster. He was seeking their advice on a new project – to set up a think-tank with the specific aim of "converting" the Conservative Party to free market ideas. The idea was Sherman's, but it was a logical culmination of Joseph's activities when he was last in Opposition.

27. Ranelagh, *Thatcher's People*, 129; *Hansard*, vol. 871, cols 990–1001, 1 April 1974; interview with Lord Prior.
28. Hugo Young and Anne Sloman, *The Thatcher Phenomenon* (BBC, 1986), 28–9; Halcrow, *Joseph*, 59; Cockett, *Thinking the Unthinkable*, 233; interview with Sir Alan Walters.

As a non-partisan organisation the IEA had no desire for intimate links with the Tories, but Harris and Seldon were happy to offer advice. Harris assured Joseph that he was untroubled by the idea of two similar organisations conveying roughly the same message; here as elsewhere competition would benefit everyone. The new body would "carry on where the IEA left off", by translating the broader analyses of IEA economists into proposals for government policy.[29]

Harris suggested that the organisation should be called the Centre for Alternative Policies; he also warned that Sherman was a powerful ally but very provocative and should be kept in the background. But Sherman had now replaced the civil service as Joseph's indispensable crutch, providing with ease the texts for set-piece speeches and articles which the ex-minister thought he could never get right. The psychological value of Sherman was even greater than his verbal dexterity. In John Ranelagh's phrase, he "put a burr under Joseph's saddle", telling him more than once that he lacked "backbone". In January 1977, for example, he remarked after reading a Joseph paper on Industrial Strategy that "unless you are prepared to make a much bolder attack it is better saying nothing at all". Some people would have been offended by such forthright comments; for Joseph, they provided a stimulating supplement to his own self-criticisms. Sherman soon emerged as the real driving force behind the new organisation, although to his own chagrin he was not immediately offered the post of Director of Studies. In private Joseph never contradicted those who pointed out his ally's eccentricities (and he could deliver a passable impersonation of Sherman in full cry). But even when he was teasing there was an unmistakable undertone of respect; he always emphasised the central role that Sherman had played in opening his eyes to the full benefits of the free market.[30]

As a member of the Shadow Cabinet, Joseph had to seek Heath's approval for his venture. He explained that he wanted to set up a research body to examine the reasons for West Germany's economic miracle. It was suggested at the time that Heath had put forward the original idea for Joseph to head a research group, seeing this as "a chemistry set with which he would hopefully blow himself up". But far from encouraging the plan Heath was suspicious from the start. What he may have done is to show genuine interest in the European aspect of the proposal. He gave his permission, but revealed his misgivings by insisting that Adam Ridley of the Conservative Research Department (CRD) should join the board. He also approved a further suggestion that Joseph and Mrs Thatcher should hold a series of dinner-meetings with leading industrialists, but the leader's allies Lord Carrington and James Prior were also included

29. Ranelagh, *Thatcher's People*, 130; interview with Lord Harris of High Cross; Arthur Seldon in *Independent on Sunday*, 12 December 1994; *Jewish Chronicle*, 16 December 1994.
30. Interview with Lord Harris of High Cross; Ranelagh, *Thatcher's People*, 174; Sherman memorandum to KJ, 5 January 1977, Sherman Papers, Box 3; private information; Andrew Denham interview with Lord Joseph, April 1991; John Hoskyns, *Just in Time* (Aurum Press, 2000), 27.

– to keep an eye on things, as Prior later admitted. This arrangement did not last very long. Meanwhile the press was told that Joseph's Shadow Cabinet brief was "to roam around Europe and the world exploring the advantages of the private sector and then to report back to the Conservative leader". He would have more freedom to "roam" than ever before, because although he maintained an office and a secretary at Bovis he did not return to the company's board after the election.[31]

Joseph's admirers have done him a great disservice by congratulating him on the "considerable guile" with which he played on the West German angle to secure Heath's permission to set up his new organisation, which was eventually called the Centre for Policy Studies (CPS). Although West Germany had a "social market" system under which the centrality of free enterprise was recognised by all the main parties, its founders accepted the case for an active state and the redistribution of wealth. The healthy West German economy depended crucially on good labour relations; ironically this owed much to the British, who after the war had forced private companies to accept worker representatives at board level, in order to punish them for supporting Hitler. Margaret Thatcher later denounced the West German model as "a kind of corporatist, highly-collectivised, 'consensus'-based economic system, which pushed up costs, suffered increasingly from market rigidities and relied on qualities of teutonic self-discipline to work at all". But it did continue to work – even under Social Democratic governments – and Lady Thatcher's remark invites the suggestion that the British character lacks the necessary element of "self-discipline" to underpin the kind of prosperous, civilised economy which Joseph envisaged. In particular, as A. J. Nicholls suggests, the West German people exhibited a "willingness to abjure short-term gains for the benefit of long-term success". The country was certainly no paradise for asset-strippers. National and regional banks treated their clients with patience and consideration even in times of recession; companies valued their employees, and benefited from a generous welfare system which provided subsidies to enable them to retain their workforce in bad times instead of just laying them off. West German capitalism, in short, was like a large-scale model of Bovis as it had been in the early days; significantly, the proportion of family owned firms in West Germany was twice as large as that in Britain.[32]

Clearly there was much to attract Joseph in both the theory and practice of the West German social market. As we have seen, he had used the phrase "social market" before the 1970 general election. One of the first things he published

---

31. Cockett, *Thinking the Unthinkable*, 236; James Prior, *A Balance of Power* (Hamish Hamilton, 1986), 97; Interview with Lord Prior; *The Times*, 14 March 1974.
32. Cockett, *Thinking the Unthinkable*, 236, 253; John Ardagh, *Germany and the Germans* (Penguin, 1991), 129; A. J. Nicholls, *Freedom with Responsibility: The Social Market Economy in Germany, 1918–1963* (Clarendon Press, 1994) 395; Will Hutton, *The State We're In* (Jonathan Cape, 1995), 264–6.

after the foundation of the CPS acknowledged that Conservatives "must take into account what kind of society our economic ideas will operate in, and how our economics will interact with our society". An early suggestion for the name of what became the CPS was "Institute for a Social Market Economy".[33] But later Joseph allowed himself to be persuaded that the phrase "social market" should be dropped from his speeches. It was felt that it "only diluted the understanding of market economics and the need for a return to the primacy of the role of the market in economic affairs". This argument (advanced by Joseph's academic friends William and Shirley Letwin) was an early sign that his combination of economic rigour and social concern could be "diluted" by ideologues even more determined than himself. The subsequent removal of the "social market" dimension did simplify Joseph's message, but only at the expense of making his rhetoric seem harsher; it led directly to the kind of thinking which inspired Mrs Thatcher's famous denial of the existence of any such thing as "society". Presumably Joseph convinced himself that Britain could not hope to replicate the West German model, because the "British disease" was too virulent to respond to such soothing therapy. Despite the appearance of one or two CPS pamphlets on West Germany the original mission-statement was soon superseded by other priorities. The most detailed study (by Konrad Zweig – like Mrs Thatcher herself, an ex-J. Lyons employee) emphasised the role of the independent Bundesbank and argued that the West German combination of economic success and progressive welfare was perfectly compatible with British socio-economic thinking since David Hume and Adam Smith. Significantly, the foreword to the pamphlet was written by Geoffrey Howe rather than by Joseph; and even Howe felt it necessary to warn against "mechanical imitation of the German prototype".[34]

But this does not mean that Joseph was showing unwonted "guile" when he emphasised comparative studies of European economies in his conversation with Heath. At the time he was perfectly sincere; certainly he had no idea when he spoke to Heath that the foundation of the CPS would be interpreted by future historians as a masterstroke in a deep-laid conspiracy to unseat the leader. Others might have known in advance that the European concept of a "social market" would "not prove particularly fruitful" (as Lady Thatcher delicately put it), but Joseph felt himself to have slipped up by paying insufficient attention to continental practice, and genuinely believed that others would benefit from the CPS research. Although the findings concerning economic management proved to be uncongenial on the whole, in January 1977 Joseph countered Lord

---

33. *Sunday Times*, 9 March 1970; KJ, "The Economics of Freedom", in *Freedom and Order* (CPC, 1975), 7; KJ letter of 18 April 1974 in Joseph Papers, 10/8, CPA, Bodleian Library.
34. Cockett, *Thinking the Unthinkable*, 253; Margaret Thatcher, *The Downing Street Years* (HarperCollins, 1993) 751; Konrad Zweig, *Germany Through Inflation and Recession: An Object Lesson in Economic Management, 1973–1976* (CPS, 1976), 50, vii.

Kaldor's claim that he had put West Germany "in the dog house", asserting that it was "in many ways an example of rational economic policies". At least the research had provided backing for his belief that competition should be enforced by the state, and there were other important lessons to be learned. For example, a meeting in February 1978 between the CRD and officials of the West German Christian Democrats (CDU) produced details of a major job-creation programme by the latter party. This was more interesting to the CRD Director Chris Patten than it was to Joseph and Mrs Thatcher, but Patten could also report enthusiastically on the primacy which the CDU gave to the family in their social policy. On education, too, West German practice made a profound and lasting impact on Joseph's ideas.[35]

Even in retirement Joseph could lapse into his old habit of appealing to the experience of "the erstwhile devastated countries in North West Europe" as if this really did support the more abrasive brand of economic liberalism with which he came to be associated. The concept of the "social market" remained attractive (if not entirely "fruitful") for others, including Patten, David Owen and Professor Robert Skidelsky. Even John Major's first Chancellor Norman Lamont used the term, and the Social Market Foundation (SMF), originally linked to Owen's Social Democratic Party (SDP), gravitated towards the Conservative Party after the 1992 general election.[36] But by then Joseph was no longer ambivalent about the social market. He had come to share Lady Thatcher's view on (the now reunited) Germany. It was vital to publicise perceived defects in the German system which would be "imposed" on Britain if it ever became part of a federal Europe. Joseph explained that:

as [West German] prosperity increased and as younger people with fewer memories of [the war] came into the positions of power, the old lessons were forgotten. Bit by bit the rules and conventions were relaxed. Public sector bodies expanded: public spending grew faster than GDP: cartels and subsidies crept back: corporate taxes grew and grew: firms demanded and obtained subsidies: pensions and social security payments soared: health services were subsidised far beyond the contributions of the citizens: unions clamoured for more pay, more benefits, shorter hours, forgetting all the enlightened self-interest of their predecessors: and the social market economy designed for a self-reliant people became slacker and slacker.[37]

35. Thatcher, *Path to Power*, 252–3; KJ, "One-Eyed Vision", *Policy Studies* **10**(2), Winter 1989, 13; *The Times*, 12 January 1977; Chris Patten, memorandum of 16 February 1978, Joseph Papers 8/15, CPA, Bodleian Library.
36. On the SMF see Denham and Garnett, *British Think Tanks*, 178–81; for the "social market" concept in British politics, see Duncan Brack, "David Owen and the Social Market Economy", *Political Quarterly* **61**, 1990, 463–76.
37. KJ, *The Social Market Economy: Containing Some Lessons from Germany* (CPS, 1992), 21.

It was a familiar tale. Instead of Britain taking its cue from West Germany in the virtuous days of the social market economy, the Germans had apparently decided to imitate Britain in the worst period of its "statist" decline. But the account was typical of Joseph's historical sketches – long on assertion and short (to vanishing point) on detail. When, exactly, did the rot set in? (it could hardly be said that Chancellors Brandt, Schmidt and Kohl had forgotten the horrors of war). And the extensive list of wrong-headed policies was followed by a rather lame conclusion: "German competitive strength is still formidable but at risk. Its productivity is still higher than ours . . .". Even if one accepted Joseph's analysis, the sad story only confronted him more starkly with the key problem faced by anyone who wishes to combine economic efficiency with social compassion. If even the Germans had failed to get the balance right, and had sacrificed efficiency for the sake of welfare, what chance was there that the British could ever fare any better?[38]

Joseph's "guile" thus extended no further than his failure to inform Heath that the new Centre would only accept lessons from Western Europe insofar as they lent support to a radical free market programme.[39] But the notion that Joseph at this time made use of a previously undetected devious streak leaves him vulnerable to further allegations about his conduct. It has been suggested – more often in private conversation than in print – that the CPS used Heath's name in fund-raising activities which resulted in the diversion of money which would otherwise have gone to the central party.[40] The ill-feeling seems to have originated within the CRD, which was itself barred from such fund-raising. During the late 1960s there had been stirrings of revolt against a small unit set up by Ernest Marples and David Howell to study the public sector; this body, which had a licence to raise independent funds, was evidently in Joseph's thoughts when he established the CPS. But while the Public Sector Review Unit (PSRU) had been so innocuous that its activities have left hardly a trace, the CPS was of a nature to encourage louder protests from those who thought that the Research Department should enjoy similar privileges.[41]

On this point the CRD had a strong case, but the more serious allegation can never be proven. Certainly Joseph remembered having a very good response to his appeals for money. "Of the first 20 firms I wrote to", he later told Anthony Seldon, "I think probably 17 or 18 immediately gave their support". The initial

---

38. *Ibid.*
39. Had Joseph been open-minded about his inquiry into European economies he could have consulted his old Magdalen friend Andrew Shonfield, whose *Modern Capitalism* (1965) was a pioneering comparative study. But Shonfield's research had uncovered some awkward facts, including the revelation that West German prosperity had been achieved despite a higher tax burden (as a percentage of GNP) than Britain's. In 1960 the British figure was 27.6 per cent, compared with 33.9 per cent in West Germany. See Shonfield, *Modern Capitalism* (Oxford University Press, 1965), Chp. 12.
40. See William Keegan, *Mrs Thatcher's Economic Experiment* (Penguin, 1985), 47.
41. Interview with Brendon Sewill; on the PSRU, see Ramsden, *Conservative Party Policy*, 256–7.

target was £90,000 for each of the first three years. Some donors to the Centre had earlier been generous patrons of the party. Joseph and Mrs Thatcher were particularly grateful to James Goldsmith, who had provided a very substantial sum for Central Office coffers in 1970. While Joseph asked each of the twenty businessmen for £1,000, one was reported to have sent £15,000 and this generous sponsor may well have been Goldsmith. Yet Goldsmith was still enthusiastic enough to undertake voluntary work for the Conservative Party in the run up to the general election of October 1974, and this was the period during which Heath was told that donations were falling well below expected levels. Party finance is always a murky area, and conclusions are particularly difficult in the case of shadowy figures like Goldsmith (who gave money at this time as a private individual rather than using the resources of his companies). If there were others who transferred their financial loyalty from the central party organisation to the CPS, no one can be sure that their donations would otherwise have gone to Central Office; had the CPS not existed, the money might have stayed in the pockets of industrialists who were obviously attracted by the radical free market message which Heath rejected. Joseph could not be blamed if people in this category decided to back their ideas with their cash when he approached them. But it might have been better for him to resign from the Shadow Cabinet rather than to exploit Heath's name and his own senior standing in the party to promote a message which was so subversive of the Conservative record, and of its existing policy line. Such a decision might even have been more helpful to his cause; certainly it would have ensured that the CPS could have been launched amid the maximum publicity, and his own personal position would have been far less complicated. But Joseph was not a natural resigner; neither, on past form, was he likely to realise the damage that he might be doing to his party's immediate prospects. Like Heath he was thinking primarily of his country's needs, however strongly they disagreed in their diagnoses.[42]

Obviously the CPS required funds to pay for offices, support staff and publications. But its most important resource was the energy of Alfred Sherman, who began work "in a cramped basement room at 8 Wilfred Street", near Westminster. A public launch for the Centre was delayed by the October 1974 election. But the first board meeting was held on 12 June 1974, by which time Margaret Thatcher had been recruited as Vice-Chairman. The only definite decision was that Joseph should once again embark on a crusade to convert his party. Sherman had already begun work on a major speech to be delivered at Upminster, East London, on 22 June.[43]

42. KJ interview with Anthony Seldon, 29; Chris Ogden, *Maggie: An Intimate Portrait of a Woman in Power* (Simon & Schuster, 1990) 118; Geoffrey Wansell, *Tycoon: The Life of James Goldsmith* (Grafton Books, 1988), 192–3.
43. Cockett, *Thinking the Unthinkable*, 240–41.

While preparing a wider appeal Joseph had continued to nag away at the Shadow Cabinet. At the beginning of May he presented a paper on inflation, which acknowledged that "Deceleration of the money supply should be very gradual if unacceptable levels of unemployment are to be avoided". The need for caution was indicated by his assertion that Labour's "squeeze" of 1969–70 had been "too severe". Nevertheless, "consistent policies – involving some unemployment, some bankruptcies and very tight control of public spending – will be needed for at least five years". The goal of policy should be "to tread, if possible, a narrow path between hyperinflation on the one side and intolerable unemployment on the other". He added that the party should retain a policy on incomes (albeit one which was "selective and involv[ing] as few decisions and as little bureaucracy as possible") while dropping any intention to control prices and dividends. Indeed, wage increases should always be passed on to the customer through higher prices; "only when the public feels the results of wage claims will they turn against them". This admission of the link between higher wages and inflation was a marked deviation from the "purist" monetarist analysis; it also conflicted with Joseph's further suggestion that key workers ("e.g. those at power stations and in water") should be identified and offered "satisfactory terms and conditions". Joseph's colleagues could not agree that prices should be allowed to rip while incomes were controlled, but they were polite in their reception of a paper which implied no radical break with the practice of the Heath government. In the ensuing discussion it was agreed that while the money supply was important, "the real difficulty arose over timing and in deciding what the actual increase should be at any particular time".[44]

Heath showed his willingness to give Joseph a full hearing by agreeing to attend a seminar on monetary policy in the early summer. Presumably this meeting took place prior to the Upminster speech, since Joseph later told Anthony Seldon that he only went public after he had "failed to persuade Ted Heath to re-examine policies". In his attempts to educate the party leader Joseph was labouring under an ironic misunderstanding. Heath had been assisted at Balliol College, Oxford, by an Organ Scholarship and since his own son James had recently secured a similar award for his music studies at Exeter College, Oxford, Joseph assumed that Heath had no academic qualifications in economics. In fact he had taken his degree in Politics, Philosophy and Economics (PPE). Heath was a Keynesian by instinct and by intellectual conviction – and he already knew the merits of the monetarist case far better than Joseph imagined.[45]

Accounts of the seminar, which was addressed by Walters, Professor James Ball (of the London Business School) and the former Treasury official Sir

---

44. LCC 74/11, Meeting of 3 May 1974, CPA, Bodleian Library.
45. KJ interview with Anthony Seldon, 28; private information. In the early days of his government Heath had held a private discussion with Milton Friedman, and found the latter wholly unconvincing; interview with Sir Edward Heath.

Donald MacDougall, are conflicting if not wholly contradictory. One right-wing author has produced a very lively story. According to John Ranelagh, after MacDougall gave a broadly sympathetic critique of the Heath government Walters attacked him on predictable lines. The party leader then invited Ball to speak, expecting him to support MacDougall. Instead, Ball exclaimed that "Alan Walters was completely right!". Heath then summed up, "absolutely refusing to concede that his economic policy had been wrong". On hearing this, "Sir Keith Joseph's eyebrows shot up; Angus Maude shook his head and looked down; Sir Geoffrey Howe looked astonished, and Margaret Thatcher sat without expression with her back to the wall". "Heath", John Ranelagh concludes, "had lost his sense of objective reality".[46]

The latter accusation could be levelled with more justice at the author and his source, whose identity is concealed but can be readily guessed.[47] Recalling the incident in his own memoirs, Heath notes that everyone had known in advance that Ball would join Walters in pressing the monetarist case, which nevertheless "failed to cut any ice with the great majority of his colleagues". Another "less than admiring" Shadow minister remembered "Once [Joseph] brought two professors along. They knew even less than he did". It was remembered that no one in the monetarist camp had any answer when MacDougall suggested that they should take account of the velocity with which money circulated. At the end of the meeting Joseph tapped MacDougall on the shoulder and asked him for help on this subject – a long-standing problem for monetary theorists. MacDougall told him to consult Walters, adding that contrary to Joseph's assumptions the velocity of money circulation had declined in recent years. To an objective observer this statistic ought to have dealt a fatal blow to the monetarist case, since it implied that inflation should have been falling. MacDougall also remembers pointing out that an exclusive concentration on the money supply as a remedy for inflation would produce unemployment of over one million. Joseph replied that Walters "had worked out that nothing like that would be necessary". The reply missed MacDougall's point, which was that whether or not such an unemployment rate was *necessary* it was the likely outcome of monetarist policies.[48]

The meeting is a further clue to Joseph's state of mind at the time. Serious theoretical and factual objections had been raised against monetarism, and a majority of his colleagues had shown their disagreement. If the argument had

46. Ranelagh, *Thatcher's People*, 126–7.
47. John Campbell has pointed out that the head-shaking Maude was not a member of the Shadow Cabinet at the time; just conceivably, however, he might have been asked along for this unusual occasion. But in an interview with the present authors Lord Howe indicated that he doubted Ranelagh's colourful account; see Campbell, *Grocer's Daughter*, 267; interview with Lord Howe.
48. Ramsden, *Winds of Change*, 416; Heath, *Course of My Life*, 521; Simon Hoggart in *Guardian*, 31 July 1980; interview with Lord Walker; MacDougall, *Don and Mandarin*, 211–12.

proceeded any further the critics could have inquired about the mechanics of an economic policy which proposed to use monetary statistics as its main indicator: even if one accepted that the money supply could be accurately measured, to avoid over-corrections at any given time a Chancellor and his advisors would have to possess powers of prediction at least as great as anyone applying Keynesian ideas. But Joseph had aligned himself with people who were skilled enough to erase any doubts, and sufficiently forceful to convince him that it would be both prudent and productive for him to air his thoughts in public. After this umpteenth failure by the Shadow Cabinet to prove themselves worthy, the way was clear for Joseph to begin his new crusade. He was not deflected by an offer from Heath on 12 June to become Shadow spokesman on Home Affairs. Presumably the timing was a coincidence; the reshuffle took place because William Whitelaw had become Chairman of the Party. But the choice of Joseph for Home Affairs does look like another attempt to keep him as far away as possible from economic questions. The gambit failed; Joseph accepted the position, but reserved his right to speak out on other matters.[49]

The Upminster speech has passed into right-wing legend. Richard Cockett has proclaimed that "for the first time a senior Conservative[ex-]minister accepted that *both* political parties were responsible for Britain's decline relative to her neighbours, as *both* parties were responsible for those Keynesian, interventionist policies which had led to Britain's crisis in the mid-1970s". But Joseph had taken out the patent on this approach during his First Crusade of 1967. If there was anything new about Upminster, it was the sharper phrasing of Alfred Sherman:

> This is no time to be mealy-mouthed. Since the end of the Second World War we have had altogether too much Socialism. There is no point in my trying to evade what everybody knows. For half of th[ose] thirty years Conservative Governments, for understandable reasons, did not consider it practicable to reverse the vast bulk of the accumulating detritus of Socialism which on each occasion they found when they returned to office. So we tried to build on its uncertain foundations instead . . . . I must take my share of the blame for following too many of the fashions.[50]

There was plenty in the speech about excessive government spending, but nothing specific as yet about the new "fashion" of monetarism.

Most of Joseph's Shadow Cabinet colleagues – including at least one with some sympathy for the monetarist message – were deeply unhappy about the

---

49. *The Times*, 14 June 1974.
50. Cockett, *Thinking the Unthinkable*, 241; KJ, text of Upminster speech, 21 June 1974, reprinted in *Reversing the Trend: A Critical Reappraisal of Conservative Economic and Social Policies* (Barry Rose, 1975), 6.

Upminster speech. Members of Heath's team had developed over the years a strong collective bond which Joseph had now burst through. As in his speeches of the late 1960s he included himself in his indictment. He singled out the social services as an area in which "we seem to have generated more problems than we have solved", and admitted that "I fought my colleagues hard for extra resources". Indeed his general explanation for recent government failure – "We have tried to take short cuts to Utopia" – was more applicable to his own pre-1974 outlook than to that of any other senior Conservative. Revealingly, only in an interview of 1988 did Joseph admit that his "utopian" outlook made him an unusual Conservative; indeed, by then he had realised that "utopianism" is "apt to be a socialist proclivity". But his main thrust at Upminster was directed against the economic policies which, to his own frustration, he had never been able to influence in government. More seriously, like Angus Maude in 1966 he seemed to be inviting Harold Wilson to convert a precarious position into a comfortable governing majority by calling a snap election against an obviously divided Opposition. Joseph's timing could scarcely have been worse from the point of view of Heath's closest advisors, who were working hard to persuade him into projecting the Conservatives as the party of "national unity". At the time of Upminster Heath and Whitelaw made speeches presenting Tony Benn's plans for industry as the gravest threat to Britain as "One Nation". Instead of following that line, Joseph merely used Benn as the cue for an attack on the record of his own party.[51]

Tony Barber was particularly hurt by the implied rebuke from a colleague with whom he had enjoyed a very good working relationship. In his memoirs he published a letter which Joseph had written after the 1971 Budget, concluding with the statement that "You with Ted's backing have given the country a new chance. If the militants don't wreck our prospects your reform may be the start of a British miracle". Barber clearly thought that in printing the letter he was landing a blow against the man who had distanced himself "from some aspects of the policy which we had been pursuing together in the Heath Government". But very few even on the Right ever complained about the 1971 budget, which introduced ambitious tax reforms, and if Joseph ever commented on later budgets Barber does not say so. What the letter does indicate, though, is that Joseph was not too distracted by the work of his own department to gauge what was happening on the economic front; and his remark about the prospects for a "miracle" implied that the greatest danger to the Heath government came from outside forces, rather than the misplaced "good intentions" of ministers.[52]

51. Interview with Lord Jenkin; KJ, *Reversing the Trend*, 7, 8. Joseph made his admission about his "utopian" outlook in an untransmitted interview for the Brian Lapping Associates television programme "The Thatcher Factor". The transcript of the full interview (conducted on 17 November 1988) is in the LSE archives, Thatcher 003/13.
52. Barber, *Taking the Tide*, 104–5.

Much attention has focused since 1974 on the question of what exactly Joseph said or did whenever the Heath government discussed economic policy. In the spring of 1974 *The Times* dismissed Joseph's chances of ever becoming party leader because he had been so engrossed in his home patch that he "refused to engage in general cabinet dialogue". Some of his former colleagues remembered that he would be silent throughout meetings, then suddenly introduce a complex problem facing his own Department under Any Other Business when everyone else was preparing to leave. In 1977 Joseph told Tony Benn that "most things were done in committees, there was a sort of inner Cabinet and the Cabinet as a whole did not discuss things very much". At the Elephant and Castle he had been physically isolated, and this must have encouraged an unusual degree of preoccupation with the business of the Department of Health and Social Security. But none of this means that Joseph was uninformed of key economic developments; on the contrary, given his conviction that civilised welfare services depend on healthy growth he would have been neglecting his duty if he did not pay special attention to economic trends. In any case, since his Department was affected by the Treasury's more drastic measures he had to be consulted; he was called to at least one special ministerial meeting after Barber had embarked on his ill-fated measures to reflate the economy.[53] In conversation with Anthony King in 1973 Joseph admitted that his grasp of government policy as a whole was imperfect, but that as "a domestic animal" he was "concerned with the economy, with the Social Services, with the affairs that go on at home". As for the suggestion that Joseph temporarily forgot the message of his speeches before 1970, one of his supporters remembered that when the subject was broached one day over lunch he remarked that he kept the texts in a drawer. In July 1972 the *Spectator* noted that Joseph "has not retreated a whit from the stern and right-wing economic doctrines" he had laid down in the speeches of 1969–70. John Biffen remembers that in private Joseph made no secret of his doubts after 1971 – a memory supported by the fact that he read and passed on to Heath Alan Walters's written complaints. Even Barber hints at an awareness at the time that Joseph was "concerned at the way events seemed to be forcing us to adopt measures which we would not have considered at the beginning of the 1970–74 Parliament". But any misgivings he may have felt were never spelt out explicitly to his colleagues, and as he admitted at Upminster he continued to raid the Treasury for his expensive programmes, whereas he now realised that "when we place too heavy a burden on the private sector, we stall the engine".[54]

---

53. *The Times*, 20 March 1974; Tony Benn's unedited diary, 24 February 1977; Andrew Roth, *Heath and the Heathmen* (Routledge & Kegan Paul, 1972), 226. The meeting was held on 3 November 1971 – the same day as the key gathering at Chequers (see note 5 above).
54. KJ interview with Anthony King; interviews with Lords Carr and Biffen; Barber, *Taking the Tide*, 104; text of Upminster speech (CCO handout), 7; Patrick Cosgrave, "The man who told the truth", in *Spectator*, September 1974; *Spectator*, 22 July 1972.

The launching of a public critique of the Heath Government confronted Joseph with the dilemma of explaining his own role in recent events. His best known account, in the foreword to a 1975 volume of speeches, attributed his new clarity of vision to a revelation only granted to him *after* the General Election of February 1974: "It was only in April 1974 that I was converted to Conservatism. (I had thought I was a Conservative but I now see that I was not really one at all)".[55]

To Joseph's admirers, the story of the "conversion" meant that he was not only right but also unusually honest for a politician. In the *Spectator* Patrick Cosgrave hailed him as "the man who told the truth".[56] But as we have seen, Joseph's account was a distortion of his own intellectual development. From the start of his political career he had made no secret of his attachment to free enterprise, and, in particular, of the need for incentives to stimulate individual effort. The only new element in his speeches after the election was his emphasis on "monetarism" as an essential element of sound economic policy; but this was only a matter of degree, since he had shown sympathy for the doctrines of Milton Friedman before the General Election of 1970.

In some disarming comments to Anthony Sampson in December 1975 Joseph demolished his own claim to have undergone a "conversion" to monetarism and the more general free market case in April 1974. "Of course in 1969 I was singing the same tune as now", he said. "But I am more humbled by experience and more sure that it's the right tune". He had overlooked his own message when in office because he was "obsessed with squalor and avoidable misery, which a minister should never be . . . we concentrated on symptoms not on men and women".[57] From his point of view the misleading version of events that he had been presenting in his speeches was unobjectionable. It would have been undignified for him to suggest that he had been more enlightened than his colleagues before their troubles began, and his quasi-religious language helped to draw attention to the country's predicament. If people chose to regard Joseph himself in a new light, as the most suitable candidate to lead the party, that was up to them; had this been his conscious intention he would not have been so insistent that he was a late-comer to the Truth. Even so, the exaggerated confessions satisfied a psychological need. He could only summon adequate "moral courage" to attempt the conversion of his countrymen if he placed himself in the ranks of the sinful. The details mattered far less to him at the time than they did to his critics; his reviews of the past, after all, were only a means to a positive end. As he put it, "self-criticism is not the end of the matter, but only the beginning".[58]

55. KJ, *Reversing the Trend*, foreword.
56. Cosgrave "The man who told the truth", *Spectator*, September 1974.
57. Anthony Sampson, *The Changing Anatomy of Britain* (Coronet, 1983), 46–7.
58. KJ, *Reversing the Trend*, foreword.

Yet to the end of his life Joseph remained highly sensitive to the notion that during 1974 his behaviour had been improper. In a 1987 interview he admitted that Heath's subsequent resentment was:

> extremely understandable. After all, I never lifted my head and protested in all his four years as Prime Minister. I had been a Cabinet minister with perfectly good opportunities had I wished to say "hey, hey, we are making things worse rather than better". I never said it *because I never saw it*. That's the shame, my shame not anyone else's, and therefore Heath was entitled to say, and to feel afterwards, why didn't he say these things earlier?[59]

If this statement contained elements of distortion, as so often with Joseph he had only introduced them with the intention of magnifying his own failings. But he had missed the true root of the offence taken by the majority of his old colleagues – and by many of those who still sat with him in the Shadow Cabinet after the change of leadership in 1975. When he wrote that he had not been a Conservative until April 1974 he was implying – whether deliberately or not – that other senior figures within the party who had not changed their minds were heretics who should reassess their political allegiances. In his 1977 book *Inside Right* Sir Ian Gilmour, the spokesman on Defence, noted that "the allegation that Toryism has been betrayed does raise some apparently awkward questions. For one thing it implies that Churchill, Eden, Macmillan, Butler, Douglas-Home, Heath and Macleod were all either grossly misguided or were not true Tories". To Gilmour this seemed "improbable". In a chapter entitled "What Conservatism is Not", he turned the tables on Joseph and those who shared his views, decrying any attempt to make the Conservative Party "explicitly and primarily a capitalist party". Ideological thinking of any kind, Gilmour felt, was alien to the party's traditions; the particular creed advanced by the monetarists would also be divisive to the nation. Conservatives, he claimed, had always been eclectic in their economic thinking, "not merely because economic theories conflict but because the British economy fits into no clearly defined category". Even if Joseph's economic thought was compatible with Conservatism, his outlook was not: "the Conservative Party is not a church or a branch of theology. It has seldom gone in for heresy-hunting".[60]

In an interview of October 1974 Joseph himself conceded at least part of Gilmour's argument, agreeing that "the Tory party has never been a business

---

59. KJ interview with Anthony Seldon, 28; our italics.
60. Ian Gilmour, *Inside Right: Conservatism, Policies and the People* (Quartet, 1978), 12, 131–2, 233, 167. For an excellent account which argues that Conservatism offers "a twin inheritance" and can include both economic liberalism and "paternalism", see W. H. Greenleaf, *The British Political Tradition: Volume II, The Ideological Heritage* (Methuen, 1983).

party", and had never understood free enterprise.[61] But Joseph had no intention of heeding Gilmour's warnings about the electoral dangers of adopting a "divisive" ideology. On economic ideas, at least, there had been no "conversion"; but Joseph now held his long-established convictions with a convert's zeal. An essay published in 1975 provides the best insights into his new approach. Denying that he was "doctrinaire", Joseph defined that outlook as "basically one which decides issues without reference to the facts, in accordance with a set of fixed beliefs". In the remainder of the essay Joseph consistently "decides issues . . . in accordance with a set of fixed beliefs". Indeed few political authors at any time have produced a better illustration of what on his own definition was a "doctrinaire" outlook. Statements of purported fact are brought into the argument, but Joseph's "facts" would only be recognised as such by those who already sympathised with his viewpoint; even a mild sceptic could take issue with almost everything he says.[62]

In short, the change in Joseph had been more psychological than ideological. He was still invariably courteous in his personal dealings, and apologetic when he sensed that he had fallen below his exacting standards of conduct. But professional observers in the press noticed one outward symptom of the fire raging within him. Even mundane questions, which he had once dealt with smoothly, were now greeted by prolonged silence. It seemed that he was wrestling with himself – "agonising" was the word which irresistably suggested itself. Ironically, when Joseph was a minister in the Macmillan government he was praised for having sensed and avoided "the malaise that arises from too much wrangling about principles and anxiety for the future".[63] But his hesitation in interviews after 1974 did not arise from an unquiet conscience, as many commentators assumed. It was his new inner certainty, rather than doubts concerning the justice of his cause, that produced the hesitation. He had never enjoyed easy relations with the press, probably because he felt that they were always trying to catch him out. Now it was more important than ever to find the crisp phrases which had always eluded him; and in a face-to-face interview he could not be prompted by Sherman. As Nicholas Wapshott put it, "He cannot relax when a notebook is out . . . He would much prefer to discuss the

---

61. KJ interview with Llew Gardner.
62. KJ, "The Economics of Freedom" in *Freedom and Order*, 19. In the paragraph that follows the definition of the "doctrinaire" politician, Joseph claims that "The market economy developed spontaneously as a result of the actions of millions of people following their self-interest as they understood it". Although (as usual) he proceeded to deny the label "laissez-faire", his description of the free market implied a rejection of *any* government interference.
63. KJ interview with Anthony Howard; *The Times*, 22 September 1964. To some, Joseph's behaviour lent credence to rumours that one of his operations had gone wrong, resulting in significant brain damage. Hints of such a problem appeared in at least one newspaper profile (*Observer*, 9 December 1984). Apparently complications *did* arise during one operation in the early 1970s (ironically, when Joseph had ministerial responsibility for Health); but friends insist that the mishap was not serious and it had no noticeable effect on his mental faculties (private information).

question than answer it directly".[64] After so many years of searching, at the age of fifty-six Joseph had found an identity for himself. In spite of fatigue, chronic ill-health, his failing marriage and the sniping of critics, he would force himself onwards in his self-appointed role, promoting the cause of economic liberalism. If his performance in interviews led to further ridicule this was something he could easily bear. What he refused to do was to buy cheap popularity by adopting any of the usual tricks of the political trade.

Given his temperament, it might have been easier for Joseph in his new martyr's guise had he been snubbed or shouted down in the Shadow Cabinet after Upminster. Instead his colleagues continued to give him every chance to air his views. A discussion on inflation and unemployment at the party's steering committee on 15 July 1974 heated up after Joseph had expressed strong disagreement with the paper written by David Howell and Terence Higgins. But Sir Geoffrey Howe stepped in to say "that despite the argument, the actual disagreement between the members of the Committee was not wide. All were agreed that inflation was the main enemy". From his own point of view Howe was right, but his rational assessment left out the emotional gulf which yawned between Joseph and the majority of his colleagues.[65] Three days later Joseph was asked to open for the Opposition in an economic debate. But the compliment was distinctly double-edged, because his brief was to criticise Labour's abolition of the Pay Board. Perhaps it was felt that the case for retaining this interventionist body would sound more effective coming from Sir Keith. If so, the idea was more astute in conception than in execution. Joseph took the opportunity to give a violent exposition of his true feelings. "Passions in the extreme are aroused by an incomes policy", he declared. "Some people pin exaggerated, almost mystical hopes on it while some regard it as economic nonsense, misguided if not mischievous and perverse". In reality, no one in the House entertained anything like "mystical hopes" for incomes policy; this was another sign that, to keep his new state of enthusiasm at boiling point, Joseph had to pretend that he was faced by an equally dogmatic foe.[66] He decided to read out quotations from Lewis Carroll's *The Hunting of the Snark* which, he felt, applied to the Employment Secretary Michael Foot. Foot intervened twice to complete the quotations from memory, prompting cries of "Encore!" from Labour back-benchers. After suffering this personal deflation Joseph concluded with a lame request for his own parliamentary colleagues to ignore his real convictions, and join him in voting "to keep this potentially modestly useful mechanism in existence".[67]

---

64. Wapshott in *The Times*, 12 October 1980.
65. Minutes of steering committee meeting, LSC/74/14, 15 July 1974, CPA, Bodleian Library.
66. Cf. Ian Gilmour, widely regarded in the 1980s as the intellectual leader of the "wets": "People get very excited about incomes policy. It is hard to understand why": *Inside Right*, 247.
67. *Hansard*, vol. 877, cols 781–9, 18 July 1974. Joseph might have been on firmer ground had he quoted from Edward Lear; "The Pobble who has no toes" was a great personal favourite (private information).

A week later Joseph made his first important Commons' speech on Home Affairs, in a debate on the decline of respect for the law. In view of what was going on in his own mind, it was ironic that Joseph should have marked his speech with an attack on "the worst follies of ideological fanaticism"; as a reporter from *The Times* pointed out, he seemed to think that this attitude was found exclusively on the Left, and had to be prompted by Labour to say a few words of complaint about the National Front on the opposite flank. Joseph, *The Times* objected, had exhibited a respect for the law which "was severely limited to matters that best suited [Conservative] party interests". The article produced a furious letter from Joseph, in which he made clear his abomination of the National Front and protested that he had always intended to discuss the extreme Right. Yet, while his image of the left-wing activist was that of a determined, lawless subversive he had kinder words for the average racist. Apart from some "very nasty people", he seemed to have learned that the National Front had recently recruited "some frustrated decent people", including trade unionists. Joseph had also included some ominous hints on the subject of capital punishment, where his remarks suggested that, without committing himself either way, he was beginning to wonder whether the public demand for the execution of terrorists ought not to be appeased. As the *Daily Telegraph* pointed out, Enoch Powell had recently given a more coherent exposition of the same argument, and the paper reported that Joseph's remarks were receiving "close scrutiny" from MPs. But the prevailing tone defies any attempt to convict Joseph of calculation. He was ready to set aside his reputation as an instinctive champion of tolerance because he genuinely thought that the occasion demanded it – that liberal democracy was under threat from a coalition comprising terrorists and left-wingers in the BBC, in schools and in universities. People whom he would once have applauded for their "good intentions" were now treated with caution. When Amnesty International asked Joseph for permission to use his photograph on a poster featuring a wide range of supporters from public life, he only agreed after hours of discussions, during which he demanded reassurance that the organisation protested as loudly about conditions in Communist countries as it did about Spain, South Africa and Iran. The insights he gained into Amnesty's work did nothing to undermine his conviction that there was an invariable connection between free market economics and democratic institutions; as late as 1978 he applauded Singapore, Hong Kong and Korea as bastions of enterprise, forgetting that not one of these would pass muster as a "free" country even by the standards of Hanoverian Britain.[68]

Parliament went into recess, but there was no rest for Joseph. On 5 August, writing from "the wilds of Fife", in a house which the family had rented for

---

68. *Hansard*, vol. 877, cols 1835–44, 25 July 1974; *The Times*, 26, 30 July 1974; *Daily Telegraph*, 30 July 1974; *Sunday Times*, 12 October 1975; Francis Wheen, "The Economics of Sir Fu Manchu", *New Statesman*, 19 January 1979.

five consecutive summers, he told Lord Alport that he and Hellen were "blissfully content – if it were not that the papers and the news were so universally depressing". He thanked his old colleague for passing on *"legitimate"* strictures on the Upminster speech, adding "I am quite clear in my own mind that Conservative govts. have erred badly. I am not alone among my colleagues in thinking this, though we are a minority". Typically, Joseph was planning to exploit his vacation to take his message to a different part of Britain, and he was about to deliver a speech at Leith Town Hall, Edinburgh. In case Alport was inclined to reconsider his own position, Joseph enclosed the text of the speech which warned that British industry was "bleeding to death". Alport was unmoved by the argument, but a few days later he learned that it had made an impression on at least one member of the public. On 9 August he was sent an anonymous letter which listed the faults of Shadow ministers, including those of Sir Keith "sob for everyone" Joseph. Before dispatching the letter Alport's correspondent scribbled a postscript: "Since writing the above I read of a good speech made by Sir Keith Joseph which has quite happily surprised me".[69]

Alport's correspondent would have been even more "happily surprised" to hear about Joseph's next speech, delivered at Preston on 5 September. The text, mainly the work of Sherman with help from Walters and Samuel Brittan of the *Financial Times*, was circulated in advance to members of the Shadow Cabinet. Jim Prior approached Margaret Thatcher, saying "You know this is a disastrous speech – can't you stop him giving it?" Sir Geoffrey Howe was also asked to intervene. If the party wanted to win the next election, the timing could not have been worse; the Shadow Cabinet was engaged in preparations for a new manifesto, and the press was already carrying well-founded rumours of disagreement. The Conservative *Campaign Guide* had just been published, denouncing Labour for spreading "myths" about the failure of counter-inflation policy under Heath. Thatcher and Howe met Joseph at the CPS offices on the morning of 3 September, and did convince him to tone down the section on incomes policy. But it was felt that nothing of real substance could be amended without destroying the central theme of the speech, and Joseph would not retreat from that. Having looked through the text, Mrs Thatcher considered it to be "one of the most powerful and persuasive analyses I have ever read". While his Home Affairs spokesman was pondering over his speech, Heath was mourning his godson – drowned on the previous day with another crewman when his yacht foundered off the Sussex coast. But he found time for a meeting with Joseph which lasted for an hour and a half.[70]

69. KJ to Lord Alport, 9 August 1974; KJ, *Reversing the Trend*, 11; Anonymous letter of 9 August 1974 in Alport MSS, Box 42.
70. Prior, *Balance of Power*, 97; Howe, *Conflict of Loyalty*, 87; Thatcher, *Path to Power*, 255; *The Times*, 2 September 1974; *Financial Times*, 4 September 1974.

Heath's PPS Kenneth Baker remembers the leader telling Joseph on another occasion that "Your analysis of the Government's record has left me heartbroken". Even if Heath ever said such a thing – and the words are so unlike him that Baker's memory has to be doubted – it seems that during these months Joseph was so engrossed in the task he had chosen that he failed to exercise his usual consideration for the feelings of others. His distraction affected allies as well as opponents. Around this time a sympathetic industrialist attended a dinner at St Ermin's Hotel near St James's Park. Joseph's invitation had contained an ominous phrase: the food would be cold, "so that we can talk before, over and after it". Yet his guest, who was offering to help with policy work, was unprepared for Joseph's method of making a newcomer feel at ease. Having arrived at the hotel after an important business meeting he was hoping to unwind a little. Instead, as he later reminded his host, "you obviously expected your guest to have done a certain amount of homework". Joseph dashed off a hasty apology: "You suffered when you dined with us from over-enthusiasm on my part. Such a sudden immersion of guests in the deep end of discussion will not occur again – thanks to you!". It was a resolution which Joseph was quite unable to keep for long – if at all.[71]

When Joseph stood up in Preston's Bull and Royal Hotel on 5 September he opened with a solemn warning. "Inflation", he said, "is threatening to destroy our society". The problem had arisen because successive governments had been induced to create excessive demand by their fear of mass unemployment. But that fear had been greatly exaggerated. Joseph had discovered that, in addition to the "frictional" unemployed (those between jobs), the figures included "the unenthusiastic, the unemployable, the fraudulent", and many white-collar workers who had to retire at sixty but were still obliged to register as unemployed. The number of truly "deserving" jobless – i.e. "people who are both willing and able to work and who have been unemployed for over eight weeks" – had never risen above 300,000 since 1945. Throughout those years the number of unfilled vacancies had varied betweeen 600,000 and 1,000,000 – which implied that even the residual 300,000 had lacked the moral fibre to take any available work. Ironically, government attempts to solve a non-existent problem provided the real threat to employment; boom conditions caused by excessive demand led to balance of payments crises, which induced deflationary policies in turn. A lasting solution to Britain's economic problems depended on "a broad but gradualist strategy to phase out excess demand", which a government must persevere with regardless of any criticism. The "beginning of the cure" would be painful. The unemployment figures would rise for a time. But before long "the balance of payments deficit, and after a lag, the rate of inflation, will start to ease". In due course, and without "any artificial stimulus or

---

71. Baker, *Turbulent Years*, 42. Correspondence of July–September 1974, in Joseph Papers, 10/8, CPA, Bodleian Library.

inflation, spontaneous in-built correctives will begin to make themselves felt". Joseph's current guess was that the process would take three or four years, although in case his audience found this time frame depressing he went on to predict that the beneficial effects would come through after "a couple of years" (the outlook had clearly improved since May, when Joseph had told the Shadow Cabinet that tough policies would be required for "at least five years"). He was willing to accept for himself the label "monetarist", but that position had been cruelly caricatured. It did not mean "that if we get the flow of money and spending right, everything will be right . . . What I believe is that if we get the money supply wrong – too high or too low – nothing will come right".[72]

The Upminster and Leith speeches had received wide publicity but Preston caused a much greater stir. Unlike race, economics was not a subject to goad dock workers into marching on Westminster. Yet the new speech provoked what by the standards of the serious press was a comparable response. *The Times* devoted a lengthy editorial to a discussion of Joseph's case, under the headline "The Sharp Shock of Truth"; its readers were treated to the full text, while other broadsheets carried extensive excerpts. Although he was responsible for very little of the final text this accolade brought lasting pleasure to Joseph; apart from the boost it gave to his message, it also tapped a deeply buried seam of vanity in the man who had won prizes at Harrow for his oratory. He could also read some supportive commentaries from sympathetic journalists, notably Peter Jay in *The Times* and Patrick Cosgrave in the *Spectator*. Others were less flattering. In the *New Statesman* Roger Opie denied that Joseph's analysis was "lucid, authoritative and, above all, honest"; rather, it was "muddled, naïve, assertive and tendentious". Opie thought that in accepting the monetarist theory Joseph had behaved like many "Clever laymen". He went on to suggest that the superficial "cleverness" of monetarism concealed insurmountable practical difficulties:

> nowhere does he explain how his policy will actually work. We must get the money supply right, he says – not too high or too low. Which money supply? How high is too high, how low is too low? . . . It is less than honest to advocate a brutal policy without telling us who will suffer, and how much, and why.

Opie might have added that when Joseph was precise in his language he had a tendency to qualify his statements in the next breath. At Preston there was the ever-changing estimate of the time needed to make his policies work, while at Leith the plight of industry was deemed to be affecting "all", "many" or "some" firms. He also seemed to have difficulty making up his mind whether all British economic policy since the war had been equally bad, or some periods better

---

72. *The Times*, 6 September 1974.

than others, and in deciding whether Keynes was "dead" (Sherman's view) or the victim of misinterpretation at the hands of his followers. Throughout the Opposition period he wrestled with the problem of the "time lag" which one could expect before a change in the money supply worked through into the inflation rate. In April 1976, for example, he told the Commons that "No one can know the lag that works on the money supply. It is somewhere between one and two and a half years. It is impossible to be more precise. There is a lag. There are consequences". These vague or contradictory remarks could not be dismissed as mere verbal slips; without a settled position, Joseph's case eluded detailed scrutiny. Even in published essays, which allowed more time for consideration, the ambiguity persisted. For example, in a key work published in 1975, "The Economics of Freedom", Joseph tried to discredit the ideals of his opponents by associating them with economic conditions within the Soviet bloc, and made tactical switches between the words "socialist" and "semi-social-ist" to describe the policies pursued in Britain since the war.[73]

To students of political thought Joseph had (predictably) fallen between two stools. By the standards of a Rawls or a Hayek his work was characterised by confusions and inconsistencies.[74] That failing hardly made Joseph unique among politicians, even those of the front rank. At the same time, he gave the impression of having formulated a reasoned case; he resembled Edmund Burke at least insofar as he sounded "too deep for his hearers". Yet the circumstances of 1974 were abnormal, and whether or not the British public entirely grasped the nature and significance of "monetarism", the word now gained much wider notice. The Conservative Selsdon Group hailed the Preston speech, and urged that Joseph should be made Chancellor when the party returned to power. While the *Guardian* predicted that Labour would seize this "golden chance to say that the Tories are hopelessly split on economic policy", Michael Foot showed his fury at what he regarded as a "wretched" slur on the unemployed (although even he acknowledged that the speech demonstrated "reckless courage and rare intellectual distinction"). Enoch Powell sneered that he had "heard of death-bed repentance . . . but perhaps it would be more appropriate to refer instead to post-mortem repentance". He offered ironic congratulations to Joseph for putting together an "admirable anthology from my speeches on [inflation] in recent years". The think-tank Political and Economic Planning (PEP) published detailed research findings which, while not conclusive against

73. KJ, "The Economics of Freedom" in *Freedom and Order* (CPC, 1975); *The Times,* 6 September 1974; *Spectator,* 14 September 1974; *Hansard,* vol. 909, col. 931, 12 April 1976; *New Statesman,* 13 September 1974.
74. Hayek himself was somewhat cavalier in his identification of economic trends. For example, he claimed that Britain took "a headlong plunge" along "the road to serfdom" in 1931. At least this was a refinement on the more typical anti-socialist case, that the country's problems began with the Attlee government of 1945–51. But it was (at the very least) an exaggeration to say that Britain's economic system had been "transformed. . . beyond recognition" in the years 1931–9; see Friedrich Hayek, *The Road to Serfdom* (Routledge, 1944), 9 and note.

Joseph, at least emphasised the fact that attitudes to work were more complicated than his abstract theorising suggested; his figures on the "real" unemployed, in particular, seemed to have been clutched out of thin air. But some moderate Conservatives thought that Joseph had harmonised his thinking with a real shift in public attitudes. As Robert Carr noted in the party's steering committee, people seemed to find the prospect of "much higher levels of unemployment" more acceptable than they had done ten years before. The question which divided the Shadow Cabinet was whether this should be regarded as a political opportunity or a matter for regret.[75]

If Heath really was left "heartbroken" by the Preston speech he made a good public show of brushing it aside. At Elgin in Scotland he identified four weapons in the battle against inflation – agreement on wages and salaries, some controls on prices, tax policies that favoured industry, and "a firm and consistent control over the money supply". Heath admitted that on this score "we may have lessons to learn from our past experience. We will not be too proud to learn them". Clearly this was an attempt to find some compromise formula to keep the party together in the short term. It worked, at least to the extent that Joseph began to make some reassuring noises after 18 September, when Wilson called the long-expected general election. Returning to the North-West for a campaign speech in Bolton, Joseph told reporters that all was "friendship and light" between himself and his leader. He also allayed fears that there would be immediate action to clamp down on the money supply after a Tory victory; "The scale of bankruptcies and unemployment would be intolerable", he thought. But Joseph's skin was sensitive, and when attacked his instinctive action was to ransack his stationery cupboard when it would have been more prudent to sit still. Almost any negative comment in the press received a lengthy answer, and he even clashed with his old colleague Reginald Maudling in the correspondence columns of *The Times*. Feeling as an ex-Chancellor that his own competence had been brought into question by the Preston speech, Maudling was more aggressive than Sir Keith in this exchange. In his memoir (published in 1978) he described Joseph as "the most articulate and intelligent exponent" of monetarism – an elegant compliment somewhat undermined by his further observation that the doctrine was "totally divorced from reality". Privately Maudling confided his belief that his antagonist was now "nutty as a fruit-cake".[76]

On the day after Preston Heath had told reporters that sacking Joseph as Home Affairs spokesman was a "preposterous" idea, and that there was no

---

75. Oliver Goldsmith, "Retaliation"; *Financial Times*; *The Times*, 6 September 1974; Guardian, 6, 19, 21 September 1974; *Sunday Times*, 8 September 1974; steering committee meeting of 15 July 1974, LSC/74/14, CPA, Bodleian Library.
76. *The Times*, 6, 9, 11 September 1974; Maudling, *Memoirs*, 209; interview with Ian Aitken.

comparison with the Powell situation in 1968. But the distinction was clearer in Heath's mind than it was to others, and there could be no more than a temporary truce within the Shadow Cabinet. Confusingly, because the money supply was mentioned at all, some commentators thought that the Conservative manifesto for the election of October 1974 represented a significant victory for the right. In an attempt to exploit this impression, Denis Healey commented that "Sir Keith is absolutely honest in saying that he does not want mass unemployment, but he is equally honest in advocating a policy which will result in that".[77] But parts of the document read as if the party was just as keen to distance itself from Joseph as it was to point up the contrast with Labour. The unsigned foreword certificated the party "free from dogma and free from dependence upon any single interest". The control of inflation was identified as the first priority for any government, but this could not be achieved "by using only one weapon". Restraint of the money supply was acknowledged to be "a vital, though not the only, part of our counter-inflation amoury". Price controls were deemed to be necessary at "a time of roaring inflation", although the Price Code would be made more flexible; an incomes policy was envisaged, and "If after all our efforts we fail to get a comprehensive voluntary policy we shall need to support the voluntary restraint that *is* achieved with the back up of the law. It would be irresponsible and dishonest totally to rule this out . . .".

In short, Heath had listened to the monetarist case but preferred to heed the lessons of his own practical experience. Only by October 1974, when it was too late, had he put his name to the form of words which would have been appropriate for his 1970 manifesto. A far more conciliatory approach was taken to questions of industrial relations, and the party admitted that "In present circumstances it would be irresponsible to promise large reductions in tax rates". The most publicised pledge, however, would have ensured that interest rates for home buyers would not rise above 9.5 per cent. It fell to Margaret Thatcher to advertise on the party's behalf this significant interference with the operations of the free market. She objected at first, not to the principle but to any idea that the compulsory rate should be lower than 9.5 per cent. Of greater concern to her was Peter Walker's plan to make the sale of council houses easier for tenants who had occupied their properties for more than three years. This, she felt, would alienate "bedrock Conservative voters", but eventually Walker got his way.[78]

While his ally was receiving attention that was not always welcome to her, for the purposes of the Conservative campaign Joseph was almost a non-person. The *Campaign Guide* mentioned him only twice, in connection with immigration and women's rights. A senior party official remembers that he and his colleagues in Central Office were on the alert before any Joseph speech, in case

---

77. Campbell, *Heath*, 640; King, *Diary 1971–74*, 383; *Express & News*, 27 September 1974.
78. *Putting Britain First* (Conservative Party manifesto), 4, 6, 12, 14, 16; Thatcher, *Path to Power*, 246–7.

the press picked up a new gaffe. But the *Guardian*'s Francis Boyd found Sir Keith "in one of his quiet and rather sad moods" at his adoption meeting in late September. First he treated his audience to a lecture on the relative merits of Marx and, in the free market corner, Hayek and Schumpeter. Suddenly he switched into nostalgic mode, drawing on his prodigious memory to flatter individuals in his audience. "How many of you here tonight were present on that fateful day 18 years ago when I was first adopted as candidate?" he asked. "You, Sidney! Dorothy! Len! Well, thank you very much for my repeated adoption eight times since then". After revealing that "when you first chose me we disagreed about almost everything" – a point which the veterans of 1956 might not have appreciated at the time – he continued, "What I had in those days was book-learning, and what you had was life experience. Bit by bit I have come to see the book-learning in the light of the judgement of life". In fact Joseph was reading more furiously than ever, and his own "life experience" was as far removed from the average resident of Leeds North-East as it had been in 1956. But after his recent antics Joseph's attempt to identify himself with the concerns of ordinary Conservative activists was enough to reassure an audience which heard him "with silent respect". A later "meet the people" tour of Leeds was impaired by a lack of people to meet, and by Joseph's ingrained reluctance to interrupt the business of the few that he encountered. Instead he went to a residential area where he delivered by hand an election leaflet which pointed out a "decline in standards of education and behaviour and weakening of the family", all of which could be attributed to "fanatical socialism".[79]

During the campaign Joseph made the usual forays outside his constituency; indeed, when Central Office asked ministers to make themselves available for "not fewer than four" of such engagements he suggested that he could manage seven.[80] But instead of speeches to rally the faithful he tended to deliver lofty "state of the nation" addresses, in keeping with the tone he had adopted after February 1974. At Luton on 3 October he reminded his listeners that:

> it was not long ago that we thought utopia was within reach . . . What has happened to all this optimism? Has it really crumbled under the weight of rising crime, social decay and the decline of traditional values? Have we really become a nation of hooligans and vandals, bullies and child-batterers, criminals and inadequates?[81]

Regrettably the answer was "yes". Quoting Arthur O'Shaughnessy, Joseph identified the culprit as ideas, "the most powerful of all forces":

---

79. Interview with Miles Hudson; *Guardian*, 25 September 1974; *The Times*, 5 October 1974.
80. Correspondence in CCO 20/17/54, CPA, Bodleian Library.
81. All quotations from CCO handout of speech by KJ at Farley Hill, Luton, 3 October 1974.

One man with a dream, at pleasure
Shall go forth and conquer a crown,
And three with a new song's measure
Can trample a kingdom down.

Joseph thought that two centuries after his death Jean-Jacques Rousseau was still trampling Britain down with his educational theories – ideas which had persuaded teachers "to dispense with the structured systems of learning which have been so successful in the past". The result was "the belief, taught by Mr Roy Jenkins, that a permissive is a civilised society"; yet:

> . . . A facile rhetoric of total liberty and of costless, superficial universal protest has really been a cover for irresponsibility. Our loud talk about the community overlies the fact that we have no community. We talk about neighbourhoods and all too often we have no neighbours. We go on about the home when we only have dwelling places containing television sets. It is the absence of a frame of rules and community, place and belonging, responsibility and neighbourliness that makes it possible for people to be more lonely than in any previous stage in our history. Vast factories, huge schools, sprawling estates, sky-scraping apartment blocks; all these work against our community and our common involvement one with another.

While others might have interpreted this as a howl of rage against the modern condition in general, Joseph was convinced that ideas were to blame. As usual, he acknowledged that left-wing theorists – and even Mr Roy Jenkins – had the very best of intentions. Ideas were so powerful, he said, that no one could estimate their effects. The Left could be reclaimed if they were honest, and recognised that events had not answered to their hopes. But Joseph failed to apply the obvious lesson to his own ideas. Might it not be the case that the more active prosecution of free market ideas in such a soulless country would lead to even deeper alienation? Elsewhere in the same speech he gave an unconscious prediction of the kind of development which might be expected:

> There is moreover a commercial exploitation of brutality in print and in film which further debases the moral climate. And how is it that a genera-tion that rejects the exploitation of man by man and promises the libera-tion of women can accept the exploitation of women by pornography? The left, usually so opposed to profitable commerce in trades beneficial to the public, systematically defends the blatant commercialism of the pornographic industry.

Unconsciously, Joseph had provided the answer to his own conundrum. To the extent that people on the Left really did try to construct principled justifications for pornography – an extent which Joseph backed with assertion rather than evidence – they were acting as the unwitting agents of a powerful and growing arm of the capitalist system. To put the argument in its mildest form, there has always been a tendency for entrepreneurs to take social norms as they find them, and to test the boundaries of public morality in their quest to make money through "blatant commercialism". As Bernard de Mandeville had shown at the beginning of the eighteenth century, what social conservatives upheld as sound morals were in reality obstacles to prosperity; in practice "private vices" turned out to be "public virtues". The logic of this argument leads to the rejection of any interference in the market, regardless of its effect on traditional morals. By contrast, Joseph's strictures on exploitation pointed to the opposite extreme. It was no accident that, in response to one of his later "moralising" speeches, *Private Eye* jumped to the conclusion that "Sir Keith has now renounced his faith in the free enterprise system".[82] Far from exploring these unpromising avenues, Joseph found it much easier simply to blame everything that repelled him on "Socialism" – ignoring the fact that the British Left has notoriously owed far more to ethics than to economics. If pressed he could affirm that the free market can only operate within a "civilised" moral and legal framework, and this would allow for occasional censorship in society's best interests. But this only opened up another paradox in his position. The "Man in Whitehall" should be kept away from the adjustment of prices and incomes, but he could be given a free hand when making windows into other men's souls. Although Hayek had argued that a "constitution of liberty" could keep this interference within bounds, constitutions are only as effective as the people who operate them; and on Joseph's own theory (as opposed to his practice in office) the servants of the state were no more to be trusted than anyone else, being driven by the desire to look after themselves and their families rather than pursuing the national interest.

The real puzzle arising from Joseph's speech is not the behaviour of a minority of left-wing hedonists, but why so many (though not all[83]) social conservatives since the 1960s have thought that they could marry Adam Smith to the social campaigner Mary Whitehouse. Noticing that the post-war period had been marked by a tendency towards "collectivism" in intellectual circles, and towards wayward individualism in social behaviour, they decided that there must be a connection between two trends which they instinctively detested. Their account of recent history could not withstand close inspection, but Joseph picked it up and ran without a moment's pause. Social conservatives had

---

82. *Private Eye*, 18 October 1974.
83. Notable exceptions were Peregrine Worsthorne and some other members of the "Salisbury Group" founded in 1977. See Chapter 14 for further discussion.

been so thrilled by Powell that they tended to overlook his frequent votes in favour of "permissive" legislation. They were happy to transfer their loyalty to an All Souls Fellow who understood their fears, convinced as he was that he was articulating the thoughts of the overlooked majority of his fellow citizens. If Joseph experienced a "conversion" of principle during 1974, it took place in his social outlook, not in his economic thinking.[84]

The Conservatives duly lost the election on 10 October 1974, although the result was closer than many had expected. On a turnout 6 per cent lower than that of February the government collected 319 seats; an overall majority of only three left it vulnerable to future by-election reverses. The Conservatives held 277 seats: Joseph retained Leeds North-East with a slightly reduced majority of 5,628. Only Heath's most vehement critics could take the outcome as an explicit vote of no confidence in the party leader. As in 1966 all the electoral cards had been in Wilson's possession, and compared to the contest of that year the Conservatives had conducted what Heath privately described as "a good containment exercise". But this was Heath's third defeat in four outings, and speculation about his position had been growing since February. As early as April, when Joseph claimed that Denis Healey had "declared war upon the middle class", Labour's Chancellor chose to interpret his words as the opening shots in a leadership battle. In June Joseph had met Lord Alport, who had been unhappy with Heath for some time and was obviously hoping for some signal that his former PPS had leadership ambitions. After the lunch, however, he lamented to a friend that Joseph was evidently "a committed Heath man". But pundits continued to speculate. In July the Labour MP John Stonehouse told Cecil King that Joseph was the most likely successor to Heath, and there was a new outbreak of gossip in the wake of the Preston speech. Other names being canvassed included Whitelaw and Christopher Soames. But there was no provision for a leadership contest under the current rules without a vacancy at the top, and Heath had no intention of creating one.[85]

Before Parliament reassembled two young back-benchers, Norman Fowler and Norman Lamont, went to see Joseph at his room in the Commons. Both had decided that they would support Joseph in the event of a leadership election, appreciating his blend of conscience and efficiency. Now they approached him to discover his intentions. According to Fowler, "He listened to what we said; thanked us for our support; but did not absolutely commit himself to the battle". At least he did not rule himself out, and the two-man deputation left feeling confident that Joseph would stand. Fowler flew off to

---

84. The further question (unanswerable without a separate lengthy dissertation) is why the British Left allowed the vocabulary of morality to be kidnapped and forced into such an unlikely partnership with free market thinking – a combination whose instability was only revealed by John Major's "Back to Basics" campaign.

85. *Hansard*, vol. 871, col. 1001, 1 April 1974; Thatcher, *Path to Power*, 263; Alport to Simon Wingfield-Digby, 14 June 1974, Alport MSS, Box 37; King, *Diary 1971–74*, 378.

Turkey for some sunshine, and in Istanbul read about a new speech which his putative candidate had made to the Edgbaston Conservative Association on Saturday 19 October.[86]

In the local evening paper Birmingham's Grand Hotel had been advertised as offering "that night out which will linger in your memory for ever". It probably did not seem like that to the 300 people who listened to Joseph in the Hotel's main hall. The speaker went through his text at "breakneck speed"; this style of delivery, "coupled with the hour and the after-dinner atmosphere", gave the members of the Association "the air of Monday morning commuters blearily watching their train flash through the station when they had expected it to stop". At the terminus there was "vigorous and fairly prolonged applause which stopped short of a standing ovation"; the Edgbaston MP, Jill Knight, was far more enthusiastic, telling the gathering that "Sir Keith has shown us the way".[87]

But the Edgbaston speech has "lingered in the memory", because of a single sentence: "The balance of our population, our human stock is threatened". Ironically, although Joseph's close allies have treated responsibility for the phrase as if they were playing pass-the-parcel with a hand grenade, it seems that this section was almost the only contribution which Joseph made to his own speech. In recent months Sherman had taken care to remove additions to the texts which he provided, but on this occasion Joseph was so attracted by a phrase that he re-inserted it.[88] The storm provoked by the remark began on the night of its delivery; the *Evening Standard* broke the press embargo on the prereleased text. The reaction took Joseph by surprise. After his death his son remembered with affection that he "*could* not understand how such a clever man could get into so much trouble". The Edgbaston speech was the prime example of Joseph's unwariness; he had every reason to expect that it would be widely discussed, and there can be no doubt that when he delivered it he thought of himself as a leadership candidate. On the previous Sunday (13th) a group of right-wing MPs meeting at Nicholas Ridley's flat in Pimlico had decided that Joseph was their man. They telephoned their champion and were told "I am a candidate for the leadership and will be a candidate whenever the election takes place. You have my authority to tell that to anybody who asks".

---

86. Interviews with Lord Lamont and Sir Norman Fowler; Norman Fowler, *Ministers Decide* (Chapmans, 1991), 10. Fowler places the meeting with Sir Keith on the day that he was sworn in, but since that was 22 October (i.e. after the Edgbaston speech) his memory seems to be at fault here.

87. Unsourced cutting in Roth archives. Following quotations taken from KJ, speech at the Grand Hotel, Birmingham, 19 October 1974; CCO handout.

88. Cf. Margaret Thatcher's loyal comment at Sir Keith's memorial service, that the offending phrase "was not his". So anxious was Joseph that the responsibility should lie with the true culprit that as late as 1989 he personally telephoned to correct a *Times* diarist who had attributed the phrase to Sherman; see *The Times*, 10 February 1989; interview with Sir Alfred Sherman.

This message was repeated on the day before Edgbaston, when Joseph wrote to Ian Gow, a back-bencher who had urged him to overcome his reluctance to stand.[89] David Mitchell, Joseph's former PPS, had put together a card-index of MPs and was taking soundings at Westminster; Margaret Thatcher had announced herself as Joseph's "campaign manager" on the day after the October election. Other MPs were canvassing an improbable "Dream Ticket", featuring Whitelaw as Leader and Joseph as Shadow Chancellor. Sherman believes that the favourable publicity after the Preston speech in September had ended Joseph's doubts about the leadership. He was certainly much changed from the man who had "shuddered away from the suggestion with something approaching genuine horror" when it was put to him towards the end of the Heath government.[90]

Joseph began his Edgbaston speech by claiming that politics was about far more than economics – although he felt sure that he would be called "unfashionable, indeed anti-fashionable" for saying so. During the two election campaigns of 1974, he continued, "discussion focused almost exclusively on economics; and we lost the election[s]". It was a clever way of reminding his audience that a change of direction from the top was urgently required by the Conservatives; but it was odd that the point was being made by a Home Affairs spokesman who only six weeks earlier had delivered the most talked-about economic speech for years. Much of what followed had been heard before from Joseph over recent months. He attacked the permissive society, the left-wing theorists who threatened social order with their "well-orchestrated sneers", the tax-funded universities which were seed-beds of anarchy. This time Joseph would not even allow that these developments had come about through the efforts of well-intentioned people, although the rapid expansion of the universities had been planned under Conservative governments of which he had been a part. The results of post-war decadence were "Drugs, drunkenness, teenage pregnancies, vandalism, an increase in drifting – now called by new names, but basically vagrancy". This was "the very opposite of freedom, which begins with self-discipline". Amidst the gloom there was one glorious example – Mary Whitehouse, from whom all Britons should take courage. Holding her banner aloft,

> We must fight the battle of ideas in every school, university, publication, committee, TV studio even if we have to struggle for our toe-hold there; we have the truth, [and] if we fail to make it shine clear, we shall be to

89. James Joseph, speech at KJ memorial service; Nicholas Wapshot and George Brock, *Thatcher* (Futura, 1983), 113–4. While Halcrow (*Joseph*, 79–80) dates the letter as Wednesday 16 October, Ranelagh (*Thatcher's People*, 132–3) suggests Friday 18 October.
90. Halcrow, *Joseph*, 79–80, 88–9; O'Sullivan, "Conservatism, Democracy and National Identity", Third Keith Joseph Memorial Lecture (CPS, 1999), 1; Peter Jenkins in *Guardian*, 12 October 1974; interview with Sir Alfred Sherman; Patrick Cosgrave in *Spectator*, 14 September 1974.

blame no less than the exploiters, the casuists, the commercialisers . . . we shall need intellectual as well as moral courage to grapple with the dilemmas inherent in the remoralisation of public life.

Up to this point it had been a very shrewd speech, a tribute to Sherman's phrase-making skill. The middle-classes had developed a persecution complex since the war, and Joseph was there to tell them that they had every reason to feel that way. But he had been carried away by Sherman's eloquence, and his closing section produced a rude collision with reality. Saying that his remarks were based on a recent article (by Margaret and Arthur Wynn) published by the Child Poverty Action Group, he argued that "a high and rising proportion of children are being born to mothers least fitted to bring children into the world". Earlier in his speech he had rejected Marxism, saying that "History is not made by abstract forces, or classes. It is made by people". But clearly some groups in society were just too poor to deserve treatment as individuals. The unfit mothers were adolescents:

in social classes 4 and 5. Many of these girls are unmarried, many are deserted or divorced or soon will be. Some are of low intelligence, most of low educational attainment. They are unlikely to be able to give children the stable emotional background, the consistent combination of love and firmness which are more important than riches. They are producing problem children, the future unmarried mothers, delinquents, denizens of our borstals, sub-normal educational establishments, prisons, hostels for drifters. Yet these mothers, the under-twenties in many cases, single parents, from classes 4 and 5, are now producing a third of all births. A high proportion of these births are a tragedy for the mother, the child and for us.

Joseph admitted that some would describe as "immoral" proposals for the extension of birth-control facilities to these unfortunates. But he asked whether this would not be the lesser of two evils? To solve the problems of society was not within the power of government; most of the effort would have to come from voluntary organisations. In conclusion he showed just how hard it was to get away from that accursed, "fashionable" subject of economics: "Are we to move towards moral decline reflected and intensified by economic decline, by the corrosive effects of inflation? Or can we remoralise our national life, of which the economy is an integral part? It is up to us, to people like you and me".

On the following day Mrs Whitehouse said that she was "tremendously grate-ful" to Joseph. "Until this speech", she told reporters, "the people of Britain have been like sheep without a shepherd. But now they have found one". Judging from Joseph's mailbag, British "sheep" had indeed recognised the man to lead them. Joseph recalled years later that he had received around 700 letters after the Preston speech. A week after Edgbaston he claimed that the tally this time was 2,000, among whom the critics were outnumbered fourteen to one. He could not resist displaying these letters for the cameras at the CPS offices; after all, they seemed to prove that he had achieved what he took to be a key goal of all politicians – to be loved. But he would have been better advised to stuff them in a drawer. On the last occasion that a political speech had aroused such a remarkable response – after "Rivers of Blood" – the heaps of fan mail had only stiffened the resolve of the recipient's enemies. Joseph had obviously struck a chord with many people; one woman wrote that he had delivered "a great, great speech . . . which all true Englishmen who hold real values have waited so long to hear". But by definition those who write to politicians in response to a speech are an unrepresentative sample of public opinion. One admirer had felt compelled to inform Joseph that "Too many Irish are breeding", and another captured the serious nature of the debate by sending a photograph of himself playing golf. Joseph proudly displayed to friends a supportive telegram from Sir Laurence Olivier –which at least proved that the speech could draw a response from a busy person engaged in an unrelated sphere of public life. Newspapers and magazines also received an impressive volume of supportive letters, but some of these correspondents had clearly misunderstood the Edgbaston message. In the *Spectator*, for example, one reader ignored all Joseph's nuances and praised him for having spoken out against the high birth-rate among those of "low intelligence"; the same lesson, he thought, could apply on a global scale at a time when the birth-rates in "advanced" nations were shrinking.[91]

But some of Joseph's critics, homing in on the "human stock" phrase, showed an equal lack of judgement. At least one Labour MP accused Joseph of hoping to create a "master race", while Paddington's Arthur Latham summarised the message of the speech as "castrate or conform". But any allegation that he had consciously peddled a racist message is unworthy even of contempt. A more telling point was that as a minister Joseph had *opposed* free prescription of birth-control supplies for all – a stand which had been reversed by his successor Barbara Castle. He had also shown far more sympathy than his officials to Leo Abse's arguments against abortion on demand; at the DHSS he had announced the establishment of an inquiry into the subject under Lord Lane, and after further promptings from Abse he extended its terms of reference. For the CPAG, Frank Field measured his response, despite his anger at what he regarded as a serious misrepresentation of the Wynns' research. The speech, Field continued, "bore all the marks of deliberately attempting to unleash a national backlash against the poor".[92]

---

91. *Sunday Times*, 20, 27 October 1974; KJ, interviews with Morrison Halcrow and Lord Lamont; see letter from R. G. W. Rickcord in *Spectator*, 2 November 1974.
92. *Sunday Times*, 20 October 1974; Abse, *Private Member*, 232–3.

Following up a critical and well-researched speech by Mrs Castle – whose civil servants had been distressed by their ex-minister's remarks – the *Sunday Times* "Insight" team stepped in to deliver the final blow. The distortion of the CPAG article, they revealed, was not the only instance of Joseph's inadequate homework. His "statements on the relationship between social class and the birth rate are just not true – and no amount of constituents' letters will make them so". In fact the number of children born to working-class parents was falling, as was the incidence of teenage pregnancy. Joseph had been wrong on almost every other count:

> there has been a marked drop in the number of sexual offences and armed robbery. The murder rate is static and burglary fell last year. Drunkenness is certainly increasing, particularly among the young, though we are nowhere near the Victorian rate of some 100,000 cases a year in London alone. Even illegitimacy, which increased rapidly in the sixties, is now on the decline.

Joseph replied that he had never cast any aspersions against illegitimacy; he had no quarrel with that, so long as the parents remained in a stable relationship. But this could not appease those of his critics who looked beyond the absurd accusations about eugenics and concentrated on the detail of Joseph's case. The Wynns had also been careful to note that illegitimacy could arise in many different circumstances; nevertheless, they concluded that "the illegitimacy percentage [is] a useful indicator of poverty and of social malaise". Poverty, indeed, "is both a cause as well as a consequence of illegitimacy". Certainly poor women were more likely to carry "unplanned" children for the full term of the pregnancy; it was far more common for their middle-class counterparts to arrange for terminations. While the Wynns acknowledged that family planning might have some long-term effect on poverty, their findings underpinned the usual CPAG assertion that "There is no cheap solution to all the problems of child poverty". At best, Joseph's speech had betrayed his anxiety to avoid this prescription, and offered a means of reducing poverty at minimal expense; at worst, in the eyes of more extreme social conservatives he had convicted the poor of immorality, thus lending some credibility to wild ideas about the withdrawal of all state assistance (or even forcible sterilization). Like Powell in 1968, Joseph had underestimated the extent to which careless words could be taken as validation for the prejudices of the ignorant. The crucial difference was that while Joseph appreciated the support he received, he was genuinely puzzled by the response. After the Edgbaston furore had died down he continued to articulate the views of a constituency which he felt to have been unjustly ignored by policy-makers, but the focus of his "remoralising" campaign returned to subjects of more traditional concern for politicians. This was a wise decision. His attempts to clarify his stance on illegitimacy proved that although he shared with the Whitehouse lobby a distaste for many aspects of "permissiveness", he was equally repelled by an unthinking intolerance. The man who as a government minister could reply to a question about the growing incidence of venereal disease by coolly distinguishing "between Gonorrhoea, the incidence of which had greatly increased and Syphillis, which had not increased" was an unlikely ally for Mrs Whitehouse, whose moral sensibility was outraged by a Clint Eastwood film because the bad guys won.[93]

Joseph had done more homework than his critics supposed. He had discussed the CPAG article with its authors, and had contacted the Central Statistical Office for confirmation of his figures. But he had spoken out before he had received more than an informal acknowledgement that he was on the right lines. It was an uncharacteristic slip, suggestive of his impatience to make an impact at this time. In the *New Statesman* Alan Watkins, while rightly defending Joseph against the cruder charges, called him "a saloon-bar Malthus". Even before a deluge of statistics buried the would-be shepherd, he issued a statement which could be read either as an apology or a howl of defiance. His critics had subjected the speech to "gross misrepresentation"; at the same time, he admitted that the section on birth control was too brief, since the subject merited a speech of its own. Revealingly, he continued that "I had thought that my record of initiative and concern for problem families and for what I have called "the cycle of deprivation" when I was Secretary of State for Social Services would have protected me from misunderstanding". But the "cycle" speech had not been delivered in the context of a looming leadership contest. Drafted by civil servants, it had been serious without introducing the kind of apocalyptic sound-bites which peppered the Edgbaston speech. Joseph could have added that the dreaded social categories 4 and 5 had made their debut in the speech he gave at Luton during the general election campaign, and not a dog had barked. He had even made more questionable references to the poor in the past, and got away with them. In March 1973 he had told the *Sunday Mirror* that one reason for the reluctance of such people to take advantage of family planning services was that they were ashamed to go out in dirty underclothes. Far from treating this grotesque remark as evidence that Joseph was well-meaning but inept in his social theorising, the interviewer in 1973 had waxed lyrical about his compassion, going so far as to refer to his "melting brown eyes". But instead of excusing his lapse about "our human stock", Joseph's subsequent protests merely explained why it had happened. Having been praised for his social concern for so many years, he had begun to assume that he could think aloud on almost any subject without suffering for it. But

---

93. Margaret and Arthur Wynn, "Can Family Planning do More to Reduce Child Poverty?", in *Poverty*, No. 29, Summer 1974, 17–20; minutes of ACP meeting, 8 November 1972, CPA, Bodleian Library.

the fact that he so obviously cared had won him admirers when it was thought that he had no ulterior motive for speaking out. Now that he had become the focus of so many leadership rumours, it was essential for him to be guided by established fact, and to deliver his warnings in careful language.[94]

A few Conservative MPs expressed their delight with Joseph's speech, but even one of his supporters muttered about "a carefully planned disaster". It was felt that Joseph's half-apology had done as much harm as the original speech. The Conservatives could not land themselves with a leader who made controversial statements one minute and retracted them the next. More confusion ensued when Joseph denied that the speech had been in any way connected to a leadership bid. He told Terry Coleman that "it wasn't intended to do more than advance the cause in which I believe", and expressed his regret that he might have done that cause more harm than good. His allies were putting it about that he had been "to some extent" pushed into making all of his recent speeches by (unnamed) people who thought that he would have a better chance of succeeding Heath if he set out his philosophical ideas. The notion that Joseph was a tool in the hands of others was hardly likely to revive his chances. Sir Geoffrey Howe, who along with Ian Gow had seconded Fowler and Lamont in urging Joseph to stand, was not alone in concluding that "Keith's judgement was too erratic".[95]

After the speech many right-wing Conservatives must have turned moist eyes towards Ulster, where Enoch Powell now sat as the Unionist MP for South Down. Interviewed by the BBC, Powell said that politicians should never preach. Showing that disappointment had not blunted his black humour, Powell admitted that "It's great fun to see somebody else getting into hot water over a speech. I almost wondered if the River Tiber was beginning to roll again". But he further undermined Joseph's position by adding that "There is something disasteful about the spectacle of men who followed [Heath] through briar and thicket turning on him now as if that had never happened". Later, in a private letter to Ralph Harris who hoped for a reconciliation, Powell ridiculed Joseph's assertion that he was "so immersed in the social services as not to know" what was happening on the economic front under Heath, although he added nothing to the force of his complaints by hinting that Joseph had only seen the light once he had been deprived of his ministerial "salary, car and chauffeur".[96]

Joseph's immediate response to his critics had been drawn up without the help of Alfred Sherman, who had another pressing engagement on the crucial day. Sherman felt that he could have extricated his ally had he been available; certainly he could have improved on the statement which was released. The

94. Halcrow, *Joseph*, 83; *The Times*, 21, 22 October 1974; *Sunday Mirror*, 25 March 1973.
95. Halcrow, *Joseph*, 86; *Guardian*, 21, 22 October 1974; Howe, *Conflict of Loyalty*, 89–90.
96. *The Times*, 22 October 1974; letter to Harris quoted in Heffer, *Like the Roman*, 741.

depths of Joseph's misery after Edgbaston can only be guessed at; presumably his own sense of having intended no harm kept him going through the inevitable round of searching interviews. Understandably his temper was frayed, and there was an angry televised clash with Ludovic Kennedy on the day after the ill-starred speech. But even before Edgbaston Joseph had shown a tendency to speak without fully realising the possible consequences of expressing his ideas. *Private Eye* (which was shortly to recognise his stance on contraception by dubbing him "Sir Sheath") revealed that during an interview with the *Observer*'s Polly Toynbee in early October Joseph had behaved very erratically, "sometimes pausing in strange silences and at other times pounding the table":

"I believe we are doomed", he is understood to have said after uttering his forebodings about the apocalypse. "We need a new prophet", he told Ms Toynbee, then went on to reflect out loud that "Jeremiah and Isaiah didn't work" . . . He spoke disparagingly of "huge industries devoted to exploiting most of the seven deadly sins", a reference perhaps to the building industry and the sin of avarice. It is understood that in his anguish, Sir Keith even exclaimed that "the cement of society is crumbling", though not we sincerely hope, the cement of the many buildings erected by Bovis. However, at one point in his interview with Ms Toynbee, Sir Keith struck a positive note reflecting his keen sense of the problems facing Britain at this time of crisis. "There'll be more lavatories. I'm in favour of lavatories. Very much in favour of them".

The *Eye* reported that the interview had been spiked by the *Observer*. In the *New Statesman* Alan Watkins made a well-informed suggestion that the newspaper's proprietor, David Astor, wanted to protect Joseph from himself. A spokesman for Joseph said that he had been very tired at the time, after a prolonged train journey. This was undoubtedly true, but Ms Toynbee had given Joseph what should have been a congenial opportunity to range beyond the political questions of the day and she had been taken aback by the response. The contrast with his equally wide-ranging interview with Anthony King only fifteen months earlier demonstrated the change in Joseph's character, wrought by the loss of office, the downfall of Bovis, and the influence of rigid ideologues. With King he had sounded like a modest man trying to iron out the remaining problems of a civilised society; now he seemed to be conducting a cavalry charge against the horsemen of the apocalypse. News of the Toynbee interview could not be suppressed, and in a discussion broadcast by ITV five days after Edgbaston Llew Gardner asked Joseph for his views on prophets, lavatories, etc. Gardner also wanted to know whether Joseph was nursing leadership ambitions. According to the unflattering transcript, the reply was

"Oh it isn't like that. There isn't um – we have a leader". The question was repeated twice more, and the answer was the same.[97]

Obviously the *Eye* had distorted the Toynbee interview, but its full publication would have led to questions about Joseph's suitability for any government office, let alone the leadership of his party. Its semi-suppression promised to give columnists in the know the chance to make fun of him for months. The *Eye* had also signalled that it would raise the issue of the Bovis connection with the now-jailed John Poulson if Joseph's candidature looked likely to prosper; during the architect's bankruptcy hearings in January 1973 Harry Vincent had been forced to deny a series of allegations, including the charge that Bovis was hoping to collaborate with Poulson in monopolising "all the available town centre development schemes in Britain". Conservatives opposed to Heath began a frantic search for an alternative champion. A small group of MPs approached Edward du Cann, the Chairman of the 1922 Committee, on the day of the Gardner interview. Significantly, Margaret Thatcher had been mentioned as a possible starter even before the Edgbaston speech.[98] Yet Joseph's course of action remained unclear, because there was still no provision for a leadership election. To announce that he was no longer a candidate in a leadership contest which might never be held would have seemed like a full repudiation of the Edgbaston speech. This he could not contemplate; however ill-phrased, it had been sincerely meant.

Instead of pulling out of the undeclared battle with Heath Joseph picked out more enemies to combat. The *Times Educational Supplement* had been deeply concerned by Joseph's remarks at Edgbaston on schools and universities. Admitting that in some places there was a problem with "the bully boys of the left", an editorial in the paper nevertheless deplored the absence of "intellectual rigour" in the speech, under the hurtful headline "A fellow of All Souls should do better than this". In a lengthy reply Joseph gave another alarming insight into his current mentality. The *TES* critique had betrayed more anxiety than animosity, but Joseph chose to regard it as an "anathema . . . peevish in tone". He thought that it reflected "the intolerance of dissent which characterises the 'new establishment'". Teachers at all levels who had been troubled by the Edgbaston speech were given cause for additional concern in Joseph's closing paragraphs. Here he expressed genuine doubts about the wisdom of the university expansion of the 1960s, noting that the size of the student population had overwhelmed "the sense of community which once made the student's life both civilising and stable". Unfortunately he interlaced these tenable debating

97. *Private Eye*, 18 October 1974; *New Statesman*, 18 October 1974; interview with Polly Toynbee; KJ interview with Llew Gardner.
98. *The Times*, 31 January 1973; Nigel Fisher, *The Tory Leaders* (Weidenfeld & Nicolson, 1977), 160; for Thatcher, see, for example, *The Times*, diary, 17 October 1974.

points with shrill political attacks on left-wing academics. Teachers and lecturers could only expect that, if Joseph were ever to be given a say in the education system, he would deny them the cool appraisal that was thought necessary after the radical changes of recent years. Those professionals who regretted the intrusion of ideology of any kind into education policy could expect no respite from Joseph. Ironically, his remarks ensured him a hot reception when he embarked on his subsequent speaking campaign in the universities; in turn, his treatment at the hands of students and staff convinced him that he had been right all along.[99]

Remaining allies such as Margaret Thatcher just hoped that the fuss would soon die down after Edgbaston, but the exchanges in the *TES* showed that Joseph could be enticed into a prolonged raking of the embers. Although he thought it prudent to spend his days at the CPS offices rather than in Parliament, the controversy could be rekindled in his absence. Mrs Castle attacked him in a debate of 1 November, pointing out Joseph's errors of fact and interpretation, and expressing her outrage at his explicit identification of socialism with the excesses of the "permissive society". Opponents within the Conservative Party also spoke out; Peter Walker ridiculed monetarism in a speech at Droitwich, and even the octogenarian Harold Macmillan joined in, taking credit for having "discovered" Joseph but pointing out the dangers of any simplistic economic doctrine. Sherman was not quite alone in refusing to think that Joseph's chances were finished after Edgbaston. As late as 12 November an opinion poll showed him running third (behind Whitelaw and Powell) as an alternative to Heath. A young Tory MP, Cecil Parkinson, tried to convince him that he should stand. However, Joseph was now "adamant" in his refusal.[100] On 18 November 1974 he wrote to Fowler and one or two others who had supported his candidature:

You have very kindly expressed your wish that I should compete for the leadership. I have told you that I have been considering whether to run. I have now concluded that I am not willing, and must therefore at once let you know ... Such a decision must, of course, be difficult and personal. It may cause some disappointment – and some pleasure! But one factor that did *not* enter into my thoughts was any unwillingness to stand against Ted. Since I've not said publicly that I would run but have simply kept my options open I am under no obligation to make a public statement saying that I am not standing. But if asked I shall reply in the sense of this letter.

---

99. *TES*, 25 October, 1 November 1974.
100. *The Times*, 2, 4, 7, 12 November 1974, *Jewish Chronicle*, 16 December 1994; Thatcher, *Path to Power*, 263; Cecil Parkinson, *Right at the Centre* (Weidenfled & Nicoloson, 1992), 126.

As a matter of courtesy, Joseph also informed Heath and the Chief Whip Humphrey Atkins that he would not be a candidate.[101]

In a 1985 interview Joseph mentioned the "clumsy" Edgbaston speech as the single factor which caused his "precipitate withdrawal". But "precipitate" was hardly the right word to describe the month's delay between Edgbaston and the decision not to contest the leadership. In fact Joseph told at least one of his colleagues that his wife had been opposed to him standing, and this had played a key role in his decision.[102] Given her desire that the family should be left in peace, and the likelihood that the press would camp out in Mulberry Walk until any contest was over, Lady Joseph's feelings were perfectly understandable. This still leaves unsolved the problem of her husband's timing, but other developments in those days provide a plausible explanation. On 14 November Heath told the 1922 Committee that he was setting up a committee to revise the party rules in order to allow a challenge to a sitting leader. Members of the 1922 were trying to pre-empt the new rule book by pressing the case for an immediate election.[103]

When he pledged himself to stand prior to the Edgbaston speech Joseph believed that the question would not arise unless Heath stepped aside to trigger a contest; in his letter of 16 October, for example, he had written that "If Ted does decide to resign, I shall certainly allow my name to go forward". After 14 November he was confronted with the full implications of a challenge to the man with whom he had worked closely since 1960, and for whom he had campaigned in 1965. Morrison Halcrow relates that "some of those close to [Joseph] sensed that what really worried him was actually the prospect of success". It was not just that the imminence of a contest forced him to assess his real aptitude for the job (with predictable, self-deprecating results). Success, after all the controversies of 1974, would leave him at the head of a bitterly divided party. Antipathy towards him extended beyond the remaining Heath loyalists in Parliament; Miles Hudson, who had briefed the party leader during the October campaign, reflected in his diary on polling day that if Joseph were to succeed Heath "he will have opposition to him at Party Headquarters which might be difficult for him".[104]

Was it worth submitting himself and his family to intrusion and stress in order to secure such a dubious prize? However hard Joseph tried to keep the contest focused on ideas, after the events of the past nine months the press was sure to drag the subject back to personalities; and once he really had thrown his hat into the ring his personal affairs would come under even closer scrutiny. Du

---

101. Fowler, *Ministers Decide*, 11–12; Fisher, *Tory Leaders*, 159.
102. Whitehead, *Writing on the Wall*, 327; Thatcher, *Path to Power*, 266.
103. Fisher, *Tory Leaders*, 156–7.
104. Halcrow, *Joseph*, 79, 91; *The Times*, 11 November 1974; Fisher, *Tory Leaders*, 162, 160; Miles Hudson's diary, 10 October 1974 (we are most grateful to Major Hudson for allowing us to consult his private record of the October 1974 general election).

Cann had already begun to waver as the press investigated his own business interests; according to parliamentary gossip, Labour officials held a dossier of damaging material. One of du Cann's chief supporters speculated that this "campaign of quiet but persistent denigration was part of the strategy adopted by some of Heath's adherents to prejudice the prospects of any potential candidate". By the end of December it was clear that du Cann would join Joseph in sitting out the impending battle.[105]

On the day that Heath addressed the 1922 Committee Margaret Thatcher, recently appointed as deputy to the Shadow Chancellor Robert Carr, gave a bravura display in the Commons' debate on Healey's post-election financial measures. A week later Joseph rang to ask if he could see her in her Commons' office. Since Mrs Thatcher had been canvassing hard on her friend's behalf it seems strange that he had not informed her of his decision not to stand at the time that he wrote to Fowler and Lamont; possibly he hoped that someone else would give her the bad news.[106] In fact, for some time individual MPs had been suggesting to Mrs Thatcher what recent events had made obvious even to the most blinkered Joseph loyalist – that she would be the more promising candidate. As far back as July David James, the MP for Dorset West, accosted her outside the Commons' tea-room and gave her the encouraging results of a private straw poll; although Mrs Thatcher looked surprised, James remembered her saying that at some point she might have to run for the leadership. When Joseph told her that he was bowing out of the contest, her reply was unhesitating: "if you're not going to stand, I will, because someone who represents our viewpoint *has* to stand".[107]

105. Fisher, *Tory Leaders*, 162. One of Mrs Thatcher's reported remarks from this time could be read as a hint that, like du Cann, Joseph was a victim of "dirty tricks" from within the Heath camp: "I saw how they broke Keith. But they're not going to break *me*". One possible opening for Joseph's more desperate opponents was his religious background. Patrick Cosgrave reported that one "senior Conservative member" raised the question of Joseph's Jewishness, claiming that if he became leader of the party it "might offend the oil companies". By contrast, Sir Alfred Sherman was astonished to hear "true blue Tories telling me that, since Disraeli was the best Tory Prime Minister ever, Keith Joseph should be given a chance". On balance it seems that the "Jewish factor" made no difference to Joseph's prospects one way or the other. See Patrick Cosgrave in *Spectator*, 6 September 1975, 14 September 1974; Sherman in *Jewish Chronicle*, 16 December 1994; interview with Patrick Cosgrave.
106. John Campbell has written that Mrs Thatcher was the first MP to be told about Joseph's decision. Possibly some dates have been confused in the published accounts, but it seems that at most Mrs Thatcher might have been the first of Joseph's colleagues to be told *in person*: see Campbell, *Grocer's Daughter*, 282.
107. Thatcher, *Path to Power*, 266; Interview with Sir Charles Fletcher-Cooke; David James, letter to *Sunday Telegraph*, 19 June 1981.

Chapter 11

"A Good Mind Unharnessed"

"Had I become party leader", Sir Keith Joseph told Anthony Seldon before the 1987 general election, "it would have been a disaster for the party, [for the] country and for me". Although he had been flattered when colleagues approached him, he was aware that he lacked "the breadth of judgement, let alone knowledge, to take on the task". For instance, he had no experience in foreign affairs. And the job of Leader of the Opposition was "overwhelmingly difficult"; as he explained on another occasion, it involved a "constant exercise in schizophrenia" in which "one wants the country to do well and the Government to do badly". So when asked if he really did harbour any regrets about the outcome of his fleeting candidature, he replied "No, none whatsoever. I know my own capacities. Adequate for some jobs, but not for others".[1]

Paying her memorial tribute to Joseph in 1995, Margaret Thatcher saw things very differently. "Keith should have become Prime Minister. So many of us felt that was his destiny . . . In 1975 [sic] we wanted him to become Leader of the Opposition . . . If only in the course of one day fate had flowed through different channels, if only . . .". For opponents of Thatcherism there is a

1. KJ interview with Anthony King, 29–30; *House of Lords Debates*, vol. 539, col. 1451, 4 November 1992. The authors are most grateful to James Douglas for reading and commenting on this chapter.

contrasting "if only". If only Joseph had challenged for the leadership, it would have remained in orthodox hands, either belonging to Heath or to someone else who broadly shared his views.[2]

The "if only" approach to history can be very entertaining, but it should be kept in reserve for dull moments at dinner parties. Some speculations of this kind, though, are more improbable than others. Mrs Thatcher was certainly wrong to think that Joseph would have become leader "if only" he had torn up the offending section of the Edgbaston speech. With or without "our human stock", one cannot imagine him becoming leader. True, he had too much support to have suffered the fate of Enoch Powell in the contest of 1965; if he had stood against Heath in February 1975 he might even have gathered enough votes to make the leader withdraw. Just conceivably, the unexpected field which lined up against Mrs Thatcher for the second ballot – Geoffrey Howe, Jim Prior, John Peyton and Whitelaw – might have faced Joseph had he progressed that far. But the result would not have been the same. Presumably the unnamed "senior Tory" was exaggerating when he told one of Mrs Thatcher's biographers that "When Keith's name was mooted, we all roared with laughter". But even before Edgbaston serious doubts had been expressed about Joseph's suitability on grounds of temperament. On 13 October 1974 the sympathetic Ronald Butt wrote that Joseph was "far too highly strung and nervy" for the top job. Most of the memoirs from this time imply that Edgbaston was the key moment, but for many people it simply confirmed what they thought already; for example, Norman Tebbit's view that Joseph lacked "that indefinable quality that makes a national political leader" apparently characterised his feelings before and after the ill-fated speech. The doubts were reflected before Edgbaston in the bookmakers' odds for the eventual succession to Heath. On 11 October Whitelaw was 5/4 favourite, followed by Robert Carr at 7/4. Joseph was available at 7/2, while the "unconsidered" Mrs Thatcher was 50/1.[3]

But this does not mean that the alternative "if only" is wholly persuasive. If Joseph was an unlikely winner even before Edgbaston, the chances of an endorsement of Edward Heath's leadership by the parliamentary party were almost equally remote. One of his supporters, Kenneth Clarke, was only exaggerating a little when he claimed that "They would have elected anybody who wasn't Ted Heath". This was not just because Heath proved to be a taciturn candidate, who defied the efforts of his campaign team to entice him into small-talk with potential supporters. He had been leader for almost ten years, and built up the inevitable stock of resentments over that time. Had he stooped to offer more knighthoods to undistinguished back-benchers he might still have won, but in addition to real or imagined slights a number of MPs

2. Margaret Thatcher, speech at KJ memorial service.
3. *Sunday Times*, 13 October 1974; Ogden, *Maggie*, 118; Tebbit, *Upwardly Mobile*, 177; *The Times*, 12 October 1974.

thought that he had been a liability for the party in October 1974 and it was difficult even for his admirers to see him as a positive asset in any future contest. The best argument for retaining Heath as leader was the possibility that, with Labour highly vulnerable in the Commons, Wilson might call a snap election before a replacement had been given time to make a mark. But Conservative MPs who had heard complaints on the doorstep could only expect that the party would do at least as badly if Heath stayed in post. "If only" Heath had decided to retire from the leadership after the second 1974 defeat his legacy might have been conserved by his successor (presumably Whitelaw, in such circumstances). But once he had followed the advice of friends who urged him to fight on, it became impossible to predict the course of events.[4]

Almost the only things that can be said with confidence about developments within the Conservative Party in 1974–5 are that there was no sudden "conversion" to Joseph's way of thinking,[5] and that without him Mrs Thatcher might not have won. There was, of course, an element within the parliamentary party which agreed with the monetarist diagnosis, but this was not substantial enough to secure victory and a successful candidate needed to convince less ideological MPs that he or she offered change which stopped short of a clean break with the past. While MPs knew that a vote for Mrs Thatcher was to some extent a leap in the dark, this looked an acceptable risk compared to what might be a plunge from the cliffs under Joseph's navigation. In defiance of the facts, one commentator has even advanced the theory that Joseph's unbridled oratory was part of a preconceived plan – that in the summer of 1974 he consciously set himself up as a kind of demented stalking-horse to make the real candidate of the Right seem sane and electable.[6] Once she had emerged as a candidate Mrs Thatcher advertised her unhappiness with the record of the government of which she had been a part, but after Joseph's Upminster speech no expression of such views was likely to cause a sensation and by comparison her tone was measured, with criticism of Labour outweighing the strictures on her own party. Before Joseph's withdrawal Mrs Thatcher had advertised her qualities as a potential Opposition leader with a parliamentary attack on the budget which was more notable for its personal sallies than for references to abstract economic ideas. On 22 January 1975 she followed up with an assault on Denis Healey which delighted back-benchers. One never knew with Joseph; instead of delivering sharp debating points he was just as likely to have treated the Commons to an extended lecture on the merits of Hayek and Schumpeter. Tactically Mrs Thatcher followed the shrewd advice of Heath's sworn personal

---

4. Andy McSmith, *Kenneth Clarke: A Political Biography* (Verso, 1994), 57.
5. For the latest research on the 1975 leadership election, see Philip Cowley and Matthew Bailey, "Peasants' Uprising or Religious War? Re-Examining the 1975 Conservative Leadership Contest", in *British Journal of Political Science*, Winter 2000. We are most grateful to the authors for allowing us to see a copy prior to publication.
6. Bruce Arnold, *Margaret Thatcher: A Study in Power* (Hamish Hamilton, 1984), 109–10.

enemy Airey Neave, who had approached Joseph soon after the October 1974 election but would have found him more difficult to manage had he remained in the race.[7] Unusual press interest focused on the fact that Mrs Thatcher had the chance to be the first female leader of a British party, and although for some this was an additional reason to oppose her, others could speculate on the electoral advantages – not just among women, but also among gentlemen of a certain age. Her physical appearance made such connoisseurs as Kingsley Amis and Woodrow Wyatt think the unthinkable. After their first meeting Friedrich von Hayek gasped "She's so beautiful", and in the wake of her victory even Geoffrey Howe found himself echoing this aesthetic judgement.[8] Fear of her declared principles might be tempered by the chauvinistic assumption that, as a woman, she would be more likely than Joseph to heed more temperate advisors. Again, some opponents scoffed at Mrs Thatcher as a stereotyped representative of her class, but her appeal to key target groups within the electorate was far more obvious than that of Joseph, whose Harrow schooling and baronetcy conjured the image of a renegade aristocrat.

In short, people who wanted rid of Heath could think of several positive reasons for supporting Mrs Thatcher without assenting to her economic and social views, and these factors came into clearer perspective in the comparison with Joseph. Not without reason did the *Economist* dub the latter a "lightning-conductor to Mrs Thatcher". When reflecting on his performance as Secretary of State for Industry in Mrs Thatcher's first government, Joseph gave a humorous twist to the same point, admitting that his reputation for eccentricity had often been helpful – he had been "a convenient madman": "I was a joke, a useful joke". In fact, this was far more true of February 1975 than for any subsequent period.[9] The final, best-known factors in explaining Mrs Thatcher's leadership victory were her courage in being the only senior figure in the party to stand against Heath – and her luck, in that some supporters of William Whitelaw were tempted to vote for her as their only means of bringing their own champion into the lists for a second ballot.[10] They succeeded only too well. While for their purposes a narrow victory for Heath would have been sufficient, Mrs Thatcher won by 130 votes to 119. In theory all the candidates

---

7. The stark contrast between the respective personalities of Joseph and Neave is neatly captured by the latter's response when in October 1974 he discovered that Joseph intended to tell Heath of the backing he had received for the leadership. "He'll kill us! He'll kill us!", Neave is reported to have exclaimed. Having a Colditz escapee at the head of one's campaign team brought obvious benefits; the (predictable) downside was the injection of a prevailing mood of paranoia into any assessment of the "enemy's" likely tactics. See Ranelagh, *Thatcher's People*, 136.

8. Cockett, *Thinking the Unthinkable*, 176; Howe, *Conflict of Loyalty*, 94.

9. *Economist*, 27 September 1975; Halcrow, *Joseph*, 149; Ogden, *Maggie*, 118.

10. To add to the confusion, at least one economic liberal voted for Whitelaw, believing that under his leadership the party's economic policy would still move in a "Powellite" direction but that this departure would be consolidated more easily under the genial Whitelaw; interview with Lord Biffen.

in the next round started again from scratch, but considerable momentum had built up behind Mrs Thatcher who suddenly looked like a winner while Whitelaw was discredited by association with the defeated regime.

Obviously Joseph gave his warm support to Mrs Thatcher; he was the only member of the Shadow Cabinet to vote for her on the first ballot. Along with Neave and William Shelton he attended a series of Sunday-night strategy meetings at her home in Flood Street, Chelsea (a short stroll away from Mulberry Walk). On the day after the first ballot showed Mrs Thatcher ahead Joseph gave a talk to school children in Hampstead, and made no secret of his delight. He seemed "overjoyed by the shock news. He spoke with irrepressible gaiety, with a broad smile on his face throughout his visit". But this was only reported locally. The national press gave no indication that he worked very hard for Mrs Thatcher behind the scenes. Patrick Cosgrave explained Joseph's low profile by claiming that he "was quite unversed in the subtleties of vote-getting in Westminster". Since Sir Keith had helped in Heath's 1965 campaign, the implication was that his speeches of 1974 had made him such a divisive figure within the party that he was more likely to hinder than to help (in any case, as he later admitted, "I really don't have any skill in tactics, none whatsoever").[11] Many of his own supporters would have switched automatically, and if anything the best service he could do to Mrs Thatcher's cause was to avoid any ideological infelicities until the election was safely over. Further musings about "our human stock" were off the agenda, and a serious problem might have arisen if Joseph had persisted with his thoughts on education. The dismal picture he had painted so recently of schools and universities reflected little credit on Mrs Thatcher's ministerial record, which she herself had found "no difficulty" in defending at the election of February 1974. To adopt a blasphemous parallel which was commonly heard on the Right after February 1975, it was as if John the Baptist had drawn attention to flaws in the Messiah's work over the past few years before introducing the people to their new leader.

It appears that there was a change after Mrs Thatcher stepped forward. In early December 1974 Joseph surprised his colleagues by presenting to steering committee an economic paper which concentrated on immediate problems rather than visionary prospects for the distant future. Even Robert Carr – who had recently been irritated to the point of offering his resignation by Mrs Thatcher's habit of consulting only Sherman and Joseph before making statements on Treasury matters – found much to agree with.[12] On New Year's Day Joseph resumed his most disconcerting form, but at least he had chosen a

---

11. Wapshot & Brock, *Thatcher*, 128; *Ham and High*, 7 February 1975; Patrick Cosgrave, *Margaret Thatcher: Prime Minister* (Arrow, 1979), 57; Thatcher, *Path to Power*, 192; KJ interview for "The Thatcher Factor".
12. Interview with Lord Carr; LSC (74) 22, minutes of steering committee meeting, 9 December 1974, CPA, Bodleian Library.

fresh subject. Opening the Camping and Outdoor Life Exhibition and Motor Caravan Show at Olympia, he attracted the attention of a mischievous diarist from *The Times*, who witnessed an "extraordinary speech":

> To get the full flavour, you have to picture it being delivered to an audience of apparently non-political campers, many with young children, who were standing in front of a mock woodland area. In this incongruous setting, the speech Sir Keith chose to deliver amounted to an attack on the Soviet Union. While the campers and their young stood speechless, he spent several minutes pointing out that it was more difficult for the Russians to move about their country than it was for us. It was only when he came to the punch line that it was clear what he was on about. "It does strike a chill", he said. "Are we sure that we shall not eventually be subject to movement permits if socialism advances here? Don't be too sure."

The leap from the joys of camping to the horrors of socialist restrictions was too much for the man from *The Times*, who was even more perturbed when, interviewed afterwards by the BBC "against a background of recordings of bird and animal calls, Joseph described his speech as 'light-hearted'". It was further proof that Joseph's sense of humour could be misunderstood outside a narrow circle of intimates. After all his scare tactics he had acknowledged that "socialists don't want movement controls", before warning that "It is not their intentions but the logic of their policies that count . . . this is all the more reason for acquiring a caravan while you can".[13]

After this jocular diversion, in Edinburgh on 10 January 1975 Joseph returned to the economy, defending his Preston speech in fairly measured terms. He admitted that his preferred policies would entail some job-losses, but reiterated that he was not recommending "a sudden tug on the reins to tighten up money supply". When a few days later he gave a speech to mark the public launch of the CPS he urged that the Conservative Party should be "doctrinal, not doctrinaire" – an interesting distinction which he did not flesh out – and spoke sympathetically of the pressures which might induce a minister to bail out companies in financial trouble. He went on to assure his audience that "We can afford to argue calmly, factually, courteously. We need not shout like the Socialists do, nor abuse opponents as they do". Not even Joseph – famed as he was for his scrupulous political manners – could maintain this code of practice in his excitable mood between 1974 and 1979. But at least the speech would have brought more restful sleep to anyone who was having nightmares about voting for Mrs Thatcher in the leadership election because of her association

---

13. *The Times*, 2 January 1975; KJ, text of speech at Olympia, 1 January 1975.

with Joseph. It featured a thoughtful exposition of the ideal of *embourgeoisement* which he had broached in 1969–70; he looked forward to a time when "middle-class values" would prevail throughout society, and the overwhelming majority would exhibit "a willingness to defer gratification, to work hard for years, study, save, look after the family future". It was a text-book description of the typical Victorian household; as Joseph pointed out, these values had once been accepted by aspiring workers as well as those who were already comfortable. In aiming at their destruction, socialists were betraying the true interests of the class that they claimed to represent.[14]

In the Commons Joseph was less restrained. One speech, in particular, showed that Edgbaston had not cured him of his habit of thinking aloud. On the day that he told Mrs Thatcher of his decision not to stand, the Birmingham pub bombings refocused attention on the terrorist menace. In response the Government rushed through the draconian Prevention of Terrorism Act, for which Joseph offered wholehearted Conservative support. On most of the issues which confronted him as Shadow Home Secretary he relied on the advice of a convenient expert – his deputy Norman Fowler, who had gained insights into law and order issues from his work as a Midlands journalist. But Joseph had resolved his internal debate over capital punishment on his own, and on 11 December 1974 he reported his detailed findings to an astonished House. Since terrorist murders were premeditated they deserved the death penalty, he said, but this should not apply in Ulster where there were no juries in terrorist trials. To confuse matters further, Joseph announced that he would support the amendment under discussion, even though this called for the reintroduction of the death penalty *throughout* the United Kingdom. To save himself the difficulty of voting for a position which he had just rejected, Joseph looked forward to Roy Jenkins's speech in the hope that the Home Secretary would produce "arguments which totally defeat what I believe at present". Barbara Castle described the argument as a "contribution of marvellous tortuousness and circumlocution", noting her suspicion that Joseph was "consumed with ambition as well as self-doubt". But Joseph had already dropped out of contention for the leadership. In reality the speech was an ill-starred attempt to express in logical terms the views that a majority of voters had reached on emotional grounds. By contrast, in his former guise Joseph had rejected any appeal to the emotions on this subject, on one occasion denying that he would want even the murderer of his own child to suffer the death penalty. The result of his rethink, in Jenkins's view, was a position "both tortured and nonsensical". Certainly Joseph was deeply troubled by the issue; the consistent abolitionist Ian Gilmour remembers hurrying down the Mall at this time, pursued by an

---

14. Speech at Edinburgh, 10 January 1975; speech at St Ermin's Hotel, 15 January 1975, both reprinted in KJ, *Reversing the Trend*, 46–64.

agitated Joseph who would not give up trying to make him appreciate the force of his argument.[15]

Fortunately for himself Joseph was soon released from the necessity of wrangling with these problems in public. After Mrs Thatcher's victory on the second leadership ballot of 11 February – by 146 votes to Whitelaw's 79 – it was widely anticipated that Joseph would finally secure the Shadow Chancellorship. Joseph himself was reported to be confident.[16] Instead (and to his own amazement) Sir Geoffrey Howe was offered the position. Lady Thatcher has described how a delay in announcing the new team led to speculation in the press that "a battle was under way to prevent Keith Joseph becoming Shadow Chancellor. In fact", she wrote, "he did not ask for the position nor did I offer it". At the time, Joseph rushed out a press statement to the same effect. But the speculation was well informed, although Lady Thatcher's words are technically correct. The new leader had *not* offered the post to Joseph – because opponents led by Whitelaw prevented her from doing so. Joseph would not have dreamed of asking her for it. It proved to be a pyrrhic victory; from their own point of view the moderates (or "wets") who constituted the clear majority of the Shadow Cabinet had been saddled with a far more dangerous foe. One of his supporters regarded Howe as "the natural political successor to Keith Joseph", but in one vital respect Joseph had followed in the younger man's footsteps; Howe had been among the first Conservative MPs to take serious notice of the IEA. If Howe had shared Joseph's temperament his actions during the Heath government would have weighed heavily on his conscience; as Solicitor-General he had played a key role in drafting the ill-starred Industrial Relations Act, and he moved on from this calamity to act as the nation's price-fixer under the terms of Heath's incomes policy. Yet from Howe there were no extravagant cries of repentence after February 1974. The mood in his memoirs is one of puzzlement that he should have contradicted his beliefs in this way, although he is careful to note that others did the same. After the February election he moved to Social Services, which he had studied for many years. Persuaded into standing for the leadership in February 1975, he had attracted support from several promising Conservatives, concentrated on the Bow Group rather than a single wing of the party. His tally of nineteen votes disappointed him, but there was plenty of quality among his backers, including Kenneth Clarke, Leon Brittan, and Fowler (who was convinced that Mrs Thatcher would project the wrong image to voters). Howe himself struck most people as being dour but diligent

15. *Hansard*, vol. 883, cols 532–7, 11 December 1974; Barbara Castle, *The Castle Diaries 1974–76* (Weidenfeld & Nicolson, 1980), 247; Roy Jenkins, *A Life at the Centre* (Macmillan, 1991), 401; Roth memorandum; interviews with Sir Norman Fowler and Lord Gilmour. Some measure of the surprise caused by the speech can be gained from the fact that Douglas Hurd remembered it better than anything else Joseph said in the Commons, although they sat in the House together for a further twenty-two years and later became Cabinet colleagues; interview with Lord Hurd.
16. Peter Jenkins in *Guardian*, 14 February 1975.

– a combination of qualities which prevented him from rising to the very top but which, in hindsight, made him the best leadership contender for those who had hoped for a permanent revolution in British economic policy.[17]

Joseph was asked to continue with his Shadow Cabinet responsibility for policy and research, in the heartening expectation that this time his ideas would be received with sympathy by the party leader. Presumably – along with a status junior only to Mrs Thatcher and Whitelaw in the Shadow Cabinet pecking order – this was ample compensation after a fourth failure to take on the leading economic role for his party. On this subject he no longer had to shout from the sidelines; he had moved to a position just behind the main striker. He was a member of the Economic Reconstruction Group, and, more important, he was a regular attender at the informal meetings, held in Howe's home on Fentiman Road near Vauxhall Bridge, where the monetarists could plan strategy away from such infidels as Prior and Gilmour. Even the Reconstruction Group was weighted against the moderates; apart from Howe and Joseph, it included John Nott, Arthur Cockfield, Nicholas Ridley, Nigel Lawson and Powell's most faithful disciple, John Biffen. Among the other members, Patrick Jenkin and David Howell were more pragmatic but still predisposed towards radical ideas.

Looking back, many of the "wets" might regret that from an early stage the initiative on economic policy was seized by the Right. But although they enjoyed their maximum influence in early 1975 the "wets" could not regard the newly elected Mrs Thatcher as a helpless prisoner; and if the limits of their power meant that they had to choose between holding a majority in the Shadow Cabinet and maintaining control over economic policy, the first option seemed irresistible. Instead of blackballing Joseph, Whitelaw might have insisted that he was restrained by a predominantly Keynesian Treasury team, but even an operator of Whitelaw's pre-eminent skills could be forgiven for missing that tactical master-stroke. Other important changes within the party machine, such as the sacking of Heath's speech-writer Michael Wolff, and the elevation of the veteran rebels Thorneycroft and Maude to the Chairmanships of the Party and the Research Department, had to be accepted as appointments in which the leader had always been allowed a free hand.

Ultimately for the "wets" everything hinged on events; and events played them a cruel hand after 1975. The "if only" school could entertain themselves by asking what might have happened if James Callaghan's daughter had decided not to marry Peter Jay. After succeeding Wilson in April 1976 Callaghan faced almost continuous economic crises. At the end of September, in the midst of

---

17. Howe, *Conflict of Loyalty*, 91–3, 94; Thatcher, *Path to Power*, 285; Fowler, *Ministers Decide*, 15. Whitelaw would probably have opposed Joseph's appointment in consequence of the latter's "disloyalty" during 1974. But if he had any doubts on the subject they must have been removed by the capital punishment debate, during which Whitelaw intervened to make clear his own opposition (and that of Heath) to Joseph's new arguments.

negotations for a loan from the International Monetary Fund (IMF), Callaghan read to his party conference a speech written largely by his son-in-law. In the most famous passage Callaghan claimed that:

> We used to think that you could spend your way out of a recession and increase employment by cutting taxes and boosting government spending. I tell you in all candour that that option no longer exists, and that, insofar as it ever did exist, it only worked on each occasion since the war by injecting a bigger dose of inflation into the economy, followed by a higher level of unemployment as the next step. Higher inflation followed by higher unemployment – that is the history of the last twenty years.[18]

This was a neat paraphrase of Sir Keith – a revisitation of the Preston speech which Jay had welcomed. It heralded the Labour government's acceptance of strict control on public spending at the behest of the IMF. It would be stretching even an elastic term a little to describe the government as "monetarist" after 1976; Chancellor Healey later claimed that "In order to satisfy the markets, I began to publish the monetary forecasts we had always made in private, and then described them as targets". In fact, like Jenkins before him the unbelieving Healey proved a better monetarist in practice than Friedman's disciples, and, as he put it, under his stewardship modest figures for monetary growth "kept the markets quiet".[19] But if Healey continued to think that the money supply was of marginal relevance to the state of the real economy, others were encouraged by Callaghan's speech to think that the present crisis marked the burial of Keynes and the enthronement of Friedman. Possibly Callaghan felt that in order to appease the IMF he had to sound as if he had undergone some kind of "conversion" – albeit a reluctant one. If so, it was an ironic way of ending the post-war "consensus", under which politicians of both parties had too often manipulated the economy for short-term gain. In order to secure Callaghan's short-term survival in 1976, Jay had provided him with a text which envisaged an indefinite political era of rigorous accountancy. Jay believed that tighter economic management was compatible with idealistic policies in other fields, but not many Labour Party members were prepared to take that view in 1976.

The consequences of Callaghan's speech were equally impressive within the Conservative Party. From being regarded as odd-ball enthusiasts on the margins of political debate, Joseph and his allies now seemed to be riding the wave of the future. If anything, events had befriended Joseph *too* warmly; it looked as though Callaghan was about to steal the monetarist clothes before the

---

18. Quoted in Whitehead, *Writing on the Wall*, 189.
19. Denis Healey, *The Time of My Life* (Penguin, 1990), 434.

Conservatives had modelled them for the public. In September 1975 Joseph proclaimed that "We are all monetarists now – except for a few die-hard inflationeers who cannot learn from experience or admit mistakes".[20] But a year later, when Callaghan indicated his own "conversion", the "die-hard inflationeers" were as strongly entrenched as ever in the Shadow Cabinet. Both factions within the Conservative Party looked to the next election as the conclusive event in their quarrel; the result would encourage remaining agnostic Tory MPs to take sides. Here too Callaghan had the decisive voice. If, as was widely expected, he had called a general election in the autumn of 1978 Labour might not have won, but at best Mrs Thatcher would have been forced to compromise with her critics in a minority administration. By delaying until he was defeated in a vote of confidence, Callaghan ensured that Labour was still in office during the "Winter of Discontent" which seemed to epitomise the failure of post-war politics. As the man who had arguably started the process of decay by opposing *In Place of Strife* back in 1969, Callaghan was an appropriate undertaker for "consensus" politics.

When Joseph began his policy work in February 1975 he assumed that Labour's economic management would be inept, but he could not expect that the government would commit such crippling tactical blunders. Even if the Conservatives won an early election, he was haunted by the fear that the old "consensus" approach would reassert itself. One of his first actions was to circulate among colleagues the memorandum which Alan Walters had drawn up in June 1972, presumably in the belief that there would now be unanimous assent to this monetarist analysis. For the Shadow Cabinet meeting of 11 April he collaborated with Maude on a lengthy paper setting out the lessons of the past and the tasks confronting the party if it were to present a credible alternative to "the inexorable collectivism of our society". Joseph acknowledged that "We shall not be able to change everything at once, not in the run-up to the next election, not in our political life-times for that matter. What is important is that we should show a way forward, away from the discredited policies and failed illusions, and that we tackle first things first".

The measured tone of these remarks was more characteristic of Maude than of Joseph's recent speeches. In the opening section, however, there could be no doubting the dominant voice. After running through the dismal Conservative record since the war, Joseph informed his colleagues that "In short, by ignoring history, instincts, human nature and common sense, we have intensified the very evils which we believed, with the best of intentions, that we could wipe away". Almost every word of this begged a question. Joseph's own view of history was idiosyncratic; his experience of human nature was relatively limited; and it seems strange that so soon after Edgbaston he could appeal to the

---

20. *Daily Telegraph*, 25 September 1975.

promptings of "common sense". Those who had hoped that Joseph would change his tune under a more congenial leader were dismayed; if anything the tune had become even more discordant. In discussion, the moderates hit back. As the restrained minutes record:

> Several members, while regarding the policy suggestions as valuable, thought the paper was too critical of the recent past and, in particular, of recent Conservative policy. They emphasised that the Party should not repudiate its previous attempts to reach a national consensus and to hold the middle ground of opinion, as this was the key not only to electoral success, on which all else depended, but also to governing and staying in power. Conservative policy should be evolutionary, and build upon the past, not revolutionary, rejecting the past. Stability in approach was also important as people became more bewildered by events.

The Shadow Cabinet "generally felt that the Conservative Government of 1970–74 had, on the whole, tried to do the right things, but had failed to explain its intentions adequately".[21]

The surprise of the meeting was not that the moderates refused to abase themselves at Joseph's bidding, but that there was no detailed criticism – indeed no minuted discussion – of the policy ideas expounded in the remainder of the twenty-page document. Presumably Joseph's opponents felt that it was too soon to start a battle over specific policies; the key point for them was to stamp on any suggestion that they should spend the next few years apologising for the past. The more convinced Keynesians on the committee, such as Prior and Gilmour, found little in the economic paragraphs with which they could agree. But at least the tone was fairly equable. The real danger signs came in the section which dealt with what Joseph called "the climate of opinion". This was used to denounce the "range of alien values – based on variants of tyranny and anarchy – which are propogated [sic] apparently[22] by some teachers and lie behind the bias shown on some television programmes. Are we defenceless against such misuse of freedoms? We need not be". "We must not fear the epithets 'McCarthyism' and 'reds under the beds'", Joseph reassured his colleagues: "The facts will support us". Television programmes should be monitored for signs of bias – presumably by objective experts like Joseph himself – and student activists should be curbed by reducing the number of postgraduates and legislating against compulsory contributions to student

---

21. KJ and Angus Maude, "Notes towards a definition of policy", paper of 4 April 1975, 5; LCC (75) Fifty-Seventh Meeting of Leader's Consultative Committee, 11 April 1975, CPA, Bodleian Library.
22. "Apparently" was a significant word. Was Joseph conceding the possibility that his hostility towards teachers might be based on the views of an unrepresentative sample of parents?

union funds. Joseph was not against free speech – only against "the hidden use of non-political opportunities for political purposes". This was a laudable approach. Yet on the previous page he had written that "It is curious that our education system does so little to teach children about the system of free enterprise that sustain[s] the pluralistic and democratic freedoms we take for granted". Like most ideologues, Joseph had convinced himself that his own views were based on "common sense"; only on this premise could he regard lessons in the virtues of the free market as anything but a prime example of "the hidden use of non-political opportunities for political purposes".[23]

Instead of helping the Shadow Cabinet to define its policy, Joseph's paper had confirmed that the period of Opposition, at least, would be marked by constant bickering. After the outbursts of 1974 it would have been sensible for him to usher in a time of healing; instead he had rubbed salt into fresh wounds. The press soon learned that Gilmour and Maudling (now recalled to the front-bench as Foreign Affairs spokesman) had led the counter-attack against Joseph; one or two personal remarks disparaging the policy supremo also found their way into the newspapers. But only in 1997 did the full story come out, when Geoffrey Lewis published Lord Hailsham's more detailed note of the discussion. Francis Pym, the Agriculture Spokesman, had called Joseph's paper "a recipe for disaster". When Gilmour denied that the "consensus" up to 1970 had been dominated by Labour, Mrs Thatcher protested, "Ian, you *do* believe in capitalism?". If the dissidents in the Shadow Cabinet felt too constrained by their positions to extend public displays beyond nods, winks and coded speeches, Peter Walker (whom Mrs Thatcher had sacked to make room for older men) was roaming unmuzzled on the back-benches as Powell had done after 1968. More than once he clashed with Joseph over incomes policy, a subject which produced more disagreement within the Shadow Cabinet than almost any other (predictably enough, after the experience of the Heath government).[24]

Ten days after the Shadow Cabinet discussed his paper, Joseph was given a perfect opportunity to show his critics that, whether they agreed with him or not, he was a parliamentary force to be reckoned with. At the end of a four-day debate on the latest Healey budget, Joseph caught the speaker's eye knowing that the press were expecting him to explain "how a Conservative government would deal with inflation, unemployment, maintenance of the social services, and all the rest". In *The Times* David Wood anticipated "perhaps the most important speech in his political career so far". But the result fell below expectations. Joseph attacked Healey for misquoting the unemployment figures, provoking (and losing) a skirmish with the Chancellor over footnotes

23. KJ and Maude, "Notes towards a definition of policy", 17–19.
24. David Wood in *The Times*, 21 April 1975; Geoffrey Lewis, *Lord Hailsham* (Jonathan Cape, 1997), 326; Thatcher, *Path to Power*, 302.

in learned economic journals. Although he made the usual pleas on behalf of Britain's hard-pressed managers – "the ulcer people – talented, job-creating, potentially wealth-creating for the country" – Joseph seemed uncertain whether to criticise the Chancellor or to congratulate him on a budget which marked the beginning of an attack on inflation. He also had a new apology to make, since by now it had become clear that his reorganisation of the NHS had produced a massive increase in bureaucracy with no noticeable improvement in services.[25]

In a stern editorial the next day, *The Times* landed an unexpected punch. While Joseph's colleagues were complaining that he was too dogmatic, the newspaper felt that it was apparent from the speech "that nothing approaching a coherent alternative economic philosophy was yet available". At best, Joseph had confused control of public spending with restrictions on the money supply, and "No monetarist could have said that". Neither would a follower of Friedman have spent so much time championing "tax-payers, entrepreneurs, the middle-classes and the owner-occupier". It seemed, in fact, that Joseph was a kind of perverted Keynesian, who wanted to use demand-management to raise the level of unemployment in order to squeeze inflation out of the system. Whatever his intentions, he had laid himself open to the charge of pandering to groups associated with the Conservative Party rather than explaining a theory which might help the country as a whole. The editorial challenged Joseph to decide "whether he is the prophet of alternative economic theories or the salesman of quite differently based political slogans".[26]

The editorial might have been regarded by non-specialists as an obscure squabble within the Church of Monetarism, but it was more than just an assault on Joseph's economic credibility; it also threatened his new sense of identity as a trustworthy friend of those liberal economists who had no patience for political expediency. If the editorial was right, either Joseph did not understand the doctrine with which he had associated himself, or he had skewed a "scientific" theory to score political points. The author – presumably Jay – had his own reasons for arguing that monetarism should be treated as a tool of policy with no ideological or partisan connotations. As an avid reader of *The Times* Joseph must have seen the article, and in the following year he restated his monetarist credentials in his Stockton Lecture entitled "Monetarism is not enough". His reply to his purist critics was that they had based their argument on a false distinction between Friedman and Keynes, who (unlike his misguided followers) was himself "a monetarist by any reasonable definition of the term". The demands for real cuts in public expenditure and for incentives to entrepreneurs did not mark a retreat from monetarism, he claimed; rather, they were an improvement on the theory. To Joseph's monetarist critics this was

25. *Ibid.*; *Hansard*, vol. 890, cols 1000–18, 21 April 1975.
26. *The Times*, 22 April 1975.

an avoidance of the main question rather than a rebuttal of the allegation about narrow partisanship. But the most important aspect of the speech is the fact that Joseph felt the challenge deeply enough to produce even the semblance of a reply.[27]

After Joseph's disappointing performance in the budget debate he left the main parliamentary battle over economics to others. He was ill-equipped for the cut-and-thrust of debate – particularly with a bully like Healey, who was able to crow after Joseph's debut performance that he would "take a wager that over the coming weeks every newspaper from the *News of the World* to the *Yachtsman's Journal* will be flooded with letters and articles by the right hon. Gentleman explaining what he meant to say this afternoon but, once again, failed to get across". After he became Shadow Industry spokesman in February 1977 close colleagues noticed that Joseph would enter the chamber with a prepared speech, but as the debate progressed the floor around him would become strewn with discarded pages as he revised his text in response to the developing argument. Another problem was the state of his nerves. Even in television studios Joseph's composure would desert him when faced with an eloquent opponent. After recording a discussion in February 1977 Tony Benn noted that "Keith is an absolutely tortured soul – he was in agony, his face twisted in anxiety, his stomach [seemed] all torn up, his head in his hands and he was scribbling and worrying, he really is a sick man". It might have been on this occasion that, as Benn recalls, Joseph was physically sick before a broadcast discussion. He had undergone another (unspecified) operation in September 1976 and was convalescent for most of that month, yet clearly problems remained.[28]

In theory, set-piece speeches would be less of an ordeal for a person of Joseph's health and disposition. There might be heckling – or worse – but a speaker had the option of sticking to his text regardless of interruptions. Even so, most doctors would have doubted the wisdom of the regime that Joseph imposed on himself during the Opposition years. In trying to change the "climate of opinion" he could count on important allies in the press, but he was determined to take the case for the free market into what he saw as the citadel of the enemy – the universities. By February 1977 Joseph was able to claim that he had visited "almost every university in England and Wales"; it has been estimated that he made 150 speeches at various educational institutions during this Opposition period. In conversation with Morrison Halcrow, he described his itinerary as "self-inflicted misery"; even so, "his face lit up" at the recollection. "It was *lovely*. (Of course it was horrible at the time.) Very large audiences

---

27. KJ, *Monetarism is not enough* (CPS, 1976), 5, 18; interview with Peter Jay.
28. *Hansard*, vol. 890, col. 1116, 21 April 1975; interview with Kenneth Clarke; Tony Benn, unedited diary, 24 February 1977; interview with Tony Benn; correspondence in Joseph Papers, 10/8, CPA, Bodleian Library.

– almost to a girl or boy convinced statists if not socialists". The tone of his recollections brings to mind an old actor dwelling on the biggest nights of his career; and while Joseph's remarkable efforts clearly tapped into that half-buried aspect of his character, it also revealed his respect for the ailing British tradition of political oratory.[29]

The "campus campaign" must have taken Joseph back to his happiest Harrow days; but instead of the Shakespeare Prize, he felt that he was now competing for the mind of a generation, and the penalty for failure was a hail of rotten eggs. He told Halcrow that he "improvised when he got to the hall", but the theme was fairly constant: "that capitalism was the least bad way yet invented – as Churchill said about democracy". Francis Wheen, then a student at London University, has left a detailed account of a typical Joseph speech, delivered at Royal Holloway College in January 1976. Joseph began by saying that he was free to criticise the post-war record of both main parties, because he had only recently discovered that he was a Conservative. He asserted that political debate since 1945 had disguised a wide gulf of principle between Conservative and Labour, corresponding to two ways of running society – the "market system" and the "command system". Under the command system the choices of individuals were determined by bureaucrats, who would continue to draw their salaries even if they failed to satisfy the public. Everything was owned by the state, which meant that there could be no place for writers, artists, inventors, critics or reformers. Without independent sources of patronage creative thinkers of all kinds would have to conform or starve: even Karl Marx had depended on the generosity of Engels. By contrast, freedom, innovation and choice were integral features of the market system. Business ventures would fail if they were inefficient or ignored public tastes; in the arts and sciences no one could be assured of a hearing unless they had something worthwhile to say. Unfortunately the British were in danger of forgetting the benefits of the market, which had served them so well in the past. "We have mismanaged our market system for generations", Joseph claimed. "Since the war we have totally discouraged decision-making and risk-taking".[30]

The typical Joseph speech would last for about half an hour, and was followed by "up to an hour of questions". This part of the proceedings might have proved awkward for Joseph, but as he told Halcrow "they didn't realise how relatively easy it was to answer questions". He was rarely stumped for a reply, because those who were most likely to shout out a question were the ideologues of the Left whose arguments were simply the mirror-image of his own. When an answer eluded him he could always ask his colleagues at the CPS for assistance before

---

29. Minutes of "KJ Committee", 23 February 1977, Joseph Papers 18/2, CPA, Bodleian Library; Halcrow, *Joseph*, 104.
30. Halcrow, *Joseph*, 104; Francis Wheen, "Adam Smith Rides Again", *Chateau*, Vol. XVI, No. 9, 28 January 1976, 3.

the next encounter. In January 1977, for example, he requested advice after reporting that "More and more I am attacked on the 'irrelevance of freedom to those who are poor'. I am also attacked because of the alleged inevitability of concentration of industry under capitalism".[31] But on six occasions feelings among student activists ran so high that they prevented Joseph from speaking at all. At Sussex University in October 1975, he left the hall with egg spattered on his suit and even when he continued his lecture outside he was shouted down. There were similar scenes in May at Glasgow University, where the man who had recently deprecated personal attacks compared Tony Benn to Dracula. At least such incidents maintained the surge of adrenalin which was necessary for the continuation of his new crusade. The worst let-down would follow speeches such as the one he gave at Kingston Polytechnic shortly after Mrs Thatcher became leader; as *The Times* reported, "Although many in the audience clearly agreed with little he had to say, he was given a warm reception by the students".[32]

In February 1977 – a few days before the meeting which convinced Tony Benn that Joseph was "a tortured soul" – the orator visited Essex University. In advance of his arrival the Students' Union had issued a public warning that Joseph was an unwelcome intruder who had been asked to stay away, since his views were "anti-working class and" – a significant rider, given his background and early reputation – "also racist". In their statement the students noted that Joseph would be offered no protection if he insisted on carrying out the engagement, although the union would "not physically prevent its taking place". To Joseph this kind of talk acted as an irresistible challenge, and the Essex Conservatives were also determined to hear him. When he arrived, eggs and other edible projectiles were aimed at him; eyewitnesses testified that a flour-bomb made contact with his back. Despite (or because of) the anticipated trouble, his audience was 500-strong; he addressed them for thirty minutes, "amid constant shouting and interruptions", on "the moral and material case for capitalism". The local reporter thought that "the content of the speech was largely forgotten" in the mêlée, but the ensuing debate ranged "through Marx, the American poor, and the fall of the Berlin Wall". The president of the Students' Union remembered enough to declare that the speaker "certainly acted in a provocative way, first by getting off the platform and walking to the front of the meeting and by making a banal speech". Few lawyers would have

---

31. Halcrow, *Joseph*, 104; KJ memorandum of 10 March 1977, Sherman Papers, Box 3. If Joseph had really found it difficult to provide off-the-cuff replies for these key (and obvious) questions, one has to wonder whether his responses to students were really as successful as he maintained. The answer that pleased him most was the challenge to left-wing students to name a country in the world where they would prefer to live; the predictable silence, he thought, settled the argument in his favour. But his comment cannot be perfectly reconciled with other statements he made at this time, about the country he loved being so hopelessly misgoverned as to resemble a "slum"; and in any case the assertion that Britain is the best nation on earth leaves uncontested the socialist position that it could be made better still.

32. *The Times*, 22 February 1975.

based a legal defence on "provocation through banal speaking", but the president went on to say that Joseph's speech "was more suited to 12-year-olds than to university students". Even so, the majority of students had applauded at the end. Afterwards Joseph commented that his reception was "not worthy of a university at all"; with his customary precision he ranked it as the fifth worst out of eighty-one meetings in the past two years. The *Sunday Times* promptly called for Essex University to be closed down, even though the "protestors and howlers" clearly represented only a fraction of the student body.[33]

There is reason to suspect that Sir Keith's performances did tend towards "banality"; after all, to maximise the impact of his message it had to be condensed and adjusted for the intelligent non-specialist. At the same time, offering only the "market" and "command" systems as alternative models of society begged the key question of whether or not a "mixed economy" could secure satisfactory levels of freedom, efficiency and social justice. Other aspects of Joseph's argument were vulnerable to serious objections. For example, he claimed at Royal Holloway that "Conservatives regard the individual as a rational being with choice; Socialists regard him as a bundle . . . a package subject to psychic and psychological pressures from without". When these abstract models were applied to the thinking of real individuals, it appeared that Joseph was saying that the ideologues of the French Revolution had actually been Conservatives, while Edmund Burke and Mary Whitehouse were both in the socialist camp. Since no one could deny that Joseph was "subject to psychic and psychological pressures from without", his own character provided excellent backing for what he had characterised as the "Socialist" view of human nature. When pressing home his familiar lesson about Britain's relative post-war economic decline Joseph chose America and Switzerland as more prosperous examples, which missed the crucial point that neither of these countries had suffered anything like the level of damage which Britain experienced between 1939 and 1945. On this occasion there was no reference to West Germany; and Sir Keith had apparently lost interest in the Netherlands, which had been his favourite country in 1973 (because of its traditional respect for the family).[34]

Joseph's university speeches have been cited as a source of inspiration by more than one future Conservative MP who was a student at this time.[35] Whatever the sceptics could say about the details of Joseph's case, his claim that intellectual freedom depended on the market was cleverly designed to appeal to these audiences. And the detail of the speeches was probably less important than the impression that a Conservative had the courage to undertake such a draining

---

33. *Colchester Evening Gazette*, 8, 14, 18 February 1977; *Daily Telegraph*, 12 February 1977; *Sunday Times*, 13 February 1977.
34. Wheen, "Adam Smith Rides Again" in *Chateau*, 28 January 1976; KJ interview with Anthony King.
35. Interviews with David Willetts and Matthew Parris.

ordeal and face rowdy critics head-on. Young and intelligent people who already leaned towards the free market case (including Peter Lilley and the young William Hague) were heartened by the feeling that in this All Souls Fellow they had living proof that the Conservative Party was prepared to take on the socialists in a "battle of ideas"; others had never dreamed that the capitalist system could be defended in this way. As Mrs Thatcher put it, "He gave us back our intellectual self-confidence".[36] In turn, the behaviour of Joseph's opponents reinforced the view – which had become more common since the late 1960s – that elements on the Left were now so intolerant that it was time for the friends of freedom to rally against them. This point was emphasised by several intellectuals who left the Labour Party in the mid-1970s.[37] It was an indirect compliment to Joseph that his campaign induced a new level of boorishness among the more militant students. Delegates to the 1976 conference of the National Union of Students (NUS) suspended their proceedings to pass a motion to expel him from his balcony seat. Even after this democratic triumph, he had to be protected – ironically, by a group of left-wing students – on his way out of the hall. In April 1978 Joseph was prevented from speaking at the London School of Economics (LSE). He was reported to have looked "shaken" after "a number of somewhat confused and emotional exchanges" outside the lecture room. Letters that subsequently passed between Joseph and the LSE Director, Ralf Dahrendorf, were published; Dahrendorf, wishing to uphold the School's traditional respect for free speech, invited Joseph to return at a later date and offered to chair the rescheduled meeting himself. The incident was given special prominence in the tabloid newspapers. One of these took the opportunity to contrast the antics of "student yahoos" with Sir Keith's "fastidious and translucent humanity". When Joseph returned to give his lecture in June there was no trouble, but the earlier incident ensured that his controversial speech received much wider publicity than would otherwise have been the case. By contrast, when Bristol University's Professor of Education banned Tony Benn from speaking on democracy in July 1979 the press response was relatively muted.[38]

Joseph's performances were not universally applauded within his own party, and the misgivings extended beyond those who disliked the content of his message. The Conservative writer T. E. Utley, for example, wrote in 1978 that "The habit which exists among many of the advocates of sensible reforms in economic policy of speaking of their 'mission' to the universities or middle

---

36. Halcrow, *Joseph*, 194; letters to authors from Peter Lilley and William Hague.
37. See, for example, Hugh Thomas's "A Letter to a Social Democrat", reprinted in Patrick Cormack (ed.), *Right Turn: Eight Men Who Changed Their Minds* (Leo Cooper, 1978), 89–104, and the account in Philip Thody, *The Conservative Imagination* (Pinter, 1993), 22–3.
38. *Manchester Guardian*, 12 February 1977. For the contrast between press attitudes to Joseph and Benn see Philip Schlesinger and John Griffith, *Free Speech for All?* (Council for Academic Freedom & Democracy, 1979). Benn was banned because his speech was judged to be political in content, and thus unsuitable for the proposed forum.

management, and of the necessity to 'convert' the electorate to capitalism is more suitable to the heirs of nonconformist radicalism than to the Tory party". Utley thought that this style of politics was based on a misunderstanding of an activity which was concerned with "the management of prejudices and reconciling of interests".[39] But for Joseph the "campus campaign" was precisely what politics should be about. He had never relished the process of bargaining and compromise which he had experienced since he first became a front-bencher. Now he was invigorated by the thrill of freedom, while preaching the virtues of that enviable condition. The new crusade (which, appropriately enough, included a speech in 1978 from the pulpit of Southwark Cathedral) was a crucial affirmation of his new sense of identity, and it was understandable that he should treasure his memories of this time for the rest of his life.

But no one ever saw his eyes light up when he spoke about his appearances at Conservative Party conferences. Nowhere in his repertoire was there anything quite "banal" enough for that forum, now that he could no longer satisfy activists with a list of departmental achievements. The civil servants who had pruned his speeches of any controversial phrases were now working for Labour; his new assistant, Sherman, was more attuned to the kind of dialectical exercises favoured by Marxists than the slogans and music hall songs which delight Conservatives when they assemble in seaside resorts. Joseph's first effort under the new dispensation, delivered on 7 October 1975, is the best illustration of his dilemma. He delivered what in advance must have seemed like an effective response to the Shadow Cabinet critics who had rounded on him in April: it was designed as a rebuke and an invitation in a single speech. While Gilmour and Maudling had asserted that the party should stick to the "middle ground", Joseph now claimed that this was illusory terrain. The middle ground was "a will-o'-the-wisp . . . As we move towards it, it moves further to the Left". This argument was not new; Lord Coleraine's elegant book *For Conservatives Only* (1970) had contained a chapter which exposed "The Myth of the Middle Ground". Appropriating another idea, this time from Enoch Powell,[40] Joseph alluded to a socialist "ratchet". The Labour Party added:

> more destruction and more damage each time they are in office, which we, for one reason or another, have not been able to reverse . . . there will only be a full flow of confidence and investment, jobs, prosperity and the freedom and social services which they underpin when the two main parties operate a mild pendulum rather than a ratchet as savage and destructive as the Labour ratchet.

---

39. T. E. Utley, "The Significance of Mrs Thatcher", in Maurice Cowling (ed.), *Conservative Essays* (Cassell, 1978), 41–51.
40. Powell spoke of "the ratchet of nationalisation", in a speech to the City of London Young Conservatives in April 1966; reprinted in John Wood (ed.), *Freedom and Reality* (Paperfront, 1969), 76.

Instead of seeking yet another compromise with socialism, Conservatives should pitch their tents in the "*common* ground". Just by changing a single word in a familiar phrase, Joseph thought, he could "reconcile the need for a national approach, the yearning for a national approach with both the realities and with the values which, whatever the differences of emphasis, unite us as a party". This time borrowing a cherished word from the "wet" lexicon, he claimed that "Common ground is the real meaning of the word consensus; common ground policies consistent with the reality and yet with the beliefs that we and others have come to hold".

It was a peculiar speech to deliver to an audience which must have been expecting some red meat from the man who had so recently pilloried the permissives. From his own point of view Joseph was making a genuine appeal for a new national consensus. But he was not the ideal Conservative to make such a gesture; far from appealing to supporters of other parties, he had alienated many of his own colleagues by the ideological fervour which he had injected into Shadow Cabinet discussions. Anyone who followed the detail of the speech could see that the invitation to share "common ground" really meant accepting Joseph's own view of the world; the message reflected his current faith in the example of West Germany, where socialists had apparently learned that "Free enterprise in a competitive, but comprehending, climate is the best friend of all, including the workers".[41] Meanwhile, to the average Tory activist it seemed that he was pleading the case for a cessation of conflict with Labour – a prospect which was unlikely to enthrall the people who thrived on combat with "the Socialists". Even Michael Foot, a favourite target for glib abuse at Tory conferences, was singled out for praise by Joseph. Although he won a partial standing ovation, the party official who guessed that the real message had failed to register with eighty per cent of the audience was probably not exaggerating. The *Daily Express* reported that even some of Joseph's colleagues on the conference platform wore "a glassy-eyed look". Certainly the representatives of the press were baffled. Ian Aitken of the *Guardian* was despatched to ask what the speech had really meant, whereupon Joseph clasped his forehead and exclaimed "My God! I have failed again".[42]

Those who found Joseph's dismay slightly excessive had forgotten the address which he gave in May 1975 to mark the publication by the CPS of his recent speeches (the collection, *Reversing the Trend*, included the famous admission that until April 1974 he had not been a Conservative). In what was called "a somewhat extraordinary publicity exercise" Joseph said that he would regard the volume as a success if it sold around 5,000 copies, and went on to confide that "I regard success as an index of virtue, in the Puritan tradition".

---

41. *Hansard*, vol. 909, col. 942, 12 April 1976.
42. Minutes of Ninety-Second Conservative Party Conference, 7 October 1975, 31–3; *Daily Express*, 8 October 1975; interview with Ian Aitken.

This attitude meant that apparent failure had to be taken as a temporary set-back, to be used as a spring board for ultimate success. If the "common ground" text had sown confusion at the conference, Joseph and Sherman would have to knock it into better shape for another speech, at a different venue. Accordingly, on 6 December 1975 the Oxford Union was treated to a more lengthy variation on the theme, which featured a new insistence that the majority of Britons already agreed with the views expressed. The press reception was relatively cordial this time, so the "common ground" and the "ratchet" duly reappeared in Joseph's speech to the 1976 party conference along with an indirect tribute to the importance of his own role within the party:

> Strategy matters. Policies matter. But behind them all stands the vision. Scorn not the vision; scorn not the idea. Man said that power grows out of the barrel of a gun. A gun is certainly powerful, but who controls the man with a gun? A man with an idea. "One man with a dream at pleasure . . ."[43]

It mattered not to the Prophet whether few or many were gathered together to hear the word. In June 1975 Joseph hired the ballroom of St Ermin's Hotel to launch another CPS pamphlet, *Why Britain Needs a Social Market Economy*. More than a hundred seats were set out for the expected throng, but only nine journalists turned up. Undeterred, Joseph descended from the platform to chat with them. His action averted what might have been a serious blow to his "Puritan" virtue-index; one reporter considered that the poor turn-out made the event all the more successful, because in that intimate setting Joseph provided clearer insights into his current thinking.[44]

These refresher-courses for the press were particularly useful in the Opposition years. There seemed to be at least one speech every week, and a new idea would pop up roughly once a month. Some took this as a sign of instability, and expected at any time to hear of a new "conversion". But Joseph's mind-set was now so fixed that everything he saw or read merely confirmed his existing beliefs. It was no accident that in the summer of 1975, on a walking-tour of Yorkshire, he felt ready to expose himself to the writings of Marx in order to know his enemy better.[45] While he made little use of this reading other authors were embraced and found their work transformed by

---

43. *The Times*, 30 May 1975; interview with Sir Alfred Sherman; minutes of Ninety-Third Conservative Party Conference, October 1976, 56–8.
44. *Birmingham Post*, 11 June 1975.
45. He had much work to do on this front. In a book review of April 1976 he had declared "Look at Marx himself, the man not the myth! He was born into a middle-class Jewish family, wealthy but socially inferior" (KJ, "Is Beckerman Among the Sociologists?", *New Statesman*, 18 April 1976). In reality Marx's family was well-connected rather than "socially inferior", and only "moderately prosperous" instead of "wealthy"; see Wheen, *Marx*, 8; interview with Rob Shepherd.

Joseph's over-affectionate touch. Samuel Brittan's attempt to clarify political language by calling the choice between "Left" and "Right" "a bogus dilemma" was made the theme of a Joseph speech, delivered to newspaper editors in April 1975. His thesis was that in the past upholders of the "establishment" had been regarded as right-wing, and the critics belonged to the Left. But now, he asserted, the Left had captured the establishment and there was a sense "in which the next Tory government, if it does its job, will be radical, anti-establishmentarian". So where did that leave the old terminology? The true answer was that although to some extent "Left" and "Right" were misleading short-hand terms, Joseph had introduced unnecessary confusion by his use of the word "establishment". Falling back on the very terminology that he was supposed to be discrediting, his case rested on an assumption that left-wingers could never be happy unless they were agitating against something. But if a society is governed in rough conformity to the ideas of the Left, left-wingers who defend the new regime – like those who fought for Allende in Chile – are hardly being inconsistent. In fact, notoriously, the Left *was* bitterly disappointed by Labour governments after 1964, and to that extent remained "anti-establishment". The most serious problem unearthed by Joseph confronted those on the Right who really *did* have an objection to radical change, on the grounds that no one can predict the final outcome of major upheavals. If political agitation was in itself anathema to many Conservatives, how much worse would be a struggle to reverse post-war policies in search of a free market utopia which had never existed in Britain? Joseph himself seemed unsettled by this problem; when Samuel Brittan pointed out that the application of economic liberalism would have a radical effect on society (as opposed to merely being "anti-establishmentarian") he "shied away from the notion".[46]

Applied to his own opinions, the terms "Left" and "Right" really were problematic for Brittan. Taking the view that liberty should be upheld in all things, his was a brand of consistent, high-principled liberalism which could not be made to fit under the old labels. But Brittan's position was too unusual to require an overhaul of the political vocabulary on his behalf. By contrast, Joseph had jettisoned the last vestiges of ambiguity by voting for capital punishment and paying court to Mrs Whitehouse; he was now in danger of becoming a stereotype of right-wing thinking on every subject of current controversy. Yet he adapted Brittan's argument in order to defend his own, very different position: "Suppose a man believes in free enterprise and in the positive value of differentials; that makes the man right wing, does it not? Suppose he only

---

46. Halcrow, *Joseph*, 114. Joseph did not borrow from a more recent production by Brittan, which suggested a significant weakness in Joseph's current thinking by pointing out that Conservatives were "fairly open to attack . . . when they argue for free enterprise, or oppose certain types of state intervention, because of a professed belief in the over-riding importance of individual liberty". Samuel Brittan, *Capitalism and the Permissive Society* (Macmillan, 1973), 356 (for further discussion, see Chapter 14).

entered politics, however, because of a hatred of poverty? Suppose his ambition was to level up; what does that make him?"[47]

Such a person might be difficult to classify, but the question had little to do with the Sir Keith Joseph of 1975. As he told Anthony Sampson at the end of that year, he now regretted having been "obsessed with squalor and avoidable misery" during the Heath government. Just before that interview he had launched a ferocious assault on Labour's Anthony Crosland, who had insisted that "levelling" was still an ideal worth pursuing (and added further provocation by pointing out that, contrary to Joseph's favourite phrase, the incidence of ulcers in manual workers was twice that among the middle classes).[48] Joseph's reference to "levelling up" sat uneasily beside other pronouncements at this time. In August 1976 the *Observer* ran an article on equality under Joseph's by-line. The published version was fairly restrained, but the original draft had stated that equality "is destructive of everything that is moral and humane. If imposed it will inevitably increase poverty and tyranny". The ambition to "level up" had not been relinquished, but it had slipped down the list of Joseph's priorities; his overriding obsession was now the perceived threat to freedom from an over-mighty state rather than "squalor and avoidable misery". In the battle against the advocates of a "command economy" Joseph soon decided that the old political labels were useful after all. As he had said himself, "Reacting to stereotypes discourages thought", and there were occasions in politics when it would be improper to provoke excessive mental activity. So at the 1976 Conservative conference he thundered against "the moral fervour and self-righteousness of the Left".[49]

Correlli Barnett was another reputable author whose work was pilfered. "I'm a Correlli Barnett supporter", Joseph affirmed in his 1987 interview with Anthony Seldon. In his follow-up question Seldon qualified this: "You are *partly* a Correlli Barnett man".[50] This showed that the interviewer, at least, had read Barnett's work carefully. In a series of scholarly books and articles Barnett had argued that Britain's economic decline could be traced to an anti-business culture whose foundations were laid by an education system which had been shaped by the model of the public school. Joseph was living evidence that Barnett's theory did not invariably hold good, and indeed some of his detailed points have been criticised.[51] There was a further problem in that Barnett was

47. Text of KJ speech at Council House, Birmingham, 11 April 1975, CCO handout.
48. Sampson, *Changing Anatomy*, 46–7; Kevin Jefferys, *Anthony Crosland* (Richard Cohen Books, 1999), 184. Before the war there had been no clear correlation between ulcers and social class; the trend noticed by Crosland had been established during the very years when Joseph was hailing managers as "the ulcer people"; see Peter Townsend and Nick Davidson (eds), *Inequalities in Health* (Penguin, 1982), 69.
49. *Sunday Telegraph*, 7 December 1975; *Observer*, 24 August 1976; draft copy in Joseph Papers, Box 18/9, CPA, Bodleian Library.
50. KJ interview with Anthony Seldon, 27.
51. See, for example, Bruce Collins and Keith Robbins (eds), *British Culture and Economic Decline* (Weidenfeld and Nicolson, 1990).

in no sense an economic liberal; the state, he felt, had not intervened enough in industry. But these minor details did not deter Joseph. Barnett had written that British power collapsed because of a pervasive anti-business culture, and for Joseph that was quite enough to make the historian "one of us". Barnett recognised the diffences of principle which Joseph overlooked, but the connection proved useful to him in the 1980s, when Sir Keith and Lord Young encouraged him to put his ideas on vocational training into practice.[52]

In 1975 (despite his instinctive constitutional conservatism) Joseph flirted with the idea of a Bill of Rights, a proposal also advocated at this time by Lord Hailsham. For both men the appeal of this bulwark against "elective dictatorship" suddenly faded when the Conservatives returned to power in 1979. In a sense Hailsham's inconsistency was the greater, because his writings on the subject were based on deep reflection and an absorption in British constitutional thought. As late as 1978 he thought that a stronger, proportionately elected second chamber would be needed to check the Commons when "a government elected by a small minority of votes, and with a slight majority in the House, regards itself as entitled, and, according to its more extreme supporters, bound to carry out every proposal in its election manifesto". Obviously Hailsham was thinking of the Labour governments formed after the two narrow victories of 1974. But, in every respect save the "slight majority in the House", the description applied to the first Thatcher Government. Although Hailsham was perturbed by right-wing ideologues (and in particular by Joseph, whom he regarded as "clever, even brilliant" but also "dotty"), his pessimism about the constitution receded after 1979. In his own brief reforming mood Joseph seemed to think that a Bill of Rights was necessary because some local housing departments misapplied their powers of Compulsory Purchase – powers which (as Joseph never stopped reminding himself and his audiences) had been greatly increased under the Macmillan government. He proceeded to deplore the decline of small shops in city centres, as if a Bill of Rights should include a special clause to protect them – unless, of course, they were driven out of business by the natural operations of the free market.[53]

Joseph's conduct during these Opposition years lends weight to the notion that he required the discipline of office to concentrate his efforts. Hailsham characterised him as "an albatross", who was "Clever-silly. Attracts Barmies". But that private judgement was delivered after more than three years of Opposition, a period in which Joseph had been surrounded by ardent activists rather than civil servants. It brings to mind a comment of "Chips" Channon after a lunch

---

52. Interview with Correlli Barnett.
53. Lord Hailsham, *The Dilemma of Democracy: Diagnosis and Prescription* (Fount, 1979), 129–30; Lewis, *Hailsham*, 326–7; KJ, *Freedom Under the Law* (CPC, 1975), 8–9. The case for small shops had been less persuasive when Joseph was supporting Heath over Resale Price Maintenance.

with another ex-minister: "the tragedy of a good mind unharnessed". Enoch Powell thought of Joseph as "a gorgeous butterfly, with a coat of many colours, alighting first on this flower, then on that . . .".[54] A more telling comparison would be with a man trying to complete a jigsaw by pulling pieces at random from any box within reach. But by the end of 1975 Joseph conjured a more dangerous image; he seemed like an untrained kamikaze pilot, who contrived to return from numerous missions but threatened one day to cause maximum destruction behind his own lines. In the month after his "Common Ground" speech he gave an interview for the *New York Times* in which, after admitting that he disliked "splashing mud on my own country abroad" he proceeded to do just that. Pronouncing the word "'socialism' in a voice heavy with anger and despair", Joseph spoke of the "slumdom" into which Britain was sinking as a result of "mischievous, wrong-headed, debilitating" ideas. The remarks were prompted by fervent patriotism, but the effect would have been greater had he toned down his language and omitted the preliminary remarks about "splashing mud". Even the *Spectator*, which thought that many of his detailed points were well-founded, was exasperated by this outburst. It warned that "Sir Keith is in need of modera-tion, not so much in his convictions or in his reading of society as in his words". Yet by some miracle the pilot guided his plane through the flames and the smoke, returning to dust down his uniform and prepare for a new mission – with the encouragement, apparently, of his Commander-in-Chief.[55]

Mrs Thatcher clearly retained in full her admiration for Joseph. But the *Sunday Express* noted that only a year after being tipped as the next leader he was regarded as "a loner, a mystery figure remote from the front-line troops in the Commons". He hardly ever spoke in debates, and MPs were beginning to wish that he would be equally tongue-tied outside Westminster. Joseph's kinder critics thought that he should go no more a'roving, and settle down with a specific portfolio. But in February 1977, when Joseph took over from John Biffen as the Conservative spokesman on Industry, he combined this with his existing role.[56] Concerns were voiced that as overlord of policy and research Joseph was bringing no tangible benefits to the party, and the *Spectator* wondered aloud why he had not merged his CPS with the Research Depart-ment – a move which would not have been a great sacrifice for Joseph, since the former body had been dogged by personal rifts and disagreements about its purpose from the outset. Lord Thorneycroft had expected a merger as soon as Mrs Thatcher became leader, but nothing had happened and although insiders

---

54. Hailsham Diary, 11 April 1975, 1/1a, Churchill College; Lewis, *Hailsham*, 326–7; Robert Rhodes James (ed.), *"Chips": The Diaries of Sir Henry Channon* (Weidenfeld & Nicolson, 1993), 471 (the ex-minister was Leslie Hore-Belisha); Halcrow, *Joseph*, 115.
55. *Sunday Express*, 7 December 1975; *Daily Mail*, 10 November 1975; *Spectator*, 15 November 1975.
56. *Sunday Express*, 7 December 1975. Rather ominously for someone with Joseph's medical history, Biffen had stepped down because of excessive stress.

spoke of increased co-operation it was impossible to conceal the spirit of rivalry between the two bodies (Sherman thought that the CRD was "staffed by a group of low calibre opportunists"). Joseph was (rightly) regarded as a partisan for the more philosophical approach of the CPS, but he was supposed to be in charge of the policy-making exercise and for this the CRD was indispensible.[57]

In this context one has to wonder why Mrs Thatcher had named Angus Maude, rather than Joseph as the head of the Research Department.[58] This decision seems to have been based on the leader's knowledge that Joseph was more at home with general ideas than with specific policy proposals. Yet that leaves unanswered the question of why Joseph was put in overall charge of the policy exercise – a post which demanded not only an eye for fine detail, but also the ability to build a team. It was always likely that in this role Joseph's doctrinal commitment would prove the master of his managerial skills – and given his deteriorating reputation among party moderates his appointment was sure to cause more tension than creativity. Lord Carrington was unsettled by the influence of both Joseph and Maude, but conceded that at least the latter was "not extreme". Mrs Thatcher could not substitute Maude for Joseph without a serious loss of face, but the result was a serious loss of focus. As early as June 1975 an MP with no ulterior motive for speaking out claimed that the process was "a shambles"; others were "both unhappy and ill-informed" about the situation. Front-benchers complained that their own efforts were not being co-ordinated with the thinking of other groups, and this feeling could only increase in tandem with the growing number of such bodies. By March 1976 there were seventy of these; by the following year there were at least ten more. Any MP with a bee in his bonnet could approach Joseph in the confident expectation that he would be allowed to accommodate fellow-enthusiasts in a new policy group, and since the CRD was supposed to provide back-up (in addition to the briefs it produced for parliamentary debates) the seemingly limitless proliferation of groups and sub-groups caused yet more friction within the party machine. The mood within the CRD was not improved when the attention of the policy supremo seemed to wander during meetings; Sir Adam Ridley remembers at least one occasion when he noticed that Joseph was reading a book under the table.[59]

The CRD's Director, Chris Patten, had been kept in post despite his friendship with the previous Chairman, Ian Gilmour, and his obvious scepticism

---

57. *Spectator*, 15 November 1975. For CPS infighting, see especially correspondence and minutes in Sherman Papers, Box 7; Sherman on CRD, memorandum to KJ, 22 April 1975, Sherman Papers, Box 7.

58. In an interview after his retirement Joseph mistakenly said that he, rather than Maude, had been Chairman of the CRD. It was a rare and suggestive memory lapse; in the same interview he described the CRD as "a nuisance" (Interview with Andrew Denham, April 1991).

59. Lewis, *Hailsham*, 326; *Liverpool Daily Post*, 20 June 1975; Robert Behrens, *The Conservative Party from Heath to Thatcher: Policies and Politics 1974–1979* (Saxon House, 1980), 49–50; interview with Sir Adam Ridley.

about the monetarist crusade. Joseph regarded Patten as an intelligent sinner whose repentance would be well worth having, and greeted him with a list of improving works by economic liberals. Patten was not as voracious in his reading as Joseph but his studies had been even more eclectic. He was able to tell Joseph that he had already consulted most of the suggested texts, which had clearly made no profound difference to his thinking.[60]

A false impression has been created, largely because Patten coined the nickname "The Mad Monk" for Sir Keith (rather than being mortally offended, Joseph regarded the tag as a great joke). There were deep policy disagreements, and the continued existence of the CPS rankled, but there was no personal antipathy. Patten soon realised that even if Joseph decided not to take advice, he would bear no grudge if it was firmly expressed. On one occasion, after reading a draft of a speech he minuted to Joseph that although the style was "trenchant", the content featured "a number of mines quite large enough to blow you out of the water. It would add quite a number of new quotations to Denis Healey's armoury". Even if he had shared Joseph's economic views, Patten would have been exasperated by the ever-swelling ranks of the policy groups. He often shared his feelings with James Douglas, a veteran of the 1960s exercise. Patten's copies of letters sent out by Joseph to the chairmen of the new groups were sprinkled with marginal comments intended for Douglas, such as "Here we go again!" and "Do you know anything about this waste of time?" Only the approach of an election could halt the flood of new areas which Joseph thought worthy of study. As late as July 1978 Adam Ridley told Patten that "our programme of publications seems to be in a state of constant flux and some of the Shadow Cabinet seem unaware of what is going on already"; since Joseph was Chairman of the Conservative Political Centre (CPC) which was responsible for publications, there was no need to look beyond the usual suspect on this occasion. By then relations had been darkened by Patten's removal from the post of Minute Secretary to the Shadow Cabinet. The official line was that Patten needed a lighter workload while he was nursing the marginal Bath constituency, but the press connected the decision with a series of policy leaks, and *The Times* reported a claim (instantly denied) that Joseph had instigated the change. Certainly Joseph did not share in full the feelings of some members of his entourage – that dissent from full-blooded radicalism was tantamount to a betrayal of Britain.[61]

---

60. Interview with Chris Patten.
61. Patten to KJ, 19 January 1979, Joseph Papers, Box 18/11; Adam Ridley to Patten, 19 July 1978, Joseph Papers, Box 18/3; various annotations in Joseph Papers, Box 18/1, CPA, Bodleian Library. Although Joseph worked himself up into a "complete flap" over a similar incident in January 1978, the most spectacular "leak" occurred in May, when the *Economist* published a report on de-nationalisation written by Nicholas Ridley. When he commissioned the report, Joseph had reflected on the abortive exercise of 1969 and promised that "It will be different this time"; Nicholas Ridley, *My Style of Government: The Thatcher Years* (Hutchinson, 1991), 15. John Hoskyns, *Just in Time: Inside the Thatcher Revolution* (Aurum Press, 2000), 162, 54.

Even Mrs Thatcher later admitted that Joseph's system "had a somewhat ramshackle feel to it". But she could tolerate the anarchistic approach to policy-making because she felt that the party should learn the lesson of 1970 and avoid an excess of detailed pronouncements. Rather than relying on the work of policy groups, she preferred to make her own commitments in television interviews – much to the annoyance of moderate Shadow ministers who disagreed with her message and her methods. In the run-up to the election broad statements of principle could be published to reassure the faithful that something was happening, but the divisions within the Shadow Cabinet meant that these had to be drawn up with a view to minimising controversy. Since the aptitude of the party's policy chief lay in the opposite direction, the trick was to give Joseph some role while ensuring that the final wording was controlled by others. The first document, *The Right Approach*, was published for the 1976 party conference. In his speech Joseph said that he felt quite free to praise *The Right Approach*, because it had been written by Patten in consultation with Maude. Yet the press greeted these emollient words with a degree of cynicism, because Joseph's latest collection of speeches had been published by the CPS on the day before the launch of the official party statement, and this volume (*Stranded on the Middle Ground?*) repeated all the arguments which had infuriated the moderates since the spring of 1974.[62]

Joseph's name appeared on the cover of the following year's Conservative offering, *The Right Approach to the Economy*, but while he took a full part in preliminary discussions he was not involved in the drafting. The document still caused a row in Shadow Cabinet, since some members felt that there should have been more advance discussion of its contents; Mrs Thatcher was also dissatisfied because of an enthusiastic section about consultation between government and unions through the National Economic Development Council (NEDC). The statement was denied official status, and appeared under the names of Joseph, Howell, Prior, Maude and Howe. Yet the last-named, at least, remained fond of *The Right Approach to the Economy*; and for good reasons, since rather than looking for confrontational statements of ideology he was now interested in devising a package which was as radical as possible without threatening further the fragile unity of his colleagues. He was very happy to envisage some role for the NEDC, and the commitment that a Conservative Government would "continue the gradual reduction in the rate of growth of money supply, in line with firm monetary targets" made a significant appearance as the first of three measures to be taken against inflation. There would be substantial tax cuts, and public spending would be reduced without causing "avoidable hardship and bitterness". Even Howe might have been disappointed by the

---

62. Thatcher, *Path to Power*, 298; Minutes of Ninety-Third Conservative Party Conference, October 1976, 56; Hugo Young in *Sunday Times*, 18 September 1977.

section on trade union reform, which (thanks to Prior) went no further than pledging to resist "firmly and decisively" any political challenge from union militants. But before *The Right Approach to the Economy* appeared a new initiative had been started which promised to deal with that problem. Much of the credit for this belonged to Joseph.[63]

Joseph's habit of collecting ideas then speaking out before thinking through their implications brought confusion and irritation rather than enlightenment. But he had always been good at collecting people, and – despite one very spectacular slip[64] – during these years he was seen at his best as a recruiting-sergeant. Some of the enthusiasts he picked up were people he already knew, or who (like the All Souls Fellow John Redwood) took little finding. But his new level of crusading zeal made him restless in his search for useful allies, and the CPS provided an excellent outlet for their energies. At the same time he felt that he had joined a very exclusive set of believers, and applicants were made to feel that a whole-hearted commitment was required before he would consider them for admission. Lord Young has provided a vivid account of Joseph's technique. On 12 May 1975 Young chaired a dinner, on behalf of the Organisation for Rehabilitation by Training, at which Joseph was the guest speaker. His speech greatly impressed Young, who had once supported Labour but was now dismayed at the declining prospects for energetic industrialists like himself. He made an appointment to see Sir Keith on 6 June, and offered his services. Joseph's immediate response was "Why? You don't believe". The astonished Young found himself mumbling "Why not try me?". The newcomer soon proved his mettle at the CPS, then embarked on an unlikely career within the party which he ended as a Cabinet minister with a seat in the House of Lords. His friendship with Joseph was only broken by the latter's death.[65]

Another celebrated piece of talent-spotting brought John Hoskyns and Norman Strauss into the policy-making team. Hoskyns, a former army captain who had built a successful computer company, was introduced to Joseph by Sherman who had heard of his attempts to analyse government failure in Britain. Strauss had worked on management issues for Unilever, and, encouraged by Joseph, wrote a paper on the need for the Conservatives to supply the public with more information. Once Sherman had brought them together, Hoskyns and Strauss formed an energetic team. Hoskyns was convinced that politicians were poor strategic planners, and with Strauss he outlined his own impressions of the task which would face a new Conservative Government. Their paper, called "Stepping Stones", was presented to Mrs Thatcher in November 1977; it argued that the trade unions were the most serious obstacles

63. *The Right Approach to the Economy* (CCO, 1977), 8–9, 20–1.
64. See page 356.
65. Lord Young, *The Enterprise Years: A Businessman in the Cabinet* (Headline, 1990), 29; interview and correspondence with Lord Young of Graffham.

to meaningful reform, and that the Conservatives should start arguing their case immediately, to prepare the ground for radical change after the next election. Joseph was delighted with what he dubbed "stepping stones to public persuasion"; Hoskyns was keen on illustrating his ideas with diagrams and with the kind of technical vocabulary which marked him down as a true expert. At first the leader was sceptical, telling Hoskyns and Strauss after a lunch at her Flood Street home that they had eaten a whole joint of roast beef and she had received nothing in return. But she changed her mind, presumably when she contrasted the "Stepping Stones" message with the approach to the unions which Prior had included in *The Right Approach to the Economy*. There was no overnight conversion of the Shadow Cabinet, and an attempt by Mrs Thatcher to stampede the party into a policy of compulsory secret ballots before industrial action was headed off by Prior. By the autumn of 1978 the initiative seemed to have stalled. But Joseph continued to press his leader, and after the "Winter of Discontent" of 1978–9 there was some movement. The voters were at least made aware that the Conservatives were prepared to take action on such key issues as secondary picketing and the closed shop, and commitments on these points were included in the manifesto. More importantly, "Stepping Stones" allowed Mrs Thatcher and her allies to believe that there was a decisive plan of action which they could deploy once an election victory had rendered irrelevant all the tiresome compromises of the Opposition years.[66]

But Joseph's undoubted gifts as a head-hunter had to be balanced against a series of public gaffes. Official unemployment stayed above one million almost continuously after 1974, reaching a peak of 1.6 million in August 1977. This was a gift to the Opposition and in the Conservative poster "Labour Isn't Working" it produced one of the most effective images of the decade. Yet instead of exploiting the embarrassing figures Joseph spent the Opposition years trying to revise them downwards. One of the first activities of his CPS was to publish the "true" tally, for the "involuntary" jobless. This was a long-standing interest for Joseph; he had broached it in the Preston speech, and in August 1975 he eagerly announced that the Department of Employment should slash the figure by a half, to around 550,000. At the same time the number of job vacancies should be reckoned at 350,000, rather than the published 130,000. To confuse matters further, Joseph denounced state subsidies to firms such as British Leyland, which kept the official jobless figure artificially *low*. If anyone cared to follow the logic of all this, they would arrive at the conclusion that Labour had decided to fiddle the figures to exaggerate the failure of its own policies; once Conservative measures were in place the dole queues would grow, but at least everyone in those queues would truly be out of work. As so often with Joseph, informed observers could understand why his thoughts had moved in this direction. But he had paid no attention

---

66. Ranelagh, *Thatcher's People*, 220–21; interview with Sir John Hoskyns; interview with Lord Joseph, April 1991; Thatcher, *Path to Power*, 420–26; Hoskyns, *Just in Time*, 39.

to the rule that headlines mean more to the average voter than small-print. He hastened to explain himself to readers of the *Sun*, claiming that unemployment was "a misery that I want to cut to the minimum . . . It is because I hate unemployment so much that I stress the reality that the monthly figures conceal". This was a laudable aim, but Joseph lacked the tools for the task. He revealed in full the methodology on which the CPS had based their conclusions; everyone should admit that scroungers exist, and benefits are relatively generous. Thus it obviously followed that "about half [of] the million registered unemployed are fit and ready for work".[67]

Instead of learning from these examples of what one commentator tactfully described as "absent-mindedness", Joseph courted more controversy as the decade progressed and Britain's problems multiplied. While a diplomatic Conservative formula on the unions was being thrashed out for *The Right Approach to the Economy*, he waded into the long-running saga which centred on the Grunwick Film Processing Laboratories in Brent, North London. A strike broke out over the sacking of a worker and the refusal of management to allow union representation in the plant. By August, 137 workers were on strike, most of whom joined the union APEX. The management refused offers of conciliation, and on 2 September 1976 the strikers were sacked. In sympathy, post-office workers stopped delivering mail to the plant. This threatened to bring the employer, George Ward, to his knees; instead, the uncompromising Ward asked for assistance from the National Association for Freedom (NAFF). The dispute involved a clash of freedoms – between the right of the employer to hire and fire at will, and the right of workers to a proper procedure for handling grievances. While NAFF could only acknowledge the first of these, Labour focused on the second and in May 1977 three moderate ministers appeared on the picket-line. Grunwick thus came to symbolise the central dilemma of post-war industrial relations; could a balance of power be struck between the two sides of industry, and, if not, which side should hold the upper hand? The fact that the majority of the workforce was Asian brought another controversial factor into the mix.

By June 1977 there had been a peaceful picket at Grunwick for many months. The dispute then escalated, as left-wing extremists realised that their counterparts on the Right wanted to make this a trial of strength. By 24 June reinforcements had arrived from Yorkshire, led by Arthur Scargill; facing the 2,000 pickets were more than 1,500 policemen. Violence broke out, and predictably each side blamed the other for provoking it. An inquiry was established early in July, under Lord Scarman. But Sir Keith Joseph had already completed his own inquiry, and decided to intervene. At the end of June he despatched an article to the *Daily Mail*, in which he admitted that he had "no

67. *Sun*, 4 November 1975.

special expertise" on the subject but still felt able to declare that "We are all under siege at Grunwick". Someone had to speak up, he claimed, in order to "save the unions from themselves".[68] This was a clear trespass on the territory of Prior, the Employment Spokesman, who had already been embarrassed by his colleague when a private meeting with the TUC degenerated into an argument between the pair. At least there were traces of a balanced approach in Joseph's first article. But his next intervention, in August, was far less temperate. He described Grunwick as "a make-or-break point for British democracy, the freedoms of ordinary men and women". While others recognised the true complexity of the dispute – and even commentators on the Right thought that NAFF's involvement was almost as sinister as that of the flying pickets – Joseph had no doubts. At best, Grunwick offered him the chance to argue general points about Labour's antagonism to wealth creation, which was driving away investment, and its failure to deal with secondary picketing which, whatever the justice of Ward's case, clearly demanded tough government action. Instead Joseph wrote as if the front line of the Cold War was now running through North London. There had always been "apologists for Soviet despotism, mass murder, denial of freedom" within the Labour Party, he informed his readers. But now these elements were in control, using moderate dupes as a cloak for their "Red Fascism".[69]

When Scarman published his report at the end of August he criticised Ward for acting "within the letter but outside the spirit of the law", and recommended that the sacked workers should be reinstated. NAFF had continued to support Ward's case in the courts, and a ruling was pending from the House of Lords. Joseph instantly delivered a speech denouncing the report, without considering that he might be exceeding his Shadow Cabinet brief. On the day of Joseph's speech an official telephoned Prior from Central Office and began to read over the text. After a few minutes Prior inquired if he was being asked to give clearance to the speech or simply being presented with advance warning of what was sure to be a new disaster. He was told that copies had already been distributed to the press.[70]

Had the Conservatives stood back from the Grunwick conflict – as Prior wanted – it would have been an unequivocal propaganda coup for the party. Television images of injured policemen, and of terrified workers who still tried to cross the picket line, needed no commentary to work their effect on public opinion. The unions were already less popular than they had been during the Heath government; in 1975 Gallup found for the first time that over a third of respondents thought the unions were a "Bad thing". Yet instead of reining them

---

68. *Daily Mail*, 28 June 1977.
69. Richard Clutterbuck, *Britain in Agony: The Growth of Political Violence* (Faber & Faber, 1978), 190–210; Interview with Lord Murray; *Conservative News*, August 1977.
70. Hugo Young in *Sunday Times*, 18 September 1977.

in, Labour had extended their rights after repealing the Industrial Relations Act and involved them more closely in government decision-making under the terms of the "social contract". It was beyond even the power of Joseph entirely to blunder away this advantage, but he had made things more complicated by his public identification with Ward. For the TUC Len Murray described Joseph as "highly idiosyncratic", while his most bitter enemies, the "wet" Tory Reform Group, believed that he was "off his head". Even Mrs Thatcher thought that her friend's remarks had been "too sharp". The *Spectator* described his speech as "maladroit". Joseph had "polarised the leadership, inflamed the rank and file, aroused suspicions about his motives", and threatened to destroy Prior's attempts to cultivate a working relationship with the unions – despite the fact that only a few months earlier he had identified as a major task for the party the need to combat "the Socialist claim that we would be unable to deal with the Unions". Even after the unhelpful meeting with the TUC in January 1977 Murray had tried to arrange further discussions; now the mood was as sour as it had been when the Heath government tried to implement the Industrial Relations Act.[71]

It looked possible for a time that Prior could not survive the feelings whipped up within the party by Joseph's intervention. The Conservative conference was only a month away, and if the debate on industrial relations went against the cautious line of *The Right Approach to the Economy* Prior would have no alternative but to resign. Under a less supportive leader the sack would certainly have loomed for Joseph himself. On 16 September Lord Hailsham drafted an apoplectic letter of protest, accusing Joseph of conduct "quite unworthy of a Conservative"; although he decided not to send this, he did show it to Mrs Thatcher. Hailsham was mortified by the imputation of political bias to Scarman, a highly respected member of the legal profession. With his own background in law, Joseph should really have known that his intervention would cause offence in such quarters. He might not have known exactly what he was doing when he associated the Conservative party with NAFF's campaign. The Federation had links with his friends in the IEA, and his spokesman on Small Businesses, David Mitchell, was a founder member. These personal contacts might have given him the false impression that NAFF was primarily an intellectual pressure group. But amongst its other roles it gave expression to a feeling of outrage, arising mainly from the self-employed, against high taxation, bureaucratic meddling, and union power. This emotion was neatly captured by the journalist Patrick Hutber, once a Keynesian who had applauded Barber's budgets and ridiculed Powell's economics, but now the author of the successful book *The Decline and Fall of the Middle Class - and how it can fight back* (1976). Whatever the merits of their case, the

---

71. Robert J. Wybrow, *Britain Speaks Out, 1937–87: A Social History as Seen Through the Gallup Data* (Macmillan, 1989), 160; *Spectator*, 17 September 1977; *Guardian*, 3 September 1977; *Sunday Times*, 18 September 1977; Thatcher, *Path to Power*, 402; Interview with Lord Murray.

object of groups like NAFF was to make the Conservative Party subservient to a sectional interest. Thus they were no different from union militants working within the Labour Party (with whom they shared the common objective of destroying the post-war "consensus"). Joseph's speeches encouraged supporters of Ward, such as John Gorst, MP for Hendon and founder of the Middle Class Association, to give vent to their feelings against Prior. As the *Spectator* commented, some of the language used was "preposterously out of place in our current domestic debates", and Prior proved that he was no appeaser by vigorously defending his position and making a private protest to Mrs Thatcher.[72]

When challenged about his own outburst Joseph protested that "'he did not think it was about industrial relations. It was', he said plaintively, 'simply about the rule of law'". This only threatened to make matters worse for Joseph; in addition to consulting Prior (and Hailsham) he should have cleared the speech with Whitelaw, the official spokesman on Home Affairs. But Whitelaw knew that his influence could not prevail with Mrs Thatcher beyond ensuring that Joseph would never become Chancellor; ironically, he was now counting the cost of his initial intervention which had left Joseph with an ill-defined role. Caught as so often between his desire for a Conservative victory and his distaste for the antics of class warriors, Whitelaw could only pray for a temporary lull in hostilities. His wish was granted, when Prior emerged from the 1977 conference wounded but alive. At the end of the debate it was thought that Joseph had "flinched a little when Mr Prior plonked his hand on his shoulder in a gesture of unity".[73]

In the wake of the Grunwick row the *Spectator* warned that although the Conservatives looked almost certain to win the next election "the capacity of some of them to lose it through fatuous misjudgement and wildly intemperate talk is not to be underrated". In the polls of late 1977 Labour narrowed the gap, and at the end of the year the two major parties were neck-and-neck. The government's resurgence owed more to apparent improvements in the economy than to worries about Conservative extremism, but government strategists believed that the Joseph factor could swing undecided voters their way. As one sketch-writer put it, an unstated aim of Labour's election platform was to pledge itself "to provoke Sir Keith Joseph into a major indiscretion before polling day". In January 1978 "Crossbencher" in the *Sunday Express* felt that the danger had been noticed and averted: "Every time [Joseph] might be pushed to the fore the Shadow Cabinet finds a pressing reason for some other subject to be debated. Or for someone else to handle the matter". But he could not be physically barred from the Commons, and although he took great care to sound reasonable during his own speeches on Industry there was always a chance that a government barb

---

72. Hailsham Diaries, 1/3, Churchill College. For Gorst and his allies, see Roger King and Neil Nugent (eds), *Respectable Rebels: Middle Class Campaigns in Britain in the 1970s* (Hodder & Stoughton, 1979); Roth memorandum; *Spectator*, 17 September 1977.
73. *Sunday Times*, 18 September 1977; *Spectator*, 15 October 1977.

would pierce his delicate skin. Callaghan and Foot took the lead in this exercise. In March 1978 it was reported that "Sir Keith's voice rose momentarily towards orbit" when he jumped to the Dispatch Box to answer a Callaghan jibe against his attitude to council housing; fortunately he soon composed himself. Labour MPs subjected his gestures and grimaces to keen observation, but in the days before televised debates these could make little impact on the electorate. Once, while telling the House that a Conservative government would gradually phase out employment subsidies rather than abolishing them all at once, Prior was disconcerted by shrieks of laughter from the Labour benches. On asking afterwards what had been so amusing, he learned that Joseph, sitting beside him on the Conservative front-bench, had evinced increasing misery during the speech and finally buried his head in his hands.[74]

Had there really been Labour sympathisers in the Research Department – as opposed to disillusioned but loyal Conservatives – it would not have taken them long to pass on a bulging dossier of promising material. Joseph's correspondence was voluminous, and the time he allocated to non-essential tasks would have horrified the most slapdash civil servant. If an obscure young woman wanted a reading list, Joseph was happy to oblige; if a retired businessman sent him poetry he was ready with advice. The views of people who would have been written off as cranks by any other MP were treated with unfailing respect; only when he realised that he had been writing to a Keynesian did Joseph recoil from further communication. Used creatively by Labour, some of the replies sent out by such a senior Conservative could have damaged the party. But other material which crossed Joseph's desk needed no distortion to spread dismay among his colleagues.[75]

Some of the ideas considered by Joseph in these years were remote from his earlier thinking; for example, he spent some time exploring the possibility of action against the sport of hare coursing, and even wrote an article on the subject.[76] One colleague remembered him as a playful hound rather than a trained hunter: "Keith was always dashing off into the woods and coming back with a stick between his teeth". But most of his enthusiasms could have been predicted from his previous experience in Opposition. He took up again the idea of education vouchers, and gave cautious encouragement to Dr Rhodes Boyson who was hoping to run pilot schemes at local level. Searching for avenues of attack against the universities, he favoured the introduction of student loans and the removal of job security from lecturers. He pondered over

---

74. Undated cuttings in Roth archives; Michael White in *Guardian*, 15 March 1978; interview with Rob Shepherd. Joseph's head was in his hands so often during this period that his action might have been entirely unrelated to Prior's speech – but that possibility did not detract from Labour's mirth.
75. See, for example, correspondence in Box 18/8, Joseph Papers, CPA, Bodleian Library.
76. Clearly the hunting community was one area of traditional Conservative support that Joseph continued to discount. The 1979 Conservative manifesto said nothing specific about hare coursing, but did contain a section on animal welfare: *The Conservative Manifesto 1979*, 18.

Health Service reform, and in April 1978 went so far as to prophesy in public that within twenty years the state's monopoly of care would be confined to what he had once called the "Cinderella services".[77] Significant tax cuts for the better off were taken for granted; the disaffected James Douglas was ignored when he suggested that beneficiaries might just use the money to fly their dogs across the Atlantic and buy gold-plated bath taps. As a wholehearted believer in the "trickle-down effect" – the process by which the conspicuous consumption of the wealthy would one day help the poor – Joseph clearly thought that something would eventually trickle down from the gold taps. But another of the "credibility gaps" which Douglas identified was the question of how to protect the poor from the effects of a shift from direct to indirect taxes. This objection was also ignored; a serious reappraisal would have imperilled the whole economic strategy being cooked up at the Fentiman Road meetings.[78]

Unemployment, though, was a favourite topic for speculation. From an early stage Joseph was preoccupied with the problem of sustaining a tough line in the face of soaring jobless figures (revised or not). One reason for hesitation in this area was the fact that the consequences of tight monetary policy might extend beyond the working class, at least in the short term. At a meeting of March 1976 Joseph discussed with three colleagues the problem of forcing people to take any available job, regardless of the fall in social status which this might involve. Aware that some "failed middle-class executives" had influence within the Conservative Party, the group decided that compulsion should not be introduced until prosperity had returned. The same awkward consideration might also have been raised had Joseph proceeded very far with another idea he floated at this time – that people dependent on benefits should be deprived of the right to vote.[79]

Joseph was convinced that the instincts of the British people had always been sound; regrettably, they had been grievously misled by the politicians, who had not listened enough. In words which he would later apply to the Left, his social vision was becoming "insular, blinkered and one-eyed" in his drive to reconnect the policies of his party with what he took to be widespread public demands. He was acutely conscious of the need for what he called "populist" policies and slogans, but his own efforts to think up punchy phrases showed scant improvement; hence his continued reliance on Sherman. While his new attitude to the question of capital punishment surprised even seasoned Joseph-watchers, his stance on immigration had been "evolving" for some time and Sherman accelerated the process. In a Shadow Cabinet discussion paper of December 1976 Joseph suggested that the party should "be ready to disappoint the expectations of immigrants if the only alternative is to disappoint the

77. Whitehead, *Writing on the Wall*, 332; *Sunday Times*, 16 April 1978.
78. "Credibility Gaps", memorandum by James Douglas, 2 November 1976, Joseph Papers, Box 18/1, CPA, Bodleian Library.
79. KJ to Paul Dean, 28 February 1976; minutes of meeting, 3 March 1976, Joseph Papers, Box 29/5, CPA, Bodleian Library.

expectations of the English. The English have rights too . . .". The best way of reasserting these rights would be to deny similar respect to outsiders; even close relatives of the existing immigrant population should be denied entry, he thought. Earlier he had asked the CRD to prepare a note for him "setting out the parameters of repatriation", and was greatly impressed when a friend returned from the Caribbean with the tale that West Indians themselves were anxious to prevent further entry of dependent children into the UK.[80]

The campus cries of "racist" which were hurled at Joseph along with the eggs and the flour-bombs reflected no inside knowledge among students; they were working on the simple-minded syllogism "all Conservatives are racist", "Sir Keith Joseph is a Conservative", therefore "Sir Keith Joseph is a racist". The refusal of LSE students to give him a hearing in April 1978 was prompted by his refusal to sign an anti-racist declaration, but his justified anger at such a blatant interference with free speech meant that he did not even bother to read the document thrust at him. Attempts to resolve the question of whether or not a particular person is racially prejudiced usually take their final refuge in humbug. Joseph's view of the immigrants themselves had probably changed little since the days when he tried to house newcomers through his Mulberry Trust, but he had always opposed mass immigration and had come to see violent opponents of racism in the context of a systematic campaign of leftist subversion, with the race relations industry as a powerful propagandist wing. Therefore it was quite legitimate to trawl for votes in this stagnant pond. At Hampstead in October 1977 he gave his own potted history of the problem. "During the 1950s", he said, "we opened the doors to immigrants – we didn't realise then that perhaps we should have shut them. But when we tried to shut them in the early 1960s the Liberals and Socialists made such a fuss that we couldn't".[81]

On 2 March 1978 a by-election was held in the East London constituency of Ilford North. Race was always likely to feature in the campaign; the previous Conservative MP Tom Iremonger had paid close attention to the interests of his Jewish constituents (who numbered around 6,000), but his narrow defeat in the election of October 1974 was attributed to the fact that his Labour opponent, Milly Miller, was Jewish. The National Front put up a candidate in the by-election which followed Mrs Miller's death, and planned a march. Before official campaigning began Mrs Thatcher made her most famous pronouncement on race, revealing in an ITV *World in Action* interview her sympathies with those people who felt themselves to be "swamped" by immigrants.[82]

On 20 February Joseph gave a speech in the constituency. He told his audience that:

---

80. KJ, "One-Eyed Vision" in *Policy Studies*, 12; "Our Tone of Voice and Our Tasks", discussion paper by KJ, LSC (76) 55; note of 22 October 1975, Joseph Papers, 18/1; KJ to Whitelaw, 12 February 1976, Joseph Papers, 16/5, CPA, Bodleian Library.
81. *Evening Standard*, 25 April 1978; *Ham and High*, 7 October 1977.
82. Alderman, *Jewish Community in British Politics*, 144.

There is a limit to the number of people from different cultures that this country can digest. We ignore this at our peril, everyone's peril. Therefore I say that the electors of Ilford North, including the Jews – who are just like everyone else, as the saying goes, only more so – have good reason for supporting Margaret Thatcher and the Conservative Party on immigration.

The "only more so" quip sounds like a suggestion from Sherman, Joseph's co-religionist. Few people who knew Sherman (or Sir Keith himself) would have agreed that they were "just like everyone else", but this was beside the point. The *Jewish Chronicle*, already agitated by Mrs Thatcher's "swamped" remarks, claimed that Joseph's appeal went "against the whole tradition of independent Jewish citizenship in Britain". Some objected on the grounds that the Jews in Britain were all either descendants of immigrants, like Joseph, or had themselves settled in the country. In fact there was a long tradition of Jews opposing further mass immigration, but this was not something people liked to talk about – particularly since the war, when the British might have saved more Jewish lives had the government not worried about being "swamped" by people "from different cultures".[83] More serious was the allegation that (although he had also referred to the voters of Ilford North in general) Joseph had appealed to a distinct "Jewish vote" in the constituency. If the Jews really were "just like everyone else", there would have been no separate lobby to address. In the *Spectator*, an anonymous critic wrote that the message of the Ilford speech "sat very uneasily on Joseph's lips", contrasted it with his conduct during Suez, and insinuated that it had all been Sherman's doing.[84] But Joseph's conduct towards his co-religionists had been of a piece with his treatment of the Conservative Party since 1974. Even if he did not write his own script on this occasion, he had read it out without first reflecting that some people would take offence (leaving aside the wider question of whether or not the strict control of immigration was consistent with his arguments for economic freedom). The Jewish establishment had no desire to be seen as representing a distinct lobby in Britain because of their desire for full assimilation. It was debatable whether opinion-leaders had always stuck to this rule themselves, and some of their outcry over Ilford reflected opposition to the Conservative party rather than a more general concern for the proprieties of debate. But the issue no longer mattered to Joseph as it had done at the time of Suez. For him, the key to identity lay in ideas, and in this sense after years of struggle his own "assimilation" had taken place. More important than questions about Jew or Gentile was whether or not one believed in the free market. If only he had discovered Adam Smith at Lockers Park!

---

83. *Ibid.*, 147–9. In happier days Joseph had himself freely acknowledged this, recognising his luck in living "in this civilised country of ours" and noting that "Had I been born in a different country it would have ended my life": KJ interview with Anthony King.
84. "A deeply impractical man", in *Spectator*, 19 May 1979.

But the tactic did not backfire, despite widespread and generally adverse press comment (*The Times*, for example, called Joseph's appeal "most un-British").[85] Although Iremonger restricted the majority by standing as an Independent, the Conservatives won the by-election on a swing of almost 7 per cent; among the Jews of Ilford North the swing exceeded 10 per cent. In asking Jews explicitly to support Mrs Thatcher and her party's immigration policy Joseph had raised another serious question, since the leader's statement on television had gone beyond Whitelaw's compromise position, prompting her deputy to talk of resignation. Yet the lack of clarity on this key issue meant less to voters than the impression that the Tories took a hard line; one poll found that immigration influenced almost half of those who switched from Labour to Conservative in the by-election.[86]

Against most expectations, Joseph had shown that he was capable of being a very popular populist. He might be hated by the Left, and cold-shouldered by many of his Westminster colleagues, but for the Tory activists in the country he was a hero. In June 1978 a poll of constituency officers found unanimous approval for him; even Mrs Thatcher collected only 69 per cent support. Twelve per cent would have liked Joseph to be leader of the party, a figure only seven per cent behind Enoch Powell. When the columnist Frank Johnson wrote a witty profile in the *Telegraph* pointing out the confusion created by Joseph's highbrow speeches, a Conservative from Hove protested that, on the contrary, his "vigorous arguments in support of free enterprise and individual freedom are like water in the desert". In September 1977, she continued, a meeting in Hove addressed by Joseph had been attended by 800 people, "at £1.50 a ticket".[87] If numbers were a reliable guide, the message was getting through. But although Joseph had convinced himself as early as September 1975 that "the climate of opinion" was turning against Keynes, he remained alert to any signs of heresy. On one occasion he detected the stigmata of unorthodox thought in a CRD brief, which had been produced for another shadow minister. Summoned to Joseph's office, the author – who, as usual, had cobbled the brief together from previous speeches and policy statements – expected a serious dressing-down. But Joseph merely pointed out the "mistake", and discussed the matter quietly.[88]

Joseph was not always so lenient. In January 1976 he reviewed a book by the Keynesian John Kenneth Galbraith, and found it "unstructured, superficial, trendy and confessedly selective". He predicted, though, that the book would "prove profitable both to publisher and to author" (the free market could move in very mysterious ways). Two months later Joseph was horrified to learn that Galbraith had been invited by the BBC to give thirteen televised talks. He

85. *The Times*, 4 March 1978.
86. Alderman, *Jewish Community in British Politics*, 148–9.
87. *Daily Telegraph*, 7, 23, 29 June 1978.
88. "Inflation: The Climate of Opinion is Changing", KJ's speech at Preston, 24 September 1975, reprinted in *Stranded on the Middle Ground: Reflections on Circumstances and Policies* (CPS, 1976), 9–17; interview with Rob Shepherd.

contacted Whitelaw, instructing him to use his influence with the Corporation in order to secure the cancellation of the series. Describing Galbraith as "about the most dangerous intellectual opponent that we have", he claimed that his writings were "half-baked and dependent upon bold and inaccurate over-simplifications". Whitelaw – who on economic matters sympathised more closely with Galbraith than with his own colleague – made a few tentative enquiries but was probably quite happy to take "no" for an answer. To Joseph it was unthinkable that Whitelaw should not share his fears, and in September he tried again. "Galbraith", he reminded his colleague, "is socialist, intervention-ist, anti-enterprise and totally indifferent to the realities of life. He is not respected by economists ["economists" was evidently now a synonym for "the IEA"] but he is a facile journalist sort of a writer with a huge lay following who believe the rubbish he propagates". If this emissary of the devil should be allowed to address the British nation, at the very least the schedules should be cleared for a reply. The difficulty lay in finding someone suitable; Joseph felt that Galbraith's "highly selective abuse of economics and misuse of so-called industrial evidence" could only be answered by somebody who was famous, articulate and robust, yet warm, witty and pungent. Fortunately, one senior industrialist fitted this demanding bill, and Joseph invited Whitelaw to share his joy at the news that Sir Frank McFadzean of Shell had been persuaded to take up the cudgels because "he recognised the danger of a rampant Galbraith". Joseph then embarked on a breathless and unnecessarily detailed encomium of a pamphlet by the same author which would soon appear under the CPS imprint, and sent copies of his letter to several other colleagues.[89]

Galbraith's series, *The Age of Uncertainty*, appeared in 1977 as planned. Joseph forced himself to watch; his splenetic letters of protest became such a regular feature of *The Times*' correspondence columns that readers could be forgiven for thinking that the newspaper had hired an additional TV critic.[90] Almost immediately filming began on a monetarist reply, delivered by no less an authority than Friedman himself. Comparing the two series, Wayne Parsons judges that while the first "was intended more as a piece of economic education than Galbraithian propaganda, Friedman's programmes were frankly designed to convert and persuade". The accompanying book, *Free to Choose* (1980), similarly made no attempt to explain the development of economic thought, and its political purpose was unconcealed. In other words, Joseph's strictures on Galbraith actually applied with much greater force to Friedman's contribution; but there is no record that he was unhappy about "half-baked . . . over-simplifications" when they came from within his own camp. Many politicians have praised pluralism while working for the complete domination of their

---

89. *Observer*, 9 January 1976; KJ to Whitelaw, 10 September 1976, Box 18/9, Joseph Papers, CPA, Bodleian Library.
90. See for example, *The Times*, 1 April, 3 May 1977.

own ideas, but few can have displayed their double standards with such refreshing naïveté as Sir Keith Joseph.[91]

Joseph's furious assault on Galbraith was provoked in part by an obscure interview in which the "rampant" economist had said "I am not particular about freedom", and offered the opinion that the Berlin Wall had helped to keep the peace in Europe. But sheer fatigue must have had some effect on Joseph's tone. He had allowed himself no respite from political work in the twenty years since his first victory at Leeds North-East. Even before Reginald Maudling was sacked in November 1976 Joseph had a longer record of continuous front-bench service in the Commons than any of his colleagues. 1976 marked his twentieth year as an MP, and into that time he had packed more activity than a normal member could manage in half a century. His health had been far from perfect since before he first entered Parliament, and although some photographs show surprisingly youthful features, by his sixtieth birthday in January 1978 most observers were remarking on the speed with which he had aged. Stress and overwork were the obvious culprits here. Remarks on Joseph's demeanour were still uncommon in serious articles, but sketch-writers and Labour MPs agreed that there was something badly amiss. If they lacked much human sympathy in their sallies, it was because Joseph was a voluntary martyr to his profession – and because ideologues are driven by inner demons which are inexplicable to normal mortals.

In April 1978, for example, Labour's Geoffrey Robinson asked if he might "inoffensively put to the right hon. Member that watching him perform from this side of the House one gets the impression that he is being tortured on the rack rather than speaking with the authority that the Dispatch Box should confer upon him".[92] Robinson's remark showed how far Labour had strayed from the normal conventions of parliamentary etiquette in Joseph's case. During a party meeting at the beginning of March, the policy guru had suddenly urged his colleagues to consider the infliction of "boredom" as a suitable punishment for some offences.[93] This was not the first time that Joseph had listed boredom among mankind's most pitiful conditions. But the suggestion of a "long, dull shock" as a suitable deterrent betrayed an unusual degree of detachment from political reality. He had every reason to be preoccupied. A few days later newspapers carried an announcement that his marriage had ended in separation. Apparently the initiative for this move had come from Hellen. Whether or not the split affected him as deeply as it might have done a decade earlier, Joseph was certainly anxious about the press response – after all, no politician had drawn more attention to "problem families" – and he asked media friends to treat him gently.[94] Reaction was in general sympathetic; the

---

91. Wayne Parsons, *The Political Power of the Financial Press* (Edward Elgar, 1989), 173–4.
92. *Hansard*, vol. 947, col. 1024, 10 April 1978.
93. ACP (78) 155, minutes of meeting on 1 March 1978, CPA, Bodleian Library.
94. Private information.

Daily Mail, for example, dwelt on the pressures of political life, and pointed out that Joseph shared Sir Harold Wilson's obsession with politics while lacking the ex-premier's ability to "switch off". An unnamed friend commented that Lady Joseph "cherished a family life and may have gradually become more disenchanted". For observers who had known about the domestic difficulties for some time the interesting question was "why now?". The family was growing up, but the youngest child, Anna, was still only thirteen. The strong likelihood of a general election in the near future was another possible factor, but if Joseph wished to avoid embarrassment he could have suggested that the couple kept things quiet until that was safely out of the way.[95]

In their statement, the couple denied that a third party was involved. Most private comment at the time concerned the facts that Joseph was only moving a few hundred yards, to 63 Limerston Street, and he continued to see his wife as often as his outside commitments allowed. This could be interpreted as another example of Joseph's eccentricity, but it provides circumstantial backing for a story which he hinted at to friends. He suggested that there had been threats against him, and that if he lived on his own his enemies would know where to find him without putting his family at risk. Joseph was certainly moving in dangerous company; Ross McWhirter of NAFF had been assassinated by the IRA, and Joseph featured on more than one death-list (he continued to do so long after he had retired from the Commons). But if security had been the overriding consideration Joseph would have taken action in 1975. In July of that year he was named along with other Jewish celebrities in connection with Carlos "The Jackal", and McWhirter was shot dead in November.[96]

To add further complexity to this murky plot, within a few months of decamping to Limerston Street Joseph was the victim of a burglary while he was in the United States. A strong-box had been forced open, but it contained no valuables; the thieves only made off with a few household items. But as the press reported, it was the third break-in involving the Conservative Party within a month; previously Patten's office at the CRD had been ransacked, and the home of Tim Bell of the advertisers Saatchi and Saatchi was also targetted. In fact Joseph himself had suffered a far more suspicious break-in while still living at Mulberry Walk. In July 1976 thieves had entered the house, but nothing at all was taken. After the latest attack party officials were particularly jittery, given Joseph's involvement with sensitive policy work. But he hastened to reassure Mrs Thatcher that the burglary seemed to lack a political dimension, and he was particularly relieved that two papers connected with the economic discussions at Fentiman Road had been left unmolested.[97]

---

95. *Daily Mail*, 31 March 1978.
96. Private information; *Daily Telegraph*, 3 July 1975.
97. *Daily Mail*, 21 October 1978; KJ to Mrs Thatcher, 25 October 1978, Joseph Papers, Box 18/ 11, CPA, Bodleian Library; *Daily Telegraph*, 22 July 1976.

The break-in was still an unpleasant scare at a time when Joseph seemed to be adjusting to his new circumstances. At the party conference in Brighton just before the burglary he made what was judged to be a successful speech – supposedly on Industry, but also featuring a blast against polytechnic lecturers and an unprecedented compliment to farmers. In the *Guardian* Simon Hoggart noted that the speech was delivered on the day after the Jewish Day of Atonement, and joked that "It is a sign of Sir Keith's growing confidence that this is thought to be the first time he has atoned for a speech before making it". Unusually, Joseph had ended his speech in an anecdotal mood:

> On Monday I was walking past a group of strikers. I do not know the rights and wrongs of the strike. One of them stepped out, pointed at me as I was passing, and said "He's a friend of the workers, that guy". He was using a narrow definition of the word "worker" and he was being sarcastic. But with humility I think that he was telling the truth. I think that I am a better friend of the workers, however they are defined, than the flat earthers who ignore the consumer, who praise conflict and who resent and obstruct the entrepreneur.[98]

Although the tone of this speech was in marked contrast to some of Joseph's policy deliberations, he believed what he was saying. Outside the hall, the strikers were an early sign that the union movement was beginning to kick against the government's policy of pay restraint; Heath told the conference that this made him "grieve for our country", but the majority of his audience preferred to gloat at Labour's discomfort.[99] Events seemed to be confirming the case put forward by John Hoskyns – that Britain was doomed unless its policy-makers could break free from a crazy logic which meant that every attempt to correct the economic situation only seemed to make matters worse. The "Labour Isn't Working" poster tapped into a widespread mood of public disillusionment with the government, although Callaghan was still far more popular than Mrs Thatcher. The Prime Minister's parliamentary pact with the Liberal Party had broken down, leaving him dangerously dependent on the support of nationalist MPs. The fact that he had decided not to call an autumn election was a good indication that Labour's private pollsters were sending negative signals, whatever the findings of other organisations. Provided that the Conservative Party kept its nerve, it looked as though Joseph would soon have the chance to put to the test of practice the ideas he had been trying to explain since 1974.

---

98. *Guardian*, 13 October 1978; Minutes of the Ninety-fifth Conservative Party conference, 12 October 1978.
99. Heath, *Course of my Life*, 569.

Chapter 12

"Really, Keith!"

In retirement, when asked whether his political influence had been greater before or after 1979, Lord Joseph replied without hesitation: "Before". He felt that "The work had been done. If you read a thing like *The Right Approach* I think the work was largely there . . . I think it was all there, agreed, blessed by Margaret Thatcher and by Willie Whitelaw".[1]

The remark implies that in hindsight Joseph judged the policy exercise to have been a success. But as we have seen, he had publicly distanced himself from *The Right Approach*. At best, that document reflected the fact that the "wets" were now on the defensive. In turn, this development was largely due to "events". Joseph's real contribution had been his speeches of 1974 and 1975, which had enthused existing believers in monetarism and convinced many agnostics that at least there was an alternative economic approach that might be worth trying. In short, from Joseph's point of view "The work had been done" before the official policy exercise commenced; the impact, combined with a prolonged run of misfortune for the opponents of economic liberalism, was still being felt at the beginning of the twenty-first century.

It was typically unassuming of Joseph to rest his claim to influence on what was (at least on paper) a collective endeavour rather than one of his many

---

1. KJ interview with Anthony Seldon, 29.

personal initiatives. But in this context he might have been expected to allude to his relationship with Mrs Thatcher. Hugo Young has described this as "one of the most formative political relationships of modern times". It was cemented by shared experiences, by mutual respect, and (above all) by the political and economic ideas which both held with equal conviction. To a unique extent in post-war British politics they were protective of each other. Critics and admirers alike were glad to think that the relationship was unusually close: the first because they saw Joseph as a potential source of embarrassment to the leader, the second because they regarded his intellectual reputation as an asset. Joseph was either Mrs Thatcher's "mentor", "policy guru", "Svengali" (or "Rasputin" for those who saw Joseph as "The Mad Monk"). In 1976 Malcolm Rifkind noted that if the press was to be believed Joseph was "a cross between an *eminence grise* and a benevolent sugar-daddy".[2]

Yet there was an obvious difference between the pair, neatly expressed by Joseph in the same 1987 interview. While he had reached his conclusions "with the help of friends", Mrs Thatcher, he suspected, "came to it by her own common sense and instinct". Thus to say that his influence was so strong that he had shaped her basic ideas would be highly misleading; there had been few if any searching intellectual discussions, he told an interviewer after his retirement. He believed that they had been "along parallel lines"; more precisely, their separate paths had now converged in the same truths, and the message could be disseminated through different channels. Joseph's intellectual approach would take care of highbrow newspapers and the universities, while Mrs Thatcher gave voice to her "instincts" through the tabloids, the television and the Jimmy Young Show. There was no doubt that the new party leader would always be grateful to Joseph for his part in the events of 1974–5, and would never cease to admire his intellectual powers. What remained to be seen was whether this complementary relationship forged in adversity would stand up to the changes which followed Mrs Thatcher's rise to the leadership.[3]

It would be a mistake to place too much emphasis on written evidence of the dealings between Mrs Thatcher and Joseph, which were likely to have been more formal than their other communications. But the tone of the surviving memos is surprisingly distant, even allowing for Joseph's innate diffidence. In January 1976, for example, he wrote:

One evening at [the industrialist] Val Duncan's you remarked to me that you thought that the day of great new industries was over – and that there

---

2. Hugo Young, *One of Us: A Biography of Margaret Thatcher* (Macmillan, 1990), 43; *Jewish Chronicle*, 13 February 1976.
3. KJ interview with Anthony Seldon; KJ interview for "The Thatcher Factor", Thatcher 003/17, LSE archives.

would not be a repetition of the sort of surge of cars, aeroplanes, television etc. that we have witnessed in our lives. Your remark worried me because while I could not produce an example to confound you I felt strongly that you were wrong . . .

Since their conversation Joseph had made enquiries, and among other things he mentioned information technology as a likely development which would prove Mrs Thatcher wrong. He concluded that there was no reason for her to reply "unless you want me to pursue any particular point".[4]

It was rather like a letter to his employer from a young nobleman's tutor. Joseph believed that he should try to supplement Mrs Thatcher's knowledge, recognising that she was destined to play a much more active part in the world. Among other things, he provided her with a list of key books by economic liberals such as Friedrich Hayek. While Mrs Thatcher did read IEA publications for herself her new role greatly reduced the time she had to spare, and Joseph could keep her in touch with the latest thinking at Lord North Street. As he put it himself, this "perhaps gave a framework to her own analysis". He knew that there were other aspects of his leader's education for which she would rely on others, such as Airey Neave for tactical advice and Gordon Reece as her hair, dress and speech supremo. And on some policy matters it seems that Joseph followed his leader's initiative. For example, in 1970 he had been a member of the Conservative Group for Europe along with several other ministers including Nicholas Ridley (but not Margaret Thatcher). Asked in October 1974 whether he would welcome Enoch Powell back into the Conservative Party, Joseph said that he would first "have to change his attitude on some subjects very important to him", notably Europe on which "I think he's entirely wrong". He proceeded to reject Powell's case on the key sovereignty issue. In the campaign leading up to the referendum of June 1975 Joseph appeared in one of "Britain in Europe's" broadcasts along with Roy Jenkins and Shirley Williams (not for the first time, he was filmed on a building site). In 1975 Mrs Thatcher agreed that Britain's economic interests lay with continued EEC membership, but her doubts were thinly concealed and during the referendum campaign she was criticised for her passive role. For the remainder of the Opposition period Joseph was reticent on Europe, and by 1979 he had come to share Mrs Thatcher's doubts about developments within the Community. Joseph also seems to have followed Mrs Thatcher's lead on the negative income tax as a remedy for poverty. As late as August 1976 he was speaking positively about this complex reform, but Mrs Thatcher was sceptical and despite continued support from within the CRD Joseph dropped the subject before the 1979 general election. The party

4. KJ to Mrs Thatcher, 21 January 1976, Joseph Papers, Box 8/22, CPA, Bodleian Library.

manifesto included only the vaguest of references, pointing out the difficulties in terms of cost and technology.[5]

During the 1979 campaign (which began after Callaghan lost a vote of confidence in the Commons on 28 March) Joseph was accused by the *Guardian* of keeping out of sight. The allegation was inspired by a report that the Conservative Party Chairman, Peter Thorneycroft, had asked him not to deliver another hard-hitting speech on the trade unions. Typically Joseph fired off a furious letter to the newspaper. Far from adopting a low profile, he wrote, he had featured in two televised discussions, attended two morning press conferences, and three of his speeches had been circulated by Central Office. In these he claimed to have "spoken controversially as I always do". At Penistone, South Yorkshire, he had predicted that under Labour Britain would become a "totalitarian slum", and in Lichfield he flung back Callaghan's allegation that unemployment would rise under the Tories.[6]

Yet the press had heard all this before; only a fresh indiscretion would be newsworthy. According to one account, Joseph would have obliged if a well-disposed newspaper editor had not prevented him from going public with an admission that economic recovery might take as long as three years under the Conservatives; instead, he recorded this prediction in his first major interview after the election had been won. An embarrassing private conversation also went unreported at the time. He was overheard saying that he expected his party to win, then "began to bang his forehead rhythmically with his hand. 'Oh God', he groaned, 'what I'm worried about is all the mistakes we're going to make. I know we are going to make mistakes. I lie awake worrying about them'".[7] His most interesting public utterance was another of his endearing attempts to inject humour into his serious message, which as usual caused more confusion than controversy. On 21 April, in a speech to his own constituents, Joseph told a parable about "two neighbouring kingdoms", one called "the Neddylands", ruled by "the good King Neb and his allies, the Quangeroos" and the other known as "Lakeland", governed by "King Laker" (named in honour of one of Mrs Thatcher's favourite entrepreneurs, Freddie (later Sir Freddie) Laker). In "Lakeland" Joseph explained, "more citizens took trouble and took risks and showed enterprise, not because they were more virtuous than the citizens of the Neddylands but because it was worthwhile to do so". Predictably, despite all the efforts of King Neb the Neddylanders "grew poorer and

5. Hugo Young and Anne Sloman, *The Thatcher Phenomenon* (BBC, 1986), 60; KJ interview with Llew Gardner; David Butler and Uwe Kitzinger, *The European Referendum of 1975* (Macmillan, 1976), 199; *Observer*, 22 August 1976; *The Conservative Manifesto 1979*, 27. Cf. Trevor Russel's claim that in Opposition Joseph led attempts to ditch the party's commitment to negative income tax (*The Tory Party: Its Policies, Divisions & Future* (Penguin, 1978), 111).
6. Thatcher, *Path to Power*, 451; *Guardian*, 25 April 1979; cf. David Butler and Dennis Kavanagh, *The British General Election of 1979* (Macmillan, 1980), 332.
7. *Observer*, 9 December 1984.

poorer". Whether or not the audience comprehended this frivolous fable, there is no record of another public outing for King Laker and the Quangeroos.[8]

The tone of the campaign was set by the manifesto, which marked a further slight sway, rather than a pronounced swing, to the Right. As with earlier policy documents, Joseph was involved in discussions but the drafting was left to others. There was a heavy emphasis on "proper monetary discipline . . . with publicly stated targets for the rate of growth of the money supply", and the trade union proposals had been toughened. But there would be "open and informed discussion of the Government's economic objectives", and although pay in the public sector would be strictly controlled there would be full consultation with the relevant unions. While monetary policy was identified as the key weapon against inflation, the party pledged nothing more than to "review the workings" of the Price Commission (which would have no place at all if the Conservatives were to abandon prices and incomes policy). In Joseph's own area of Industry, the manifesto echoed virtually every Conservative document since the war in promising to reverse the most recent Labour nationalisations (in this case aerospace, freight transport and shipbuilding). Far from ruling out further subsidies to "lame ducks", the manifesto merely noted that "such help must be temporary and tapered". It was hoped that firms which were already being succoured by the taxpayer would soon be fit to stand alone. But since the section on regional aid stressed that government assistance should be related to the number of jobs at stake it seemed that Mrs Thatcher's party had learned an important lesson from the early months of the Heath government.[9]

The moderate tone of the manifesto was explained by the line-up of spokesmen who appeared at the launch on 11 April. Mrs Thatcher was joined by Whitelaw, Pym, Prior, Thorneycroft, Howe and Joseph (who was seen to be nodding with unusual vigour whenever the leader spoke). Of these only the last two were economic "dries". On balance the "wets" (and "damps" like Thorneycroft) had reason to be satisfied with a document which contained enough radicalism to allow them to blame Mrs Thatcher for defeat, but not enough to make it easy for her to talk of a "mandate" for fundamental change if she should win. But, as they well knew, Prime Ministers are notoriously inconsistent in their adherence to the doctrine of the mandate. If the party won even a narrow victory, the prestige of Mrs Thatcher's office would weaken her opponents, even if they still commanded a majority in her cabinet. The room in which the press conference took place was unusually hot, and as noticed by the press, the temperature was not the only reason for the discomfort.[10]

---

8. "The Charlton Interview", BBC Radio 4, 30 July 1979; *Observer*, 9 December 1984; KJ speech in Leeds, 21 April 1979 (CCO handout).
9. Hugo Young in *Sunday Times*, 4 May 1980.
10. *Guardian*, 12 April 1979.

Joseph knew that this would be the most important election of his life. Mrs Thatcher was convinced that she would be toppled if she lost, but defeat would not necessarily mean her disappearance from the Conservative front-bench. Joseph was seven years older than his leader, and highly vulnerable to the suggestion that retirement would benefit his health. Whether in the form of a gentle hint or a brusque instruction, that was the message he was likely to hear from any of those who were best placed to succeed Mrs Thatcher.

As election day approached the opinion polls were (in Lady Thatcher's phrase) "all over the place", NOP finding a slight Labour lead on 1 May, less than ten days after another organisation had placed the Conservatives twenty points clear. At least Joseph's position in Leeds North-East was fairly secure, although the number of immigrants and their British-born children had almost doubled during the 1970s and they were unlikely to be much impressed either by their MP's Ilford speech or by Mrs Thatcher's talk of being "swamped". After the latter outburst the local agent admitted many people in the constituency "had a great fear that somebody would knock on their doors at four in the morning and ship them off where they allegedly came from". But they had been offered reassurance in the local press. Joseph felt confident enough to spend most of his time campaigning outside the constituency, and to help (among others) Teddy Taylor, fighting the marginal seat of Glasgow Cathcart. This visit offered Joseph the chance to inspect at first hand areas of serious social deprivation, but as he was being driven through a particularly run-down district it was noticed that he seemed more interested in the book he was reading – an academic study of poverty in Chicago. On the train journey to Scotland Joseph had received several urgent requests for anecdotes which could form the basis of an article in Rupert Murdoch's *Sun*. Although at this time one journalist called Joseph "the most charming bogey-man in British politics", his warmth was only recognised by people who had the chance to speak to him in person.[11] Mrs Thatcher had lunched with the *Sun*'s editor, Larry Lamb, who told her that "Keith's reputation as a cold intellectual, remote from the people, was a hindrance to the Tory campaign". This could be rectified if the *Sun* ran a piece showing "The Human Side of Sir Keith Joseph". Joseph refused to co-operate at first, saying that "he had done nothing to help the poor and unfortunate. All his efforts had been in vain or even counterproductive". When the train reached Carlisle Joseph was shown a third telegram, this time begging for just a single helpful anecdote. He relented, describing his work on behalf of widows after the Second World War, then retracted his story after remembering that "the Treasurer ran off to Brazil with all the money".[12]

---

11. Thatcherl, *Path to Power*, 439; *Observer*, 29 April 1979; interview with Richard Shepherd; Graham Turner in *Sunday Times*, 6 May 1979.
12. O'Sullivan, "Conservatism, Democracy and National Identity".

Teddy Taylor turned out to be one of a handful of Tory casualties in an election which gave the Conservative Party a comfortable cushion of forty-three seats. Joseph's own majority fell very slightly; his vote increased by 1,500 compared with October 1974, and this almost compensated for a marked swing from the Liberals to his Labour challenger. As Mrs Thatcher proudly recorded, the party did much better nationally; the 5.6 per cent swing from Labour was the biggest shift in the vote between the two main parties since 1945. Even before the poll, James Callaghan had detected what he called "a sea-change in politics"; whatever he had said during the campaign, he thought, the country had already decided that it wanted Mrs Thatcher. More accurately, the electorate had already judged that it no longer wanted Labour. There could be little public faith in the economic competence of a government which was driven by expediency rather than any coherent strategy, even if the actual record was rather better than subsequent commentators have assumed. But Labour's most obvious weakness was its inability to tackle union power. In a much later interview Joseph described the unions at this time as "uncomprehending, suicidal". But Callaghan had given them a rope with which to hang both themselves and his government, by postponing the election until union patience with pay restraint had been exhausted. The result was nightly news bulletins throughout the winter of 1978–9, featuring picket lines outside hospitals, uncollected rubbish, and bodies left unburied due to industrial action by gravediggers. There were even instances of workers going on strike before their pay claim had been submitted. Raucous press support carried this message to areas beyond the reach of the Conservative Party's skilful advertisers, Saatchi and Saatchi. Lamb at the *Sun* came up with "the Winter of Discontent" to sum up the industrial mayhem; on the day of the election the newspaper which in Murdoch's early days had introduced "Maggie Thatcher – Milk Snatcher" made amends by telling its readers that a Tory victory was "the only way to stop the rot". When so many things were going wrong people were unlikely to be scared by Labour predictions that they might get even worse under the Conservatives, and trying to portray Mrs Thatcher as an extremist before she had been given a real chance to prove the point was equally ill-judged. For the purposes of reassuring an electorate which fed on images rather than ideas, all her advisors had to do was to force a calf into her arms. 1979 marked no more of a "sea-change" in British politics than 1970 (when the Conservatives actually won a slightly higher percentage of the vote). Even within the parliamentary party, there was little discernible change (although regardless of their private views a high proportion of the newly elected members could be relied upon to support a winning leader). Another interesting trend for the future was the party's performance in the south of England where (including London) its representation increased by twenty-seven seats; now almost 200 of the 339 Conservative MPs were elected from this area. But none of this would have mattered had the Conservatives lost the next election – which they seemed very likely to do for more than half of the 1979–83 Parliament. The real "sea-change" in British politics occurred in December 1981, when General Galtieri seized power in Argentina.[13]

Mrs Thatcher would have liked to have been in a position to offer Joseph the Treasury after her victory, but evidently the internal opposition was still too great. Once again it seems that the main obstacle was Whitelaw, who did not trust or understand Joseph (by contrast, the latter always entertained the highest regard for Whitelaw, whose loyalty to the Prime Minister he regarded as indispensable).[14] In *The Downing Street Years* she rationalised the situation by noting that although Joseph had no doubts concerning the right economic decisions, "he knew that they meant unviable firms would collapse and over-manning become unemployment, and he cared about those who were affected – far more than did all our professionally compassionate critics". This account would be more convincing had Mrs Thatcher not offered Joseph the Industry portfolio; at that Department he, rather than Chancellor Howe, would be confronted directly with any adverse results of economic policy. Mrs Thatcher's decision seemed to confirm that Joseph would never be Chancellor himself, but he made no complaint. His thoughts were already ranging beyond economic matters. On the night after the election a celebration was held at the Research Department (shortly to be deprived of its cherished independence and merged into the Central Office machine). Joseph dropped in for a time, and was remembered to have asked one reveller whether teacher-training courses were really necessary.[15] It was a peculiar setting for this kind of chit-chat, but it was not so strange that the new Secretary of State for Industry should be asking such questions. Despite his repeated warnings about the state of the economy, he had repeatedly placed education at the top of his list of priorities in the run up to the election. He had not been given that post – as yet. But throughout his political career he had been aiming to educate the public. In his new job he would have to persuade employers, unions and the general public that "socialist" propaganda had led them all to expect too much of governments since the war. As he put it years later, "the very first words that a British baby is apt to be taught to utter are that 'The Government should do something about it'". To change these attitudes was a vital task – yet he had never been trained to teach.[16]

---

13. Thatcher, *Path to Power*, 461; Bernard Donoughue, *Prime Minister: The Conduct of Policy under Harold Wilson and James Callaghan* (Jonathan Cape, 1987), 171, 191; Andrew Denham, interview with Lord Joseph, April 1991; Peter Chippindale and Chris Horrie, *Stick It Up Your Punter! The Rise and Fall of the Sun* (Mandarin, 1992), 55–61; Thompson, "Economic Ideas and the Development of Economic Opinion" in Coopey and Woodward (eds), *Britain in the 1970s*, 78.
14. Interview with Lord Brittan.
15. Thatcher, *Downing Street Years*, 26; Interview with Rob Shepherd.
16. *The Scotsman,* 1 April 1978; *House of Lords Debates*, vol. 494, col. 205, 2 March 1988.

After the election the pressure of government business ruled out a resumption of the Campus Campaign. But Joseph could still hope to reach a significant audience through the printed word. One of his favourite lessons in recent years had been the evils of egalitarian thinking. Back in 1967 he had urged that the defenders of the free market should show that their preferred system was superior in every respect to the "statist" alternative. In his university speeches he had concentrated on the proposition that capitalism was morally superior to socialism because it could provide resources for the poor while not asking too much of human nature. It continued to irritate him that the Left claimed a monopoly of virtue – particularly when such claims were advanced by people like Anthony Crosland, who made no secret of his relish for the good things in life. Joseph wrote several articles on equality during the opposition years, and gave a long lecture when finally allowed to speak at the LSE in June 1978; but even that format denied him sufficient scope for a thorough inquiry into a complex subject.[17]

Less than a month after the 1979 election the publisher John Murray produced a short book entitled *Equality*, which bore on its cover the names of Joseph and of Jonathan Sumption, an associate of the CPS and a former Fellow of Joseph's old college, Magdalen.[18] This was a new departure for Joseph, whose work had previously been issued in pamphlet form under the imprint of bodies associated with the Conservative Party. Joseph had been approached by the publisher, but the man who had left unfinished his dissertation on toleration could not be expected to reveal new levels of productivity on this equally ticklish topic. Sumption wrote most of the text, although the full contents were agreed with Joseph. The book was ready for publication before the election, and to maximise sales this might have been the ideal timing. But Joseph asked for a postponement, concerned that parts of the book might be quoted against him and his party during the campaign. The publication date was pushed back, on the understanding that he would help with a post-election publicity drive. It was a compromise typical of Joseph; while most politicians would refuse to allow their names to be linked with a book which might be used against them at any time, his sole concern was that nothing should impair his party's chances of winning the election. After that, his opponents could quote it to their heart's content, because the consequences would fall on him alone.[19]

Once the election had been won Joseph was far too busy to give the promotional help he had promised. There is no evidence that *Equality* was ever quoted against him in debate during his ministerial career, and the book was not discussed by his first biographer. But what Joseph's friend Jock Bruce-Gardyne described as "a treasure-house of a book" deserves more attention, as an

---

17. KJ speech on "Equality", LSE, 8 June 1978 (CCO handout).
18. Sumption is now a noted lawyer and prolific historian.
19. Private information; internal John Murray memorandum reporting conversation with KJ, 10 April 1979. We are most grateful to Virginia Murray for locating this correspondence in the company archives.

indication of Joseph's thinking at a time when he was preparing to take on a key government position.[20] Even in a country where philosophical reflections rarely catch the headlines, the contents were sufficiently controversial to win wider notice. As Ralf Dahrendorf pointed out, *Equality* represented "a deliberate and radical break" from the British tradition; the LSE Director felt that even the nineteenth-century Manchester School was "more compassionate, more oriented to the tradition of solidarity" than Joseph and Sumption. The authors presented an uncompromising philosophical argument, in fluent prose. But their claim that "A society which had achieved a high degree of economic equality would be horrible to live in" was of marginal relevance to the inter-party conflict of 1979, or the immediate concerns of the British electorate; if anything, it had more bearing on the internal debates of the Labour Party. The argument was concentrated against the advocates of *complete* equality of incomes, who in the Britain of 1979 were either rare or extinct. The main-stream Left felt that British society was still disfigured by *excessive* inequality despite improvements over the previous half-century;[21] but it was possible to hold that view without dreaming of a society in which everyone enjoyed exactly the same living standards. The message of *Equality* was confusing; by turns, the authors argued that redistribution had gone too far, that it had not worked at all, that it had only worked at the expense of the rich and of economic growth, or that redistribution *per se* was "morally indefensible". Joseph and Sumption relied heavily for their arguments (and some of their analogies) on Robert Nozick's *Anarchy, State and Utopia*. Since Nozick's libertarian position was radical even in the context of the United States, this begged the question of whether that country, with its long tradition of individualism, was a suitable model for Britain.[22]

At least *Equality* fell in line with most twentieth-century British thinking in its support for the principles of equality before the law and equality of opportunity. But their enthusiasm for Nozick took Joseph and Sumption too far in their attacks on the state. Ultimately, the logic of their case for inequality

20. *Sunday Telegraph*, 3 June 1979.
21. Ralf Dahrendorf, *On Britain* (BBC Publications, 1982), 125. According to an authoritative study, "The inequality of personal wealth distribution had reduced substantially between the 1920s and the mid-1960s, and narrowed again between the early and mid-1970s". However, there were still "substantial inequalities in the distribution of income and wealth" when the Thatcher government came to power; ironically, the post-war trend of diminishing inequality had stalled *before* Joseph and Sumption began to write their book. Reviewing the evidence, A. H. Halsey concludes that "The activity of the state makes for no dramatic reduction of market inequalities". See John Hills (ed.), *New Inequalities: The Changing Distribution of Income and Wealth in the United Kingdom* (Cambridge University Press, 1996), 1–5, and A. H. Halsey, *Change in British Society: From 1900 to the Present Day* (Oxford University Press, 1995), 45.
22. See Keith Joseph and Jonathan Sumption, *Equality* (John Murray, 1979), esp. 13–18. In the year before the appearance of *Equality* William Waldegrave (who had worked for Heath but later served as a Cabinet minister under both Thatcher and Major) accused Nozick and those who thought like him of "fanaticism"; see William Waldegrave, *The Binding of Leviathan: Conservatism and the Future* (Hamish Hamilton, 1978), 50.

(concentrating on the infringement of liberty represented by taxation) destroyed the rationale for even the most basic state welfare provision. This contradicted their acknowledgement that no society, "free or unfree, [can] tolerate differences between its members so extreme as to undermine its security and stability". Thus, after all, a degree of redistribution from rich to poor was necessary. This admission brought the debate down from the philosophical plane to more practical questions; how much redistribution was needed, and how, in the modern context, should poverty be defined?

The latter question produced the key argument of the book. Those who spoke of poverty in relative terms were wrong. "An absolute standard means one defined by reference to the real needs of the poor . . . A family is poor if it cannot afford to eat". Thankfully, "By any absolute standard there is very little poverty in Britain today". The remaining problems affected "those who, like the old, the disabled, widows and some one-parent families, have special needs". Joseph had revised his view rather sharply since July 1976, when he had confidently asserted that "poverty is relative". He had not changed his mind about the most "deserving" categories. But the end of his argument was incompatible with the beginning. If no society could "tolerate" "extreme" inequality, surely it was permissible to talk of relative poverty after all – and to justify government help even above subsistence level if the gap between rich and poor was dangerously wide? As with his enthusiastic embrace of monetarism, Joseph had grasped at a theory because of "its apparent clarity and its moral force". But he had not worked through its practical implications; nor, apparently, had he consulted the work of Adam Smith, who defined "necessities" as "not only commodities which are indispensably necessary for the support of life but whatever *the custom of the country* renders it indecent for creditable people, even of the lowest order, to be without". In a later interview Mrs Thatcher inadvertently revealed the hazards of applying even Joseph's narrow definition of poverty to social policy at a time when the government hoped to restrain welfare spending. "Capitalism", she said in 1987, "works by increasing what used to be the privileges of the few to become *the daily necessities* of the many". For her, the new "necessities" included "all mod cons". In July 1976 Joseph had agreed with his leader: "As the general standard of living rises", he had declared "so does the definition of poverty".[23]

The book had some other puzzling features. In a review for *Labour Worker*, Barbara Wootton noticed the authors' underlying assumption that "human beings (especially in the richer classes) are overwhelmingly, if not exclusively, motivated by pecuniary considerations". The Joseph-Sumption emphasis on

---

23. KJ and Sumption, *Equality*, 27–8; Adam Smith, *Wealth of Nations*, quoted in Carey Oppenheim and Lisa Harker, *Poverty: The Facts* (CPAG, 1996), 9; Thatcher quoted in Kenneth Hoover and Raymond Plant, *Conservative Capitalism in Britain and the United States: A Critical Appraisal* (Routledge, 1989), 263 (our italics); KJ speech to the Bow Group, 25 July 1976, reprinted in KJ, *Stranded*, 62.

economic explanations for human behaviour, thought Wootton, "would do credit to any Marxist". Yet the writing of *Equality* could not have been prompted by pecuniary considerations.[24] Wootton might have added that some of Joseph's allies had recently been behaving with equal eccentricity; Hoskyns, Young and others had made significant financial sacrifices by working voluntarily for the cause. While these concrete examples might have been deployed to show that even wealthy people can rise above material concerns, Joseph and Sumption followed Nozick in using fictional illustrations which read like an accidental libel on the rich. One of these invited the reader to sympathise with a well-paid surgeon, who would refuse to work an extra hour if he lost most of the pay in tax. Yet the number of nurses willing to put in long hours for little reward was, "fortunately, quite large".[25] Why nurses should be more capable than surgeons of putting the interests of their patients first was left unexplained, but consistent with this the authors argued that the tendency of Victorian writers like Samuel Smiles to equate material success with moral desert was "plainly untrue as well as morally repellent". Yet Joseph himself had shown a tendency to attribute success to virtue. Actually, he had not yet read *Self-Help*, Samuel Smiles's classic eulogy to the entrepreneurial ethos; when he did so, in the 1980s, it became one of his favourite books.[26]

Other passages clearly owed much more to Joseph's personal experience, and echo his vocabulary. The property boom of the early 1970s, for example, resulted from an explosion of credit "designed with the best will in the world to sustain employment. But its most noticeable symptom was that a relatively large number of people, mostly young men, made exceptionally large sums very quickly by speculating in land (and in most cases lost it when the bubble burst)".

Clearly Joseph had forgotten the "dynamic" young entrepreneurs who had helped Bovis to *lose* "exceptionally large sums very quickly" in the early 1970s. Envy of those who had done well out of the property boom, the authors felt, explained an "abrupt leftward lurch of the English middle class in the early 1970s". This "lurch" is difficult to trace; certainly the Labour Party won a smaller percentage of the vote when winning the two general elections of 1974 than it had done when losing in 1970. There were other strange passages on the "envy" theme. It was "capable of serving the valuable social function of making the rich moderate their habits for fear of arousing it. It is because of the existence of envy that one does not drive Rolls-Royces through the slums of Naples

24. *Labour Worker*, 13 July 1979.
25. KJ and Sumption, *Equality*, 24, 75.
26. *House of Lords Debates*, vol. 536, col. 327, 26 February 1992. Among his numerous attractions for Joseph, Smiles shared his exalted view of the role of ideas, believing that "The solitary thought of a great thinker will dwell in the minds of men for centuries, until at length it works itself into their daily life and practice"; Samuel Smiles, *Character* (John Murray, 1888), 21.

. . .". This piece of psychological reasoning sounded most unlike Joseph; evidently he did not anticipate the behaviour of wealth-flaunting "yuppies" in the 1980s.[27]

Despite such gratuitous invitations to Joseph's critics, counter-attacks from Labour's intellectuals were slow in coming. Roy Hattersley dismissed one section of *Equality* as "a rag-bag of sophistry, half-truths, and logical errors"; another was "an unchallenged absurdity".[28] There could never be "common ground" between Hattersley and Joseph; while the latter had resolved his dilemma of the 1950s and now accepted that "freedom" entailed merely the absence of intentional, external constraint of the individual, Hattersley worked from the characteristic position of the British Left, which denies that one can be truly free while lacking the means for a life of reasonable comfort.[29] But Hattersley's attack was not published until 1987 – on the eve of Mrs Thatcher's third election victory, by which time Joseph had retired from the government. Another critique from the Left, by the philosopher Ted Honderich, appeared in the year of Mrs Thatcher's downfall.[30] Joseph escaped lightly at the crucial time because of events outside his control. In the intervening years between the publication of *Equality* and the appearance of these attacks the British Left was preoccupied with the Labour schism which led in 1981 to the foundation of the Social Democratic Party (SDP) (and, later, to the "witch-hunt" against the Militant Tendency). This is not to say that *Equality* "won" a crucial argument by default. The authors themselves noted that egalitarianism is "a moral judgement of a kind which is not susceptible [to] careful, logical criticism", and recognised that very few authors had tried to justify it in principle. At best, *Equality* could only help to generate the same intensity of feeling among existing opponents of egalitarianism. Yet Joseph and Sumption wanted to show that believers in equality were not only unwitting advocates of evil, but also unsound in their reasoning. The fact that Joseph could associate himself with such an enterprise lends further support to Leo Abse's identification of him with Jung's "introverted thinker", constantly "searching for intellectual solutions for what are properly emotional problems".[31]

In putting his name to *Equality*, Joseph had caricatured his own message. But that was nothing new. In October 1976, for example, he had lashed out at people who regarded entrepreneurs as "anti-social self-seekers". While it was

---

27. *Equality*, 16–18.
28. Roy Hattersley, *Choose Freedom* (Penguin, 1987), 4, 54.
29. The CPS Treasurer Nigel Vinson had shown himself to be closer to Hattersley than to Joseph when he wrote that "freedom starts when you have a thousand pounds in the Bank"; Vinson memorandum, 26 November 1974, Sherman Papers, Box 7. Among other things, Joseph's definition of "freedom" knocked away the principled underpinnings of his treatment of the elderly, and most of the disabled, as especially "deserving" cases. People who cannot provide for themselves because of "natural" impediments are just as "free" as everyone else.
30. Ted Honderich, *Conservatism* (Hamish Hamilton, 1990).
31. KJ and Sumption, *Equality*, 2–3; Abse, *Margaret*, 156.

indeed absurd to assume that all wealth-creators fell into this category, to claim that they were without exception "inspired, bold, thoughtful, adventurous individuals" (as Joseph did) was equally sweeping. He had come across some corrupt businessmen in his time; Mr Rachman, for example, he can scarcely have forgotten. But often he spoke as if honesty was a defining characteristic of the entrepreneur. Typically, this distortion would be introduced when Joseph was in "populist" mode, apparently in the belief that provoking a strong reaction was the best way of sparking a public debate. But he could have introduced an element of realism without blunting the force of his message. In a speech of August 1978 he had found the right formula, admitting that "Entrepreneurs are not heroes. They are no better than anyone else. But they are indispensible". That speech, though, was delivered to the Bow Group, which had always been sympathetic to economic liberalism. The same speech, published by the CPS as *Conditions for Fuller Employment*, included a rare recognition of the "despair, indignity and impoverishment" that so often accompany the loss of a job, and an acknowledgement that "most of the unemployed are desperately seeking work". Compared to Joseph's more provocative efforts the speech won little publicity.[32]

Equality duly appeared on a new reading-list, which Joseph prepared for the civil servants in his new Department of Industry. As he told the sympathetic Patrick Hutber, he often recommended specific books to guide his officials when they replied to enquiries from the public. His secretary asked for a list of these books, to save time; whereupon somebody in Joseph's Private Office requested a more general list so that everyone in the Department could be better informed. When the press heard of this – apparently as a result of "an unguarded conversation with a civil servant in a Turkish bath" – they considered it to be a great joke, particularly since nine of the twenty-nine titles had been written wholly or in part by the minister himself.[33] It was certainly a break with precedent; normally politicians asked civil servants for this sort of guidance. Joseph spoke without embarrassment when asked about the list; perhaps he thought that the press attention would help to publicise some of the classics of economic liberalism. But the relevance of several titles to the work of the Department of Industry in 1979 was tangential at best. Alexis de Tocqueville would have been baffled at the appearance of his great *Democracy in America* (first volume 1835) alongside Frank McFadzean's attack on Galbraith and Jock Bruce-Gardyne's morality tale about Meriden, the motor-cycle co-operative which Tony Benn had tried to rescue when he was at Industry in the 1970s. It was certainly odd that de Tocqueville found a place while living acquaintances like Hayek and Friedman were spurned. The recent books and pamphlets were written from the same (narrow) perspective, but the older publications deviated sufficiently from the Joseph hymn-sheet

---

32. *Sunday Telegraph*, 31 October 1976; KJ, *Conditions for Fuller Employment* (CPS, 1978), 1, 6, 10.
33. *Sunday Telegraph*, 10 June 1979; Halcrow, *Joseph*, 137.

to have induced philosophical confusion in open-minded readers. Even Adam Smith, whose name was so often yoked to "Thatcherism", was out of tune with the entrepreneurial drive which Joseph hoped to inspire from his new Department. Smith's *The Theory of Moral Sentiments* (1759) argued that a life of moderate comfort was far better than a restless quest for riches. Applied at the macro level the *Theory* could be read as an endorsement of the anti-Thatcherite view that, in a choice between evils, the "civilised" management of relative economic decline was preferable to a divisive attempt to re-ascend the ladder. In any case, there is no evidence that anyone at the DTI struggled very far through the list; most of the senior officials were already very familiar with the more theoretical literature, and they hardly needed reminding of the problems they had experienced over Meriden.[34]

Mrs Thatcher had given Joseph half of the job which he would have taken in 1970, had Heath not plumped for Geoffrey Rippon. The first union between the departments of Trade and Industry was short-lived; for reasons of political expediency rather than administrative convenience Harold Wilson had set the two asunder in 1974. It was anticipated that Joseph's career at Industry would be nasty, brutish, and short; despite the relatively emollient 1979 manifesto, it was no secret that he wanted the Department of Industry to be shorn of its powers and reincorporated with Trade – if not abolished outright. The Department (situated on Victoria Street – very convenient for Westminster and the CPS offices) was seen as the haunt of obsessive interventionists, who allegedly had never recovered since 1975 when Tony Benn was demoted to Energy. It was therefore a surprise when, a month after his appointment, Joseph told Patrick Hutber that although it was too early to be sure of lasting harmony he was working well with his new colleagues who had "behaved with great enthusiasm and propriety". In fact he had discovered that the image of the Department propagated by right-wingers was a caricature; there may have been scepticism about Joseph's free market approach, but few officials were interested in seizing control of the commanding heights of the British economy. Joseph had worked with his shrewd Permanent Secretary, Sir Peter Carey, when he was at the Board of Trade in the early 1960s. Carey admired Joseph's intellect, and knew that the private man was very different from the public image. The pair soon established a good working relationship.[35]

Even so, it was said that the atmosphere when Joseph first went to the Department had been "distinctly edgy", something akin to a "phoney war". At

---

34. Edward du Cann, *Two Lives* (Images, 1995), 125. Morrison Halcrow reprints the full list in *A Single Mind*, 136–7. Joseph read *The Theory of Moral Sentiments* in 1979; if he was troubled by any of the contents he never showed it, and insisted that readers of the *Wealth of Nations* should never forget that Smith "was a two-book man". See also KJ's interview with Patrick Hutber in *Sunday Telegraph*, 10 June 1979.
35. Hennessy, *Whitehall*, 432–3; Hutber in *Sunday Telegraph*, 10 June 1979; interviews with Sir Alfred Sherman and Sir Peter Carey.

his first meeting with the CBI Joseph questioned whether there was any need for his own Department to exist; understandably, the attendant officials "just stared and sat there glassy-eyed".[36] Knowing that their minister enjoyed strong backing from Downing Street, the civil servants had few weapons with which to resist the new regime. But leaks soon became a problem inside the Department. Within days of the election Joseph wrote to the Chief Secretary to the Treasury, John Biffen, evidently to congratulate him on his appointment but also to point out a potential target for cuts:

> I have lovingly kept on my file against this very opportunity the possibility of making some savings in state spending in connection with something called the School for Advanced Urban Studies. May I diffidently direct your attention to this expensive minnow, which seems to me to teach town planning with practically no reference whatsoever to supply and demand or to market forces or to choice.

Presumably Joseph had heard about the School on his campus campaign. But he had been poorly briefed. Whether or not its teachings were as woefully unsound as his second-hand knowledge indicated, when the School was set up under the Heath government Bristol University had agreed to pay its running costs only after reaching a binding legal agreement that the Department of the Environment would cover any financial deficit. Nothing could be done about the "minnow" after all, and the press heard all about Joseph's fishing expedition once it had swum clear of his net.[37]

Stories soon began to appear in the press which apparently confirmed Joseph's reputation for eccentricity. In June Hutber had protested that "the public has been presented with some very odd and distorted pictures of this eminently reasonable man". But the avalanche of leaks and whispers about his conduct had only just begun, and at least some of these must have come from within the Department. The press learned that Joseph's obsession with unnecessary public expenditure had inspired him to write his departmental memos on scraps of used paper and the backs of envelopes. A few months later *Private Eye* was told that to accompany his reading list "Sir Sheath" (or the "Mad Mullah" as the *Eye* now called him) had drawn up a feeding list, which was sent ahead of the Secretary of State whenever an engagement included an invitation to eat. Unnamed officials were said to be alarmed by his dietary habits, and by the fact that the list of acceptable foodstuffs had allegedly been registered as "classified information". The reason for this precaution was Joseph's chronic digestive condition, but mischief-making journalists preferred to connect the

---

36. Hugh Stephenson, *Mrs Thatcher's First Year* (Jill Norman, 1980), 36; Martin Holmes, *The First Thatcher Government 1979–1983* (Harvester Wheatsheaf, 1985), 155.
37. *Guardian*, 13 November 1979.

symptoms with his image as the unbalanced wild man of the Right. Tales soon emerged of Joseph ordering single boiled eggs at lavish business lunches – on one occasion sending back the spartan refreshment because it was too runny – and of the meal he gave for the press, at which Fleet Street's finest gorged themelves on exquisite dishes while Joseph hesitated over ordering a slice of "British Rail cake". Concern allegedly spread to his Special Branch detectives, who witnessed distressing scenes on the King's Cross to Edinburgh express after Joseph had been told that there was no tea at the buffet.[38]

Joseph's public demeanour lent support to these rumours. Although his contribution to the debate on the Queen's Speech on 21 May 1979 was taken as a sign that he would be more "pragmatic" in office than expected, he spoke of "a Luddite trade union movement" which was one of "six poisons" afflicting Britain. Replying from the Opposition back-benches Tony Benn congratulated Joseph on being "the architect of the Conservative philosophy and its most articulate exponent"; he proceeded to argue that the philosophy was unworkable, illustrating his point with historical examples. Joseph intervened twice, first to deny that the new government was intent on "sweeping away the inheritance of the past" but later (in what was described as "almost a high-pitched scream") protesting that socialism and public ownership had always led to "evil, totalitarianism, cruelty and poverty". Benn had been quoting those feared commissars of the extreme Left – Hugh Gaitskell and Clement Attlee. "Even allowing a certain amount of poetic licence", felt Malcolm Rutherford of the *Financial Times*, "visual observation alone is enough to suggest that those are not the remarks of a reasonable man". The unions protested against the "poison" remark and Jim Prior had to mollify them, but it became a favourite slogan with Joseph and a year later it provoked a public row with Jim Callaghan.[39]

Looking back on this period, Joseph emphasised the size of his task at Industry. "It was a mammoth inheritance from previous governments", he complained. "I had a whole mews of augean stables". Soon after the upbeat Hutber interview, the *Sunday Telegraph* expressed concern that the cleaning job might prove too much for Joseph, who was, "by all accounts, having an exceptionally difficult time. To some of his colleagues, he looks both burdened and preoccupied, as if he were not enjoying office as much as he should. The fact that he drives himself at a demonic pace does not help". Joseph's opponents within his own party were unmoved by this spectacle, and probably helped to publicise it by tipping off the newspapers. He was under tremendous pressure; his performance, like that of Howe at the Treasury, was subjected to special

---

38. *Sunday Express*, 3 June 1979; interviews with Colette Bowe and Simon Hoggart; *Private Eye*, 28 March 1980; Holmes, *First Thatcher Government*, 155–6. There was a simple explanation for the story about the tea; Joseph was obviously showing once again his irritation when confronted with inefficiency.
39. *Hansard*, vol. 967, cols 714–24; *Financial Times*, 25 May 1979;

media scrutiny from the outset. As the leading theoretician within the new government, Joseph knew that any deviation from his own stated approach would be seized upon as (in the impoverished vocabulary of the day) a "U-turn". As Michael Foot mockingly put it shortly after the election, "he carries, Atlas-like, the full weight of the [government's] intellectual case". Allies on the Right were alarmed at the thought that, in the cheery words of *The Economist*, Joseph would "bend under the twin pressures of his responsibilities and his civil servants". There were warning signals even in the Hutber interview, in which Joseph had expressed his joy at being "pampered. After tubes and taxis there is an official car. There are plenty of secretaries and so on". He had been sucked into a cocoon, and no one could be sure what changes might be wrought before he re-emerged.[40]

Immediately after the election the new government had settled down to the task of reducing public expenditure. In July Joseph made his first detailed announcements, but only (as the *Observer* reported) "after considerable hesitation". He had encountered stiff opposition from the Secretaries of State for Wales and Scotland, because he planned a reduction of over one third in the £500 million regional aid budget. This measure produced one of the government's first semi-public squabbles; at first Joseph hoped to make the announcement through a written parliamentary answer, but – apparently after an intervention by Mrs Thatcher herself – he had to face the Commons with news which affected the constituencies of many in his audience. Cuts were also announced in shipbuilding, (reduced) funding for British Steel would be reviewed from month to month, and the Meriden works would no longer be supported. After another protracted battle, Joseph pledged that £100 million would be raised from the sale of state assets over the coming year.[41]

All this was compatible with the manifesto, and with Joseph's contribution to the debate on the Queen's Speech when he spoke of a "transitional period" in which spending would be reviewed. For the first year, at least, he was bound "morally and legally" by commitments carried over from the previous government. Two months later he confided that his overall purpose was to attack the "anti-business culture", but "particular tactical decisions at any one moment in order to achieve that purpose must be for that moment". The savings Joseph announced were impressive enough to anger the Opposition, but they scarcely affected the overall range of government intervention, and even the complicated three-tier system of regional assistance – Special Development Areas, Development Areas and Intermediate Areas – was left intact. Judging Joseph by

---

40. Holmes, *First Thatcher Government*, 162; Hutber in *Sunday Telegraph*, 10 June 1979; *Observer*, 22 July 1979; *Hansard*, vol. 967, col. 989, 22 May 1979. Joseph might have added that after his run of bad luck in terms of accommodation, his new room in Ashdown House at least featured "a good view of Westminster looking west"; Young, *Enterprise Years*, 36.
41. *Observer*, 15 July 1979.

his reputation rather than by the manifesto commitments, the Right regarded the announcements as a retreat.[42] For the same reason, the Department of Industry was delighted. "It's the same instrument, only playing a slightly different tune", crowed one official. In his account of the government's first year, Hugh Stephenson dated the feeling of senior civil servants that "they had got the guru under control" to the middle of June. The mood lightened further in August, when it was reported that Joseph and his equally "dry" colleague at Trade John Nott were resisting suggested staff cuts of 20 per cent in their respective departments. Soon many of the officials who had been so "edgy" in May were feeling protective towards their fragile minister, although continued disquiet in some quarters is indicated by the fact that reports of Joseph's more unusual deeds still filtered through to the public. In December 1980, for example, he was said to have reprimanded a Department receptionist for not smiling enough.[43]

At first sight, the taming of Joseph looks like a last hurrah for the old civil service establishment – an achievement worthy of the fictional Sir Humphrey Appleby, who, ironically, was entertaining the nation in *Yes, Minister* while Mrs Thatcher was seeking to replace his real-life representatives with more dynamic characters sharing her outlook (if not, contrary to legend, her policies). Some radicals had been hoping for stern and immediate action against the civil service. Leslie Chapman, author of *Your Disobedient Servant* (1978) had been consulted by Mrs Thatcher and by Joseph, who had marked almost every idea in his book "with an enthusiastic tick". Joseph hoped for a reduction of "50,000 to 100,000" in civil service numbers; this target had been exceeded by 1984, and there had also been a successful efficiency drive headed by Sir Derek Rayner. Ian Bancroft, the Head of the Civil Service when Mrs Thatcher arrived in Downing Street, was deeply concerned that the new government intended to "deprivilege the Civil Service". He believed that Joseph himself had coined the latter phrase, which he thought "populist and silly"; it "did [Joseph's] luminous intelligence less than justice", and "showed terrible confusion". Morale in the service was reported to have slumped to an all-time low soon after the 1979 general election.[44]

While change seemed dramatic to those inside the civil service many of Mrs Thatcher's advisors felt that an opportunity had been wasted. In Opposition Joseph himself had admitted that "we are still too fresh from our last mistakes to be convincing as anti-bureaucrats", and the radicals were still looking for conclusive proof of a new outlook. Leslie Chapman was quickly

42. *Hansard*, vol. 967, col. 707, 21 May 1979; "The Charlton Interview", BBC Radio 4, 30 July 1979; Ivan Fallon in *Sunday Telegraph*, 22 July 1979.
43. *Observer*, 22 July 1979; *Financial Times*, 15 August 1979; Stephenson, *Thatcher's First Year*, 37; Interview with Colette Bowe; *Guardian*, 18 December 1980.
44. Peter Kellner and Lord Crowther-Hunt, *Civil Servants: An Inquiry into Britain's Ruling Class* (Macdonald, 1980), 287–8; Hennessy, *Whitehall*, 600, 629.

disillusioned, and the perceived failure was an important reason for Norman Strauss's departure from the Downing Street Policy Unit in 1982. Later Strauss complained that Mrs Thatcher's ministers were no different from their predecessors; for them, he felt, the companionship and support of civil servants was their greatest reward for winning an election. Strauss believed that Mrs Thatcher had listened to her own advisors in Opposition and turned to the civil service once she had become Prime Minister. Alfred Sherman thought that the same process had transformed Sir Keith Joseph. He had argued in Opposition for a "Territorial Army" of several hundred advisors who would flood into ministries to counteract the influence of "statist" civil servants, but although Joseph recruited a couple of trusted friends (including Lord Young, and Jeffrey Sterling from P&O) his practice was not a radical departure from that of the previous Labour government. In an outspoken memorandum to Mrs Thatcher Sherman warned that, as on previous occasions, Joseph had been "swallowed up" by his Department. But it made more sense to turn this argument on its head, and conclude that Joseph had been "swallowed up" by Sherman between 1974 and 1979. It was not that Joseph was excessively cautious as a minister; rather, he had been excessively outspoken in Opposition. He soon realised that the staff of his own Department were more necessary than he had previously thought, and apologised to Sir Peter Carey for even the limited cuts which were forced on him. As time went on, he found that he had no alternative but to act against his stated principles because of economic conditions that were far worse than expected. But Joseph had also been introduced to an important and undeniable fact – that other Western European governments subsidised their industries on a scale that, in some cases, exceeded that of Britain even under "Socialism". In his early months at Industry this lesson was brought home during a conversation with a West German minister. "Why does your government intervene and try to pick industrial 'winners?'", Joseph asked. "Because it works", was the crisp reply.[45]

It was an accelerated version of what the civil service used to call "an education in the realities", and anyone who remembered that the CPS had supposedly been set up to examine the factors that had brought about an economic "miracle" in post-war West Germany would have appreciated the irony. In fact, the Centre's first Director of Studies Martin Wassell had warned in June 1976 that "the party has to face the fact that all industrialised countries subsidise their industries"; the point was that other countries did this more effectively than the British.[46] But Joseph could not accept that other countries

---

45. Hennessy, *Whitehall*, 646; Sampson, *Changing Anatomy*, 47; Halcrow, *Joseph*, 157; interview with Sir Peter Carey; John Elliott in *Financial Times*, 1 August 1980.
46. Martin Wassell, memorandum on Industrial Policy to KJ, 23 June 1976, Sherman Papers, Box 3. An indication that his was a minority voice at the CPS is his later light-hearted comment in the same memorandum that colleagues would "garrotte" him for spelling out such heretical thoughts.

were right in what they were doing. He continued to deny that he had developed anything which could be described as an "industrial strategy" – as Francis Pym discovered to his surprise when he asked for a briefing on the subject in January 1981. But in the short-term, reality had to be allowed to affect his decisions. If Britain took a vow of self-denial while competitors were busy preserving their own flocks of lame ducks the political consequences could be devastating to the Thatcher government. Once this insight had registered, other reasons were close at hand to prompt a more pragmatic approach. Enterprises rescued under Labour – notably the gargantuan British Leyland, which Harold Wilson had salvaged in 1975 – might be notorious for their union militants, their hideous "overmanning" and their limitless capacity to soak up taxpayers' money, but they stood at the end of a supply chain which included numerous small businesses – the very enterprises which the Conservative manifesto had promised to nurture. The result of these considerations was a reversal of the normal process, where the head dictates hard-line decisions and the heart pleads for the soft option. Joseph's commitment to the free market was emotional, and given a free hand he would have cut the legs from any state-supported business. But he soon realised that such gratification had to be deferred. Meanwhile he could not give up the rhetorical fight – the "battle of ideas", as he liked to call it – even if his most important deeds belied his words. So, in Stephen Wilks's phrase, to the end of his tenure at Industry he "maintained a commitment to ideological positions and policy options which were blatantly at odds with his own operational decisions and the actions of his Department".[47]

In retirement, Joseph blamed himself for once again lacking "conviction and moral courage" in a Cabinet post, and felt that his achievements had been overshadowed by his treatment of the big nationalised industries. He did, though, make significant inroads into the problem of "overmanning". In August 1979 British Shipbuilders announced that 10,000 jobs were to go; in the following month, Michael Edwardes, the Chairman of British Leyland (BL), warned that 25,000 workers would be sacked. Just before Christmas, Sir Charles Villiers of British Steel announced a cull of 50,000.

Joseph was back in his old role of "numbers man". Where housing completions had once been the yardstick, success was now measured by staff reductions in state industries. But in every case the price of victory was a promise of another hand-out, to cover existing debts, pay for redundancies or even to finance new developments. This process reached its climax in January 1981. In Opposition Joseph had given a guarded response to planned investment in British Leyland, but spoke about breaking up the company and gave notice that "It may be necessary to rescue British Leyland from the British Leyland rescue".

---

47. Francis Pym, *The Politics of Consent* (Sphere, 1985), 161; Stephen Wilks, *Industrial Policy and the Motor Industry* (Manchester University Press, 1984), 57.

The company had already absorbed more than the £1 billion suggested by Lord Ryder after the initial salvage operation, and Edwardes thought he had convinced Joseph that further expenditure was justified. There were plans for collaboration with Honda, and industrial relations seemed to be improving. Before Christmas in 1980 Joseph presented a paper drafted by his officials, which conceded the BL argument for an additional £1 billion; a later revised document contained few changes of substance. The statement which Joseph proposed to deliver to the Commons was attached to this new paper. But when he spoke to the paper at the Cabinet of 22 January 1981 he pleaded with his colleagues to tear it up and allow the company to go into liquidation. In the past Cabinet ministers had made it clear that they were unhappy with their proposals – for example, John Davies had made no secret that he shared the misgivings of his colleagues about the proposed rescue of Upper-Clyde Shipbuilders in the early 1970s. But a complete *volte-face* of this kind was unprecedented. Jim Prior felt that over the festive period Joseph's "more extreme and out of touch friends" had persuaded him to perform this bizarre somersault. No doubt he was thinking of Sherman, who back in 1977 had stigmatised the non-committal Conservative approach to BL as being "tantamount to unconditional surrender".[48] But the "out of touch friends" had intervened too late; intense discussions had been going on for weeks, and as the BL Chairman noted "almost everyone around that table was a supporter or had been converted" to the position which Joseph was now urging them to reject. The Environment Secretary Michael Heseltine demanded to know what was going on in the Department of Industry; Howe merely remarked that the cost of liquidation to the Exchequer would be too high if Joseph was right in his prediction that only a third of the existing BL was viable. Joseph appealed to the Prime Minister for a decision, clearly hoping that she would side against the majority of his colleagues (and his own Department). But after further discussions with Edwardes the Secretary of State told the House of Commons on 26 January that another rescue package had been agreed. He could not conceal his personal unhappiness with the decision.[49]

In a television interview Mrs Thatcher said that "I never want to take on another British Leyland", and explained why this was not the right time to "chop [them] off at the stocking tops". But she had good reason to be concerned at the performance of her "guru", who had involved her in his own embarrassment by his appeal in Cabinet. His conduct had forced her to contradict an earlier asser-

---

48. Prior, *Balance of Power*, 128; Sherman, memorandum of 9 November 1977, Sherman Papers, Box 3.
49. *Hansard*, vol. 927, col. 435, 2 March 1977; Michael Edwardes, *Back from the Brink: An Apocalyptic Experience* (Collins, 1983), 239–40; Wilks, *Industrial Policy*, 218–20. Cf. the account in Hennessy's *Whitehall* (432–3), in which Sir Keith is depicted as presenting a hardline paper then retreating from its conclusions. The full truth awaits the release of the papers, but the account here is based on the recollection of several witnesses. Significantly, the story given to Professor Hennessy tallies better with the prevalent image of Sir Keith as a soft-hearted man who could not bring himself to follow up his ideas with action.

tion that "In a properly run govenment" matters concerning nationalised industries were nothing to do with the Prime Minister.[50] The BL fiasco was not the first time that she had been disappointed by the Secretary of State for Industry. In the spring of 1980 Joseph had submitted a memo on the high-tech company Inmos, which had been promised £50 million of aid by Labour. The first tranche of £25 million had been paid, and the Department armed Joseph with a rationale for continuing the assistance. It was said that the paper was returned to the Department with a hand-written note from Mrs Thatcher – "Really, Keith!". Her attitude was understandable; after all, when Labour announced the initial cash injection Joseph had told the then Industry Secretary Eric Varley of his fears that "this venture will simply be the first instalment in a costly failure". Jim Prior felt that in Cabinet the Prime Minister continued to "mother" her ally, but others remembered that her treatment of him was surprisingly harsh; she whispered disparaging comments to neighbours and, on one occasion, forced him to make a miserable protest at his treatment. Even Prior remembered that under her cross-examination "poor Keith used to have sweat all over his face as he contorted himself and his conscience".[51]

Mrs Thatcher's bullying of Joseph was not confined to the relative privacy of Cabinet meetings. Edward du Cann remembered being embarrassed by a brutal dressing-down in his presence. In conversation with colleagues Joseph made light of this treatment, telling Norman Lamont that Mrs Thatcher "deals in destructive dialogue. When I feel the lash they have to send a stretcher". It would be taking the idea of Joseph as an "emotional masochist" too far to claim that he secretly enjoyed such treatment. The last thing he wanted was to be seen as a political liability for Mrs Thatcher. For her part the Prime Minister never wavered in her respect for Joseph's intellect, but even before the BL incident press reports had indicated that his influence at the centre was fading.[52] A compromise would have to be struck which kept Joseph in the Cabinet (where his ideological support was essential) while trying to steer him away from banana skins. When (against her wishes) Mrs Thatcher had appointed Prior to Employment, she insisted that Patrick Mayhew should be his junior minister because, as she put it, "I'm determined to have *someone* with backbone in your Department". After the election Joseph had surprised many when, instead of securing places at Industry for his shadow aides, Kenneth Clarke and Lamont, he allowed them to be snapped up for other posts.[53] His first junior ministers, Adam Butler and Lord

---

50. Edwardes, *Back from the Brink*, 243; Halcrow, *Joseph*, 138.
51. Stephenson, *Thatcher's First Year*, 37; *The Times*, 21 June 1978; Interviews with Lords Prior, Howell and Jenkin; Prior, *Balance of Power*, 125, 128.
52. Interview with Lord Lamont; Max Hastings in *Evening Standard*, 12 November 1979.
53. Michael White in *Guardian*, 26 March 1980; Prior, *Balance of Power*, 114. Cf. Mrs Thatcher's alleged comment, reported by the *New Statesman* in 1976, that "My job in cabinet is to keep Keith's spine straight" ("Prophet without Honour", 29 October, 1976). If the wording was exactly as printed Mrs Thatcher must have made the remark in the 1970–4 period.

Trenchard, were not known for their radical zeal; indeed when Butler was first appointed an unnamed enemy told the *Spectator* that his job was "to find out what Keith is up to and tell him to stop". In the reshuffle of January 1981 Mrs Thatcher stiffened Joseph's spine with Norman Tebbit, grafted from Trade. Tebbit was told that Joseph needed some protection from Labour in Commons' debates. But the tough new recruit soon took over the more intricate tasks within the Department, and within a month of his arrival he had concluded a deal which introduced the first Nissan car plant to Britain.[54]

Shortly after the arrival of the Tebbit reinforcement the Prime Minister ordered Joseph to take a brief rest. But this was an unappealing assignment, and when he returned he seemed even more agitated. In February 1981 it was reported that his colleagues "find his habit of tearing out articles from the *Financial Times* in the middle of important committee meetings disturbing and distracting". At a meeting of the NEDC Joseph was unable to keep still and had to keep leaving the room, a symptom of internal discomfort which he frequently exhibited. Prior felt that Joseph's time at Industry proved that "This thoroughly honourable man was not suited to being a departmental minister". Others felt that appointing Joseph to Industry had been "an unconscious act of cruelty" on the Prime Minister's part. Certainly a less battle-scarred minister with the same radical instincts – a Tebbit, for instance – would not have been reduced after less than twenty months to such an invertebrate condition. Yet Joseph was right to protest that even Hercules would have buckled a little under the strain, and far from resenting the appointment of Tebbit he appreciated the help from a person he admired, despite their contrasting backgrounds. The legacy of the previous government was far more complicated that it had seemed from the Opposition benches. For example, Joseph was saddled with the task of compensating shipbuilding firms that Labour had nationalised; at the same time he was planning their liquidation or return to the private sector. In August 1980 he had to concede that there was no possibility of improving the "grossly unfair" compensation terms offered by Labour in 1977. He also had to shelve plans to sell off the profitable warship yards, while closing down the loss-making parts of British Shipbuilders. Conservative back-benchers were furious, particularly since the news reached them by means of a written parliamentary answer. *The Times* thought that "the wholesale dismissal of ship-yard workers in areas already suffering from exceptionally high rates of unemployment would betoken a social ruthlessness altogether harder than is the nature of the Conservative Party of today". But in Opposition Joseph had taken the lead in promising that his party would never again flinch from difficult decisions, and the rationale for mercy in 1980 was no better than it had been

---

54. du Cann, *Two Lives*, 212, 227; Jock Bruce-Gardyne, *Mrs Thatcher's First Administration: The Prophets Confounded* (Macmillan, 1984), 18; Tebbit, *Upwardly Mobile*, 218–9; *Spectator*, 19 May 1979; interview with Lord Tebbit.

when Upper-Clyde Shipbuilders was rescued in 1971. At that time there had been no dissent in Cabinet; on this occasion there was a fierce battle, and Joseph lost. He ought to have considered when making his speeches after 1974 that he would have to continue working with at least some of Heath's allies, and that it would be best to tone down some of his rhetoric to insure himself against the time when he might need their co-operation in Cabinet. Back in office he gave further ammunition to his critics. This tendency was illustrated by three major incidents, all of which could have been far better handled even if the ultimate damage to the government was less severe than it threatened to be.[55]

The first concerned the workings of the National Enterprise Board (NEB), which was established under Labour's 1975 Industry Act. Tony Benn envisaged that it would secure state control, either through direct ownership or stringent planning agreements, of the "commanding heights" of British industry – starting with the hundred biggest firms, ultimately extending to "about half of Britain's manufacturing output". With justice, Benn felt that this had been foreshadowed by Labour's radical programme of 1973, but Harold Wilson placed a very different interpretation on policy proposals approved by left-wing conference delegates. Even before Benn's removal from Industry, the Prime Minister set out to "castrate" the scheme. The result was another of those post-war bodies like the ill-fated IRC – to right-wingers, an advanced staging post on the road to serfdom, to the left an inadequate prop for a capitalist system ripe for collapse. The initial budget (£700 million) was relatively large, but Wilson ensured that the NEB was hedged about by strict operating rules and appointed an orthodox businessman, Sir Douglas (later Lord) Ryder, as its first Chairman.[56]

By 1979 the NEB had overspent its budget; more than half of the £1.3 billion it disbursed under Labour was lavished on British Leyland, and it also gave generously to the American-owned Chrysler car company. "Good King Neb" looked a prime target for the incoming Thatcher government; the manifesto only promised a reduction in its powers, but the same had been said before the abolition of the IRC in 1970. Joseph did order the NEB to reduce its holdings by £100 million over 1979–80, but the Right was bitterly disappointed that the Board had survived in any form. This view was forcefully expressed by John Redwood, who co-wrote a pamphlet (published by the CPS) on the subject. Redwood was soon brought in to the Downing Street Policy Unit, reinforcing the impression that the CPS was more important as an ideological recruitment agency rather than in itself a potent source of workable ideas. But in government Joseph "completely cut himself off" from the Centre, feeling that it had

---

55. Prior, *Balance of Power*, 125; Tebbit, *Upwardly Mobile*, 220; Adam Raphael in *Observer*, 15 February 1981; *The Times*, 8 August 1980. To complete Joseph's embarrassment, on the same day as his announcement over British Shipbuilders Norman Fowler told the Commons that the National Freight Corporation was to be returned to the private sector.
56. Keith Middlemas, *Power, Competition and the State: Volume 3, The End of the Post-War Era: Britiain Since 1974* (Macmillan, 1991), 80–4.

already served its main purpose of promoting economic liberalism within the party. It certainly had not been established to prescribe to its founder the purist programme which he had found impossible to carry out. According to one well-placed witness, Joseph could not always conceal his irritation with his extra-parliamentary allies.[57]

Among the companies under NEB supervision was the engine manufacturer Rolls-Royce (1971), which had been taken over by the state after its bankruptcy under Heath. At the time of the 1979 election Rolls-Royce's Chairman, Sir Kenneth Keith, was in dispute with the NEB. He resented interference in his operational decisions, and found it easier to deal directly with the Department of Industry; naturally this met with resistance from the NEB Chairman, Sir Leslie Murphy. At first Joseph was inclined to side with the Board in this dispute – as were Prior and Geoffrey Howe – but the balance of the argument suddenly shifted when Sir Kenneth, who was approaching retirement, let it be known that his chosen successor was none other than Sir Frank McFadzean, the doughty opponent of J. K. Galbraith and a close friend of Margaret Thatcher. McFadzean was equally opposed to interference from the NEB. In November Joseph told the astonished Sir Leslie Murphy that Rolls-Royce was to be removed from NEB control and returned to the direct supervision of the Department of Industry. Sir Leslie and his colleagues offered to resign *en bloc*, and Joseph accepted the suggestion, despite his intitial fears that the row might result in his own departure from office.[58]

After his resignation, Sir Leslie wrote that it was "quite extraordinary that a Conservative Secretary of State should have come to the conclusion that the monitoring of Rolls-Royce would be better carried out by civil servants rather than by an independent board composed of senior industrialists and trade union leaders backed up by an expert staff". But this was not the conclusion that Joseph – or rather, Mrs Thatcher – had reached. When the Prime Minister visited the DoI early in 1980 she was asked how a great company could be run from the Department's offices in Victoria Street. "She replied that the job was impossible. The only thing to do was to let Rolls-Royce get on with the job". By "Rolls-Royce" Mrs Thatcher meant "Sir Frank McFadzean". The new Chairman was evidently regarded as a more trustworthy ally than the NEB in preparing the company for de-nationalisation; but this example of personalities overcoming principles meant that Rolls-Royce remained under the nominal control of civil servants until its sale in 1987. To right-wingers any decision which undermined the hated NEB was welcome, but the reconstituted board

---

57. Cockett, *Thinking the Unthinkable*, 291–2; Interview with Lord Waldegrave. Joseph's irritation was fully justified, because different members of the CPS gave him conflicting advice. Martin Wassell, for example, had argued in June 1976 for the retention of an "NEB-type body", just as Joseph himself had made the case for the IRC before 1970; see Wassell's memorandum of 23 June 1976 in Sherman Papers, Box 3.
58. Private information.

was left with seventy companies to oversee. In February 1980 it was announced that the target of £100 million sales of NEB assets within a year had been relaxed.[59] Amity was short-lived; more messy resignations from the NEB were announced at the end of 1980. Before Joseph left the DoI, he approved a merger of the NEB with the National Research and Development Corporation, to form a British Technology Group. The final outcome might have satisfied the Right, but they would have preferred Sir Keith to have taken the clinical approach pointed out by Redwood.

Joseph's second crisis was the national steel strike, which began in January 1980 and lasted thirteen weeks. The steelworkers' leader, Bill Sirs, was a moderate, but the programme of plant closures and job losses had already provoked a militant mood among his members when the Chairman of British Steel, Sir Charles Villiers, offered a pay rise of only 2 per cent. Although the industry was losing £7 million every week, the miners had just been offered a 20 per cent rise and British Steel's management failed to produce a convincing explanation for the disparity. In fact, the government's behaviour was explained by the report of a policy group set up by Joseph under the chairmanship of Nicholas Ridley. This had been leaked in May 1978, at a time when relations between the party leadership and the CRD were particularly bleak; it showed that the Thatcher government dreaded a coal strike above all else. John Hoskyns advised that at this early stage the steelworkers should also be appeased, but Joseph and Mrs Thatcher agreed that they should back Villiers, while maintaining a public pretence that the matter concerned the unions and British Steel, and was nothing to do with the government.

Joseph refused to negotiate directly with the unions, although he did meet Sirs once in the company of Jim Prior. This "hands-off" approach, Prior felt, was "contradictory and unconvincing"; the government could hardly claim to be standing aloof from nationalised industries at the same time that it was dictating price increases to British Gas. In one angry exchange, Len Murray of the TUC told Joseph that "talking to you is like trying to teach Chinese to a deaf mute". Joseph, who had previously tried to teach Murray capitalism by giving him suitable pamphlets, seemed hurt by the remark.[60] In February the dispute escalated. Hadfields, a Sheffield firm owned by Lonrho, was the scene of picket line violence reminiscent of the worst days of the Heath government. Like Saltley Coke Works in 1972 the plant was closed on police advice, and Mrs Thatcher passed an awkward hour discussing the crisis with representatives of the private steel industry. A *Daily Telegraph* leader claimed that the fate of the government was hanging in the balance, and demands were heard for a more hard-line approach in industrial relations. The immediate pressure fell on Prior, but he conducted an able defence of his gradualist trade union strategy at a

59. *Daily Telegraph*, 29 November 1979; Stephenson, *Thatcher's First Year*, 106–7.
60. Prior, *Balance of Power*, 126; Interview with Lord Murray.

meeting of the 1922 Committee on 7 February. Mrs Thatcher's frustration was growing, and a week later she gave notice that supplementary benefits to strikers' families would be reduced, whether or not trade unions made good the difference. Joseph had been hesitant about this measure in the early 1970s, but he had been converted to the idea and argued for it in a "stormy" Cabinet meeting of December 1979. Thwarted on that occasion, the Cabinet hard-liners won in 1981, and rather than allowing the change to be debated in isolation the Chancellor pushed it through as part of his March budget. But right-wing radicals outside the Cabinet were pressing for even stronger action, and on 22 April forty-five back-benchers voted to include provisions in Prior's first industrial relations Bill for a secret ballot in advance of any industrial action. By then the steel strike had been settled when a three-man committee appointed by British Steel and the unions came up with an offer of 18 per cent. This looked like a defeat for the government, but the productivity agreements built into the package meant that over the next five years the workforce was reduced by 90,000.[61]

In hindsight the steel dispute looks like a well-planned engagement with the union enemy. Mrs Thatcher soon learned that supplies from abroad were getting through, and production in the rest of British industry was barely affected. Lord Young thought that the outcome was a turning-point: "for the first time we had proved that the country was governable".[62] Since the strike had been resolved without recourse to over-hasty and heavy-handed legislation, Prior's strategy had been vindicated. Yet, to the pleasure of the Right, his political position was weakened. Early in the dispute he had expressed his dissatisfaction with Villiers, and earned a public reprimand from the Prime Minister (although he had already apologised in Cabinet for the error of judgement).[63] After more than a decade of almost incessant industrial strife the public was far more willing to contemplate radical trade union policies than it had been in 1970, but a more hawkish minister than Prior might have dissipated this mood by acting with undue haste and severity. After the steel strike the way was clear for fresh initiatives – and a new Secretary of State for Employment.

Yet far from deliberately courting the strike as an early test of strength, the government had blundered into it with good reasons to expect a defeat. More than one of Joseph's monthly "state of the union" meetings within his Department was plunged into gloom by pessimistic assessments of the chances for survival. Far from acting with hard-nosed realism, more than ever the Secretary of State seemed a stranger whenever he ventured outside his Department. On 11 February 1980 he decided to go ahead with an official visit to South Wales,

---

61. Stephenson, *Thatcher's First Year*, 73–6; Middlemas, *Power, Vol. III*, 290; Lewis, *Hailsham*, 328.
62. Young, *The Enterprise Years*, 43.
63. Ian Gilmour, *Dancing with Dogma: Britain under Thatcherism* (Simon and Schuster, 1992), 80.

apparently hoping for a rational talk with the striking steelmen. Instead, at Port Talbot his car was pelted with eggs and (a new weapon of choice among his opponents) tomatoes. One demonstrator held a placard with the welcoming message "Sir Keith, you are mad and we hate you". In Ebbw Vale he was prevented from entering a factory by 400 pickets, and he was mobbed in a local council building. Reporters noticed that he looked ill and tired during the fracas. A helpful psychiatrist thought that (like his Departmental receptionist) Joseph should "smile more" if he wanted a better reception; as it was, "He has a very erect posture which, in most animals, signals hostility". Whether his posture or his policies were to blame, the man who had once impressed a Welsh audience with his knowledge of the language was now *persona non grata*; on another venture into the country in June he was attacked again. In the follow-ing month the egg and tomato roadshow reached the North-East of England, where the giant Consett steelworks had been condemned to closure, despite Joseph's efforts to promote a takeover by a private consortium. One protestor reported that the Secretary of State had "just seemed dazed" amid the placards and the chanting. Reports of such incidents lend credence to the view (expressed by one of Joseph's colleagues) that the "hands-off" approach to pay negotiations might have been an enforced solution, arising from well-founded doubts concerning his ability to conduct talks with tough union officials. To succeed in such dealings it was not necessary for one to admire the unions as institutions; Joseph however, seemed quite unable even to *understand* them.[64]

At the end of April 1980 there was a third incident which seemed to confirm Joseph's detachment from political reality. After a lengthy search for qualified and available candidates Prior had suggested that Villiers should be replaced on his retirement by Ian MacGregor, an experienced Scottish steelman who had made his career in North America. Surprisingly MacGregor wanted the job, but he was under contract elsewhere and protracted negotiations were necessary before the appointment could be announced. As Joseph told the Commons, there would be a down payment of £675,000 to MacGregor's present company, plus performance-related compensation of up to £1,150,000. He failed to mention that a considerable bounty had been awarded to the firm of "head-hunters" who had managed to track down a candidate whose qualities were so well known in Whitehall that he had been sounded out for the same job in the mid-1970s. It was an early example of the post-1979 tendency of governments to reward consultants handsomely for stating the obvious. Joseph carried on with his Commons' statement, apparently thinking that the incredulous gasps from the Labour benches were unrelated to the figures he was reeling off. In subsequent exchanges he agreed that the government was paying what amounted to a transfer fee, and claimed that in football the largest sums were

---

64. *Birmingham Post*, 15 February 1980; *Newcastle Journal*, 12 July 1980; Private information; inter-view with Peter Hennessy.

paid for the best players – a statement which even in those days reflected blind faith in the wisdom of the market rather than intimate knowledge of the game. After some coaching from Prior, MacGregor picked up the theme in his own interviews, only tripping once when he confused Manchester United with Manchester City. He performed much better than Joseph, whose display showed why he had previously avoided making controversial statements in the House. It was described by the Chief Whip Michael Jopling as "Disastrous". The episode scarred MacGregor's reputation, making him look mercenary even though his salary was in line with other bosses in the state sector. Memories of this fiasco did little to help him when he later moved to the National Coal Board.[65]

Morrison Halcrow has written that MacGregor's appointment showed "courage that in any other minister might have been dismissed as foolhardiness" (the same judgement could be passed on the Port Talbot trip). Joseph was only acting on ideas about the remuneration of bosses in the nationalised sector which he had expressed in his maiden speech back in 1956. In a curious way it could be argued that Joseph's presentation of the decision helped his personal campaign to shock the nation into its senses; by maximising the outrage he ensured that the government seemed more determined when it confirmed the decision to appoint a man who was certainly well equipped for the job at hand. But at the time the press showed no inclination to differentiate Joseph from "any other minister"; the unanimous verdict was that he had scored another spectacular own-goal. Lord Trenchard produced a remarkable defence for his DoI boss: "with his very quick mind he sometimes follows a complicated path with very great clarity, and it sometimes takes time for the rest of us to absorb the process of his actions and his reasoning; so we fail, initially at least, to understand his correct conclusions, and they are very often correct". The *Daily Telegraph* proved particularly slow to "absorb" Joseph's message. It thought that MacGregor would be worth the money if he did a good job; but since that was impossible, he was another example of wasteful government expenditure. In the *Sunday Times*, Hugo Young reported that many Tory MPs were asking "just how long can Keith go on?" The probable answer, Young thought, was "quite a long time", because Joseph was a veteran of numerous gaffes and enjoyed "a very special bond" with the Prime Minister which gave him "a dispensation from the rules of normal political behaviour". Even so, he continued, "a graceful departure by Sir Keith after all these years would be an event the nation could sustain with equanimity". On the same day, the *Observer* reported that Joseph had apologised to Tory back-benchers for his handling of the MacGregor affair, although he felt no regrets about the expensive signing. He survived a Commons' debate on 14 May, but on the following day found himself attacked with an unexpected argument from a different quarter. In *The*

---

65. Prior, *Balance of Power*, 129.

Times Alfred Sherman marked his increasing disillusionment with his old ally by predicting that MacGregor's appointment would ensure new funds for British Steel. So it proved; a £1.5 billion package was announced in June, followed by over £4 billion at the end of the year, although the industry continued to be "slimmed down" in MacGregor's capable hands. One predictable result of continued state support was that the private companies which had survived during the long years of gross inefficiency at British Steel now started to close. More jobs were lost, and at least one company, which had been a generous donor to the party, announced that its contributions would cease.[66]

Over the summer of 1980 Joseph's bountiful mood continued. The shipbuilders Harland and Woolf were given £66.5 million over two years, Dunlop received £6 million, and having tricked Labour into subsidising his Belfast plant the American sports car manufacturer John DeLorean prised a further £14 million out of the government. Meanwhile Joseph urged Mrs Thatcher to fulfil Labour's promises to Inmos. The delay in reaching a decision was not entirely due to the reluctant Prime Minister; one official complained that "it's like Alice in Wonderland. The NEB is waiting for Inmos's corporate plan. Inmos's corporate plan is waiting on a decision by Sir Keith. Sir Keith is waiting for the reappraisal by the NEB". Joseph also lingered over his response to a report presented by a Labour-appointed committee on the engineering industry. Headed by the former Chairman of British Steel, Sir Monty Finniston, the committee was determined to boost the prestige and quality of British engineering. The key proposal was to set up by statute an Engineering Authority, which would co-ordinate the work of the numerous existing professional institutes. This idea should have appealed to Joseph. British engineers had been complaining since the mid-nineteenth century about the superior status of their German counterparts, and an effective Authority, imposing uniform standards in training and qualificiations, could strike a blow against the alleged "anti-business culture" diagnosed by Correlli Barnett and others. At first Joseph gave positive signals, even suggesting that he would accept the case for additional public spending if this proved necessary. Yet he became bogged down in negotiations, keenly aware of opposition from vested interests who preferred the existing, fragmented structure. Doubts expressed by others triggered misgivings related to his previous ministerial record; he was reported to have asked "Do you really want me to do for the engineers what I did for the National Health Service?". Although the report was presented in November 1979 negotiations about the nature and powers of the new Authority continued into the spring of 1981. Sir Peter Carey was placed in charge of the discussions in March; the result was a chartered body, with no statutory powers to give

---

66. *Daily Telegraph,* 2 May 1980; Halcrow, *Joseph,* 155; *Sunday Times, Observer,* 4 May 1980: *The Times,* 15 May 1980; *The Times,* 18 February 1981.

teeth to its proposals. As Finniston complained, "What I wanted was an engine for change. Instead we have got a shunter moving along disjointed lines". Even the "shunter" had arrived well behind schedule. A new Whitehall quip dubbed Joseph the "Secretary of Wait for Industry".[67]

By August 1980 Joseph had at least won his battle over Inmos. In Opposition he had predicted that new technologies could pave the way to a new industrial revolution, and far from being shamefaced about the state help for Inmos he told John Elliott of the *Financial Times* that the possibilities of intervention in this area were "rather exciting from my point of view". The NEB had already invested £12 million in biotechnology. "I hope you've noticed what they're doing", enthused the sworn enemy of "statism", giving the lie to suggestions that his new initiatives had been forced on him by the more pragmatic Prime Minister.[68] Joseph now felt that the individual entrepreneur, "left to himself, is likely to under-invest in state-of-the-art research from the point of view of society in general". In May he had travelled to California and Mexico, on the first of several "busman's holidays" to gather new ideas. He told his hosts in Silicon Valley that it was now safe to invest in Britain; industrial relations were far better in this developing field, and skilled labour was much cheaper than it was in North America. But Joseph's own mastery of technology was open to doubt; a disgruntled CPS staff member had once accused him of not knowing how to operate an electric fire, and on one factory visit he had inquired whether television was really "here to stay". In January 1981 direct ministerial responsibility for information technology passed to Edward Heath's former aide Kenneth Baker, now working his way into Mrs Thatcher's favour. Before the 1979 election Baker's alienation from the Right had been such that he confided to Tony Benn his hope that Joseph would be given the deeply improbable post of Defence Secretary. Now Baker found that Joseph could be an excellent colleague after all; he was given a free hand, and flourished the Department's cheque book for worthy causes such as fibre optics, robotics, and computers for schools. Mrs Thatcher signalled her approval of the new initiatives by telling the Welsh CBI that the government would be "stimulating industries which do have a future, rather than shoring up lost causes: helping to create tomorrow's world rather than to preserve yesterday's". Ideological purists wondered why the state had to give a helping hand if the new businesses were going to succeed anyway; opponents with a sense of history will have remembered that this rationale for intervention was identical to that which

---

67. *Sunday Times*, 15 June 1980; *The Times*, 17 January, 8 August 1980, 25 March 1981; A. G. Jordan and J. J. Richardson, "Engineering a Consensus: From the Finniston Report to the Engineering Council", in *Public Administration*, Vol. 62, Winter 1984, 390–2; Sampson, *Changing Anatomy*, 251–2; *Guardian*, 25 June 1980.
68. See Stephen Wilks, "Conservative Industrial Policy 1979–83", in P. M. Jackson (ed.), *Implementing Government Policy Initiatives: The Thatcher Administration 1979–83* (RIPA, 1985), 131.

Peter Walker had brought to his work at the DTI after Heath's supposed U-turn.[69]

Since Norman Tebbit was also brought in at this time – in his own words "to take a good deal of work from [Joseph's] overloaded shoulders" – it was difficult to see a meaningful role for the Secretary of State. As Tebbit tactfully put it, "Keith had no taste for the wheeler-dealer negotiating world of the [EEC] Council of Ministers" (although he had been popular among his continental counterparts). So his deputy even took his place in European discussions – a development which led to something less than a lasting love affair. Lord Tebbit remembers that when Joseph took part in negotiations he played a skilful hand, but he tended to participate when the issues were particularly clear-cut. Even before Joseph had been at Industry for a year it was said that "The matters which concern him more – and which he would far prefer to spend time discussing – are his longer term reforms", which included "breaking the monopoly of the Post Office, taking private capital into State businesses like aerospace, encouraging financial institutions to invest in small companies, and improving the system of public purchasing". Joseph gave "the impression of a man searching after eternal truths who would prefer not to be diverted by the day to day problems". One of the brightest young DoI officials, Colette Bowe, was assigned the task of acting as a "Devil's Advocate" during lengthy debates with the Secretary of State. Both participants found these meetings enjoyable and fruitful, but the suspicion remains that they had been instituted to keep Joseph away from more practical concerns. In April 1981 *Private Eye* claimed that officials at Industry were now referring to Joseph as "His Insanity"; it noted that during one recent radio interview listeners "thought that they had lost the sound because of the long silences between the questions and Sir Keith's answers", while on ITV's *Weekend World* the minister was observed to be "staring transfixed either into the middle distance or down at his shoes". Interviewed on the day that British Leyland launched its flagship Mini Metro after much state expenditure, Joseph replied "You've got the wrong man" when asked about the car's potential, and attributed his ignorance to the fact that he had not owned a vehicle since his last one was stolen several years before. Despite his long exposure to the electronic media, certain procedures still eluded his comprehension; on one occasion, feeling dissatisfied with the replies he had given on a television programme which had been broadcast "live", he found it hard to accept that it was now too late to conduct the interview again.[70]

---

69. *Financial Times*, 1 August 1980; Tony Benn, *Conflicts of Interest: Diaries 1977–80* (Hutchinson, 1990), 430; Baker, *Turbulent Years*, 58–62; *Financial Times*, 6 January 1981.
70. Tebbit, *Upwardly Mobile*, 220, 225; interview with Lord Tebbit; *Financial Times*, 25 February 1980; interview with Colette Bowe; *Private Eye*, 24 April 1981; Simon Hoggart, *On the House* (Robson Books, 1981), 116, and *Back on the House* (Robson Books, 1982), 100; interview with Michael Mates.

Hardly a week now passed without some new Joseph story appearing in the satirical press or the columns of newspaper sketch-writers. In *Punch*, Simon Hoggart related that the minister was regularly assailed on his way to and from the Chelsea shops by a punk (who turned out to be Sammy Miller, son of the literary critic Karl). On these occasions the punk would loudly express his dissent from the government's policies. Joseph would regard these as opportunities to enlighten a wayward soul, and try to start an earnest conversation. Once, when travelling in his mother's car, young Miller made a rude gesture towards Joseph; his mother was stunned by what she thought was a reciprocal movement by the Secretary of State (probably she was mistaken; this would have been entirely out of character). On another occasion, when Miller criticised MacGregor's appointment, Joseph was seen by his neighbours "bellowing down the street 'Take that back! You must take that back!'". In the early 1970s reports like this would have been taken as evidence that Joseph, though undoubtedly eccentric, was keen to investigate a broad cross-section of opinion. After his "conversion" Joseph's human qualities were submerged in press reports under the too-effective image of "The Mad Monk". Eye-witnesses claimed to have seen him banging his head against walls, obsessively tying and untying his shoe-laces – even singing in a deserted railway compartment. Hoggart's best story concerned a visit by Joseph to a bird sanctuary. "How on earth do the birds know it's a sanctuary?", he asked. In fact this was an example of his sense of irony; but his image of other-wordly innocence was such that it was interpreted as a serious question.[71]

Some of these stories were obviously embroidered to entertain readers; certainly they contrast with other reports of Joseph between 1979 and 1981. During his American trip in May 1980 Joseph spent some time with Nicholas Henderson, the British Ambassador. Remarkably acute even by the standards of his profession, Henderson had not been impressed by Joseph when, soon after the 1979 general election, he had asked for guidance on the government's intentions in the industrial field. Joseph had "flung his hands in the air but revealed little". At their next meeting Henderson noticed that Joseph was tired, and recorded some interesting mannerisms; his "explosive" laughter seemed at odds with his "buttoned up" character, and his facial expressions clashed with his apparent thoughts, like "an unsynchronised soundtrack in a film". But Henderson found him thoughtful, courteous and sensitive, being particularly struck by his obvious unease whenever his name was mentioned at a press conference. He seemed like a man who took no pleasure from his work, regarding his present task as a painful duty. Discussing the British situation over a drink, he told Henderson "I don't think there's an alternative to what we are doing". The words he used suggest that, contrary to the public perception and

---

71. Hoggart, *On the House*, 25, 108–10, 140; interview with Alan Watkins.

in spite of all that he had invested in its success, Joseph was at least trying to keep an open mind on the monetarist "experiment".[72]

The most alarming press reports appeared at the beginning of 1981, when Mrs Thatcher told Joseph to rest. At about this time the Prime Minister's Press Secretary, Bernard Ingham, noticed that Joseph was unable to walk properly, so severe was his latest chest infection.[73] Yet in February he was able to conduct a lengthy debate with Tony Benn, when they met by chance on the train from Bristol to Paddington. During their wide-ranging discussion, Joseph revealed that he no longer saw much of Enoch Powell, but he confided his view that "Enoch was right in the sense that we shouldn't have had immigration without consulting the people". When they reached Paddington they encountered a student who shook Benn's hand, but refused to acknowledge Joseph. Benn's enthusiastic account suggests that although he doubted the rationality of Joseph's policies – and felt that he "could knock him into a cocked hat in argument" – he regarded the man himself as perfectly sane and, apparently, in better health than he had been in 1977.[74]

But the sheer volume of Joseph anecdotes is impossible to resist, and a vivid eye-witness account shows that his meetings with Henderson and Benn had taken place on two of his better days. In December 1979 a by-election was held in South-West Hertfordshire. As the first such contest since the general election it was a crucial battle, and several ministers visited the constituency on behalf of the Conservative candidate, Richard Page. Despite his numerous commitments Joseph found time to attend a rally at Chorleywood Village Hall. Just before this event a local party member was told by his son that the chairman had appeared at his front door with "a strange man wearing one slipper and one shoe and looking quite untidy". The "strange man" turned out to be the Secretary of State for Industry who had been delayed in London and now wanted to make a telephone call to America (presumably the footwear was induced by an injury and the "untidyness" was temporary; in the following year Joseph was voted joint runner-up to Kevin Keegan in a poll for Britain's best-dressed man). He made the call, and gave his temporary host £5 which more than covered the cost. Joseph went on to speak at the rally, but collapsed after a few minutes. An ambulance was summoned, and it was found that Joseph was suffering from "exhaustion". The incident occurred just after the clash with the NEB, but before the steel strike.[75]

---

72. Nicholas Henderson, *Mandarin: Diaries of an Ambassador 1969–1982* (Weidenfeld & Nicolson, 1994), 273, 343–5.
73. Interview with Sir Bernard Ingham. Typically, Joseph refused the offer of an official car to take him home to bed, and insisted that he was quite well enough to fulfil a speaking engagement that evening.
74. Benn, *The End of an Era: Diaries 1980–90* (Arrow, 1994), 93–5; unedited diary entry for 20 February 1981. Ironically, Joseph had thought in 1975 that Benn could be "converted" to economic liberalism; Hoskyns, *Just in Time*, 19.
75. Information kindly supplied by John Oakey-Smith, JP.

Joseph had always driven himself on all six cylinders, but these had begun to misfire long before 1981 and only his inner conviction could keep him going. He might not have been experiencing a repetition of his breakdown in the late 1940s, but he was verging on that condition. Under the continuing stress of business, the situation was hardly likely to improve. During a two-hour Commons' meeting on British Leyland in May Joseph was said to have exhibited "a formidable repertoire of distress signals. He twitched his eyebrows, shuffled his papers, buried his face in his hands, squeezed his brow between thumb and forefinger until the veins throbbed purple. Even his voice, deep, unnaturally calm, seemed to emanate from a spirit beyond the grave". At the end of the meeting, one MP said "I thought we were going to have a corpse on our consciences".[76]

A government reshuffle was expected in September, and even Joseph's friends must have hoped that he would be given a chance to rebuild his life. His personal affairs had continued to go badly after the separation from his first wife in 1978. Martin Bendelow, a high-flyer at the CPS who had been placed on the Conservative Party candidates' list at Joseph's urging, was charged in July 1980 with having taken his entrepreneurial flair outside the law; he was later jailed for trafficking in cocaine. Joseph told the *Sunday Times* that he was "devastated" by the arrest of a man who had driven him to many engagements and accompanied him on a 1978 visit to the United States. Unnamed sources claimed to have found Bendelow "boorish", which at least implies that Joseph's powers of discrimination deserted him when he was confronted with a character very different from his own. There was further embarrassment when Joseph appeared on television with a bogus businessman who had convinced him that he was about to purchase the Talbot car plant at Linwood; like Bendelow, this exemplar of the entrepreneurial spirit ended up in prison.[77] In April 1981 there was a far greater blow when Joseph's mother died. He had continued to visit her almost every day, and apart from the obvious emotional shock her passing can only have increased his sense of isolation. But despite the personal courtesy which continued to impress almost everyone, Joseph's behaviour since 1974 had left him with enemies who felt too deeply to spare much sympathy for him. There might have been a favourable reaction had his true condition been revealed to the public, but the same ideological drive which his opponents deplored prevented him from owning up to any physical weakness. He continued to accept engagements only suitable for a much fitter minister, provided that they gave him more opportunities to bear witness to his faith. During his "campus campaign" of the 1970s he had spoken at Cambridge

---

76. David Lipsey in *Sunday Times*, 31 May 1981.
77. *The Times*, 11 July 1980; *Sunday Times*, 13 December 1981; *Daily Express*, 7 May 1982. In August 1979 Joseph had recommended Bendelow to the Home Office as someone who could advise on drug-related matters.

University, and the only noteworthy incident had been his accidental upsetting of a jug of water over an undergraduate, just as he was denouncing Denis Healey for "soaking the rich". Now it was impossible for any university to guarantee a safe haven for him. In January 1981 he returned to Cambridge to defend the government against a motion of no confidence. He arrived with egg spattered over the back of his head. The students rejected Joseph's case and passed the motion, which had been proposed by the hated John Kenneth Galbraith. One of the eggs had hit Galbraith; Joseph immediately apologised, assuring his rival that he had been the real target. Two months later Joseph was once again the involuntary recipient of food – this time in Colchester, where chips were added to the menu laid on by his assailants.[78]

In the month after his mother's death Joseph was attacked in *Crossbow*, the journal of the Bow Group which had once provided his loudest support within the party. Now he was named as "the most dismal disappointment of this administration", whose "transfer to a less demanding post is clearly long overdue". Although *The Times* had been calling for Joseph's head since February, this criticism from inside the party triggered feverish speculation. Ironically, it was felt that the clamour would only increase Mrs Thatcher's determination to retain Joseph in the Cabinet; leaving aside her personal feelings, for tactical reasons the Prime Minister who defiantly rejected any thought of a policy U-turn could not suddenly ditch her supposed court philosopher. This prophecy was verified when the reshuffle was announced in September. The moderate contingent of the Cabinet was reduced by three, as Gilmour, Christopher Soames and Mark Carlisle were dismissed. Prior was removed from Employment, but the offer of Northern Ireland meant that if he resigned the Right would be able to accuse him of cowardice. He remained on condition that he would keep his place on the government's Economic Strategy Committee – rather an empty concession, given the increasing domination of the right-wing.[79]

On 14 September 1981 Lord Young was told by a Downing Street official that he should go to see the Secretary of State. At first it seemed to be a routine meeting, but at 4.50 pm precisely Joseph said that he was now free to inform his visitor that he was leaving his job. He had not even tipped off Sir Peter Carey, who only had prior notice from a well-informed ministerial chauffeur. Typically punctilious, Joseph was anxious to spare the feelings of colleagues who were about to be sacked. He would be staying in the government. Presumably Mrs Thatcher had told him that he had fulfilled his task at Industry (although he would have preferred to stay). He had asked for the post of Education Secretary – "When it was clear that there was going to be a vacancy".

---

78. Letter to authors from John Kenneth Galbraith.
79. *The Times*, 20 February, 26, 29 May 1981.

If the question of his health was mentioned at all, presumably Joseph was able to offer some reassurance; in August he had undergone a long-overdue hernia operation. His nerves, however, could not be helped. Soon after his move a friend sitting next to him before he made one speech was alarmed by his condition; he seemed to be fighting for every breath, and had it been anyone else she would have called a doctor. But when he addressed the meeting he showed no sign of discomfort.[80]

The reshuffle took place after months of bad news for the government. Anticipating his imminent departure from office, Sir Ian Gilmour had told a reporter that there was little point in throwing men overboard when the ship was so clearly heading for the rocks. Unemployment had stood at 1.22 million in May 1979; by July 1981 it was 2.85 million, and set to rise further. During 1980 manufacturing output fell by 15 per cent, and company profits by 20 per cent. Inflation began to fall in May 1980, but only after reaching a peak of 22 per cent. After his 1981 budget Geoffrey Howe was the least popular Chancellor on record, and the Prime Minister was plumbing similar depths in the polls. When Gallup conducted its end-of-year survey for 1980, only a fifth of respondents expected that 1981 would see an improvement on the past twelve months – which in truth had been grim enough. More than three-quarters thought that unemployment would rise, only 5 per cent expected increased prosperity, and the same puny proportion believed that taxes would continue to fall. Just before his death in February 1981 Andrew Shonfield speculated that the Conservatives had only persevered with their experiment because they assumed that "there was no possibility of violent opposition". But Hayek had warned many years before that any monetary policy which produced "extensive and protracted unemployment" must be avoided because it would be "politically and socially fatal". During the summer of 1981 inner-city rioting added a law and order crisis to the country's existing economic problems. Before the 1979 election Joseph had denied that there was anything special about the problems of Merseyside, pointing instead to an economic malaise affecting Britain in general. After the riots – and an enquiry headed by Sir Keith's *bête noire* Lord Scarman – Mrs Thatcher appointed Michael Heseltine as "Minister for Merseyside".[81]

The government had conducted an economic experiment at almost the worst imaginable time. Oil prices rose nearly three-fold after the Iranian Revolution of 1978, and although this helped Britain's balance of payments as a net exporter of the fuel it raised industry's costs and plunged the world economy into recession.

---

80. Interview with Lord Young; interview with Sir Peter Carey; KJ interview with Anthony Seldon, 30; private information.
81. Figures in Wybrow, *Britain Speaks Out*, 153–65; *Liverpool Daily Post*, 7 March 1979; Andrew Shonfield, *The Use of Public Power* (Oxford University Press, 1982), 107; Friedrich Hayek, *A Tiger by the Tail* (IEA, 1972), 84.

Yet the monetarists in the Cabinet acted as if these considerations were irrelevant, taking that position even before Geoffrey Howe discovered, at the Tokyo Summit in July 1979, that the other major powers were adopting a similar line. The attack on inflation had become a worldwide priority, but Britain was unusual in following a rigid economic prescription rather than a calculated assessment of the national interest. Exchange controls had already been lifted by Howe, allowing sterling to rise; a policy of high interest rates set in accordance with dogma rather than the economic needs of industry accentuated the trend, so that exporters already faced with deteriorating market conditions found themselves unable to sell abroad. According to Prior, Joseph often spoke in terms of sorting out "the lean meat from the fat" in British industry, but high interest rates emulated the dietary preferences of Jack Sprat and his wife. British Leyland was just one of many companies whose forward plans were destroyed by the policy. Ironically, in Opposition Joseph had written that one of government's few justified economic activities was to provide "a stable framework of expectations" for businesses. Following another course laid down during the Opposition period, Howe almost doubled VAT in his first budget, to 15 per cent. At least social security benefits were now linked to price increases rather than wage rises, but this only widened further the income differentials in a society increasingly fixated with material status. At the same time, voters were encouraged to mistake a shift in the distribution of tax for a cut in the overall burden. This confidence trick was one of the greatest achievements of the Thatcher years; it put into practice Powell's cynical remark at Morecambe in 1968 ("I believe in 'letting the dog see the rabbit', and there's no better way than letting him see a good large chunk of his income"). But in the short term the VAT increase added to inflation, as did the government's decision to honour a manifesto commitment to public sector pay rises recommended by the Labour-appointed Clegg Commission. In turn, high inflation increased the pressure on exporters and destroyed more manufacturing jobs.[82]

All of this was done in the name of a dogma which soon proved unworkable. In 1980 the Medium Term Financial Strategy was unveiled, setting targets for money supply and public sector borrowing over the next four years. Die-hard Thatcherites still treat this innovation as if writing out the desired figures was the same thing as achieving them, but the targets were comfortably missed in each of the first three years. Nothing daunted, in 1982 Howe established new targets. As Ian Gilmour has written, "This was not so much a matter of moving the goalposts as of erecting them all around the pitch"; since the monetarists could already deploy "time-lags" of varying lengths to "prove" that their theory worked, they were now potentially invulnerable to any empirical evidence.

---

82. Prior, *Balance of Power*, 123; for the economic record 1979–81, see Gilmour, *Dancing with Dogma*, 9–29; KJ, "Freedom and Order", 20; Powell, *Income Tax*, 27.

When Joseph had said that "monetarism was not enough" he was referring to the need to control public expenditure, but due to the recession and the huge rise in unemployment the Public Sector Borrowing Requirement (PSBR) increased during 1980–1, from 4.75 per cent of GDP to 6 per cent. The fact that inflation fell after mid-1980 in spite of excessive growth in the money supply must be attributed not to the rigorous application of Friedmanite theory but to interest rates which peaked at 17 per cent, and the knock-on effects in terms of the exchange-rate, investment, output and employment.[83]

Years later, Joseph told Anthony Seldon that "in the first two or three years of government we were almost, to a man [*sic*] I think, surprised by the extent to which unemployment rose". This "surprise" led to ever-deepening splits in the Cabinet, with the previously reliable Biffen and Nott becoming more restive. But Mrs Thatcher could always depend on Joseph in Cabinet. After all, not only had he argued for the experiment before 1979, but he was also involved in the design and implementation of economic policy. With the usual band of believers he attended regular breakfast meetings at 11 Downing Street, was a member of the Economic Strategy Committee, and had to stray into "Neddyland", since the NEDC surprisingly escaped the government's axe at this stage. Joseph also chaired the sub-committee on public sector pay which had allowed the Clegg increases to go through. Prior remembered looking on "in amazement" as this forum sanctioned the pay rises, although he was well aware of the reasoning behind Joseph's relaxed attitude. Increases in the money supply, not wages, caused inflation; if people lost their jobs because they demanded too much that was their own fault, and eventually the magical free market system would force supply and demand into equilibrium.[84]

At first Joseph stuck to the approved line in his public pronouncements. In March 1980 he told the Commons that inflation had been caused by the previous government, which in its final year had allegedly lost control of the money supply. The high exchange rate was necessary until inflation came down; for the time being it had to be regarded as a stimulus to manufacturing efficiency. When Nigel Vinson, a close CPS ally and businessman, asked him if anything could be done to help industry, Joseph replied that he had no influence on economic matters. In fact, as he disarmingly admitted in a 1988 interview, he had made a conscious decision not to interfere, even though neither he nor his colleagues had realised "quite what pressure would be brought upon business". Although, as Nicholas Henderson had noticed, Joseph was capable of expressing a degree of uncertainty about the effects his recommended policies were having, his conviction that the results would be advantageous in the longer term helped him to suppress any feelings of guilt. He was

---

83. Gilmour, *Dancing with Dogma*, 22; Christopher Johnson, *The Economy Under Mrs Thatcher 1979–1990* (Penguin, 1991), 44; Hutton, *State We're In*, 70–71.
84. KJ interview with Anthony Seldon, 30; Prior, *Balance of Power*, 121.

fully supportive of the interest rate policy; in Opposition he had told John Redwood that if necessary the rates should be raised to 100 per cent. In June 1980, he caused a stir by arguing that people should consider pay-cuts, to price themselves into jobs. Had the government not itself been responsible for much of the unemployment problem this idea might have provoked a constructive discussion. But by September a different note was emerging. On a visit to the West Country he expressed the view that "industry is having to pay too high a price. It would be healthier if we had reduced the demands of the public sector . . . so far we have not done a very good job in cutting public expenditure". Then in Basingstoke on 23 November – after protestors had thumped his car – he conceded that the government had "lost the first year". This followed a speech by the CBI Director-General Terence Beckett, who conveyed the swelling discontent of his members with a pledge to embark on "a bare-knuckle fight" with a government which refused to address the exchange rate situation.[85]

To the outside observer it might have seemed that Joseph was about to get his blow in early this time, and condemn his own government *before* it had fallen. Apparently some senior back-benchers reached this conclusion. In December 1980, when Mrs Thatcher met the executive of the 1922 Committee, she was warned about "public agonising" by unnamed people. In her memoirs she loyally implies that this referred to Prior and the "semi-detached" Biffen, but that was not the impression at the time. In the Commons Michael Foot had recently depicted Joseph as "walking around the country, looking puzzled, forlorn and wondering what has happened". But his talk of losing the first year was acceptable to his leader, because his discontent arose from a successful rearguard action against spending cuts, conducted by the "wets" and their new allies at a series of meetings in early November. To compensate, in an autumn statement which finally reduced interest rates by 2 per cent Howe increased Employees' National Insurance Contributions, and introduced a new tax on profits from North Sea oil. Despite all that Joseph had said in Opposition about the difference between "real" and "artificial" jobs – "Dead Sea fruit", he called the products of government job creation – Mrs Thatcher thought that a simultaneous announcement of more places for the Youth Opportunities Programme was "good news".[86]

The March 1981 budget, which contradicted previous ideas of economic rationality by reducing public spending during a recession, was seen as the Thatcherites' revenge for their defeat in November. In fact the inspiration was

---

85. *Western Morning News*, 16 September 1980; private information; KJ interview for "The Thatcher Factor", 17 November 1988, Thatcher 003/13, LSE archives; interview with John Redwood; *The Times*, 25 November 1980.
86. Thatcher, *Downing Street Years*, 130, 129; *Hansard*, vol. 991, col. 607, 29 October 1980; John Cole, *As It Seemed to Me* (Weidenfeld & Nicolson, 1995), 204.

far more complicated than this. Mrs Thatcher was now desperate for further reductions in the interest rates which had only been raised so high in the first place because of monetarist theory. Deeply concerned that industry might be suffering unnecessary pain, Alfred Sherman had commissioned the Swiss economist Professor Jurg Niehans to examine the situation. His report confirmed that monetary policy was far too tight. Urged on by Joseph and Alan Walters, Mrs Thatcher pressed Howe for a more drastic reduction in public spending to make room for an interest rate cut. Although Walters suggested an increase in the rate of income tax, the Chancellor chose the less unpopular (but more regressive) course of freezing allowances. On hearing that the budget would be "astonishingly perverse" Gilmour, Prior and Peter Walker (who had been grudgingly appointed to Agriculture) contemplated resignation; the first two later regretted that they had not jumped when they might have made a difference, rather than waiting for the inevitable push.[87]

The 1981 budget is often taken as confirmation that "the lady was not for turning". Although 364 professional economists wrote to denounce the measures in *The Times*, they inadvertently helped Mrs Thatcher to establish her real point. The budget was turned into an assertion of political virility designed to make the critics "put up or shut up". Yet the behaviour of the Cabinet dissidents presents an interesting contrast to that of Joseph and Mrs Thatcher in the Heath government; Norman Tebbit's remark that they "were trying to duck their collective responsibility" could form the basis of an interesting dissertation on the Thatcherite theory and practice of Cabinet government. More important, while Mrs Thatcher absurdly felt that she was engaged in a "second Battle of Britain" in 1981, preparations for surrender were already well advanced. Kenneth Baker relates that around this time he was involved in devising "a package of industrial support" which Mrs Thatcher could announce if she was threatened with defeat in a Commons' censure motion. In fact, officials had been working on such a contingency programme since the summer of 1980 – at Joseph's request. In February 1981 he had taken his itch for intervention to new levels, when he pleaded with the Talbot company not to close the loss-making Linwood plant which it had inherited from Chrysler; humiliatingly, this entreaty was rejected. In April he tried to reassure the Bow Group that the government was on course, "despite the occasional detours". A few days later it was reported that he was working to persuade public bodies to "Buy British" wherever possible, although in heroic days he had claimed that this approach would damage domestic industry by taking away the incentive to become more efficient. This creative use of public purchasing was called "intelligent clientship"; Howe and his Treasury officials regarded it as a subsidy by other means, and anything but "intelligent". By June 1981 Joseph was taking

---

87. Thatcher, *Downing Street Years*, 132–7; Gilmour, *Dancing with Dogma*, 36–7.

the lead in ministerial whistling to keep up public spirits, telling a radio audience that the outlook on unemployment would start to improve within nine months (despite many attempts to massage the figures, they did not peak for another sixty months – until July 1986). His forecasts of brighter weather became even more erratic, varying from months to years to decades depending on his audience or whether he was talking about the first steps to recovery, the conquest of inflation, better living standards or the final defeat of the "anti-enterprise culture". The truth was that neither he nor anyone else had any idea how or when the experiment would end. As Michael Foot pointed out in one of the greatest speeches of the 1980s, Joseph was like a hapless magician-conjuror, who smashes a watch then forgets the rest of the trick.[88]

In the wake of the *Crossbow* attack David Lipsey wrote that "At 63, Joseph's face has crumpled under the strain. It is a shock to look back at photographs of him in his forties and fifties". No one can be sure how much of Joseph's troubled state of mind and deteriorating appearance should be attributed to fears that the "watch" might never be reassembled. As always he belittled his personal difficulties; when one colleague referred to the strain that the whole Cabinet was under Joseph merely replied that it must be far worse for the Prime Minister. But for Joseph personally the spell at Industry had been a time of virtually unrelieved gloom. Almost the only moment of light relief came in March 1980, when the man who scorned his aptitude for the job of party leader was required to deputise for Mrs Thatcher at Prime Minister's Question Time. It was an unmissable opportunity for the "actor" Joseph to emerge from hibernation. Inspired by the cheers which greeted his appearance (from Labour, of course, these were tokens of gleeful anticipation), he was evidently in a "positively genial mood": "He grinned, patted MPs heads, complimented his colleagues, and exuded an air of bonhommie. Even neatly-laid traps by Mr Michael Foot and Mr Peter Shore, from the Labour front-bench, were swept aside with precision".[89]

It was as if Joseph was making the best of what he already knew would turn out to be a fleeting glimpse of sunshine. Ironically, the hair shirt Treasury policies to which he gave rigid support in Cabinet had forced him to be flexible as Secretary of State. Headlines in the serious press such as "A Warden for Lame Ducks", "The Last of the Big Spenders" and "Sir Keith Looks for Winners" were embarrassments to the government which it would have avoided had the job been given to someone with a milder line in rhetoric. On paper the old excuses for the industrial slump could be trotted out indefinitely; whenever it

---

88. Thatcher, *Downing Street Years*, 155; *Financial Times,* 1 August 1980; *Birmingham Post*, 13 April 1981; *Daily Telegraph*, 7 November 1980; *The World this Weekend*, LWT, 21 June 1981; *Guardian*, 3 April 1981; *Turbulent Years*, 58 (rather confusingly, Baker writes as if the merger of Trade and Industry had already taken place); *Hansard*, vol. 991, col. 607, 29 October 1980.
89. Private information. *Western Morning News*, 26 March 1980. Normally Whitelaw would have stood in for Mrs Thatcher, but on this occasion he was unavailable.

was said that the recovery was taking too long, it could be argued that this merely showed how bad things had been before Mrs Thatcher liberated the country from "socialism". Sceptics could then be asked if they really wanted to return to the Winter of Discontent, as if those desperate months had proved that there was "no alternative" to the present government's policies. As Tony Rudd predicted in the *Spectator* during the dismal autumn of 1980, "the rhythm of the recession" would lead to a recovery whatever the government did; and at that time the "monetary Canutes" in the Cabinet would be able to dry off their clothes and claim that "because they plotted the tides, they turned them".[90]

Yet Joseph's remarks in late 1980 proved – to anyone who needed more evidence – that he was far too honourable to hail the success of his doctrine when any doubts remained. A more emollient figure was required to present the government's case at Industry. Joseph's successor, Patrick Jenkin, could strike some positive notes for the conference of October 1981, even though the SDP was soaring towards 50 per cent in the polls and was on the verge of winning by-elections at Croydon and Crosby. Productivity was rising (unsurprisingly, given the decimation of the workforce) and under tough management losses were being reduced in the nationalised industries. More exciting was Jenkin's revelation that "the commanding heights of the economy are being handed back to the people". De-nationalisation had not progressed very far under Joseph – Sherman accused him of failing to engage "in the basic thinking which is a pre-condition" for this process. But British Aerospace had been sold off, as had state holdings in Ferranti and ICL (unfortunately the latter had to be bailed out to the tune of £200 million soon afterwards), and in many cases state concerns had been restructured as a first step. The list of candidates for imminent return to the private sector included British Airways, the National Freight Corporation, and Cable and Wireless. One of Joseph's first actions as Secretary of State had been to separate British Telecommunications from the Post Office; this new entity was also embarking on "the process of liberalisation and privatisation". Jenkin paid a generous tribute to Joseph and his junior ministers, but despite some fast and efficient work by Tebbit the new Secretary of State was still faced with a massive task; and, as had always been expected, the real attack on the state sector only began after the 1983 general election.[91]

When the inevitable recovery came, and successive election victories made all the early struggles of the Thatcher government seem worthwhile (at least to those who had never faced redundancy) colleagues could write of Joseph with indulgence and even offer some faint praise for his performance at

---

90. *Sunday Times*, 31 May 1981; Tony Rudd, "Monetarism in a Muddle", *Spectator*, 20 September 1980.
91. Patrick Jenkin, speech to 1981 Conservative Party conference; interviews with Sir Norman Fowler and Lord Jenkin.

Industry.[92] But in September 1981 they were less forgiving. At that time it seemed most unlikely that the government would be re-elected. Later it could be appreciated that Joseph had laid some important foundations for success at the DoI; but when he left he looked sure to be condemned as one of the foremost architects of defeat. Before 1979 James Callaghan had described him as "the Dr Strangelove of the economic world", and placed him at the forefront of those who hoped to create the mass unemployment which had now come about. There could be no forgiveness from the "wets", even though many of his actions might have won their approval had he not continued to dismay them with his rhetoric. But on the other flank of the party his reputation was now almost as bad. In the wake of his departure, one colleague was quoted as saying that he had turned his Department into "a soup kitchen". What he would do at Education and Science was anyone's guess. Despite his attacks on the profession in the 1970s, the *Times Educational Supplement* extended "the best welcome politeness can muster". But politeness was clearly in short supply as Joseph moved across Whitehall; the headline of the editorial recording the changes was "Mrs Thatcher shows her low opinion of the DES".[93]

---

92. The predictable exception was Lady Thatcher, who wrote that "he did the vital job that no one else could have done of altering the whole philosophy which had previously dominated the department". But that warm tribute only disguised her feeling at the relevant time that Joseph had been emasculated by his officials. See *Downing Street Years*, 26.
93. Callaghan quoted in *Daily Telegraph*, 16 May 1979; *The Times*, 15 September 1981; *Times Educational Supplement*, 18 September 1981.

Chapter 13

The Last Examination

Undoubtedly Mrs Thatcher *did* have a low opinion of the Department of Education and Science (DES). On her appointment as Secretary of State by Edward Heath in June 1970 she had presented officials with a list of eighteen demands, of which the most urgent was the withdrawal of circulars issued by Labour to enforce the comprehensive system on local authorities. Although she was acting in accordance with the party manifesto, DES officials seemed reluctant to comply. Tempers rose, and Heath had to invite Mrs Thatcher and her Permanent Secretary to Chequers for a meeting which established an armed truce. Before the fall of the Heath government Mrs Thatcher had driven through significant improvements to nursery and primary education; the conference of the National Union of Teachers (NUT) had given her a warm ovation; the *Guardian* had applauded her progress towards "a respectably socialist education policy"; she had fought tenaciously in defence of her Departmental budget; and a record number of schools had turned comprehensive. But her respect for DES civil servants remained roughly on a par with her feelings towards student unions, several of which burned her in effigy in response to her suggestion that they were ripe for reforms.[1]

---

1. Thatcher, *Path to Power*, 165–91.

By the time that Mrs Thatcher left the Department it had moved from "its splendid old quarters in Curzon Street", to Elizabeth House, "a hideous new office block at Waterloo". Ironically, the unappealing edifice had been designed by John Poulson; like the DHSS at the Elephant and Castle, it was too close to a railway line and double-glazing had been installed, turning the Secretary of State's room into an oven during the summer.[2] Education had not been regarded as a key government post since Rab Butler's Education Act of 1944, despite the fact that in October 1976 James Callaghan had used a speech at Ruskin College, Oxford, as an attempt to launch a "Great Debate" on standards in British schools. But although Education might have been perceived as another "Second XI" job, Joseph was excited by a new challenge which demonstrated Mrs Thatcher's continuing faith in his courage and abilities rather than her disdain for the Department. Of all his appointments, Education came closest to fitting the man with the hour. It could almost be said that Joseph's previous ministerial life had been a rehearsal for a position which offered his best chance of affecting the nation's long-term future, for good or ill. Always fascinated by the development of young minds, he was convinced that education was a major reason for Britain's economic decline. He let it be known that he considered this last examination to be the peak of his career, and took to referring to "my beloved Education service". One commentator remembered being told by Joseph as early as 1973 that the job was strongly appealing. He was troubled only by his imagination, which proved to be inspired: he confided that he had a "terrible vision of the teachers marching round and round the building in protest".[3]

As usual, Joseph's first meeting with his civil servants soon passed into Whitehall legend. This time there was no list of demands, and the recommendations for bedtime reading went no further than a single (albeit relatively lengthy) CPS pamphlet which he had commissioned himself – Max Wilkinson's *Lessons from Europe: A Comparison of British and West European Schooling*. Joseph was unsurprised to discover that his officials had not read this objective and well-researched study, although it had been available for four years. On the following day, Joseph remembered, his senior officials confessed that "it was rather more interesting than they had thought". A delegation from the Department was sent to study the situation on the ground; this had never been done before, and the findings supported Wilkinson's arguments for reform.[4]

---

2. *Ibid.,* 165; Baker, *Turbulent Years,* 166.
3. *New Society,* 28 January 1982; Peter Jenkins in *Sunday Times,* 29 September 1985; Joe Rogaly in *Financial Times,* 8 April 1987.
4. Andrew Denham, interview with Lord Joseph, April 1991; *House of Lords Debates,* vol. 523, col.706, 21 November 1990. Wilkinson remembers receiving little feedback from Joseph – only a recognition that the completed pamphlet was "jolly interesting". Alfred Sherman had also contributed, requesting changes after seeing the first draft; interview with Max Wilkinson.

After handing out their homework, Joseph astonished his new colleagues by asserting that 50 per cent of British school leavers received no benefit from eleven years of education "in terms of learning, skill, work-habits, character or preparation for adult life, earning and citizenship". He was persuaded that for public consumption, at least, it would be better to reduce the estimate to 40 per cent. On the bare figures, Joseph was marginally closer to the dismal truth; in 1979, of 915,000 school leavers at sixteen years of age 434,000 departed without a single "O" level. Having stressed the size of the task which faced the Department he fired off several questions, ranging from the philosophical ("What is the purpose of education?") to the alarmingly specific ("How do you close a University?").[5] The answer to the second question was relatively simple. The universities were independent in theory, but they were funded by the taxpayer via the University Grants Committee (UGC) and bankruptcies could be arranged by a Secretary of State with the requisite "moral courage". Joseph's predecessor Mark Carlisle had been appalled by the cuts he was asked to impose on higher education; according to his political advisor Stuart Sexton he "came back bleeding" from his bouts with the Treasury.[6] By contrast, Joseph felt that the expansion of higher education which started in the 1960s had gone too far – more precisely, that there were too many universities and polytechnics offering similar courses. It was impossible for him to forget that many of their students seemed to be more interested in protest than in learning – that instead of being the haunt of open-minded scholars seeking truth, these institutions bred subversion and intolerance on a diet of taxpayers' money. Radical reforms were in order, and Joseph's question was seriously meant. If they did not change, many institutions of higher education would have to die.

When challenged himself Joseph had difficulty with his first question about the underlying rationale for education, but he was convinced that it should be geared to the needs of a free market economy and that the present system was failing in this respect. Indeed education in Britain had always been unsatisfactory; as he put it, "we have had compulsory, coerced, conscripted education in this country for 110 years". He had no romantic vision of a "golden age", but he felt nevertheless that the introduction of the comprehensive schools (which catered for more than nine-tenths of pupils) had been a mistake, which sacrificed the needs of children to the wrong-headed pursuit of equality, regardless of their abilities. On this point he enjoyed powerful backing from Wilkinson's work.[7] The comprehensive ideal had also been attacked in the polemical *Black Papers*, the first of which had appeared in March 1969. The various authors

5. KJ, "One-Eyed Vision" in *Policy Studies* **10**(2), Winter 1989, 12; Nicholas Wapshott in *The Times*, 12 October 1981; John Fairhall in *Guardian*, 13 October 1981; Shirley Robin Letwin, *The Anatomy of Thatcherism* (Fontana, 1992), 93; *Observer*, 1 June 1986.
6. Quoted in Timmins, *Five Giants*, 419.
7. *TES*, 12 February 1982; Max Wilkinson, *Lessons from Europe: A Comparison of British and West European Schooling* (CPS, 1977), 10.

(who included Ralph Harris) identified and lamented a breakdown in school discipline, a decline in standards, and the prevalence of "trendy" ideas about active rather than passive learning in mixed ability classes. As opposed to what they regarded as the sterile conformity of the comprehensives they called for greater diversity of provision and more parental choice. This approach led an early adherent of the movement, Dr Rhodes Boyson, to embrace the idea of education "vouchers" which would force schools to compete with one another for the "custom" of parents. Although "paternalism" was a word that the voucher lobby refused to utter in polite company, their proposed system (devised by Milton Friedman) was literally paternalist;[8] the prospects of all children would ultimately depend on the decisions of their parents, and power would be wrested away from teachers and other representatives of the educational "establishment". When Joseph came to the DES Boyson was a junior minister. Although he regretted the departure of Mark Carlisle, Boyson thought that the new Secretary of State "brought a breath of fresh air intellectually into the Department, and ministerial meetings became rather like postgraduate seminars". There was good reason to hope for a renewal of the radical impetus that Boyson had generated in the Opposition period.[9]

At the Conservative Party conference of October 1981 Joseph signalled his approval of parental choice and diversity of provision in education. "It is vital", he said, "that we remember that our education system should offer a series of social and educational ladders to all children". Carlisle was congratulated for having brought in the Assisted Places Scheme (under which the taxpayer enabled gifted children from poorer backgrounds to attend public school) and for having increased parental choice through "open enrolment". Joseph continued:

> Now I must speak personally for a moment. I have been intellectually attracted to the idea of seeing whether *eventually* a voucher might be a way of increasing parental choice even further – (Applause) – let me finish please. It is not as easy as all that. There are very great difficulties in making a voucher deliver .... It is up to the advocates of such a possibility to study the difficulties, and they are real, and see whether they can develop proposals which can cope with them.[10]

Despite the initial rush of excitement when his audience heard the sacred word "voucher" pronounced from the platform, experienced Joseph-watchers noticed the significant qualifying clauses. The *TES* thought that these amounted to an acknowledgement that the voucher "was likely to prove a dead end for him as it

---

8. This point is also made by Nicholas Bosanquet in *After the New Right* (Heinemann, 1983), 173–5.
9. Rhodes Boyson, *Speaking My Mind* (Peter Owen, 1995), 159.
10. Ninety-Eighth Conservative Party conference, October 1981.

has for other enthusiasts faced by the realities of administration, finance and the powerful interests behind the status quo". A subsequent parliamentary answer drafted by the DES pointed out that there would have to be an experiment in a limited area before the question of a national voucher system arose. Even this pilot scheme would require legislation, and several Conservatives had promised all-out opposition (Edward Heath believed that the idea was nothing more than an attempt to subsidise private education). A summary of objections was sent by the DES to the two main pressure groups advocating vouchers; the document asserted that "the Secretary of State . . . has made it clear that he has no plans for the general introduction" of such a system.[11]

In February 1983 it was reported that a Cabinet committee had given the go-ahead after all, but this was premature. Geoffrey Howe, himself a long-standing supporter of the principle of vouchers, had established a Policy Group on Education under the All Souls Fellow Lord (Max) Beloff, to report in time to help deliberations on the next party manifesto. In April 1983 the Group's findings were leaked. It had accepted one of Boyson's ideas – that parents should have the right to set up their own schools in certain circumstances – and urged an extension of the Assisted Places Scheme. But it decided against the voucher. It was felt that "its cost would be hard to justify to a highly sceptical public at a time of stretched resources". According to a government advisor Howe was suitably impressed by this argument, but in her memoirs Lady Thatcher says that it was Joseph himself who persuaded her that vouchers should be dropped, on the grounds that the same objective could be reached (albeit more gradually) through measures already in place. There was no mention of vouchers in the 1983 manifesto, and at the party conference of that year Joseph announced that the idea was "at least in the foreseeable future, dead". At a question and answer session he pleaded that die-hard supporters should at least "give me credit for trying". A similar fate had befallen another radical initiative which had looked a definite runner in January – that student grants should be topped up by loans, as was the case in most other Western nations including West Germany and Sweden. When Carlisle had taken this idea to a Cabinet sub-committee Joseph seemed to be more interested in studying his watch than in helping Boyson, who had invested much time and effort in an investigation of schemes already in operation. The idea was revived during discussions of the 1983 manifesto, but it was shelved after a Chequers' meeting at which Cecil Parkinson claimed that working-class families would be deterred by the thought of incurring so much debt.[12]

11. *TES,* 16 October 1981; *The Times,* 15 October, 18 December 1981.
12. Christopher Knight, *The Making of Tory Education Policy in Post-War Britain: 1950–86* (Falmer Press, 1990), 161–3; Clyde Chitty, *Towards a New Education System: The Victory of the New Right?* (Falmer Press, 1989), 163–6; Thatcher, *Downing Street Years,* 591; John O'Sullivan in *Daily Telegraph,* 13 October 1983; *Observer,* 2 January 1983; interview with Sir Rhodes Boyson; Parkinson, *Right at the Centre,* 59. Joseph was still having to explain to the Commons as late as the summer of 1984 the reasons for his rejection of the voucher idea; see *Hansard,* vol. 62, col. 290, 22 June 1984.

In retirement, Joseph clarified his position on vouchers. He had indeed been "attracted" by the idea, but *"believing in the philosophy is not the same as judging the consequences of the philosophy"*. He came to see that even a pilot scheme would have involved "hugely controversial and complex legislation, splitting the Conservative Party, as well as creating a tumultuous split between parties, alienating most teacher unions, most local authorities, perhaps the churches, and leading if we went for a pilot scheme possibly to a mouse at the end". To override this opposition and impose a nationwide scheme "called for more moral courage than I had".[13]

The Department, Joseph acknowledged, was generally opposed to vouchers; but he thought that it had not been obstructive. When Sir Alfred Sherman accused "thoroughly unscrupulous senior officials" of scuppering the idea, Joseph issued a sharp rebuke. "I find it hard to believe", he wrote, "that, if your remarks have been reported accurately, you have any evidence whatsoever to support them". His advisor Oliver Letwin noticed that officials were quick to point out difficulties but less helpful when it came to solutions; had their attitudes changed, he felt, something might have been achieved. There were many administrative headaches, and several variations of the voucher scheme were developed to combat them.[14] Nicholas Timmins has summarised some of the main difficulties:

> Would the voucher cover the full cost of a state education or would parents have to supplement it? Would it be a fixed sum, but means-tested? Could parents top it up if they wanted to? Could it be spent in private and independent schools, or only in state schools? If only in state schools, was it any more than the open enrolment – the freedom to choose their child's school and the school's freedom to fill all its available places – which the 1980 Act theoretically provided? If it could be spent in independent schools was it worth the dead-weight cost of subsidising the 5 per cent of parents who already opted for the private sector, a sum sufficiently large to cause the Treasury permanent concern? Would the voucher be a flat sum or a relative one, given that education costs varied by 50 per cent between schools? The list went on and on.[15]

Inevitably this led to complications, with advocates of the general principle of vouchers lining up behind their favoured alternative. But the greatest obstacle to progress was Joseph himself. Letwin recalled being invited with Sexton to

---

13. *Contemporary Record*, Spring 1987, 30–1 (our italics).
14. Interviews with Sir Rhodes Boyson and Oliver Letwin; *TES*, 5 October 1984; Timmins, *Five Giants*, 420–1.
15. *Ibid.*, 420. See also Mark Blaug, "Education Vouchers: It All Depends on What You Mean", in J. Le Grand and R. Robinson (eds), *Privatisation and the Welfare State* (Allen and Unwin, 1984).

argue over the points with senior civil servants, led by the Department's Deputy Secretary Walter Ulrich. A later Secretary of State remembered Ulrich for his "formidable intellectual bullying"; by contrast, Joseph admired his analytical powers, and accepted that the raising of objections was an essential part of a civil servant's job. When Joseph was present at meetings he merely listened to the contesting parties; often he was not even there. The languid "post-graduate seminars" soon proved irksome to Boyson (who had completed his own doctoral thesis in four years while running a large comprehensive school). After a while he detected that they were being made into a substitute for the radical action that he desired, and he stopped attending. Drafted into a discussion group on student loans, Ralph Harris had much the same experience. Sitting around an enormous table heaped with papers, the group would hear Joseph examine points of detail from every angle.[16]

For the radicals of the IEA it was a familiar story – a re-run of 1970–4. In 1986 the Institute published *The Riddle of the Voucher*, in which Arthur Seldon blamed the lack of progress on "official feet-dragging and political under-estimation of potential popular acclaim". Seldon continued to number Joseph "among the most scrupulous and upright politicians of the age"; criticism of the minister himself was muted and oblique. Yet the true "riddle" of the voucher is not why Joseph failed to implement it, but why he allowed himself to acknowledge that he was "intellectually attracted" in the first place, thus stimulating a level of expectation which was difficult to control, and highly embarrassing when he decided that it could not be satisfied.[17]

The advocates of the voucher argued that it would raise standards at all levels of ability. Under the imperious sway of market forces, schools which failed their pupils would soon close; the best would prosper, and others would fight to catch up. In theory, then, the worst off in society would benefit as much as the richest – Milton Friedman, indeed, thought that they would benefit the most.[18] Yet in practice this vision would only be realised if all parents were both able and willing to inform themselves of relative school performance, and sufficiently rational to take the right decision on the basis of their researches. The choices of the wealthy would hardly be affected, whether or not the voucher scheme included a means-test. But some upwardly aspiring middle and working-class families, willing to make sacrifices yet reluctant to bankrupt themselves, would seize this opportunity to offer their children a headstart in life. Among these groups, implementation of the voucher would indeed have

---

16. Interviews with Oliver Letwin, Sir Rhodes Boyson and Lord Harris of High Cross.
17. Arthur Seldon, *The Riddle of the Voucher: An Inquiry into the Obstacles to Introducing Choice and Competition into State Schools* (IEA, 1986), 97; Arthur Seldon, *Capitalism* (Blackwell, 1990), 299.
18. Milton and Rose Friedman, *Free to Choose* (Penguin, 1980), 203. In fact the version of the voucher advocated by Friedman would allow parents to "top up" the amount they received from the state. It would be difficult to see how this could bring special benefits to the poor, and Friedman provides no evidence to substantiate his claim.

been greeted with "political acclaim" – at least until the best schools became oversubscribed. The remainder, presumably, would have to wait for standards to rise in the schools which were shunned by the more affluent and the better motivated. But these were precisely those people, predominantly from the lower classes, who were trapped in what Joseph had called "the cycle of deprivation". Enthusiasts like Boyson – himself from a working-class background – were confident that all parents could be trusted to make the right choices. By contrast, Joseph's own social theory suggested that, badly educated themselves and transmitting their lack of ambition to their children, they would fail to make the effort. Help for these families could not be delayed during the (unpredictable) interval before the benefits of the market trickled down to them; while standards remained low, and staff disillusioned, new generations would be fed into the "cycle", creating what Vernon Bogdanor called a system of "educational apartheid".[19] At the same time, a steep decline in the demand for "unskilled" labour presented a gloomy outlook for anyone who left school without qualifications. The only way to break the cycle would be for the state to pour extra resources into these "sink" schools, offering attractive terms to recruit the best teachers and compensating for the fact that costs per pupil would be significantly higher for as long as such schools remained undersubscribed.[20] But, apart from endangering the whole point of the exercise by introducing a serious market distortion, this expedient would involve an administrative task pregnant with complexities and political risks. How would one decide which parents were fit to use a voucher? Perhaps submit the whole population to an intelligence test, and deny the voucher to the bottom 50 per cent?

Joseph had certainly not forgotten about the cycle of deprivation, and the research which had questioned his theory had made little or no difference to him. He came to the Department anxious to help those whom he identified as victims rather than beneficiaries under the existing dispensation. To underline the poor public image of the Education Department over recent years, Joseph's emphasis was welcomed as an important new departure. But he never mentioned his fears for the already deprived as a reason for rejecting the voucher; the closest he came to making the connection was his admission in an interview that "Some parents won't take advantage of choice. But that's life".[21] Perhaps he was so impressed by the administrative complexities that he never had reason to consider in full the possible "consequences of the philosophy"? Yet there are other explanations. At Education he seems to have shied away

---

19. Vernon Bogdanor, "Education", in Robert Blake and John Patten (eds), *The Conservative Opportunity* (Macmillan, 1976), 124–5.
20. Letter to the authors from Sir David Hancock. We are most obliged to Sir David for reading and commenting on this chapter.
21. Interview with David Lister, *TES*, 12 February 1982.

from speaking out on the subject of social deprivation, which had brought embarassment to himself and endangered his "cause" in the wake of the Edgbaston speech. There was another potent factor, which threatened to affect Joseph's personal relationships and the future of his party. If he had realised the dangers, a gulf of principle would have been revealed between himself and the economic liberal allies who were so important to him. Still worse, pressing on with vouchers would have exposed the frailty of the ill-assorted intellectual coalition (social conservatives and libertarian individualists) that offered support to the Conservatives; it might bring to light contradictions in the thinking of those who hoped for a more orderly society *and* the "rolling back of the state".[22] Undoubtedly some advocates of the voucher saw it as a means of benefitting people who subscribed to "Victorian Values", such as thrift and rational self-interest; those who failed to conform could be left to their fate. Others, like Boyson, had an optimistic view of human nature, and thought that liberation through market forces would in itself break the poor out of the dismal cycle. Joseph fell somewhere between the cynics and the optimists; he had a utopian vision of a bourgeois society, but when put to the test he could not risk the introduction of a scheme that, on his own view of the poor, might easily (and permanently) worsen their plight. If he really was conscious that the voucher exposed these crucial differences, it would have been typical of Joseph to deflect attention by referring to his inadequate "moral courage". But a more calculating minister would simply have kept quiet about vouchers in the first place. It was highly characteristic of Joseph that he brought extra pressure to bear on himself, blurting out his statement of sympathy while giving fair warning that the expectations he aroused would be disappointed in the end.

At the DHSS Joseph had canvassed radical options at the outset, only to discover on inquiry that a clean break from traditional practice would merely produce new difficulties. Whatever his true reasons for rejecting the voucher, he was left (as he had been in 1970) with the problem of finding an alternative route to his goal of raising the quality of public provision. Success would depend above all on co-operation from teachers (a point noted by Callaghan in his Ruskin speech).[23] As Joseph told the 1981 party conference, "It is the quality of teachers that matters; it is the skills of teachers that matter; it is the quality of head teachers that matters, and it is the skill of head teachers that matters". It followed that a responsible Secretary of State would nurture these qualities and skills, and motivate the staff of Britain's schools to greater efforts.

In the same month as his first Party conference speech on Education, Joseph travelled from St Pancras station to address a union meeting at Sheffield. The

---

22. On the latent tensions between "traditionalists" and "individualists" see Andrew Denham, *Think-Tanks of the New Right* (Dartmouth, 1996), 111–9.
23. Kenneth O. Morgan, *Callaghan: A Life* (Oxford University Press, 1997), 540.

day began badly; he caught the wrong train, and ended up in Doncaster. When he finally arrived to give the speech his audience – the Assistant Masters' and Mistresses' Association, traditionally one of the more moderate teachers' bodies – was alienated by his denial that there was a correlation between class size and academic performance. The message, greeted by one cry of "codswallop!", was that quality could be improved without an increase in resources. After the meeting Joseph stepped on a different set of toes, speculating to reporters that subsidised pre-school nursery provision was unnecessary; mothers should stay at home and look after their children, he thought.[24]

It was a poor start to a relationship which, despite occasional hints of rapprochement, ended up a great deal worse. Once or twice Joseph apologised to those who felt that he had undermined morale within the teaching profession – and at every opportunity he pointed out that he lacked the ability to do the job himself – but some demon inside him kept whispering that teachers were the enemy. The same prompter has been at the ear of Education Secretaries (and Prime Ministers) ever since; it dictates phrases like "The vast majority of teachers in Britain today do a first-rate job. Nevertheless . . ." In Joseph's case the evil spirit had a clinching argument. To widen the debate, and discuss social problems that would help to explain the plight of the failing "50 per cent", might lure him into repeating Edgbaston themes. It was much safer to talk about the teachers as if they really could have a decisive influence over youthful minds; after all, this was taking some of the earlier rhetoric of the profession at face value.[25] At the 1984 Conservative conference Joseph provided an interesting variation. "Just out of interest", he enquired matily, "how many teachers and ex-teachers are there in the conference hall today? I am sure that we all recognise that it is a hard job and it is probably harder now than it has been for a long time . . . So the first thing that the Government set itself to do was to raise the quality of those *coming into* the teaching profession". Statements of that kind maximised the fear and suspicion felt by teachers at the prospect of the regular performance appraisals that Joseph wanted. The teachers and ex-teachers in the hall would not have been consoled by the thought that even if they had proved inadequate themselves, their failings would be corrected by the next generation.

When Joseph handed over his Department to Kenneth Baker in 1986, his parting advice was "Don't make the same mistake as I did of attacking the teachers". Baker acknowledged the wisdom of this, but for insight it can only be compared to warning a football manager not to put drawing-pins in his cen-

---

24. *The Times*, 27 October 1981.
25. The assumption that schooling was a more important influence on character than family background also allowed social conservatives to side-step the left-wing argument that capitalism encouraged decadent behaviour. The late Shirley Letwin, for example, claimed that under the guidance of "trendy" teachers "pupils were encouraged to pursue instant gratification of desires and to resent any discipline that interfered with 'spontaneity' or 'self-expression'" (*Anatomy of Thatcherism*, 231).

tre-forward's boots. Back in 1962 Joseph had referred to teaching as "the finest profession in the world". To betray such a worthy calling would indeed be unforgivable. But Joseph seems to have made up his mind that the betrayal had already taken place, before he had properly investigated the evidence; indeed, when he met teachers in their schools he usually came away saying "If all teachers were like that there wouldn't be a problem". During one radio interview he admitted that he would have liked to have praised teachers more often, but claimed that had he done so parents would have said "That man's talking rubbish". This was particularly feeble; after all, the reassurance of parents was as much a part of Joseph's job as was the crucial task of cajoling the teachers. Perhaps Joseph's "mistake" arose from a feeling that at some point he was bound to clash with the unions, so he might as well take his gloves off from the outset. Here as in so many aspects of Joseph's approach to education Max Wilkinson's pamphlet may have been a factor. Wilkinson had urged that standards in the teaching profession should be improved by raising the necessary qualifications and introducing a new pay structure to reflect this.[26] Even Joseph, with his limited experience of negotiating with the unions, must have guessed that this desirable goal could only be reached after a protracted struggle. An indispensible first step would have been patiently to assure the teachers that he was on their side – that he wanted to enhance their prestige within the community. Regrettably he never deployed this tactic. To the teachers his attitude implied that he considered public servants in general to be demotivated human beings; otherwise they would never have entered those poorly rewarded professions in the first place. This ran counter to one of his earliest political pronouncements, when he told the voters of Leeds North-East in February 1956 that "although teaching was a vocation it must be properly paid". But it echoed the message of *Equality*, and chimed in with the thinking of other members of the Thatcher Cabinet. Often Joseph was accused of treating the teachers as if they were stupid, and there was something in that too. Their "stupidity" took the form of failing to understand the laws of supply and demand, which meant that they could be treated differently from (say) the police force because (Joseph assumed) there were long queues of people waiting to enlist as teachers while would-be constables were thin on the ground. Head teachers, for some reason, he decided to treat differently, although if standards were really slipping badly they should have been first in

---

26. For once Wilkinson seems to have been carried away by the ingenuity of his reasoning at this point. He argued that "most youngsters are attracted to professions which are difficult to enter, partly for no other reason than that they are difficult". This might have appealed to Joseph, whose decision to compete for an All Souls Fellowship seems to have been made on these grounds. But few people set themselves such challenges unless they expect a considerable reward at the end of the process; and at a time of financial stringency Wilkinson's plan could only bring disaster to the profession if applied across the board. See *Lessons from Europe*, 101. Baker, *Turbulent Years*, 161; *Hansard*, vol. 664, col. 920, 2 August 1962.

the firing line. When John Redwood pointed out to him that Heads might have to roll, he at first seemed to ignore the message, then showed interest, and finally allowed officials to convince him that all was well. To outside observers it seemed that the laws of the market were being made to operate to coincide with the current wishes of many Tory activists, and Joseph took no steps to allay these fears.[27]

The story is particularly puzzling because Joseph had a reasonable case to present, particularly on staffing levels in secondary schools. Intake had been falling due to demographic change, and spending per pupil was at record levels despite the recent cuts. But the argument for redundancies was badly handled, against a background of incomprehension and hostility. One possibility that only registered with Joseph after the damage had been done was that teachers in the most "vocational" subjects would accept redundancy and run to better-paid jobs. The inevitable result was, before long, a desperate shortage of staff in the key subjects, notably mathematics. Before the end of 1981 a figure of 13,000 job losses was announced; nearly a quarter of these would be compulsory. If local councils increased the pay of those who remained by more than 4 per cent they would incur financial penalties. In January 1982 Joseph urged local authorities to sack incompetent teachers; in March he abolished the teacher-dominated Schools Council, and replaced it with two quangos whose members were to be nominated by himself. The President of the militant NUT claimed that these early moves betrayed "a death-wish for the education service, and, therefore, the whole nation". In this context, Joseph's recruitment of extra staff to HM Inspectorate of Schools, and his drive to publicise indicators of school performance, were inevitably regarded as unfriendly acts. The teaching unions also resented the constructive work of David Young's Manpower Services Commission (MSC) in promoting and financing vocational training after 1982. Young's Training and Vocational Education Initiative (TVEI), which introduced a range of courses "from agriculture and catering to computer studies, office technology and design technology", fell outside the influence of local councils and the DES. As Young reflected, the arrangement ensured that Joseph "would be subjected to a shower of abuse by the whole of the educational establishment". Educational "traditionalists" were also appalled by the appearance in schools of charts explaining to the children how "learning chemistry was linked with a window-cleaning job, geography with bus-driving, English with being a traffic-warden", etc. But Joseph felt that this was the only way to cater for young people who were unsuited to what Wilkinson had described as the "old academic aims of broadening the pupils' intellects and providing a general grasp of facts". At least it was a new phenomenon for a politician to be criticised for

---

27. *Yorkshire Post*, 2 February 1956; Ted Wragg in *TES*, 30 May 1986; interview with John Redwood; private information.

going too far in his drive to prepare young people for their working lives. But Joseph also drew attacks from a more familiar source, when he chose a political advisor (Oliver Letwin) who was a product of Eton.[28]

If Joseph disappointed his fellow-ideologues through his unwillingness to push through vouchers, he was determined to compensate for this (and for his record at Industry) by keeping firm control of expenditure at his new Department. Carlisle had felt education cuts like a wound, but even when Joseph recognised the need for extra resources he knew that his own speeches before 1979 had provided unsympathetic colleagues like Whitelaw (who chaired the key "Star Chamber" committee on spending) with excellent reasons for turning him down. Joseph's tactics resembled the situation at Industry; like the hand-outs to lame ducks, pay offers to teachers came with strings attached. This might have worked if the wage increases had been sufficiently generous to compensate for his demands; but they were not. And the national economy could survive the closure of British Leyland – or even the disappearance of the steel industry – but that ultimate sanction was not available in dealings with the teaching profession. It would not be possible to call in new supplies from Sweden if British teachers went on strike or deserted the profession. Yet Joseph was attracted by "crude industrial analogies". He was quoted as saying "Teachers don't realise how lucky they are. They don't even have to pay for their raw material. Nor do they have any notion of the insecurity of industry". This analogy was not simply "crude", but palpably false; Joseph seemed to think that shop floor workers in car factories customarily paid for the frames and windscreens. The idea that teachers might perform better in the classroom under constant threat of redundancy led one head teacher to accuse Joseph of "personnel mismanagement, which any reputable commercial organisation would condemn out of hand". Given Joseph's frequent lectures on management skills the blow was shrewdly placed – even if it overrated the quality of management in the British private sector, which during the 1980s deteriorated in response to "fashionable" ideas about the right to "hire and fire".[29]

After the campus battles of the 1970s staff in institutions of higher education had good reasons for unease when Joseph's appointment was announced. Again, the figures justified some action. It was estimated that during the 1980s the number of nineteen year-olds would fall by 30 per cent. But the expenditure White Paper of March 1981 had envisaged cuts amounting to over 10 per cent in real terms between 1980–1 and 1983–4. When the UGC made public the effects on individual institutions there was an "explosion of dismay". New

28. Wilkinson, *Lessons from Europe*, 10; *Guardian*, 22 January 1982; *Daily Mail*, 23 April 1982; Timmins, *Five Giants*, 424; Letwin, *Anatomy of Thatcherism*, 255. On the TVEI, see Jeremy Moon and J. J. Richardson, "Policy-Making with a Difference? The Technical and Vocational Education Initiative", *Public Administration*, Vol. 62, Spring 1984, 22–33.
29. George Walker in *TES*, 19 July 1985.

universities such as Aston and Salford (ironically, institutions which had forged strong links with industry and were committed to "vocational" courses) were to lose between a quarter and a half of their total budgets; Oxford and Cambridge, with all their advantages in attracting private funding, for some reason emerged virtually unscathed. Outside Oxbridge, Vice-Chancellors had been horrified by a "quite extraordinary decision", which gave them no time to plan a gradual run-down in staffing levels through "natural wastage". When Joseph arrived at the DES he was thus in a position to dictate terms of surrender to institutions that after years of complacent expansion suddenly found themselves friendless. He offered some help with redundancy payments, but in return Vice-Chancellors were expected to modify their statutes, to remove job security from academics. These provisions had been inserted to guarantee freedom of expression, a principle of particular importance to Joseph. But he had not been extended the same rights on his university visits, and too many academics were abusing their positions by clinging on to outdated "pseudo-Keynesian" ideas.[30]

The best illustration of Joseph's approach to higher education was his treatment of the Social Science Research Council (SSRC), which distributed grants for research in sociology and other subjects of ill repute with most Conservative activists. Carlisle had already trimmed the Council's £20 million budget by £1.5 million, but after his departure rumours circulated in academia that more drastic action could be expected. It was claimed that Joseph had a personal grudge against social scientists and the SSRC in particular; he felt that they had not taken seriously enough his own ideas on the cycle of deprivation, despite the fact that as Secretary of State at the DHSS he had arranged the funding of exhaustive SSRC research.[31] On 10 December 1982 Joseph wrote to Sir Geoffrey Howe, suggesting a further cut of around £2 million in the Council's budget and informing the Chancellor that he had set up an inquiry under Lord Victor Rothschild to decide whether projects might be funded by the private sector in future. If so, Rothschild was asked to consider whether "there would be any continuing justification for the Council's existence". Evidently Joseph was confident that Rothschild would reach the right conclusions, and he pointed out to Howe the benefits "of proceeding with a tried and respected

---

30. Maurice Kogan with David Kogan, *The Attack on Higher Education* (Kogan Page, 1983), 46–8, 86–7; Peter Scott, "Higher Education" in D. Kavanagh and A. Seldon (eds), *The Thatcher Effect: A Decade of Change* (Clarendon Press, 1989), 200.
31. This was unfair. Andrew Shonfield, who had been Chairman of the SSRC, remembered that in 1970–1 he contested Joseph's view that the social sciences were "packed with people committed to the left in British politics". At most, then, Joseph's disappointment over the response to his speech reinforced an existing antipathy. But certainly the SSRC research rankled. As late as November 1991 Joseph alluded to Rutter and Madge's preference for the phrase "cycles of disadvantage", and claimed that "No one denied the thesis". See *The Times*, 21 November 1975, and KJ, *The Importance of Parenting* (CPS, 1991), 5.
32. *New Society*, 7 January 1982.

operator".[32] Five days later an attempt was made to soften up public opinion, when Lord Beloff launched a stinging attack on the Council in the Lords. Perhaps this co-ordinated attempt to give the SSRC a bad name before hanging it persuaded a civil servant to be careless; Joseph's confidential letter found its way to *New Society*, along with Howe's encouraging reply. Rothschild had been an eccentric choice for a hatchet-job in any case; his high standing arose from his reputation for objectivity as well as his formidable intellect. But even if he had been persuaded of the need for action by stories of some of the SSRC's more outlandish acts of generosity, the leak compromised his position. His report, published on 19 May 1982, was typical of the man; "pithy, sharp, full of interesting nuggets". One of these "nuggets", expressed in the polished prose of an experienced public servant, betrays Rothschild's real feelings about the task Joseph had invited him to perform:

> The need for independence from Government departments is particularly important because so much social science research is the stuff of political debate. All such research might prove subversive because it attempts to submit such policies to empirical trial with the risk that the judgment might be adverse. It would be too much to expect ministers to show enthusiasm for research designed to show that their policies were misconceived. But it seems obvious that in many cases the public interest is served by such research being undertaken.[33]

This argument cut no ice with Joseph; even in retirement he could express his incredulity that among the 364 economists who had criticised the 1981 Budget were many academics on the public pay roll. But at the time he was forced to retreat; even the cut in the SSRC budget fell short of his initial target. As a paltry token he secured a change in the name of the quango, which would now be known as the Economic and Social Research Council (ESRC). The rationale for this rebranding was that Joseph considered the word "science" to be "misleading for a subject that cannot provide testable answers". At least this was a respectable proposition for debate, but it was highly dubious coming from Joseph, given his enthusiasm for testing Milton Friedman's economic theories on the people of Britain (Friedman himself claimed that his work was "scientific"). The new name provoked an outburst of sarcasm from Lord Rothschild, who described Joseph's initiative as "timely, creative, logical, apposite, epistemologically unassailable and psychologically desirable".[34]

---

33. Quoted in Paul Flather, ""Pulling through" – Conspiracies, Counterplots, and How the SSRC Escaped the Axe in 1982", in Martin Bulmer (ed.), *Social Science Research and Government: Comparative Essays on Britain and the United States* (Cambridge University Press, 1987).
34. KJ interview for "The Thatcher Factor"; *The Times*, 23 October 1982; Ian Gilmour, *Britain Can Work* (Martin Robertson, 1983), 154.

Joseph's higher education strategy dictated a reduction of student numbers in the universities; in the polytechnics, by contrast, increases were encouraged despite cuts in funding. The real value of grants awarded to students by local authorities was also reduced to discourage applications. Joseph felt that many young people merely continued in education to defer decisions about their careers; his determination to close this option was a risk on both economic and political grounds, since the taxpayer ended up subsidising many of the would-be students, who joined the swelling ranks of the unemployed. But the "scientific" laws of supply and demand failed to operate as expected. In 1981 there was a 4 per cent increase in applications, to which the universities were forced to respond by imposing a 3 per cent cut in the number of places. The following year saw a further 4 per cent rise in applicants. For those fortunate enough to secure a place, demonstrations against the cuts became a regular feature of the academic calendar. Apart from the major gatherings in London, *ad hoc* protests could be assembled whenever Joseph ventured near a university town. Grumbling students were often reinforced by other groups with their own grievances from the past. Unluckily, the 1982 party conference was held in Brighton, near the University of Sussex. Joseph was spat upon at the station, and during a break in proceedings he wandered down the wrong side of a security barrier into the midst of a hostile crowd. Although research conducted a few months later showed that only 1.7 per cent of schoolchildren could name the Education Secretary (one thought the post was held by "Sir Kenneth Williams") these protestors were better informed. An eye-witness said that "Anyone who was near enough to dive in, dived in". Before he could be rescued Joseph had been punched in the face and on the shoulder. He tried to make light of the encounter, telling reporters that "it was merely an intellectual argument", but when he returned to the conference platform he was visibly shaken, if not bruised.[35]

Even before this disgraceful incident Joseph's friends were reported as saying that he might not stand at the next general election. At that time his radical flagships, vouchers and students loans, were still afloat. In the speech which he had delivered to the party conference before the attack he suggested that the voucher system could work in tandem with a policy of "open enrolment", which allowed schools additional resources for expansion if they were oversubscribed. But not all of the faithful were cheered by these radical ideas. A journalist overheard "a middle-aged Lancashire matron" in the hall whispering "'E doesn't inspire you at all.' 'He was very nice at that meeting', her neighbour remonstrated. 'Nice isn't enough', said the matron grimly."[36]

Mrs Thatcher disagreed with these critical noises from the grass roots. Although the arrival of determined supporters such as Tebbit, Nigel Lawson

---

35. *TES*, 4 February 1983; *Birmingham Post*, 9 October 1982.
36. Michael White in *Guardian*, 6 October 1982.

and Cecil Parkinson had produced a more congenial Cabinet, the Prime Minister still felt reassured by Joseph's presence. Before 1979 ideological agreement had been enough to win Mrs Thatcher's favour, but suspicion is an inevitable companion of power and Joseph's unflagging personal loyalty meant more to her than ever. He was hardly equipped for the kind of instant decision-making required during the Falklands crisis, and was not among the small group of ministers picked for the War Cabinet. But he was consulted whenever his advice was deemed to be relevant; for example, he was included in the key Family Policy Group set up by Mrs Thatcher to devise a strategy for a second term, and he was one of only five ministers who read the whole of the 1983 manifesto prior to publication. Overall that document was regarded as "smooth, self-congratulatory and unmenacing"; from the point of view of Education, it was most notable for the omission of loans and vouchers (although there was a temporary scare when the latter proposal was included in one edition of the *Daily Notes* issued by the party during the campaign). Another notable proposal was the erasure of two of Joseph's youthful indiscretions. The GLC and the Inner London Education Authority (ILEA) were both to be scrapped. The government was already in the process of unpicking an acknowledged error from 1970–4, Joseph's NHS reorganisation.[37]

The unwritten rule of "One Nation" politics had decreed that the Conservatives could only hope to win elections if they governed in the general interest. Mrs Thatcher had obeyed that rule when she promised in 1979 to bring harmony out of discord. She had claimed in opposition that her party would have been "drummed out of office" if it had presided over unemployment of 1.3 million. But by the time of the 1983 election, despite convenient changes in statistical methodology, it was above 3 million. Yet when asked who was to blame for this, only a quarter of respondents replied that it was "mainly" the government's fault – despite the opinion of Friedman himself, who in March 1983 suggested that Britain had suffered "a much more severe recession than would have been necessary" because the government had failed to implement a coherent monetary policy. Whether or not Friedman was right, a significant section of the British people felt that the Thatcher government had shown the resolution which had been lacking during the 1970s. The conduct of the "Iron Lady" during the conflict with Argentina was now regarded as a vivid symbol of her performance in other fields. In reality, as Samuel Beer had noted before the war transformed public perceptions, "the Government had executed not one but several U-turns" compared to its pre-election commitments. But even so its most controversial measures had been carried out in obedience to doctrinaire considerations, so there was sufficient truth behind the "inflexible"

37. David Butler and Dennis Kavanagh, *The British General Election of 1983* (Macmillan, 1984), 40.

image to convince Conservative voters that Mrs Thatcher had laid to rest the memory of Heath's alleged vacillations.[38]

The "Falklands Factor" certainly helped to secure the Conservative victory of 9 June 1983, but the opinion polls had marked a slight revival before the islands were recaptured. A slow rise in manufacturing output began in the last months of 1981; over 1982 GDP grew by 1.5 per cent. Yet the recovery had been delayed by government policy which (as Peter Jay had feared in 1975) had turned out to be a form of "inverted Keynesianism" rather than monetarism as strictly defined. If the monetarists had been correct in their original view that Sterling M3 was the key indicator, inflation should have been above 10 per cent at the time of the election. But, as David Howell later explained, "the monetary aggregates were being shot to pieces by computerised banking, by far more sensitive and rapid movements of funds in and out of different financial institutions, and by the maddening perversity of the public in switching their funds around so as to seek the best rate of return". In short, it proved impossible to gain an accurate measure of Sterling M3, largely because of the policies of deregulation pursued by the Thatcher government and the tendency of many members of the public to behave as "rational" economic agents (i.e. in conformity to "Thatcherite" assumptions about human nature[39]). Thanks to the factors which really mattered – rising unemployment, high interest rates, falling world commodity prices and an over-valued pound – inflation was down to 3.7 per cent by May 1983. Monetarists could attempt a defence of their creed by reference to "time-lags" between changes in the money supply and adjustments in the inflation rate. As one commentator wrote in the *Spectator*, "a certain amount of innocent amusement can be derived from the sight of monetarists refudging figures, rephrasing their arguments and generally re-arranging the pieces"; but none of this would benefit the economy. Besides, the theory of time-lags rested on assumptions about economic causation derived from faith rather than reason. As Nicholas Kaldor had argued after the original monetarist "experiment" under Roy Jenkins, "Christmas may follow an expansion of the money supply but that does not mean that the latter is the cause of the former".[40]

Joseph's own faith was still unshakable. In September 1982 he flew to the United States to justify his government's actions before the Mont Pelerin Society (the elite international group for economic liberals). Joseph's paper on "The British Experiment in Monetary Policy" was judged "not entirely convincing" by an audience which included Hayek and Friedman. But the fate of a theoretical experiment was less important than a renewed sense of prosperity among many people who had retained their jobs. Relatively stable

---

38. Young, *One of Us,* 140, 319; Samuel Beer, *Britain Against Itself: The Political Contradictions of Collectivism* (Faber & Faber, 1982), 215.
39. David Howell, *Blind Victory: A Study of Income, Wealth and Power* (Hamish Hamilton, 1986), 33.
40. Tony Rudd in *Spectator*, 20 September 1980; Kaldor quoted in Thompson, "Economic Ideas and the Development of Economic Opinion", 67.

prices lured them back into the shops, and the removal of hire-purchase restrictions in July 1982 led to "a massive expansion of consumer and business credit". The ceiling on the tax relief for individual mortgage-holders was increased from £25,000 to £30,000 in Howe's 1983 Budget. As a result of these alluring concessions, "the period after mid-1982 saw an old-fashioned pre-election mini consumer boom of the classic post-war kind"; it heralded the British debut of what J. K. Galbraith later called "the culture of contentment". Galbraith's critique applied with greater force to Ronald Reagan's America, where most of the better-off voters received significant tax cuts (at the expense of a yawning Federal deficit). In Britain, only the top 1 per cent had solid grounds for feeling "contented". For everyone else, increases in indirect taxation wiped out any gains from the reduction of income tax. But a million new owner-occupiers had reasons to be cheerful; half of this increase was accounted for by the sale of council houses at up to 50 per cent discount under the terms of the 1980 Housing Act.[41]

The election produced an overall majority of 144 for the Conservatives. It seemed that the change in the "climate of opinion" that Joseph had worked for had come about. But the government's share of the vote had actually fallen by 2 per cent compared with 1979. Hailsham had worried about an "elective dictatorship" carried out by a party with a small parliamentary majority and minority support in the country. With hindsight that scenario looked relatively benign, because it offered the possibility that a few back-bench dissidents could veto extreme measures. Now the British voting system had produced a result which handed a controversial government the power to do almost whatever it liked. Yet since 1922 no Conservative administration had been returned with such a small percentage of support (42.4 per cent), and the size of the majority re-flected the fact that non-Conservatives were more divided than they had been since the days of Lloyd George, Asquith and Ramsay MacDonald. The new SDP/Liberal Alliance won more than a quarter of the vote, almost pushing Labour (27.6 per cent) into third place. In Leeds North-East, where Joseph was returned for the ninth time with a majority of almost 9,000, the SDP/Liberal Alliance pipped Labour as runners-up. Providing dramatic support for their own policy of electoral reform, the Alliance came second in 313 seats but returned only twenty-three MPs. Labour, fighting under Michael Foot on a platform broadly similar to that of February 1974, was perceived to be divided and extreme (a message which the Tory-dominated press was keen to disseminate).[42]

One feature of the 1983 election was the record number of Jewish Conservatives (seventeen) who were returned to the House of Commons. This

---

41. Gilmour, *Dancing with Dogma*, 54–5; Keegan, *Economic Experiment*, 177–8; Peter Riddell, *The Thatcher Government* (Martin Robertson, 1983), 72–3, 155.
42. Alan Sked and Chris Cook, *Post-War Britain: A Political History 1945–1992* (Penguin, 1993), 432.

was a product of a dramatic shift since 1966, when there were thirty-eight Jewish Labour MPs; by 1987 the figure was reduced to seven. The growing attractiveness of the Conservative Party to Jews has been explained by reference to "socio-economic influences", and a reaction against left-wing support for a Palestinian state. This is not to say that anti-Semitism had been eradicated within the Conservative Party, either at Westminster or among grass-roots activists. In January 1986 Leon Brittan, the Secretary of State for Trade and Industry, resigned after failing to secure back-bench approval of his role during the crisis over Westland Helicopters. He was described by "very senior Conservatives" as "behaving like a cornered rat" at the crucial meeting of the 1922 Committee; Peter Jenkins detected "unpleasant ripples" of racist sentiment among Brittan's tormentors. Undoubtedly Brittan had personal enemies inside the parliamentary party, and not all of the ill-feeling could be attributed to jealousy at what (until September 1985 when he was demoted from the Home Office) had been a rapid rise within the ministerial ranks. Nearly two years later Alan Clark reported a conversation in which a junior minister and a young back-bencher both denied that Nigel Lawson could become Foreign Secretary "as a Jew". Ian Gow, Mrs Thatcher's former PPS, became "very indignant" at this, but subsided into the limp protest that "he's not a practising Jew, anyway". Joseph remained unconscious of any anti-Semitic feeling against himself, and by this stage of his career he was recognised by critics and detractors alike for his beliefs rather than his background. But at least one politician had not forgotten Joseph's origins. When protesting to Lord Whitelaw about the effect of education policy on Scotland, Lord Boothby referred to Joseph as "a Jew from London". Boothby (himself a pro-Zionist of long standing) received a very brusque reply. But according to Clark, Whitelaw himself had been present at a private dinner during which someone had claimed that there were "too many jewboys in the Cabinet" (at the peak in early 1986 there were five, comfortably outnumbering the Old Harrovians (one)).[43]

Joseph scarcely featured in the 1983 campaign. He made one verbal slip, admitting that the last few days were "very nerve-wracking", and predicting that "It could still crumble". His remark betrayed a lack of confidence in the government's record; he, more than anyone, knew how vulnerable to searching analysis its performance had been.[44] But by now such exhibitions of brutal honesty were expected from Joseph, and compared to Rab Butler's similar

---

43. Geoffrey Alderman in *THES*, 10 July 1987; Peter Jenkins, *Mrs Thatcher's Revolution: The Ending of the Socialist Era* (Pan, 1988), 201; Rhodes James, *Boothby*, 445–6; Alan Clark, *Diaries* (Weidenfeld & Nicolson, 1993), 185, 133. Presumably Francis Maude's point about Lawson reflected the long-held notion that a Jewish Foreign Secretary would antagonise opinion in the Arab states.
44. Halcrow, *Joseph*, 176; In later years he could only say that the government's economic experiment had been conducted "within the electorate's tolerance": KJ, obituary of F. A. Hayek, *The Times*, 25 March 1992.

judgement of 1964 the remark barely registered with the press. His best-publicised contribution came late in May, when he refused to join a walkabout in Stockton South with the Conservative candidate Tom Finnegan. Finnegan had been a member of the National Front, an awkward fact that was not revealed until the morning of Sir Keith's visit. At another time Joseph might have hailed Finnegan as evidence for his claim that even "decent" people could flirt with the Front; after leaving the organisation Finnegan had become "a churchwarden, pillar of the local Rotary Club, and active in a host of local charities". But Joseph had to consider opinion within his constituency, and the wider interests of his party. He did, though, make a supportive speech in Stockton South. The press made much of the fact that he jumped down from the platform to deliver it, as if he would be contaminated by standing next to Finnegan. In fact, as Morrison Halcrow has rightly noted, Joseph often indulged in this kind of mobile oratory.[45]

Speculation about Joseph's future resumed after the election. A reshuffle sent Howe to the Foreign Office; Lawson took over at the Treasury, to be replaced at Energy by Peter Walker whose political skills helped the govenment to survive the year-long miners' strike of 1984–5. It was rumoured that Joseph might be appointed Chancellor of the Duchy of Lancaster or Minister Without Portfolio. But he was confirmed in his existing post, while Boyson left for the DHSS. In March 1984 Hailsham, the Cabinet's other survivor from the Macmillan years, delivered a speech at Cambridge that journalists interpreted as a plea for a well-deserved rest (less coverage was given to his characteristic quip that for him M3 was "only the designation of a motorway"). The close of the Lord Chancellor's long career of public service might have provided an appropriate opportunity for Joseph to step down, but Hailsham's remarks had been misinterpreted and both veterans stayed in the Cabinet. It was thought that an informal agreement had been reached with Mrs Thatcher; Joseph would continue in office for as long as the Prime Minister needed him.[46]

For a few months after the election little was heard from the DES. Joseph was faced with difficult decisions, on proposals to merge into one examination the "O" Levels and (much-criticised) CSE's currently taken by sixteen-year-olds, and on possible changes to the school curriculum. On the first of these his misgivings were fully endorsed by the Prime Minister; unless it was carefully managed, the introduction of continuous assessment in the new "GCSE's" could lead to a dilution of standards. Joseph was criticised for indecision since his predecessor had accepted the need for reform back in 1980, but eventually he allowed the change to go ahead, feeling that whatever the dangers the new examination would allow a better comparison of pupil performance across the

---

45. Halcrow, *Joseph*, 176–7; Parkinson, *Right at the Centre*, 230. In the event, Finnegan was narrowly defeated.
46. *New Society*, 28 January 1981; *Sunday Times*, 15 March 1984.

country.[47] The second issue presented an even greater dilemma for Joseph, who was troubled by the implications of state interference in the content of lessons. Problems with individual schools, brought to his attention by the Inspectors, led to further agonising and daily meetings with officials. Joseph was also plagued by proposals from local authorities to teach sixth-formers in separate colleges. Although this expedient was usually mooted as a means of saving money, Joseph instinctively disliked the trend and rejected several applications, regardless of whether the council was under Labour or Conservative control. Yet another time-consuming problem was whether or not to allow "voluntary-aided" status to single-religion schools – a decision which would qualify them for assistance from local authorities. In March 1984 he was criticised for denying this status to an Orthodox Jewish primary school in North London (an affirmative decision would have cost the ILEA £500,000 per year).[48]

An indecisive minister is rarely popular in his department, and Joseph's habit of asking the Treasury for extra cuts was unlikely to endear him to his officials. But his courtesy, combined with "his manifest integrity and intellectual honesty", ensured that relations at the DES were generally good, and some officials became fiercely loyal to their Secretary of State. David Hancock, who became Permanent Secretary in 1983, was impressed by Joseph's diligence; he thought that he had read every report from the Inspectors "which was more than I could claim". Determined to brief himself for every decision, Joseph was found on one occasion sitting at home reading biology textbooks in advance of a meeting on science funding. "You know, what these people have found is magnificent", he exclaimed when a friend intruded on his studies. On another occasion, after a tip-off that a key Open University (OU) social science course showed a clear Marxist bias (and said some rude things about monetarism) he requested and read all of the relevant teaching materials.[49] It might have been less time-consuming – and more useful – simply to visit the university. When he finally got round to this in July 1985 he seemed greatly impressed. But by then the OU, which Mrs Thatcher had saved from the axe in 1970, had suffered particularly severe cuts. Some of Joseph's fact-finding activities were less orthodox; often he slipped away from his officials to quiz schoolchildren about the abilities of their teachers, and on one occasion he asked a class of astonished thirteen-year-olds for their considered opinion of "integrated humanities in the middle years". He informed many groups of sixth-formers that instead of seeing employment or unemployment as the only alternatives for their future lives, they should also consider "self-employment and one day perhaps employer-ment" – i.e. taking on employees themselves. As he later

---

47. J. R. G. Tomlinson, "The Schools" in Kavanagh and Seldon (eds), *The Thatcher Effect*, 189.
48. *Sunday Times*, 16 March 1984.
49. *Sunday Times*, 1 July 1984; letter to authors from Sir David Hancock; Colin Hughes in *The Times*, 13 September 1984.

admitted, "That concept seemed unfamiliar to them". Interested in anything that might affect young minds, Joseph ordered a video of the BBC's *Grange Hill* when his chauffeur alerted him to the iniquities of that programme. He had no complaints after his viewing, but he remained ill at ease with the medium. When he visited BBC studios, for convenience his hosts provided him with five-minute excerpts from a variety of children's programmes. Joseph indicated his approval, "but was slightly bothered that the programmes were so short". Apart from obvious worries that television might provide poor guidance for the conduct of children, Joseph was concerned about grammar. "But surely it should be *You and I*?" he pointed out after sitting through a programme entitled *You and Me*.[50]

At the beginning of 1984 it seemed that Joseph had taken stock of his experiences and decided to pursue new tactics. Speaking to the North of England Education Conference in Sheffield, he surprised his audience with an address "literally decked with olive branches" for the teachers. Admitting that he had not fully appreciated at first the difficulties facing teachers – particularly those in inner-city schools – he asked "teachers, governors, local authority elected members and officers" to join him in a collective effort to achieve "constructive reform". It was a new version of his old "common ground" appeal; the remainder of the speech showed that Joseph was asking his opponents to share his own objectives, rather than offering a compromise with his critics. Education, he felt, should be geared to the needs of employers. Influenced by Lord Young and Correlli Barnett, he called for clear objectives and more "relevant" teaching.[51] Scepticism was expressed in some quarters, but the general response of the teaching unions provided further evidence that up to this time Joseph had badly misjudged the situation. There was widespread relief that everyone concerned might now move forward under a flag of truce. In an editorial comment, the *TES* claimed that "This was a new Sir Keith Joseph, and one who needs to be greeted with applause, not snide recollections of past insensitivity". Ted Wragg, previously one of Joseph's leading academic critics, admitted that "He's very close to uttering sense".[52]

But Joseph continued to listen to advisors who told him that education was failing Britain, and statistical evidence seemed to prove that the nation was lagging further behind its competitors. Despite his declared reservations about social science methodology, Joseph was easily convinced when confronted with figures that backed his intuitive judgements. In 1984 these were refreshed when his PPS George Walden told him "that British schools were self-indulgent, that

50. *Open House*, 7 August 1985; *The Times*, 20 May 1986; *Sunday Times*, 27 April 1986; *House of Lords Debates*, vol. 539, col. 232, 15 July 1992; interview with Ted Wragg. We are most grateful to Professor Wragg for reading and commenting on this chapter.
51. Knight, *Tory Education Policy*, 169.
52. *TES*, 13 January 1984; *Sunday Times*, 22 April 1984.

they were anti-business and anti-industrialist".[53] The "new" Joseph turned out to be a prototype, which was locked in the hangar after its maiden flight. By the time of the 1984 Conservative conference at Brighton he was back to his old form, praising "the good intentions and the hard work of teachers" before presenting the prosecution case:

> There are complaints of lack of discipline; there are complaints of illiteracy; there are complaints of innumeracy; there are complaints . . . of bias. Employers complain that young people do not have an understanding attitude towards the imperatives of work, the imperatives of satisfying the consumer. Her Majesty's Inspectors of Schools are constantly emphasising in their reports, which we now publish, that teachers have far too low expectations of what pupils should be able to achieve.

Some allies had warned Joseph that the Inspectorate was itself "infected" with "progressive" ideas.[54] For Joseph this suspicion merely added weight to its findings when these turned out to be critical. In showing his faith in the Inspectorate Joseph was setting another trend for his successors, although he cannot be blamed for the animosity towards the teaching profession that the body evinced after its privatisation in the early 1990s. Given his views on public spending Joseph could not admit that better funding was a key element in solving the education crisis he perceived. Even when he witnessed at first hand the deteriorating fabric of Britain's schools he refused to be moved; he remembered being taught in surroundings which were less than perfect, and no one ever suffered. He once even denied that education ought to be regarded as an "investment" for the future, without giving any reasons for rejecting this basic rationale for any system of education, public or private. No doubt this was another example – like his earlier question about television being "here to stay" – of the All Souls Fellow challenging accepted wisdom, not in order to subvert it but to force others to think through their unreflective assumptions. But when reported out of context such comments increased concerns about Joseph's long-term vision. Even a Conservative MP who knew him well wondered if he was serious when he speculated in private about the abolition of all state education.[55]

By the time of the 1984 party conference at Brighton Joseph's performance at Education was approved by only a quarter of voters (although at least he was two points ahead of Tebbit (back at Industry) and Whitelaw (Deputy Prime Minister)).[56] Trouble with the teachers erupted before the end of the year; the wonder

---

53. Quoted in Knight, *Tory Education Policy*, 172.
54. Letwin, *Anatomy of Thatcherism*, 234.
55. John Fairhall in *Guardian*, 4 June 1985; letter to authors from the late Sir Robert Rhodes James.
56. *Sunday Times*, 7, 14 October 1984.

was that it had been so long delayed. A less predictable blow had fallen just before his speech at Brighton, when an IRA bomb exploded in the Grand Hotel on the night of 11 October. The device was placed in a sixth-floor bedroom; the killed and injured were staying directly above and below the blast. Joseph's room was on the sixth floor, but some distance from the site of the bomb. Although the first reports in America named him among the fatalities, he was entirely unscathed. He slept through the explosion – probably having taken sleeping pills – and was escorted from the shattered building. Watching the immediate aftermath on television, Alan Clark was struck by the image of an "indestructable" Joseph "wandering about in a burgundy-coloured dressing-gown, bleating". Semtex was no more likely to daunt "Smokey Joe" than the eggs, flour and chips had done; but though he held his own life cheaply he was stunned by the unexpected assault on the lives of colleagues, their wives, and, above all, his leader. Half-way down the fire escape Joseph remembered his dispatch box, which he retrieved and used as a seat on the promenade. The fabric of his elegant dressing-gown (mistakenly identified as silk) provided some light-hearted relief for commentators on such a dreadful day. Once the immediate shock subsided, "tremendous grief" for dead and injured friends took over. Joseph's speech had been lost, and while a new one was being drafted by officials he found it difficult to read through his tears. As the victims recovered, Sir Keith was among their most regular visitors.[57]

The Brighton outrage strengthened still further the emotional ties between Joseph and Margaret Thatcher. "I beam at the very sight of her", he gushed a few months later.[58] Back-benchers might have shared Clark's sympathy with Joseph, begowned and bewildered on Brighton promenade. But within two months of the bomb they were laying down a murderous barrage of their own against the Secretary of State, and the Prime Minister's loyal friendship was more important to him than ever.

Back in the summer of 1984 Joseph had discussed his Departmental budget with Peter Rees, the Chief Secretary to the Treasury. Although in a well-functioning market economy scientific research would have been far more likely to attract private money than the subjects covered by the ESRC, Joseph had listened to protests from academics that the funding cuts they had suffered would have catastrophic effects on the future of British industry. He had always been vulnerable to the voice of expertise, and he was easily convinced in an area of which he knew only enough to be aware of his ignorance. Having decided to protect the science community from these "grievous" cuts he looked around for compensatory savings within his overall budget, rather than asking the Chancellor to dip into his war-chest.[59] The idea he hit upon had been floated

---

57. Clark, *Diaries*, 99; private information; interview with Stuart Sexton.
58. *THES*, 11 January 1985.
59. "Grievous" was the word Joseph used when discussing the cuts in private conversation; interview with Ted Wragg.

in his first few months at Education. The minimum student grant of £205 per year, awarded to those from the most affluent families, would be scrapped. The contributions to maintenance due from others "in the middle and upper reaches of the income scale" would be increased, and the richest would have to pay up to £520 per year towards the tuition fee. The latter proposal breached an important principle of British higher education – that the teaching should be provided free of charge, whatever the parental contribution towards living expenses. The overall saving was estimated at around £40 million, half of which would be put towards protecting the worst-off from earlier grant cuts, with the rest going to science. The Treasury was always glad to do business with a minister who offered to finance his own initiatives, and the package was agreed without much discussion.[60]

As soon as Joseph announced the changes, on 12 November 1984, protests poured in to Conservative MPs from infuriated middle-class parents. Their elected representatives – who in many cases would be hit equally hard by the measure – made known their grave dissatisfaction. The party was attacking its own core supporters; as one minister put it, "We've now managed to shoot ourselves in both feet". A motion deploring the changes was tabled, and eventually signed by 180 MPs – more than half of the parliamentary party. Although the question presented Labour with some tactical difficulties – as one ex-MP argued, Joseph could be regarded as a "secret socialist" for proposing a measure which "could well have been introduced by a Labour minister of education" – the Opposition parties sensed the mood and joined the attack. An embarrassing Commons defeat loomed before the government – and a key by-election was pending in Enfield, Southgate.[61]

Very late on the evening of 3 December Joseph spoke on the Local Government Bill which would abolish his own creation, the GLC. He had fought for, and secured, a reprieve for the ILEA, which would now be directly elected; a single education authority in London was needed, he felt, because so many pupils attended schools outside their home boroughs. But in isolation it was difficult enough for him to explain his views on the GLC; the fact that while he was speaking the Whitehall gossips were predicting his own abolition made it an appalling test of nerve. But he met the challenge without flinching, despite a tricky moment early on when he recalled a book from his childhood called *Gobbo Bobbo – or the One-Eyed Griffin* – relevant because it had contained a brisk attack on the old London County Council. He hastily abandoned his story when, in response to his revelation that the book featured a witch named "Bordibus Skulibus", Labour members yelled "She's not here tonight".[62]

---

60. *Hansard*, vol. 69, col. 360, 5 December 1984.
61. Christopher Price in *The Times*, 8 December 1984; *Financial Times*, 1 December 1984.
62. *Hansard*, vol. 69, col. 126, 3 December 1984; Ian Aitken in *Guardian*, 7 December 1984.

Joseph had met the Conservative back-bench education committee earlier that day to discuss his student grant proposals. It was reported that the minister was "non-committal and gave no indication of any compromise". During Education Questions on 4 December "he seemed almost relaxed" as he replied to his Conservative critics "with the objectivity of a university don conducting a tutorial".[63] But on the same evening he once again faced the education committee, and this time the meeting, in the "cavernous" Committee Room 14, was thrown open to all Tory MPs. Around 250 accepted the invitation; it was thought to be the largest such gathering since the Falklands. Back in April 1982 a vicious attack had prompted the resignation of the Foreign Secretary, Lord Carrington. After the meeting of 4 December 1984 it was generally agreed that although the treatment meted out to Carrington had been the worst in living memory Joseph had suffered a comparable mauling. MPs had been angered by another opaque address from the Secretary of State, who promised a new statement but concealed its likely contents. When William Benyon told Joseph to scrap the whole idea his colleagues regressed to their own student days, cheering and banging on desks. One former minister declared afterwards that he could "still smell the blood"; another, dragging himself away early, reported that "It is going very well; they are 99 per cent against him". Judged by those who actually spoke this arithmetic was slightly inaccurate; of the thirty-three contributions, three were thought to have offered the minister "guarded support". Later, while casting a series of votes on the GLC Bill, Joseph was subjected to further harassment by Tory MPs demanding a climb-down on the grants issue.[64]

"Bordibus Skulibus" and her Chancellor, Lawson, were ready to come to terms with the back-bench rebels. Lawson was particularly discomfited by the furore, feeling that the original agreement between Joseph and the Treasury had slipped past the usual Cabinet machinery for detecting "banana skins". He believed that Joseph's role in the affair had made matters worse, because the back-benchers "had always suspected that Keith had no political judgement".[65] Now there seemed to be no way of avoiding a serious slip. The back-benchers were demanding an immediate retreat and had the numerical strength to defeat the government, but the Prime Minister was sensitive to any hint of a U-turn and on this occasion Labour would be able to claim that she had flinched from conflict with "her own people", who were held to have benefitted so much from her tax cuts. To add a further complication, Mrs Thatcher had no desire to help students, who had held a demonstration in London which led to over a hundred arrests and ugly clashes with police. Those who marched on that day

---

63. John Hunt in *Financial Times*, 5 December 1984.
64. Ian Aitken in *Guardian*, 5 December 1984; Anthony Bevins in *The Times*, 5 December 1984; Adam Raphael in *Observer*, 2 December 1984.
65. Nigel Lawson, *The View from No.11: Memoirs of a Tory Radical* (Bantam, 1992), 309.

remembered that the students were more sinned against than sinning, but the reaction of the Conservative press showed that the revolt of Middle England against Joseph's measures was not based on deep sympathy for youngsters who were assumed to have more money and independence than was good for them.[66] As one of Joseph's lonely champions had pointed out to his fellow back-benchers, it would be difficult to defend cuts that affected pensioners "when the Conservatives refused to contemplate charging more to the better-off members of the community". For some, the furore over a few million pounds exposed problems that went to the heart of the government's programme. During the rowdy meeting one speaker was cheered when he questioned the overall strategy of paying for tax reductions through expenditure cuts. In the *Guardian* Peter Jenkins emphasised this general theme, claiming that "the Government is the victim of its own dogma and the crude procedures it has devised for their implementation".[67]

Joseph's future once again seemed to hang in the balance. Conflicting stories appeared in the press about his intentions should he be forced to give way. Years later he confirmed that he offered his resignation because he was proving an embarrassment; apparently the Prime Minister told him "not to be ridiculous".[68] At a meeting held at Number 10 on the morning of 5 December a face-saving formula was devised. As Joseph told the House that afternoon, the proposal to charge tuition fees would be withdrawn, at a cost to the Treasury of £21 million. But he stood by the rest of his package, and more than half of the cost of his concession would be covered by additional cuts. To the dismay of the scientific community – whose "desperate plight" Joseph had recently acknowledged in public – they would lose £3 million from their augmented research budget. Latching on to arguments advanced in previous debates, Joseph explained that his partial retreat had been made in consideration of the need for the parents of students to plan their financial commitments in advance. Some critics, including Joseph's former PPS Patrick Cormack, were not deflected by his arguments (which were a little ironic, at a time of high and rising unemployment when confident forward planning was already impossible for so many families). But a majority of back-benchers was strongly supportive. Joseph's warm reception testified not to the generosity of his concession but to the elation of back-benchers who were astonished at their ability to bend the government's will even slightly. Andrew MacKay, who had made the point about the hardship facing parents on the previous day, hailed a "very healthy day for democracy". According to Ian Aitken, other back-benchers now felt thoroughly ashamed of the "*auto-da-fé*" in Committee Room 14. The relief spread to Enfield, Southgate, where Tory canvassers had joined the pleas for a

---

66. Private information.
67. *Guardian*, 5 December 1984.
68. Halcrow, *Joseph*, 183.

change in policy, and the Liberals had distributed leaflets that exaggerated the likely costs to an electorate with a majority of middle-income families. The Conservative candidate Michael Portillo retained the seat for his party.[69]

According to the *Observer*, "it was hard not to feel sorry" for Joseph as he delivered his statement. Although Lawson and Mrs Thatcher emphasised their support by sitting on either side of him on the front-bench, "His head was bowed, and his hoarse voice held a familiar note of plangent regret, like a toff down on his luck asking the Bench for one last chance".[70] The husky voice was the product of another of Joseph's marathon duels with the common cold; the posture might have been meek, but the spirit was undaunted. When Tory MPs recovered from the intoxication of victory, it dawned on them that they had hardly gained a foot of ground. They noticed that having defused one booby-trap for the party Joseph had promptly laid another one, promising a review of the whole system of student finance – which might lead to the introduction of loans. Certainly Joseph had avoided the anticipated drubbing without having to consume more than a medium slice of humble pie, and once the ordeal was over he thanked Lawson "for helpfulness at a crucial time – and for decisiveness". The Chancellor was grateful for this characteristic message, but resolved to prevent any similar fiascos by bringing "politically controversial savings" to the attention of the full Cabinet in future. At the time of the crisis Mrs Thatcher's mood was described as "sulphurous"; on 4 December, she had travelled to the Commons after a Dublin summit meeting, and engaged in some angry exchanges with Joseph's critics. Now she felt that she had discharged her duty. Four months after the dust had settled she told a reporter that she had been away when Joseph made his first announcement, and realised his mistake as soon as she had a chance to look at the details. She had no desire to reopen the battle over loans, and when in the New Year Joseph worked out a new proposal with Lawson's assistance they found her "implacably opposed". Joseph, Lawson recalled, "had a terrible time" at this meeting. It was another reminder of the difference between the Prime Minister and her friend; the "instinct" which had led her to embrace economic liberalism was also able (on occasion) to tell her when she should let go.[71]

The public rumpus over the campus lasted less than a month, but it was immediately succeeded by a classroom rift of far longer duration. While Joseph was battling to save his plans for student grants, talks with the teaching unions broke down on a 4 per cent pay deal, offered in return for clearly defined contractual duties and a revision of the career structure to reflect more closely

---

69. *Hansard*, vol. 69, cols 360–1, 5 December 1984; *Guardian*, 5 November 1984; Michael Gove, *Michael Portillo: The Future of the Right* (Fourth Estate, 1995), 123–4.
70. *Observer*, 9 December 1984.
71. *Hansard*, vol. 69, col. 361, 5 December 1984; Lawson, *View from No. 11*, 309, 601; *Guardian*, 7 December 1984; *The Times*, 11 April 1985.

the abilities of individual teachers. The dispute was still unsettled when Joseph left office a year and a half later. Teachers were prepared for a long war of attrition, and devised a plan of school disruption which avoided any loss of pay. Joseph's bargaining position seemed weaker, given the imminent introduction of the new GSCE courses and his drive for higher standards, re-emphasised in March 1985 with the publication of his ambitious White Paper, *Better Schools*. Even an expert negotiator with a flair for public relations would have struggled to find a satisfactory settlement; the unions were divided amongst themselves, and disagreements between their local authority paymasters increased the complexity of Joseph's task. Memories of his adamantine conduct during the steel strike, and grievances arising from his first years at Education, reduced the chances of a compromise to vanishing point. Joseph was soon accused of blocking the local authorities in their attempts to secure a deal; later he stood out against arbitration (although it was urged on him by his predecessor, Carlisle), and reduced union representation on the official negotiating body, the Burnham Committee. Whenever Joseph came up with better terms – as he did after a tense Cabinet meeting in July 1985 – teachers could be certain that a less miserly minister would have asked for more. The presentation of his case was not helped by decisions outside his control. In July 1985 he spoke to a local authority conference in the wake of a 48 per cent pay award to top civil servants. Struck by the contrast with Joseph's handling of teachers, his audience (which included councillors of all parties) punctuated his address with cries of "shame" and "crap". When Joseph visited a school in Berkshire towards the end of the first year of deadlock, a hundred parents offered to take the place of teachers demonstrating outside. Asked on his arrival whether he had seen the *ad hoc* picket-line, Joseph replied that he had been asleep in his car; he was getting less than four hours' sleep every night, he confided. When he spoke to the teaching staff he seemed to be on the verge of tears. But his opponents were unmoved by his pleas on behalf of Britain's children; they felt that these arguments would be better used in negotiations with the Treasury for a better pay deal.[72]

Constant rumours of a government reshuffle did nothing to mollify the teachers. As the months dragged by, resentment at Joseph's surprising durability was added to the ill-feeling aroused by his policies. Lady Thatcher's memoirs indicate that Joseph was ready to retire in September 1985; at that time it seems that she offered the Education post to Lord Gowrie, but he declined. Four months later Joseph took unilateral action. At the end of January 1986, in a "cold and crowded Scout hut" in Leeds, he announced that he would not be standing at the next election. It was his constituency Annual General Meeting, and he felt that he could not allow the meeting to pass without making his intentions clear. Fittingly, the weather was as bleak as it had been thirty years

---

72. *The Times*, 20 July 1985; *Guardian*, 26 November 1985.

before, when Joseph had first won Leeds North-East. The news had leaked out in advance, and prior to his speech Joseph strayed near a television set which was showing a potted summary of his career. "It's like watching my own obituary!" he remarked as he hurried out of the room. At the venue several photographers had gathered, and as they rushed around on the ice to secure the best vantage points Joseph asked them to be careful because he would not like to have any injuries on his conscience. Clearly enjoying himself, Joseph then embarked on one of his more convoluted speeches, ensuring that most of the reporters had gone home before he came to the announcement of his impending retirement.[73]

But even this decision failed to persuade Mrs Thatcher that her servant should be allowed to depart in peace. It was rumoured that Joseph would not leave Education until he had achieved a settlement with the teachers, a suggestion which infuriated union leaders who were praying for the appointment of a more flexible successor. When Joseph spoke to the National Association of Schoolmasters/Union of Women Teachers (NAS/UWT) union in Scarborough on 3 April 1986, feelings boiled over against the weary minister. Struggling with yet another cold, Joseph told his audience that he was "appalled by the damage to the education of children deliberately inflicted by some teachers". When he had finished, applause came only from one "lonely, hesitant" delegate, who was soon hushed. During questions Joseph was told that he had "completely lost the confidence of the teaching profession"; a motion to that effect had been passed during the morning session, when one of the less civilised speakers had compared him to "a drowned rat". He tried his usual approach, saying that he had "constantly praised good teachers", but this evaded the main point, which was that he had always given equal emphasis to the supposed failings of an unquantified minority. He asked his audience "if it would be right to seek the confidence of the teaching profession and forget the interests of the children", as if conflict between the two were inevitable.[74]

It seemed that this sterile encounter could be the final straw for Joseph, who was being badgered on his other flank by the die-hard voucher supporters (Mrs Thatcher had rather tactlessly refloated the idea back in July 1985). During Education Questions in the House five days after the Scarborough conference, he referred to the DES with curious detachment, as "the department of which I am at present the head". At the same time Mrs Thatcher, in a scornful reply to a demand from Labour's Giles Radice for Joseph's resignation, claimed that her friend had done more to raise standards and to promote debate about education

---

73. Thatcher, *Downing Street Years*, 420; *The Times*, 4 April 1986; private information. Among those who wrote privately to Joseph after the announcement was Lord Stockton, the former Harold Macmillan, whose references to the loss which British politics had incurred showed that despite all his criticisms of monetarism, and his regular quips about his former colleague, he had retained a high opinion of Joseph's abilities (private information).
74. *TES*, 11 April 1986.

than any of his predecessors – a list which included Rab Butler, not to mention the Prime Minister herself. Given the persistent speculation, this eulogy could be taken as the verbal equivalent of a gold watch for Joseph. It was uncontestable that he had lasted longer than most of his predecessors – longer, indeed, than anyone since George Tomlinson who ended an anonymous stint in November 1951, and a year longer than Butler. In *The Times* Ronald Butt argued that Joseph should now retire to the pavilion to reflect on his long innings, and to give a successor the chance to play himself in before the next election.[75]

Yet Joseph's choice of words in the Commons had no more significance than proving once again that he had a strange way of talking about himself in light-hearted moments. On other occasions he had gone still further, referring to the House of Commons as his address "for the moment". While others were writing him off he was planning future initiatives. He told a Cabinet sub-committee of his intention to launch radical new proposals in advance of the next party conference. In an interview for the BBC on 6 April 1986 he revealed the tendency of his thoughts, grumbling that "the holder of my office has very, very much less influence than he or she had in 1944 and the years following that . . . I do think that the Government, which is accountable to the public for the performance of education, should have more influence than it does now". These sentiments echoed a recent speech by Chris Patten, once again in harness with Joseph as Minister of State at the DES. At a teachers' conference, which recorded one last vote of no confidence in the Secretary of State, Patten made a significant allusion to other countries (such as France) that had "a national service, centrally directed and controlled".[76]

Taken together, these statements made explicit a trend in education policy which had alarmed "decentralisers" like Boyson throughout Joseph's tenure of the office. In *Accountable to None* Simon Jenkins describes Sir Keith's time at Education as a "passive phase" before the arrival of Kenneth Baker. Certainly Joseph argued in Cabinet against the idea of removing local authorities from the education system. But while Baker undoubtedly whizzed up several gears – and others, notably Nigel Lawson, wanted to go even faster – Joseph set the juggernaut in motion. The man who pronounced the word "statist" with a shudder presided over "a massive shift towards central control of education"; one expert has even described Joseph as resembling "nothing so much as some modernising and absolute monarch of the eighteenth century" at Education. Joseph had announced himself as a hands-on Secretary of State from the outset, and his fingers were always fidgeting. Soon after his appointment a journalist asked him how he was settling into his new job; "I haven't found the levers

---

75. *The Times*, 9 April 1986; *Guardian*, 7 April 1986; Butt in *The Times*, 27 March 1986.
76. *The Times*, 7 April 1986; *TES*, 11 April 1984.

yet", he replied. In another early interview he had admitted that he was "perturbed by things which I do not control". Had the DES dealt directly with the education system, instead of acting through "intermediate bodies" like local authorities, the "levers" would not have been so elusive; the solution, for someone as determined as Joseph to leave his mark on Britain's children, was to increase his powers of intervention. As one of Joseph's successors put it, the Secretary of State for Education merely existed "to hand out the money and to take the blame". In these circumstances central government, rather than the local authorities, the unions or individual schools, should have a decisive influence over the training, pay and working conditions of teachers. Under Joseph, the Department of Education began to attach conditions to its funding to Local Education Authorities; money would only be disbursed if it was used for specific purposes.[77]

While the Thatcher governments have often been criticised for their centralising tendency, in Education the logic seemed irresistible. Yet Joseph was still reluctant to dictate the content of lessons. At a Politics Association conference in Brighton he expressed agreement with Bernard Crick's advocacy of political education, adding that he thought that this should be included in the curriculum along with economics, "social service and volunteering". A blind teacher challenged Joseph to make these subjects compulsory. "'God forbid', Sir Keith replied, 'that any English minister of Education should ever make any subject complulsory'; but he hastily added, as his private secretary leapt at his ear, 'except religious observance, of course'". After the conference Joseph and the teacher, David Blunkett, travelled home in the same standard-class railway carriage; their debate, conducted at high volume, continued for the entire journey.[78]

But Joseph found it difficult to live within the terms of his self-denying oath. Merely by setting guidelines for the curriculum he established a precedent for the compulsion subsequently introduced by Baker. He had always been ready to offer an opinion on certain courses, notably the "Peace Studies" which produced regular protests from the Right. On his last day in office he gave at length his views on "ethnically-mixed education", acknowledging that the British tradition was a blend of many cultures but that every school should now "transmit to all its pupils a sense of shared national values and traditions" rather than focusing on minority cultures. Back in 1973 he had told the Zionist Federation Education Trust that he saw no difficulty with separate schools for Jewish children; if he still held that view, his pronouncement of May 1986

---

77. *Sunday Times*, 22 April 1984; Simon Jenkins, *Accountable to None: The Tory Nationalisation of Britain* (Hamish Hamilton, 1995), 115; *TES*, 12 February 1982; Lawson, *View from No. 11*, 603; Ken Jones, *Right Turn: The Conservative Revolution in Education* (Hutchinson Radius, 1989), 18; *Guardian*, 27 May 1986; Peter Riddell in *The Times*, 12 December 1994; interview with Kenneth Clarke.
78. Information kindly supplied by Bernard Crick.

implied that such schools ought to include lessons on British culture in their curricula.[79] He began the process which would lead to the regular testing of students and national "league tables" of school performance, and also broke new ground by advising teachers on the setting of homework for their pupils. Other centralising measures being discussed within the DES in the spring of 1986 included the establishment of direct-grant schools outside local authority control, an extension of the Assisted Places Scheme (by this time covering 25,000 children) and the vocational training provided by the MSC, a new system of state funding for the polytechnics, more control over teacher training, and plans for a much greater involvement of businessmen in education.[80] Most of these ideas had Joseph's warm approval; to others he would only have put up a half-hearted resistance. Max Wilkinson's "Lessons from Europe" had not been thrown away on Sir Keith Joseph; the lack of central direction was identified in that pamphlet as the overriding reason for Britain's educational shortcomings compared to the performance of its European neighbours, and there is a remarkable coincidence between Wilkinson's proposals and DES policy initiatives under Joseph.[81]

During his final months in government Sir Keith mused about the legacy he would leave at the Department. Many of his remarks to interviewers began with the phrase "I would like to be remembered as the Secretary of State who . . .". With typical modesty, in retirement he thought that he had done no more than to "lay the foundations" for an improvement in standards. This judgement was echoed by a senior civil servant, who predicted that "in 30 years' time people will think differently about him". *Better Schools* was designed as a blueprint for education in the twenty-first century. The key points were further revisions of the examination system, more emphasis on vocational learning, better teacher training, more consistency in the curriculum, and greater influence for parents on school governing bodies. Much of this was implemented in the 1986 Education Act, which also abolished corporal punishment (in line with European law, but in opposition to Joseph's own wishes). In the *Sunday Times* Peter Wilby hailed a "coherent, consistent programme that tackles the major weaknesses in the educational system". The Secretary of State had transcended the simplistic

---

79. *Guardian*, 21 May 1986; among other things, his statement indicated yet another ground for disagreement with the voucher lobby, since that system of funding would encourage people from minority backgrounds who wished to set up separate schools that would transmit distinctive cultural ideas. It was typical of Joseph that he should only produce this argument when he was about to leave the Department of Education. Cf. *Jewish Chronicle*, 22 June 1973.
80. Raison, *Tories and the Welfare State*, 132; Lucy Hodges in *The Times*, 21 May 1986; Baker, *Turbulent Years*, 124; 160–1.
81. For example, Wilkinson suggested regular formal testing; national guidelines for the standards expected of children between the ages of seven and thirteen; "detailed curricular guidelines in different subjects, including suggestions for a common core of studies for the majority of children"; a more intrusive role for HM Inspectorate of Schools; and advice on homework. See *Lessons from Europe*, 123.

debates between "traditionalists" and "progressives" which had continued in spite of Callaghan's pioneering speech; he had distanced himself from those who demanded "excessive direction" from teachers, and called for pupils to be given the opportunity "to express their own views and to develop their ideas through discussion". But Wilby understood the hostility that Joseph's plans had inspired in teachers, for five reasons. Joseph had "tried to do too much at once"; where other ministers might have given in to opposition from vested interests he had imposed decisions; he had allowed ideology to drive some of his detailed suggestions (predictably, his suggestions on economics had been "littered with references to 'entrepreneurship', 'markets' and 'profits'"); he had concentrated too much power at the centre; and, above all, even in the well-received White Paper he had been unable to resist gratuitous digs at the teaching profession. With its mixture of insight and insensitivity, *Better Schools* was a fitting memorial to Joseph's spell at Education.[82]

In higher education Joseph's legacy was enshrined in the Green Paper of May 1985, *The Development of Higher Education into the 1990s*, which called for an increase in the proportion of graduates studying "vocational" subjects such as engineering, and envisaged a decline of 14 per cent in the student population between 1990 and 1997. It was difficult to see how this projection squared with Joseph's efforts to raise standards in schools; if the drive produced the desired results, there would be a dramatic rise in the number of bright, qualified young people who would have to abandon their studies at eighteen. In a document which David Watt described as "uniformly grey, narrow, niggling, and bureaucratic", it was deemed "not improbable that some institutions of higher education will need to be closed or merged at some point over the next 10 years". Those institutions which survived would be divided into two tiers, with research concentrated in selected "centres of excellence". Joseph had pointed the way towards the determination of funding levels for departments by measuring the relative quality of their research output; the system was to be applied across the board, even in arts and social sciences where the problems of appraising research are particularly acute. According to one recent study, this process has imposed a "Stalinist culture" in higher education; in a general context of spending cuts, it has meant that more academics are producing books and articles but university libraries lack the money to buy them. Academics who felt that they should not intrude their thoughts on the world before prolonged reflection were shouldered aside by colleagues who were more productive, although not necessarily more erudite. And the appraisal system gave free play to old jealousies, so that in some subjects the greatest value was placed on publications of least interest to the general reader.[83]

---

82. KJ interview with Anthony Seldon, 30; *Sunday Times*, 31 March 1985.
83. Ferdinand Mount (ed.), *The Inquiring Eye: A Selection of the Writings of David Watt* (Penguin, 1988), 247–9; Peter Dorey (ed.), *The Major Premiership: Politics and Policies under John Major 1990–97* (Macmillan, 1999), 162.

Although David Watt thought that Joseph's proposals betrayed a "bleak accountant's view of higher education", some attempt was made to counter critics who accused the government of "philistinism". If education failed to service a dynamic economy, it was argued, there would be no money to support "education for pleasure and general culture". Joseph had forced higher education to "take a hard, cool look at itself and its role in society". This was not sufficient to protect Joseph from the wrath of Enoch Powell, who asked his former colleague "to recognise that it is barbarism to attempt to evaluate the contents of higher education in terms of economic performance, or to set a value upon the consequences of higher education in terms of monetary cost-benefit analysis". The Fellow of All Souls could find no better response than to jeer that Powell's attack convinced him all the more that his existing policies were right. The MP and scholar Robert Rhodes James resigned from his post as an advisor to Joseph in disgust at a Green Paper which he considered to be "not only illiterate but innumerate". The DES, Rhodes James stormed, had no understanding of the purpose of a university. In April 1986 the *Salisbury Review* carried an article by the philosopher, Anthony O'Hear which denounced an educational "utilitarianism" that was "likely to be destructive of humane sensibility". Joseph stood accused of "seeking to produce a population ready only to fulfil technological functions". The *Review* was the authentic voice of social conservatism – the constituency which had applauded Joseph since his Edgbaston speech. Later it was suggested that Joseph had been upset by the reaction to the Green Paper, and that he "secretly feared" the destruction of a long British tradition of academic achievement. This was true; but he had kept his secret very effectively. Although Joseph did allow the UGC to protect a whole generation of academics from annihilation by the introduction of "New Blood" posts, this was made into a back-door attack on the independence of the universities, which had to bid for the money and were told to forget any thought of recruiting new social scientists. Rhodes James thought that Joseph's attitude to academic staff was as negative as his view of school teachers; while one enthusiast claimed that Thatcherism "insisted that the skills of businessmen were as worthy of respect as those of dons", the record suggested that the latter were esteemed even less than other public servants. By the time that Joseph left office, the pay of a junior lecturer had fallen behind that of the police and nurses at comparable levels. In a speech on the theme of technology, a senior official from Joseph's old Department of Industry joked that there was a new test for artificial intelligence, which any computer would pass if it recognised that there was a missing letter "i" in the fourth word of the sentence "Sir Keith Joseph runs British universities".[84]

---

84. *Hansard*, vol.79, col. 861, 21 May 1985; *THES*, 23 May 1986; *Sunday Times*, 22 December 1985; correspondence with the late Sir Robert Rhodes James; Letwin, *Anatomy of Thatcherism*, 343; Anthony O'Hear, "Education Beyond Present Desire", in *Salisbury Review*, April 1986; Scott in *The Thatcher Effect*, 203, 208; Jenkins, *Accountable to None*, 141; *Guardian*, 2 April 1986.

Understandably, Joseph would have liked to depart when a few more bricks had been placed on his foundations. But a reshuffle was planned for the autumn of 1986, and having lamed himself by announcing his intention to leave the Commons it was unthinkable that he should hobble on through yet another round of Cabinet changes. Much later it emerged that Joseph had wanted to retire from the government at the same time as his announcement at Leeds North-East.[85] He had only agreed to stay on because the Prime Minister was more desperate than ever for his staunch support. The Conservatives, and Mrs Thatcher in particular, had started 1986 with a near disaster. Michael Heseltine's resignation over Westland in January, and the subsequent recriminations, left the Prime Minister deeply unsettled if not quite unseated. In the same month the government published another Green Paper, which recommended a community charge to replace the rates. Already dubbed the "poll tax", this reform was received with the strange fatalism that seems to have affected the British electorate in the mid-80s; if the immediate outcry had been greater, perhaps the ultimate consequences would have been less dramatic. In a Cabinet sub-committee Joseph applauded the element of accountability in the new tax. But he did register some unease, to the extent of arguing (unsuccessfully) that students should be exempted.[86]

Mrs Thatcher encountered fresh trouble in February, over the proposed sale of Land Rover and other profitable parts of BL. By early 1986 the company's performance had been transformed, due to energetic management and a collaboration with Honda of Japan which had been planned while Joseph was at Industry (Joseph, indeed, had wanted Honda to buy the company outright). But the Thatcher government, so used to the taste of policy failure, now discovered that success can turn sour. Two American companies, General Motors and Ford, wanted to buy Land Rover, but the sale was called off after a rebellion by thirty Tory MPs, for whom "nationalism proved a more potent ideology than privatisation". Another mutiny, against a Bill to legalise Sunday trading, led to a defeat for the government on 14 April. That same night, American planes flew from British bases on a mission to bomb Libya.[87]

As Party Chairman Norman Tebbit was bound to be uneasy at repeated blows to the government's standing, notably a resounding defeat on 11 April at a by-election in Fulham, near Joseph's home. But there were more personal reasons for grievance. In particular, Tebbit had not been consulted about Libya, which he felt had given Mrs Thatcher's opponents the chance to make capital out of her perceived deference to President Reagan. Sensational rumours began to circulate, that furious ministers who had only been informed about Libya twelve hours after the raid had begun were planning a *coup* against Mrs

85. Baker, *Turbulent Years*, 160.
86. *The Times*, 14 January 1986; Baker, *Turbulent Years,* 124.
87. Young, *One of Us*, 500; private information.

Thatcher. Whoever was behind the stories, they made fascinating reading. On 22 April, for example, the *Sunday Times* cleverly connected Tebbit's discontent with Joseph's precarious Cabinet perch. It was reported that rumours about the succession at Education were "affecting party morale", and that the reshuffle would be brought forward if the Conservatives performed badly in May's local elections.[88]

The elections, held on 9 May, brought "the Government's most dismal night at the polls since 1979". Two parliamentary by-elections had also been held; in one, Derbyshire West, the Tories hung on by 100 votes, but the other, Ryedale, saw a 16,000 Conservative majority transformed into a 5,000 lead for the Lib–Dem Alliance. The local elections registered defeats for the government across the country; the net loss for the Conservatives was 705 council seats. In London the party only controlled eleven boroughs, and the new ILEA was dominated by Labour. Given Joseph's Departmental responsibilities – and the fact that he had pressed for a directly elected Education Authority in the capital – the latter result was taken by some panicky MPs as a referendum on his stewardship. The press picked up renewed calls for his replacement. At the same time, significantly, there was a new move to settle the teachers' dispute, with a back-dated pay offer of around 6 per cent.[89]

The Party Chairman was also criticised after the May defeats, and more tittle-tattle appeared in the newspapers. Among his alleged offences, it was claimed that Tebbit had upset the Prime Minister by "demanding" Joseph's sacking.[90] This choice of phrase was particularly wounding for Tebbit; evidently someone close to Number 10 was briefing the press in order to discredit him. As Chairman he had to make objective judgements in the best interests of the party, regardless of his personal feelings. Mrs Thatcher still agreed with her husband in regarding Joseph as "England's greatest man"; "a darling man", as she remarked to her Press Secretary one day when she spotted him scurrying through the London streets. But not even she could rate him as a significant electoral asset, and with her mind turning once again towards vouchers she realised that he was not the man to carry out a programme of radical reform.[91] Since the various Conservative factions were agitating on behalf of rival candidates for the succession it made sense to end the uncertainty as soon as possible. But Tebbit had always entertained a warm personal regard for Joseph, and recognised his increasing value within a Cabinet where personal loyalty to the Prime Minister was in short supply. In fact, if anyone had been speaking about Joseph out of turn it was Mrs Thatcher herself. She had discussed her friend's

---

88. Tebbit, *Upwardly Mobile*, 186–8; *Sunday Times*, 22 April 1986.
89. *The Times*, 10 May 1986.
90. *Mail on Sunday*, 11 May 1986.
91. Carol Thatcher, *Below the Parapet: The Biography of Denis Thatcher* (HarperCollins, 1996), 4. Interview with Sir Bernard Ingham.

future at a private meeting with the journalist John Junor before Libya and Fulham, and later even invited the garrulous Woodrow Wyatt to suggest possible dates for Joseph's departure. The fact that the least conspiratorial of men was now being used as the football in a disorderly kick-about among team-mates was a telling symptom of the rift between the Prime Minister and the Party Chairman which continued to dog the party even during the 1987 general election campaign.[92]

On Wednesday 20 May it was reported that Joseph had won additional money for the universities – or at least, he had argued that there should be no more cuts for the time being. *The Times* predicted that he would leave Education before the end of the week, but would remain in the Cabinet as Minister without Portfolio. In fact he departed that same day. The announcement, it was said, was brought forward "to give him the chance to bow out gracefully, with a statement he takes to be a landmark in the history of higher education: the imposition of quality control on the research done in universities, and therefore on the money handed out to them". Yet this "landmark" had already been fore-shadowed. More likely, the timing was intended to spare him the difficulty of having to explain the ninth annual Her Majesty's Inspectorate of Schools (HMI) report, which estimated that a quarter of schools were suffering from inadequate resources. The finding was more damaging to Joseph because clear warnings about the situation had been included in the previous year's report. While it was possible to measure the standard of school buildings and the supply of library books with some accuracy, appraisals of teaching quality could only be subjective. However, the inspectors asserted with confidence after visiting more than 1,500 schools that 30 per cent of lessons were unsatisfactory. Understandably the teaching unions focused on the first statistic, regarding it as a suitable epitaph for Joseph's ministry; one union leader protested "Just as he flies the coop the political chickens are coming home to roost". The *Guardian* felt that the report revealed the existence of "two nations in education"; if schools in affluent areas were short of money, the parents could dip into their own pockets. In response, Joseph repeated his familiar arguments about teaching standards, and implied that local authorities should divert a greater proportion of their budgets from the payment of staff to the repair of buildings. But the timing of his resignation meant that the report was seen more as a challenge to his successor than an indictment of his own performance.[93]

In the ensuing exchange of letters, the sentiments expressed by Joseph and Mrs Thatcher were obviously more genuine than is customary on these

92. John Junor, *Memoirs: Listening for a Midnight Tram* (Pan, 1991), 305; Sarah Curtis (ed.), *The Journals of Woodrow Wyatt: Volume One* (Macmillan, 1998), entries for 6, 20 April 1986. According to Wyatt, Mrs Thatcher now felt that although Joseph could compose great speeches he was unable to get his message across to voters; she also reflected Sherman's view that he was "too much governed by officials".
93. Hugo Young in *Guardian*, 21 May 1986; *The Times*, 22 May 1986; *Guardian*, 22 May 1986.

occasions. The Prime Minister hailed "a unique career", and paid tribute to her friend's "passionate concern for the future of our country and its people . . . Your integrity, selflessness and thought for others are an example to us all". Joseph had always shown "rare intellectual grasp of policy in all fields", and more than anyone else he was "the architect who, starting from first principles . . . shaped the policies which led to victory in two elections". Joseph's letter was a model of quiet dignity. He promised that from the back-benches he would "enthusiastically support you and the Government's policies to encourage enterprise and competitiveness". Apparently the post of Minister without Portfolio had been formally offered at some point, but he had turned it down. Had he taken such a post in 1979 he might have spared himself much trouble. But now, having devoted so much energy to two demanding Departments over the past seven years it would not have been fitting for him to end his career in a position which offered influence without responsibility. Besides, he was now far more exercised than he had once been by the prospect of spending more time with his family. Mrs Thatcher consoled herself by naming Joseph as a Companion of Honour, and by promoting a controversial kindred spirit, Nicholas Ridley, from Transport to Environment. Another personal favourite, John Moore, began a spectacular but brief ascent by taking Ridley's place. The indefatigable Hailsham stayed on until after the 1987 general election. The Right had wanted Boyson at Education, but the job was given to Baker. This appointment proved how successful Joseph had been in moving education up the political agenda, because Baker was regarded as one of the best communicators in the government. The ambitious new Secretary of State found plenty of ideas on his desk, and since Joseph had been so parsimonious it was easy for Baker to press the case for a significant boost to Departmental resources. In October 1986 a Cabinet committee agreed in principle to a deal on teachers' pay which would cost more than twice the amount that Joseph had offered.[94]

On hearing of Joseph's departure one senior minister remarked "Marvellous man but a terrible politician". Ferdinand Mount reported his fear that Joseph's retirement "stirs a sensation of relief among his colleagues. The sound of breaking crockery has made them nervous". Some of his old antagonists could afford to be generous in public, but there were some sincere expressions of mixed feelings. Professor Ted Wragg of Exeter University, who had once described Joseph's approach to education as comparable to that of a Martian arriving in the middle of a rugby match, now regretted that "most teachers never saw him relaxed and good-humoured"; for his own part, "each time I met him I liked him more and more". The *TES* wrote of "Sir Keith's highly creative term of office", and acknowledged his success in focusing public attention on the work of his Department (although at times he had been

---

94. *The Times*, 21 May 1986.

"almost unbelievably incompetent for so experienced a politician"). Even after the successive upheavals in education policy that the Conservatives forced through after Joseph's departure it remained difficult to reach firm conclusions about his "legacy". One perceptive critic wrote that Joseph had proved to be a man of strange contradictions – "the anti-centralising interventionist, the enterprising traditionalist, the public service free-marketeer". In himself he carried all the conflicting tendencies to be found within the broad coalition of Conservative support. While Labour had been in power the tension between economic liberalism and social conservatism had been obscured by the need to confront a common enemy. By the end of Mrs Thatcher's second term there were ominous signs that the fragile alliance was falling apart, and education exposed the cross-purposes better than any other policy area. According to Shirley Letwin, in education "the Thatcher Government adopted policies most blatantly at odds with its fundamental commitments". "Fundamental commitments", of course, were in the eye of the individual Thatcherite beholder, and since the unelected critics were free from the responsibilities of decision-making they could pick their grounds for attack according to whim. Back in the mid-1970s, when Mrs Letwin had helped to persuade Joseph that he should stop referring to the social market, she had clearly been working on the assumption that Britain's economic needs took precedence over all other considerations. "Intellectually attracted" as he was to both of the broad "New Right" tendencies, Joseph found himself torn between incompatible demands. It was hardly surprising that his successors proved to be more decisive – if not necessarily more adroit.[95]

Ten months before Joseph's departure the *Guardian*'s Hugo Young had reflected the general ambivalence about Joseph's record. While conceding that no recent Education Secretary had "exhibited a more sincere and credible devotion to the improvement of education than he has", Young deplored the "staggering failure of persuasion and presentation" which thwarted Joseph's good intentions. On the day of the resignation he agreed that Sir Keith was a "thoroughly decent man". But Young pointed out that he personified another interesting paradox. The government claimed to have changed the "climate of opinion" in Britain. As Education Secretary Joseph had an ideal opportunity to cement the supposed victory in the "Battle of Ideas"; he could "carry the revolution into the universities, fusing his intellectual arguments with the world of the intellectuals". This constituency was not large, and its influence was certainly a great deal less than in other European countries, such as France. Yet without significant support from intellectuals it was hard to substantiate the

---

95. Ferdinand Mount in *Spectator*, 31 May 1986; *TES*, 30 May 1986; Richard Johnson, "A New Road to Serfdom? A Critical History of the 1988 Act", in *Education Limited: Schooling, Training and the New Right in England since 1979* (Unwin Hyman, 1991), 64; Letwin, *Anatomy of Thatcherism*, 228.

notion that the government had triumphed in "the Battle of Ideas". As it was, the 364 economists who registered their dissent from the 1981 Budget, and the Oxford dons who refused to award Mrs Thatcher an honorary doctorate in 1984, symbolised an opposition which, if anything, was swelling. It was not enough to base claims about the state of public opinion on the support of right-wing newspaper columnists – a miniscule minority of the population, even if they monopolised a lofty soap box in what was formerly Fleet Street. The conversion of one or two irascible writers from socialism could not be taken as proof that there really was "no alternative". According to Young, the record showed "how narrow Josephism's base continues to be, how small the sect that really believes in it, how few of its propositions command support, and how ineffective the prophet has been in making sense of his own message". His remark was backed by surveys of broader opinion, which showed a rising demand for better public services as opposed to tax cuts, and even a resurgence of support for nationalisation. There was overwhelming agreement with the proposition that the gap between rich and poor had grown too large, and by the end of the second Thatcher government less than half of the population accepted the message of *Equality* – that the only measurement of poverty was the ability of a family to feed itself.[96]

If Joseph read Young's piece it would not have surprised him. He was well aware that there had been little real change in the "climate of opinion". More than ten years after proclaiming that "we are all monetarists now", he protested that "research workers, policy proposers, opinion formers and journalists – both those who work for newspapers and those who work for television – shy away from unfashionable realities and are insular, blinkered and one-eyed". The use of such language, it might be quibbled, was not the best way to win more converts. But although Joseph's ministerial career closed with his departure from Education there was no question of retirement. He would continue to fight the Battle of Ideas for as long as he felt that his services could be useful.[97]

96. *Guardian*, 25 September 1985, 21 May 1986; Ivor Crewe, "Values: The Crusade that Failed", in Kavanagh & Seldon (eds), *The Thatcher Effect*, 239–50; Hoover and Plant, *Conservative Capitalism*, 276, 279. For an excellent overview of social attitudes under Mrs Thatcher, see John Rentoul, *Me and Mine: The Triumph of the New Individualism?* (Unwin Hyman, n.d.).
97. KJ, "One-Eyed Vision" in *Policy Studies*, 12.

Chapter 14

"If you seek his monument . . ."

In August 1986, three months after his resignation, Sir Keith Joseph was spotted on the Number 22 bus travelling along the King's Road in Chelsea. When he was in the Cabinet his preference for public transport had sometimes caused unease among his security staff, and after his return to the back-benches he was frequently sighted on buses going to and from central London. He refused, however, to take advantage of that unselective subsidy, the pensioners' bus pass. On meeting old acquaintances during these journeys he would often engage in conversation on topical issues; when he visited his local supermarket he continued to quiz the staff, as he had done as a minister, and the residents of Chelsea were well accustomed to seeing him on his way home, loaded with plastic bags full of groceries. On this occasion he was engrossed in a book, which turned out to be Gabriel Garcia Marquez's novel *One Hundred Years of Solitude*.[1]

The title seemed appropriate to Joseph's circumstances at the time. By the standards of a normal person he was still extremely busy. In addition to relatively new business interests, including consultancies for Cable & Wireless and Trusthouse Forte, he rejoined the Bovis board as a non-executive director, and continued to give the company full value for his services. In the 1990s he

---

1. Interview with Lord Harris of High Cross; *The Times*, 10 August 1986.

helped to negotiate the contract for the £3 billion Canary Wharf development, and the new chairman Sir Frank Lampl remembered his embarrassment on the occasions when Joseph sat quietly waiting outside his office until he was free.[2] He could never be anything less than a full-time politician while he remained in the Commons. But as a minister he had gone far beyond the commitment that lesser mortals consider "full time". Now removed from the bustle of Whitehall, the mountains of red boxes, the constant attendance of civil servants, advisors and interest-group deputations, he must have felt strangely disorientated. It was thought within the CPS that he was interested in resuming an active role in the day-to-day activities of the Centre, but this came to nothing.[3] And although he was in close touch with his family, he now had more free time to spend alone in the house on Limerston Street. One day, after meeting an old friend in the street he invited her to lunch at his home. The friend was rather surprised by Joseph's skills in the kitchen, but felt sure that he was lonely (his marriage had been dissolved in 1985). Although Joseph had never thrown himself into the social life offered by the House of Commons, after his departure from the Cabinet he enjoyed conversations over a cup of tea with like-minded individuals like Frank Field (now a Labour MP and far more sympathetic to Joseph's ideas than he had been in 1974). Field remembers that they discussed their shared interests in welfare reform, and that Joseph continued to recommend books. But he has a more vivid memory of gossiping with Joseph about colleagues in their respective parties, and watching his friend laughing until tears streamed down his face. Such light-hearted interludes could not protect Joseph against melancholy. On the day that they both retired from the House of Commons, he expressed some jealousy of his parliamentary "pair" Leo Abse, who at least could fall back on a settled home life.[4]

Yet although Joseph had often been physically alone at Limerston Street, for some time before he left office he had been sustained by a sense of companionship crucial for a man of his temperament. He had known Yolanda Sheriff (née Castro) since the late 1940s, when they had a brief romance. Geographical factors were too much of a handicap at that stage – Yolanda lived in Egypt – but there had been earlier connections between her family and the extended Joseph-Gluckstein clan and they kept in touch after Yolanda married an American. In the early 1980s that marriage had ended. There was a natural sympathy between

---

2. Sir Frank's reported remarks included an ironic twist. Having praised Joseph for his "clear economic views" which were "an enormous help", he reflected that "He used to say he went into politics to improve the lot of the people, but didn't seem to have achieved it". Certainly Joseph's advice was not always based on narrow economic calculations. Although Bovis was involved in overseeing the privatisation of the Public Services Agency he felt that the company should not bid for any of its constituent parts, in case this produced allegations of a conflict of interest. As Bovis's historian notes, the advice robbed the company of what would have been "a marvellous acquisition"; Cooper, *Building Relationships*, 155, 194, 208.
3. Interview with David Willetts.
4. Private information; interview with Frank Field; Abse, *Margaret*, 160.

long-standing friends in similar circumstances, and Joseph began to see more of Mrs Sheriff. Yolanda now lived on a farm in Connecticut, and this presented a dual obstacle to her friendship with Joseph, who had never been drawn to the rural life and who had limited opportunities for travel while he was at Education. He was not even an enthusiast for flying. But he could force himself onto a plane, when these transatlantic missions did not interfere with serious government business. And he adjusted to the farm so readily that at one time he helped with the difficult delivery of a calf, expressing delight and awe when the young animal emerged. In later years, when friends visited the farm he took a special pleasure in pointing out his favourite views over the landscape. In November 1992 he even took part in a House of Lords debate on agriculture, confessing that "a number of noble Lords expressed surprise" on seeing his name on the list of speakers. At least he claimed to be speaking as a consumer, not as a farmer.[5]

For Joseph, the new situation produced a tug-of-war between his highly developed sense of family privacy and his natural desire to share the joy of the rekindled friendship. For once he was forced to strike a compromise. Somewhat skittishly, he would tell friends that he was "going a-wooing" – even when that explanation for his sudden absences was not strictly necessary. But the target of his courtship was concealed even from some of his closest friends. The secrecy amused his Cabinet colleagues (and Labour opponents), but they were discreet and no hint of a liaison appeared in the newspapers until after the couple were married in August 1990. Even then the subterfuge continued; few were invited to the ceremony, which took place at Alnwick in Northumberland, near the home of Lord (Nigel) Vinson, Joseph's old friend from CPS days. It was rumoured that Sir Keith (by then Lord Joseph) booked into his hotel under an assumed name; when a fellow guest pointed out his resemblance to the former Cabinet minister, the prospective bridegroom retained his composure and replied "So they tell me", suggesting that the strange resemblance entitled him to a drink.[6]

At the time of his marriage Joseph informed friends that he was "a very lucky and happy man", and when he introduced them to Yolanda after the long embargo they were touched by his unambiguous love and pride. When the press finally caught up with the new Lady Joseph she responded with typical modesty and charm, informing them that "He's the interesting one" and divulging little more about herself than the fact that she could drive a tractor. One telling symptom of a new serenity in Joseph's life was the fact that for the first time he began to read the novels of Trollope (although he pursued this new interest with typical fanaticism, reading several of the volumes more than

5. Private information; Henderson, *Mandarin*, 344; *House of Lords Debates*, vol. 540, cols 831–2, 24 November 1992.
6. Lord Tebbit speech at KJ memorial service; interviews with Lord Harris of High Cross and Giles Radice; private information.

once). At Joseph's memorial service several speakers paid warm tributes to Yolanda's contribution to his last years. His son felt that "it was as if he had been granted an extra life". An American friend recalled that, as his health failed, his frailty "weighed on him, because he felt it was an imposition on the lady he loved above all else". On her last visit, the friend had remarked that Joseph looked particularly happy. "'I am', he whispered. 'You see, we are on our honeymoon'". By that time he and Yolanda had been married for four years. The sentiment was beautiful, and revealed a romantic side to Joseph's nature which only a handful of close friends had ever appreciated during his lifetime.[7]

Joseph had left the government at an intriguing moment. The early part of Mrs Thatcher's second term was dominated by the miners' strike, which was resolved to the government's satisfaction in March 1985. After this the Prime Minister's worst problems arose mainly from personality clashes, which had previously been kept in check by the need for unity against the most dangerous of the "enemies within" – the wets. However bad things had been in the first three years, recent improvements allowed the government to claim that events had refuted the warnings of Heath, Prior and their remaining supporters. Noting the contrast with the gloomy days of the late 1970s, some incautious commentators were beginning to acclaim an "economic miracle". Inflation had continued to fall, almost touching 2 per cent in the summer of 1986. Unemployment at last began to recede three months after Joseph's departure, in response to a boom in part-time work (and twenty changes to the methods of counting). But the long years of gloom seemed to be ending; even manufacturing output was picking up. None of this, though, had much to do with monetarism. Between 1983 and 1988 the money supply increased by an annual average of almost 15 per cent; the corresponding figure for inflation was below 5 per cent. Not even the monetarist theory of "time-lags" could explain away this discrepancy. The Chancellor, while persisting officially with his monetary targets, now regarded the exchange rate as the real key to economic management. In the run-up to the general election of 11 June 1987 Lawson delighted most Conservatives by cutting interest rates to 9 per cent, and the basic rate of income tax to 27 pence. Consumer demand was soaring, and the City of London was buoyant; between the elections of 1983 and 1987 the *Financial Times* share index quintupled in value. When the party stormed to its third consecutive election win with an overall majority of 101, Lawson was hailed as the architect of victory. His swift actions after the Wall Street Crash in October 1987 seemed to have averted the worst repercussions of a development which illustrated the new inter-dependence of world markets.[8]

---

7. Speeches at KJ memorial service by Margaret Harrison, James Joseph and Patricia Labalme; *Evening Standard* (no date); private information.
8. William Keegan, *Mr Lawson's Gamble* (Hodder & Stoughton, 1989), 172–99; Young, *One of Us,* 502; Hutton, *State We're In*, 73; Lawson, *View from No.11*, 745–51.

But the "architect" had ignored the biblical advice on house construction. In his 1988 budget he stunned even the government's supporters by reducing the higher rate of income tax to 40 per cent. Lawson had greatly simplified the tax system, but the result was a further boost to the prosperity of those who had already gained disproportionately from the Thatcher years. The "poll tax", which meant that in local taxation a Duke paid no more than a dustman, had the same effect; the government's argument that the new system would force voters to consider their choices more carefully in future local elections could not withstand the impression that the Conservatives had now gone too far in their attempt to redress the post-war social balance. The same feeling was provoked by a series of legislative measures to shackle the trade unions, whose militancy had already been curbed more effectively by job insecurity. The government pressed on with its course despite clear evidence of public unease. Six months before the 1988 Budget Gallup had found that only 11 per cent of voters wanted further tax cuts; in May 1979 the figure had been 37 per cent. By the end of 1987, 71 per cent thought that trade unions were a "good thing"; the figure for 1979 had been 51 per cent.[9]

Those government supporters who paid attention to the polls assured themselves that attitudes would swing back once the public was faced with real choices at the ballot box. But this complacency rested on the assumption that the "miracle" had corrected the underlying economic problem of post-war Britain: that the good times would be followed by a slump. The consumer boom was already running out of control when Lawson delivered his budget, and British industry had not recovered sufficiently to satisfy demand. Imported goods filled the gap. The balance of payments deficit for 1988 was £15 billion; for 1989 it was £20 billion. Inflation rose once again towards the double figures which the government thought it had banished forever. To combat this alarming trend, interest rates were pushed up, reaching 15 per cent by October 1989 – the month of Lawson's departure from the Treasury.

As Ian Gilmour has pointed out, the situation bore a close resemblance to the conditions of 1971–3 associated with the name of Tony Barber. The result this time was more drastic: the longest economic slump since the 1930s. In 1990 the CBI reported that 15,000 companies had gone bankrupt. Trapped in houses which were now worth less than the mortgages they had taken out, thousands of individuals faced the prospect of losing everything they had worked for in the 1980s – and more (this development caused Lord Joseph particular concern).[10] After all the upheavals of the early 1980s Britain was once again facing the "stagflation" of the previous decade; in response, the new Chancellor John Major increased public expenditure. Simon Jenkins regarded Major's 1989

---

9. Ivor Crewe, "Values: The Crusade that Failed", in Kavanagh & Seldon (eds), *The Thatcher Effect*, 246; Wybrow, *Britain Speaks Out*, 160.
10. Letter to authors from Bob Bessell.

autumn statement as "the final triumph of the wets over the forces of Thatcherism". This was improbable; at least, there were very few "wets" left in the Commons to enjoy their "triumph", since the younger generation by this time had accommodated itself to the new dispensation. But the Prime Minister was increasingly unpopular, and isolated within the Cabinet. Whether or not his presence would have affected policy outcomes, Joseph's dogged loyalty was missed as much as the advice of Lord Whitelaw, who retired in January 1988.[11]

After the 1987 general election a party was held to celebrate Joseph's contribution as a member of the Commons over thirty-one years. As Arthur Seldon remembered, "praise from friends . . . drew tears he tried to disguise". He was elevated to the Lords, as Baron Joseph of Portsoken, in the Dissolution Honours list of 1987, and in October was introduced to peers by Lords Vinson and Young. He delivered his maiden speech on 19 February 1988 – the month before Lawson's budget. It was a characteristic effort, in a congenial debate on the recent White Paper issued by his old Industry Department, which had merged with Trade since Joseph's time and was now being relaunched as "DTI – the department for enterprise". After the preliminary remarks expected on such occasions, Joseph informed his audience that he had "entered politics in order to try, however modestly, to reduce the widespread poverty of many people. At the time, and for many years after, I was an unreflecting statist seeking short cuts to Utopia. Over time I have come to realise that perhaps the state can do better by setting the right framework and by intervening little".

The Conservative governments of the 1980s, he contended, had made progress towards "*embourgeoisement* – that is, towards a state in society where most people own and earn enough to have choice and scope and where everyone has the attitudes and time-horizons to make use of them". However, he freely admitted that there was more to do; there was, he reminded the House, the small matter of 14 million people on benefit, 2.7 million unemployed, "with very much crime and with low standards of education". Despite everything that the government had done, the remedy was still "more millionaires and more bankrupts". Lord Young, now running the DTI, had pointed the way forward with his new White Paper. The Department was busy selling off the remaining state industries; it seemed only a matter of time before it could retreat to a "nightwatchman" role, enforcing necessary regulations on industry rather than running businesses itself. This was very similar to the regime that Joseph had envisaged in the late 1960s. His only objection to Young's White Paper was that there should have been more emphasis on productivity, which had improved since 1979 but not nearly fast enough.[12]

---

11. Gilmour, *Dancing with Dogma*, 59–68; Edgar Wilson, *A Very British Miracle: The Failure of Thatcherism* (Pluto Press, 1992), 168; Seldon, *Major*, 104.
12. *House of Lords Debates*, vol. 495, cols 873–5, 19 February 1988. A BBC reporter covering the speech assumed that Joseph had made a verbal slip, and had really meant to appeal for *fewer* bankrupts. Joseph immediately telephoned the Corporation to put the record straight; interview with Ted Wragg.

The speech showed that Joseph retained his idealist streak; the virus of the late Thatcher years – "Triumphalism" – had failed to infect him. But he was not proof against a salmonella bug which swept through the Lords in May 1988, also felling the Leader of the House, Lord Belstead, and three junior Whips.[13] By that time Joseph had established himself as a regular speaker, and the malady was only a temporary check although for a time his condition was grave. In the late spring and early summer of 1988 he contributed regularly to debates on Kenneth Baker's "Great Education Reform Bill" (GERBIL). This mammoth piece of legislation – eventually running to 238 clauses – brought closer to fruition many of Joseph's own aims, giving schools the right to opt out of local authority control and extending the principle of "open enrolment". In passing, the Bill swept away academic tenure, severed the connection between local government and polytechnics, and scrapped the recalcitrant ILEA – a measure which Joseph now felt able to support. In theory, parental power was boosted, but the Secretary of State was a much greater beneficiary.

While other commentators reflected on the strange tendency of the Thatcher governments to centralise power while talking loudly of curbing the state, Joseph was unable to detect such ambiguity. Joining a debate on the power of government (after making copious notes, as usual)[14] he listed education among the areas in which the state had been "rolled back", along with de-nationalisation, the end of incomes policy, and the removal of "beer and sandwiches" from the Number 10 menu. Among Baker's achievements in higher education was the introduction of student loans (beginning in 1990); Joseph must have been amused to read in the *THES* that the case for loans, which in 1984 had turned Conservative MPs into a lynch-mob, had now developed "an unstoppable momentum". But one aspect of Baker's Bill did worry him. The imposition of a national curriculum by statute went far beyond his own wishes. As he explained, he would not have objected if the Bill had introduced statutory backing for three "core" subjects – English, science, and mathematics – but he balked at its extension to seven or eight more "foundation" subjects. The rigidity of the curriculum, he felt, would damage the prospects of non-academic children; the system would also be bureaucratic, imposing "a quite intolerable burden" on "those people who know the child's needs best – the teachers". The strain on such people was great enough already; in 1988 nearly 14,500 left the profession before retirement age.[15]

Joseph's misgivings on the national curriculum were shared in full by Mrs Thatcher.[16] So when he voted for an amendment which sought entirely to

---

13. *The Times*, 12 May 1988.
14. *Financial Times*, 3 March 1988.
15. *House of Lords Debates*, vol. 494, cols 204–7, 2 March 1988; vol. 496, cols 380–2, 3 May 1988; Wilson, *Miracle*, 150; Baker, *Turbulent Years*, 240.
16. The Prime Minister's ideas, Baker felt, were more suitable for a nineteenth- than a twenty-first-century school system: *Turbulent Years*, 196.

remove the statutory element he was making a gesture in favour of his leader against a member of her Cabinet. But he was the only Conservative to do so, and in the lobby he was joined by some unlikely allies, including Baroness Blackstone (with whom he clashed on an almost daily basis) and his old CRO boss, Lord Alport, who had lost the Conservative whip because of his regular rebellions. By this stage in the life of the Thatcher government the Lords was almost the sole remaining refuge for dissidents; in part, the Prime Minister's own successes had ensured this, because so many "wet" ex-ministers had by now been transferred there from the Commons. The Education Bill gave the ageing rebels much sport, but not on this particular issue. As Joseph reflected sadly two years later, "I failed completely to persuade the House or my former colleagues in government". The Bill's main features remained intact, leaving a new government quango, the National Curriculum Council, with the unenviable task of devising from scratch one of the most detailed and intrusive learning programmes in the industrialised world. After Mrs Thatcher's departure, Baker's successor Kenneth Clarke announced that only the three "core" subjects would be compulsory up to GCSE level after all; ironically, this was seen as a concession to the teachers, for once in unison with the former Prime Minister.[17] But the decision did not put an end to controversy over the curriculum – nor did it make life easier for the teachers, who might have developed a hankering for the days of Sir Keith Joseph.

Joseph was troubled by other developments after his departure from Education, notably the planned increase in the size of the student population and the permission granted to polytechnics to apply for the status of universities. On the latter subject he had seen no reason to change his mind since November 1974, when he had urged that some universities should be turned into polytechnics. He also evinced some doubt about the wisdom of his own GCSE system, clearly fearing that it might have helped to disguise a dilution of real standards. The new examination had been attacked by the think-tank the Social Affairs Unit (SAU – formerly linked to the IEA), and Joseph's own CPS had published a series of critical pamphlets. His ally Shirley Letwin lamented that the GSCE had been designed "by the same old educational establishment who continued to make the new scheme serve the old orthodoxy, indeed to entrench it". For the sake of friendship Mrs Letwin admitted that "These consequences were not what Sir Keith Joseph had intended"; as usual, the allegedly all-powerful DES could be paraded as a scapegoat. But Joseph had no intention of concealing his own sense of failure.[18] On 21 November 1990 he delivered a reflective speech to the Lords, admitting that his party had not succeeded in raising standards in schools. But he argued that Labour had done less than nothing, and although he welcomed signs that the Opposition were paying more attention to the issue he aimed several

---

17. *House of Lords Debates*, vol. 523, col. 707, 21 November 1990; Timmins, *Five Giants*, 442–3; McSmith, *Clarke*, 187.
18. Letwin, *Anatomy of Thatcherism*, 256–7.

blows at Lady Blackstone: he thought that she had not done justice "either to herself or to the House in riding so easily off on the panaceas that Labour *will* introduce". His choice of the word "will" was significant, and other remarks in his speech suggested that he now saw a change of government as inevitable. On the previous day Mrs Thatcher had narrowly failed to secure a sufficient majority to knock out Michael Heseltine in the first round of the Conservative leadership contest. A week later she left Downing Street.[19]

Joseph was devastated by the events of November 1990. In May he had written an article for the *The Times*, in which he complained of "vicious verbal personal abuse" directed against a Prime Minister who remained the best conceivable candidate for the job (at the same time he betrayed his euphoria at the imminent prospect of his marriage by sprinkling the piece with uncharacteristic exclamation marks). On the day of the first ballot he sent a letter to the same newspaper, informing possible floating voters that although some of Mrs Thatcher's achievements were secure there was still "no substitute for her insights and" – significant phrase – "her moral courage". Heseltine, by contrast, wanted to return to "the soft options of the 1960s".[20] Joseph would have delivered a longer rallying-cry in the *Evening Standard*, but after Sherman had left him with a polished text he inserted a five-hundred word attack on Geoffrey Howe, whose resignation speech had triggered Heseltine's challenge. This diatribe, of marginal relevance to the current situation, ensured that the piece was never published. Sherman is convinced that the original article might have made a difference, given that Mrs Thatcher would have won outright on the first ballot had only two MPs changed their minds. Realistically, though, to survive she needed to detach a larger number of Heseltine supporters than Joseph could possibly have reached; if he ever listed her fall among his political failures he was doing himself more injustice than usual.[21]

By now Joseph's identification with Mrs Thatcher was so complete that he imagined her to have shared his motives when he entered politics – i.e. to help "the poor and downtrodden".[22] He attended a special lunch to mark Mrs Thatcher's retirement from office, and at the end told her that "You have done more than any of us ever thought possible and ever hoped to do. You were a great leader, a giant. 'A beautiful giant'". In early December he encountered Howe at a public gathering. According to Howe he "turned courteously but firmly away" (but one bystander remembered that he rebuffed a friendly gesture with the words "Go away Geoffrey. I don't love you any more"). If Joseph recognised that Howe's departure from office had arisen from a genuine disagreement of principle with the Prime Minister, he overlooked this and

19. *House of Lords Debates*, vol. 523, cols 705–8, 21 November 1990 (our italics); *The Times*, 15 November 1974.
20. *The Times*, 7 May, 20 November 1990.
21. Interview with Sir Alfred Sherman.
22. *Independent*, 23 November 1990.

interpreted Howe's critical resignation speech as an act of personal revenge. He could no longer be friends with his best friend's enemy – even though Howe had accompanied him in so many battles in the past – and although Howe thought that the breach lasted for three years (which was long enough), others maintain that Joseph never forgave him. Undoubtedly his reaction was over-dramatic. Like his challenge to Lord Young ("You don't believe"), it was another glimpse of the Keith Joseph who had struck his Harrow contemporaries as an accomplished actor in his personal dealings. Other old friendships, though, were now fully repaired. Joseph attended Enoch Powell's eightieth birthday party, and later dined with him in the Lords even though Powell was a very rare visitor to Westminster after he lost his seat in the 1987 general election.[23]

The fall of the "beautiful giant" gave Joseph the chance to judge the performance of her governments, in an article for the *Independent*. The main achievements, he felt, were the taming of the trade unions, a shift in the political "centre of gravity", and a dramatic improvement in Britain's world status. The reality (and value) of these achievements he took for granted, although like so much of the Thatcher record they will continue to be debated by others. It would have been easy for Joseph to claim that although serious mistakes had been made these were easily outweighed by the gains for Britain since 1979. But most of his article was devoted to an analysis of "what went wrong"; or rather, the factors that ensured that "one of the greatest prime ministers in British history" was leaving office "before completing the tasks that she is best fitted to fulfil". Joseph felt that he and his colleagues "knew what we rejected in the post-war economy and society, but we never worked out clearly enough our disengagement strategy" (an opinion which echoed Sherman's long-held view). He felt that problems over Europe had only overwhelmed the Thatcher governments because "early successes in the economy" came to an end; for this he blamed Nigel Lawson, who had allowed the boom to rage out of control. "Mrs Thatcher's mistake was in not dismissing Mr Lawson despite his popularity", he wrote. But Joseph acknowledged other factors which could not be blamed on a single person. Most significant was the fact that although productivity per head had greatly improved since 1979 the gap with "our neighbours in North West Europe" remained because they had also improved their performance.[24]

Much of this was predictable; even the image of a Prime Minister who could not restrain her Chancellor might have been anticipated, because it was the only way in which Joseph could deplore Britain's renewed economic difficulties without directly implicating Mrs Thatcher herself.[25] In later speeches Joseph

---

23. Baker, *Turbulent Years*, 415; Howe, *Loyalty*, 676; interview with Simon Heffer; private information.
24. KJ, "We did not go far enough; we failed her", *Independent*, 23 November 1990; KJ, "One-Eyed Vision" in *Policy Studies*, 13.
25. The same device was employed by Nicholas Ridley, in his hagiographical *My Style of Government*.

loaded Lawson with additional criticisms; he had increased Capital Gains Tax, and his fiscal strategy had penalised marriage. On 24 September 1992 – only a week after a fresh economic disaster, "Black Wednesday" – he blamed himself "for not reacting strongly" against Lawson's abandonment of the Medium Term Financial Strategy after 1984. It was the latest of many myths about the recent past; he implied that monetarism had been working perfectly well, and that Lawson had wilfully discarded his most potent weapon in the fight against inflation. Yet in an unpublished interview of November 1988 Joseph had candidly admitted that monetarism had been a mistake; money, he said, could not be measured after all.[26] On this view the only conceivable benefit which might have arisen from a continued preoccupation with the money supply figures was the psychological one of convincing the public that the government was sticking to its economic strategy; but even that would have been of dubious value in the face of so much evidence that the key element of the strategy had proved unworkable. As well as being unfair to Lawson, Joseph's strictures ran the risk of undermining Lady Thatcher's reputation for strong leadership. If Joseph, who had only been Secretary of State for Education at the time, felt that his inadequate protests after 1984 made him culpable, what share of the blame was attributable to the First Lady of the Treasury?

Lawson himself branded as "superficial commentators" those critics who believed that his 1985 Mais Lecture marked the end of the monetarist experiment. Nevertheless, the lecture had included a recognition that "intermediate targets", notably the exchange rate, were more useful indicators of a successful anti-inflation policy than measurements of the money supply itself.[27] Lawson was naturally interested in the Exchange Rate Mechanism (ERM) of the European Monetary System, as an alternative means of controlling inflation without reverting to any of the old "statist" methods such as prices and incomes policy. But Mrs Thatcher, spurred on by the inevitable Sir Alan Walters, regarded the new approach as an unwarranted "interference" in the laws of the market. In this quarrel she could rely as usual on Lord Joseph, who as far back as October 1979 had expressed his opposition to ERM membership.[28] Like the Prime Minister, he now feared that the British might be "swallowed up into a super-state" and convinced himself that in the debates over membership of the Community in the early 1970s "we disclaimed political union and a federal Europe".[29] However, when Mrs Thatcher finally allowed

26. KJ interview for "The Thatcher Factor"; *House of Lords Debates*, vol. 539, col. 459, 24 September, 1992.
27. Lawson, *View from No. 11*, 480–2.
28. Thatcher, *Downing Street Years*, 691–2.
29. *The Times*, 7 May 1990. When Lady Thatcher gave the first Keith Joseph Memorial Lecture in January 1996 she concentrated on European matters, and denounced Europhiles in her own party as "No nation Conservatives". There is no reason to think that Lord Joseph would have disapproved. See *The Times*, 12 January 1996.

Britain to join the ERM in October 1990 Lord Joseph had made no public comment.

Joseph's views on Europe had evolved since the early 1960s, when he had argued that the political benefits of closer union were even greater than the economic advantages. In 1974 he had established the CPS, supposedly to learn lessons from other European nations; but the lessons he learned only convinced him that the Europeans were inveterate "statists". Mrs Thatcher's Bruges speech of 1988 seems to have deepened his scepticism, and the contribution of Europe to her fall produced an outburst of wrath which surprised even the closest observers of his career. Like Mrs Thatcher Joseph was a Conservative at least in his constitutional thinking; the man who had decried the thought of a strong regional tier of government in Britain was unlikely to have any sympathy for the concept of "subsidiarity".[30] In his *Independent* article he referred in passing to "Euromaniacs", but that was only a warm-up. Almost a year to the day after Mrs Thatcher's resignation he gave the Lords a more sustained insight into his new thinking. The concept of "federalism", which he had treated with respect in his contribution to Lionel Curtis's *Open Road to Freedom,* was now so offensive to him that – in an interesting variation on the growing trend of "political correctness" – he preferred not to hear the word. He was "wistful for stable money", and to that extent had some sympathy with the idea of a European Central Bank modelled on the German Bundesbank. But the only realistic prospect was for a Bank with "a board containing Greeks, Portuguese and Italians". "They are noble people in their way", he added hastily, "but not ideal people to put in charge of a single central bank". The notion of allowing these Mediterranean types a decisive say in British economic policy was hateful enough to Lord Joseph, but his real fear was that the establishment of a Bank "would involve a single central government". On the question of whether or not Britain might be damaged if the other eleven member states went ahead with monetary union regardless, he admitted that he was not an expert, but thought that the input of the Greeks, Portuguese and Italians, would ensure the project's failure. In *The Times* the former Conservative MP Matthew Parris thought that Lord Joseph's speech was "winning, thoughtful and somehow delightfully batty, as usual". He had good reason for this charitable assessment, having inspired one of the best of all Joseph anecdotes when the great man mistook him for a Westminster lift-attendant. This had not spared Parris an intense cross-examination on the merits of "East–West trade linkage" as the lift ascended.[31]

---

30. See interviews with Alastair Hetherington, 24 February, 17 March 1964, Hetherington Papers, 5/4, 6/20, LSE archives.
31. *House of Lords Debates*, vol. 532, cols 1171–3, 25 November 1991; *The Times*, 26 November 1991; interview with Matthew Parris. In his Keith Joseph Memorial Lecture of 1998 Frank Field placed the incident at "a long distant Tory party conference", but Mr Parris confirms that it happened at Westminster in the late 1980s.

By this time Joseph was a member of the "Conservative Way Forward" group, dedicated to keeping alight the "Thatcherite" torch. He continued to speak outside Parliament, and to publish occasional pamphlets. In the Lords he adopted much the same tone that he had used in his great university campaign of the 1970s – to the annoyance of some of his new colleagues who were unwilling to be instructed in that way. From some of his remarks, it seems that Joseph was aware of disquiet at his regular interjection of party-political points. In May 1991 he displeased peers by speaking against a Bill which affected the interests of a business friend; with typical candour he had admitted at the outset that the friend had invited him to join the board of his company, and that he was likely to accept in due course. If not a breach of the rules of the House in the letter, his somewhat rambling speech certainly contravened its spirit. As so often on these occasions, he denied that he had any need for guidance on proper procedure.[32]

The impression that the House did not love Lord Joseph was no deterrent to him. Through constant repetition of his favourite themes, he hoped that he could still exert some influence over "the climate of opinion". The entrepreneur was praised on numerous occasions, and the scarcity of these market place gladiators was bemoaned in speech after speech. Joseph had searched the dictionaries – "in Partridge, in the slang dictionaries as well as Oxford and Chambers" – to find out whether "barrow boys" could be used as an impeccably English alternative. Certainly there seemed to be no closer approximation, a deficiency in the lexicon which bore a dreadful significance for Joseph. Much of his time in the Lords was taken up by a search for *mots justes*. He made several attempts to encapsulate the work of the entrepreneur – "the character who works the magic, the Aladdin who creates jobs".[33] In May 1988, speaking to his own motion which called attention to the remaining productivity gap between Britain and its European competitors, he cried "I should love to be able to create an aphorism that would ring round the country" to prove the point that "it is customers who provide jobs". He never could; perhaps because, as he told the Lords in February 1990, entrepreneurship "is not a gift that I have".[34]

But Joseph showed in other speeches that his thinking had moved on since the campus campaign, and from his time at Education. His main concern after leaving the Commons was to develop further his thoughts on "the Cycle of Deprivation". Nearly twenty years after he had first used that phrase, he

---

32. *Financial Times*, 22 March 1991; interview with the late Lord Alport; *House of Lords Debates*, vol. 528, cols 1548–53, 14 May 1991.
33. *House of Lords Debates*, vol. 529, col. 279, 22 May 1991; vol. 536, col. 326, 26 February 1992; vol. 529, col. 279, 22 May 1991. Before the 1979 general election Joseph had been advised by Martin Bendelow of the CPS to omit the reference to Aladdin, in case journalists exploited it to describe Joseph as "the mad lamp-rubber". After 1987 Joseph saw no need for such self-restraint; Halcrow, *Joseph*, 110.
34. *House of Lords Debates*, vol. 515, col. 867, 7 February 1990.

thought that it was more difficult than ever to be a good parent. As he put it, "The extended family has been dispersed. The framework of religious belief has been weakened. The influence of television may be baleful" (Joseph continued to resist the latter trend; during one stay with Lord Young he refused all invitations to relax in front of the "baleful" invention and instead refreshed himself by reading Dickens). Government could help to stave off threats to the family, he argued, particularly by recognising through the taxation system the efforts of mothers who worked in the home. But the main hope for society was the work of a growing number of charities. Joseph singled out for praise "Home-Start", which had been partly inspired by the "Deprivation" speech and whose founder Margaret Harrison had become a close friend. In November 1992 he outlined the work of this organisation in the Lords. Helped by 4,000 volunteers, it protected 20,000 children per year "from what would otherwise be the prospect of family break-up and a life in care leading probably to criminality, addiction and all the other miseries". Its approach was based on the idea that volunteers should befriend families, providing more intimate assistance to those struggling to bring up children. He was conscious that his advocacy would be badly received in some quarters, notably among those who thought that social work should be left exclusively to state agencies. But on this subject his earnestness was compelling, because it was untainted by any overt party-political slant. Noting the importance of "a solid, loving and guiding base" for children, he called on employers to introduce "flexible working arrangements for mothers and also for fathers". One can interpret his interest in Home-Start as a recognition that his drive for improved standards at Education was based on a false premise; even his "intellectual attraction" to the voucher had finally been quashed by his old theory of "deprivation". He now saw that however skilful their teachers, children cannot be expected to succeed if they receive no encouragement at home. Reading his work (which was published in two pamphlets by the CPS) one can only wonder whether Joseph had taken the right course back in the early fifties. Perhaps without party politics he would have lacked such a prominent platform. But he retained to the last his talent for encouraging others, using his extensive network of contacts to put workers in the voluntary sector in touch with potential sources of funding in private industry. Had he devoted all of his energies to the organisation and publicising of voluntary work, his message would have been heard with more respect across the boundaries of Westminster and beyond: and all those eggs and tomatoes would have been propelled at more robust (and deserving) targets.[35]

When the Lords debated a motion on voluntary organisation funding on 3 February 1993, Joseph took the opportunity once again to applaud Home-Start,

---

35. *House of Lords Debates*, vol. 540, cols 237–8, 11 November 1992; interview with Lord Young; KJ, *Importance of Parenting*, 17.

whose activities were continuing to expand. His attendance, and his contributions to debates, had increased markedly in recent months. But this was to be his last appearance in the House for more than a year. A few days after his speech he suffered a stroke which affected the left side of his body. He joked that this aspect of his attack would allow people to say that he was more right-wing than ever.[36] He was unable to attend the Lords for some months, and could write only with difficulty. But he could still dictate his thoughts. In June 1993, while the Conservative Party was tearing itself apart over the ratification of the Maastricht Treaty, he despatched a long letter to *The Times*. It represented the best contribution he could make to Lady Thatcher's campaign for a referendum on Maastricht. His attitude to this constitutional device had changed in tandem with that of the ex-premier since the Conservative Party deplored its use by the Wilson government in 1975. But the letter contained one or two surprising thoughts. He denounced the "sinister" phrase "ever closer union", and was (rightly) aghast at "the low level of discussion" of its implications for Britain. Even so, he thought that most people recognised that the greatest interference in their lives came not from Brussels but from "our own parliament with its avalanche of laws and regulations". This seemed to knock much of the wind out of his own argument, and cast ironic light on Mrs Thatcher's use of a Joseph phrase to boast at Bruges that her government had successfully "rolled back the frontiers of the state".[37]

Joseph's words betrayed a sense that, after all, he had failed – a view he expressed more than once to his close friend Lord Young, who tried his best to reassure him.[38] His depression about the political and economic situation – such a bleak contrast to the contentment in his domestic affairs – reflected his unease about the general approach of the Major administration. He was not close to the new Prime Minister (who failed even to mention Joseph's name in his memoirs), but he paid a couple of visits to the then Chancellor, Norman Lamont. Europe was an obvious point of difference at that time; Lord Lamont remembers dutifully struggling to outline a positive case for the ERM, to which his visitor replied with gentle irony.[39] As with Edward Heath's Shadow Cabinet, the main problem Joseph perceived was the lack of faith within Major's ministers. Certainly he believed that one key audience had remained deaf to his arguments. In *The Social Market Economy* (1992) he wrote that "the popular perspective amongst intellectuals remains that markets are vulgar, wasteful, corrupt and enriching only [of] a few".[40] Instead of consoling himself with the thought that his failure to win over the intellectuals had not prevented his party from

36. Interview with Lord Harris of High Cross.
37. *The Times*, 7 June 1993. Geoffrey Goodman remembers Joseph using that phrase in private conversation in the late 1960s; interview with Geoffrey Goodman.
38. Interview with Lord Young.
39. Interview with Lord Lamont.
40. KJ, *The Social Market Economy: Containing Some Lessons from Germany* (CPS, 1992), 23.

winning three elections, he was haunted by the fear that the run of success would come to an end before a lasting change had been effected. Whether or not he saw the opinion polls which suggested that, after all, there had been no significant change in the underlying beliefs of most Britons, Joseph sensed that there was far more work to be done. Most commentators agreed that Labour's more positive approach to the market under Neil Kinnock and John Smith should be credited to the Conservatives. The thesis of Lord Joseph's "common ground" speech of October 1975 – at the time the subject of so much ridicule – seemed to have been verified. There were even signs of superficial success in a task that Joseph had considered to be still more difficult – "to persuade the trade unions to see that their prosperity is best assured by a market system". But Joseph denied that there had been any real movement on the key issues. He still suspected that Labour's policies would "so qualify their acceptance of the market that they wreck its dynamism". One of the last things he wrote – an unpublished article designed to attack "the shallowness of the Labour Party's attitude to unemployment" – characterised the Opposition as "Marxist".[41]

On 23 February 1994 he was well enough to return to the Lords, where he took part in a debate on the family. He expressed his gratitude for what he sensed as "a wave of silent sympathy" for his condition. Speakers had been allocated a maximum of nine minutes each; having thought about these issues for most of his adult life, Joseph regarded this restriction as a sore trial. But he promised that he would pay attention to "the discipline of the Clock", and would waste no time attacking the speech of Labour's Baroness Dean, who had introduced the debate.

Lord Joseph expressed his pleasure that Labour seemed at least to have moved from its former stance of automatic hostility to any cause supported by Lady Thatcher. Apparently "common ground" had been established on the advantages to children of being raised in stable, two-parent families. Yet, as Baroness Young had noted earlier in the debate, in contemporary Britain the number of marriages and divorces each year was almost equal. Joseph pointed out that in a recent year around two-thirds of Britain's babies had been born "out of wedlock". As his time ticked away, he recommended an IEA pamphlet on the subject, describing its authors and its contents in lavish detail. When he began to lecture the House on the work of an obscure eighteenth-century sociologist who "used to write of the globe being invaded each year by about 10 million uncivilised barbarians", his Conservative colleague Viscount Astor rose to remind him that he had already exceeded his time limit. Joseph acknowledged the hint, but continued until he had spoken for almost twenty minutes, attacking his party for having "nibbled at the tax concession available to a

---

41. *House of Lords Debates*, vol. 515, col. 865, 7 February 1990; KJ, "The economics of freedom", 18; KJ to Lord Harris of High Cross, 16 September 1993. We are most grateful to Lord Harris for showing us this correspondence.

married couple" and imploring MPs to vote against such moves in the future. As he was recommending the work of Home-Start to the Home Office spokesman in the Lords, he was interrupted again by Viscount Astor. This time he decided to give way, thanking the House for their courtesy.[42]

Observers in the Lord's gallery recalled their embarrassment as Joseph, speaking from his wheelchair, ignored "the discipline of the Clock". Above all, they remembered the speech as yet another occasion on which he had provided a plug for an IEA pamphlet; this sort of thing was all very well when the audience was made up of one's civil servants, but it was not quite "form" to instruct experienced legislators in this fashion. A former colleague wryly remarked that many of Lady Thatcher's allies – not to mention the ex-premier herself – seemed to think that time limits only applied to lesser beings.[43]

But Lord Joseph was now under the watchful eye of a more august Time-Keeper. It turned out to be his last speech in the Lords. Intensive physiotherapy had alleviated some of the effects of his stroke, and he proudly demonstrated to his friends that he could lever himself out of his wheelchair. But in May 1994 he suffered a further attack, less serious than his first, but even more debilitating after his previous attack. Now his eyes could no longer focus well enough to allow him to read. Towards the end of 1994 it was clear that the bright flame was fading; as he admitted himself, he felt "Oh so tired". He retained his keen interest in politics and could still chuckle over current gossip. To stave off that worst of all human conditions – boredom – a rota of readers was organised for him when he stayed at Yolanda's farm (he had become something of a local hero). In London his devoted friend Michael Alison read to him. As Alison remembered, he was particularly appreciative of the Book of Psalms. Bob Bessell, who had remained a close friend since their first meeting in 1972, continued to visit him more than once a month "to discuss everything under the sun". In early December Lady Thatcher arrived for what turned out to be a two-hour visit. If the pair had wanted to discuss the past this final meeting would have lasted far longer. Instead they looked to the future, rehearsing the themes of the family and the social services which had absorbed so much of Joseph's time since 1970. Apparently what must have been a remarkable conversation was further invigorated by some pink champagne. When Lady Thatcher was preparing to leave Joseph smiled and asked if he should send her a note of his suggestions. No doubt this was intended to be light-hearted, but perhaps he remembered that in 1971 he had brought a list of ideas back from a visit to Lady Reading's sick-bed. Lady Thatcher said that it had been such a useful meeting that they should hold another one soon; Joseph replied that "he had nothing more to say". For a man whose whole life had been devoted to a search for truth it was an ominous remark. Fittingly, the last thing Joseph wrote was a light-

---

42. *House of Lords Debates*, vol. 552, cols 647–50, 23 February 1994.
43. Interviews with Matthew Parris and Lord Jenkin.

hearted message to Lord Harris of High Cross, who had just reached the age of seventy. The message was that Harris was still a young man: "you have yet time to make your mark".[44]

Two weeks after the poignant visit from Lady Thatcher Lord Joseph of Portsoken died in the Royal Brompton Hospital, Chelsea (near Mulberry Walk and Limerston Street) with his beloved family around him. The end was peaceful; the cause of his death was given out as "chest complications". He was just over a month short of his seventy-seventh birthday. Ironically, the man who had always called for more millionaires died on the day that the new National Lottery distributed its first bumper jackpot, of £17.5 million. His body was flown to Connecticut, accompanied by all of his four children, with whom he had enjoyed much more fulfilling relationships in his final years. About half a mile from Yolanda's farm is a small cemetery, past which the couple had often strolled on a favourite walk. Several of the first settlers to the area had been buried there. It was a quiet setting: a place undisturbed by the applause of the party faithful, or the angry shouts of demonstrators. In that scene it was possible to forget that in life there are questions which torment the intellect, and rack the conscience. It was a fitting burial-place for a man who in life had deliberately spurned the more gentle paths that he could have chosen. It would be comforting to think that after his years of seeking the truth Joseph had found the answer to the greatest question of all, but he had some difficulty with the concept of an after-life. The inscription on the simple gravestone was equally apposite. Unadorned by Joseph's many titles, it read: "Husband, father, scholar, patriot".[45]

In Britain senior Conservatives lined up to hail Lord Joseph's achievement. Returning an old compliment, Lady Thatcher described him as "a political giant"; she dedicated a volume of her autobiography to his memory, and never lost an opportunity to acknowledge her devotion or her debt. John Major, who must have known of Joseph's deep reservations about the record of his Government, still recognised "one of the foremost Conservative thinkers since the second world war". Lord Carrington, seen as a representative of a different style of Conservatism, pointed out that the uncaring image had been an illusion, although his reservations were made clear in his remark that Joseph "was a man doing what he thought was right". For Labour, Lord Healey paid tribute to "a very nice man" but added that "his political ideas were bizarre and damaging". Lord Tebbit's praise was unequivocal: "There are too few like him".[46]

While making no attempt to disguise Joseph's complexities, the obituarists agreed that he had been an ornament to public life, and that even his political enemies would feel a void in politics without his presence. The *Sunday Times*

---

44. Hoskyns, *Just in Time*, 404. Speeches at KJ memorial service by Michael Alison, Baroness Thatcher and Margaret Harrison; letter to authors from Bob Bessell; private information; interview with Lord Harris of High Cross.
45. The funeral service included some elements of Judaic ritual; private information.
46. *Sunday Times, Independent on Sunday*, 12 December 1994.

commemorated someone who was "kind, diffident in the extreme, courteous and an agonisingly scrupulous man". In an editorial the newspaper acknowledged that Joseph might have "lacked the administrative skills and common touch needed to translate ideas into practical politics", but that his "honesty marked him out from most of his contemporaries". Despite reservations which he made no attempt to conceal, Arthur Seldon wrote of "a saintly character". In the *Jewish Chronicle*, Sir Alfred Sherman recognised "a man of intellect and conscience". The *TES*, which had published so many critical articles in the past, felt that Joseph's death "leaves a sense of loss in the education world" which was "quite astonishing" in view of the continual struggles between 1981 and 1986 (although the mood of forgiveness in the teaching profession had only been fostered "as the impact of less intellectually honest successors manifested itself"). Perhaps the most significant tribute of all was given years after Joseph's death. After listing all his reasons for disagreement, his Labour Shadow at Education Giles Radice added that Joseph was "rather splendid" all the same.[47]

The headlines on the day after Joseph's death emphasised a link that he would have been proud to acknowledge, even if he would have toned down the phrasing: "Thatcher's guru dies"; "Father of Thatcherism dies"; "Lord Joseph: the principal architect of Thatcherism". But while these epitaphs were inevitable, given Joseph's personal loyalty to Lady Thatcher, they were inadequate indications of his true legacy. For all their close collaboration over so many years and their agreement on many issues, it remained the case that Joseph and Lady Thatcher had always complemented each other: their thinking was not identical. Over the years, existing differences of temperament had been accentuated by the nature of the offices they had held. Joseph could never have said, as Mrs Thatcher did in her last speech as Prime Minister, that "we on this side have never flinched from difficult decisions". In his view his friend was entitled to mythologise the recent past; after all, he believed that she had shown the requisite "moral courage". But he could not avoid brooding on the collective and individual failings which had left "Thatcherism" as an incomplete project.[48]

In retirement Lady Thatcher's main focus was on global developments – as it had been for most of her time in office. Here the "Thatcher myth" inspired her claim to have played a significant role in ensuring the worldwide defeat of socialism, symbolised by the destruction of the Berlin Wall. By contrast, Joseph's preoccupation with the domestic scene convinced him that the "Battle of Ideas" had yet to be won. His speeches emphasised that the British economy was still fragile; but his unmistakable subtext was that the socialist threat would remain until the benefits of the market reforms were much more widely shared. He could not forget the continued existence of poverty. In this respect,

47. *Sunday Times, Independent on Sunday,* 12 December 1994; *TES,* 16 December 1994; *Jewish Chronicle,* 16 December 1994; interview with Giles Radice.
48. Thatcher, *Downing Street Years,* 860.

ironically, the approach of John Major was closer to that of Joseph. It can be argued that Major represented a more voter-friendly version of Sir Keith – a Brixton boy with something of the "common touch", who combined economic rigour with obvious social compassion, while suffering from none of Joseph's intellectual agonising. Major's early assertion that he believed in a "classless society" was subjected to various interpretations, but the most plausible explanation was that he shared Joseph's ideal of wider *"embourgeoisement"*. At the same time, he believed that a Conservative Britain should be "Genuinely compassionate – because some people do need a helping hand to enable them to enjoy a life full of choice and independence".[49]

Throughout his premiership Major was dogged by internal party divisions, and his social agenda was always overshadowed by the European issue. Yet his call for "a nation at ease with itself" after the upheavals of the 1980s had lost none of its potency, provided that it could be delivered with conviction. Since his election as Labour leader in the year of Joseph's death Tony Blair has exploited the opening on domestic policy created by the Conservative civil war over Europe. Major was clearly enraged when Blair appropriated the "One Nation" slogan, but he was wrong to attribute this shrewd move to cynical opportunism. In part the change in Labour's thinking was prompted by electoral considerations; but to a far greater extent it reflected a sincere belief that while Mrs Thatcher's reforms had improved Britain's economic prospects, the social cost had been unacceptable and a more "caring" approach was urgently needed. In short, whatever "New" Labour's supporters thought that they were going to get after 1 May 1997 the leadership intended to give the country the "Thatcherism with a human face" which Major had hoped to offer.

Mrs Thatcher's governments polarised British intellectuals to such an extent that Tony Blair's search for the thinkers who might validate his "Third Way" has not been an unmixed success. Yet only the odium that the Left attached to his name could obscure the claims of one obvious candidate. While this book was being written Blair's advisor Charles Leadbeater noticed the parallels between the words and actions of "New" Labour and the ideas of Lord Joseph. Leadbeater thought that Joseph should be classed among the "intellectual godfathers" of the Blair government – which at least made a change from the too familiar word "guru". It was unlikely that any Cabinet members had actually studied Joseph's work, and Leadbeater might have been claiming too much even to say that Joseph's message had been "ingested . . . albeit unconsciously". The transmission of political ideas can rarely be traced with confidence. But what is beyond dispute is the coincidence between "New" Labour's priorities and those which Joseph endorsed at a time when he was regarded by the Left as a wild reactionary.[50]

---

49. John Major, *The Autobiography* (HarperCollins, 1999), 204.
50. Charles Leadbeater in *New Statesman,* 10 May 1999.

If Joseph's economic message could be boiled down into one central proposition, it would be that only private enterprise could create the wealth without which no amount of compassion could help those members of society who were unable to support themselves. To the despair of the "old Left" – the people who have now joined the Conservative "wets" in the political wilderness – the economic strategy of the Blair government is everything that Joseph could have wished for. In Gordon Brown's lexicon "prudence" took the place of Joseph's "monetary continence", but the meaning was identical to both men. In his pre-budget statement of November 1999 Brown unveiled a package of business incentives of which Joseph would have approved; he also hoped to "encourage the next generation of entrepreneurs" through links between schools and local companies. Further tax incentives followed in the Budget delivered in March 2000, which laid special weight on small businesses; among other reforms, Capital Gains Tax was to be progressively reduced to 10 per cent. Even Brown's new spending pledges chimed in with Joseph's personal preferences. Special help was to be given to pensioners over the age of seventy-five. The only problem for Joseph would have been the precise nature of that assistance; elderly pensioners were to be exempted from paying the television licence fee.[51]

Brown's concentration on the "micro" economic level, while leaving interest rate policy in the hands of a newly independent Bank of England, indicated that far from returning to "Socialism" the government had opted to leave Keynes in his coffin. The Chancellor's obvious comfort with the word "entrepreneur" was another ironic testament to Joseph's legacy. As late as November 1992 his conviction that Britain had clung to its anti-enterprise culture was so deep that he wondered whether women's magazines should be asked to carry positive messages about careers in "trade" for the nation's children. But by that time the political division that he had identified in 1967 – between "those who believe in a collectivist economy with a relatively small private sector" and "those who believe in a private enterprise economy with a relatively small public sector" – had all but disappeared. He continued to plead his case at the end of a decade which saw the establishment of 500 small businesses per week. In 1999, an official document was published in support of Britain's bid for the 2006 World Cup. When searching for a suitable phrase to capture the spirit of the country at the end of the twentieth century, it chose "Britain is a nation of entrepreneurs . . .". All that was lacking was an acceptable English equivalent of the word that Joseph had so often pronounced, but by now that seemed unnecessary because the original term had become a common-place of political and economic discourse.[52]

---

51. *Hansard*, vol. 337, cols 883–91, 9 November 1999. In the Spring of 2000 Brown even took up Joseph's old tactic of comparing the unemployment figures with job vacancies, and deducing from the close match that Britain really had "full" employment after all.
52. *House of Lords Debates*, vol. 540, col. 194, 11 November 1992; KJ in *Spectator*, 19 May 1967; *Guardian*, 11 October 1999. The word even became familiar to sporting enthusiasts; Joseph would have smiled had he lived to see the Michael Stoute-trained "Entrepreneur" win the 1997 2,000 Guineas at Newmarket.

The coincidence between Joseph's ideas and "New" Labour thinking was also evident in the field of education. Joseph took pride in the fact that he had succeeded in drawing greater public attention to Britain's schools. When Tony Blair named "education, education, and education" as the three most urgent problem areas requiring attention from a "New" Labour government Joseph would have been delighted; although Blair accused the Conservatives of having failed the nation's children, Joseph had always recognised that the reversal of Britain's post-war decline in this field would be a long-term undertaking. The Secretary of State David Blunkett, who had once argued so vehemently with Joseph, reminded commentators of his predecessor in his tendency to tackle educational policy questions from a philosophical angle. In practice, he pressed on with Joseph's strategy. The schools' inspectorate (re-branded as the Office for Standards in Education (OFSTED) in 1992) was more powerful than ever, national testing was rigorously enforced, and Blunkett, presiding over the newly merged Department for Education and Employment, shared Joseph's view that education should be regarded as a preparation for the world of work. Blunkett even seemed in danger of repeating Joseph's mistakes; he clashed with teachers over performance-related pay, and called for a revival in discipline and politeness – a very worthy aim, but one which overrated the influence of schooling compared with other factors in the shaping of character. Elsewhere there were signs of a more realistic approach, similar to that of Joseph after his retirement. In April 2000 the government welcomed a report which focused on the problems of children under four from impoverished backgrounds. Their parents would now be offered special advice, on the assumption that children who are ill-prepared for schooling can never recover the lost ground. The Health Minister Yvette Cooper echoed Joseph when she argued that increased benefits alone could not compensate for other factors affecting disadvantaged children. In its report on the issue the *Guardian* referred to the government's desire "to break the cycle of deprivation", and introduced the kind of statistics that had landed Joseph in so much trouble after the Edgbaston speech (for example, "Girls are nine times more likely to become teenage mothers if they come from a low skill background").[53]

Yet in spite of the fact that "New" Labour was pursuing Joseph's agenda in so many key policy fields few people recognised the link. Presumably this owed something to the hatred which he had inspired through his connection with Mrs Thatcher; another likely reason was the speedy departure from the government of Frank Field, the Labour MP most intimately associated with Joseph. Critics alleged that Field had been too radical in his proposals for welfare reform; but he might have been allowed more scope for action had he not been widely portrayed as a man with a penchant for "thinking the unthinkable". The

---

53. For Blunkett on "politeness", see *Guardian,* 28 April 2000; on "deprivation", see Patrick Wintour in *Guardian*, 11 April 2000.

impression that Field's offences had concerned his image rather than his ideas was reinforced when the government continued to enrage the Left by pushing through a Joseph-like welfare agenda, of greater selectivity and regular crack downs on "benefit cheats".

Meanwhile there were few signs that the Conservatives were any more willing to recognise their obvious debt to Joseph. William Hague was, like Joseph, a graduate of Magdalen College, which by his day had become a hot-bed of economic liberalism. Joseph had offered him some friendly advice after his youthful speech to the 1977 party conference, but there was no further contact between them.[54] Charles Leadbeater thought that by 1999 Joseph was "unmourned and hardly remembered even by his own party". Here too "the Thatcher factor" was an important handicap because the ex-leader was still a potential source of disunity. Also, in their search for "clear blue water" to distinguish their ideas from those of "New" Labour the Conservatives were unlikely to find Joseph's work very helpful, precisely because so much of this formed the new "common ground" between Government and Opposition. Although talk of the transformation of the old aristocratic Conservative Party into the exclusive preserve of secondhand car dealers and estate-agents is exaggerated, Joseph had been one of an increasingly rare breed of gentlemen amateurs, and his exemplary manners were somewhat out of place at a time when the word "charm" was almost invariably preceded by "old-world". But the most important reason for Joseph's personal eclipse was the fact that his own political fortunes after 1974 had not mirrored the success of his message. The speeches of the 1970s had empowered Margaret Thatcher, giving her the confidence to deride highbrow critics who scoffed at her instinctive beliefs. Yet, ironically, the propaganda effort on behalf of the free market had enfeebled Joseph himself. Had he retired from the front-bench in October 1974 and refused Departmental office under Mrs Thatcher, he would still have retained his high profile as the foremost advocate of the economic approach adopted by successive Conservative governments. His past performances at Housing and at the DHSS would have been open to criticism – not least from himself – but on balance he would have been regarded as a capable and energetic administrator who had more practical achievements to his name than the average minister. Even at one remove from the political fray he would have enjoyed media coverage for his views after his retirement: whether people agreed with him or not they would not have been able to deny him lasting respect as a "Tory sage".

But Joseph's ambition for solid achievement was far too great for him to consider premature retirement; and very soon after his return to office it became clear how damaging the speeches of the late 1970s could prove to a man

---

54. Jo-Anne Nadler, *William Hague: In His Own Right* (Politico's, 2000), 74; correspondence between authors and William Hague.

of his character. Enoch Powell was close to the truth when he drew a comparison between political "butterflies" and "hawks", declaring that Joseph was fated to be "a butterfly broken on the wheel". But he was less perceptive when he proceeded to argue that butterflies could never be effective if they tried to speak like hawks.[55] The sequence of events after 1974 lent crucial assistance to Joseph's message, but this was also helped by the fact that he *was* a "butterfly". Powell could rarely make a speech without his words being explained by reference to his ambitions, yet on this score Joseph was invulnerable. Ambition was only awakened *after* his speeches had created a sensation, and it proved short-lived. But during that brief interlude he delivered the fatal Edgbaston speech. A "hawk" like Powell might have recovered from this, and once back in office he could have spied out the political landscape before pouncing on specific objectives. By contrast, the Edgbaston speech conjured up rough winds from which Joseph could never find shelter; indeed, he increased their force by continuing to speak (as he proudly put it in 1979) "controversially as I always do". While Mrs Thatcher relished the fight with her internal party critics Joseph was far less robust. The "Mad Monk" could still count on devoted admirers on the Right of his party, and even among opponents who knew him well; but outside this limited circle he had made himself into an easy target for mockery, his reported antics providing light relief for those who hated his ideas. Mrs Thatcher might not have regretted placing him in charge of policy in 1975, but for Joseph it was a disastrous appointment. Powell had ended his frontbench career in 1968 by making a controversial speech in someone else's policy area; the fact that Joseph was under special protection from the leadership and was able to repeat Powell's offence with impunity only increased his unpopularity with the majority of his colleagues. At Industry and at Education it might be argued that his genuine achievements were obscured by a reputation for ideological excess which after 1979 was bolstered by the symptoms of illness. But it would be more accurate to say that his reputation prevented him from achieving more than a fraction of what he had hoped. As in his previous jobs he tried to do too much; and now, because of his image, he faced additional distractions from an intrusive media and angry protesters. All too often Joseph caused trouble for the government when he tried to satsify the demands of his creed, and when forced to back down he disappointed allies who did not have to face the burdens of office. The BL fiasco and the apparent "U-turn" on vouchers were only the most spectacular examples of "banana skins" which Joseph threw in his own path.

The fact that his career ended in something of an anti-climax should not blind historians to Joseph's "towering role in the Thatcherite revolution".[56] But

---

55. Ranelagh, *Thatcher's People*, 137.
56. *Sunday Times*, 12 December 1994.

the peculiar nature of his contribution also helps to explain why the record of Mrs Thatcher's governments continues to arouse such fierce controversy. Almost the only thing on which commentators can agree is that this was a period in which ideas played a central role in the conduct of policy. Joseph himself thought that the fate of an idea was more important than the political fortunes of any individual, but a close examination of his career provides strong grounds for doubting whether he was really equipped to furnish any programme for government with theoretical coherence. In normal times this would have been unimportant, since British governments typically "muddle through" in the hope that practical achievements will satisfy even their most demanding ideological supporters. But this was a government that habitually (if not invariably) acted in obedience to ideas; hence it was crucial that its thinking should not be fundamentally flawed.

Although Joseph was always anxious to play down his own intellectual credentials, the All Souls Fellowship ensured that others would attribute his disclaimers to his famous self-deprecation. Yet he was telling no more than the truth when he referred to his lack of economic expertise. Even as a young man his strength lay in his remarkable ability to memorise facts and quotations. His failure to complete the All Souls thesis on Toleration had indicated that he was far less adept at creative thinking; at the same time, however, it showed that in intellectual matters his enthusiasm was able to overcome even his acute awareness of his own limitations. In the 1960s his exposure to the Institute of Economic Affairs, and his fascination with Enoch Powell, convinced him that the Conservatives lacked a sound philosophical foundation for their policies. Even before Powell's sacking he had convinced himself that it was his duty to make some contribution. His early efforts provoked in his more pragmatic colleagues perplexity rather than anger, but they should not have been surprised: his previous record had betrayed a strong tendency for him to grasp at simple solutions – he was, after all, in a quest for "utopia". Even so, if Labour had implemented *In Place of Strife* – or if the public had rallied behind Heath's version of trade union reform – Joseph would have remained as he was in 1967: economically on the right wing of his party but still content to look for answers to political problems within the broad framework of the post-war "consensus". Instead, after the failure of the Heath government an exaggerated sense of personal responsibility convinced Joseph that his whole political career had been based on false premises. Monetarism now provided him with the certainty he had always craved. His intellectual reputation, and the courage he showed in his "campus campaign", encouraged his fellow-believers to reject any sceptical voices, and to follow the dictates of the theory when they returned to office – even when this seemed likely to destroy much of British industry and to consign the Conservatives to ignominious electoral defeat.

Joseph's philosophical short-comings can also be detected in his failure to come to terms with the tension between the economic and social priorities of the "New Right". He resembled many critics of "Thatcherism", in overlooking the incompatibility of the varied ideas and attitudes which were lumped together under that single word. He was not the only thoughtful Conservative to argue that a programme of economic liberalism could be carried out without endangering traditional institutions and social practices.[57] Unusually, though, he never gave any explicit acknowledgement that there might be a problem – even when (at Education) he was confronted with the most acute policy dilemmas arising from the clash between "libertarians" and "social conservatives", at a time when traditional family life in Britain was being placed under severe stress by economic insecurity and the explosion of part- (and full-) time work for women. Given the stir caused by his speeches at Preston and at Edgbaston in 1974, one might have expected Joseph to have spared some time for this difficulty long before he returned to office; after all, it attracted comment at the time, even in the *Economist* (which he probably still read even though he was dismayed at its consistent support for the economic policies of the Heath government).[58] At the 1976 party conference, in a debate which Joseph had opened, one "libertarian" extolled the new leadership because like him it believed that people should have "the right to spend our money the way we want to, the right to do the things we want to . . .".[59] In a 1978 collection of essays including contributions from John Biffen and Shirley Letwin, the then Associate Editor of the *Sunday Telegraph*, Peregrine Worsthorne, warned Joseph and Thatcher that their policy ideas ran directly counter to the real demands of Conservative activists, who feared "not so much the lack of freedom as its excessive abundance".[60] Certainly the problem should have struck Joseph by

---

57. See, for example, David Willetts's evocation of his home in Havant, situated between two pubs, one of which commemorated the great nineteenth-century campaigner for free trade, Richard Cobden, and the other called "The Prince of Wales". Willetts claims that "a Conservative can happily drink in both establishments" – i.e. economic liberalism is perfectly compatible with social conservatism. But he offers no further argument to indicate that the revellers would continue to get along if one of them broached a controversial subject. Presumably if another round of drinks was suggested, the economic liberal would refuse to pay and the social conservative would say that his companion had drunk too much already. See Willetts, *Modern Conservatism* (Penguin, 1992), vii.
58. See *Economist*, 26 October 1974: Joseph "is too intelligent to miss the paradox of advocating moral discipline with economic permissiveness". In discussing the "unresolved tension between the liberal-conservative economic ideal, on the one hand, and its cultural ideal, on the other", Noel O'Sullivan also drew specific attention to the Edgbaston speech. Joseph, he felt, had been "clearly puzzled by the fuss, largely because he was unaware of the tension under discussion". Yet even this perceptive comment, in the work of an academic with close links to the "New Right", had no effect in persuading Joseph that he should re-examine his position. See Noel O'Sullivan, *Conservatism* (Dent, 1976), 147.
59. N. Linacre, contribution to debate on "Party Policy and Public Relations", Ninety-Third Conservative Party conference, October 1976, conference minutes, 59.
60. Peregrine Worsthorne, "Too Much Freedom", in Cowling (ed.), *Conservative Essays*, 141–54. In the same collection another "Tory Sage", T. E. Utley, stressed that a free market economy

the mid-1980s, when it was possible to find supporters of Mrs Thatcher who advocated the legalisation of heroin and incest, alongside others who wanted to sweep away all vestiges of the "permissive society".[61] Both of these groups could cite Joseph's work as lending theoretical support to their views; the extreme "libertarians" could point to his endorsement of Robert Nozick, while the social conservatives still cherished their memories of Edgbaston.

It would not be convincing to suggest that Joseph had appreciated these difficulties all along, only to decide that the need for change in Britain was so desperate as to outweigh the demands of logical purity. More likely, his undiscriminating advocacy was another product of his intellectual innocence. Hayek and Friedman have been criticised for assuming that "the self whose liberty and spontaneous realization they defend is a fundamentally virtuous self".[62] Believing that the failure of the "consensus" had been both moral and economic, Joseph seized on a theory which implied that the maximisation of freedom would of itself bring about a moral reformation, without pausing to consider that Hayek and Friedman might have been unduly optimistic in their reading of human nature. From this mistaken viewpoint, Joseph saw no difficulty after 1974 in making pronouncements designed to mobilise support for his party from everyone with a grievance against "socialism". Whether or not this was a praiseworthy tactic, it did not lend itself to the construction of a rival theory that could withstand the test of practice. When the Conservatives returned to office they were certain to be pushed in different directions by their diverse collection of allies, all of whom felt confident that their conflicting demands would be satisfied by legislative action. Even after Mrs Thatcher's fall Joseph failed to recognise the difficulty. Writing Hayek's obituary in March 1992, he assumed that the economist "must have sympathised with Mrs Thatcher in confronting the problem of how to tackle, within a free society, the cataclysmic effects on moral restraint of television and permissiveness". Yet Mrs Thatcher only "confronted" these problems in occasional rhetorical excursions; she did nothing to restrain the commercialisation of television, and she was notably

---

"will only work properly in a cohesive society whose members are willing to temper self-interest with enlightenment". Utley's essay reads like an attempt to persuade Joseph to return to the "social market" line which, ironically, had been subverted by Shirley Letwin, one of his fellow contributors. See *Conservative Essays*, 47–8.

61. In a 1978 profile of Joseph, Frank Johnson claimed that while critics might consider Joseph's social conservatism to be "inconsistent with his belief in freedom in economic matters", such strictures betrayed "a misunderstanding of the free market; Joseph would have no difficulty in rebutting [them]". It would have been useful for Johnson's readers to have been given an idea of how Joseph might have brushed the critics aside; regrettably, he chose not to enlighten them; see *Daily Telegraph*, 23 June 1978. For the wilder shores of "Thatcherism" see the controversy over the Federation of Conservative Students (FCS), which resulted in their expulsion from the party in November 1986. The FCS stood accused of "a fanatical belief in personal freedom", and among their other offences was the physical intimidation of Edward Heath in October 1985. See *The Times*, 30 March 1985, 13, 14 November 1986.

62. O'Sullivan, *Conservatism*, 146.

"liberal" in her attitude to the personal indiscretions of her ministers. There was nothing like the government-led crusade against "permissiveness" that social conservatives had hoped for. Ironically, circumstances dictated that the incoherence of "Thatcherism" was not really exposed until after John Major's "Back to Basics" speech of October 1993.[63] The result was a catastrophe for the Conservative Party, instead of the sustainable setback, followed by a quiet rethink, which might have occurred had defeat not been delayed for so long.

If success should be measured by the adoption of broad political ideas by mainstream parties, few politicians have left a mark to rival that of Keith Joseph. But while other members of his party could feel that their "revolution" had succeeded once direct taxation had been reduced and other obstacles to personal enrichment dismantled, Joseph's ideals were far more demanding. When policy *outcomes* since 1979 are judged in the context of his life-long abhorrence of "undeserved" poverty, his pessimism was fully justified. On the view expressed in *Equality* – that poverty is absolute rather than relative, and that a family is only poor if it lacks the resources for adequate food and shelter – Joseph lived to see the virtual conquest of the British poverty that he had entered politics to alleviate. But he also believed that "inequality and the high levels of income that a free economy generates make generous help practicable and raises the standard of living and minimum levels of income". By the time of Joseph's death this crucial assumption had been exposed as yet another of the dubious "panaceas" which had raised unrealistic expectations among the British public since 1945. Between 1979 and 1993 average earnings rose by 34 per cent in real terms; but 25 per cent of the population (more than 14 million people) were receiving less than half the average income compared to 9 per cent when the Thatcher government came to power. A book published by the Child Poverty Action Group concluded that "whichever way you measure it, poverty has grown significantly over recent years". If the Conservative rhetoric about a "dependency culture" had any validity, the 14 million people on benefit constituted a social disaster which would have a knock-on effect for future generations; to Joseph, with his theory of a "cycle of deprivation", the prospect must have seemed particularly chilling. Statistical evidence about poverty could be disputed in detail, but there was a widespread impression that under Conservative rule Britain was divided once again into the "Two Nations" which Disraeli had discerned in the mid-nineteenth century. In 1984 Gertrude

---

63. See KJ in *The Times*, 25 March 1992. The distortions of Major's speech by members of his own party should be interpreted as the product of the demand for a return to "prepermissive" values, which had been left unsatisfied by the Thatcher governments. In practice, the policies of those governments always placed economic liberalism well above the demands of social stability and those "Victorian values" which emphasised sexual morality. See Martin Durham, "The Thatcher Government and the Moral Right" (*Parliamentary Affairs*, Vol. 42, No. 1, January 1989) and Joan Isaac "The Politics of Morality in the UK" (*Parliamentary Affairs*, Vol. 47, No. 2, April 1994).

Himmelfarb (herself a favourite author for Thatcherites) wrote of that period that poverty was not in itself the main problem; rather there was a "recurrent complaint . . . that individuals and classes no longer felt responsible for each other, that human relations had been reduced to calculations of interest, that the only social reality was the 'cash nexus'".[64] By 1990 exactly the same complaint was being voiced too often for the government's supporters to brush it aside as nothing more than the jaundiced opinion of the "chattering classes". Even if the British had learned to tolerate evidence of poverty (such as the increasing problem of homeless people in inner cities), they were repelled by the salaries which were "earned" by top managers. The crushing defeat of the Conservatives at the 1997 General Election was caused in part by a widespread identification of the party with boardroom "fat-cats". Stories of financial irregularities by Conservative MPs only increased the feeling that governments since 1979 had devoted themselves to the interests of a few, at the expense of the general population.

At least one old acquaintance thought that in his last years Joseph was less eager to defend his theories than he had been when in office.[65] After all that had gone before it was difficult for him to make an explicit declaration of misgivings, and his post-retirement writings yield only a few hints, compared to which the "coded" speeches of the wets were models of transparency. For example, Joseph's 1986 introduction to *Self-Help* congratulated Samuel Smiles on having "lauded individualism not as a means to worldly gain but as the path to independence and to self-fulfilment". It was the closest Joseph ever came to denouncing the "yuppie" culture of the 1980s. There followed one of his rare admissions that entrepreneurs should not be regarded as heroes; a belated recognition that "free" enterprise can thrive in countries where political liberty is unknown; and an astonishing attack on economists who "appear to have misled themselves by their own highly abstract model of perfect competition – which exists nowhere". In other contexts, Joseph's regular acknowledgements that Britain was still lagging behind its competitors read like demands for additional doses of the pure Thatcherite medicine. In this thoughtful and little-known piece, the lament that "we are at the bottom of the league of developed nations" leaves room for the thought that Joseph had begun to detect serious flaws in a "revolution" that had already entered its eighth year.[66]

---

64. KJ and Sumption, *Equality*, 27; KJ in *Observer*, 22 August 1976; Oppenheim and Harker, *Poverty: The Facts* (CPAG, 1996), 24–5; Gertrude Himmelfarb, *The Idea of Poverty: England in the Early Industrial Age* (Faber & Faber, 1984), 528.
65. Interview with Geoffrey Goodman.
66. KJ, foreword to Samuel Smiles, *Self-Help* (Sidgwick & Jackson, 1986), 8, 12–13, 15. Cf. his (belated) return to the debate on the "social market", in which he attributed the fact that "We have high unemployment and far less widespread prosperity than we should have" to the misdeeds of governments before 1979 – an excuse which surely even he must have regarded as a bit thin by 1992. See *The Social Market Economy*, 12.

Michael Foot had been right all along: Joseph was indeed a conjuror who had forgotten the second half of his trick after smashing the wrist-watch. More exactly, his life-long weakness for "utopian" thinking had deluded him into the belief that the watch would miraculously rebuild itself without any further intervention. It remains to be seen whether it is possible in a consumerist society to combine the drive for prosperity with an ethic which regards individualism as something more than "a means to wordly gain". Although Tony Blair's "Third Way" is a notoriously obscure concept it seems that "New" Labour aspires to something closer to the outward-looking individualism that Joseph applauded in Samuel Smiles than to the "uncomprehending" greed of the Thatcher years. In November 1999 Gordon Brown claimed to be demonstrating through his economic measures "that enterprise and fairness can go hand in hand". There was much work to do if the government was to achieve its stated aim of abolishing child poverty within twenty years; a Treasury report published two decades after Mrs Thatcher first won power revealed that two out of every five British children were born in households receiving less than half of average income. If Brown's strategy meets with even moderate success in tackling this problem, he will have proved to be a far better "Josephite" than Keith Joseph himself.[67]

---

67. *Hansard*, vol. 337, col. 891, 9 November 1999; *The Times*, 30 March 1999.

Bibliography

Primary sources

All Souls memorial service in honour of Lord Joseph, 3 June 1995, All Souls College, Oxford.

Alport Papers (papers of Lord Alport), Albert Sloman Library, University of Essex.

Boyle Papers (papers of Lord Boyle of Handsworth), Brotherton Library, University of Leeds.

British Library of Political and Economic Science Archives, London School of Economics (LSE).

Butler Papers (papers of Lord Butler of Saffron Waldon), Trinity College, Cambridge.

Conservative Party Archives (CPA), Bodleian Library, Oxford. (The authors wish to thank James Walsh, Director of the Conservative Policy Forum, for permission to quote from documents in the CPA).

Conservative Party Conference Proceedings (various dates).

Correspondence between Keith Joseph and Michael Hargreave (various dates), private possession.

Clark Papers (papers of William Clark), Bodleian Library, Oxford.

Curtis Papers (papers of Lionel Curtis), Bodleian Library, Oxford.

Family Record Centre, London.

Government Papers, Public Records Office (PRO), Kew.

Hailsham Diaries (diaries of Lord Hailsham), Churchill College Archives, Cambridge.

Hansard (House of Commons and House of Lords Debates).

Harrow School Archives, Harrow.

Heath Papers (papers of Sir Edward Heath), personal possession.

Jewish Chronicle Archive, London.

Interview with Sir Keith Joseph by Terry Coleman, *Guardian*, 12 November 1973.

Interview with Sir Keith Joseph by Anthony King, "Talking Politics", BBC Radio 4, 4 August 1973.
Interview with Sir Keith Joseph by Llew Gardner, Thames Television, 24 October 1974.
Interview with Sir Keith Joseph by Anthony Seldon, *Contemporary Record*, **1**(1), Spring 1987.
Interview with Sir Keith Joseph for Brian Lapping Associates television programme, "The Thatcher Factor", 17 November 1988, LSE archives.
Interview with Lord Joseph by Andrew Denham, April 1991.
Joseph Papers (papers of Sir Keith Joseph), Bodleian Library, Oxford.
Lockers Park School Archives, Hemel Hempstead.
Mansion House Papers, Guildhall Library, London.
John Murray (publishers) Archives, London.
Roth Archive (papers of Andrew Roth), Open University, Milton Keynes.
Roth, Andrew, Memorandum on Sir Keith Joseph, unpublished.
Sherman Papers (papers of Sir Alfred Sherman), Bedford Library, Royal Holloway and Bedford New College, University of London.
Townsend Papers (papers of Peter Townsend), University of Essex.

Books and pamphlets by Keith Joseph

[and various authors] *Automation and the Consumer*, CPC, 1956.
[and various authors] *The Challenge of Leisure*, CPC, 1958.
[and various authors] *The Responsible Society*, CPC, 1959.
Changing Housing, CPC, 1967.
Caring for People, CPC, 1972.
"The Economics of Freedom", in *Freedom and Order*, CPC, 1975.
"Foreword", in *Self-Help*, S. Smiles, Sidgwick & Jackson, 1986.
Freedom under the Law, CPC, 1975.
Reversing the Trend: A Critical Reappraisal of Conservative Economic and Social Policies, Barry Rose, Chichester and London, 1975.
Stranded on the Middle Ground: Reflections on Circumstances and Policies, CPS, 1976.
Monetarism Is Not Enough, CPS, 1976.
Conditions for Fuller Employment, CPS, 1978.
Solving the Union Problem is the Key to Britain's Recovery, CPS, 1979.
[with Jonathan Sumption], *Equality*, John Murray, 1979.
"One-Eyed Vision", *Policy Studies* **10**(2), Winter 1989.
Rewards of Parenthood, CPS, 1990.
The Importance of Parenting, CPS, 1991.
The Social Market Economy: Containing Some Lessons from Germany, CPS, 1992.

Newspapers and periodicals (various dates)

Birmingham Post; The Builder; City Press, Colchester Evening Gazette; The Connoisseur; Conservative News; Contemporary Record; CPC Monthly Reports; Crossbow; Daily Express; Daily Mail; Daily Notes [CRD]; *Daily Telegraph; The Economist; Evening Standard; Express & News; Financial Times; The Guardian; Ham and High; The Independent; Independent on Sunday; Jewish Chronicle; Labour Worker; Leeds Searchlight; Liverpool Daily Post; London Gazette; Magdalen College Record, Mail on Sunday; Newcastle Journal; New Society; New Statesman; The Observer; Open House; Private Eye; The Scotsman; The Spectator; The Sun; Sunday Express; Sunday Mirror; Sunday Telegraph; Sunday Times; Time and Tide; The Times; Times Educational Supplement; Times Higher Educational Supplement; Western Morning News; Yorkshire Post; Yorkshire Evening Post.*

Secondary sources

Abse, Leo, *Margaret, Daughter of Beatrice: A Psycho-Biography of Margaret Thatcher* (Jonathan Cape, 1990).
Abse, Leo, *Private Member* (Macdonald, 1973).
Alderman, Geoffrey, *The Jewish Community in British Politics* (Clarendon Press, 1983).
Alderman, Geoffrey, "Converts to the Vision in True Blue", *Times Higher Education Supplement*, 10 July 1987.
Alexander, Andrew, and Watkins, Alan, *The Making of the Prime Minister 1970* (Macdonald Unit 75, 1970).
Ardagh, John, *Germany and the Germans* (Penguin, 1991).
Aris, Stephen, *The Jews in Business* (Jonathan Cape, 1970).
Arnold, Bruce, *Margaret Thatcher: A Study in Power* (Hamish Hamilton, 1984).
Ashley, Jack, *Acts of Defiance* (Reinhardt Books, 1992).
Baker, Kenneth, *The Turbulent Years: My Life in Politics* (Faber & Faber, 1993).
Baldwin, Stanley, *On England* (Philip Allen, 1927).
Banting, Keith, *Poverty, Politics and Policy: Britain in the 1960s* (Macmillan, 1979).
Barber, Anthony, *Taking the Tide* (Michael Russell, 1996).
Barnett, Correlli, *The Collapse of British Power* (Eyre Methuen, 1972).
Barnett, Malcolm Joel, *The Politics of Legislation: The Rent Act 1957* (LSE, 1969).
Beckett, Francis, *The Rebel Who Lost His Cause: The Tragedy of John Beckett, MP* (London House, 1999).
Beer, Samuel, *Britain Against Itself: The Political Contradictions of Collectivism* (Faber & Faber, 1982).
Behrens, Robert, *The Conservative Party from Heath to Thatcher: Policies and Politics 1974–1979* (Saxon House, 1980).
Bellairs, Charles, *Conservative Social and Industrial Reform* (CPC, 1997).
Benn, Tony, *Office Without Power: Diaries 1968–72* (Hutchinson, 1988).
Benn, Tony, *Conflicts of Interests: Diaries 1977–80* (Hutchinson, 1990).
Benn, Tony, *The End of an Era: Diaries 1980–90*, (Arrow, 1994).
Berkeley, Humphrey, *The Odyssey of Enoch: A Political Memoir* (Hamish Hamilton, 1977).
Bevins, Reginald, *The Greasy Pole: A Personal Account of the Realities of British Politics* (Hodder & Stoughton, 1965).
Blaug, Mark "Education Vouchers: It All Depends on What You Mean", in Julian Le Grand and Ray Robinson (eds), *Privatization and the Welfare State* (Allen & Unwin, 1984).
Bogdanor, Vernon, "Education", in Robert Blake and John Patten (eds), *The Conservative Opportunity* (Macmillan, 1976).
Booker, Christopher, *The Neophiliacs: A Study of the Revolution in English Life in the Fifties and Sixties* (Collins, 1969).
Bosanquet, Nicholas, *After the New Right* (Heinemann, 1983).
Boyson, Rhodes, "Prologue", in Rhodes Boyson (ed.), *Down with the Poor: An Analysis of the Failure of the "Welfare State" and a Plan to End Poverty* (Churchill Press, 1971).
Boyson, Rhodes, *Speaking My Mind* (Peter Owen, 1995).
Brack, Duncan, "David Owen and the Social Market Economy", *Political Quarterly* **61**, 463–76, 1990.
Brittan, Samuel, *Capitalism and the Permissive Society* (Macmillan, 1973).
Brittan, Samuel, *Capitalism with a Human Face* (Edward Elgar, 1995).
Broackes, Nigel, *A Growing Concern* (Weidenfeld & Nicolson, 1979).
Bruce-Gardyne, Jock, *Whatever Happened to the Quiet Revolution?* (Charles Knight, 1974).
Bruce-Gardyne, Jock, *Mrs Thatcher's First Administration: The Prophets Confounded* (Macmillan, 1984).
Bruce-Gardyne, Jock and Lawson, Nigel, *The Power Game: An Examination of Decision-Making in Government* (Macmillan, 1976).
Butler, David, *The British General Election of 1955* (Frank Cass, 1969).

Butler, David, and Kavanagh, Dennis, *The British General Election of February 1974* (Macmillan, 1974).

Butler, David, and Kavanagh, Dennis, *The British General Election of 1979* (Macmillan, 1980).

Butler, David, and Kavanagh, Dennis, *The British General Election of 1983* (Macmillan, 1984).

Butler, David, and King, Anthony, *The British General Election of 1964* (Macmillan, 1965).

Butler, David, and Kitzinger, Uwe, *The European Referendum of 1975* (Macmillan, 1976).

Butler, David, and Pinto-Duschinsky, Michael, *The British General Election of 1970* (Macmillan, 1971).

Butler, Lord, *The Art of the Possible* (Hamish Hamilton, 1971).

Calder, Angus, *The People's War: Britain 1939–1945* (Jonathan Cape, 1969).

Calvocoressi, Peter, and Wint, Guy, *Total War: Causes and Courses of the Second World War* (Pelican, 1974).

Campbell, John, *Edward Heath: A Biography* (Jonathan Cape, 1993).

Campbell, John, *Margaret Thatcher: Volume One, The Grocer's Daughter* (Jonathan Cape, 2000).

Castle, Barbara, *The Castle Diaries 1974–76* (Weidenfeld & Nicolson, 1980).

Castle, Barbara, *Fighting all the Way* (Macmillan, 1993).

Chippindale, Peter, and Horrie, Chris, *Stick It Up Your Punter! The Rise and Fall of the Sun* (Mandarin, 1992).

Chitty, Clyde, *Towards a New Education System: The Victory of the New Right?* (Falmer Press, 1989).

Churchill, Randolph S., *Winston S. Churchill: Volume I, Youth 1874–1900* (Heinemann, 1966).

Clark, Alan, *Diaries* (Weidenfeld and Nicolson, 1993).

Clutterbuck, Richard, *Britain in Agony: The Growth of Political Violence* (Faber & Faber, 1978).

Cockett, Richard, *Thinking the Unthinkable: Think-Tanks and the Economic Counter-Revolution 1931–1983* (HarperCollins, 1994).

Cole, John, *As It Seemed to Me* (Weidenfeld & Nicolson, 1995).

Collins, Bruce, and Robbins, Keith (eds), *British Culture and Economic Decline* (Weidenfeld & Nicolson, 1990).

Conservative Party, *Prosperity with a Purpose*, CCO, 1964

Conservative Party, *Putting Britain Right Ahead*, CCO, 1965.

Conservative Party, *Action not Words*, CCO, 1966.

Conservative Party, *A Better Tomorrow: The Conservative Programme for the Next 5 Years*, CCO, 1970.

Conservative Party, *Firm Action for a Fair Britain*, CCO, 1974.

Conservative Party, *Putting Britain First*, CCO, 1974.

Conservative Party, *The Right Approach to the Economy*, CCO, 1977.

Cook, Chris, and Ramsden, John (eds), *By-Elections in British Politics* (Macmillan, 1973).

Coombes, David, *The Member of Parliament and the Administration* (Allen & Unwin, 1966).

Cooper, Peter, *Building Relationships: The History of Bovis, 1885–2000* (Cassell, 2000).

Corina, Maurice, *Trust in Tobacco: The Anglo-American Struggle for Power* (Michael Joseph, 1975).

Cosgrave, Patrick, *Margaret Thatcher: Prime Minister* (Arrow, 1979).

Cowley, Philip, and Bailey, Matthew, "Peasants' Uprising or Religious War? Re-Examining the 1975 Conservative Leadership Contest", *British Journal of Political Science*, Winter 2000.

Crewe, Ivor, "Values: The Crusade that Failed", in Dennis Kavanagh and Anthony Seldon (eds), *The Thatcher Effect: A Decade of Change* (Clarendon Press, 1989).

Critchley, Julian, *The Palace of Varieties: An Insider's View of Westminster* (Faber & Faber, 1989).

Crossman, Richman, *Diaries of a Cabinet Minister, Volume I, Minister of Housing 1964–66* (Hamish Hamilton and Jonathan Cape, 1975).

Crossman, Richman, *Diaries of a Cabinet Minister, Volume II, Lord President of the Council and Leader of the House of Commons 1966–68* (Hamish Hamilton and Jonathan Cape, 1976).

Crossman, Richard, *Diaries of a Cabinet Minister, Volume III, Secretary of State for Social Services 1968–70* (Hamish Hamilton and Jonathan Cape, 1977).

Curtis, Lionel, *The Open Road to Freedom* (Basil Blackwell, 1950).

Curtis, Sarah (ed.), *The Journals of Woodrow Wyatt: Volume One* (Macmillan, 1998).

Dahrendorf, Ralf, *On Britain* (BBC Publications, 1982).

Deakin, Nicholas, *The Politics of Welfare: Continuities and Change* (Harvester Wheatsheaf, 1994).

Denham, Andrew, *Think-Tanks of the New Right* (Dartmouth, 1996).

Denham, Andrew, and Garnett, Mark, *British Think-Tanks and the Climate of Opinion* (UCL Press, 1998).

de Rothschild, Edmund, *A Gilt-Edged Life* (John Murray, 1998).

Dicey, A. V., *Law and Opinion in England* (Macmillan, 1914).

Donoughue, Bernard, *Prime Minister: The Conduct of Policy under Harold Wilson and James Callaghan* (Jonathan Cape, 1987).

Dorey, Peter (ed.), *The Major Premiership: Politics and Policies under John Major 1990–97* (Macmillan, 1999).

du Cann, Edward, *Two Lives* (Images, 1995).

Dunleavy, Patrick, *The Politics of Mass Housing in Britain 1945–1975* (Clarendon Press, 1981).

Durham, Martin, "The Thatcher Government and the Moral Right", *Parliamentary Affairs*, Vol. 42, No. 1, January 1989.

Edwardes, Michael, *Back from the Brink: An Apocalyptic Experience* (Collins, 1983).

Endelman, Todd M., *Radical Assimilation in English Jewish History 1656–1945* (Indiana University Press, 1990).

Field, Frank, *Poverty and Politics* (Heinemann, 1982).

Field, Frank, "Social Policy: A Thirty-Year Journey", Second Keith Joseph Memorial Lecture (CPS, 1998).

Fisher, Nigel, *Iain Macleod* (Andre Deutsch, 1970).

Fisher, Nigel, *The Tory Leaders* (Weidenfeld & Nicolson, 1977).

Flather, Paul, "Pulling Through – Conspiracies, Counterplots and How the SSRC Escaped the Axe in 1982", in Martin Bulmer (ed.), *Social Science Research and Government: Comparative Essays on Britain and the United States* (Cambridge University Press, 1987).

Fowler, Norman, *Ministers Decide* (Chapmans, 1991).

Friedman, Milton, and Rose, *Free to Choose* (Penguin, 1980).

Garnett, Mark, *Alport: A Study in Loyalty* (Acumen, 1999).

Gilmour, Ian, *Britain Can Work* (Martin Robertson, 1983).

Gilmour, Ian, *Dancing with Dogma: Britain under Thatcherism* (Simon & Schuster, 1992).

Gilmour, Ian, *Inside Right: Conservatism, Policies and the People* (Quartet, 1978).

Gilmour, Ian, and Garnett, Mark, *"Whatever Happened to the Tories?"* (Fourth Estate, 1997).

Gove, Michael, *Michael Portillo: The Future of the Right* (Fourth Estate, 1995).

Grant, John, *Member of Parliament* (Michael Joseph, 1974).

Greenleaf, W. H., *The British Political Tradition: Volume II, The Ideological Heritage* (Methuen, 1983).

Griffiths, Richard, *Fellow Travellers of the Right: British Enthusiasts for Nazi Germany 1933–39* (Oxford University Press, 1983).

Hailsham, Lord, *The Dilemma of Democracy: Diagnosis and Prescription* (Fount, 1979).

Halcrow, Morrison, *Keith Joseph: A Single Mind* (Macmillan, 1989).

Halsey, A. H. (ed.), *British Social Trends Since 1900* (Macmillan, 1988).

Halsey, A. H., *Change in British Society: From 1900 to the Present Day* (Oxford University Press, 1995).

Harrington, Michael, "Sir Keith Joseph" in T. Stacey and R. St Oswald (eds), *Here Come the Tories* (Tom Stacey, 1970).

Harris, Ralph, and Sewill, Brendon, *British Economic Policy 1970–74: Two Views* (IEA, 1975).

Hattersley, Roy, *Choose Freedom* (Penguin, 1987).

Hayek, Friedrich, *The Road to Serfdom* (Routledge, 1944).

Hayek, Friedrich, *A Tiger by the Tail* (IEA, 1972).

Healey, Denis, *The Time of My Life* (Penguin, 1990).

Heath, Edward, *The Course of My Life* (Hodder Headline, 1998).

Heffer, Simon, *Like the Roman: The Life of Enoch Powell* (Weidenfeld & Nicolson, 1998).

Henderson, Nicholas, *Mandarin: Diaries of an Ambassador 1969–1982* (Weidenfeld & Nicolson, 1994).

Hennessy, Peter, *Whitehall* (Fontana, 1990).

Hill, Charles, *Both Sides of the Hill* (Heinemann, 1964).

Hills, John (ed.), *New Inequalities: The Changing Distribution of Income and Wealth in the United Kingdom* (Cambridge University Press, 1996).

Himmelfarb, Gertrude, *The Idea of Poverty: England in the Early Industrial Age* (Faber & Faber, 1984).

Hoggart, Simon, *On the House* (Robson Books, 1981).

Hoggart, Simon, *Back on the House* (Robson Books, 1982).

Holmes, Martin, *The First Thatcher Government 1979–1983* (Harvester Wheatsheaf, 1985).

Honderich, Ted, *Conservatism* (Hamish Hamilton, 1990).

Hoover, Kenneth, and Plant, Raymond, *Conservative Capitalism in Britain and the United States: A Critical Appraisal* (Routledge, 1989).

Horne, Alistair, *Macmillan, 1894–1956* (Macmillan, 1988).

Hoskyns, John, *Just in Time: Inside the Thatcher Revolution* (Aurum Press, 2000).

Howard, Anthony, *Crossman: The Pursuit of Power* (Jonathan Cape, 1990).

Howe, Geoffrey, *Conflict of Loyalty* (Macmillan, 1994).

Howell, David, *Blind Victory: A Study of Income, Wealth and Power* (Hamish Hamilton, 1986).

Hutton, Will, *The State We're In* (Jonathan Cape, 1995).

Ignatieff, Michael, *Isaiah Berlin* (Chatto & Windus, 1998).

Inglis, Brian, *Poverty and the Industrial Revolution* (Panther, 1972).

Irving, Clive, Hall, Ron, and Washington, Jeremy, *Scandal '63: A Study of the Profumo Affair* (Heinemann, 1963).

Isaac, Joan "The Politics of Morality in the UK", *Parliamentary Affairs*, Vol. 47, No. 2, April 1994.

Jefferys, Kevin, *Anthony Crosland* (Richard Cohen Books, 1999).

Jenkins, Peter, *Mrs Thatcher's Revolution: The Ending of the Socialist Era* (Pan, 1988).

Jenkins, Roy, *A Life at the Centre* (Macmillan, 1991).

Jenkins, Roy, *Gladstone* (Macmillan, 1995).

Jenkins, Simon, *Accountable to None: The Tory Nationalisation of Britain* (Hamish Hamilton, 1995).

Johnman, Lewis, "The Conservatives in Opposition, 1964–70" in Richard Coopey, Steven Fielding and Nick Tiratsoo (eds), *The Wilson Governments 1964–1970* (Pinter, 1993).

Johnson, Christopher, *The Economy under Mrs Thatcher 1979–1990* (Penguin, 1991).

Johnson, Richard, "A New Road to Serfdom? A Critical History of the 1988 Act", in *Education Limited: Schooling, Training and the New Right in England since 1979* (Unwin Hyman, 1991).

Jones, Harriet, "The Cold War and the Santa Claus Syndrome", in Martin Francis and Ina Zweiniger-Bargielowska (eds), *The Conservatives and British Society 1880–1990* (University of Wales Press, 1996).

Jones, Ken, *Right Turn: The Conservative Revolution in Education* (Hutchinson Radius, 1989).

Jordan, Grant, and Richardson, Jeremy, "Engineering a Consensus: From the Finniston Report to the Engineering Council", *Public Administration* **62**, Winter 1984.

Junor, John, *Memoirs: Listening for a Midnight Tram* (Pan, 1991).

Keegan, William, *Mrs Thatcher's Economic Experiment* (Penguin, 1985).

Keegan, William, *Mr Lawson's Gamble* (Hodder & Stoughton, 1989).

Kellner, Peter, and Crowther-Hunt, Lord, *Civil Servants: An Inquiry into Britain's Ruling Class* (Macdonald, 1980).

Kelly, Richard, *Conservative Party Conferences: The Hidden System* (Manchester University Press, 1989).

King, Cecil, *The Cecil King Diary 1965–1970* (Jonathan Cape, 1972).

King, Cecil, *The Cecil King Diary 1971–74* (Jonathan Cape, 1975).

King, Roger and Nugent, Neill (eds), *Respectable Rebels: Middle Class Campaigns in Britain in the 1970s* (Hodder & Stoughton, 1979).

Klein, Rudolf, *The Politics of the National Health Service* (Longman, 1983).

Knight, Christopher, *The Making of Tory Education Policy in Post-War Britain 1950–86* (Falmer Press, 1990).

Knightley, Philip, *The First Casualty* (Prion, 2000).

Kogan, Maurice, with Kogan, David, *The Attack on Higher Education* (Kogan Page, 1983).

Kynaston, David, *The City of London, Volume III: Illusions of Gold, 1914–1945* (Chatto & Windus, 1999).

Lamb, Richard, *The Failure of the Eden Government* (Sidgwick & Jackson, 1987).

Lawson, Nigel, *The View from No. 11: Memoirs of a Tory Radical* (Bantam, 1992).

Layton-Henry, Zig, *The Politics of Immigration* (Blackwell, 1992).

Leadbeater, Charles, "New Labour's Secret Godfather", *New Statesman*, 10 May 1999.

Letwin, Shirley Robin, *The Anatomy of Thatcherism* (Fontana, 1992).

Lewis, Geoffrey, *Lord Hailsham* (Jonathan Cape, 1997).

Lindsay. T. F., and Harrington, Michael, *The Conservative Party 1918–1970* (Macmillan, 1974).

Lipman, V. D., *A History of the Jews in Britain since 1858*, (Leicester University Press, 1990).

Loewe, L. L. *Basil Henriques: A Portrait* (Routledge & Kegan Paul, 1976).

Longford, Lord, *Dairy of a Year* (Weidenfeld & Nicolson, 1982).

Lowe, Rodney, *The Welfare State in Britain since 1945* (Macmillan, 1993).

Lowe, Rodney, "The Replanning of the Welfare State", in Martin Francis and Ina Zweiniger-Bargielowska (eds), *The Conservatives and British Society 1880–1990* (University of Wales Press, 1996).

Lowe, Rodney, "The Social Policy of the Heath Government", in Stuart Ball and Anthony Seldon (eds), *The Heath Government 1970–74: A Reappraisal* (Longman, 1996).

MacDougall, Donald, *Don and Mandarin: Memoirs of an Economist* (John Murray, 1987).

Macmillan, Harold, *At the End of the Day* (Macmillan, 1973).

Major, John, *The Autobiography* (HarperCollins, 1999).

Marr, Andrew, *Ruling Britannia* (Michael Joseph, 1995).

Maudling, Reginald, *Memoirs* (Sidgwick & Jackson, 1978).

McAlpine, Alistair, *Once a Jolly Bagman: Memoirs* (Phoenix, 1988).

McSmith, Andy, *Kenneth Clarke: A Political Biography* (Verso, 1988).

Mellor, Hugh, *London Cemeteries* (Scolar Press, 1994).

Middlemas, Keith, *Power, Competition and the State: Volume 2, Threats to the Postwar Settlement: Britain 1961–74* (Macmillan, 1990).

Middlemas, Keith, *Power, Competition and the State: Volume 3, The End of the Postwar Era: Britain since 1974* (Macmillan, 1991).

Mitchell, Yvonne, *The Family* (Heinemann, 1967).

Moon, Jeremy, and Richardson, Jeremy, "Policy-Making with a Difference? The Technical and Vocational Education Initiative", *Public Administration*, Vol. 62, Spring 1984.

Morgan, Kenneth O., *Callaghan: A Life* (Oxford University Press, 1997).

Mount, Ferdinand (ed.), *The Inquiring Eye: A Selection of the Writings of David Watt* (Penguin, 1988).

Nabarro, Gerald, *Exploits of a Politician* (Arthur Baker, 1973).

Nadler, Jo-Anne, *William Hague: In his own Right* (Politico's, 2000).

Nicholls, A. J., *Freedom with Responsibility: The Social Market Economy in Germany, 1918–63* (Clarendon Press, 1994).

Nicolson, Nigel, *Long Life* (Phoenix, 1988).

Nind, Philip F., *A Firm Foundation: The Story of the Foundation for Management Education* (Foundation for Management Education, 1985).

Ogden, Chris, *Maggie: An Intimate Portrait of a Woman in Power* (Simon & Schuster, 1990).

O'Hear, Anthony, "Education Beyond Present Desire", *Salisbury Review*, April 1986.

Oppenheim, Carey, and Harker, Lisa, *Poverty: The Facts* (CPAG, 1996).

O'Sullivan, John, "Conservatism, Democracy and National Identity", Third Keith Joseph Memorial Lecture (CPS, 1999).

O'Sullivan, Noel, *Conservatism* (Dent, 1976).

Parkinson, Cecil, *Right at the Centre* (Weidenfeld & Nicolson, 1992).

Parsons, Wayne, *The Political Power of the Financial Press* (Edward Elgar, 1989).

Parton, Nigel, "The Natural History of Child Abuse: A Study in Social Problem Definition", *British Journal of Social Work* **9** (1979).

Piltch, Michael, "Saving for Retirement", in Rhodes Boyson (ed.), *Down with the Poor* (IEA, 1971).

Pimlott, Ben, *Harold Wilson* (HarperCollins, 1992).

Ponting, Clive, *Breach of Promise: Labour in Power 1964–70* (Hamish Hamilton, 1989).

Powell, Enoch, "Conservatives and the Social Services", *Political Quarterly*, Vol. XXIV, No. 2, April–June 1953.

Powell, Enoch, *Income Tax at 4'3 in the £* (Tom Stacey, 1970).

Powell, Enoch, "Is it Politically Practicable?" in *The Rebirth of Britain: A Symposium of Essays by Eighteen Writers* (Pan, 1964).

Prior, James, *A Balance of Power* (Hamish Hamilton, 1986).

Pym, Francis, *The Politics of Consent* (Sphere, 1985).

Raison, Timothy, *The Tories and the Welfare State: A History of Conservative Social Policy since the Second World War* (Macmillan, 1990).

Raison, Timothy, *Why Conservative?* (Penguin, 1964).

Ramanathan, Sugana, *The Novels of C. P. Snow: A Critical Introduction* (Macmillan, 1978).

Ramsden, John, *The Making of Conservative Party Policy: The Conservative Research Department since 1929* (Longman, 1980).

Ramsden, John, *The Winds of Change: Macmillan to Heath 1957–1975* (Longman, 1996).

Ranelagh, John, *Thatcher's People* (HarperCollins, 1991).

Rentoul, John, *Me and Mine: The Triumph of the New Individualism?* (Unwin Hyman, [no date]).

Rhodes James, Robert, *Anthony Eden* (Papermac, 1987).

Rhodes James, Robert, *Bob Boothby* (Headline, 1992).

Rhodes James, Robert (ed.), *"Chips": The Diaries of Sir Henry Channon* (Weidenfeld & Nicolson, 1993).

Richardson, David, "The History of the Catering Industry, with Special Reference to the Development of J. Lyons & Co. Ltd to 1939", unpublished PhD thesis, University of Kent, 1970.

Riddell, Peter, *The Thatcher Government* (Martin Robertson, 1983).

Ridley, Nicholas, *My Style of Government: The Thatcher Years* (HarperCollins, 1991).

Roth, Andrew, *Heath and the Heathmen* (Routledge & Kegan Paul, 1972).

Rothschild, Lord, *Meditations of a Broomstick* (Collins, 1977).

Rowse, A. L., *A Cornishman at Oxford* (Jonathan Cape, 1965).

Russel, Trevor, *The Tory Party: Its Policies, Divisions and Future* (Penguin, 1978).

Rutter, Michael, and Madge, Nicola, *Cycles of Disadvantage: A Review of Research* (Heinemann, 1976).

Salter, Lord, *Memoirs of a Public Servant* (Faber & Faber, 1961).

Sampson, Anthony, *The Changing Anatomy of Britain* (Coronet, 1983).

Schlesinger, Philip, and Griffith, John, *Free Speech for All?* (Council for Academic Freedom & Democracy, 1979).

Scott, Peter, "Higher Education", in Dennis Kavanagh and Anthony Seldon (eds), *The Thatcher Effect: A Decade of Change* (Clarendon Press, 1989).

Searing, Donald, *Westminster's World: Understanding Political Roles* (Harvard University Press, 1994).

Seldon, Anthony, *Major: A Political Life* (Phoenix, 1998).

Seldon, Arthur, *Capitalism* (Blackwell, 1990).

Seldon, Arthur, "Conservatives and the Welfare State", *Crossbow*, August–September 1972.

Seldon, Arthur, *The Riddle of the Voucher: An Inquiry into the Obstacles to Introducing Choice and Competition into State Schools* (IEA, 1986).

Sharp, Evelyn, *The Ministry of Housing and Local Government* (Allen & Unwin, 1969).

446

Shepherd, Robert, *Enoch Powell: A Portrait* (Hutchinson, 1996).

Shepherd, Robert, *Iain Macleod: A Biography* (Pimlico, 1995).

Shonfield, Andrew, *Modern Capitalism* (Oxford University Press, 1965).

Shonfield, Andrew, *The Use of Public Power* (Oxford University Press, 1982).

Short, Edward, *Whip to Wilson: The Crucial Years of the Labour Government* (Macdonald, 1989).

Sked, Alan, and Cook, Chris, *Post-War Britain: A Political History 1945–1992* (Penguin, 1993).

Skidelsky, Robert, *John Maynard Keynes: The Economist as Saviour 1920–1937* (Macmillan, 1992).

Smiles, Samuel, *Character* (John Murray, 1888).

Smile, Samuel, *Self-Help* (Sidgwick & Jackson, 1986).

Smith, Adam, *The Theory of Moral Sentiments* (Chapman, 1809).

Smith, David, *The Rise and Fall of Monetarism* (Penguin, 1987).

Smith, Janet Adam, *John Buchan* (Rupert Hart-Davis, 1965).

Snow, C. P., *The Conscience of the Rich* (Penguin, 1961).

Souhami, Diana, *Gluck 1895–1978: Her Biography* (Pandora Press, 1988).

Stephenson, Hugh, *Mrs Thatcher's First Year* (Jill Norman, 1980).

Stewart, Michael, *Life and Labour: An Autobiography* (Sidgwick & Jackson, 1980).

Stewart, Michael, *Politics and Economic Policy in the UK since 1963: The Jekyll & Hyde Years* (Pergamon Press, 1978).

Taylor, A. J. P., *The Struggle for Mastery in Europe 1848–1918* (Oxford University Press, 1971).

Taylor, Robert, "The Heath Government, Industrial Policy and the 'New Capitalism'", in Stuart Ball and Anthony Seldon (eds), *The Heath Government 1970–74: A Reappraisal* (Longman, 1996).

Tebbit, Norman, *Upwardly Mobile* (Futura, 1989).

Templewood, Viscount, *The Unbroken Thread* (Collins, 1949).

Thatcher, Carol, *Below the Parapet: The Biography of Denis Thatcher* (HarperCollins, 1996).

Thatcher, Margaret, *The Downing Street Years* (HarperCollins, 1993).

Thatcher, Margaret, *The Path to Power* (HarperCollins, 1995).

Thody, Philip, *The Conservative Imagination* (Pinter, 1993).

Thomas, Hugh, "A Letter to a Social Democrat", in Patrick Cormack (ed.), *Right Turn: Eight Men Who Changed Their Minds* (Leo Cooper, 1978).

Thomas, Hugh, *The Suez Affair* (Pelican, 1970).

Thompson, Noel, "Economic Ideas and the Development of Economic Opinion", in Richard Coopey and Nicholas Woodward (eds), *Britain in the 1970s: The Troubled Economy* (UCL Press, 1996).

Thorpe, D. R., *Alec Douglas-Home* (Sinclair-Stevenson, 1997).

Thwaite, Ann, *Waiting for the Party: The Life of Frances Hodgson Burnett 1849–1924* (Secker & Warburg, 1974).

Timmins, Nicholas, *The Five Giants: A Biography of the Welfare State* (HarperCollins, 1995).

Tomlinson, J. R. G., "The Schools", in Dennis Kavanagh and Anthony Seldon (eds), *The Thatcher Effect: A Decade of Change* (Clarendon Press, 1989).

Townsend, Peter, and Davidson, Nick (eds), *Inequalities in Health* (Penguin, 1982).

Utley, T. E., "The Significance of Mrs Thatcher", in Maurice Cowling (ed.), *Conservative Essays* (Cassell, 1978).

Waldegrave, William, *The Binding of Leviathan: Conservatism and the Future* (Hamish Hamilton, 1978).

Walden, George, *Lucky George: Memoirs of an Anti-Politician* (Allen Lane, 1999).

Wansell, Geoffrey, *Tycoon: The Life of James Goldsmith* (Grafton Books, 1988).

Wapshot, Nicholas, and Brock, George, *Thatcher* (Futura, 1983).

Webster, Charles, *The Health Services Since the War: Volume II, Government and Health Care: The National Health Service 1958–1979* (HMSO, 1996).

Weight, Richard, *Patriots: National Identity in Britain 1940–2000*, (Macmillan, 2001).

Weiner, Martin, *English Culture and the Decline of the Industrial Spirit 1850–1980* (Pelican, 1985).

Wheen, Francis, "Adam Smith Rides Again", *Chateau*, Vol. XVI, No. 9, 28 January 1976.

Wheen, Francis, *Karl Marx*, (Fourth Estate, 1999).

Whitehead, Phillip, *The Writing on the Wall: Britain in the Seventies* (Michael Joseph, 1985).

Wilkinson, Max, *Lessons from Europe: A Comparison of British and West European Schooling* (CPS, 1977).

Wilks, Stephen, "Conservative Industrial Policy 1979-83", in Peter M. Jackson (ed.), *Implementing Government Policy Initiatives: The Thatcher Administration, 1979–83* (RIPA, 1985).

Wilks, Stephen, *Industrial Policy and the Motor Industry* (Manchester University Press, 1984).

Willetts, David, *Modern Conservatism* (Penguin, 1992).

Wilson, Edgar, *A Very British Miracle: The Failure of Thatcherism* (Pluto Press, 1992).

Wilson, Harold, *The New Britain* (Penguin, 1964).

Wilson, Harold, *Final Term: The Labour Government 1974–1976* (Weidenfeld & Nicolson, 1979).

Wood, John (ed.), *A Nation Not Afraid: The Thinking of Enoch Powell* (Batsford, 1965).

Wood, John (ed.), *Freedom and Reality* (Paperfront, 1969).

Worsthorne, Peregrine, "Too Much Freedom", in Maurice Cowling (ed.), *Conservative Essays* (Cassell, 1978).

Wyatt, Woodrow, *Confessions of an Optimist* (Collins,1985).

Wybrow, Robert, *Britain Speaks Out, 1937–87: A Social History as Seen Through the Gallup Data* (Macmillan, 1989).

Wynn, Arthur and Margaret, "Can Family Planning do More to Reduce Child Poverty?", *Poverty*, No. 29, Summer 1974.

Young, Hugo, *One of Us: A Biography of Margaret Thatcher* (Macmillan, 1990).

Young, Hugo, and Sloman, Anne, *The Thatcher Phenomenon* (BBC, 1986).

Young, Lord, *The Enterprise Years: A Businessman in the Cabinet* (Headline, 1990).

Zweig, Konrad, *Germany Through Inflation and Recession: An Object Lesson in Economic Management, 1973–76* (CPS, 1976).

Index

Biffen, John 249, 285, 302+note, 360,
  361, 433
Birch, Nigel 85
Blackstone, Tessa 415–16
Blair, Tony x, xi, 427, 429, 437
Blake, Robert 31, 33–4, 36, 47, 54–5, 183
Blenkinsop, Arthur 70
Blunkett, David 398, 429
Body, Sir Richard 163
Bogdanor, Vernon 373
Bolton, John 140
Booker, Christopher 136
Boothby, Robert 58, 73–5, 385
Bovis 8–11, 25–6, 29, 37, 40, 43–4, 49–50,
  52, 86, 92, 101–2, 140, 146, 185, 202,
  217, 234–6, 240, 272, 273, 332, 408
Bovis, Charles 8–9
Bow Group 118–19, 138, 284, 334, 357,
  362
Bowe, Colette 353
Boyd, Francis 261
Boyd-Carpenter, John 60, 113, 116, 123,
  129, 146
Boyle, Sir Edward 70, 73, 75, 100, 111,
  120, 123, 157, 160, 169–72, 181, 184
Boyson, Dr Rhodes 210, 312, 369, 370,
  372–4, 405
Brighton Bomb 390
British Leyland (BL) xii, 341–2, 345, 353,
  356, 359, 378, 402, 431
British Steel 167, 338, 341, 347–51
Brittan, Leon 284, 385
Brittan, Sam 193note, 255, 299
Broackes, Sir Nigel 141, 235note, 236
Brocklehurst, John 16–17, 20–4, 30–31
Brooke, Henry 88, 90–3, 96, 102, 107,
  111, 113, 131
Brown, George 131
Brown, Gordon 428, 437
Bruce-Gardyne, Jock 329, 334
Buchan, John 2
Burke, Edmund 258, 294
Burn, Duncan 167
Burnett, Frances Hodgson 2
Butler, Adam 343
Butler, Rab 62, 75, 76, 86, 95, 96, 99, 100,
  103, 119, 120, 126, 131, 145, 281, 363,
  385, 397
Butt, Ronald 210–11, 278
Byron, Lord 22

Cairncross, Sir Alec 166
Callaghan, James 125, 127, 129, 146, 155,
  180, 285–8, 312, 320, 324, 327, 337,
  365, 367, 374, 400

Campbell, John 211, 246note, 276note
Carey, Sir Peter 335, 340, 351, 357
Carlisle, A. F. A. 17+note, 20
Carlisle, Mark 357, 368, 369, 370, 378–9
Carr, Sir Raymond 55
Carr, Robert 158, 170, 199, 237, 259, 275,
  278, 281
Carrington, Lord 214, 239–40, 303, 392,
  425
Carstairs, Sir George 184
Castle, Barbara 110, 176, 186, 209, 218,
  228, 268, 269, 274, 283
Centre for Policy Studies (CPS) 238–41,
  243–4, 255, 268, 274, 282, 292, 297,
  298, 302, 304, 306, 308, 317, 334, 335,
  340, 345–6, 352, 356, 360, 367, 409,
  410, 415, 419, 421
Chamberlain, Joseph xi
Channon, 'Chips' 301–2
Chapman, Leslie 339
Child Poverty Action Group (CPAG)
  162, 181, 200–3, 222, 267–70, 435
Churchill, Winston 20, 38–9, 57, 58, 69,
  91, 292
Clark, Alan 385, 390
Clark, Colin 157
Clark, William 73
Clarke, Kenneth 143, 278, 284, 343, 398,
  415
Cockett, Richard 247
Cockfield, Arthur 175, 285
Coleman, Terry 271
Coleraine, Lord 296
Compton Carr, William 224–5
Conservative Research Department
  (CRD) 127, 129, 137, 182, 239, 242,
  243, 285, 302–4, 312, 314, 316, 319,
  327, 347
Cooper, Yvette 429
Cormack, Sir Patrick 84, 217, 393
Cosgrave, Patrick 177, 250, 257, 276note,
  281
Costain, Albert 102
Crick, Bernard 398
Cromer, Lord 192
Crosland, Anthony 300, 329
Crossman, Richard 50, 87–8, 101, 110,
  125note, 142, 143, 146, 195–7, 200–1,
  204, 208–9, 212, 214
Crowder, Sir John 90note
Curtis, Lionel 46, 52, 55, 77, 97, 419
'Cycle of Deprivation' 219–25, 231, 270,
  373–4, 420–21, 429, 435

Dahrendorf, Ralf 295, 330